中華文化大綱

Edited by John Meskill
with the assistance of J. Mason Gentzler
Columbia University Press · New York and London

An
Introduction
to
Chinese
Civilization

Clothbound edition published by Columbia University Press

Portions of this work were prepared under a contract with the U. S. Office of
Education for the production of texts to be used in undergraduate education. The
texts so produced have been used in the Columbia College Oriental Studies
program and have subsequently been revised and expanded for publication in the
present form. Copyright is claimed only in those portions of the work not submitted
in fulfillment of the contract with the U. S. Office of Education. The U. S. Office of
Education is not the author, owner, publisher, or proprietor of this publication, and
is not to be understood as approving by virtue of its support any of the statements
made or views expressed therein.

Paperback edition published simultaneously in Canada.
Printed in the United States of America.

Paperbound International Standard Book Number: 0-669-73502-7
Clothbound International Standard Book Number: 0-231-03649-3
Library of Congress Catalog Card Number: 72-9410

The calligraphy for the title was prepared by Chiang Yee.

10 9 8 7 6 5 4 3 2

Contributors

KWANG-CHIH CHANG
Professor in Anthropology, Yale University

NAI-RUENN CHEN
Associate Professor of Economics, Cornell University

YU-KUANG CHU
Professor Emeritus of Asian Studies and Education,
Skidmore College

MORTON H. FRIED
Professor of Anthropology, Columbia University

J. MASON GENTZLER
Professor of Far Eastern Studies, Sarah Lawrence
College

CHI-MING HOU
Charles A. Dana Professor of Economics, Colgate
University

CHARLES O. HUCKER
Professor of Chinese and of History, University of
Michigan

CHU-TSING LI
Professor of Art, University of Kansas

JOHN MESKILL
Professor of Chinese and Japanese, Barnard College

RHOADS MURPHEY
Professor of Geography, University of Michigan

BURTON WATSON
Professor of Chinese and Japanese, Columbia
University

C. K. YANG
Professor of Sociology, University of Pittsburgh

Preface

This book consists of a brief history of China and ten essays on major aspects of Chinese civilization. It is meant to be an introduction, primarily for undergraduates. Portions of the work were prepared under a contract with the United States Office of Education for the production of texts to be used in undergraduate education. The material so produced has been used in the program of the Columbia University Committee on Oriental Studies and has subsequently been revised and expanded for publication in the present form.

While the book has been written with the thought that a new single text for a short course of study would be useful, it need not be read from cover to cover. Most courses follow a historical outline of some sort, such as is presented in the first half of the book, but points and subjects of emphasis vary from course to course. The topical essays in the second half of the book offer a choice of subjects from which selections may be made to suit different needs. Nor need the book be the only source of reading, though it can stand on its own if necessary. One particular subject for complementary reading, for example, would be the thinkers, for they have been given little space in proportion to their intrinsic interest, partly in the knowledge that a growing number of good source readings are now in print. More generally, almost any topic touched on in the book may seem to someone worth pursuing further. The reader is directed to J. Mason Gentzler, *A Syllabus of Chinese Civilization* (Columbia University Press, 1968), which includes descriptions of other textbooks and suggestions for additional reading.

Among those who helped to make the book better are Professor Gentzler, who edited various drafts of the first three chapters and several of the topical chapters; Laura Doeringer, who corrected many infelicities of style in the course of typing the successive drafts; and Johanna M. Meskill, who provided perspective, from her breadth of knowledge and ideas, for the planning of the book.

J.M.

Most of the Chinese words used in this book are spelled according to the Wade-Giles system, which is the most common system of romanizing standard, or Mandarin, Chinese. Each word is pronounced as one syllable. When there is a combination of vowels, they are sounded as diphthongs: ai like my, ao like cow, iao like miaow, ei like day, and ou like low.

The Vowels:
   a as in father
   e as u in up
   i as in ring
   o at the end of a word, usually as o in lofty
   u as oo in moo; much shortened as a final following the double conso-
      nants ss, sz, tz, or tz'
   ih rather like a New Englander's ending of "Americer"

The Consonants: Pronounced generally as in English, with the exception of a group that may be aspirated or unaspirated, indicated by the presence or absence of the ' sign.

ch'	as in char	ch as in jar
k'	as in kill	k as in gill
p'	as in pat	p as in bat
t'	as in tell	t as in dell
ts'		ts
tz'	as in knots	tz as in nods
j	is something like English r	
hs	is something like English sh	

Contents

AN INTRODUCTION
TO CHINESE
CIVILIZATION

PART ONE

History of China

BY

JOHN MESKILL

I

*Ancient Times
and Classical
Period*

Prehistory

Long before the rise of *Homo sapiens,* or man as we now know him, manlike creatures were living in China. The most ancient remains thus far found in China by modern archaeologists, the bones of Peking man (*Sinanthropus Pekinensis*), found in a cave in the village of Chou-k'ou-tien about 30 miles southwest of present-day Peking, date from something like 350,000 or 400,000 years ago. Peking man was what is called a hominid, on the evolutionary scale somewhere between the "highest" apes and *Homo sapiens.* He is distinguished from other hominids in that he possessed and used fire, but his cranial capacity was considerably less than that of *Homo sapiens.* (For a fuller discussion of Peking man and the evolution of early culture, see Chapter XIII.) Although Peking man had some physical traits resembling traits common among present-day Mongoloid peoples, and not usually found among non-Mongoloid peoples, it cannot be assumed, as has been done by many patriotic Chinese historians, that the history of the Chinese people's occupation of the territory now known as China began with Peking man. We know too little of the early history of man to make any firm generalizations. In the case of China, this is all the more true since there are no direct links between Peking man and the next oldest traces of man, which date from about 20,000-10,000 B.C., and show not only Mongoloid traits, but Caucasoid and Negroid traits as well. The verifiable history of the Chinese people begins with the Neolithic period, when they occupied a large area of north China. How they came to be there is still unknown.

Between them and Peking man came the Ice Age, and thereafter great winds from Central Asia, which scoured up vast quantities of earth and deposited them in dust storms over north China. This seems to have been the origin of the fine, powdery yellow earth, called loess, which covers much of north China, although another explanation that has been offered is that the loess may originally have been deposited by the Yellow River, and carried south and east by winds.

At any rate, the earliest communities appeared along the middle reaches of the great Yellow River, and some of its tributaries. In the Neolithic period, this part of China was warmer and moister than it is now, and thus suitable for the farming communities that grew up there. To the north were steppes that thinned to deserts, and forested hills that rose to mountains, colder, drier, and steeper than the Yellow River valley. The terrain to the south was more mountainous, interspersed with plains and rich alluvial valleys, later to become the most important agricultural region of the empire, but at first perhaps more difficult to penetrate and hold against natural dangers and rival tribes. Geography alone is no doubt insufficient to explain why a civilization began where it did, but in China the Yellow River valley offered advantages easy to see.

The long, preliminary phase of that civilization in the Neolithic period, perhaps 10,000 years ago, had one important result, that the Chinese were farmers from the very beginning, as we know it. Gradually, over centuries of experience, farming became a great anchor of the civilization, in its mental as well as its physical life, helping to establish the feeling of a fundamental cultural thread connecting one age to another. Moreover, discovering the Chinese as farmers at the very beginning of the archaeological record suggests an originality in the civilization, for there is no good evidence of an earlier pastoral phase or of an epoch-making invasion of foreigners, with the different culture that would imply. Chinese civilization seems to have grown essentially in accordance with a spirit of its own, even though it received stimulation from outside both before and after history began.

This is not to say that China was always the same culturally. Variations thrived, among regions and through time, beginning with the Neolithic Age. The earliest culture that we can identify was named the Yang-shao culture, after a key site, by the modern archaeologists who discovered it. It is also known as the Painted Pottery culture, after the style of pottery, covered with geometric designs, that is one of its chief characteristics. It was succeeded by the Lung-shan culture, again named after an important site discovered in the twentieth century. Slash and burn agriculture was replaced by methods that permitted more permanent settlements, including villages surrounded by walls of stamped earth similar to those that later were to be so typical of Chinese villages and cities. Wells were dug to provide the water necessary for the settlements. This new culture is also known as the Black Pottery culture, after the thin-walled black clay vessels that are associated with it, which, although different in weight and color from the painted pottery, are found in many shapes and forms similar to the earlier pottery, thus attesting to continuity as well as change. Other traits of the Lung-shan culture are domesticated animals, some of which date from Yang-shao times, and the practice of scapulimancy, or use of scapulae or collar bones of cattle, or other bones, to predict the future. This was done by applying a hot, pointed instrument to the bone, making it crack. The cracks were then interpreted, presumably by some sort of priest, to divine the future. As we shall see, scapulimancy is an important link between the Neolithic settlements and the succeeding Bronze Age.

The Emergence of History: The Shang Dynasty (ca. 1523-1122 B.C.)

The archaeological evidence just reviewed records the prehistory of China. It was not discovered until the twentieth century, and hence was never a part of the traditional Chinese view of their own history. The next period, the Bronze Age, is both found in the traditional Chinese historical record and confirmed by modern archaeological discoveries.

The material civilization of China followed the sequence common elsewhere in the prehistoric world. A Paleolithic Age, marked by the existence of hominids using crudely altered stones as tools, was succeeded by a Mesolithic and then a Neolithic Age of *Homo sapiens* living in village communities, making utensils of clay, and possessing refined tools and domesticated animals. As elsewhere, too, in China the Neolithic Age was followed by the Bronze Age. The manufacture of bronze was known much earlier both in western Asia and in the Indus valley culture of northwest India. The earliest evidence of bronze in China appears in the Shang dynasty, the first dynasty for which we have archaeological evidence, although, according to traditional Chinese accounts, the Shang was preceded by a Hsia dynasty, for which no evidence has yet been found.

Of the origins of the Shang, we have no sure knowledge. The cities that have been unearthed, the capital city of An-yang in present-day northern Honan and two other major cities, plus dozens of smaller settlements, all provide evidence of a civilization developed remarkably beyond anything previously known in China. Of these urban centers, it is convenient to turn first to the one in the vicinity of Chang-chou, in northern Honan, where excavations have provided enough evidence to permit a fairly complete material history of the site. Two preliminary stages show objects resembling objects associated with the Lung-shan culture mixed with others just as clearly belonging to the new Shang culture. These seem to indicate a transitional period. A third period followed, marked by a sudden enlargement of the scale of the settlement. A city wall, estimated to average 30 feet in height and 60 feet in width, surrounded the settlement, forming a rough rectangle, about 2,385 feet in perimeter, enclosing an area of about one and one-quarter square miles. It has been estimated that it would have taken 10,000 workers 18 years to build this wall, which suggests that, although the level of technology was low, the Chinese had already devised effective methods of organizing manpower.

Within the walls was, apparently, an administrative and ceremonial center, which, if we can generalize from the pattern of An-yang (for here the evidence of Chang-chou is as yet inadequate), included rectangular houses, as large as 80 feet by 24 feet, built on stamped earth foundations with wooden pillars and divided into halls and rooms. These were the mansions of the rulers and nobility, and perhaps a few were temples. Outside the city walls were other residences, and workshops, including bronze foundries, pottery kilns, bone and stone workshops, and possibly a winery.

For historical study, the most fruitful objects found at Shang sites, preponderantly at the capital of An-yang, are tens of thousands of bones, used for scapulimancy. Unlike the bones found at Lung-shan sites, these are inscribed; they are the earliest examples of Chinese script. The questions asked by the diviner were written on the bones before heat was applied, and sometimes after the bone had been cracked and interpreted the answer was recorded on it. The most usual questions dealt with weather, or the outcome of hunting excursions, journeys, ceremonies, or battles. Combining the rich store of information derived from the oracle bones with the material yielded by archaeological excavations, we can hazard a sketch of the life of the rulers, the nobility, and the people of Shang times, and of Shang religion.

RULERSHIP

The highest ceremonial and administrative power resided in a king, who came from one royal house. The succession was hereditary in this house, most frequently passing to a son, but also often to a brother. The king and the royal family, as well as other hereditary nobles and priests, lived and worked in the center of one of the Shang settlements. We know that there were a number of capitals, of which An-yang was one of the later ones. The most important function of the ruling family seems to have been conducting religious sacrifices, principally to the royal ancestors. Major ceremonies, such as the burials of kings, sometimes included human sacrifices. The principal celebrant in the sacrifices may have been the king himself, advised by more specialized priests, presumably those who divined with the oracle bones.

A second occupation of the ruling nobles was warfare, for conflict with other peoples was frequent. The nobles fought with spears and bows and arrows from horse-drawn chariots. While the chariots no doubt made the most powerful striking force, the bulk of the armies consisted of footmen, frequently 3,000 to 5,000 strong. Captives became either slaves or sacrifices. During times of peace, the nobles used their chariots for hunting expeditions.

The third major function of the nobles was administration. The Shang domain contained many settlements besides the one in which the ruler lived. Each of these was in the charge of a lord, often a relative of the king or a great lieutenant, rewarded for his meritorious services to the ruling house, or else a local magnate of sufficient independent strength to encourage the king to sanction his *de facto* power, in return for which he sent tribute to the king. Such tribute, we may assume, was expected of all such subject settlements. What other obligations they had toward the ruler is not clear.

But it is clear that the essential form of government was a limited monarchy, which delegated in some fashion considerable authority over outlying parts of the realm to others. Distances within the Shang territory were not so great as to preclude a rather close communication, but, as more territories were added, there probably appeared a slackening of solidarity along with a diminution of the coercive power of the king. In short, the system was not suited to controlling a large territory under a single authority.

THE PEOPLE

We know little of the ruling class, but much less of the artisans and peasants who comprised the vast majority of the population. Artisans, especially bronze craftsmen, seem to have been esteemed by the ruling class, for, although their residences lay outside the city walls, some of them, though smaller than the residences of the nobles, were of considerable size and also built on stamped earth foundations. The technical craftsmanship of the bronze workers can be seen from the extant pieces from their hands. One vessel found at An-yang weighed 1,500 pounds; others are delicate works of a few ounces. The casting and fitting of the parts was so precise that until recently it was believed each vessel had been cast as a whole. Incised decorations were cut so surely that they remain sharp today. (For a more detailed discussion of the bronzes, see Chapter XIV.) In addition to these ceremonial vessels, the bronze workers made chariot fittings and weapons.

Somewhat farther from the city walls than the artisans' quarters were villages and hamlets of farmers. The farmers lived in round or rectangular semisubterranean houses, from nine to fifteen feet in diameter, which were entered by a flight of descending steps. To the extent that the size of the houses suggests the size of the families, we are drawn to the conclusion that farming families were much smaller than those of the nobles, a difference which we know to have existed in later times.

The farmers planted millet, rice, and wheat, and cultivated them with hoes, spades, and sickles of stone, as well as with a wooden digging stick that may have been the ancestor of the plow. The crops were probably irrigated, although as yet no extensive irrigation system has been discovered. Farming seems to have been a common effort of the entire village rather than the work of separate individuals or households. Two crops were harvested a year, a good yield even by modern standards.

Of the animals of the farming economy, the pigs, dogs, cattle, sheep, horses, and chickens had been domesticated in earlier times, and the water buffalo was added in Shang times. The farmers also fished.

SHANG RELIGION

Inscriptions on the oracle bones and on some of the bronzes, supplemented by other revelations of archaeology, enable us to draw a general outline of the religion of the Shang rulers.

Important events were believed to depend on the assistance or cooperation of spirits or gods. Most of them were probably gods of nature, such as spirits of the river, the sky, the wind, and so forth, perhaps numbering in the hundreds. Other gods, such as the Eastern Mother or the Western Mother, are more mysterious. In general, three types of gods stand out prominently: the royal ancestors, the earth, and Shang-ti.

The Shang rulers sacrificed to their ancestors more often than to any other gods, from which we can see that the ancestor worship for which Chinese civilization is famous was already firmly established. Next to animism (the belief that spirit-forces reside in objects of nature), ancestor worship has been one of the world's most common forms of religion. It has seemed to many people, trying to explain what happened after death, that when those close to them had lost their breath, color, and movement, their life force or spirit must have gone elsewhere, and it was concluded that this spirit needed care after it joined the gods, just as it had when it inhabited the now lifeless body. Moreover, it was believed that the spirit could aid the living, especially those who had formerly been close to it. The Shang rulers sacrificed, that is, they ritually offered some substance presumed to be desired by the ancestors, such as animals or drink, in return for which they requested material blessings from the spirits. Later ancestor worship was less flagrantly materialistic, but it became if anything stronger in its symbolic sense, that of the primary role of the family in the life of the sacrificer.

Judging from evidence of a somewhat later period, in Shang times the Chinese sacrificed to spirits of the earth wherever a social grouping was established. There were gods of the hearth, of the locality, and of larger domains as well. In later times these gods of the earth were symbolized by earthen mounds. The Shang rulers, at the top of the social and political pyramid, sacrificed to Earth, thus confirming their authority over the whole Shang territory. The belief that the ruling house in some way was the possessor of the territory of the empire never disappeared in later times, and from time to time affected questions of property and of the relationship between the state and its subjects.

The third important object of sacrifices was a god known as Shang-ti. The meaning of the term, and thus the significance of the god, is unclear. *Ti* may have meant "ruler" or "sacrifice." *Shang* means "upper" or "above." Some scholars think that Shang-ti may have been the sacrifice itself deified and placed above the other gods, similar to the deification of the sacrifice in ancient India. Others suggest that Shang-ti was the first ancestor of the Shang ruling house. Shang-ti seems to have been especially concerned with warfare and the crops, both obviously of the greatest importance. Like the royal ancestors and Earth, Shang-ti accepted sacrifice from the kings alone.

It is apparent that the Shang religion implied great authority for the ruler, a theoretical authority which, from the evidence available, does not seem to have been translated into equivalent administrative power over the whole of the Shang domain. Moreover, this power was based on kinship ties, which were bound to diminish in solidarity as new territories and new peoples came under Shang rule. It was the task of the next period of Chinese history to produce a better system of government for the ever-expanding territory of China.

China's Classical Age: The Chou Dynasty (ca. 1122-256 B.C.)

A combination of internal weakness and invasion by a stronger force, the Chou people, led to the downfall of the Shang. The picture of the Chou before their conquest of the Shang is deep in shadow. For some four generations they lived west of the Shang domains in the Wei valley in modern Shensi, behind mountain passes that looked down on the north China plain. Some of their customs differed from the Shang (for example, they buried their noble dead in earthen pyramids rather than pits), but on the whole the similarities were deeper than the differences. Indeed, strata of Yang-shao and Lung-shan cultures have been found beneath Chou remains, showing that before the conquest as after it the Chou was more of a continuation than an innovation.

According to later accounts, three great leaders brought Chou to glory. King Wen (The Cultivated) consolidated Chou power in the Wei valley and planned the campaign against the Shang. His son, King Wu (The Martial), directed the campaign leading the Chou to victory. After his death, his brother, the Duke of Chou, governed as regent for the infant son of King Wu. By about 1122 B.C. (according to one tradition; another commonly used date is 1027 B.C.) the Chou had taken the Shang capital and reduced the ruling family to subject nobles. The Chou conquest soon extended beyond the limits of the former Shang territories, especially in the east and south, creating a kingdom larger than that which had previously existed.

The Chou period (ca. 1122-256 B.C.) has conventionally been subdivided in a way that corresponds to the successive reduction of the power of the Chou kings:

1. Western Chou 1122-771 B.C.   Subject nobles installed by Chou kings.

2. Eastern Chou 771-256 B.C.   Independent political power of regional nobles sanctioned by Chou kings.

a. Spring and Autumn   Title of a chronicle of the period cov-
   Period 722-481 B.C.   ering these years.
b. Warring States   Name taken from the history of the
   Period 403-221 B.C.   period.

WESTERN CHOU (1122-771 B.C.)

After the conquest, the Chou, like the Shang, assigned different regions (according to one tradition, 70 new states) to members of the ruling family, lieutenants, and existing rulers who promised obedience. The king expected the local ruler to see that the land was put to agriculture, to send periodic tribute and pay periodic attendance at court, and to provide armed assistance when needed. Beyond that, the lord went pretty much his own way. The king had little machinery of control, since an army large enough to control all of north China required methods of organization not yet devised. The major source of unity remained the feeling of solidarity of the regional lords with the ruling house. Yet both space and time worked against this solidarity.

The organization of society within the domains, too, probably resembled that of Shang times, the noble lord keeping a staff of fighting men, who also assisted in administration. They must usually have lived in the walled enclosures apart from the farmers, and enjoyed distinctive social and economic privileges, but in some instances the gap between the lower ranks of the military and the plebeians may not have been very wide.

The lord possessed certain fields which the farmers worked under the supervision of his bailiff, tilling the lord's lands before turning to whatever plots they had themselves. They produced a varied diet and other products: two kinds of millet, rice, wheat, hemp, beans, dates, melons, gourds, and vegetables, as well as silkworms; they also kept sheep and cattle.

THE QUESTION OF FEUDALISM

The question whether there are universal patterns in history has long interested thinkers and scholars. In recent years, some of them have asked whether or not China ever passed through a feudal period essentially like that of Europe. Certain characteristics of the Western Chou period were similar to important features of European feudalism: dependence on personal loyalties, decentralized administration of territories by appointment, and fragmented political and economic authority in the hands of a minority of warriors over a majority of peasants. Any closer comparison runs up against the lack of unanimity among experts about the essential characteristics of European feudalism.

Other features were different. The ties between lord and vassal in the Chou, unlike those of Europe, did not develop as a system separate from kinship but rather, on the whole, resulted from kinship. At the outset the Chou system sprang from a superior authority and, as long as this authority lasted, was probably more hierarchical and systematic than the European system. In the Chou, the small group of rulers possessed not only political and economic authority, but religious power as well, unlike medieval Europe, where in varying degrees there were separate oligarchies of priests and warriors. Again, while in both cases lord-vassal ties were meant to maintain social order, the origin, symbols, and material support of these ties differed. The European lord and vassal bound themselves to one another, at least in the beginning, by a voluntary, contractual association, symbolized by gestures (the joining of hands and a kiss), and the subordinate was given a fief by the lord in return for his promised service. The tie being voluntary and personal, it could be broken under certain circumstances, including, of course, at the latest the death of one of the men, and elaborate stipulations of the conditions of the relationship eventually were formulated. On the other hand, in the Chou case, the superior and his subordinate were bound by blood-ties, rather than by voluntary agreement, and the relationship was symbolized by a sacrifice to the common ancestors of the family. The gift of land to the subordinate as a fief seems to have been more like a division of responsibility by a family elder. The differences between the two systems seem too great for them to be considered essentially of the same type.

CHOU IDEAS AND SOCIETY

Aside from military power, the communities of the Chou were held together by subtler bonds—the ceremonies tying them to the gods. As in the Shang, the gods worshiped most often were the ancestors of the nobles. Sacrifice to the ancestor was a means through which concrete satisfactions were requested—long life, pious sons (so that the family and the sacrifice might be continued), a girl to produce sons, and many kinds of material rewards. Essential to the success of the ceremony, in addition to sacrificial food and drink, were perfect ritual manners. Performing the rites without the slightest mistake was the best way to communicate with the spirits.

In addition to the ancestors, there were other gods. For the Chou rulers, one diety seemed supreme. This was Heaven (*t'ien*), the origin of which is unclear. Perhaps he was a great man, or the first ancestor, who after departing from the world ascended to the sky and became identified as Heaven, gradually becoming to some extent an abstract force. The old Shang god, Shang-ti, apparently struck the Chou as being the same as Heaven, and they used both terms. Heaven gave a mandate to rule, and could withdraw it if the ruler behaved improperly or immorally, as had the last king of Shang. This is the core concept of the theory of the Mandate of Heaven, so immensely important in later political thought. The highest authority was ascribed to Heaven, not to men, and Heaven could either bestow or revoke its mandate according to its evaluation of the conduct of the officers to whom the government of men had been entrusted—conduct both in the performance of the sacrifices to Heaven and in behavior as rulers of men. Thus two important means to insure order in the polity were postulated: order by strict adherence to ritual, and order by the personal character of the ruler as reflected in his behavior.

EASTERN CHOU (771-256 B.C.)

The traditional version of the end of the Western Chou illustrates these ideas. Like earlier kings, the Chou king in 771 had a number of wives, probably a principal one and several secondary ones, which was the usual arrangement. He was so infatuated with one of these wives that he spent most of his time thinking of ways to amuse her, and found that she liked to see his subject lords come marching to the capital with their armies when he lit the military warning beacons. Therefore he lit the beacons so often that when barbarian armies really did invade the country and the king lighted the beacons in earnest, the disgusted subject lords simply stayed at home. The defenseless court was forced to flee east, where it established its new capital in the area of modern Loyang. The moral of the story was: irresponsibility breeds disaster.

The Western and Eastern Chou differed in more than the location of the capital. During the Eastern Chou, the regional lords no longer obeyed the Chou kings. Although the kings were not overthrown, their domain became the smallest in the land. They were not entirely ignored, and continued to perform some religious functions, but the regional lords decided policy questions without consulting them. The Chou kings retained the practice of confirming new lords to the succession in their lands, but they had no say in determining who actually succeeded; they merely acknowledged the *de facto* successor. Nevertheless, this power to bestow legitimacy on a ruler, which depended on the Mandate of Heaven of which the Chou house was the custodian, shows the persistence of the religious factor in Chou rule, and helps to explain why the powerless Chou kings were not overthrown sooner. The religious sanction was valued, or perhaps feared, for the Chou kings, though largely ignored and helpless, remained the titular chiefs of the kingdom for over 500 years after their flight to the east.

With the decline of the Chou house, the significant development of Chinese institutions shifted to the regional domains, or states, as they now came to be called. We can see this in the names of the two subdivisions of the Eastern Chou period. The first, The Spring and Autumn period (722-481 B.C.), is named after the title of a chronicle of the state of Lu, in present-day Shantung. The chronicle, attributed to the most famous native son, Confucius, records events by the seasons—spring, summer, autumn, winter—and two seasons are used in the title *Spring and Autumn Annals* as an abbreviated suggestion of the chronological organization of the work. Other states had similar chronicles, which have not been preserved. The central role of the states appears even more clearly in the name of the second subdivision of the Eastern Chou, the Warring States period (403-221 B.C.). A suggestion of another characteristic of this period is found in the title of a famous book of the period: *The Intrigues of the Warring States.*

For the rulers of these states, the maintenance and enlargement of their territories, mostly at the expense of other states, were the great preoccupations. The usual way of pursuing these grand goals was war, although efforts were sometimes made to avoid this. At times one of the most powerful rulers would designate himself *pa* (hegemon or overlord), and pretend to superintend some of the states on the authority of the Chou king. Sometimes alliances were formed in an attempt to achieve a peaceful equilibrium of power. The efforts were largely unsuccessful, however, for peace was valued less than new territory. For almost five centuries only one year in four was free of warfare among the major states.

Warfare was not only frequent; its scale constantly grew. During the Eastern Chou the major states increased their fighting power many times over. Armies had numbered roughly 3,000 to 5,000 men in Shang times, but they sometimes reached 10,000 in the Spring and Autumn period, a growth the more significant because there were more armies in the Chou than there had been during the Shang. Yet this growth was modest compared to what happened during the Warring States period, when armies may have numbered as many as several hundred thousand men. To the growing size of the armies was added, sometime around the end of the Spring and Autumn period, additional power in the form of cavalry. The idea of mounting men on horses for speed and maneuverability apparently came first to the northwestern states from their chronic enemies, the nomads of the north. The mounted warrior, armed with the old Chinese compound bow and a new invention, the powerful crossbow, put an end to the majestic but clumsy war chariot. At about the same time (the exact dates of these innovations are not known, but it is perhaps best to think of them as occurring in the fifth century B.C.) iron began to be worked, providing heavier and stronger weapons and more of them. The larger, more mobile, better equipped armies were effectively employed by commanders who devoted their minds to the science of warfare. About 500 B.C. a strategist and tactician named Sun Tzu wrote a short work, *The Art of War (Ping-fa)*, a compact treatise on the principles of warfare, which in later generations was followed by other works on the same subject. Warfare was obviously very much on the minds of the ruling class.

The remarkable changes of the period were not limited to military matters, nor is it likely that military requirements determined all the other changes. Changes in one sphere, whether military, administrative, technological, or intellectual, affected other spheres. Perhaps one underlying condition favoring change was the uncertainty each state felt about its own survival in a community of roughly equal, independent states, most of them ambitious. Ambition led to growth in the size of many states through incorporating new lands on the frontiers and through gobbling up other, usually smaller, states. At the beginning of the Spring and Autumn period there were probably over 100 states; at the end, about 40. Less than a century later, at the beginning of the Warring States period, there were seven important states. At the end there was only one. Even before the number was reduced to seven, some of the states were quite large, with territories the size of Ohio or France, capital cities of perhaps tens of thousands, and total populations of hundreds of thousands of people.

*Bronze figure of a man of the
Warring States Period.*

Cities, which previously had comprised religious and administrative centers within a walled compound, around which specialized manufacturing quarters were grouped, began to enclose their specialized suburbs as well as residential and commercial sections within the walled areas. This suggests that the state recognized the increased importance of certain manufacturing and commercial activities. Walls of vaster scale also began to appear along the borders of some states, in particular those facing the nomadic and predatory northern tribes. The border walls testify to a capacity for great works projects. This can also be seen in irrigation canals in some of the states. Irrigation was a sign that new means of increasing crops had begun to be developed, perhaps owing to the intense rivalry among the states and the realization that there was a connection between agricultural productivity and the political and military power necessary for survival.

Administration began to be restructured to increase the control of the lord and his staff over the entire state. These changes were in the direction of "rationalization," that is, increasing the central adminis-

17

tration's ability to pursue its aims, which implied the end of the former decentralized system. One change of lasting consequence was the substitution of appointive offices for hereditary ones. In a hypothetical model domain at the beginning of the Western Chou, the lord of the domain ruled with the aid of high ministers, great officers, and perhaps some "knights," all of whom were members of his family, a collateral family, or a family which had old and close ties with his own. The high ministers and great officers or their families received a city or a region from the lord as a fief. In turn, knights may have received portions of land from the high ministers and great officers. These holdings were transmitted hereditarily, the lord merely confirming the inheritors in their right.

The Eastern Chou introduced the principle of appointment to office to replace the previous hereditary principle. Perhaps beginning slightly before the fifth century B.C., and continuing through the fourth and third centuries, lords (or ministers who had become the real powers in all but name) slowly acquired a central staff and regional force of officials who served by appointment. New activities, such as the building of walls and canals, may have provided opportunities for appointments to new offices, which at first existed side by side with the old hereditary ones, and then slowly encroached on their functions. New territory, either virgin land on the frontier or conquered lands, had to be administered, and into such areas the newer forms of administration might be introduced. At the capital and elsewhere new kinds of office titles began to appear, indicating the growth of a staff divided according to functions, signifying the beginnings of bureaucracy. All this was done to enable the rulers of the states to pursue their goals more efficiently. At the same time, although office by appointment eventually became the standard practice, and the Chinese bureaucracy became one of the most thoughtfully devised, the principle of inherited right to at least some positions was never eliminated.

Another administrative change dating from about the fifth century was the beginning of regular taxation. In earlier times, apparently, a noble's income was the produce of the land he administered, plus "tribute" or gifts he received from subordinate nobles. The landed nobles apparently received the produce of their farmers, and clothed, housed, fed, and equipped the farmers in return, although it is also possible that farmers had plots of land from which they were expected to provide for themselves. By the fifth century the farmer's delivery of all or most of his produce to the noble, and the noble's delivery of goods of a certain value to the lord, had begun to give way to the payment to the superior of an amount of goods depending on the amount of land held, or the size of the annual yield of that land. The earlier "tribute" of the noble and delivery made by the peasant were replaced by a tax or rent. This varied according to time and place; in the region of Shantung, for example, the payment was said to be normally 20 percent of the yield.

To pay a proportion of the wealth at one's disposal implied that one was an owner, a radical change for the farmer, who had formerly appeared to be himself a possession, incapable of possessing anything. For the noble the change was hardly less radical, since it implied, or could be taken to imply, that he was being paid for something, either a service or the use of his land, rather than merely receiving tribute. Although it would be an exaggeration to say that this clearly was the beginning of a concept of private ownership of land, there was, since a tax on land or its produce replaced service or tribute, no objection to the sale of the land to anyone who would continue to pay the tax; in fact, records show that land began to be bought and sold at about the same time that taxes first appeared.

From the point of view of the government, a tax or rent on land promised a more regular revenue, for a schedule of amounts or percentages due from specific plots could be established. At the same time, revenue collection would be better guaranteed since specific families could be held responsible for individual plots. In addition, the farmers assumed the obligation of feeding, clothing, and housing themselves. At some point, it must also have been observed that men were more productive when they regarded the land and its fruits as their own.

These innovations brought pronounced changes in the fortunes of the different classes. We know least about the peasantry, but it seems likely that the increasing variety of crops and methods to increase production, combined with the buying and selling of land, brought about a wider range of wealth and poverty among farmers than had previously existed. Some may have found themselves landless and impoverished, while others may have been able to accumulate enough land to afford them a comparatively comfortable life. We have scarcely more evidence concerning the artisan class, which does not seem to have changed greatly since earlier times, although the fact that the industrial suburbs of the cities were now enclosed within the city walls seems to indicate that the services of the artisans were valued by the city officials.

There were marked changes in the life of the merchants. Rarely mentioned in earlier times, they seem to have flourished in Eastern Chou. In the cities there were quarters with shops dealing in jewelry, fabrics, furs, foods, and other goods, as well as inns, restaurants, and brothels. The widespread use of copper coins beginning in the sixth and fifth centuries is an indication of the interest that governments were taking in commerce. Officials had discovered the merchants as a source of revenue for the state. The relationship between commercial wealth and the state was to become a vexing and complicated issue in Chinese history.

Generally, shifting conditions were most detrimental to the nobility. Although glory attended the lord who conquered his neighbors, demotion or disgrace awaited him who did not. Developments within the individual states often endangered the nobility's position. The tendency toward filling offices by appointment rather than through heredity meant that the nobility had to compete with others for positions in the government.

The lowest group of the nobility, the class of knights (*shih*), benefited most from the changing conditions, which gave them an opportunity to demonstrate their abilities in warfare and in the expanding governmental bureaucracies. Many knights rose in rank, some to positions customarily held by members of the upper nobility, whom they began to replace. It is thought that the chief reason for their rise was their special competence in administration.

Among the knights were men who saw in the issues of the time much more than administrative problems. What was needed, some asserted, was wisdom, and they offered themselves as teachers and advisers. In large measure, Chinese philosophy was founded upon the ideas they expressed, and it is to these that we now turn our attention.

The Classical Age: The Philosophers

The instability and chaos that pervaded China in the Warring States period troubled many thoughtful men. They saw their states challenged by powerful neighbors and weakened by poverty and disloyalty within. It seemed to them that the Eastern Chou had fallen far below the condition of order and contentment they attributed to an earlier, ideal age. They were thus more concerned about social and political questions than about higher abstractions such as Nature, the universe, or Pure Being, and this concern set the tone for most of later Chinese thought.

Most of the philosophers whose works have survived traveled from state to state offering their services to rulers or, as teachers, expounding their views when their ambitions of government service were frustrated. Their main ideas are introduced briefly below. For a fuller account of the effects of some of them on later society, see chapter XXI. For treatments of the schools of thought as creeds, see the "Note on Bibliography and Selected Readings."

LEGALISM

The most influential thinking in Eastern Chou, although it appeared as a coherent doctrine later than other schools, was Legalism (*fa-chia*), the emphasis of which is suggested by two translations of its name: the School of Systems and the School of Methods. The Legalists were concerned wholly with making the state a powerful instrument for achieving whatever the ruler desired. They were primarily interested not in what the goals of the ruler were (although they usually assumed them to be the creation of a strong and aggressive state), but in methods of achieving them.

As a fundamental means they proposed techniques of concentrating the power of the state in the ruler's hands so that he could control everyone else. A major principle was that of the "Two Handles," by which the ruler was to steer his subjects as he wished. The two handles were proportional rewards and harsh punishments. In theory, by consistently using these handles, he would make his ministers perform their duties precisely. In practice, severe punishments for relatively minor misdemeanors seem to have been more frequent than rich rewards for work well done. In any event, the principle appealed to two presumably basic human drives: greed and fear.

In order that rewards and punishments might determine everyone's actions, it was necessary to define standards against which to measure performance. The second major element of the Legalist scheme was therefore laws and regulations, clearly setting out everyone's duties and prescribing strict penalties for failure to perform them. For the Legalists, law was not the supreme authority in the state but an instrument of the ruler. They realised that no large state could be governed rationally without clearly stated standards and sanctions to protect these standards. In imperial China law became an important element in government, not as an authority to which the ruling dynasty was subject, but as a body of directions by which it controlled the people.

In concentrating on fear and greed, the Legalists largely ignored other human traits, such as faith, intelligence, or loyalty. They rejected the concept that actions should be judged according to standards established by the ancient sages, since circumstances changed with the times, and what had been right centuries before was not necessarily right forever. To prevent any disagreement about what was right, they would suppress ways of thought that differed from the ruler's. They were especially sensitive to the forms that political power could take. Any group whose interests might conflict with the ruler's, such as professional philosophers, high officials, palace women, or the ruler's own family, had to be either eliminated or carefully watched. Under their doctrines religious and familial solidarity declined as the basis of power, and a new, single-minded search for methods to increase the power of the government arose.

One of the most famous Legalists in action was Lord Shang, or Shang Yang (d. 338 B.C.), minister of the state of Ch'in and responsible for a great growth of power in that state. Lord Shang vigorously encouraged farming, weaving, and a warlike spirit among the people through the use of rewards and punishments. He is said to have abolished the old, manorial divisions of land and assigned land to individual farming families, to insure that the state would benefit through taxes from the increased productivity. Among the strict laws and regulations he promulgated was a system of joint responsibility. The people were divided into groups of five and ten households, each of which was responsible for the behavior of each individual member.

Under Shang Yang, Ch'in grew rich and strong, but after the death of its ruler, the patron of Lord Shang, some of the many enemies Lord Shang had made by his ruthless measures had him tied to two chariots and torn apart. A century later, when the Ch'in tried to enforce Legalist policies throughout the empire it had created, it too was torn apart by men who had suffered from the harshness of the Legalist system.

The most coherent statement of the Legalist theory came a century after Shang Yang, in the writings of Han Fei Tzu (d. 233 B.C.). For him the goal of the state was wealth and power, to be pursued with a singleness of purpose by the means already described. He warned, with a vividness and an air of cool cynicism that make his writings fascinating, of the dangers of human feelings. Han Fei Tzu seems to have believed that men could be controlled and manipulated like marionettes by rewards and punishments. The failure of the Legalists to acknowledge how complicated human beings are, and to foresee situations in which immediate material self-interest might be overridden by other considerations, weakened their theory. Nevertheless, Legalism, which made important discoveries about the psychology and mechanisms of power, had a great appeal to rulers. Thus Legalist ideas were to be influential throughout Chinese history. Both severe punishments and lavish rewards, for instance, found important places in later Chinese government, perhaps owing to the force and clarity of Legalist arguments.

THE CONFUCIANISTS AND THE CLASSICS

Preoccupied with the strengthening of the state, which they believed could be achieved exclusively through pragmatic means, the Legalists appealed little to any love of continuity, legitimacy, or ethical vision. In just these areas Confucius and his followers made their profound and lasting contribution to Chinese life.

What we call Confucianism the Chinese call the learning of *ju*, a word of very uncertain derivation, meaning at first something like "unwarlikeness," which may have set its followers off sharply in a class of professional warriors. Later, the word was applied to those who devoted themselves to certain classical books, specifically to the followers of Confucius.

The distinguishing marks of Confucian thought can be seen in the character of the Confucianists. They were, first, private teachers and scholars, which is to say that they put great value on knowledge of the records of the past. They taught the sons of the aristocracy, the *chün-tzu* (literally, sons of the rulers), to prepare them for the exercise of the authority that was theirs by heredity. Second, therefore, the Confucianists were aristocrats, legitimists, and conservatives. Finally, they envisaged the fruit of their teaching to be great, moral men, who by their efforts and example would return society to the halcyon state of harmony and peace that they asserted had existed in a previous Golden Age. The Confucianists were thus humanists and visionaries. They appealed to what was noble in their audience—a belief in individual perfectibility and in the merits of the ruling class, and a vision of an ideal society. In this way, the Confucianists were reformers, for they realized that much had deteriorated since an earlier more peaceful time, and hence that, in order to restore the earlier conditions, great changes had to be made. The approach and recommendations of the Confucianists may be considered in connection with the three major figures of classical Confucianism, beginning with the Master himself.

Confucius. Very little is known of Confucius. The traditionally accepted dates of his life are 551-479 B.C. He was a native of the state of Lu (in present-day Shantung), traditionally the domain of his hero, the Duke of Chou. Confucius belonged to the class of knights, perhaps to the highest level, though apparently his family was poor. His greatest ambition was to advise a ruler, but he attained only a modest appointment as a criminal judge in the latter part of his life, and exerted far more influence as a teacher than as an official, even in his own lifetime. He lived to be more than seventy, but felt that he had achieved complete development only at that advanced age.

The major source of the teachings that spread so far is a slim collection of brief sayings, the *Analects* (*Lun-yü*), part of which was put together perhaps a century after Confucius' death.

Confucian comment on society and politics begins with the assertion that conditions had once been much better. For Confucius, this had been half a millenium earlier, in the time of King Wen, King Wu, and the Duke of Chou, and, still earlier, Yao and Shun, figures who do not appear in writings before Confucius' time but are represented thenceforth as sage rulers of great antiquity. According to the *Analects* they, like the early Chou rulers, reigned over a society which was practically perfect. Confucius, although he asserted that he was no innovator, merely a transmitter of the past, seems to have created a splendid character for this past in order to contrast it with the inglorious present. He was reinterpreting the past, as others for whom history has held some timeless principle have also done.

Confucius' attempt to reestablish the cohesion and harmony of earlier times seems to us to impart new meanings to old forms. To begin with, although Confucius clearly regarded kinship as a crucial social bond, emphasizing filial piety and other family-centered virtues, his stress was new. Merely providing material necessities for one's parents no longer could be considered a sign of filial piety. That was done by everyone; the important thing was the attitude of love that accompanied the prescribed behavior. Similarly, in other relationships, Confucius stressed the emotional and ethical content.

The same moral emphasis was applied to the whole ruling class. Government would continue to be by the aristocracy, the *chün-tzu,* but the true *chün-tzu* was no longer simply a man of noble pedigree. He was a cultivated and moral man, a "gentleman" in every way. In this idea was the power to change the very character of society and government. Confucius no doubt expected virtue to appear most often among men of the right blood, but he made it clear that birth was not enough, that the ruling class should be an aristocracy of merit. He would define the bonds linking men in terms of moral conviction rather than simple kinship.

Confucius also retained the religious practices and the ritual of earlier times but infused them with an ethical emphasis. He acknowledged the power of Heaven to influence men and the world, but he advised his followers to avoid too much speculation about the supernatural and to concentrate their attention on man and society, about which they could do something. The same concentration on man marked Confucius' love of ritual. Ritual (*li*) included a wide variety of actions devised to express feelings appropriate to events ranging from the most hallowed sacrifices to such everyday acts as sitting properly on a mat. (Chairs had not yet been invented.) Rites, which thus included everything from sacred ceremonies to good manners, were for Confucius outward signs of an inward attitude. In addition, they were the forms of harmonious and graceful human relationships. Though the rites might no longer magically influence the gods, they still had an extraordinary power, that of harmonizing the social and emotional life of the men who performed them.

The proper way of government, then, called for gentlemen (*chün-tzu*) to hold office and to use their influence to improve the world, or to "civilize" it, as the Confucians preferred to say. The moral power of the *chün-tzu* was to be exerted through example, which would sway others as certainly as the winds swayed the grass. The way of reform, then, was to obtain good men, not to alter institutions. Ritual was regarded as the basic instrument, far more important than law, which could only make men outwardly obedient, not inwardly better.

In most matters, moderation, a subtle perception of human feelings, and a reluctance to interfere excessively with established ways seemed to guide Confucius. Nothing could have been farther from the basic Legalist approach.

Mencius. We know as little about Mencius, Confucius' most famous follower, as we do about the Master. Mencius was born in

Ch'i, another state in what is now Shantung Province. According to tradition, he lived from about 372 to 289 B.C. His family, which was of the knight class, was apparently rather poor, and Mencius' childhood was made more difficult when his father died soon after his birth. Like Confucius, Mencius yearned to serve a promising lord but obtained only minor posts and gained his great fame as a teacher.

Mencius' sayings, entitled simply *Mencius* (in Chinese *Meng-tzu,* of which Mencius is the Latinized form, just as Confucius is the Latinized form of the Chinese *K'ung-fu-tzu*), concur with most of the basic ideas of Confucius, and elaborate on several of them. First of all, Mencius assigned great importance to the common people. In what can only be called a reversal of the usual political and social priorities of the time, Mencius argued that the king who wins the people will win the empire. By this he meant that kindness to the people and attention to their welfare would assure the king of their loyal support, as well as spread his fame abroad. His benevolence would thus become a key not only to internal stability but also to a foreign policy which might be called "benign aggrandizement," since the people of other states would yearn to be taken under his protection. In Mencius, the Confucian ideal of the humane and righteous king as the fundamental answer to all questions of government began to take definite shape.

Mencius' insistence that the king concern himself with the people had a religious motive as well. Mencius connected the king's behavior in this respect with the old idea of the Mandate of Heaven. No more than Confucius did he question the right of hereditary rule, but he emphasized that the ultimate authority was Heaven's. The actions of the people signified whether or not the king continued to hold the Mandate of Heaven. If the people were acquiescent, presumably the king possessed the Mandate. If they were rebellious, it was a sign that Heaven might withdraw its Mandate. In this, Mencius did not imply any doctrine of human rights; he merely said that Heaven could express itself though the people's action. Yet his stress on the people was radical enough to make kings uneasy. He suggested what is now called a "right of revolution." Although in fact the "right" was no more than approval by Mencius of the assassination, by ministers, of two ancient kings who, through villainous conduct, had lost all claim to their position, it offered a useful line of argument for rebels. It advanced the Confucian tendency to require of a king qualities beyond royal birth.

From Mencius' conviction of the importance of the people followed his attention to their material welfare. The people, he said, must have the necessities of life before they can be expected to concentrate on being good. He gave considerable space to discussing the economic arrangements best for the people and the state. He described, for instance, what he asserted to have been the earlier system of landholding, the so-called well-field system, thus named because the plots of land were arranged in a shape similar to the Chinese graph for "well," which looks something like a ticktacktoe graph. The central field was supposed to be the lord's land, while each of the surrounding fields was cultivated by a peasant family, which also contributed labor to the cultivation of the lord's land. It seems doubtful that this system ever existed, but the principle is clear: the ruling class, in return for governing, was to be supported by the labor of the people, who worked principally at farming and were provided with sufficient land to support themselves.

Mencius urged equally lenient treatment of merchants. Goods should be taxed only in the markets, which should be well administered to provide favorable conditions for trade. The merchants would no doubt still be told by the officials where and when to do business. Moreover, the world was divided into "gentlemen," who were guided by ethical considerations, and "small men," who were motivated by personal profit. Thus the merchants, like the farmers, were considered unqualified to rule.

In other parts of his economic program, Mencius also stressed the material welfare of the people. He advised the king to avoid extravagance at court and to open his parks and other state lands to the people so that they might gather wood and herbs. He also urged that public funds be used for the care of the aged, the poor, and orphans, and for relief when natural disasters struck.

Provision of the material necessities of life was not the end of the state's responsibility toward the common people. If the people had the necessities and then were not educated, Mencius said, they would be no better than domestic animals. He proposed a revival (as he puts it) of the ancient system of public schools. These schools would, in Mencius' view, be a further means of providing that "constancy of mind," by which he meant contentment and acquiescence, that his welfare measures were designed to promote.

No discussion of Mencius can ignore his famous doctrine of human nature. Human beings, he asserted, had a basic tendency to do good. This goodness, to be sure, was at first no more than an instinct to feel sorry for another human being in distress, to consider one action right and another wrong, and to feel ashamed if one did something wrong, but it was capable of being sufficiently cultivated and strengthened to guide one constantly. Mencius' optimism led him to say that anyone might become a Yao or Shun, that is, a perfect or near-perfect man.

Hsün Tzu. The third great classical Confucianist, Hsün Tzu, who lived in the third century B.C., was also a teacher. Like other Confucianists, he taught the importance of the virtuous gentleman for successful rule, the value of the support of the people, and the need for education to improve morality. Where he differed frequently proved to be a matter of emphasis rather than of fundamental view. He thought material incentives and administrative sanctions more important than had earlier Confucianists, and favored the use of rewards and punishments. While the true gentleman remained the keystone of good government, good laws and regulations were also required. That two famous legalists, Han Fei Tzu and Li Ssu, studied under Hsün Tzu suggests an affinity of temperament, though Hsün Tzu opposed the immorality and narrowness of the Legalist approach.

Hsün Tzu's interest in systematic discipline was perhaps sustained by his conviction that men were by nature evil. Rather than seeing like Mencius evidences of budding compassion and other social impulses in men, Hsün Tzu found the most significant, crude human traits to be propensities for selfishness, envy, and greed. He spoke more than Mencius about mechanisms to maintain social order while training man to be good. He was equally optimistic about the power of education.

On two subjects, Hsün Tzu elaborated and strengthened opinions already familiar. One is the rightness of social inequality. Without inequality, and by extension hierarchy, order would be impossible in society, equal contending against equal, each intent on his selfish interest. Hsün Tzu seemed even to argue that the human ability to rationalize inequality—to "make distinctions"—was the basic intelligence that permitted men to impose order on themselves.

His second stress was on ritual. Hsün Tzu insisted that the events of Heaven and earth followed a regularity quite independent of anything man does. Men's religious acts affected nothing but men themselves. Yet rites, religious and otherwise, were the very crux of order in society and balance in the human heart. Insofar as rites were the way of perfect human behavior, they became the principle harmonizing mankind with the other components of the universe, Heaven and earth, each following its own way, each perfectly complementary to the others. In Hsün Tzu's teachings, we might say, the ritual that once formed a magic bond between men and the gods was redefined as the role men play in the Way of the Universe.

The Confucian Classics. It should be clear from this brief account that the Confucian philosophers pictured themselves as lovers of the past, which had set eternally valid standards of behavior. Owing to the emphasis of the Confucianists on tradition, and to their success, by the first century B.C., in attaining recognition as the teachers of the nation, the books that they thought contained the essential truths of the past survived and were exalted as the Classics, works written in an earlier age that propounded timeless principles. Although all the Confucian Classics recorded pre-Confucian times, all were said to owe something to Confucius, whether as compiler, commentator, or author. Confucius indeed may have had a hand in the composition of these works, but modern scholarship has demonstrated that the Classics consist of parts widely separated in date, some perhaps written as early as the Western Chou, others dating from Han times, so that Confucius' contribution, if any, was a limited one.

The first of the Five Confucian Classics, in the customary order, is the *I ching* (*Book of Changes*). It is composed of a highly laconic and ambiguous principal text, which seems originally to have been a handbook of divination, and commentaries which are almost as enigmatic as the text itself, for which they attempt to give a cosmological explanation. The *I ching* became for some a key to a metaphysical design governing events, and as such its presence among the Classics warns us to avoid too secular and irreligious an evaluation of Confucianists in general.

The second Classic is the *Book of Documents* (*Shu ching*), sometimes translated as the *Book of History*. Both translations are justifiable, since it is a collection of documents, mostly speeches and other declamations, purporting to deal with ancient history. There is no particular unity to the work, aside from the fact that all the documents were believed to embody important ethical principles. Although modern scholarship has disproved the authenticity of much of the work, most educated Chinese of the past accepted it all as true.

The third Classic is the *Book of Songs* or *Book of Odes* (*Shih ching*), a collection of 305 songs divided into four sections: "airs of the states," which are mostly lyrics of love and other emotions and festive songs; the "lesser odes" and "greater odes," which in general deal with more public and even official subjects, such as political satire and royal hunts and feasts; and "hymns," mostly in praise of the Chou dynasty and the accomplishments of Chou kings. The Confucianists' admiration of the songs of political content is easy to understand, but their attention to the simpler poems, the folk ballads and love lyrics, might seem beneath them as lofty ethical philosophers. They justified the inclusion of such material by interpreting much of it as political allegory, no doubt distorting the meaning but in any event preserving a fresh and vigorous poetry. The literary qualities of the Odes are discussed in chapter XX.

Fourth among the Classics is the *Ritual,* three texts counted as one—the *Rites of Chou (Chou li),* the *Ceremonial Rites (I li),* and the *Book of Rites (Li chi).* They contain a great variety of matter: philosophical essays, idealized descriptions of systems of administration, and detailed instruction on proper behavior in the home. The administrative systems described in the *Rites of Chou* were later cited by reformers in support of proposals to "restore" the way of the ancient sage kings.

The fifth Classic is the *Spring and Autumn Annals (Ch'un ch'iu).* It is a chronological record, season by season, of the important events in principal states from 722 to 481 B.C. It notes laconically events such as the accession and death of rulers, wars, and diplomatic missions. The brevity of the notices makes it difficult to discover the general truths one expects to find in a Classic. It owes its great reputation partly to the tradition that Confucius himself compiled it from records of his native state of Lu. Later scholars devised elaborate interpretations to prove that Confucius had used subtle phrasing and a technically precise vocabulary to express "praise and blame" of rulers and ministers. These attempts to explain Confucius' message in the *Annals* resulted in several commentaries, three of which still exist, though they are by no means mutually consistent. Of the three, the most important is the *Tso Chuan* (Tso commentary), probably compiled in the third century B.C. Today it is of more importance as an independent narrative history, the longest and most detailed history of the Chou, than as a commentary on the *Annals.* For its literary qualities, see chapter XX.

For centuries, all educated Chinese read and studied the Five Classics. In response to an increasing attention to education, from the twelfth century of the Christian era onwards students devoted themselves also to the Four Books, namely, the *Analects, Mencius, The Great Learning (Ta hsueh),* and the *Doctrine of the Mean (Chung yung).* The last two were short philosophical sections from the *Book of Rites,* singled out because of their trenchant statement of key Confucian ideas.

TAOISM

A way of thinking strikingly different from anything considered so far was Taoism, named after its central notion of the Tao, or Way. The classical authors of the school were a shadowy figure called Lao Tzu and a philosopher named Chuang Tzu. Almost nothing is known about either, aside from the possibility that Chuang Tzu was a contemporary of Mencius.

The book traditionally considered to be by Lao Tzu takes his name as its title: the *Lao Tzu,* and is also called the *Tao te ching,* or *The Way and Its Power.* A brief, enigmatic work that may have been written or compiled in the last century of the Chou dynasty, its primary and fundamental notion is the Tao, or Way, which extends well beyond the early Confucian idea of a right way of government or conduct and signifies a universal force or principle of the natural world. The Tao cannot be defined, it can only be intuitively sensed or felt and heeded. When men are attuned to the Tao, they cooperate with the processes of nature, respond directly to experience rather than reflect on it, invent no mental abstractions, and live and die quietly according to the standard of *wu-wei,* an obscure term meaning "non-action" and apparently implying "non-striving." Such, at least, is the kind of understanding the symbolic, paradoxical language of the *Lao Tzu* permits. As for its political implications, the best government would be that which governed least, the best society a "natural" one of small villages whose members lived in peace with each other and nature and gave no thought to the outside world. The Legalist empire builders, the vicarious Confucian judges of humanity, and the social planners were only thwarting the universal harmony.

Chuang Tzu concentrated more on the liberation to be gained by mystical union with the Tao. He exposed the limited truth and fragility of manmade standards and aims, the narrow bounds of conventional knowledge, and the artificiality of logic. Remember the limits of all conventional thinking, Chuang Tzu says, embrace the universal Tao, and be free. He meant, of course, a psychological freedom, a mental independence of the world of men, not freedom from political, social, or economic forces. At times he seems to say that the sage will conform outwardly to conventions for the sake of convenience, since they cannot touch him at the true center of his life.

Although Taoist political ideas were not subsequently developed and had no major influence on systems or organizations (aside from certain instances of imperial patronage and religious cults, to be mentioned below), Taoist points of view refreshed and inspired Chinese indefinitely. The Taoist attraction to nature, the linking of oneself with a perfect universe, the exposure of the vanity of the world, and the emphasis on spontaneity, intuition, and freedom vitally enriched the spiritual and cultural resources upon which Chinese could draw.

MO-ISM AND OTHER SCHOOLS

During the three centuries from Confucius to the time of Han Fei Tzu, many schools of thought flourished. Of these, Confucianism, Taoism, and Legalism were by far the most influential in later centuries, but a few other schools may be mentioned, if only briefly, for what they add to the character of classical thinking.

A school which seems to have challenged Confucianism for a time was founded by Mo Tzu (470-391 B.C.?). Famous for his readiness to sacrifice his own comfort for the welfare of all, a tactician and defender of weak states against strong, free of the aristocratic pride of the Confucianists, Mo Tzu lacked also their interest in the individual personality and stressed instead a comprehensive social organization, its officialdom to be chosen perhaps more rigorously on the principle of individual merit than the Confucianists would have done, and held together by a more absolute requirement of obedience to superiors in the hierarchy. Like the Legalists, Mo Tzu was interested in over-all plans, uniform patterns, and standardization, and defined the good in a similarly utilitarian way as that which increases wealth and population; but he opposed aggrandizement of the kind the Legalists took for granted and introduced the striking concept of universal love, in opposition to what he called the Confucianists' graded love or "partiality." Yet even universal love, like obedience and other measures for stability, should be enforced. His propensity for combining genuine concern for the people with strict control of them would be seen in others later.

Another school was that of the Logicians, or Dialecticians, who discussed such propositions as whether a white horse was a horse.

(The answer in this instance was no, since the quality of whiteness introduced a separate category.) The paradoxes of language that this school exploited were a source of entertainment for later Chinese, but logical analysis for its own sake never became important in Chinese thought.

One other mode of thinking, which did influence a great deal of later Chinese thought, should be mentioned. This was a form of naturalism known as *yin* and *yang,* after its twin key principles. *Yang* first meant the sunny side of a hill, while *yin* meant shadow. More generally, the pair of terms came to stand for a ceaseless alternation of opposites throughout all nature: day and night, sun and moon, summer and winter, dry and wet, male and female. Some time later, another naturalistic theory emerged to complement the *yin-yang* dualism. This was the "five agents" theory, according to which five elements—wood, metal, fire, water, and earth—underlay and determined all natural events. These ideas became the basis of much later Chinese thought about the physical universe.

II

The First

Imperial Period

CH'IN DYNASTY
221-209 B.C.
FORMER HAN DYNASTY
206 B.C.-A.D. 8
LATER HAN DYNASTY
A.D. 23-202

Ch'in Establishes the Empire

During the constant strife of the Eastern Chou, no practical or theoretical arrangement for a stable community of equal states ever won much support. To the contrary, the idea of unity, or rather of ultimate domination, preoccupied the minds of all the great territorial lords. In retrospect, the idea of a single empire seems a major and ancient theme of Chinese government.

The final triumph went to Ch'in, the state that had adopted a more rational administration through the reforms of Shang Yang and later Legalists. In addition to efficient organization, Ch'in possessed the advantages of a favorable geographical position, improved military and agricultural techniques, and, not least, singlemindedly ambitious rulers. Far in the northwest, the land of Ch'in straddled the Wei River, the same vantage point from which the Chou had conquered the Shang. The mountainous terrain protected Ch'in from rival armies, while easily guarded passes in the mountains were gates through which her forces could strike out against her neighbors. Ch'in early learned the art of mounted warfare from the nomads on her northern border and increased her agricultural production by constructing irrigation canals, one of which in the Wei Valley was said to have been 100 miles long.

In the third century B.C. Ch'in rapidly completed the conquest of her rivals. The Chou house was destroyed (256 B.C.), and in rapid succession the major states of Ch'u and Ch'i fell. In 221 B.C. the king of Ch'in declared that the world was united under his sovereignty. This first period of unification lasted through three dynasties, the Ch'in (221-209 B.C.), the Former Han (206 B.C.-A.D. 8), and the Later Han (A.D. 23-202).

In the course of the First Imperial Period, the boundaries of the territory under central administration, ignoring some large unsubjugated pockets, came near to what would be China Proper, extending in the north to the Great Wall, the southern boundary line of present-day Inner Mongolia, and the Jade Gate (Yü-men) in Kansu Province; in the west to the foothills of the Himalayas and the basin of the Salween River; and in the south to the border of modern Vietnam. The capital of the Ch'in, Hsien-yang, was near the site of the Western Chou capital, and later under the name of Ch'ang-an was to be a capital of the Han dynasties.

Four Great Figures of the First Imperial Period

One of the most important sections of traditional Chinese histories was the Annals of the Emperors, for the crucial decisions of the government turned, or were supposed to turn, on the will of the emperor. Moreover, in theory—and this was the theory held by the historians—the quality of the reign reflected the character of the ruler, and thus indicated the grip of the dynasty on the Mandate of Heaven. A summary of the work of a few important rulers whose reigns put their stamp not only on their own time but on the imperial government for centuries afterwards may be a useful introduction to the First Imperial Period.

CH'IN SHIH HUANG-TI (REIGNED AS EMPEROR 221-210 B.C.)

Ch'in's creation of the empire assured the king of Ch'in a special place in history. Even at the time, the sense of an epoch was so strong that the king thought it necessary to devise a new designation for his position. The Chou rulers had called themselves "king" (*wang*), a term used also by the Confucianists to designate the best and highest type of ruler. In the later Chou, lords of the warring states had signified their independence by appropriating this title, which had thus lost much of its significance. According to the accepted legends, in the most ancient times there had existed sage kings and emperors, sometimes grouped as the "Three August Sovereigns" (*San Huang*) and the "Five Lords" (*Wu Ti*). The victorious king of Ch'in, who desired to show that his position was superior to that of the many kings who had existed in the past, combined the two terms for awesome lordship and called himself *Huang-ti*. Until the end of the empire in the twentieth century, the word stood for the emperor of China. The Ch'in ruler prefixed the cardinal number "First" to his title, in order to indicate that he anticipated a long line of successors, who would be called "Second," "Third," and so on for centuries. The full title thus became Ch'in Shih Huang-ti, or First Emperor of Ch'in.

The First Emperor created additional symbols of his majesty. One of the most famous was his enormous palace, which was said to be capable of seating ten thousand. His tomb, built during his own lifetime, was filled with treasure, lined with bronze, and decorated with the constellations of heaven on the ceiling and a map of the empire on the floor. To this day, the earth mound built over it looks like a small mountain.

Many of the First Emperor's measures were inspired by his chief adviser, the Legalist Li Ssu. Li Ssu pointed out, for example, that it would be dangerous to follow the earlier method of dividing the kingdom into domains put in charge of relatives, for experience showed that the enfeoffed relatives would become enemies. It would be better, he argued, to extend the system of centrally controlled and taxed territorial units instituted by earlier Legalists throughout the entire empire. Accordingly, the emperor divided the country into 36 commanderies (*chün*), which were subdivided into many more prefectures or districts (*hsien*). Each was put in charge of officials who were responsible to the central government for collecting and forwarding taxes and exacting from the common people labor on public works, or *corvée*.

The First Emperor attempted to eliminate all possible opposition. He promulgated an elaborate set of laws which included severe punishments for infractions. He moved great numbers of rich and powerful families (120,000 according to one record) from their home districts to the capital, where they could be watched. On his orders many city walls were razed, and all weapons except those of the Ch'in armies gathered up and melted down to make harmless bells and statues. All these measures were devised to weaken the former ruling groups in the various states and strengthen the new central government.

Another important measure prohibited two adult males from living under the same roof, on pain of extra taxation, and required that upon the death of the father the land be distributed among all the sons. This was obviously meant to prevent the growth of large, close-knit families, potential rivals of the state. Although the decree is sometimes described as the abolition of primogeniture, it seems more likely that primogeniture had not yet become a universal custom and that the law merely served to discourage its further development. Conversely, it encouraged the fragmentation of land tenure, a pattern that was to be characteristic in the Chinese countryside.

Political and administrative control promoted standardization and unification in other spheres. Weights, measures, coinage, and even axle-lengths were standardized, the last to help carts travel over the dirt roads of north China, where ruts were deep. A standard form of script was also adopted, the principle inspiring by the second century

B.C. the basic style still used today, a fact of importance for our appreciation of the Chinese sense of tradition.

Unification also touched the realm of thought. Li Ssu argued that the various books and teachers in circulation caused dissension, which undermined imperial power. The solution was simple: the state should tolerate only one doctrine. In accordance with Li Ssu's recommendations, in 213 B.C. all historical records but those of Ch'in, all copies of the *Book of Songs,* the *Book of Documents,* and other philosophical texts were to be burned, with the sole exception of copies to be preserved in the Ch'in imperial library. The only teachers were to be those employed by the state. This famous event, the "Burning of the Books," followed by the burning of the capital a few years later when the Ch'in fell, dealt a cruel blow to history. Many works (at the time mostly written on strips of wood or bamboo) disappeared forever. Fortunately, others were preserved in secret hiding places, or in the memory of scholars who later reproduced them in writing during the following dynasty. Nothing blackened the name of Ch'in more than the burning of the books, but the First Emperor was not the last to ban books nor were the Legalists the only thinkers to try to suppress rival schools. No classical school exalted freedom of thought. Yet the Chinese intellectual tradition has been basically far more tolerant than the Ch'in policies and persistently more diverse than strong governments would have wished.

With the use of *corvée* labor, Shih Huang-ti also undertook massive public works projects. He built a system of roads, radiating out from the capital and bringing the central government and outlying regions into closer touch. On the northern border, he joined together walls built by earlier states to guard against nomadic incursions and made the famous 1,400-mile-long Great Wall, which, properly manned, put an end to casual barbarian raids and invasions. It also established the boundary between China and the "barbarians."

Corvée and convict labor put heavy burdens on the people, and we are told that huge numbers died. Nor was this the only source of grievance, for heavy taxation and harsh punishments roused reactions. Bandits and rebels appeared even before the death of the First Emperor, but his death in 210 B.C. released forces that brought an end to the Ch'in—struggles for power within the highest levels of the court, latent animosity among the remaining aristocracy of the old states, and popular discontent. The tremendous personality of Ch'in Shih Huang-ti had held the state together, but a man of his mold cannot be expected to appear often. His rightful successor fell victim to factional struggles at court and an infant was placed on the throne. Uprisings in the commanderies soon led to full scale civil war and the end of the dynasty.

HAN KAO-TSU (REIGNED AS EMPEROR 202-195 B.C.)

The man who won the civil war and put the empire back together again named his dynasty Han, and was posthumously called Han Kao-tsu (First Ancestor of Han), the name by which he is known in history.

The Chinese have invented several categories of names to identify an individual, depending upon his various roles, positions, and other circumstances, and generally growing more numerous as his status rises. The founder of the Han dynasty, for example, was called simply Liu (his surname) and Pang (his given name) when he was a plain peasant. Liu Pang as a ruler would never be addressed or indicated by his name. Any one of a number of reverentially oblique forms would be used instead, terms like "His Highness," "The Throne," or more intimately, "10,000 Years." In the late dynasties emperors might be identified by the names given to the period in which they reigned. In the fifteenth century, for example, one reign was named Yung-lo or "Perpetual Pleasure," and the emperor the Yung-lo Emperor (also frequently Emperor Yung-lo). Emperors were also given "shrine-names," like Kao-tsu, after their deaths. Even an ordinary, educated man would usually have, in addition to his given name, a name he chose to suggest his principles and to use in writing (*tzu*) and a name by which colleagues or friends outside the family might refer to him (*hao*), not to mention other possibilities. The multiplicity of names may have been connected with a Chinese stress on keeping names and reality matched, and it might help the reader in his efforts to attune to the Chinese point of view, if he were required to trace one man through his changing names, as in Chinese sources. Nothing would be more certain to drive away all but the most fanatical scholars, however, and in this book the rule will be one man, one name (with a few unavoidable exceptions).

Kao-tsu differed in many ways from the First Emperor of Ch'in: he was a self-made man, the son of peasants, with remarkable qualities as a leader, especially an ability to take advice from the many capable men he chose as subordinates, and to win the allegiance of men of all levels.

The government that Kao-tsu founded after his victory maintained the Ch'in institutions and developed them in many respects. At first he parceled almost two thirds of his territory into kingdoms and marquisates and put them into the hands of his brothers, sons, nephews, and lieutenants. This return to the pre-Ch'in system did not last long. Kao-tsu kept much of the land himself, ruling it through a centralized bureaucracy like that of Ch'in. By the end of his reign he had taken back control of most of the kingdoms he had previously delegated to his lieutenants. Half a century later the most powerful of the remaining kingdoms, provoked by the central government, revolted, but were rapidly defeated and their autonomy ended. Kao-tsu promulgated a legal code much simpler and more moderate than that of the Ch'in, yet, like the old code, it was based on the principle that law was an instrument of coercion of the ruler.

EMPRESS DOWAGER LÜ (IN POWER 195-180 B.C.)

When Han Kao-tsu died the prestige and power associated with him did not evaporate, as the First Emperor's had seemed to do. The imperial house had a glorious name and loyal supporters. Kao-tsu's young son succeeded to the throne, to be followed by two boy emperors. It grew apparent, however, that the real power resided in the empress dowager. Empress Lü had shared life with Kao-tsu from the time when he was a minor village official and she had to weed the fields. Able and ruthless, she used her position next to her husband to benefit herself and her family, and put out of the way many who opposed her. After Kao-tsu's death she had a woman who had caught the emperor's fancy mutilated and thrown into a privy, a vengeance so shocking to her mild son that he went to bed and took to drink, abandoning any further involvement in state affairs. When Kao-tsu died, Empress Dowager Lü could invoke, in addition to the loyalty of old followers, the bonds of filial piety, for it was becoming understood that emperors revealed their moral force particularly through that virtue. She prevailed upon her puppet emperors to place her brothers, sisters, and other relatives in high offices within the central government and the kingdoms and marquisates. She herself issued decrees in the manner of an emperor. Her behavior abetted divisions and hatreds in officialdom and, when she died, forces hostile to her had their day. Virtually the entire Lü family was murdered. Yet the extraordinary power of emperors' consorts, increased when as mothers they could call upon filial piety, would appear many times again.

EMPEROR WU (REIGNED 140-87 B.C.)

The second great emperor of the Early Han was Emperor Wu, the "Martial Emperor." Among the marks of his greatness was the interest he displayed in learning. He favored Confucianists more than his predecessors had done and appointed scholars to look into the reconstruction of the Classics and to teach them in the Imperial University that he established. He agreed to a proposal to suppress doctrines not acceptable to the Confucianists. Graduates of the Imperial University could qualify for employment in office by means of examinations. All these steps increased the influence of Confucianism within the imperial government.

Yet Emperor Wu's motives must have been mixed. He was by no means a Confucian purist himself—there were few in his age—and for personal advice leaned towards magicians and clairvoyants. Perhaps in part he wanted a staff of learned and polished men to ornament his administration, for style and pomp were important. Perhaps he believed that men of relatively humble birth would be more compliant than scions of capital families and the older landed rich, who had proud traditions of their own. In any event, the men he selected by his examinations distinguished themselves more as yes-sayers and sycophants than as strong-minded counselors. Emperor Wu's character encouraged little else.

For another of his distinctive marks was love of glory. He had enormous energy, ambitions, and little patience with delay or obstruction. He furthered the policy of reducing the power of the kingdoms and weakening local interests. He extended Chinese influence beyond the borders in all directions. In the north, he attacked and weakened nomadic tribes known to the Chinese as the Hsiung-nu (probably ancestors of the Huns who later invaded the West), who had threatened the borders periodically since the fifth century B.C. He sent armies into northern Korea, and established there commanderies and districts that introduced many features of Chinese civilization. He sent an ambassador, Chang Ch'ien, into Central Asia in search of allies against the Hsiung-nu and as a result learned something about not only Central Asia but the Roman Empire as well. Chinese armies campaigned in Central Asia, bringing the small states that skirted the Tarim Basin under Chinese influence and reaching as far as Ferghana, almost one half the distance to Rome. In the far south, Chinese political and cultural influence extended to present-day North Vietnam, a region that Ch'in had previously controlled.

As much of this would imply, a third feature of Emperor Wu's administration was its notably despotic style. All theory recognized, of course, that the emperor had absolute political power, but in practice that power might be asserted more or less vigorously. Emperor Wu elaborated the laws and applied them more harshly. He exploited the labor of masses of convicts and peasants for works projects. Like Ch'in Shih Huang-ti, he held his ministers in almost constant suspicion, and deposed and had put to death no fewer than five chief ministers. Yet forces that made Chinese autocracy far more complicated in fact than in theory were in play at the same time. We shall look briefly at some of these forces next. (For a discussion of the growth of political institutions, see chapter XVIII.)

Constituents of Politics, Economics, Reform, and Rebellion

THREE FACTORS IN POLITICS

In the Han, there were three forces at work in the political arena: the emperor, the bureaucracy, and powerful families. We have seen how the organization of a centralized state gradually increased the power of the ruler to unprecedented proportions. Here, it need only be added that, while the emperor claimed absolute power by right, how fully he could direct events depended largely on his own character and that of groups that in one way or another affected his government.

The emperor could not devise and administer policies for the vast empire all by himself. Inevitably, those he chose to assist him were in a position to influence his acts, sometimes by dissuading him directly from a harsh decision or goading him into a harsher one, sometimes by watering down his orders in practice or pursuing private interests in his name.

By nature, the bureaucracy tended to check the power of the emperor in one way or another. In the Han period, officialdom grew to truly imperial proportions—one estimate was 130,285 men. Regular methods of recruitment began to develop, including the recommendation of capable men by local officials, and the examination of them in the capital. A fully developed examination system as the chief means of recruitment did not emerge until centuries later, but the important principle of recruitment on the basis of individual ability was established in the first imperial period. Moreover, ability was defined in terms of knowledge of the Classics and moral character. The role of the Classics in determining qualification for office gave the Confucianists and Confucianism a special advantage. Confucianists could begin to view the large bureaucracy as an organization for men like themselves devoted to assisting the emperor to achieve Confucian government. Officialdom thus acquired its own standards against which to measure the emperor.

The bureaucracy became an elaborate structure of many offices, in a regular hierarchy of ranks and responsibilities, with the emperor at the top. Along with the ranking system, corresponding insignia and graduated scales of remuneration were established. The functions of three senior executives, called the "Three Lords" during the Han, indicate the organization of power. The Chancellor assisted the emperor generally in administration and acted as head of officialdom. The Imperial Secretary was principally concerned with the supervision and disciplining of officials. The third, the Grand Commandant, was in charge of military affairs. Immediately below these officials were the Nine Ministers, some of whom dealt with matters relating to the imperial household, while others dealt with the administration of the empire. For one of the indications of the power of the bureaucracy was its ability to separate these two spheres of authority of the emperor, in administrative organization and in finance as well, where there was an imperial treasury for the emperor's own use and a state treasury for official purposes.

Although it is convenient for the moment to treat the bureaucracy as a unitary force, it actually tended to include any number of shifting and competing factions, an aspect that became more obvious in later dynasties. One group that might well be mentioned here was the eunuchs. Precisely speaking, eunuchs were functionaries of the palace precincts, commonly called the Inner Court, not members of the regular bureaucracy, which occupied the Outer Court. They came, it is thought, from prisoners of war or boys taken in rebellions, and they served in the women's quarters and eventually in other parts of the palace, such as the kitchen. Coming into touch with influential women and the emperor, often in relatively intimate circumstances, eunuchs sometimes seemed appropriate for special administrative assignments, particularly when the emperor found fault with the regular bureaucracy. The recourse to eunuchs and other protégés of the palace, often through the offices of the women, might be called "Palace Government" to distinguish it from the regular bureaucratic practices. It usually aggravated factional hostility.

The third force, the great families, was probably the oldest form of political organization, an intimate connection between families and political power dating from the Shang and Chou. In spite of the attempts of Shih Huang-ti and, to a lesser extent, later emperors to decrease the influence of powerful families, the principle of politics according to kinship remained strong. It was especially apparent outside the Court in the countryside, where great wealth and prestige were concentrated in large estates, many of them gifts of the emperor to members of his family, favorites, and officials. The estates were clearly political factors in their regions, where their sheer wealth and size, or their known connections with the Court, assured them of privileges and immunity from the demands of minor regional officials. Great families might also dominate the very center of government, as we have seen in the behavior of Empress Lü, who placed relatives in high positions and liberally endowed her family with land in the provinces.

AN ECONOMIC SYNDROME

Especially after the reign of Emperor Wu, the growth of estates became more obviously part of a pattern of development that, though most visibly economic, indicated a many-sided weakening of the Han order. Even in Emperor Wu's time, a Confucianist scholar had submitted a "memorial," that is, an opinion on a point of policy, asserting that, since Ch'in and Han had allowed the people to buy and sell land, the rich had bought up huge tracts and had encroached on resources traditionally treated as the state's, such as those found on mountains and in waters. The common people suffered directly and indirectly, even to the point of being enslaved. The scholar suggested a limitation on the ownership of land and a prohibition of slavery.

Although little was done at the time, it is useful to be as clear as possible about what was happening, for similar issues rose repeatedly later. The families involved in aggrandizement were apparently those of officials, nobles, and probably local magnates who took every opportunity to increase their wealth, especially in its principal form of farmland. Branches of even the imperial Liu family, for example, eventually spread far and wide and were to be found not only living off estates but also engaging in commerce and even maintaining troops of followers whose business was banditry. Inevitably their growth infringed on the freedom and prosperity of weaker neighbors, some of whom faced a choice between losing the land entirely or becoming tenants, sometimes under conditions amounting to serfdom. Local officials seem to have contributed to the misery of many of the common people by excessively harsh treatment. Harassed by landlords and officials, some peasants took to the hills and found a free if dangerous living in banditry. Others joined the private troops, hardly distinguishable from bandits, of a great family. Bandits became especially prevalent towards the end of Emperor Wu's reign.

Intelligent officials could therefore see several needs, none easy to supply. One was the general aim, prompted by Confucian values, of insuring the welfare of the people. That the people were turning to crime was, in the enlightened Confucian sense, the shame of the government, for economic despair had driven them to it. The second need surely was to eliminate bandits, who disturbed the security of the countryside and could, if they grew, become rebels. The third need was to curb great families, who by their arms challenged the ability of the ruling house to control the countryside and, by their encroachments, bled the dynasty's source of revenues.

Acquiring sufficient revenues was another perennial concern of the state. A supplementary source of funds for the government was a monopoly on certain products, such as iron and salt. A debate over the monopoly illuminated some of the issues and attitudes.

THE DEBATE ON SALT AND IRON (81 B.C.)

In 81 B.C., soon after the death of the strong-willed Emperor Wu, his milder successor convened a court conference on economic problems. It became a debate between Confucianists who opposed the monopolies established in the previous reign and other ministers who favored the monopolies. Although the latter did not call themselves Legalists, Legalism having been largely discredited by Confucian attacks on the excesses of Ch'in, many of their arguments resembled those of the Legalists.

The Confucianists argued that the wars which created the need for larger revenues, which in turn had led to the monopolies, were unnecessary and unwise. Furthermore, in seeking to make a profit through the monopolies, the state was setting a bad example for the people. The arguments were based on the familiar Confucian assumptions that the aim of the state was to encourage a harmonious and moral society by benevolent and frugal means, and that it should place the welfare of the common people before its own aggrandizement.

The ministers who defended the monopolies argued that the wars were meant to defend the country against threatening barbarians and therefore necessary. Hence revenues to finance the wars were also necessary. If the state made money from the people, it at least protected them from the greater avariciousness of private merchants and powerful families. As to the example set by officials, what kind of example was that of the sanctimonious Confucianists, so full of piety and so empty of practical ideas?

The debate brought some relaxation of the monopolies, as the Confucianists wanted. It did not bring lasting economic health. Rather, it proved to be an incident on the way toward a great crisis, in which the state attempted to intervene in the economy at the expense of the wealthy, for its own political benefit and the economic welfare of the common people.

WANG MANG AND HIS "NEW" DYNASTY

(A.D. 9-23)

One sign of rising political instability was a growing tendency, from the end of Emperor Wu's reign, toward a form of Palace Government characterized by the use of regents. The men appointed were mostly relatives of the empress dowager. They became powers behind the throne, actually appointing emperors. At last one of them, Wang Mang, took the throne himself. He called his dynasty Hsin, or "New." The name suggests turning away from the recent past, but Wang Mang was careful to describe his policies in terms of the practices of a golden age as depicted in the *Rituals of Chou* and other classics. By "New," he did not mean to convey dissatisfaction with the way of the ancients.

Among Wang Mang's policies, the most fundamental was to declare all land the ruler's—an act today often loosely callled nationalization of the land—and to prohibit the buying and selling of land by private families. He set limits on the amount of land that any one family was permitted to hold and ordered the land in excess of these limits to be confiscated and redistributed to families who did not have enough, following the model of the well-field system described by Mencius. At the same time he forbade private families to own slaves.

A second policy of Wang Mang gave the state control of certain important commodities. The administration monopolized the minting of coins; the sale of salt, iron, and fermented liquors; and the right to the products of mountains and marshes, such as pelts, timber, and fish. All these measures had precedents, notably during the reign of Emperor Wu, when similar monopolies had been established in order to increase government revenues to meet rising expenses.

A third important act was the establishment of grain storehouses in major cities, through which officials were to buy goods when prices were low and sell them when prices were high, in an attempt to stabilize prices, to obtain surpluses that could be used to relieve famine when necessary, and to supplement the revenues of the government. Like the monopolies, therefore, the "ever-normal granaries" would serve at least in part to profit the government. That, as we have seen before, was a matter of suspicion to less interventionist officials and gave a clue to the opposition to be expected.

It proved impossible to realize the reforms. The failure is not adequately understood, but perhaps too many groups felt threatened. The redistribution of land and prohibition of slavery was revoked only two years later. It seems likely that, after decades of weak leadership following Emperor Wu's death, the central government did not have suficient political power to enforce radical change against the interests of the great families throughout the land. The rest of the program soon collapsed, too, and there was a general political disintegration. Officials in the capital and in the provinces, perhaps frightened for their own future under the new radical program, stopped cooperating with Wang Mang. Banditry spread. Famine and pestilence broke out in several places, probably in part the result of decades of official neglect of flood control and grain storage, as well as the rapacity of great families.

REBELLIONS AGAINST WANG MANG

The rebellions that led to the downfall of Wang Mang and his New Dynasty arose from various sources. First came roving peasant bands from communities that had suffered severe economic distress. Some of the most desperate were in Shantung, where flood and famine had been aggravated by a shift in the course of the Yellow River. Among them arose a cult of the imperial Liu family of the Han. They dyed their eyebrows red, the color of the Han, as an indication of their loyalties, and thus came to be called the Red Eyebrows. At first small in size, the bands gradually grew, and were able to raid villages and towns, and to defeat armies that Wang Mang sent to suppress them. As they roamed over north China toward the capital, they widened the existing unrest and disorder.

In an atmosphere of general rebelliousness, it was members of the Liu clan who led the organized opposition that eventually brought about Wang Mang's downfall. In various sections of the empire Liu families led uncoordinated uprisings against the usurper. Sometimes they took the initiative in rebelling; sometimes they found themselves pressed into positions of command by peasant rebels. Only the surname of the Han house seems to have possessed the ring of legitimacy that satisfied both gentry and peasantry.

Eventually, the capital was taken, Wang Mang and his followers were killed, and Wang Mang's head was displayed in a market place. Yet the fighting did not end, for the various Liu pretenders struggled among themselves for the succession to the throne. The winner, known to history as Emperor Kuang-wu, defeated his rivals and took the throne as the first ruler of a restored Later Han dynasty (A.D. 25).

The Eastern (or Later) Han
(A.D. 25-220)

The new emperor established his capital in Lo-yang. During his reign and those of his immediate successors, for about 80 years, China was relatively free from disturbances. The stability may have followed, unfortunately, on what was reported as a drastic reduction of the population from the famine, pestilence, and fighting of the last years of Wang Mang's reign. With a smaller population, land may have been easier to find, and many surviving farmers may have made a fresh start. The same unsettling conditions may have shaken up the provincial social structure in some beneficial way. Certainly some of the great families who had opposed Wang Mang were absorbed into the administration of the rejuvenated Han government, while other dissidents were eliminated during the years of fighting.

The foreign threat had diminished, too. Fortunately for Han, although the Hsiung-nu raided north China from time to time, the federation split into contending northern and southern camps. The Han took advantage of this situation and used the southern Hsiung-nu against the northern group. The strategy, "using barbarians to restrain barbarians," as it was called, became a principle of Chinese foreign policy throughout history. In addition to playing off the Hsiung-nu against one another, a commissioner, Pan Ch'ao, was sent into Central Asia, and the states there submitted and acknowledged Chinese suzerainty. Trade routes to the west, which had been closed since the time of Wang Mang, were reopened and the Northern Hsiung-nu were apparently forced to begin their migration toward the west.

During the Han dynasty, Central Asian merchants traded in goods that occasionally linked the two great empires of the day, Chinese and Roman. There were no significant direct contacts, but each knew of the other. In Rome there was a taste for Chinese silk—indeed, the Romans called China "Serica," or "The Land of Silk." In Ch'ang-an and Lo-yang no Roman product was in similar demand, but the Chinese had heard of "Great Ch'in" (their name for the Roman empire) and recorded it in their histories.

DISSOLUTION OF THE FIRST EMPIRE

Within a century after the defeat of Wang Mang, some of the old centrifugal forces working against the central government once again became strong. Relatives of empress dowagers began to occupy powerful positions, and their families grew rich. Soon, the families were fighting among themselves. On several occasions, in attempts to regain central control, emperors relied on eunuchs to suppress the powerful families. Officials and scholars protested openly against the "usurpation" of power by corrupt and cruel eunuchs. Nevertheless, the eunuchs had their way. They imprisoned and killed many of the most outspoken opponents within officialdom. Yet the emperors, far from being freed by their allies, fell more under their sway and had to look elsewhere for assistance.

Meanwhile, in the countryside, the familiar process of expansion of the power of great families at the expense of the peasantry, either by resisting local officials or in collusion with them, led to misery and discontent, and then to slavery, flight, banditry, and finally rebellion. The dispossessed even turned up in cities: Lo-yang had gangs of hired toughs. Popular religious cults, in which a magical kind of Taoism was blended with Five Agents naturalism, became widespread over East China. The leader of one of these cults taught what was called "The Way of Great Peace," which seems to have implied some kind of social and political change in favor of the poorer segments of the population. Rebellions broke out in 184. The rebels wore yellow kerchiefs, yellow being in the Five Agents scheme the color of Earth, which they believed was to succeed red Fire, the agent of Han. The rebels thus came to be known as the Yellow Turbans. They were suppressed, but in Szechwan another Taoist-inspired cult rebelled and was able to defy imperial authority for decades. These peasant rebels never became strong enough to overthrow the dynasty, but they further weakened the already declining central authority, and contributed indirectly to the fall of the dynasty by creating the need for strong military forces, the leaders of which were eventually to replace the Han.

Faced with the peasant revolts, the court was forced to turn for assistance to military leaders in the provinces, for imperial armies proved inadequate. In the main, the provincial military leaders came from great local families. Eventually, they became "warlords" in their own areas, their power being based as much on military strength as on economic wealth or social prestige. This new group of professional generals owed some of their power to the official positions that they held, which put armies at their disposal. In this, they reflected the power of office as distinct from the private power of family and wealth that previously had been so important. In later centuries a military career was often to be one road to political power and influence.

THE THREE KINGDOMS

The last emperor of the Han was a puppet of one of these generals. In 220 he was deposed and a new dynasty was proclaimed, but at the same time two rivals also proclaimed themselves emperor in other parts of China. In control of north China, the richest and oldest part of the country, was Ts'ao P'ei, who called his dynasty Wei after one of the states of Chou times. In the west, in what is roughly present-day Szechwan, was Liu Pei, who traced his ancestry back to an emperor of the Early Han and thus claimed to be the legitimate emperor. Naturally enough, he called his dynasty Han, but it soon became clear that the name no longer had all its old virtue. In the valley of the Yangtze, and to the south, was Sun Ch'üan. His dynasty was named Wu after a state that had existed in the same region in Chou times. Its capital was at the site of present-day Nanking, which became the capital of a number of states during the period of disunity that followed. The warring Three Kingdoms were succeeded by a regime that worked briefly and vainly for unity. Then China dissolved into many small and short-lived dynasties.

Han Civilization

The political disintegration of the first empire did not mean that civilization reverted to the conditions of the Warring States period.

There had been an extension of civilization in many areas, beginning with administration and settlement, which spread especially toward the south and west. Canals, irrigation systems, roads, and cities all grew. New materials began to be used, the most famous being paper, the invention of which was recorded about A.D. 100. From China this commonplace but crucial invention spread westward. The Arabs, who captured some Chinese papermakers in the eighth century, began to manufacture paper in the ninth century, and by the eleventh it had been introduced to Europe. It was many centuries before paper became cheap enough for common use, but no other medium approached its value for spreading information.

It was also during the Han that the technique of making porcelain was developed. As with paper, the discovery spread in the course of the next thousand years to the Middle East, and from there to Europe. The origin of the invention is preserved in the English word, *china.* Other technical inventions were a shoulder collar that enabled the horse to be used as a draft animal, and a water wheel, which although it required much human labor to operate, must have contributed to higher yields of food.

LITERATURE

Of the literary achievements of the age, the most important was history, which ever after held a high place among the literary arts. The first great figure was Ssu-ma Ch'ien (145? B.C.-90? B.C.), who inherited his father's position as historian in the court of Emperor Wu, and completed the *Records of the Historian (Shih-chi),* which he conceived as a comprehensive history up to his day. Ssu-ma Ch'ien's first concern was to record events and put them in proper order, chronologically and sometimes topically. Much more space was devoted to the record of the recent past, that is, of the Ch'in and the first century of the Han, than to earlier periods. Ssu-ma Ch'ien's history was made up largely of excerpts from original sources, and in this sense his labors were more compilation than composition. Yet he made the work his own by his decisions about what to include and what to reject, and his comments on the actors and incidents of his history. For a fuller discussion of the work, see chapter XX.

The *Records of the Historian* was the first in a long series of officially sponsored, Standard Histories (numbering 25 at the present time). History came to mean a great deal to the Chinese; we have seen that two of the five Confucian Classics were histories. The Chinese

Pottery model of an upper-class house of Han times.

defined what they were as a people and a civilization by what they had done in the past. The noble potentiality of mankind and the deeds of great and ignoble men were recorded, providing a kind of immortality in this world. History also served as a manual of government, for it told what policies had been devised in the past to deal with recurring issues, and described the results of the policies. The knowledge led to more than administrative techniques, it led to wisdom. The historian showed how moral rulers and moral officials benefited the government and the people, and how immorality in government tended to bring about disaster. The concept was connected with a general theory of history that became accepted in China. It was a cyclical theory, whereby each successive dynasty conformed to a pattern of rise and decline. The idea of lineal progress, which underlies most of modern Western historical writing, was weak in China. On the other hand, Ssu-ma Ch'ien and the better later historians, while accepting the notion of a general cyclical pattern, did not rely heavily on the role of supernatural forces. The moving force of history was to be found in the actions and characters of men.

Ssu-ma Ch'ien's history of events extended from the most ancient times to his own day. The next major historical work, the *History of the Former Han Dynasty,* limited itself to the history of one dynasty. It set the pattern for the later Standard Histories, which because of this scope are also known as the Dynastic Histories. Although the limitation had certain practical advantages, it tended to prevent historians from seeing long-term trends, or basic continuities, that cut across the boundaries set by the rise and fall of dynasties.

The major form of poetry during the Han, called the *fu,* was a special kind of rhymed prose, which combined a richness of language with an exuberance of feeling in descriptions of beautiful places, either real or imaginary, or of the emotions of the poet. Although the main body of the *fu* was generally descriptive, a moral lesson was usually drawn at the end, for already the Confucian scholar-officials tended to believe that the purpose of literature was to convey some moral truth, that is, some Confucian precept.

While the literary qualities of the *fu* are taken up in chapter XX, we may note here that the didactic quality was part of a growing style of life. There are, for example, *fu* on the two Han capitals, Ch'ang-an and Lo-yang, written during the Later Han. Within the passages celebrating the beauty and magnificence of both capitals, the grandeur of the palace and the royal activities, and the delightfulness of the scenery, distinctly moralistic comparisons are made. The early emperors loved the hunt, and the courtiers later inspected with delight the long lines of slain animals, the ladies even returning for a second little thrill of pleasure. The later emperors hunted less and enjoyed the pageantry more than the slaughter. The early emperors built a huge palace and filled it with women. The later emperors enjoyed more modest living. Though the first capital was magnificent, the second capital delighted in the beauty of ritual, and it boasted excellent schools. The Confucian lessons—urbane decorousness, frugality, modesty, and learning—are deftly made. We may suspect that more than a little poetic license has touched the descriptions, but the sentiments of the poets show unmistakably the growth of a Confucian mode among the lettered class. The fashion of coming up to the capital from the provinces to study had been apparent even in Wang Mang's time. By the Later Han, teachers and schools had appeared in the provinces. Learning had become all the fashion, a great stimulus to civilization in the period.

While different men certainly took to the learning in different ways, officials who rose high seemed often to have learned both the Confucian rhetoric and the more instrumentalist, or Legalist, tactics that the life of the capital also encouraged. Here is a description of a prominent "Confucian" statesman: "[Chai] Fang-chin was full of wisdom and ability; he was versed both in [Confucian] learning and the laws. In his administrative work he decorated the laws with Confucian elegance. He was regarded as the most understanding and the wisest chancellor. The Son of Heaven esteemed him highly. None of his requests failed to please the throne."[1] Moreover, he "secretly sought for the hidden desires of the ruler of men in order to secure his position," and was accused of destroying a large reservoir when denied permission to appropriate the farmers' fertile lands around it. An intricacy of character was one of the products of the richness of the civilization.

1. As translated by Wang Yü-ch'üan, in "An Outline of the Central Government of the Former Han Dynasty," *Harvard Journal of Asiatic Studies,* 12(1949): 183.

III

The Period of

Disunity

The disastrous end of the Han did not deter ambitious men from attempting to found another dynasty. The rivalry had begun well before the last Han emperor came to his powerless throne. Among the rivals, however, none had the strength to overcome the others. Instead of becoming a new unified empire, China moved slowly toward disintegration. For over three hundred years there was only a kaleidoscope of states, which were less important for their separate political histories than for developments that passed through and beyond them. Chart 1 presents the political changes in simplified form.

This diagram shows how numerous and diverse the political structures of the period were, in contrast to the long unity that had preceded it. Almost all the states lasted only briefly—the average age of the cluster of 16 states founded by barbarian leaders, for example, barely reaching 25 years, or roughly the length of one man's rule. Even among the dynasties founded by Chinese in the south (the south beginning on the Huai River), though ruling houses succeeded one another with relative order, the average span was not much more than 58 years, enough for a few reigns at most. Notably, the state that lasted longest was the Northern Wei, under a non-Chinese house, whose achievement will be discussed later.

One other feature, partly apparent on the diagram, was the choice by every state, barbarian or Chinese, of a name associated with the Chinese past. Frequently a state chose the old Chou name of the territory in which it rose, as did, for example, Wu, Chin, and Wei. Some of the barbarian states even chose the old name of Ch'in. The practice perhaps suggests the power in the Chinese political tradition.

Political Forces

Throughout the constantly changing arrangements of states there were three major political forces: the military men who founded Chinese dynasties, great families that held more or less autonomous local power, and the barbarian tribes that controlled large parts of north China.

CHINESE GENERALS

In an age when the struggle for political power was as blatant as it was in the Period of Disunity, military force rapidly attained great importance. Not only were the usurpers of thrones frequently military men, but their principal achievements after they had established a

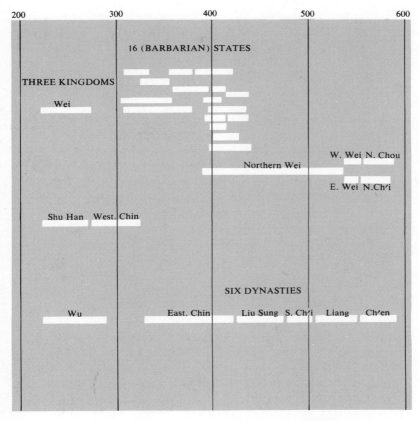

Three Kingdoms, Barbarian States, and Six Dynasties.

new dynasty were also often military. The soldier was the key figure of the period. This was true of both Chinese and barbarian dynasties, but among the Chinese it was the more remarkable for its contrast with the civil tendencies of Han times. The word "martial" (*wu*) appears in imperial titles and reign names of the period at least twenty-one times, compared to only two appearances during the Later Han.

As a rule, the generals who rose to power through their military exploits, frequently in wars against the northern barbarians, and who then usurped the throne, had no strong, dependable political or economic backing. They tended to be self-made men, not from the great families, and it was the great families that controlled large territories in the state. The usurping general's main source of support would be his army, but it was difficult to transform military power into long-lasting political power. In the long run, the great families were the key to political power.

GREAT FAMILIES

Great families, already influential in the Han, helped shape even more the character of the Period of Disunity. The prolonged civil strife at the end of the Han ruined many of the large cities, such as Ch'ang-an and Lo-yang, and drove many townsmen out into the countryside. In contrast to the cities, the estates of great families appeared relatively secure. They attracted townsmen as well as peasants who were fleeing from predatory armies or who, with the disintegration of central political power, voluntarily submitted themselves to the leading local authority. The lack of a strong political authority encouraged the great families to make their estates into largely independent domains, self-sufficient economically and militarily. Some of the estates eventually grew to include several thousand families, who were in effect the subjects of the great families, not of the state. With such large populations, it became possible for the great families to have their own private armies, composed at times of their tenant farmers, but more notably of professional soldiers who became the retainers of the families. The great families made up the social elite. They were careful to educate their sons, in a society in which education was a key sign of elite status, and they intermarried, demonstrating at once a pride in status and a desire to establish ties based on mutual interests.

NORTHERN BARBARIANS

China had suffered from the barbarians off and on for hundreds of years, but during the Period of Disunity barbarian tribes were not content with an occasional foray for booty. They came as conquerors and occupiers of much of north China, establishing dynastic states and attempting to exercise permanent political and economic control over the Chinese who lived in their territories. The shift in their aims from raiding and looting to permanent control has not been clearly explained. There must have been a gradual change, as increasing intercourse with the Chinese gave the barbarians the opportunity to become acquainted with and attracted to the splendors of Chinese court life, for it was the ruling groups who became captivated by the high style and pleasures there.

The barbarian rulers faced a number of problems. The conquerors were few in number compared to the Chinese population. They might be vastly superior in warfare, but how were they to exploit the huge population in a systematic, orderly fashion? Furthermore, the Chinese way of life conflicted with the nomadic way of life in many ways. Would they force the Chinese to change their habits, or try to force their own people to adopt Chinese habits?

For these and other questions of equally great consequences, solutions were sought during the centuries of the Period of Disunity. During that time the historical development of China divided into two streams, those of the barbarian states in the north and the Chinese states in the south, the border line between the two being roughly the Huai River.

Developments North and South

In the south, no change had greater consequences than the great influx of Chinese from the north. A marked movement southward had

Pottery figure of a warrior of the Northern Wei Dynasty.

begun as early as the Later Han, but in the Period of Disunity it so accelerated that large parts of north China became sparsely populated. A comparison of the population figures for A.D. 2 and 742 shows the extent of this trend:

	A.D. 2	A.D. 742
North of Huai River	34.5 million (80%)	30.5 million (60%)
South of Huai River	9.5 million (20%)	21.5 million (40%)

The flight from the north included people from all classes, high and low, some of whom moved in groups of hundreds and thousands. Most of the migrants settled around the lower valley of the Yangtze River, in modern Kiangsu, Anhwei, Hupei, and northern Kiangsi. This area presented valuable opportunities for development. The alluvial soil was among the richest in China, the climate superb for agriculture, and in addition the region was watered by a labyrinth of streams and rivers that fed into the Yangtze. Furthermore, a new method of cultivating irrigated rice, to which this region was especially suited, began to be employed from late Han times. It was the transplantation method, basically the same as that used today, in which rice seedlings were grown thickly bunched together in nursery beds and later transplanted into wider fields to mature. Transplantation permitted more efficient use of space and water, and a more intensive yield. The south began to produce a surplus of rice that could be shipped north. By the seventh and eighth centuries rice had become the favorite staple of the upper classes all over China.

Another distinctive development in the south assured the great families a preponderant role in government. In the Han, one of the ways candidates entered the Imperial University and became eligible for office was through the recommendations of local officials, who frequently made their recommendations in consultation with the great families of the region. In the early centuries of the Period of Disunity, a new system of recommendation, called the Nine Ranks Grading System, became prevalent in several Chinese dynasties. The system varied with time and place, but generally, in provinces, commanderies, and districts, men from the most prominent local families were appointed graders. They had the responsibility, or the opportunity, of grading the men in their region into nine ranks according to their promise as officials. In theory, this was another attempt to discover the best men for government. In practice, it strengthened the power of the great families, for although the grader made his selections in a number of ways, sometimes on advice of high ministers in the government, he usually took into account the opinion of the great families of the region; eventually he tended to rank the men according to the status of their families rather than by any standards of individual merit. The Nine Ranks Grading System confirmed the power of the great families in the state.

On the whole, the great families were able to hold their own in contests with the government. When the Ch'in dynasty briefly reunited China after the period of the Three Kingdoms, for instance, it was able to register only 16 million people in its census for taxation in A.D. 280; in A.D. 157, the registration figure had been 56 million. To be sure, avoidance of registration was not the sole reason for the precipitous decline; war, famine, and epidemics took their toll as well, but the difference clearly reflects a sharp decrease in the power and authority of the central government.

NORTH CHINA

It was in the north that the foundations for the renewal of the empire were laid. Whereas the south was being transformed by the influx of newcomers, in many parts of the north the distribution of the population was so uneven, or changed so frequently, that agricultural production suffered, which meant that the state collected less in taxes. Yet the barbarian dynasties were based on military rather than economic power. The greater effectiveness of the barbarian armies gave the emperors in the north more potential control over their territories. As a rule, however, owing to their preoccupation with fighting other states, they failed to achieve any kind of political stability. One remarkable exception was the Northern Wei (386-535), founded by the T'o-pa group of the Hsien-pei, probably a proto-Mongol people, a dynasty that lasted longer than any other during the Period of Disunity. The success of the Northern Wei seems to have come from combining Chinese methods of civil administration with a style of leadership and control more characteristic of a military conqueror.

The T'o-pa group went further than other nomadic invaders in adopting Chinese ways. Even before proclaiming the Wei dynasty, they had for some decades used an administration partly Chinese in methods. Two decades after the beginning of the dynasty, the court disbanded the tribal confederation of which the invading group had been formed. Tribal chiefs were made nobles and given Chinese titles such as Prince or Duke, as well as agricultural lands with peasants and slaves. The settlement was lavish, but it meant that the autonomous tribal leaders had been deprived of their independent power and subordinated to administration in the Chinese style. The Wei even began to repair the Great Wall, to keep out "barbarians." As Wei armies conquered most of north China, men from the great Chinese families were brought into the government. Eight chief T'o-pa families and four great Chinese families were declared to be of equal status in a formal aristocracy. The court adopted the Chinese language, Chinese styles of dress, and other Chinese customs, and moved the capital to Lo-yang, the old eastern imperial capital.

Yet the policy of sinification had its limits. The court was careful to see that T'o-pa men had a preponderant role in the central government. Above all, military command remained in T'o-pa hands. Thus, the T'o-pa put Chinese elements of administration at the service of their own power, as no Chinese dynasty in the south was able to do.

The Equal Field System. An example of how the Northern Wei state used its power to its own advantage was the Equal Field System, a system of land tenure first enforced in 486. Although it underwent many modifications in the following three centuries of its existence, in essence the Equal Field System provided an allotment of land to each adult farmer, with the aim of increasing the revenues of the state and restricting the economic growth of the great families.

An adult was defined as a male between the ages of twenty and sixty, although from time to time changes were made in these ages. The major portion of the land given each adult by the state (usually 80 percent) was for ordinary grain cultivation; the usual name for this was "personal share land." This land reverted to the state by stages as the farmer grew too old to work it all, any of it that remained going to the state at his death, to be redistributed to others who had become eligible. The rest of the land was intended for permanent crops, originally mulberry trees, the leaves of which were used to feed silkworms. This portion did not revert to the state as long as it was cultivated and silk produced by the family; it was therefore called "land held in perpetuity." In addition to male adults, old people, widows, monks, and nuns were granted smaller allotments, tax-free, for their own support.

Ordinary adult farmers who received land under this system paid taxes and performed labor service for the state in return for the land.

There were three basic taxes: a *tsu* tax in grain on the "personal share land," a *tiao* tax in kind, usually cloth, from the housewife's product from her silkworms, and a stint of *corvée* labor, which might be avoided by a tax payment called *yung*. In general, the allotments were generous and taxes relatively small, amounting, on paper at least, to less than one thirtieth of the total crop. The *corvée* requirement was twenty days of labor service a year.

The original motives of the system were to establish state control over large tracts of abandoned or newly opened land, allot it in a way to assure the common people of a living and the state of revenues, and, without diminishing the size of the estates already founded, to prevent great families from encroaching further. The ability of the Northern Wei and succeeding northern dynasties to maintain the system demonstrated their relative strength against great families. It was also an example of the age-old theory that the land belonged to the sovereign, and that he had the right and responsibility of providing for the economic well-being of all the people in some sort of equitable fashion. Yet it is clear that in practice his own interests came first, as was shown by another policy enforced by the government in 488. One tenth of the people were made state tenants. They were exempted from regular taxes and service obligations, but had to pay a heavy rent each year, probably amounting to fifty or sixty percent of an individual's produce. In effect, the state established a huge estate for itself, and charged its tenants a heavy rent.

The Militia System. Although the ruling class of the T'o-pa took the lead in sinification, eventually the lower classes also were affected; the former warriors became farmers and gradually lost their skill and pride in warfare. The change made for dissatisfaction among some T'o-pa leaders, expressed in opposition to sinification and armed revolt against the court. Most of the revolts were suppressed, but eventually the dynasty was split into two lines of rival successor states, constantly fighting each other.

The endemic warfare led one line of successor states (the Western Wei and the Northern Chou) to devise a militia system to strengthen their military power. Like the Equal Field System, the militia system became a standard institution, lasting well into the second imperial period. Essentially it made every man, or at least every farmer, a soldier. A certain proportion of the adult males—eventually one of every three who received land under the Equal Field System—was designated for a term of military service, lasting several years. During that time they ordinarily farmed their lands in season and trained at a garrison in idle times. They might also be sent to imperial bodyguard garrisons, or when needed to the frontier. In its fully developed form, as many as 600 garrisons were established throughout the country.

The system offered an alternative, or supplement, to the T'o-pa mounted warrior armies. It also promised to be less expensive than a standing professional army, for the farmer-soldiers would be self-supporting—or so it seemed. Actually any benefit would be qualified, for it depended on there being little fighting, as no one could fight and farm at the same time. Yet the system apparently offered real advantages in recruiting, maintaining, and controlling a fighting force.

Cultural Growth

As important as the political amd administrative aspects may have been, the intellectual and cultural vitality of the age was more striking. The connection between the political and social instability and the remarkable cultural achievements is difficult to determine. In general, it can be said that the decline of the influence of the central government permitted greater freedom of individual expression, and the disintegration of society impelled thinking men to question previously accepted ideas and to explore new fields of inquiry. Yet thinking followed a new direction; much less effort went into social, political, or moral thought than into questions concerning the mind, the spirit, and the ultimate state of the individual.

ECLIPSE OF CONFUCIANISM

The difference appeared, for instance, in the decline of Confucianism. With the disorders of the later Han, men began to question the validity of many Confucian concepts. Confucianism had become closely associated with the Han state, and the decline and collapse of the state seemed to reflect the inadequacy of Confucianism to achieve the harmonious order it promised. In addition, the fall of the Han and the emergence of the Nine Ranks Grading System meant that a mastery of the Confucian Classics was no longer an important road to official preferment. Moreover, the instability of the states that succeeded the Han meant that political life could be dangerous. When a dynasty was overthrown, a loyal official could easily lose his position, and not infrequently his head as well. Men turned their thoughts from ideal forms of government to fundamental problems of individual existence.

This does not mean that Confucianism disappeared. To be educated still meant that one had read the Classics, and Confucius continued to be acknowledged as a great sage. Confucian ideas, however, were no longer the keystones of wisdom. Having already been linked to larger cosmological schemes in Han thinking, they tended to become secondary in the intellectual amalgamations of the new period.

NEO-TAOISM

One of the most prominent trends during the early centuries of the Period of Disunity was Neo-Taoism, a name given by modern scholars to describe two streams of thought that derived from classical Taoism, one philosophical and one religious. Although the two were interrelated, they were distinct enough to be discussed separately, provided the reader remembers that men of the time might happily follow both simultaneously.

Philosophical Neo-Taoism was known at the time as "Mysterious Learning," a term which suggested that there was a deep, hidden meaning to life and the world. This central mystery obviously had connections with the ineffable Tao of Lao Tzu and Chuang Tzu, and like the Tao could not be adequately expressed in words.

One important theme of the Mysterious Learning was spontaneity. Lao Tzu had said, "Being and Not-Being grew out of one another," and there were many similar statements in the *Lao Tzu* and *Chuang Tzu*. The inference was drawn that things were produced by no other thing, in other words, that each thing came into existence spontaneously. Spontaneity and freedom thus became one of the aims of those influenced by this stream of thought. A knowledge of the unchanging laws of the universe, it was believed, would enable a man to understand what was "natural," and make him free. Such a person would spend his life, whether within society or withdrawn from it, spontaneously conforming to his own nature, mystically identifying himself with Nature and forgetting all distinctions—even the distinction between life and death, since both were seen as natural processes.

An instinct for the central mystery of Nature suggested different kinds of action to different men. For some of the refined aristocracy, these abstruse ideas were the topic of polished and witty discussions, known as "pure conversation." For others, a simple and quiet life would do. Still others carried the idea of spontaneity to extremes, in which being natural meant flaunting all social conventions. A fifth-century record contains the following description of some of their behavior:

> At the end of Wei, Juan Chi used to indulge himself in wine and wild abandonment. He would uncover his head, let loose his hair, take off his outer clothes, and lie sprawled on the ground. Later on the youth of the nobility, such as Juan Chan, Wang Teng, Hsien Ku, and Hu-mu Fu-chih, were all followers of his example. They said this was the way to attain the origin of the great *Tao*. Therefore they would get rid of their caps, pull off their clothes, and exhibit shameful behavior, as if they were birds and beasts. Doing this to an extreme degree was called "understanding"; doing it to a lesser degree was called "comprehension."[1]

Juan Chi and his companions, we are also told, found drinking from cups unnatural. They used to sit around a big bowl of wine on the ground and sip from it in common; occasionally they were joined by a curious pig. Such behavior was the very antithesis of that prescribed for the ideal Confucian gentleman. Although Juan Chi and his friends were by no means typical, the story nevertheless indicates the great changes that took place in the ideals of life among the educated classes in the Period of Disunity.

The second stream of Neo-Taoism was a mixture of various elements of popular religion, some of which originally had nothing to do with Taoism. The existence of popular religious sects in connection with the Yellow Turban and other revolts in the last decades of the Han dynasty has already been mentioned. Religious Taoism was a blend of many such cults, holding a few key beliefs in common, such as worship of the Yellow Emperor and Lao Tzu, and the idea that it was possible to attain long life, or Immortality. The leader of one of these cults eventually became known as the Heavenly Teacher, a title inherited by his descendants until 1927. Although the Heavenly Teacher was called the Taoist Pope by Westerners, the title was quite inappropriate, as there was no well-organized church for him to oversee, he had no special authority in doctrinal matters, nor was he very influential outside his own local area. This was also true of other Taoist cults, for the general pattern of organization was made up of countless small local shrines and temples, run by one priest, or at the most several priests, supported by the contributions of the local faithful, and receiving neither assistance nor directives from any

---

1. Fung Yu-lan, *A History of Chinese Philosophy,* translated by Derk Bodde (Princeton, 1953), II, 190.

higher organization. For the diffused quality of Chinese religion, see chapter XXI.

The nature of religious Taoism can be suggested by a description of several of the more common practices. There were, for example, breathing exercises. Breath (*ch'i*) was believed to be the vital force, and controlling and conserving the breath was seen as a means to preserving the vital force and prolonging life. The adept would lie in bed, before dawn, holding his breath for more and more heartbeats as he mastered the art. The captured breath he guided through his body, "refreshing" it, especially in three vital centers in the head, chest, and abdomen. He also swallowed saliva, which along with breath was believed to be adequate nourishment for the "Immortal," the purest of beings. The ultimate aim of the practice was immortality on earth, or at least in some corner of Nature, for those who became Immortals were thought to pass into obscurity.

Another practice was gymnastics, believed by some to preserve the vitality of the body. Usually mild exercises were devised for this purpose, one performed even to the present day being a stylized boxing. Though put forward occasionally as an art of serious combat, it is actually a therapeutic exercise, as anyone sees immediately who comes upon a dignified professor in his garden, dancing gracefully in his underwear in the cool of the morning.

Diet was also important, the usual emphasis being on the avoidance of harmful foods rather than the consumption of beneficial ones. Some adepts refrained from wine and meat while others did not eat the five grains, which it was believed nourished worms that lived within the body and caused disease, old age, and death. Yet some found wine a help rather than a hindrance. One adept was said to keep two servants constantly at his side, one with a flask and the other with a spade, to bury him where he fell. Still others considered the vital spirit to be nourished by sexual exercises, while some sought an elixir of immortality, experiments by the latter contributing to the development of alchemy in China, though sometimes at the cost of the health of the experimenters.

One last Neo-Taoist idea should be mentioned: the belief that, in addition to inner hygiene and elixirs, leading a virtuous life was necessary to attain immortality. Eventually there was a long list of prescribed and prohibited actions, each of which entailed accumulating merits or demerits that affected the length of one's life. The mechanical aspect of the idea stressed that each man was subject to the inexorable Tao, but he was judged as an individual equal essentially to all other individuals, not according to his level of education or status. In that sense he was somewhat freer than a Confucianist.

The condition of the individual was also the concern of the other most vital school of thought at the time, Buddhism.

BUDDHISM

Buddhism was at least as powerful a force as Neo-Taoism in the cultural growth of the period. There was a Buddhist community in China as early as A.D. 65, and almost immediately Neo-Taoism and Buddhism tended to become involved with each other because of apparent similarities. Yet Buddhism was an original and profound religion centuries before it reached China, and it established a distinctive importance there.

The story of the development of Buddhism begins with a combination of fact and legend about the Buddha Gautama, who probably lived in northeast India between 560 and 480 B.C. He is referred to by many names: Gautama was his family name, Siddhārtha his given name; he is also called Shakyamuni, "the sage from the tribe of the Shakyas." The Buddha, "the Enlightened," is the name of a type of which he was an embodiment. Later believers looked on him in at least three different ways—as a historical figure, as a magical, godlike being, and as a symbol of basic truth.

In history, Buddha's life reflected his search for truth and his method of attaining it. His father, a prince of the Shakya tribe, worried over a prophecy that his versatile son would become either a great ruler or a great ascetic, kept him inside the splendid palace, so that he might not be drawn to the life of asceticism. Nevertheless, curiosity drove the prince to make several brief excursions. He was deeply disturbed by three things he saw—an eighty-year-old man, a man with an ugly disease, and a corpse. The harsh discovery of aging, sickness, and death turned his accustomed pleasures to ashes in his mouth, and, realizing that he too would sooner or later suffer the same afflictions, the young man decided to leave his beloved wife and son for the life of an ascetic in the forest. That life, too, he had to give up when he discovered that self-punishment was as distracting as self-indulgence. At last, after intense meditation, he perceived a solution to the sorrows of life, the Middle Path. He taught it until he died, aged about eighty, apparently from food poisoning.

The essential insight he had gained he summed up in highly

compact form in his first sermon as the Four Noble Truths: 1. *All life is characterized by suffering.* Suffering pervades life, in the Buddha's view, not simply in the critical events of birth, aging, sickness, and death, but even in moments of apparent joy, which involve anxiety that they will soon end, or pleasure at the expense of others, or some other condition bound to produce suffering. 2. *Suffering originates in craving (or desire).* Seeking delights and satisfactions creates suffering, for craving for experiences must inevitably end in frustration, in the sense that desires can never be completely and finally satisfied. One chronic and fundamental kind of craving is the desire to perpetuate oneself, a desire that is especially pernicious, for it is based on the illusion that there is a "self." According to Buddhism, no permanent "self" (or "soul," or "I") exists to be perpetuated. The individual, insofar as he exists (different schools vary widely in their positions on this key question), is only a temporary composite of many components in perpetual flux. To be ignorant of this is to permit all sorts of false attachments to be sought. 3. *Suffering is stopped by the complete stopping of craving.* 4. The steps in the stopping of suffering are the *Noble Eight-fold Path.* The path consists of right views, right intentions, right speech, right conduct, right livelihood, right effort, right mindfulness, and right concentration. It will be noticed that in highly abbreviated form the list describes a course leading to complete absorption of the follower into a religious state, beginning with acceptance of the Four Noble Truths (the "right views"), moving through moral disciplines, and ending with a meditative state or trance ("right concentration").

The end result of this was to be the attainment of Nirvana, a condition said to include the complete extinguishing of desire and pain and the rise of perfect peace and bliss. It is not clear whether the Buddha achieved Nirvana with his enlightenment while still alive or postponed it until he died.

To a large extent the fact that death is not necessarily the moment of the advent of Nirvana stems from a world outlook that Buddhism shared with earlier Indian schools of thought, in which neither life nor death was final. The universe is made up of innumerable "world systems," each of which, although of enormous length, is finite and eventually dissolves only to be followed by new systems that come into existence. In a somewhat similar fashion, living beings are compounds of everchanging components, to which accrue merits and demerits as a result of the actions of the being. When the individual being "dies," the components re-form on higher or lower levels, depending upon the weight of these merits and demerits. This process is called "rebirth," although there is no soul to be reborn, only components to be regrouped. The force of acquired merits is called karma, a fundamental concept of Indian thought that underlies Buddhism as well as most other Indian systems. It can be seen that the concepts of karma and rebirth make the death of an individual being a less decisive event than we normally think, since it is merely a transition to another stage of existence. According to Buddhist statements, rebirth continues until ignorance is dispelled, the burden of karma lifted, and Nirvana attained.

Two centuries or so after the time of Gautama, Buddhism split into two branches, Theravada ("the Doctrine of the Elders") and Mahāyāna ("the Great Vehicle"). Theravada took the position that it was closer to the teaching of the historical Buddha. Today it remains the dominant form of Buddhism in Ceylon, Burma, Thailand, and Cambodia. Mahāyāna included teachings that, in the view of its adherents, made the doctrine more truly universal. It was the Mahāyāna branch that eventually dominated East Asian Buddhism in Tibet, Mongolia, Japan, and Korea, as well as China.

Mahāyāna Buddhism expanded on key concepts of earlier Buddhist teachings. To emphasize, for instance, that nothing has a permanent essence, Mahāyānists repeated in hundreds of writings, so that it became a key article of faith, that all things are empty. Emptiness became, for some, the ultimate reality. The enlightened individual "dwelt in emptiness," realizing that no object, himself included, had any permanent core. Yet everyone was the same in this respect; indeed, everyone shared, had he the wisdom to realize it, the Buddha-nature. Ultimately everyone was Buddha.

Another major concept was the Bodhisattva (Enlightened Being), a man who postpones his own attainment of Nirvana in order to save others. He does so out of compassion, a virtue that has equal weight with wisdom in Mahāyāna. The ideal Buddhist figure of action thereby embodies a paradox, the formula of the Bodhisattva being "Never to abandon all beings and to see into the truth that all things are empty." The Bodhisattva's virtuous acts enable him to accumulate great amounts of merit, which help to reduce the suffering in the world.

Devotion to and faith in the Bodhisattva became sources of help for the ordinary believer. Among the Bodhisattvas, a famous one was

Avalokitesvara, a great embodiment of compassion, who, known in China as Kuan-yin, was believed to be especially helpful to those in certain kinds of danger and to women who wanted sons. Buddhas, too, in their magical-godly aspects, responded to devotion. Amitabha (known as O-mi-t'o-fo in China and Amida in Japan) was the Buddha of the Pure Land or Western Paradise, who had vowed to bring anyone who called on his name in faith to that paradise, which appeared as a far more concrete place of bliss than the largely negative earlier concept of Nirvana.

Even this brief survey of a few key Buddhist doctrines suggests how different they were from earlier Chinese thought. The Chinese had not felt that life was characterized by suffering, nor, with the possible exception of some Taoists, had they conceived of renunciation of the world as the answer to the human condition. Even the Taoist reservations about society were clearly different from the Buddhist renunciation of the world.

When Buddhism began to be the subject of interest early in the Period of Disunity, some of its doctrines were mistakenly identified with Neo-Taoist ideas then current. The Taoist state of "not-being" was seen as equivalent to Buddhist "emptiness"; the Taoists' "natural" response, although its emphasis was on spontaneity, was associated with the rigid causal relationships of Buddhist karma. It was several centuries before accurate translations of Buddhist scriptures and the efforts of missionaries cleared up these confusions.

If Neo-Taoists found Buddhist positions at least superficially congenial, the reaction of the Confucianists tended to be less favorable. They objected to Buddhism's rejection of this world, to the idea of rebirth, and to the celibacy of Buddhist monks, for to fail to produce sons was considered to be unfilial. Yet the greatest conflicts occurred in the realm of practice, not of theory, as can best be shown by turning to a brief survey of the early growth and spread of Buddhism in China.

A reliable source mentions a Buddhist community in China in A.D. 65, but rapid growth did not begin until after the end of the Han or, more specifically, after the expulsion of the weak Chinese successor states from North China by the nomadic invaders in the fourth century. How much the growth of Buddhism owed to the conditions of the age and how much to the intrinsic appeal of the teaching is difficult to decide. The physical destruction and the disruption of the social order surely impressed the idea of impermanence on the shocked literati, in addition to disillusioning them about the efficacy of Confucianism. For the common people, any teaching that gave comfort and reassurance in face of the catastrophes they experienced was attractive. Yet Buddhism appealed to all classes, not merely the oppressed peasantry or the uprooted literati, but also imperial houses at the height of their success. Furthermore, it spread both in the north under barbarians and in the south under Chinese rule.

Like social development, Buddhism differed sufficiently in north and south to make a separate analysis of its growth in each area useful. In the southern Chinese states, the teaching became popular among the literate elite who had been interested in philosophical Neo-Taoism. The abstract speculations of the Mysterious Learning became a bridge spanning the gap between traditional Chinese learning and the abstruse metaphysics of Buddhism. Some who had been Neo-Taoists were converted to Buddhism and became monks. Larger numbers of the literati interested themselves in the intellectual problems of Buddhism and frequented the monasteries to converse with the monks. By the end of the Period of Disunity, there were well over a thousand of these monasteries, many built in secluded and beautiful places, which doubtless attracted visitors of all classes.

Southern rulers and southern court circles were indulgent toward Buddhism. True, Buddhist monks and the growth of the Buddhist establishment inspired opposition from the beginning, but when it was charged that Buddhist monks ought to bow before the emperor, on the orthodox assumption that the emperor was the first among men, the southern emperor accepted the Buddhist response that the clergy had cut all finite ties and dwelt in another domain, and therefore owed nothing to this world. A particularly famous patron, Emperor Wu of Liang (sixth century), "gave" himself as a menial to a Buddhist temple several times, requiring his ministers to "redeem" him with princely sums. In addition to this means of raising funds for temples, the emperor himself financed the construction of several new ones. He also attended assemblies at which sutras were discussed, issued general amnesties as acts of compassion, and decreed that Taoist temples should be destroyed and their inhabitants made to return to lay life. He enjoyed such titles as "Emperor Bodhisattva" and "Bodhisattva Son of Heaven." However, when he suggested that he might add to his temporal power control over the Buddhist establishment, he was rebuked by a monk, and abandoned the attempt.

In the north, too, the generosity of pious emperors added to

Buddhist wealth. Beginning with land not normally cultivated, as in mountains, Buddhist communities tended to make their land productive, and then to acquire more land, including regular farm land. Devout emperors either gave land to monasteries, or sanctioned their acquisition of land by giving them name-plaques as signs of imperial patronage, a patronage which often included exemption from taxes. By the sixth century a movement of "peasant monks" was noted, large numbers of farmers entering Buddhism in order to avoid taxes and *corvée*.

On the other hand, the emperors of the Northern Wei appointed prominent monks to the official post of chief of monks, charged with conveying orders from the government to Buddhist communities throughout the state. The state, in other words, asserted its control over the Buddhist establishment. In the south, when a Buddhist monk refused to rise as Emperor Wu entered an assembly, everyone, including the emperor, approved of his spiritual independence. In the north, when the chief of monks of Northern Wei tried to square his position as a civil servant with the doctrine that the monk does not bow down before a king, he decided that all could be solved by considering the emperor the Buddha, and acting accordingly.

In even sharper contrast with the south, northern emperors twice repressed Buddhism. The first time, it was done on the advice of a Taoist priest and a Confucian minister, each of whom had both the ear of the emperor and personal reasons for disliking Buddhists. A number of decrees were promulgated that aimed at destroying the independence of Buddhist communities. Anyone under the age of fifty was prohibited from becoming a monk, and private support of monks and monasteries was forbidden. To make matters worse, a monastery in Ch'ang-an was implicated in a local rebellion. Furthermore, when it was charged that monks had attended bacchanalian parties with ladies and gentlemen of the capital, the emperor decreed that all Buddhist religious objects be destroyed and all Buddhist recluses executed. The idea of killing all monks seems to have horrified even the Buddhists' worst enemies, and the decree was never put fully into effect, but some temples and sutras were destroyed and probably some monks killed.

The second repression, which occurred in the sixth century, resembled the first in several ways. Again, Taoists and Confucianists precipitated the attack by making the emperor suspicious of Buddhists. An edict of prohibition was issued calling for the destruction of temples and religious objects, the confiscation of the wealth of monasteries, and the return of monks and nuns to lay life. In addition, since on consideration the emperor decided that the Taoists stole sutras from the Buddhists, and fleeced the people of money and property, he prohibited them as well. Without doubt, Buddhism had suffered another serious check.

It revealed something of the state's attitude toward Buddhism that the emperor who ordered the second repression explained the faults of Buddhism almost entirely in terms of its practices. It did not observe filial piety, he said and it went so far as to condone self-mutilation, such as shaving the head, which defied the obligation of sons to respect the body given them by their parents. The emperor accused Buddhists of coveting riches, referring to the accumulation of wealth by monasteries and perhaps also to the loss of production when farmers left their land to take monastic vows. He further accused Buddhism of instigating rebellion, a charge probably arising from the occasional implication of a monastery in a revolt, and also because some peasant rebels were sustained by Buddhist beliefs. Finally, as the champion of a Chinese tradition to which he may have been more rigidly attached because of his foreign origins, the emperor said that Buddhism had to be destroyed because it was foreign. All of the charges stressed political, social, and economic considerations, over which the state considered itself the arbiter. Doctrinal matters might be the subject of debate, but practices belonged under the supervision of the government. If the practices were associated with an organization, even more vigilance was necessary, for in the concern with conspiracy that almost obsessed the rulers any organization could be a threat.

Yet the repressions brought out a quality of the state different from the systematic totalitarianism this might imply. The repressions did not emerge from any long-term policy of opposition to Buddhism in principle. They were circumstantial, resulting from the combination of an emperor ambitious to extend his power, of advisers hostile to Buddhism, and of bureaucratic and court factionalism brought to a crisis by some trumped-up or real misdemeanor by Buddhists. In contrast to the hostility of some Confucianists and Taoists who exploited such opportunities, there were always moderating tendencies as well, such as the habit of intellectual syncretism and tolerance of other schools of thought. This could permit a man to be a Buddho-Confucian, stressing Confucian models in official conduct and a

Buddhist vision of the life to come, or even a Tao-Buddho-Confucian, who might believe in filial piety, practice careful breathing exercises, and look forward to being reborn in the Western Paradise. As to policy itself, emperors could not always be depended on to defend or condemn consistently any one faith. If wise, they pursued their main aim, that of keeping firm control of the country, pragmatically. If foolish, they listened to whichever adviser caught their fancy at the time.

The sequel to each of the repressions demonstrated the absence of a consistent policy. In the first case, a new emperor came to the throne eight years after the repression. He reversed the prohibition and even encouraged the revival of the religion, so that soon a period of lavish patronage began. Similarly, in the second case the repression died out with the death of the emperor who had ordered it and was followed by a period of intense religious fervor. It would be rash to say that the repressions had no effect, for the attacks must at least have created an undercurrent of insecurity in the Buddhist communities. On the whole, however, the vitality of the religion seemed at the time only to grow.

VARIETIES OF LIFE IN THE PERIOD OF DISUNITY

In the circumstances outlined above, life followed an unprecedented variety of styles and activities. We can imagine some of the scenes associated with Buddhism. In strictly disciplined monasteries, monks followed a schedule of meditation, study, and prayer. Buddhism was a fashion as well as a religion, however, and in some monasteries the salons of the "pure conversation" movement existed, or graceful rites were conducted by handsome monks while the elegant society of the capital watched.

Most suggestive of the deepest Buddhist feelings were the pilgrims and missionaries who, beginning in this period, crisscrossed the eastern half of Asia. One of the most famous was Kumarajiva, who reached Ch'ang-an from Central Asia at the beginning of the fifth century. Working with a team of translators, he made some of the most important Buddhist documents available in Chinese, helping to raise the Chinese understanding of Buddhism to much greater accuracy. At the same time, one of the greatest of Chinese pilgrims, Fa-hsien, reached India. He was the first Chinese monk to do so. He studied and collected texts and returned to Nanking after fifteen years abroad, having visited parts of Central Asia, India, and Ceylon. Upon returning, he not only translated the texts he had collected but wrote a *Record of Buddhist Kingdoms,* a source of information about the Indian world of that time.

Another way of life partly inspired by Buddhism was the attempt to get away from the attractions or distractions of the world. Such was the purpose of monasticism, which in China was often centered in some handsome site in the mountains or countryside. Seclusion or rusticity of this sort appealed, moreover, to those of Taoist disposition as well as to Buddhists, so that the embrace of nature became another way of life, an ideal perhaps encouraged by the many examples the age offered of human vanity frustrated. Some of the best poetry of the period expressed the pleasure of dwelling in the country, heightened by an awareness of the impermanence of life. For a discussion of examples and of other literary achievements, see chapter XX.

Nothing expresses more directly the turn to nature than the development of gardens, which in this period perhaps began for the first time to be made solely for enjoyment. Gardens, created according to a growing body of technical skill and theory, which included the idea that a garden should represent a whole world, no matter how elementary, of vegetation, rock, and water, became a universal minor art among Chinese of means.

The fine arts also grew greatly, though it is hard to say which were the major conditions aiding this growth—the migration to the south and the extraordinary beauty of the lower Yangtze country, the turning toward nature, the many intellectual and esthetic innovations of Buddhism, or the evolving native tradition. Quickened by some combination of these, the period produced a major canon, or theoretical standard, of painting by Hsieh Ho; the first great painter known by name, Ku K'ai-chih; and the first man to establish calligraphy as a fine art, Wang Hsi-chih. Thousands of religious sculptures, ritual objects, and paintings added a whole new world of art based on Indian examples and iconographic rules modified according to Chinese taste. For an analysis of this art, see chapter XIV.

One other way of life may be mentioned that, although it contrasted sharply with religious seeking, seclusion in nature, or absorption in the arts, was always to be characteristic of some groups in China: the way of extravagant and engrossing pleasure. Many of the rich apparently devoted themselves neither to eradicating nor to sublimating their appetites but to satisfying them as fully as possible. Some patronized and stimulated the arts; some probably adapted certain discoveries of Neo-Taoism, whose experiments in lengthening life included the use of exotic and rare herbs, spices, drugs, and minerals. Growing contacts with India and Southeast Asia which had rich stocks of such goods increased the opportunities to spend money on them. Possibly the growth of knowledge especially of spices but also of other new edibles stimulated the art of cooking, which eventually became one of the most common Chinese pleasures. (Little is known, however, about the origin of the modern elaborate cuisine, which may have been developed only later.)

For some, the deepest pleasure of wealth and possessions lay in flaunting them. The famous Shih Ch'ung (third century), for example, furnished the privy of his mansion with beautiful mats and red curtains and stationed there ten or more perfumed maidservants dressed in silk. When a guest came out, they gave him a complete change of clothing. Shih Ch'ung had a rival, Wang K'ai, a relative of the emperor. When Wang stretched a screen of purple cloth ten miles along his property, Shih stretched one of brocade fifteen miles along his. When Wang showed off a big piece of coral, one of the imported treasures prized in the houses of the rich, Shih showed six pieces twice as big.

Luxury and ostentation were but the outward signs of what was held in greatest respect, money. A recluse described its marvelous powers:

Money flies without wings and walks without legs. When even a stern man sees money his face breaks into a smile. When even a silent man of goodness sees it his mouth falls open. Those who have much of it become lords, those who have none slaves. No place is too far for it to go, none too secluded for it to reach. Scholars and the "pure conversers," both are mad about it. High office, fame, all are the results of it. Make no mistake about, money is divine.[2]

The disparity between intellectual ideals and the power of wealth that is here expressed satirically became one of the characteristic issues of social thought. Though theory consistently deplored and attacked private enrichment at public expense, wealth and luxury were characteristically considered normal human desires. The potential conflict between the two extremes, the moral man and the rich man, was usually joined only when a man simultaneously rose to public prominence and displayed enormous wealth. In the Period of Disunity, however, social constraints had so weakened that the display of wealth became a fashion.

2. The essay paraphrased here is taken from Kyoto University's *Chūgoku-shi*, pp. 195-96.

IV

The Second

Imperial Period:

Phase I

SUI DYNASTY
589-618
T'ANG DYNASTY
618-907

Before describing the new political unity it may be helpful to review briefly the changes that had taken place during the long Period of Disunity. Students often feel that the second empire (and the third) merely reenacted the first. The impression is not entirely baseless; some scholars have considered basic Chinese institutions essentially the same for two thousand years. The government remained autocratic and bureaucratic, Confucian notions and pragmatic self-interest contended in the determination of policy, the economy continued to revolve around agriculture, and even the drama of the life of dynasties seemed to repeat a rough pattern from glorious beginnings to gradually accelerating decline—to name only a few obvious similarities. Yet changes occurred and were no less significant for being different, as they often were, from what we are accustomed to noticing in the history of the Western world, with its marked transformations in government, ideology, and economics. During the Period of Disunity, for example, the population shifted southward heavily, so that by the middle of the eighth century some forty percent lived south of the Huai River. Great families increased and consolidated their social, economic, and political influence. Neo-Taoism and Buddhism invaded many areas, including the world of ideas. Life in the seventh century could never be wholly contained in the ancient molds.

Reconstruction of the Empire by the Sui Dynasty (589-618)

The founder of the dynasty that finally reunified China, Sui Wen-ti, was the son of an enfeoffed nobleman in the military service of the Northern Chou dynasty, one of the successor states to the Northern Wei. Wen-ti's surname, Yang, was Chinese, but there is some reason to believe that his family had barbarian blood. Intermarriage between Chinese and T'o-pa aristocrats was not uncommon during the latter part of the Period of Disunity. In addition, Wen-ti's wife seems to have come from a barbarian family.

After usurping the throne from a young Chou emperor, Wen-ti appealed to a wide range of sympathies. He invoked both the classical intellectual tradition and the memory of the greatness of Han, signifying that his goal was the restoration of the ideals of the past, not progressive innovation. Yet he also showed favor to Taoism and Buddhism, abandoning the repressions of his predecessors and encouraging the growth of both, within limits. He established an office in the central government to supervise Taoists, permitted 2,000 adepts to be ordained, and allowed monasteries and nunneries to be built in the capital. Similarly, he set up an office to supervise Buddhism and encouraged the building of Buddhist temples and monasteries, even subsidizing more than eighty pagodas throughout the empire. Wen-ti cited as his ideal the Indian Buddhist emperor Asoka of the third century B.C., who was said to have ruled by righteousness, and he accepted the epithet "Bodhisattva Son of Heaven." By such measures Wen-ti indicated, in addition to some degree of personal belief, a desire to win the support of various groups within the state, while at the same time placing the groups under the administrative authority of his new government.

The emperor also embarked on a number of grandiose projects to demonstrate to all the splendor and power of the revived empire. Close by the site of the old Han capital of Ch'ang-an he built a great new city, which became the capital of China and the marvel of East Asia for over 300 years. It was laid out on a grid pattern, with nine great avenues running north to south and twelve east to west, dividing the residential city into 112 blocks. A wall six miles by five ran round the whole city and was pierced by 17 gates, some of monumental proportions. Inside the city, backed against the north center wall, was another walled space, for the "Palace City," and around it yet another walled space, the Imperial City, containing most of the administrative offices. Since each of the residential blocks was also walled, the arrangement resembled a complicated set of Chinese boxes, bespeaking the government's concern with keeping the people in order and protecting itself.

Other projects included, to the north, the reconstruction of the Great Wall, and its extension in the northwest. Within China, a canal was built from Hangchow on the lower Yangtze to Lo-yang, the second capital, in the northeast. An extension ran northward to the vicinity of modern Peking. This system of water transportation, which in a later form was called by Westerners the Grand Canal, was of great importance in shipping the produce of the south to the capital as revenue, and in supplying the armies along the northern frontier.

Of the modifications in government, perhaps the most important was in regional organization. During the Period of Disunity the influential great families had tended to monopolize high regional offices. Sui Wen-ti abolished both the commanderies, the highest regional administrative unit, and the practice of appointing local men to regional offices. His aim was to reduce the power of local magnates and to prevent officials from abusing state power for their private interests, which they could do, for example, by arranging a reduction in taxes or a favorable legal decision for their families. For precisely these reasons, a "rule of avoidance," as it came to be called, whereby no official might serve in his native province, became standard practice in later dynasties.

This infringement of the long-held privileges of the aristocracy no doubt struck them as outrageous, and consequently was a dangerous step for the emperor to take. Yet it was necessary in order to reunify China under a central government whose supremacy was unquestioned. Other policies of the Sui were just as dangerous but far less justifiable. Much of the extravagance in construction, especially in the two capitals, which pleased only the emperor and his courtiers, wasted economic resources and manpower.

In foreign affairs the Sui also combined reasonable initiatives with costly arrogance. The Turks to the north and northwest were kept in check through threats and the policy of "using barbarians to control barbarians." An eastern group of Turks, based on the region of present-day Outer Mongolia, and a western group, occupying territory through which the caravan route south of the T'ien-shan mountains passed, were kept divided, the Eastern Turks being incited to war against the Western Turks. A Sui campaign into present-day Vietnam had to be withdrawn in the face of native hostility and tropical diseases, but nevertheless Chinese suzerainty over the region was acknowledged. Envoys were exchanged with Japan, and an expedition reconnoitered Taiwan and brought back prisoners and exotic booty. None of these endeavors was ruinously costly. It was Korea on which the aggressive foreign policy foundered.

Three campaigns against the Korean state of Koguryŏ failed. Moreover, the suffering of the Chinese conscript soldiers became intolerable. Thousands died on the roadside for lack of adequate provisions, and those who remained were poorly led by the officers, who were intimidated by their cruel and capricious sovereign.

The blame for many of the excesses, above all for the Korean campaigns, falls on the second Sui emperor, Yang-ti. When rebellion broke out in several areas of the overtaxed, oppressed country, Yang-ti sailed down the Grand Canal to his villa at Yang-chou and shut himself in with his women and other pleasure seekers. The government disintegrated, and Sui fell after only three decades of power. Ironically, as with the even shorter Ch'in dynasty, the costly projects that led to the collapse of the Sui also laid a firm foundation for the longer and more glorious dynasty that followed.

T'ang Dynasty (618-907)

That dynasty, the T'ang, completed the picture of China as an enormous power among the nations. Like the Sui, the T'ang attended especially to its northern frontiers, but with more force. Chinese arms defeated first the Eastern Turks and then the Western, and a ceremony was arranged at Ch'ang-an, where northwestern nomadic chieftains declared the Chinese emperor their Great Leader. The oasis states along the northwestern silk route fell into line, and the Chinese influence was felt even beyond the Pamirs, as illustrated in the arrival of a Muslim ambassador in Ch'ang-an in 651. T'ang also impressed itself on the Tibetans, by a kind of subliminal diplomacy. When the Tibetan king married a Nepalese princess who was a Buddhist, the emperor sent him a Chinese princess, who was also a Buddhist, and Tibetan civilization was said to develop under these Indian and Chinese influences. A Chinese princess, no matter how beautiful, could not, of course, assure the good will of the Tibetans indefinitely, and they as well as other peoples later attacked the Chinese. At first, however, the record attests to the success of the Chinese approach.

Even Koguryŏ, which had warded off the Sui armies, and at first warded off the T'ang as well, eventually fell. T'ang, allied with Silla, a state in the southeastern part of the peninsula, defeated Paekche in the southwestern part, and, at a time when Koguryŏ was weakened by internal disturbances, attacked successfully (668), leaving Korea unified under the government of Silla.

T'ang domination of the northern coast of Vietnam was marked by the establishment near the present Hanoi of a commandery called An-nan, or Annam, "pacifying the South." From An-nan relations with Southeast Asian states were also administered. A hint of the cosmopolitan spirit of T'ang administration is contained in the fact that at one time an expatriate Japanese was assigned as governor of An-nan.

T'ang also had diplomatic relations with several states, including Japan, and certain features of the Chinese view of a proper international order were emerging. The Chinese regarded the emperor, for example, as supreme among all officers of mankind, so that when foreign embassies came to communicate messages to him from their ruler, he spoke not as an equal but as a subordinate. Communications, goods, and ritual gestures all took the form of "tribute" from the outside state on one hand and "edicts" and "gifts" from the emperor on the other. Sometimes the smaller countries neglected to observe the correct forms, as in 607, when a Japanese ruler addressed a message from "the Son of Heaven where the sun rises to the Son of Heaven where the sun sets." More often, however, China seemed too colossal a neighbor, and too much a leader in every way, not to be given at least nominal deference.

DEVELOPED MACHINERY OF GOVERNMENT

Conquest and domination expressed only partly, and superficially, the vitality generated by the second imperial unification. Domestic developments were more constructive and enduring. The government of the Second Imperial Period was more highly organized than that of the first, although patterns of the first remained obvious. They were seen, for example, in "Nine Courts" resembling the Nine Ministers of Han, but the center of administration seemed no longer to reside in those offices as it had done in Han.

The main business was conducted in a group of offices designed specifically for the administration of the state and separated from management of the imperial family's affairs. The major new offices of the state bureaucracy—the Secretariat, Chancellery, and Department of State at the top; the Six Ministries (or Six Boards) under the Department of State; and the Censorate—are described in chapter XVIII. They or bodies like them remained the backbone of the bureaucracy until the twentieth century.

Another achievement of lasting significance was the code of law published by the T'ang dynasty. It embodied such useful principles and broad applicability that it became a model for other codes in East Asia, such as those of Japan and Annam, as well as the basis of later Chinese codes. It is also discussed in chapter XVIII. As pointed out there, the philosophical basis upon which it rested gave law a different place and different functions from those with which we are familiar. Over-all, the main regulator of conduct was meant to be custom, or ritual decorum. An appeal to law often had the connotation of a failure in virtue. The resort to law meant not so much a confirmation of rights as a way of reaching a decision when more civilized means had failed.

Moreover, law was more an instrument of the state than its constitution. The emperor, who decreed the code, was in effect above it, not subject to it—even though ministers might argue at times that he was bound by certain laws, or at least by customs incorporated in the laws. There was no independent judiciary, though there was a court of review, and no statement of rights of the defendant. Trials, which were commonly conducted at the first level by district magistrates, tended to presume the guilt rather than the innocence of the defendant. It was common to threaten or to inflict pain on the defendant to elicit the truth from him.

METHODS OF RECRUITMENT INTO STATE SERVICE

When the first dynasties of the Second Imperial Period put a final end to the Nine Ranks Grading System, they acknowledged several other regular means of qualifying to be an official. One method was through schools. An Imperial University was founded in the tradition of the Han dynasty university, but more elaborately organized. It had several schools, some for special subjects such as law and accounting, the higher ones colleges for the study of classical and literary subjects. The students of these colleges were mainly the sons of officials and were grouped in the colleges according to the ranks of their fathers. Although a sizable proportion of the places was open to men whose fathers were not officials, the colleges in the main worked in favor of official status by heredity. The right of heredity was also acknowledged in the adoption of a device called "*yin* privilege," by which the son of an official might apply for position according to the rank of his father. No doubt a majority of the ranked officials—those, let us say, commissioned by an imperial edict—owed their position, at least early in the Second Imperial Period, to birth or relationship.

At the same time, the principle of qualification by individual merit and education, an idea rooted in political thought as old as the Classics, gained new strength through a regular examination system. The crucial examinations were those given in the capital to candidates sent up by regional officials, who had already administered preliminary examinations modeled on those of the capital. At the capital the candidate chose any one of several examinations, which were divided between what may be called specialized examinations and general types. The specialized examinations included ritual, law, lexicology (knowledge of the contents of certain dictionaries), mathematical literature (a knowledge of certain books on mathematics), and others. The general examinations were those for the degrees of Perfected

Talent, Classics, and Presented Scholar, the last of these more famous under its Chinese name *Chin-shih*. Each of the general examinations tested literary abilities, but the first stressed skill in writing on political topics or other current subjects; the second, mastery of the Classics; and the third, proficiency in prose and poetry. From the start, the general examinations seem to have commanded greater respect than the specialized examinations, and it was recognized that only the former opened the way to the highest offices. Moreover, the *Chin-shih* examination, which demanded primarily scholastic and literary competence, became relatively quickly (by the end of the T'ang dynasty) the one chosen in preference to all others, and it remained the most important intellectual institution of pre-modern times. It is discussed more fully in chapter XVIII.

In the early part of the T'ang dynasty the examination system had only begun to exert its influence. Although examinations were held annually (later they were held every three years), relatively few major degrees were awarded, rarely more than fifty a year, often far fewer. Moreover, the degrees, although conferring nominal rank, only qualified men to hold office; actual appointment to a particular post, or subsequent promotion of junior members of officialdom, usually depended on further examinations, administered by the Ministry of Personnel. These "selection examinations" apparently included not only written exercises like the qualifying examinations, but also evaluation of the candidate's physical appearance and speech, and perhaps recommendations by superior officials. The bureaucracy, still staffed mainly by men chosen because of family or other influential connections, underwent no abrupt change of atmosphere or outlook in the early years of the system.

A change was taking place, nevertheless, to judge from the way men rose to prominence as time passed. By the middle of the T'ang dynasty at least one quarter of the regular officials mentioned in a standard history had entered the government through examinations. In some ways more important than the growth of the proportion of officials enlisted through examinations was the honor and prestige conferred on successful candidates. A connection between the examinations and fame became obvious. Among the very highest officials throughout the dynasty, over three quarters had passed the examinations.

Developing the idea of methodical recruitment, the early dynasties of the Second Imperial Period also introduced military examinations. They consisted mainly of tests of fighting skills, such as shooting a bow on horseback and handling a lance. As tests of potential leaders of fighting men, and even tacticians and strategists, they seemed less than adequate, and that may help explain why the military examinations never ranked with the civil examinations in esteem or effect on the civilization. A more basic reason, however, seems to have been the preference of most talented young men for the civil service; the ideal of the civil minister overshadowed that of the military leader.

POLITICAL BEHAVIOR

Political events continued in the first part of the Second Imperial Period to involve familiar groups: aristocratic great families, the imperial family, and others in the palace. When the Sui authority began to disintegrate, and groups rose in rebellion throughout the country, some of the strongest contenders were former Sui officers. One among them, the commander of a garrison in a strategic region between the northern border and the capitals, prevailed, and founded the T'ang dynasty. The man's family tree was very lofty. His father, named Li, was descended from an emperor in the Period of Disunity. His mother was the sister of a Sui empress.

The main inspiration to rebel was said to have come not from the head of the house, though he ruled as the first T'ang emperor, but from a younger son of his, famous by both his personal name, Li Shih-min, and his shrine name as second emperor, T'ang T'ai-tsung (r. 626-49). It was he who urged his father to take up arms and he who became the driving force in campaigns to bring the country under control and later to assert T'ang domination abroad.

Among the handful of officials of the highest rank who devised policies and systems that gave the dynasty much of its early strength, most appear to have belonged to families which had long been prominent, some of whom had served the Sui dynasty or were the sons of Sui officials. One was T'ai-tsung's brother-in-law. The men at the top probably looked upon authority as their inherent privilege.

The struggles within the palace for power revolving around the throne which were observed earlier continued to occur in the first part of the Second Imperial Period. Before T'ang T'ai-tsung could succeed to the throne, he thought it necessary to kill two of his brothers, whom he suspected of a plot. Two months later he succeeded his father, who abdicated, some thought under pressure from his strong son. Two of T'ai-tsung's own sons in turn planned to take the throne from him but were thwarted.

When T'ai-tsung's great reign ended, the son who succeeded him

Women of the T'ang palace ironing. Detail of a twelfth-century copy, by Emperor Hui-tsung of the Sung Dynasty, of an eighth-century painting, Ladies Preparing Newly Woven Silk, *by Chang Hsüan.*

proved a weak ruler, whose reign introduced another familiar factor in palace politics, the powerful empress and her family. T'ai-tsung had taken a fourteen-year-old beauty, Miss Wu, into his harem, and when he died she had been placed in a nunnery. The succeeding young emperor, however, who had noticed her even when he was crown prince, called her back from the nunnery to the harem. She maneuvered her way to the top, resorting to any means, even, it seems, killing her own baby when political advantage required it, and became empress. She had the old empress thrown into a wine vat.

As the emperor's health failed, Empress Wu began to speak for him, and when he died she put two of her sons, one after the other, on the throne as her puppets. In 690 she abandoned the last signs of loyalty to the T'ang house and declared the founding of a new dynasty, the Chou. She remained its first and only ruler until 705, when she was too old (eighty-three) and sick to resist one of her sons, who forced her to abdicate. He took the throne, restoring the name of T'ang.

Empress Wu's rise to power in many ways resembled earlier

90

political manipulations. She used her special position near the emperor, clearly, to influence him and eventually to dominate him. As she succeeded, she placed many of her family in government; her relatives continued to exert influence even after her death. Like other strong-willed rulers who turned from the regular bureaucracy in search of an instrument more suited to their ideas, Empress Wu made greater use of eunuchs, a group which grew to overwhelming strength later. Since she was a devout Buddhist she also put numbers of monks to use, seeing in them another alternative to the normal officials. Most significantly of all, she accepted many more men into government by way of the examinations than before, apparently having recognized in the system a source of capable men who might make her less dependent on the nobles and aristocrats around her. The step represented a gradual reform of the bureaucracy into a nonhereditary, widely recruited organization and the beginning of a characteristically ambivalent political relationship between the ruler and the bureaucracy.

SYSTEMS OF LAND TENURE AND ARMED SERVICE

The first dynasties of the Second Imperial Period followed the example of the Northern Wei of the Period of Disunity in establishing an equal-field system of landholding. However, the original equal-field system had been put into effect under a particular and special condition, namely, the underpopulation of one part of the country. The Sui and T'ang dynasties diverged from their predecessors on this important point, applying the system in parts of their much larger domain where conditions were quite different. In addition to allotting fields where relatively few people lived, they tried to do so in densely settled regions, apparently intending to prevent rich landholders from acquiring too much more even where they were already well established. The Sui and T'ang also seem to have applied the system to a much greater area than the earlier northern dynasties had, if only because the Sui and T'ang controlled so much more.

Adopting another system compatible with the earlier imperial precedents, the Sui and T'ang based their armed force on a militia composed of men who had received land under the equal-field system. For the first part of the T'ang dynasty the militia seemed to work excellently. Yet it remained a question whether a militia could long serve the needs of a far-flung and adventurous empire; and whether the men could in fact be both good soldiers and good farmers.

A Creative and Splendid Age

With the establishment of great central institutions the Second Imperial Period enjoyed a flowering of civilization in many other forms as well, so much so that T'ang life became famous throughout East Asia. In Korea, Japan, and Annam, the leaders of society looked to China for the latest styles in many things, from government and religion to clothing and furnishings.

The most tangible symbol of T'ang civilization was the main capital, Ch'ang-an, which seemed to surpass even its Later Han splendor. Within it and the surrounding prefecture lived some two million people. The magnificent city plan, described previously, was embellished by monumental gates, parks, and Buddhist and Taoist temples; and life was quickened (though against the efforts of an administration disposed to keep the merchants under firm control) by the busy energy of two great markets, in the eastern and western halves of the city. As the terminus of trade routes from Central Asia, the north, and the south, Ch'ang-an had a cosmopolitan quality, imparted both by the goods found in its markets and by its foreign quarters, where Chinese gentlemen liked to stroll, sampling exotic food or trying on foreign clothing. In the streets were to be seen many of Asia's peoples—Koreans, Japanese, Annamese, Turks, probably an Indian now and then, Syrians, and Central Asians of different kinds— and here and there a temple, built under state license, serving some part of the foreign community—Manichaean, Zoroastrian, Nestorian Christian, and possibly others. There were Muslims and perhaps Jews in Ch'ang-an in T'ang times, but we do not know whether they built mosques or temples.

Yet the foreigners and foreign ways, though they added color to the city, were only part of its pleasures. The buildings of government, awesome in both the good and the bad sense of the word, were of course another, as was the beauty of many spots. But best of all, Ch'ang-an stood out as the place where the most imaginative, perceptive, and responsive men gathered and could enjoy each other's company.

PRINTING

A new technique, printing, increased the impact of the cultural achievements of the early Second Imperial Period. When texts began to be printed, probably by the seventh century, the components of the process were already familiar. Paper had been invented in the First Imperial Period (about A.D. 100), and ink made from lampblack had been known since antiquity, so that the basic materials had long been at hand. The method, too, was familiar, for the Chinese printed by drawing a broad brush across thin paper laid on inked blocks, rather than using a press; they had already done this in principle for some time in taking "rubbings," that is ink prints, from inscribed stones, friezes, and statues, and in stamping objects with seals as a mark of ownership and the like. Perhaps the only fundamental discovery involved recognizing how valuable it would be to apply the known methods to reproducing texts.

The need for copies may have spurred the development of printing, as printed works appeared when Buddhism was enjoying a phase of marked growth and enrichment. One of the common acts of Buddhist piety, we know, was copying texts and images. This encouragement to reproduce, as well as a more general enthusiasm for spreading the doctrine, may have favored the idea of printing especially among Buddhists. All the earliest printed matter we have now is Buddhist and comes from the edges of the Chinese world. In Korea, for example, there is a sutra printed on paper during the reign of Empress Wu (r. 690-705). The earliest printing we have from China proper is also a sutra on paper, dated 868, which came from Tun-huang, a town in the far northwest through which many travelers to and from Central Asia must have passed. In Tun-huang a library of several thousand documents and paintings, sealed in caves about 1035 as protection against raiders, was rediscovered in 1900.

The impetus to print need not have been Buddhist alone, for other forces, such as the examination system and the demand it created for books, probably worked toward the same end. Books were still relatively rare—only in recent times have large numbers of them reached the villages of the common people—but the printed word had become available for the transmission of information among the large, literate, upper class. Great consequences in the spread of ideas and organization of human efforts were inevitable.

TAOISM

Life continued to be colored in the new period by Neo-Taoism, so that everywhere men of all classes interested themselves in the many beliefs and practices described previously. As a particular source of additional strength in the early part of the period, the patronage of the ruling house of T'ang was enjoyed by Taoism. The T'ang rulers, whose family name was Li, traced their ancestors back to Lao Tzu, who was also held to have been named Li. Although no solid evidence existed on which to base genealogies of such antiquity, families then and later found it satisfying to think of themselves as very old. For an imperial family, the claim to legitimacy could also be strengthened by the idea, derived from a theory of cosmic cycles, that the agent or force associated with the ancient sage had come full circle and brought the rise of the descendants. In giving honorific titles to the great worthies of the major teachings, the early T'ang ranked Lao Tzu above Confucius and Buddha, calling him Emperor of the Supreme Superior Mysterious Origin. The Taoist classics were added to the material on which questions in the state examinations were based, a change that could have had great consequences for education, had it not proved to be only temporary. The favorable climate of several powerful reigns and the inner vitality of many Neo-Taoist movements aided religious Taoism in becoming much more elaborate than before; a measure of its activity was its canon, which had reached 3,744 chapters by the middle of the eighth century.

CONFUCIANISM

The examination system put Confucianism on a footing that promised advantages, for the Confucian point of view was embedded in the texts the aspiring students read for their general education. In addition, the state patronized the teaching, as it did Taoism, by subsidizing Confucian shrines in all major regions. Of original Confucian thought, however, or even Confucian scholarship, there seems to have been little. Perhaps the atmosphere of the Period of Disunity, inimical to the Confucian temper, had given other intellectual currents a momentum that carried them into the new period of unity. After the debacle of the late Han disintegration, Confucian interpretations of the world only gradually became compelling again.

BUDDHISM

The great adventures of mind and spirit occurred in Buddhism, which had grown into a powerful religious and social factor since the Period of Disunity. By the beginning of the Second Imperial Period, Buddhism was able to enter what has been called a period of independent growth.

In doctrine, the growth produced distinctive schools or sects. To mention only the most prominent, a school was founded in the sixth century in the southeast, in the territory of the modern Chekiang, and was known as T'ien-t'ai, after the mountain on which the original monastery was built. Although characterized by its intellectual profundities, T'ien-t'ai also approved of meditation and even simple piety as ways toward enlightenment, thus appealing not only to the learned but also to many others of a devout nature. The Pure Land School put even more emphasis on devotion. It taught that the Buddha Amitabha, who has been mentioned before as presiding over a Pure Land or Western Paradise, would bring there anyone who before dying meditated or called sincerely upon his name. Invocation of a name, meditation on a figure, and other uncomplicated acts of devotion were possible for anyone, and Chinese of all classes followed the Pure Land practices. A third important school, the Meditation School or Ch'an (Japanese: Zen), began to appear as a distinctive sect in the eighth and ninth centuries. It stressed meditation, of course, equating it with wisdom, which could be achieved best, however, with the aid of a teacher. It depended on "mind-to-mind transmission," which communicated the psychic preconditions, as it were, for enlightenment. Ch'an interested the mystical-minded, who seemed to include many artists and intellectuals. A fourth important school was the Esoteric School (Chen-yen; Japanese: Shingon), which pushed to a more radical degree the general Mahayana idea of Buddhahood being immanent in all by teaching that Buddha and the world are identical. The faithful must realize this identification by various means, including, as the name of the school indicates, the understanding of certain secrets, such as syllables and rituals, received from a master. Used for this were a number of graphic and ritual symbols, for it was believed that beautiful representations guided the disciple on his way toward identification with perfect bliss. Those who expected to follow the path of this school gave up ordinary life for the monastery, but the influence of the school extended far beyond its clergy, thanks to the value it placed on the beautiful as symbolic. From court circles especially the Esoteric School received lavish patronage for works of art and ceremonies. In accounting for the extent to which Buddhism won a place in Chinese civilization, the role of beauty and spectacle, the contribution of works of art and ceremonies carries great weight. A remarkable amount of this was owed to the Esoteric School.

Buddhist Travelers. Like some other great religions, Buddhism inspired men to undertake journeys, either in quest of the teaching at its source or, on the other hand, to carry the word to those suffering in ignorance abroad. In the early Second Imperial Period, Buddhists were afoot everywhere from India east, spreading religious and secular knowledge. The most famous of all was probably Hsüan-tsang (d. 664), a Chinese monk who left Ch'ang-an in 629 and spent more than a decade in Central Asia and India. When he returned to Ch'ang-an in 645, he is said to have come home with 657 Buddhist books, 150 relics, and many images and pictures; he is usually portrayed carrying all this on a huge baggage rack strapped to his back. By the time he died he had contributed to Chinese knowledge of Buddhism fully 75 translations, amounting to 1,335 Chinese chapters (*chuan*). He also wrote *Hsi-yü chi* (A record of the western regions), a detailed account of conditions in India and adjacent regions. It not only widened Chinese knowledge of the world at the time, it proved a major account of seventh-century India in any language. Hsüan-tsang captured the popular imagination, which delighted in stories of his life, embellished with touches of the miraculous; and some nine centuries after his pilgrimage an enduring work of fiction, parts of which Arthur Waley has translated into English under the title *Monkey,* was written, based on the Hsüan-tsang stories. To the universality and vitality of Buddhism, as exemplified in Hsüan-tsang and other travelers, was owed much of the cosmopolitan spirit of the early Second Imperial Period.

Growth of Buddhist Organizations. Evidence from many sources points to the fact that there was a great number of Buddhist establishments. Although many details are still unclear, three main types of establishment have been suggested: great monasteries of "official" Buddhism, which the court patronized, sometimes lavishly, while also supervising them as practically an official cult; private monasteries of various sizes patronized by the rich and noble; and small monasteries supported by donations of the common people. We have only the crudest estimates of the numbers. There were perhaps 4,000 great monasteries, a much smaller number of those privately patronized by the rich, and tens of thousands of little monasteries. The number of regularly ordained monks and nuns is equally obscure. It was at least several tens of thousands and at most several hundreds of thousands.

Buddhist influence, of course, extended much further. Some monasteries became rich. Often beginning on a mountain site, they first developed such resources as they had—in some cases, apparently,

Scenes of a journey to the West at the time of the great Buddhist pilgrimages. At the top, scenes on the road; in the center, a pilgrim being received by a high personage at the right and two monks listening to a master expound at the left. Painted about A.D. 660 on a wall in one of the caves at Tunhuang, the gateway to Central Asia.

lumbering—and increased their holdings as opportunities arose. Some acquired extensive farm lands as well as woods and mountains and eventually administered large estates, much like those wealthy laymen possessed. The great monasteries owed their good fortune partly to the emperor, who made them gifts of land as well as other valuables. No doubt they also benefited by being exempted from some of the customary obligations, such as taxes and *corvée*. Great monks at court used their influence to extend the privileges and exemptions monasteries enjoyed.

The imperial patronage of Buddhism reached its peak under the usurping Empress Wu. She seems to have been very devout, in a superstitious way, and she took a personal interest in a number of monks and nuns. Besides appealing to her beliefs, they offered to justify in part her seizure of power. Her favorite monk and his followers showed her passages in a work they may have forged called the Great Cloud Sutra, which referred to a female universal ruler. Agreeing that the universal ruler was none other than herself, she had the sutra distributed throughout the empire and Great Cloud monasteries built in all the prefectures. At the height of her ardor, she even decreed that, contrary to previous policy, the court would rank Buddhism before Taoism. Rich palace chapels were established, eventually to be served by hundreds of monks, and some Buddhist establishments reached new heights of wealth and privilege.

As they themselves grew, Buddhist monasteries fostered practices that affected life around them. They operated charities, helping the sick and the hungry, apparently setting an example for others, including officials. They served as meeting places and hostels for travelers. They gave rise to societies of laymen, organized to support the monasteries, for example, by arranging occasional vegetarian banquets for the monks and nuns, assisting with new buildings, donating needed supplies, and making other pious gifts. Some societies also developed mutual financing arrangements among the members, making one of the earliest credit systems known in China. Buddhist monasteries also seem to have established some of the earliest pawnshops and auctions. Such institutions were likely to affect the life of nearby communities if only because the innovations were tied to new social groupings based on the religion, which sometimes encouraged departures from old patterns of behavior.

In the most general and pervasive way, Buddhism affected the outlook and behavior of great numbers of people of all classes. The enthusiasm of the court, already discussed, took the shape of lavish expenditure as well as devotion, and many of the works of Buddhist art of the period owe their existence to imperial subsidies (see chapter XIV). Among intellectuals, as has also been noted, a new spirituality, richer in concept if not previously unknown, touched the lives of many. For millions of farmers, and others in every class, there was faith in the saving power of O-mi-t'o-fo and Kuan-yin. During major festivals, such as the showing of a relic of the Buddha, all kinds of people might be swept up in the excitement, some even entering a state of delirium in which they mutilated their own bodies. Exceptional though such behavior no doubt was even among Buddhists, it was evidence of the power of the teaching, for no native beliefs had ever awakened such passion among all levels of humanity.

Development of Economic Organization

Another sign of the vitality of the Second Imperial Period was a more elaborate economic life. Some of the conditions contributing to it have been mentioned. The continuing migration to the south led naturally to a greater exploitation of resources, including some of the country's richest land. New products came into more general use. Tea, for example, though noted as early as the third century in the western part of the country, became a common drink, and wet-field rice, by its nature a southern crop, apparently began to be enjoyed by at least the upper classes of the north, where wheat was the common cereal. New techniques helped to produce more goods and better ones. The water mill, which had been known earlier, now led to an important industry in the grinding of wheat to flour and the polishing of rice. The manufacture of porcelain reached a high level of skill. Chinese probing of the outer world and the enterprise of foreign merchants developed a trade that introduced many luxuries and curiosities into upper-class life, even though it probably had little effect on the economy as a whole. The greatest single force in economic development was the strong and effective government, which not only maintained the general peace that encouraged production, but was also the greatest single consumer of goods. It could, moreover, affect economic life considerably, for good or ill, by various political decisions.

Nevertheless, a well-balanced description of economic activities would have to begin with the small farmer, who accounted for much the largest part of what was produced and consumed per capita; but we know little about his life, either in his family or in his village. The closest we can come to a basic economic unit is through our knowledge of the estate. As before, the stronger families and religious groups strove to increase their holdings of land, legally or illegally, and to enjoy the wealth that came to them in the form of rents from the farmers. In addition, parts of estates were sometimes put into commercial crops, such as tea, or included valuable natural resources, such as lumber. Estates sometimes also took up manufacturing, especially pressing oil and milling or polishing grain. There is not much evidence that estates took the lead in agricultural innovations, but they may well have been among the more efficient producers, owing to their scale and unified management.

In the cities and towns there were more visible signs of growing economic organization, including market quarters with a great variety of shops and stalls. Furthermore, merchants dealing in the same goods often joined together in guilds. In and near certain towns, the state's role in economic life appeared, as in state industries supplying the court with fine textiles, paper, chinaware, and other goods of the highest quality. Moreover, in all major towns, from district capitals up, the government designated certain quarters as markets and confined trade to them, fixing business hours and generally supervising activity, partly no doubt to make it easier to collect taxes but partly, too, to keep business literally in its place. In foreign trade as well, the administration asserted an interest, designating official points of entry, such as the port of Canton, and establishing the equivalent of customs and purchasing offices there.

One illustration of the opposition between the commercial world and the political world was the development of financial mediums. In private circles there seems to have been a notable growth of such systems as mutual financing or lending associations. There were also deposit shops, a kind of simple bank which accepted valuables— copper coins called cash, gold, and silver—for deposit, charging a fee, and would honor checks written by the depositors. Merchants also developed a system of credit vouchers called "flying money." Depositing money they had received for their goods in the capital, they would take a voucher back to their own region and present it at a certain office for reimbursement, thus avoiding the danger of carrying large amounts of cash long distances. The "flying money," though apparently not freely negotiable, was one forerunner in commercial circles of paper money.

The state, however, at first showed little interest in new instruments of finance. At best it cooperated in the "flying money" system, which it adjusted somewhat to its own purposes. Individuals of the imperial house found pawnshops interesting profit-making devices, and owned some. Yet the state, despite concern about copper cash and a recognition of its usefulness, frequently debased the coins. Despite the fact that silver and gold, in bulk form, were becoming widely used as mediums of exchange, the state never coined them, as an active interest in commercial growth might have recommended. More characteristically it hoarded them for itself. Though money was becoming an important feature of the private economy, it received only limited recognition in the public economy.

Stresses and Strains in the Empire

That the early Second Imperial Period made so great an impression, both at home and abroad, of brilliance and power attested to the success of the government. Apparently, by adapting old imperial ways to modern conditions—notably by continuing certain types of control introduced under the northern barbarian administrations—the government had built a system which could last for centuries. In fact, enough of the system lasted to maintain one dynasty, the T'ang, for almost three centuries (618-906). But, even so, stresses and strains had begun to weaken the original system within a century or a little more of its founding. Although the faults were not at first of critical importance, in time they undermined the whole administration, interrupting the Second Imperial Period until adjustments could be made.

BREAKDOWN OF THE EQUAL-FIELD SYSTEM

Several features of the equal-field system and of related conditions began to eat away its effectiveness within perhaps a century of its beginning. In adopting the system, which had been connected in the Period of Disunity with a relative abundance of available land, the governments of the Second Imperial Period imposed it as well on more densely settled regions, with the result that the portions of land there assigned had to be smaller. In some of the most densely populated regions, such as those around the capitals, for example, the equal-field allotment apparently amounted to less than half of what was normal. So reduced, the allotments probably fell below the amount needed to support a family and pay taxes, so that the landholder would have to find other ways to make ends meet. It appears that in considerable part the migration of northerners to the south previously mentioned comprised farmers who could not make a living on the land alloted to them. In moving, they reduced, of course, the number of taxpayers in one region and even, on the whole, as they tended to avoid registration, to become what the government called "runaways," in the place where they settled.

On the other hand, there was a natural urge to hold on to land received under the system, even to augment it, and to pass it on to heirs if possible. Other subjects succeeded in having more and more of their allotment classified as land held in perpetuity, so that the administration would not insist on reallocating it as the holders aged and died. Similarly, the building of estates worked against the system to a degree, some estates taking up land that had belonged to the system. Both the "runaways" and those who undermined the system from within deprived the government of tax revenues, and the former group added to the difficulties by escaping routine state control altogether.

SHIFTS IN MILITARY ORGANIZATION

In another basic sphere, that of military organization, changes were considered necessary within a century of the establishment of the system. The chief military power had been centered in a militia system, manned by farmers who had received equal-field allotments. Although the hope of maintaining a reasonably cheap and willing defense force had at first seemed to be fulfilled by successful campaigns, the militia eventually proved an irksome duty to farmers, apparently falling more heavily on certain northern regions, where there was more need, and on poorer farmers, who could not pay for a replacement. Desertion became more common. There was probably also doubt about the effectiveness of part-time fighters.

From early in the Second Imperial Period the Chinese had employed as mercenaries certain foreign chiefs and their tribes. As the militia grew less satisfactory, foreign fighting forces, and Chinese troops raised as professional forces, gradually took up many of the strategic positions once held by militia garrisons.

Regional Military Governors. Over forces stationed in the most dangerous border regions, especially the frequently raided territories in the north, from Manchuria to what is now Sinkiang, were commissioned regional military governors (*chieh-tu-shih*), who were given full command of the forces in their territories. Like the forces, many of the military governors were foreigners. Entrusting the defense of contested borders to foreigners might seem a risky game to play. In fact it was, as later events proved, but high figures in the court argued the usefulness of barbarians in fighting barbarians. We have some reason to believe that the officials who argued so were aiming to please an emperor whose heart was set on the glory of conquest—and thus to advance their own future—rather than to give the wisest advice. In any event, one effect of commissioning the military governors was to shift the balance of military power away from the capital region in which it had at first been concentrated to the border regions.

FAILURE OF LEADERSHIP AT COURT

After the reign of Empress Wu, dynastic politics hinged on coups and nepotism. A son of Empress Wu succeeded her and restored the name of T'ang, but his wife, Empress Wei, apparently was ambitious to become a second Wu. She started to build her own power, using at first some of the old favorites of Empress Wu's time, and, when the emperor got wind of her schemes, had him poisoned and put her own son on the throne. Another prince then killed her and her family and, assuming control over other branches of the imperial family, took the throne. He is known as Hsuan-tsung (r. 712-55), and it was in his reign that the stresses mentioned above led to disaster.

As he came to the throne he seemed to promise a renovation of government. He hinted at an interest in economy, reducing the subsidies alloted to certain nobles and Buddhist establishments. He employed outstanding officials, some of whom had refrained from taking office in previous inauspicious reigns.

Somewhere in the course of his long reign, however, interests other than statecraft seem to have diverted him, resulting in a lack of leadership at a crucial moment. He patronized the arts lavishly, and indulged a taste for beautiful things of all kinds. His most famous love came to him when he was in his sixties and, according to the tradition, was lonesome. His first wife had been put aside because she bore no children; his second had died because she bore too many. Of the thousand girls in the rear apartments none could keep his attention. Then his chief eunuch found, in the harem of one of the princes, an astonishingly beautiful girl in her twenties, with hair like a cloud and a face like a flower. She quickly became Royal Concubine Yang, or Yang Kuei-fei, so enchanting the emperor that he not only neglected his sovereign powers but abused them, using the official postal service, for example, to speed exotic southern fruits to his beloved. Of more consequence, it was not long before status and wealth began to be showered on the Yang family, and Yangs began to hold offices near the throne, following the nepotistic pattern that had appeared earlier. The factional rivalries that must have followed ill prepared the court to deal with the catastrophe that soon occurred.

THE AN LU-SHAN REBELLION (755-63)

In the northeast a leader of great native competence and ambition had attained power as one of the regional military governors. He was An Lu-shan (d. 757), who was born of mixed northern parentage, perhaps Iranian-Turkish, and made his way up in the world apparently as a broker in the trade between northerners and Chinese. Coming to the attention of a local military governor, his qualities were recognized and he was advanced up the military hierarchy, eventually even appearing in audience before the emperor. There he established himself as a favorite, not least in the eyes of Yang Kuei-fei, whom he insisted, as the story has it, on regarding as his mother. We are asked to imagine the enormously fat and tough chieftain bowing down before the silky courtesan and saying, "I am a barbarian, and it is our custom to pay respects to our mother even before our father." Shrewdness and, no doubt, competence—the people of his region remembered him long afterwards as a sage—brought him concomitantly three military governorships in the northeast.

We are not certain what touched off his revolt. Possibly the immediate reason was a shift in the political forces at court, for we know that factions were jockeying for position, and we may assume that questions of security, and thus, openly or by implication, the throne's relations with An Lu-shan, were topics of dispute. In any event, his army moved from the region of modern Peking toward the center of T'ang power, taking Lo-yang within the year and Ch'ang-an in the year following. Although An Lu-shan was murdered by his son in 757, perhaps as a result of rivalry for leadership, first a lieutenant and then his son carried on the rebellion through much of north China.

As the court attempted to rally its forces, the emperor had to flee the capital. Before the troops would protect him in retreat, the story goes, he was obliged to execute Yang Kuei-fei and her brother, who had secured a prime ministership. Eventually, by a combination of the aid of foreign troops and the cooperation of local forces, some of whose leaders were appointed regional military governors, the dynasty regained the capitals (763).

As this implied, the T'ang government which returned to Ch'ang-an was a much smaller political power than the great dynastic name implies. The regional military governors, including some who had been wooed away from the rebels by the court, which had given concessions in return for help, staked out domains of their own. The T'ang administration was reduced to being one power among several. It was still something to be reckoned with, and regional military governors affirmed their allegiance to the Son of Heaven whenever the subject came up, but in fact the T'ang emperor could no longer collect taxes in many parts of the country, or freely appoint officials there. Although a T'ang emperor would sit on the throne for over a century, he could impose his will on only parts of China, while governors who were his officers in name lorded it over the rest of the country in fact.

Adjustments in the Second Imperial Period

As the stresses and strains hampered the T'ang administration, and especially as the great rebellion reduced its domain from a whole empire to only certain regions, changes occurred in administration and in the intellectual climate. In both spheres the aim was to correct faults and restore the vigor and soundness of earlier times. The results in fact amounted to new adjustments, rather than a restoration.

THE REVENUE PROBLEM

Of all the troubles of the T'ang government, the most central seemed to be lack of funds. Several expedient measures illustrated the habit of imperial administrations of seizing immediate profit at the cost of long-term gains. The grain in the "charity granaries," for example, which had been established with such admirable purposes at the beginning of the period, was appropriated to pay court expenses, meeting an immediate crisis but reducing the government's power to help the common people. The state mints debased the copper currency—by substituting cheap metal for part of the copper in the coins or shaving them slightly—achieving a quick saving of copper at the expense of a subsequent instability of prices in the market. Another characteristic practice was the state sale of certificates of ordination to the Buddhist and Taoist priesthood and titles to rank and office.

Other less foolish measures became a standard element in the imperial fiscal pattern. After the An Lu-shan rebellion, the state reimposed the salt monopoly. The proceeds permitted the straitened state, under an energetic minister, to restore the Grand Canal, which had been left useless after the rebellion, and devise a more efficient handling of canal transportation, so that for a time a regular supply of grain again reached Ch'ang-an. The Canal and the revenues it brought from the south became a regular consideration in fiscal thinking.

THE TWO TAXES (LIANG-SHUI) SYSTEM

The fiscal change that carried the most profound implications was the abandonment of the Threefold Tax and the adoption in 780 of the Two Taxes System as the fundamental method of collecting revenue. The Threefold Tax had been based on the equal-field system, which grew less effective as peasants deserted their land, registers failed to remain accurate, and land changed hands illegally. It can be readily imagined that the great rebellion, putting greater numbers of people to flight and no doubt leaving records and rights of possession in chaos, to say nothing of the confusion and hardship brought by many special taxes and tax collectors, had wrecked the Threefold System in those northern territories over which the T'ang reasserted its control.

The system adopted in its place in 780 acknowledged in effect that the equal-field system and the uniform Threefold Tax were no longer realistic. Instead, the actual amount of land and size of dwelling of each household were to be discovered by regional commissioners and every family assigned to one of several brackets scaled according to wealth. The tax levied on this basis was called the Two Taxes (*Liang-shui*) because it was collected in summer and autumn. Implicit in it was the idea that reducing the number of taxes, which had come to include many separate charges—taxes on land and households, and obligations of miscellaneous labor services, for example—was itself an improvement. Fewer visits from the tax collector would reduce the annoyance to the people and might simplify accounting for the funds. Simplification appeared again later as an ideal of tax reforms, but, in the event, it remained as elusive under the Chinese bureaucracy as elsewhere.

The Two Taxes System also replaced the old implicit principle that expenditure would depend on revenue with the principle that expenditure, or need, would determine revenue. In all regions local financial needs were to be calculated on the basis of previous experience and combined with the remittances due the court. The households of each region were then assessed, according to the bracket in which their wealth had put them, at a rate high enough to meet the needs. For the first time, too, the tax was, in principle, to be collected in money, a sign of the increasing use of this medium in society.

The reform showed an administrative advance in fiscal competence. To base the tax on the major premise of differences in wealth, instead of the old premise of equality, corresponded more to reality and promised a greater yield. To begin by determining financial needs and then fix taxes accordingly—to introduce a kind of budget system—allowed the administration to pursue its programs more consistently. To accept money as at least the nominal medium of taxation showed some appreciation of how much more convenient it could be than collecting in kind, though it was to be seven centuries before another comparable advance toward an official money economy was taken. All later dynasties sooner or later found their revenues less than they wanted, but the Two Taxes System was satisfactory enough to remain the basic system for the next 700 years.

The significance of the reform went beyond technical improvements. From the point of view of larger developments in society, most significant of all was the shift in attitude implied in a tax based on assessed wealth. In effect, the administration was relinquishing its attempt to administer the tenure of land. The tax reform marked a shift from state-controlled tenure to tenure by private enterprise. The shift was the more remarkable because it followed the original decision of the Second Imperial Period, influenced by practices in the Period of Disunity, to reestablish after a period of private tenure in Ch'in, Han, and later states what we may take as the classical pattern of controlled land tenure. It had now been proved that this was beyond the ability of the state to enforce. The alternative—free or private tenure—had been accepted, subject to the state's power of taxation. The state never relinquished its ultimate right of disposal of land that it wished put to a certain use, and state reservations for soldiers, estates for princes and the favored, and many other examples of preemption appear in later history. Nevertheless, private ownership became the most general characteristic of the economy thereafter, and with it concentrations of private wealth, poverty, and the state's relations with both became recurrent factors in history.

The Development of Palace Government. The disintegration brought about by An Lu-shan's rebellion appeared most obviously in the form of a country divided into practically autonomous regions under intractable military governors. While this was clearly the greatest political dislocation in the eyes of the court, it was accompanied by, and probably stimulated, a new period of what we have called palace government, referring to a tendency of the emperor to use irregular and, in the beginning, his own "private" bodies to carry out his will effectively, as he felt the regular offices did not do. One of the groups called upon was that of the palace eunuchs, who had increased their political influence in earlier governments. In the present instance they began to be used as supervisors of imperial military forces, reflecting the mistrust of the military, and as advisers to the emperor and even executors of some of his decisions. By the last anarchic decades of the dynasty they had become the makers of those decisions and indeed the makers of emperors. Their activities were formalized in a new office, the Privy Council (shu-mi yuan). Another body, which had been created for relatively nonpolitical purposes, became a source of confidential advisers to the emperor. It was the Bureau of Scholars (han-lin yuan), and its influence on the emperor, going far beyond its original purpose of furnishing literary elegance and the like as needed, also marked the perennial desire for better instruments of the imperial will.

THE REVIVAL OF CLASSICAL TRADITIONALISM.

Intellectually, the most important adjustment of the period was a turning toward worldly and moral questions, leading to a new emphasis on the Classics. The rebellion and subsequent events at court seem to have promoted serious thinking about political and social questions, even among some who had been known before for their preoccupation with the religious and psychic life. There was a review of history, as in two encyclopedic works on institutions, which their authors hoped might lead to explanations of current economic and administrative troubles. There were discussions of economic theory, some prompted by the economic measures described above, and of methods of recruiting officials, a sign that the examination system had grown sufficiently important for its implications to provoke debate. In fact, graduates of the examination system took a prominent part in the discussions, often to champion traditional and classical values. There was a movement of new criticism of the Confucian Classics, subjecting the standard interpretations to fresh scrutiny in an attempt to penetrate to the true meanings.

Another side of the reassertion of the classical tradition appeared in the movement to return to the ancient prose style (*ku-wen*). Parallel prose, or tandem prose, the style that had predominated for centuries, seemed in its concern for elaborate balance and structure to have become an end in itself. Too often, style dominated content. For some kinds of writing, especially exposition, the simpler, more explicit ancient style, it was argued, would restore the power of expression which the great ideas demanded.

The greatest advocate of the ancient style was Han Yü (768-824), whose vigorous ancient-prose writing became a model for centuries. Less immediately and universally appreciated than his prose was his message, but he would insist that the prose was in the service of the message. That, essentially, was the whole living truth of Confucianism. All achievement of the highest aspirations of mankind had depended on the Confucian way up to the time of Mencius. After Mencius it had not been transmitted; were it to be followed again, all would be well. With Confucianism raised high, it followed that Buddhism and Taoism must be laid low:

> What should be done now? I say that unless [Taoism and Buddhism] are suppressed, the Way will not prevail; unless these men are stopped, the Way will not be practiced. Let their priests be turned into ordinary men again, let their books be burned and their temples converted into homes. Let the Way of our former kings be made clear to lead them, and let the widower and the widow, the orphan and the lonely, the crippled and the sick be nourished. Then all will be well.[1]

REPRESSION AND DECLINE OF BUDDHISM.

Even a Han Yü, whom a history of the dynasty later called twice Mencius in energy, could not of course turn the tide of Buddhism and Taoism alone. In his time the court lavishly indulged a taste for esoteric Buddhism, under the influence of a powerful monk from Ceylon, and a great preacher brought pietistic Buddhism to many in the south. Some of the very men who were reviving Confucianism did not share Han Yü's exclusive bias and continued to be interested in Buddhism as well. In fact, it was to be characteristic later of the Neo-Confucian movement, as we call it, to maintain a rather paradoxical relationship with Buddhism—a formal hostility existing together with

1. As translated in Wm. Theodore de Bary, Wing-tsit Chan, and Burton Watson, comps. *Sources of Chinese Tradition* (New York, Columbia University Press, 1960), p. 434.

intellectual interests that would have been unlikely without the stimulation of Buddhism.

Yet hostility was there, and the movement back to Confucianism proved one factor in a combination that ended Buddhism's great period in China. Another factor was probably the atmosphere of factionalism and machination that grew in the court following the An Lu-shan disaster and other signs of decline. The state's financial and military weakness, for example, probably contributed to a search for causes, even scapegoats, outside the government as well as inside it.

The Repression of 845. The Buddhist establishment began to suffer in this atmosphere when in the middle of the ninth century the throne was occupied by an emperor who was absorbed in the search for Taoist immortality. He was naturally partial to his Taoist advisers and listened to them as they cast aspersions on their Buddhist rivals. Gradually he imposed limitations on Buddhist orders and confiscated parts of their property, culminating in an edict in 845. In it were repeated age-old—mainly practical and xenophobic—charges that had never been laid to rest. Buddhism was foreign, still (after over five centuries in China) a "religion of the far western wilderness." It impoverished people who donated work and wealth to it, lured men away from their lords, parents, wives, and fields, and then expected the remaining farmers to feed them. It poisoned the customs of the nation. The impoverishment and corruption that beset states of the Period of Disunity were all caused by Buddhism.

The edict declared a thorough dismemberment of the Buddhist organization: 4,600 major monasteries and 40,000 smaller establishments destroyed; 26,500 monks and nuns returned to lay life and, together with 150,000 of their slaves, put back on the tax rolls; tens of millions of acres of fertile land confiscated to be returned, presumably, to tax-yielding status. Related documents speak of the lumber of the monasteries being used for post stations and the bronze images and bells melted down for coins. In short, an attack was mounted which, though not universal, surpassed even the great repressions of the Period of Disunity. It affirmed the lesson of the earlier repressions that the state would not tolerate a religious institution which seemed to threaten it.

The threat, as the edict put it, consisted mainly of economic and social dislocation and moral confusion. In fact, however, the grounds for complaint were not wholly reasonable, for, according to one modern estimate, not more than one percent of the population dwelt in Buddhist establishments, and these establishments worked no more than four percent of the cultivated land. A systematic survey of the material situation would not necessarily show that Buddhism was bringing the nation to financial ruin—although a question might remain about its spiritual influence. The repression had something of the quality of an attack on an alien minority in a time of divisiveness and illiberality. The spirit of illiberality and parochial envy was illustrated in the inclusion in the repression of several thousand Nestorian and Zoroastrian priests, who were also foreign—in fact more literally so than most Buddhist monks—and whose temples, no doubt concentrated in the metropolitan centers to serve commerce-minded Central Asians, also seemed unjustly wealthy. The impulsiveness of the act was clear when the succeeding emperor, a year after the edict, reversed the repression and encouraged the growth of Buddhist establishments—under the eye of the state, of course.

This is not to say that the repression had no lasting effects or contributed to no larger movement. Buddhism had suffered a severe blow to its physical body, for its material wealth was centered in its monasteries, and when they were attacked little other property remained. Moreover the richer Buddhist properties, in the capital region, seem to have fared worst—relatively little movable Buddhist art from metropolitan monasteries remains today, for instance. After the repression the most extensive Buddhist lands were to be found in the south, no longer near the capitals, a shift which also implied diminished political influence. Buddhism's intellectual vitality must also have been wounded, as the monasteries were the centers of thought, and so violent and unpredictable an attack, however temporary, must have demoralized or intimidated many monks. Moreover, the repression came at a time when the intellectual tide was turning against Buddhism.

In the long run, profound changes followed the repression. Parts of Buddhism revived, particularly the Ch'an sect, which enjoyed new growth, owed in large part to a vigorous discipline that gave the sect's monasteries great resiliency. More characteristically, other sects declined, some of their beliefs and practices merging in the many cults of the popular religion. By little more than a century after the repression, Buddhism had lost forever its place as the foremost spiritual force of the civilization.

THE HUANG CH'AO REBELLION AND THE FALL OF T'ANG

In the second half of the ninth century, as the court became increasingly disordered, with eunuchs the emperor-makers, the countryside as well began to show the classical signs of disintegration—rebellions by overpressed farmers and mutinies among dissatisfied troops. Sometime around 875 the most destructive of the rebellions developed. It showed certain characteristics that, though not necessarily visible in all rebellions, recurred frequently enough to suggest that the social and political environment encouraged them. In the first place, its leader, Huang Ch'ao, was a cut above the simple peasant by virtue of his education and ambition. He had taken the examinations leading to official status but had failed. His occupation—salt bootlegging—suggested both aggressiveness and alienation from conventional life. It also suggested something about his following, which may have formed around a core of outlaws and grown with the addition of peasants sufficiently driven by officials and landlords to throw their lot in with that of the rebels. Eventually mutinous troops may also have joined, but the rebellion was still quite different from a military rising like that of An Lu-shan. Huang Ch'ao led his forces from Shantung, where they had originally risen, down eastern China all the way to Canton, laying waste region after region, and then turned around and moved northward into the central regions, destroying Lo-yang, entering Ch'ang-an, and killing many of the imperial family and officials. In 880 Huang Ch'ao declared himself emperor, but his attempt to shift his energies from military campaigns to stable government was as unsuccessful as that of many other devastating rebels. In part, probably, his trouble lay in failing to attract men of experience in administration, the old officialdom being repelled or holding back until there were clearer indications of what the final outcome would be, and in insubordination among the rebel leaders. The T'ang house, trying to play one military band off against another (as it had Central Asians against An Lu-shan), managed to have Huang Ch'ao driven out, but went down itself in the process. A military governor declared himself emperor of a new dynasty in 907.

The Five Dynasties and Ten Kingdoms

The disordered interval that followed brings to mind the sequel to the fall of the Han seven centuries earlier. Two great periods of unity, both marked by distinctive and monumental achievements, had given way to times which lacked the old grand and simple order. Chart 2 shows the principal states that were proclaimed following the formal extinction of T'ang. Like the Period of Disunity following the First

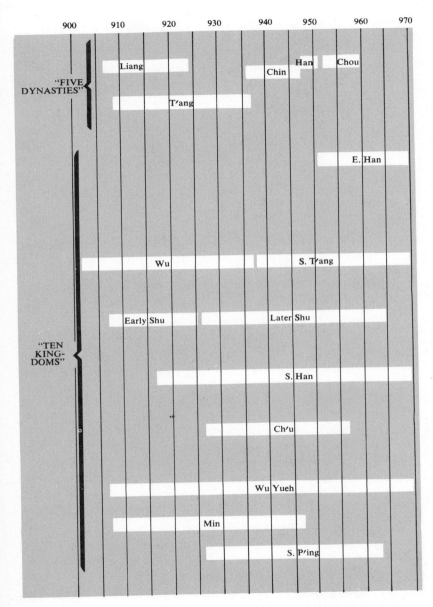

Five Dynasties and Ten Kingdoms.

Imperial Period, China again concurrently comprised several states, not one; and there were again remarkable differences between north and south. In the north there were relatively few states (quite the opposite of the Period of Disunity), and all the Five Dynasties, as they are called, had short lives, on the average fourteen years each. The Ten Kingdoms in the south did somewhat better, lasting on the average thirty-nine years each. To these rough similarities to the earlier period could be added one more, not apparent on the chart: that most of the northern rulers had barbarian ancestors.

Nevertheless, the years following the T'ang had on balance only a shade of the distinctiveness of character and influence that marked the years following the Han. The new disunity lasted hardly two generations, not ten. The total number of separate states was smaller, so that by at least one measure there was less disintegration and instability. The barbarian component in the northern ruling houses seems to have counted for less, though this is hard to measure. In any event, no potentially revolutionary ideas such as Buddhism struck the region afresh just at a time of political weakness; and no longer was the frontier as rich as the lower Yangtze Valley, with its far-reaching effects on the vital center of the civilization.

To the extent that disunity encouraged change, it was probably in directions already set rather than new ones. The differences between the north and south probably grew, especially the economic differences. As the chart shows, the Ten Kingdoms (all in the south except Eastern Han) on the whole maintained a degree of stability throughout the period. Most were produced from the dispersal of power during late T'ang. The strength of the leaders rested largely in their own armies, held together by a network of personal loyalties. In at least some of the states, government was good enough, or perhaps unobtrusive enough, to allow people to live normally. For many of the states, commerce, including "foreign trade" with other states, became an important source of wealth and power. All the states valued copper coins, both minting them and hoarding them. Perhaps especially in the south, the use of silver as a medium of exchange increased. All the southern states established their capitals in cities which have remained important commercial centers to the present day.

Among the northern Five Dynasties, warfare and hardship seemed more characteristic than stability. As under the system of regional military governors and the militarism fostered by them, the Five Dynasties generally spent much of their energy fending off rivals and holding territory. They usually controlled little more than the Yellow River basin, while around them, especially in the northeast, the old bastion of An Lu-shan, other would-be heroes staked out their own territories and looked for more. The center of most of the Five Dynasties, notably, was the region of modern Kai-feng, farther east along the Yellow River than the old capital region and near the junction with the Grand Canal. The shift of capitals down-river from the ancient site may have been both an easing of access to the great grain-growing regions to the south and a strategic adjustment in the face of the prevalent military threat from the northeast.

V

The Second

Imperial Period:

Phase II

NORTHERN SUNG
960-1126
SOUTHERN SUNG
1127-1279

The man under whom unity was restored was the founder of the Sung dynasty, Sung T'ai-tsu (r. 960-76). Coming from the northeastern military environment mentioned in the last chapter, he was the son of a general and himself a regional military governor under the last of the Five Dynasties. Tradition has it that he took the throne when his own army, to his surprise, urged it on him. Be that as it may, he proved unusually competent and flexible. He became known for his love of Confucian virtues and his ambition to be judged favorably by history. His brother, who succeeded him, though a lesser man in some respects, was also competent, and the first two emperors in their four decades on the throne revived the imperial system.

To do so required first of all putting an end to the insubordination by which the military had kept North China unstable and divided for two centuries. Sung T'ai-tsu began with his own army, transferring some of his most important lieutenants to relatively weak positions outside the capital or persuading them to retire. In addition, T'ai-tsu used one of the organs that had been developed in the latter part of T'ang as a "personal" instrument of the emperor, the Privy Council, to keep field commanders under independent supervision. Officials in the Privy Council, which became in effect a council of military affairs, might be either soldiers or literati but they were not given command of armies in the field.

As to other parts of the country, T'ai-tsu and T'ai-tsung brought all the independent states except one (a satellite of a neighboring state founded in the north by Khitans, a people to be discussed later) to submission by 979. The best of their armies were transferred to the capital region. The jurisdiction of regional military governors was narrowed, and civil officials were appointed as opportunities arose to parallel or supersede old military administrations. The first Sung rulers used their fresh power to bring government under more central control than had existed for centuries. In doing so, they consciously favored civil officials over military. From a founder's point of view, the decision provided an answer to an immediate problem of control. From a longer perspective, it contributed to the superiority of the civil spirit over the military in government.

The Administration

To govern the reunited country the Sung established in the capital an organization much like the one that had evolved by the second half of the T'ang dynasty. That is to say, a group of the highest ministers counseled the emperor (and in effect proposed policies) and through a secretariat-chancellery transmitted decisions which were administered by the Six Ministries and other offices. Since the secretariat-chancellery took the place of two separate T'ang bodies, the secretariat and the chancellery, the merger has been seen by some as a diminution of checks on the emperor's autocracy, on the grounds that it struck at a separate chancellery, which had traditionally been the preserve of the old aristocratic families. Nevertheless, it seems clear that the central administration, which in theory was meant to support autocracy, was growing more elaborate, so that the red tape and rivalries intrinsic in a bureaucracy in practice impeded autocratic effectiveness to some extent. In addition to the standard administrative departments and ministries, there were several offices of information and supervision meant to act as the eyes and ears of the emperor. The most important of these, the Censorate, kept emperors alert, if not always dispassionately informed, by means of their reports and outspoken opinions. The Privy Council retained something of the character of a special instrument of the emperor, even though its makeup had changed from a kitchen cabinet of eunuchs to a military council. The Bureau of Scholars, of which the Hanlin scholars were the most famous members, remained, as it had become in T'ang, an alternative source of advice at the disposal of the emperor. Another high office, the Finance Authority (*San-ssu*), also traced its origins to the T'ang dynasty and its existence indicated the importance accorded to an increasingly complicated administration of finance. At the same time it provided an example of overlapping or very finely divided functions, as the Ministry of Revenue historically had done some of what the Authority now did, leaving the Ministry with only certain clerical tasks. In other branches of administration as well, such as the military mentioned before and the civil service, several offices shared or divided overlapping responsibilities. In most instances, a reason for division could be found. That several offices had a hand in the appointment and promotion of civil servants, for example, reduced the opportunities for favoritism. Similarly, other offices exerted checks on each other, to the benefit, theoretically at least, of established policies and principles. Yet inertia and conservatism must be taken into account as well. Numbers of offices continued to exist because they had an honorable history and a place in the ritual tables of organization, and few rulers or chief ministers thought of government solely in terms of efficiency, without regard to the greatness of the past and harmony of the present. The multiplicity of offices signified two conflicting sentiments—a desire for a more satisfactory machinery and a reluctance to remove superfluous but honorable pieces from the structure.

THE CIVIL SERVICE

In a culmination of the movement that had begun in the T'ang dynasty, the examination system became by common understanding the most honorable avenue to office and the surest prerequisite for the highest positions. Examinations came to be given once every three years (the standard fequency thereafter), at three levels. Tens of thousands of candidates presented themselves at the lowest level, at which it is estimated no more than ten percent passed. Of those about ten percent passed the examinations at the second level and were finally ranked in the last examination, which was conducted at the palace. The emperor invested the few hundred successful with the degree of *chin-shih* at the climax of a season of celebrations, which included the calling out of each candidate's name, with an accompanying fanfare, in the main courtyard; an imperial banquet; and the donning of official dress. In the eleventh century there were probably fewer than 13,000 regular officials (another 6,000 military officers held corresponding rank), but hundreds of thousands of young men studied for the examinations.

In recent years scholars have discussed at length whether the civil service was in fact freely open to talent or was the preserve of a privileged class. It hardly need be said that having the means to pay for an education gave the wealthy as a class an enormous advantage. Yet the small amount of statistical evidence available suggests that considerable numbers of successful candidates—at least thirty percent or more—may have come from households that had not produced officials in the immediately preceding generations. If such a large proportion of men could regularly achieve a new, higher status, the system must have kept privilege relatively fluid. Even at the time, neither the examination system nor the civil service procedures as a whole satisfied everyone, though the criticisms then centered more on the quality of the service than its composition, more on the traits the examinations encouraged in officials, such as empty elegance in writing rather than personal wisdom and virtue. The adoption of a system of sponsorship, in which higher officials attested to the qualities of younger officials they knew, reflected the reservations some held about the adequacy of the examinations.

THE NONCOMMISSIONED BUREAUCRACY

The Sung paid more attention than the T'ang to another important class of workers in government, the clerks and those who performed the simple duties. The ranked officials described above were, on the whole, enclosed in the official world, preparing plans and giving orders to underlings, reporting to superiors, and making such judgments as their humanistic cultivation was supposed to prepare them to make. Not many in the capital dealt directly with the common people, and even the district magistrates, those closest to the masses, ordinarily came into touch with only a small fraction of the thousands in their care. The workaday duties, within offices and in direct connection with the common people, including filing, recording, bookkeeping, copying; computing and actually receiving taxes; guarding offices, supplies, and revenues; receiving, attending, and directing visitors to offices; carrying messages and orders; policing, and much else—all these fell to the clerical and service staffs. According to one estimate, in the whole country the service staffs employed more than a million men.

Much less thought went into the recruitment and assurance of quality of this large, noncommissioned bureaucracy than into that of officialdom. Part of the service staffs comprised ordinary subjects performing their obligatory service, which the state exacted together with tax payments. The service was no longer *corvée* proper, or hard labor, which it had become possible to commute to a tax payment with the enactment of the Two Taxes system; rather it was simple service, typically the guarding of storehouses or transporting of revenues. It generally worked hardship on the subject, as it took him away from his ordinary work, subjected him to the exploitation and harassment of the more experienced on the service staff, and, far from offering him any remuneration, exposed him to financial ruin, since he was held responsible for any losses suffered by the stores in his charge. Those who could, therefore, evaded the service obligation by bribery or even by moving into a city. The obligation fell increasingly on the poorest of the farmers, who were likely neither to provide good service nor to become more reconciled to their miserable condition.

Other parts of the noncommissioned bureaucracy made it their life's work. Recruited rather unsystematically at first, the full-time clerks and service men established the custom of nominating their own successors, who were usually their relatives. The contrast with the nonhereditary principle of the regular officialdom inspired an ironic aphorism, "Clerks may be enfeoffed, but not officials." Aside from the faults that nepotism and hereditary rights encouraged, corruption of the clerks and service men was practically assured by the methods of compensation. Although clerks in the capital apparently received salaries, these must have been very low. Others of the noncommissioned bureaucracy usually received, instead of a salary, some proportion of revenues from a state enterprise, like a brewery or a ferry, or from small miscellaneous taxes. Obviously, some of these arrangements resembled in effect the commission system for salesmen, for example, encouraging those who collected taxes to squeeze as much as possible out of the payer, in order to pocket more. Clerks and service men were understood, moreover, to exploit their access to financial records, legal documents, and the like to help or intimidate members of the public, the choice depending on what promised to be more profitable. Presumably no one understood the customary and uncustomary opportunities for gain better than officials, who sometimes exacted their share. No doubt the connivance of officials made it more difficult to correct many of the abuses. It is also true, however, that the noncommissioned bureaucracy by its permanent tenure of positions often learned indispensable specialties (accounting, for example) and knew more than the commissioned official about its own region. Much could be done behind his back. Those who recognized the harmful effect on government of the noncommissioned bureaucracy had to acknowledge at the same time that government would not work without it.

A Developed Society and Economy

If the reconstituted government seemed in many ways the same as before, the two major realms in which it was obliged to act, domestic and foreign affairs, had changed remarkably. Domestically, the character of the major groups of society and their relationships with each other seemed different.

THE OFFICIAL ELITE

The old aristocracy faded away. In the early part of the Second Imperial Period, it had been common to find in powerful positions men whose fathers and grandfathers had also been powerful. With power went, often, titles and lands. In recognition of the importance of the hereditary aristocracy, the T'ang administration compiled genealogies of the great families.

Through the latter part of T'ang and into early Sung, the ravaging of the old aristocracy's land on the north China plain by military regimes and the admission of new men to power through examinations combined to erode the old class and bring forth a new elite. Hereditary wealth and status did not disappear entirely, but government through very old family lines did disappear, except for the dynasty itself, and prominence stemmed from a *chin-shih* degree rather than a pedigree. A phrase from classical times that was revived to designate the new official elite suggested its relatively modern social origins. The phrase was *shih-ta-fu,* literally "knight-officials," a term used in the *Rituals of Chou* for officials from the lowest noble class. By Sung times the phrase connoted "officials qualified by virtue of their scholarship."

The new official was still connected more often than not with landed wealth. As observed before, a prosperous family more often than a poor one could provide its sons with the conditions, including tutoring, that success in the examinations required. Land being the chief form of wealth, it was not surprising that the sons of landlords should crowd the *chin-shih* lists.

THE LANDLORD CLASS

The landlords to whom many of the new officials were related themselves differed from the once proud great families. Probably most landlords owned less land. (We depend here on inferences from the literature; there are no reliable statistical studies, and land tenure is still one of the most vexing issues.) There remained estates of the older type, holdings of perhaps several hundred acres; but much smaller tenure had become the rule and remained so thereafter. All the same, the landlord families whose men had won their way into officialdom, or at least had reached the first rungs of the ladder of the examinations, could look after their interests by means not only of material and economic resources but also of status. As "official families" they, or at least those males who held office or an official degree, were exempt from service obligations. Apparently capitalizing on their great prestige, they could often face down the poor local tax collector, or reach some advantageous agreement with him. Most important of all, they had lines to the administration. By conversations with the right officials, as well as thoughtfully chosen gifts, they might hasten actions that would benefit them and delay or stop those that would not.

We speak of them as landlords because rents or produce provided the core of their wealth, but they could invest as well in other parts of the regional economy, such as moneylending and even commercial and industrial enterprise. In addition to economic preeminence, once they had become comfortable enough they assumed social leadership, mediating disputes; organizing public works; contributing to shrines, charities, and schools; and displaying other signs of the social virtues that their Confucian education recommended. Viewed from their economic and social position as a class, they have been called by scholars in the West the "gentry," a term that well enough suggests rural economic and social prominence but may fail to convey the crucial importance of official standing. The heart of the Chinese gentry was composed of families of officials, former officials, and would-be officials who had passed one of the examinations. The evidence suggests that the possession of local status and money meant less. Certain doors opened only to rank or title, and wealth itself slipped more easily from those who could not guard it politically. The Chinese phrase that became current, though not until much later than the Sung dynasty, and received the English translation "gentry" was *shen-shih,* which meant those who stuck the tablets of office in their belts and wore the gowns of official students.

CURTAILMENT OF THE FREEDOM OF WOMEN

The life of upperclass women apparently became more hedged about by restrictions than before. During the T'ang, for example, highborn women were occasionally divorced and remarried without great scandal. They also may have moved rather freely outside the house—enemies of Buddhists, for instance, claimed that monks joined aristocratic ladies in wild parties in underground hideaways.

It is not clear what brought about the change. The revival of Confucianism that had begun earlier gained momentum, and its concern for social order according to traditionally defined roles may have strengthened the classical idea of discriminating between husband and wife. The reaction against Buddhism and its relative indifference to status, including that of men and women, may have played a part. The rise of new classes to prominence may have meant that the dominant pattern of female life was set by families whose ways differed from those of the old aristocrats.

Among the signs of declining freedom were discourses by scholarly men on keeping women in their place, a renewed emphasis on chastity in widows, and apparently a strengthened convention that respectable women did not go outside their houses casually. Most curious of all was the spreading custom of binding women's feet. It apparently had begun earlier, in the court, where dancing girls tried to catch the emperor's eye by wrapping their feet tightly in silk strips. During the Sung, the love of small feet carried the custom beyond the court and into the upper classes, where the technique became more constrictive, until grown women had very arched, delicately pointed "golden lotuses" as they were called, about half the normal size of feet. The fashion had a great success; men grew so excited fondling them and helping to wrap and unwrap them that the scene became standard in erotic novels. The short, swaying gait enforced by the tiny feet looked attractively helpless, and in fact it impeded independent movement in the outside world. For once, fashion served a prudish morality.

TENANT FARMERS

It has also been suggested—although again many questions are unanswered—that tenant farmers of relatively different condition, essentially that in which they remained until modern times, appeared in this period. Even on the estates of earlier times, of course, farmers had worked as tenants, in that they made payments, either fixed sums or a proportion of the yield, for the use of the great families' land, and in addition served the estate through work. So too did the tenants of later times, but, it is argued, under harder conditions. The new landlord frequently lived in the city (another peculiarity of the Chinese gentry) and regarded his property more exclusively as a source of income than had the old great families, who held themselves responsible in a broader sense for their domains. The combination of absenteeism and the profit motive, it is suggested, dulled the landlord's awareness of the plight of the farmer and the vicissitudes of farming, which often provided only a marginal living and left the farmer chronically indebted. Furthermore, there were many tenants. Estimates of tenancy in the south, where it was more common, set it as high as half the farmers.

The unanswered questions about tenant farmers need not raise doubts about the miserable lives of many of them. Certainly the farmer's dream of owning his own land, fostered by the new era beginning with the enactment of the Two Taxes, that made tacit acknowledgement of private ownership, must have sharpened the discontent of the unfortunates. However, whether tenancy alone should be considered a sufficient cause of distress among farmers, who also had to contend with such banes as usury (frequently handled by landlords), arbitrary taxation, and extortion by minor authorities, is uncertain.

THE GROWTH OF COMMERCIAL LIFE

In a continuation of the mercantile vitality noted earlier in the Second Imperial Period, a great variety of goods, apparently in greater amounts than before, stimulated trade and no doubt was stimulated by it in return. Certain technical changes probably contributed to the growth. Coal, for example, became widely used in the north and, together with the knowledge of coking, played a part in the production of large quantities of iron and steel. Foreign trade also shared in the vitality, large quantities of tea and fabrics going to northern peoples and new ports being designated for others who came by sea. One intimation of the volume of the Chinese export trade comes from Japan, where between the tenth and twelfth centuries Chinese coins became the major medium of exchange. Slightly later (in the thirteenth century), the profits possible from the coin export, for which Japanese gold used to be brought back to China, where the exchange ratio of gold to copper was much higher, have been estimated as about 600 percent.

Potentially as significant for the civilization as the volume of trade itself was a new degree of Chinese participation. Until this time foreigners—Persians, Arabs, Koreans, and others—had carried on almost all the trade. In the Sung dynasty large numbers of Chinese joined them and in some areas—Japan, for example—emerged as the dominant merchantmen. They sailed in junks that by the end of the Second Imperial Period were the best ships afloat, the largest of them able to accommodate several hundred men and many months' store of grain and equipped with such advanced devices as a balanced rudder and compass. The balanced rudder was Chinese. The compass probably grew out of the magnetic needle, which the Chinese had long known, though its application to sailing may have owed much to West Asians. The commercial and technical advances launched coastal Chinese among the world's sailors. Yet it was a sign of the limits of this movement as a cultural force that the literati on the whole found little excitement in these new activities. The enthusiasm of the traders did not inspire a corresponding shift of thinking.

The absence of new ideas about trade was the more striking in that the growth of commercial life did not comprise transactions involving a few relatively luxurious products demanded only in the capital and overseas; it extended to more modest and local levels as well. Its pervasiveness accounted for the development of special commercial instruments or facilities. Of these, the most significant was money, the use of which increased rapidly. The figures available indicate that by the end of the tenth century over twice as many copper coins were being minted as in the eighth century, and by the eleventh century, ten times as many. Paper currency also became widely used, especially for distant transactions, the state reserving to itself the right to issue bank notes in the eleventh century. By that time, the state sometimes received as much as one half its tax revenues in cash.

THE GROWTH OF CITY LIFE

In no sphere of life did a combination of social and economic changes merge so strikingly as in cities. Regions of dense population, usually centering on a large city, increased, forty-six districts reporting 100,000 or more households in the late eleventh century, as compared to thirteen districts in the middle of the eighth century. (The pattern in most censuses indicates that registered households averaged four or five members each.) There were probably five or more cities of one million in population. Especially significant to commerce was the growth of a whole secondary level of cities, which had not been of sufficient size to merit that description early in the Second Imperial Period. Having arisen largely from commercial need, growing out of fair grounds that had originally served only periodic markets or existed around small garrisons, they differed from the older cities, which had developed around civil and military administrations. Moreover, even inside the older cities the order and neatness imposed by earlier administrations broke down. Trade, no longer confined to segregated quarters, spread into many parts of the city, and shops appeared everywhere. The hours of business, no longer regulated by officials, extended far into the night. The inner walls that used to divide the city into wards came down, and the house gates of rich commoners, not just titled families, began to open on main streets. City pleasures and services grew. In Kaifeng, the capital, for example, the day started at four o'clock in the morning, with the booming of temple bells. Peddlers began to make their way up and down the streets, calling out the foods they had for sale. From outside the walls carts laden with meats and vegetables moved in toward the markets. Businesses of all kinds opened. Many of these, such as the tailors, hairdressers, dealers in paper and brushes, and caterers, served the city's taste for luxury. As night fell, lanterns lit up taverns and restaurants, the largest of which had staffs of hundreds, including women entertainers skilled in singing, dancing, playing instruments, and carrying on witty conversation. In the theater district dozens of houses offered varied bills, including the latest songs, puppet shows, acrobats, wrestlers, storytellers, and comedians.

As has already been implied, many of the landlord class lived in the cities, the richer ones, it would seem, in the larger, walled, administrative cities, the capitals of districts and higher divisions. There were several reasons for them to do so. Cities offered protection from bandits and robbers, and a greater chance to evade state service obligations. More positively, cities promised the kind of life that all who could afford it sought—a life made comfortable by good food, drink, clothing, housing, and servants; and embellished by books, works of art, private gardens, gatherings of friends for conversation and the sharing of pleasures, the colorful street scene, and occasional outings in the country. Upper-class life depended upon cities; and the canons of taste usually depended on upper-class men of the city.

Foreign Pressure

After economic and social changes at home, the second major factor affecting the Sung government was the pressure of militant bordering states. Seldom, if ever, had a unified China faced neighbors of comparably unified organization. One of them, the Liao dynasty, founded among upper Manchurian tribes called Khitan in 907, brought Manchuria and lands to the north, east, and west under its control. In 936 it even received a swath of land (sixteen prefectures) within the Great Wall in return for helping the founder of one of the Five Dynasties. When the first two emperors of Sung tried to take this Chinese territory back they were badly beaten. But the Liao lacked either the will or the strength to destroy the Sung dynasty or occupy more land, for at the beginning of the eleventh century, after moving an army almost as far south as the Yellow River, they faltered before a Chinese strongpoint, Shan-yuan. The two sides negotiated and agreed, in the Treaty of Shan-yuan (1004), that they would exchange envoys periodically, neither would harbor fugitives, the border would remain as it had been, without fortifications, and Sung would pay Liao annually a certain amount of silk and silver. Trade centers would also be established along the border. Some forty years later Liao exploited the threats of another state against Sung and exacted a large increase in the annual payment. In effect, the treaty forced a Chinese government to pay tribute to a neighbor. This was contrary to the direction in which China thought tribute ought to go. Even more remarkably, relations based on the treaty continued more or less smoothly for over a century, an unprecedented form of international

Scene in a major city, showing a shop, working men, and, at the lower left, a sedan chair carried by donkeys. The detail is from a Ming Dynasty copy of a twelfth-century painting, Spring Festival on the River, *by Chang Tse-tuan. For another detail from this painting, see chap. XIV, fig. 24.*

experience in the Chinese world. It might be inferred that as neighboring states acquired the capacity for more stable organization and strength, and China seemed less determined to impose vassalage on them, a new, multi-state system was emerging. Theory, however, did not change so quickly. No Chinese suggested that a new principle had been established. The payments were regarded as blackmail; the treaty, imposed and backed by force, as being without moral sanction.

The second state to challenge Sung took shape in the northwest, where a people called Tangut, who were apparently related to the Tibetans, took control of Kansu, the Ordos, and parts of Inner Mongolia. In 1038 their leader declared himself emperor, using the Chinese term, and proclaimed the Great Hsia dynasty, which the Chinese records more modestly call Western Hsia, or Hsi Hsia. Upon hearing of these titles, which signified the end of the tributary relationship Hsi Hsia had observed earlier, Sung broke off relations and stopped trade. Forces of the two states fought sporadically along the border, but neither side could strike a decisive blow. In 1044 a treaty of peace like that with the Liao was signed, but it brought no general peace.

Along both borders the Chinese maintained large armies in face of the distrusted neighbors. By the middle of the eleventh century, Sung had taken on some 820,000 men as soldiers. If a force of military laborers is also counted, the total reached well over a million. Paying these men even the little that they received and supplying the armies took approximately 80 percent of the state's revenues. The heavy financial burden impelled the administration to try to wring more from the economy, but the effort produced, instead of more revenue, a kind of recession in which merchants withdrew from the market, so that revenue from commercial taxes fell sharply. Receipts from tea and salt monopolies also fell, and in the rich Yangtze delta a black market in tea and salt flourished. The bootleggers threatened to attract potential rebels. In the capital many high officials, contemplating an army of oppressive cost, an economy that resisted attempts to tap it, and a society that seemed on the verge of disorder, were convinced that change was imperative and looked on with approval as a new emperor chose a prime minister willing to enact reforms.

The Reforms of Wang An-shih

The emperor's choice, brought in 1069 from a provincial post into the capital as chief councilor, was Wang An-shih (1021-86). He had already won a reputation among his seniors for his intellect and competence, in part on the basis of a customary report, called a "Ten Thousand Word Memorial," which he had submitted earlier. In it, he analyzed the central issues confronting the government and, basing himself firmly on the Confucian Classics, asserted that the government needed most of all to return to the principles of the ancient kings. The power of the Neo-Confucian revival gave great force to his words, which evoke the memory of the last great reformer in an ardently Confucian milieu, Wang Mang. Like Wang Mang, Wang An-shih aroused the opposition of many who had originally supported him when he disclosed concrete plans for reforming institutions.

Among his reforms, all decreed by the emperor, some aimed to strengthen the state's finances and relieve the mass of the people of certain economic burdens. The Tribute Transport and Distribution System, for example, was meant to correct the methods of procuring supplies for the court. For years, certain regions had been charged with supplying a fixed amount of goods, which sometimes the region itself no longer produced and therefore had to buy, only to ship the goods to a court which had no need of them that year and sold them to merchants at sacrifice prices. The new system empowered a procurement office at Yangchou, at the intersection of the Yangtze River and the Grand Canal, to buy goods, according to a schedule made up annually, in the cheapest market, and, if it acquired goods that were not needed, to sell them wherever a profit might be made for the state. Another plan, the Farming Loans System, offered state loans to farmers at an interest rate of 20 percent annually, much less than the rate charged by private moneylenders. The Hired Services System substituted a graduated tax on families for local services that they had previously been obliged to perform for the administration. So onerous were the services that the better-off families tried to avoid them. By substituting a graduated tax, it was reasoned, the contribution of such families could be regained and oppressive demands lifted from the poorest people.

Other reforms would have the effect of increasing the safety of the country while reducing the cost of the army. The *Pao-chia* System, for example, established a responsibility for mutual policing in neighborhoods. Households were grouped in tens (called a *pao*), fifties, and five hundreds, with a leader for each group and a man from each household with two or more able-bodied males to serve as a *pao*-man or local policeman. It was thought that the *pao*-men, given further training, might comprise a militia, backing up a much reduced army, and apparently funds began to be diverted from the army to this program. Under the Horse Breeding System, the state provided a horse to any household that agreed to care for it, using it for farm work until the day when a *pao*-man would mount it and ride off to battle.

Still other reforms aimed at improving officialdom, which Wang An-shih implied was the key instrument of his program. He placed renewed stress on the Imperial University, for example, on the theory that men trained there under supervision would surpass in both competence and character the merely clever graduates of the examination system. He also revised the examinations themselves, to emphasize issues of judgment and government rather than poetry and rhyme-prose. To guide students to the general and abiding principles of the Classics he wrote new commentaries, and to measure the breadth of their understanding he devised a new form for the examination essays. Turning to the lower level of the state's administration, the noncommissioned clerks, he moved to improve their performance by use of the carrot and stick (or "rewards and punishments" in Legalist language), paying them a regular salary while subjecting them to much harder punishment if they misbehaved. He also opened the prospect of advancement to them, setting up examinations by which qualified clerks could be promoted to the lower ranks of the regular officialdom.

The opposition to these reforms and several others arose from doubt about their moral rightness and practicality and fear for vested interests. Among the prominent statesmen some argued, in the time-honored way, that economic acts like the Tribute Transport and Distribution System and the Farming Loans System put the government into a profit-seeking business, which compromised the moral integrity of officialdom and competed unfairly with the common people. Moreover, several of the reforms, such as the *Pao-chia* System and Horse Breeding System, not only gave arrogant underlings license to impose upon and harry the people, but were ill-conceived. Mild farmers were not likely to make fierce soldiers, nor were horses accustomed to pulling a plow likely to turn into spirited chargers.

As for other voices that officials could report as "public opinion," there were those of merchants who saw their trading opportunities growing smaller and landlords who found the Farming Loans System an intrusion on the moneylending from which many of them profited. Officials' families also had reason to resent the Hired Services System, for it taxed them for services from which they had previously been exempt. Even farming villages grumbled, we may suppose, for the *Pao-chia* System decreed an organization that must have disturbed the customary local self-government.

The disturbance of officialdom itself, however, hurt the effort at reform most. Many important officials who had originally supported Wang An-shih turned against him. He had a tendency, perhaps connected with his strongly theoretical and analytical mind, to be overbearing and contemptuous of critics. He haughtily ignored them or vehemently attacked them, according to whether their remarks had stung him or not; and he offended them in other ways as well. He was charged with a kind of misconduct that was beginning to be spoken of more often in bureaucratic circles, that of forming a "faction," especially as he had created a new commission whose members he handpicked to administer the reforms. The most serious charge that could be made against a faction—that it conspired to gain its own private ends regardless of the consequences for the emperor's government—reached the emperor's ears both formally in memorials and privately by way of the empress dowager. It suggested that Wang An-shih was disturbing the internal equilibrium of officialdom too much to permit the realization of his plans.

Although the emperor did not dismiss Wang An-shih, as the outcry against him continued, Wang resigned in 1076, after seven years as chief councilor. The emperor retained the reform policies, though under the direction of less able and more opportunistic men, until he died (1085). Then opponents gained the upper hand in court councils and repealed the whole program. In the following decades, policies swung back and forth as anti-reform and pro-reform factions fought for power.

This erratic course makes difficult any judgment of the effects of the reforms, for though so radical a program was expected to produce far-reaching results, it in fact had time for little. Of the few bits of direct evidence available, some point to success and some to failure. More funds began to enter the treasury, giving the state its first surplus in years. There was some agreement that clerks worked less dishonestly here and there. The *Pao-chia* System somewhat increased order in the countryside. Yet several of the economic measures gave corrupt officials and their subordinates opportunities to profit at the expense of the people. A land survey and some new tax programs were subverted by collusion between the well to do and dishonest officials and clerks (not all the clerical workers had been uplifted morally). Wang An-shih's program was not intact and competently directed long enough to prove itself conclusively as either help or hindrance to the state or society. Perhaps the brevity of its life pointed to the most significant fact: that the radical reform of administrative systems faced a predominantly conservative elite in charge of the very systems to be changed. To win the acquiescence of that elite would require political persuasiveness of a kind foreign to Wang An-shih. It would probably also need a sequence of several reform-minded leaders, not just one, that is to say, a strong, sustained era or atmosphere of change. Without this, an officialdom of men who found contentment in their achievement and station in life would not be fired to make a new world. Wang An-shih alone could not open such an era.

Southern Sung (1127-1279)

Fifty years after Wang An-shih retired, the armies of a new nation came out of the north and reduced the Sung by half. For several decades a people called Jürched had been growing in solidarity and ambition, until they dared to attack their erstwhile masters, the Liao. In 1115 the leader of the Jürched declared himself emperor of the Chin dynasty (1115-1234). Once Liao was defeated, Chin sent two armies south, capturing Kaifeng in 1126 and eventually agreeing to a border with Sung approximately along the Huai River. At the same time (1141) Sung agreed to pay Chin annual tribute of about the same value previously paid Liao and to address Chin in the language of a vassal. The peace that followed, although occasionally disturbed by one side or the other, defined the territory of the Sung dynasty thereafter. Putting an imperial prince on the throne, the Southern Sung ruled China proper south of the Huai, building its palaces on the site of present Hangchow, which it called the "temporary capital," Marco Polo's marvelous Quinsai, "where so many pleasures may be found that one fancies himself to be in Paradise."

ECONOMIC AND CULTURAL RICHES

Although the territory held by the Southern Sung was much smaller than before, it included China's most fertile land and most of the greatest cities. The economic and cultural developments described earlier, far from being stunted, continued, so that in some respects the Second Imperial Period entered maturity at its very end.

The country's wealth may have surpassed any level achieved in the region earlier. It was during the Southern Sung, for example, that the foreign trade previously discussed rose to new heights of activity. Sung coins became the principal currency in Japan, and great numbers of them even reached the coasts of Persia and Africa, despite prohibitions of the Sung administration aiming to keep its money at home. Sung junks, the biggest of them capable of carrying between 500 and 600 men, appeared in ports all over Asia. As indirect evidence of wealth, the country tended to bear a heavier tax burden than had Northern Sung. Taxes supported large military forces, including for the first time a full-fledged navy, consisting of several fleets with thousands of men in each, to protect the trading ports of the southern coast and the Yangtze cities.

As such a use of wealth would imply, the economy was not always stable or beneficial to the people. Yet even economic crises suggested a more elaborate fiscal world. For example, the administration, in attempting to fill its treasury after a particularly expensive attack against Chin had failed, issued a great deal of paper money inadequately backed by hard cash. As the people hoarded reliable copper cash and discounted more the face value of the paper, a runaway inflation of prices plagued city life toward the end of the dynasty.

PARTISAN POLITICS

Factional quarreling came down to the Hangchow court as a legacy from Northern Sung, with the difference that invective cut deeper than reason and posturing passed for dedication. More often than before, to lose a political battle meant to lose one's reputation or even one's life. The hired assassin constituted one of the perils of political life. Most of the time, the battleground included the palace apartments as well as the court, empress dowagers and other well-placed women abetting factions in pursuit of their own rewards. One of the weapons in their arsenal may have been the encouragement of the emperor in a life of refined pleasure; several emperors in this period abdicated in favor of their successors and ended their lives in elegant retirement.

The most debated issue was policy toward Chin. Chin had occupied the traditional heart of China and could claim, with arguments of some force, to be the legitimate successor of Northern Sung to the Mandate of Heaven. Southern Sung ministers could not avoid facing the question of how or when to dispute the claim.

On balance, the government accepted the situation tacitly, or in any event did not constantly challenge it. The reasons for this may have included, first, a preference of the emperors and their high ministers to concern themselves, despite rhetorical implacability against the foe, with matters of internal political harmony. Second, under an aggressive foreign policy, the armies unleashed might be as great a threat to the administration as to the enemy. So it appeared, for example, just before the major peace agreement with Chin. At that time a Chinese army under General Yo Fei was winning important battles against the Chin forces, and Yo Fei claimed that Chin was so hard pressed that its leaders were considering withdrawing north of the Yellow River. On the other hand, an important minister, Ch'in Kuei, was leading an effort at the Sung court to strike a bargain with Chin and end the fighting. In the end Ch'in Kuei won the emperor's open support and concluded an agreement by which both states accepted the boundary along the Huai and Sung agreed to pay Chin a large sum annually, in addition to making a ritual show of subordination. Yo Fei obeyed the emperor's command to withdraw his army. Soon afterwards, he found himself removed from command and imprisoned on a charge, almost surely trumped up, of conspiring to revolt. He had not been in jail two months before Ch'in Kuei had him killed.

The episode became famous as a story of patriotism frustrated by treachery, Yo Fei living up to noble principles and Ch'in Kuei stooping to cynical expediency; but there was probably more than that to the story. At times Yo Fei, though purporting to carry out the imperial will, conducted campaigns of daring independence. At other times, as when he withdrew from the last great campaign, he may have considered not the emperor's orders alone but also strategic dangers threatening his army. He behaved somewhat like those centrifugal figures of earlier times, the regional military governors, a title which he held among others. The history of the ambitiousness of overmighty generals at the head of victorious armies, especially before the founding of Sung, gave emperors good reason to be cautious in military ventures.

NEO-CONFUCIANISM AND MORALITY

During the Northern Sung the revival of Confucianism had progressed under a number of major figures who contributed various and often conflicting interpretations of the Classics and history, discoursing on morality and political action, and speculating on the governing forces of the universe. At the beginning of Southern Sung all these subjects came under the scrutiny of one of the greatest of the Neo-Confucians, Chu Hsi (1130-1200). He was famous enough in his own day to be courted by the administration, though he usually refrained from taking important offices, disliking the atmosphere of politics. His influence grew even greater after he died, as the genius of his scholarship and the plausibility of his teachings attracted the respect of students and governments alike, gradually making his views the main approach to study.

He has correctly been called the greatest synthesizer of Neo-Confucian theory, and his interpretations were known, because of their characteristic emphasis, as the School of Principle, or Reason. Principle (*li*) was an unchanging law that governed the operation of every single thing or event. In the broadest sense it was the Tao, the principle of the universe. As manifested in man it was his original, good, essentially moral nature. Men pursued their highest destiny when they attempted to understand principle to the utmost. This—the extension of knowledge—they achieved by investigating things, that is, reading about and discussing philosophy, people, and past and present events in order to discover the workings of principle. Handling affairs properly also could lead to understanding. The man who understood principle to the utmost achieved the complete development of his own nature—he became perfectly moral and enjoyed a sense of complete harmony, and even identity, with the principle of the world.

In effect, Chu Hsi reinforced morality as the measure of all human affairs. Considering him representative of the temper of Neo-Confucianism in his day, we find it easier to see how, in many of the factional disputes characteristic of the time, appeals to the emperor to rectify himself, and the impugning of advisers and their programs on moral grounds, should have been common topics.

PROTESTING STUDENTS AND SECLUDED ACADEMIES

The Neo-Confucian morality represented by Chu Hsi inspired two movements, both expressing dissatisfaction with tendencies of the day, but in curiously different ways. One (in which Chu Hsi took no part) was that of students of the Imperial University and other schools in the capital, who organized to express their opinion on political affairs. Sometimes many of them joined in signing a memorial to the emperor; sometimes they sent individual memorials, one after another, so that the emperor received dozens in succession on the same subject; and sometimes they gathered as a group in front of a public office, demanding to be heard. In the most heated incidents, the students printed their petitions and circulated them, led demonstrations that brought thousands into the streets, and even beat and killed official representatives. Although the subject of controversy might be as broad as the question of war or peace or as narrow as the conduct of a single official, typically the students aimed directly at the chief minister or a group of high officials, charging them with breaking one or another moral law. It was a style appropriate to the Confucian revival, with its reaffirmed and abstracted constellation of moral virtues.

If the Neo-Confucian spirit thus tended to inspire the young to hasten into politics it also encouraged the growth of an institution that in theory delayed involvement in politics. That was the academy, a center of higher learning usually founded on the initiative of some local official or former official. Chu Hsi himself established and organized one of the most famous academies when he was a local official. The more important academies kept a master teacher in residence, provided libraries, and invited renowned scholars to lecture. Their main purpose was to inculcate the classical truths, to put students in pursuit of sagehood. In this, although it accorded with the age-old aims of education, was an implied rebuke to the official educational system, for academies would have filled no need if the examinations had been discovering a true moral elite. Academies offered sanctuary from a world too devoted to wealth and fame. The most famous were located in hills and woods rather than cities. As Neo-Confucian thought reaffirmed basic Chinese truths over Buddhism, yet was formed partly under Buddhist influence, academies replaced monasteries as the chief intellectual communities, yet halfway withdrew from the world.

LEARNING AS A STYLE OF LIFE

The latter half of the Second Imperial Period ranked as a great age of scholarship by any standards. Essentially it was a scholarship that attempted to preserve the past. It included, for example, a considerable vogue for collecting old inscriptions or rubbings. In the world of books the attempt resulted in surveys of an unprecedented comprehensiveness. One, for example, was *Tzu-chih t'ung-chien* (A comprehensive mirror for aid in government), the first work since the *Records of the Historian,* a thousand years earlier, to cover the entirety of political history (in this instance from 403 B.C. to A.D. 959), in 294 chapters. Most characteristic of the age, however, was the prevalence of the love of books throughout the upper classes. Correspondingly, the bookish style of life produced a great growth in the number of volumes printed.

中華文化大綱

VI

An Era of

Foreign Rule

In attempting to understand the place in Chinese history of the foreign invaders who held parts of China from the tenth century to the fourteenth, it is well to keep in mind the limits of their occupation. The Khitans of the Liao dynasty held only sixteen prefectures in northeast China, with only two major towns, the modern Peking (a town with a history but not yet in the first rank of Chinese cities) and Ta-t'ung. The Khitan occupation lasted a century and three quarters, but it was followed by that of two more conquering peoples. The Jürcheds of the Chin dynasty held the northern half of the country, the land of the great tradition, a little more than a century; and the Mongols, who called their dynasty the Yüan, replaced them and ruled there approximately another century and a half, in the last 108 years of that period occupying the south as well and governing all China. The foreign occupation therefore weighed heaviest in North China, as it had in the Period of Disunity, but in most of the region it lasted approximately two and a half centuries, a much shorter time than before. Moreover, North China was no longer the center of the society as it had been; and the south, with greater concentrations of people and wealth and on the whole greater continuity of cultural development, lay under foreign control only a century. Nor at the time of the later invasions, was there a simultaneous spiritual challenge comparable to Buddhism.

In broad terms, the new era of foreign rule, although it revealed a striking failure of self-defense, did not last as long, or seem to be as disintegrative, as the early Period of Disunity. That certain features of Chinese civilization were affected seems reasonable, but which features, and in what way, is difficult to determine.

The Liao Dynasty (907-1124)

The population of the Liao empire was relatively small, in keeping with the inhospitality of much of the northland. It is estimated to have been 3,800,000 at the end of the dynasty. Of that number a majority were Chinese (2,400,000) and a good part of the remainder other subjugated peoples (650,000). The dominant Khitan made up only about one fifth of the population (750,000). They faced first an issue common to all three of the conquering states, how to rule an empire comprising a foreign majority when no more than a limited number of experienced leaders could be counted upon, and even those were without a native tradition of elaborate government.

Furthermore, culture divided conquerors and conquered even more than numbers. The Khitan spoke another language, one related to Mongolian, and had no writing until their great unification, when they invented two scripts, one based on Chinese and the other on a Central Asian alphabet. They put their religious faith primarily in spirits of nature, reached through medicine men or shamans, and when the greater religion of Buddhism reached them they responded more to its magical and miraculous aspects than to its psychology or ethics. Their political, social, and economic life contrasted with that of the Chinese at many points. (In view of such differences, it was ironic that the name Khitan made its way westward and came to stand for China in its European form "Cathay.") Where the Chinese had developed a tradition of staffing government on the basis of individual merit, the Khitan gave great weight to the principle of hereditary office, in keeping with their hereditary aristocracy of lineages or "clans" that formed the core of their tribes. Contrary to Chinese rules regarding affinity in marriage, a Khitan might marry his aunt. If the Chinese conceived of everyman as cultivating his fields in the village of his fathers and reckoning his wealth by the land he owned, the Khitan thought of him as one who herded his flocks from one grazing land to another according to the season and counted the horses and sheep he owned. As settled farmer, the Chinese trained his sons to help him on the land, unless he could afford to send them to school, and generally regarded soldiering as a lamentable fate, often the refuge of vagrants and outlaws. As nomadic herder, the Khitan put his children on a horse as early as possible and taught them to shoot, for life was sure to require them to fight, and they would learn to rank victory in combat among the greatest human satisfactions.

The Khitan worked out a military organization and set of tactics that gave full play to their spirit. Their basic striking force was the *ordo* (from which came the European word "horde"), the leader's bodyguard cavalry. Apparently this included all adult Khitan males, so that the whole society was in effect an armed camp, whose men were ready on short notice to leave the herds to the women and go after the enemy.

If the martial quality in Khitan life made conquest easier, other cultural differences from the Chinese made governing difficult. A great political reorganization of the empire in the first half of the tenth century revealed the solution chosen by the Liao, the principle of which succeeding conquerors continued to follow. It was to establish

Two horses of the Central Asian breed much prized by the T'ang and later dynasties. The groom is also Central Asian. Although attributed to Han Kan, an eighth-century painter, the work may be a free copy of the tenth or eleventh century.

a dual form of government, in which an administration Chinese in form as well as mainly Chinese in staff applied to the Chinese subjects, while native traditions continued to be observed among the conquerors, who of course retained ultimate control over the Chinese sector. The Liao way of embodying the principle appeared, for example, in a double central administration, consisting of northern and southern divisions, or regions, each with its hierarchy of offices headed by prime ministers residing in the supreme capital. (Reflecting the nomadic tradition the Liao established five capitals, the supreme capital being in northern Jehol and two of the remainder south of the Wall in China proper, at the site of modern Peking and near Ta-t'ung. The emperor resided in each in season, when he was not out hunting and fishing.) The northern division administered mainly the affairs of the Khitan tribes, and most Khitan who served in government were attached to it. The southern division administered mainly Chinese affairs, and Chinese officials were prominent in it. It followed the

T'ang pattern, with its six ministries and other offices, and Chinese were appointed to them following examinations and by other conventional means. In establishing a dual system the Liao rulers meant to secure their own advantage, not to promote any idea of equality between the communities. The Khitan people were the privileged elite. Khitan, not Chinese, leaders made the major decisions in government; membership in a tribe conferred a respected social status, while Chinese were subject to degradation, including enslavement; and the Khitan were taxed more lightly and received more state aid than the Chinese. Yet to rule the majority of the subjects who were Chinese, Chinese administrative patterns seemed best.

At the same time, the very closeness of the two communities gave rise to imitation, beginning, apparently, with Khitan adoption of Chinese tastes and ways. In the Liao court, where history recorded the process in greatest detail, the imitation appears to have begun consciously with certain specific objects of admiration. For example, the court imported Chinese musical instruments and silk; Chinese women and eunuchs were also introduced into the palace. It adopted reign titles, invented a script on the Chinese model, and practiced Chinese court ritual. It also imported ideas, in the form, for example, of the Chinese Classics, not to mention Chinese advisers; and Confucian terms began to appear in the record of court discussions. In many ways the court was becoming sinified. How far into the Khitan population the changes extended, and how much further unconscious acculturation spread, we do not surely know.

Not everything Chinese was admired, for the Chinese were first of all a conquered people, proof of the Khitan's superiority. The Liao sought to preserve their quality—what they might have called "Khitan spirit" if they had been in the habit of abstract thought—by protecting certain characteristic features. Especially important to them was their language, as would be the language of later conquerors. The Liao also continued certain distinctive religious observances and forbade Khitan men to take the Chinese civil service examinations, perhaps sensing the danger of an education in foreign values as well as that of compromising their authority as victors by competing with the conquered. In these and other ways the Liao expressed their native pride. They certainly were never absorbed wholly into Chinese civilization, as is shown in the arduous flight of many of them westward to Central Asia upon the final defeat of the dynasty. There they continued an independent existence as the Western Liao, or

Kara-Khitai (1124-1211). Yet many of the upper classes must have been changed by the Chinese experience, for Khitan descendants served later conquering dynasties by coaching the less urbane barbarians in Chinese culture and government.

The Chin Dynasty (1115-1234)

The differences between Jürched and Chinese were in most respects as striking as those between Khitan and Chinese. The Jürched, too, spoke a different language and had at first no way of writing it. They differed in religion, and in social patterns and rules of social status; on the whole they had been more hardened by a harsh environment and fighting than the Chinese. Only in one major respect, the relatively larger role that farming played in their lives, did they approach Chinese ways. That similarity may have helped the Chin dynasty to grasp administrative problems of the Chinese countryside more quickly than the Liao had.

Whatever the sum of reasons—the deeper penetration of Chinese territory and the much greater Chinese population presumably also counted—the Chin administration took on somewhat more of a Chinese cast. It was reorganized along the lines of the T'ang, at first with certain offices serving native Jürched concerns but eventually becoming almost wholly Chinese in style. The political capitals were shifted southward, what is now Peking becoming the central capital and Kaifeng the southern capital. Most of the population paid a variation of the old Chinese Two Taxes. Jürched men began to take examinations for office, while Chinese became soldiers. Some Jürched took Chinese surnames and dressed in Chinese style.

Although these and other signs of sinification meant that the invaders were changing greatly, the principle of their administration was nevertheless dualistic, in much the same sense as that of the Liao. The Jürched conquerors remained separate in many ways. They reserved key administrative positions for themselves. Although the Chin rulers, in imitation of the Chinese system, administered examinations to their own people, the examinations were simpler than those for the Chinese and included tests of military skill. The Two Taxes and a heavy burden of surcharges fell only on the Chinese, not the Jürched, who paid light taxes when they paid any at all. The dualism between conqueror and conquered was symbolized most clearly by the military reservations established throughout the country. There, land was taken from Chinese owners and given to Jürched warriors, who were arranged in groups under leaders directly responsible to the central administration. This system of military reservations, supporting hereditary garrisons that were meant to live, as it were, with one hand on the plow and the other on the sword, became a permanent feature of government in China.

The Yuan Dynasty (1260-1368)

After about a century of foreign rule, the north of China, instead of returning to a native dynasty, fell to another barbarian invasion, that of the Mongols, a group of tribes who in the twelfth century lived as pastoral horsemen on the steppes of what is now Outer Mongolia. In 1206 they elected a leader by their customary congress or meeting of the tribes and entitled him Chinggis Khan, which meant something like "ruler of the world." With his *ordo,* the supreme example of its kind, though still, by Chinese standards, a modest army between 100,000 and 250,000 men strong, he went from conquest to conquest, striking the Hsi Hsia, the Chin, Kara-Khitai (Western Liao), and Central Asian kingdoms to the west. His successors expanded the empire across most of Asia, until it comprised four main parts: the Great Khanate, extending from Mongolia in the north to Vietnam in the south and from Korea in the east to Tibet in the west; a khanate in Central Asia; a khanate in Persia; and a khanate in most of inhabited Russia. This division resulted from Chinggis Khan's settlement of his empire upon his four heirs, and the khanates continued to be linked together, the three to the west acknowledging the suzerainty of the Great Khan, who ruled East Asia directly. The relations and politics among these divisions counted for much in the history of the Mongol empire, and ultimately affected the fate of China under the Mongols, but the domain and administration of the Great Khan concern us most directly.

The Mongol armies won China only slowly, the north falling with the defeat of the Chin, but the south remaining not fully subdued for some forty-five years after that. Part of the time, it is true, the Mongols were engaged elsewhere, or hampered by disputes within the leadership. For the rest, when they mounted major attacks against the Chinese, they found stubborn resistance, exemplified at the very end in 1279 when a Sung commander, seeing the hopelessness of the cause, his loyal force having been driven aboard a fleet off the southernmost coast, took the token emperor—a mere boy—on his back and jumped into the sea. When South China was brought for the first time under barbarian rule, the importance of China to the Great Khan's government became clear. Khubilai Khan, the grandson of Chinggis, who directed the conquest of South China, adopted familiar symbols of Chinese government, including a Chinese dynastic name, Yuan, and era names in the Chinese calendrical style. He moved the capital from Karakorum, in Outer Mongolia, to the site of Peking, calling the magnificent new city he built Khanbaliq in Mongolian, Tai-tu in Chinese.

The Mongols differed from the Chinese as had the foreign conquerors before them, and probably in greater degree. It is estimated that the Mongol population did not exceed 2,500,000, much of it spread across the known world. In addition to speaking a different language, believing in their own tribal-centered religion (increasingly overlaid by Buddhism), and being more wholly pastoral and perhaps more devoted to conquest than any of the earlier barbarians, they were used to treating their captives as booty. When the difficulties of ruling North China began to force themselves on the Mongol warriors, a conservative group among them favored simply annihilating the population and turning the land to pasture. An experienced adviser, who was descended from the imperial Liao house and had served the Chin, argued that more could be had from the Chinese by exploiting them than by killing them. He prevailed in this, and established the general principle of rational exploitation as opposed to destruction, but many Mongol habits remained inappropriate to the government of China.

Mongol Administration

The Mongols administered China in a manner as dualistic as that of the previous conquering dynasties. Mongols kept a firm grip on all high offices and any positions that might affect their major interests, while they allowed the general form of administration, especially at the lower levels, to become ever more Chinese as they extended their occupation of the country, and Chinese came to fill the mass of lower positions. Necessity rather than choice impelled this development. In many instances the Mongols employed, instead of Chinese, foreigners—from the earlier barbarian dynasties, from Central Asia, and even from Europe—so that the administration had an international quality. Yet it became obvious eventually that only an infusion of Chinese would provide a staff adequate to govern the conquered population, even in North China. The experienced and cultivated Khitan adviser mentioned above gained permission to conduct a massive civil service examination. Although it qualified 4,030 Chinese, far more than had ever passed an examination before, it was the only examination the Mongols held until late in the dynasty. The successful Chinese, moreover, were assigned on the whole to positions that gave little opportunity to exercise independent authority.

The fact indicates one feature of possible significance in the Mongols' version of dualism: they seemed to distrust especially the established Chinese elite in government. Not content merely to keep checks on the normal authority of the regular bureaucracy, the Mongols made more use of the lowly noncommissioned clerks. The policy unsettled the old elite, but it also probably underscored a truth for any would-be military ruler, that the bureaucracy could be considered a pliant instrument only if carefully controlled.

THE LIMITED DURATION OF MONGOL POWER

The Yuan exerted its greatest power over much of China probably only in the first third of its century of life, or during the reign of the greatest of Chinggis' grandsons, Khubilai Khan (r. 1260-94), who seemed to lay the foundations of a powerful dynasty. In addition to adopting the Chinese forms mentioned before, he established or brought to completion basic administrative systems, including, for example, regional subdivisions that were the forerunners of the modern provinces, and faced a typical question of Chinese government, the transportation of revenue, by experimenting with a system of sea transport and authorizing a major renovation of the Grand Canal.

While apparently laying foundations internally, the dynasty at the same time exercised its abundant military strength in attempts at further conquest. The capital of Southern Sung fell, and the remaining Sung forces eventually capitulated or were dispersed. Korea came grudgingly under control. Beyond that lay a wholly new kind of challenge, an amphibious assault on Japan. The Mongols tried twice, assembling large fleets on the Korean and Chinese coasts and succeeding in putting men on Japanese soil, only to suffer defeat both times in the face of typhoons and Japanese bravery. Mongol armies also met with frustration in Vietnam, where successes in battles in open country eventually gave way to losses from disease, the climate, and perhaps the elusiveness of the hidden enemy.

Yet the intense force that Khubilai seemed to have at his disposal was baffled by the political problems of ruling a huge agrarian society. In the fourteenth century, which opened not long after his death, the Mongols struggled not only against the subject people but also within their own court. Chinese revolts began to break out across large regions of the country. At court, seven emperors occupied the throne in the last twenty-two years of the dynasty. Their average reign of three years each suggests the instability of the leadership, which was further hurt by one of the Mongols' great faults, an inability to devise rules of succession suitable in their new circumstances as rulers of a sedentary society. A result was ruthless factional disputes, aggravated by other splits in the Mongol community, such as those between proponents of the old, nomadic virtues or attitudes and those who embraced more Chinese ways of leadership. The combination of internal dissension and popular rebellion drove the Mongols at the end into a remarkably swift retreat back into the northern desert. The effects of Mongol rule on China were necessarily qualified by the fact that their full vigor was brought to bear on Chinese society for only a relatively short period.

Effects of the Conquering Foreign Dynasties on Chinese Life

Several of the effects of Mongol rule amounted to an extension or reinforcement of conditions associated with the earlier conquering barbarians. The most general of these was the disturbing of traditional patterns of life in the north. There, invaders had ruled for at least two centuries in most places and as many as four in others. Physically, farm lands gave way to pasture on the large tracts the foreigners set aside for animals. Reflecting both the dislocation of life under invasions and the reduced place of agriculture in the eyes of the invaders, certain arduously built features, like irrigation systems and reforestation projects, were destroyed or let fall into ruin. In the first half of the fourteenth century, nature seemed to conspire with the human forces of disruption, bringing years of drought, famine, plague, and locusts, and at midcentury cataclysmic breaks in the Yellow River dikes.

Socially, also, foreign rule stimulated disruptive changes. One was the uprooting of people. Some migrated, fleeing before the menacing invaders. Others deserted their villages out of poverty or oppression and sought some other way to live, even by banditry. The movement of people, and economic insecurity, though difficult to measure, could not but diminish order in several respects. Land records must have fallen into confusion, opening the way to fighting over land. The dispossessed and discontented more readily joined dissident organizations, especially secret societies, some of which already had a long tradition and could now appeal to hatred of the foreign rulers, so that secret societies were prominent in the widespread rebellions toward the end of the Yuan dynasty. The influence of barbarian rule and the atmosphere of uncertainty probably contributed to a loosening of traditional morals and manners. More than a century after the barbarians had left, a Korean traveler deplored what he saw in North China:

In the streets, they revere the Taoist gods and the Buddha, not Confucius. They work at business, not farming. Their clothing is short and tight, and men and women dress the same. Their food and drink are rancid. The high and the low use the same implements. There are still habits that have not been obliterated, and that is regrettable.[1]

In addition to the disparity of wealth that had long been in the making between north and south, the period of foreign occupation appears to have shaken conventional custom and order visibly.

Its effects on government were more difficult to discover with certainty. The Mongols, and the northern conquerors preceding them, came to power with no adequate ideas of their own on how to rule a great settled empire. They made do, on the whole, with one form of dualism or another, placing themselves in positions of control in an administration largely Chinese in form and staffed mainly by Chinese. One side effect of this may have been to aggravate certain faults of the Chinese sort, for the domination of foreigners may have justified various malpractices in excess of what was tolerated normally. At times, for example, subjects and low officials seemed to collude even more industriously than usual to avoid paying taxes. If the ordinary Chinese magistrate found it difficult to ferret out such practices or unwise to expose them, the unaccustomed foreigner was at an even greater disadvantage.

1. John Meskill, tr., *Ch'oe Pu's Diary: A Record of Drifting Across the Sea* (Tucson: University of Arizona Press, 1965), p. 135.

A more important effect, however, was most likely a matter of attitude and style. The barbarians long remained conscious of themselves as conquerors and apart from their subject people. We have seen the clearest evidence of this in the care with which they segregated the physical source of their power, their main armed forces, often providing the troops with separate reservations of land and keeping them free of Chinese. It was apparent also in the capital that the Mongols built in Peking, where the old system of internal walls and shutting in the population at night, little enforced under Chinese governments since T'ang times, was restored. A Mongol device of establishing "branches" of the central administration in the provinces may also be seen as an attempt to keep stricter control over society. While it is also true that groups within the conquering people grew used to Chinese ways, the assimilation was never complete, and when the dynasty fell to other attackers the sense of identity as aliens was still strong enough for many to flee elsewhere instead of seeking to sink into the Chinese population. A style of government that implied mastery over the society more than responsibility for it was, in fact, already familiar; but the barbarians, in their habitual reliance on military power, their organization to control the society for their own practical ends, and their frequently displayed contempt of the conquered, behaved in that style perhaps more nakedly than any rulers had done before. It was a style that northern Chinese had the opportunity to observe for at least two centuries. If there is any truth in the law of the great Tunisian historian of conquest dynasties, Ibn Khaldun—that conquered people tend to imitate the strength of the conquerors—we should not be surprised to find in the subsequent Chinese dynasty traces of that more single-minded despotism.

On the face of it, the barbarian style seemed to favor certain features that might change important characteristics of Chinese civilization. As an example, the outstanding characteristic of the barbarians was their superior fighting force and their esteem of martial virtues. If these qualities had deeply impressed the Chinese elite and in consequence been cultivated by them, later Chinese history would surely have been different. Yet the conquerors repelled the old literate elite and cultivated no new military elite, assigning the Chinese a secondary role at best in military affairs. The attitudes of the old Chinese elite itself, standing off from rough soldiers and actual fighting, also helped to keep a barrier between the ways of the conquerors and the conquered. As a result, the barbarian period seems to have had little effect on dominant Chinese ways of life in the area in which the barbarians were preeminent.

Another kind of far-reaching change was conceivable in regard to economic life. Students of Western history would be sensitive particularly to the consequences of a changed attitude toward trade. It has been pointed out that the northern invaders took an open interest in the material benefits of trade. The Mongols especially stimulated the movement of goods in commerce, both by means of their own demands and by making it relatively easy and for a while safe to travel. They patronized a great association of Central Asian Muslim merchants to supply wanted goods, for a time even exempting them from taxation. They allowed merchants to use certain of the facilities of a great system of courier roads that were provided with stations all across Asia. Maritime trade also seemed advantageous to them, and they provided traders with ships and capital. The conditions seemed to promise a new status to merchants in the social and perhaps even political order.

But the results fell far short of that. The court's openness to commerce, together with its blocking normal careers in officialdom for probably thousands of Chinese, may well have disposed many families of substance to pay more attention to their business interests. To some extent the Mongol administration, and the conquerors before them, probably furthered the involvement of what we have called "official" families in the life of the market place. The Korean traveler cited above a century after the retreat of the Mongols noted of both north and south, "Everyone does business; even some successful officials and men from powerful families carry balances in their own sleeves and will analyze a profit of pennies." Yet the spread of tacit commercial attitudes, profound though its effect may have been in the long run, ignited no social revolution, much less a political one. In fact, the Mongols (and the other conquerors) patronized the merchant mainly to exploit him. They did not regard the merchant as a useful ally against rivals for power or a necessary source of wealth, for they recognized no rivals and found much more wealth elsewhere. The merchant was valuable for what came out of him, and the Mongols not only bought his goods readily but also taxed him heavily. In return for providing ships and capital to maritime traders, the Mongols took 70 percent of the profits. The merchant had no more opportunity to assert his independence of the barbarian overlord than of the Chinese emperor. The Mongol ruler exercised his despotism over the merchant with less self-righteousness but no less ruthlessness.

In the arts, the effect of the barbarian period seems to have been to further some growing tendencies rather than introduce new ones. Under Yuan rule there was a notable production of vernacular prose fiction and opera. Prose fiction was rooted in earlier forms, as chapter XX shows, and the rudiments of the opera were known in the capital even before the Mongols. The spread of popular literature, in short, probably depended on conditions with which the barbarians had little to do, but the barbarians possibly encouraged in various ways a climate of opinion more favorable to the pursuit of pleasures commonly associated with urban, commercial societies. The exclusion of many lettered men from officialdom, especially by the Mongols, has been proposed as the cause which turned creative but frustrated minds toward writing fiction. However uncertain this may be, disgust with government was indeed growing among literati, and it is true that some of the popular literature shows the marks of a cultivated hand; it may be that the barbarians convinced some to follow a way of life more congenial to their talents than orthodox ambition would once have required.

Perhaps the same exclusion and alienation from government contributed to developments in painting. Chapter XIV relates the development, beginning in Sung times, of individualistic or subjective artistic aims. Nothing like this seemed to thrive under the Khitan or Chin governments, whether because the foreign occupation inhibited painters or because the south had already become the center of painting as a result of its cultural and material advantages, it is impossible to say. In any event, the only painting of importance under the conquerors was done in Yuan times and, very largely, was restricted to the region between the Yangtze River and Hangchow, the old Sung capital. Yet in that small region and brief dynasty, "literati painting" produced some of the most remarkable works of that tradition. While the government could hardly be said to have contributed to this, the attitudes it engendered could, for the great majority of important Yuan painters were self-conscious "recluses." Had the old ideal of government and social leadership cherished by the literati not been frustrated, the way of life and distinctive perspective of these great artists would have been less likely to come into being.

In certain kinds of world knowledge, on the other hand, the barbarian occupation, especially the Mongol occupation and the revulsion it engendered against everything associated with it, contributed to a strain of self-centeredness among Chinese. This was so even though the extent of the Mongol empire, linking China as it did with Europe and the Near East, made possible greater intercourse than ever before. The Mongol court attracted an international retinue. Even when still at remote Karakorum it included at one time a Hungarian servant, a Greek soldier, a woman from Lorraine married to a young Russian, a Parisian goldsmith, an Armenian monk, Nestorian Christian priests, and many Chinese and other Asians. Indeed, one of the most famous descriptions of this court was written by William of Rubruck, a Franciscan friar sent by Louis IX of France (Saint Louis), who observed the Mongol capital in 1254. After the capital had been moved to the site of Peking, the international character of the court became even more marked. It is best represented for us by Marco Polo, the Venetian merchant who was received by Khubilai Khan in 1275, spent years in China, and after returning to Italy composed a description of Asia that had great influence in Europe. Columbus, for example, regarded it highly.

While it is possible to trace European excitement about the world partly from the opportunities of exploration opened up by the Mongols, no comparable Chinese curiosity seems to have been awakened. We know that Chinese specialists traveled the length of Asia, as far as Novgorod and Moscow, for example, to serve the Mongol conquerors. A Nestorian cleric born in Peking visited Byzantium and Europe and wrote an account of what he had seen. Roman Catholic missions established churches in the capital and in such rich southern cities as Yangchow and Hangchow. Yet as to religious knowledge, though the Mongol administration was marked by eclectic credulity and toleration, the mere presence of foreign religious establishments was no sign that foreign religious ideas were penetrating Chinese society. In fact, the foreign religions had very little touch with the Chinese community, for they were generally practiced in physically segregated foreign quarters. As to ideas carried by merchants, much the same was true, for when foreign traders took up residence in China they lived, as they preferred and as had long been customary, in separate districts, and they presumably had little opportunity to impress the important literati class, even if they had been the type of cultivated man to make the most of such an opportunity. Merchants met, of course, fellow Chinese merchants, but there is no sign that foreign mercantile attitudes or techniques altered native ways.

In no kind of world knowledge was the disproportion between

promising conditions and meager results greater than in science and technology. China had already a long history of science and technological discovery, the greatest original achievements of which included sericulture, papermaking, printing, and porcelain making. In the Sung dynasty, technology seemed to gain in momentum. Gunpowder, which had been known earlier, began to be used in weapons, leading to a barrel gun early in the twelfth century. At about the same time, paddle wheel warships (driven by manpower) appeared. An advance in astronomy, as important for the mathematical skill it implied as for its use in celestial measurements, was the armillary sphere, which was manufactured with a clock drive by the end of the eleventh century. The clock drive was in turn evidence of the development of an astronomical, mechanical clock.

The Mongol conquest opened the way to a stimulation and reinforcement of such efforts by introducing knowledge from some of the great Muslim cities, which at the time served as repositories of much Mediterranean and Persian science and technique. As if in response, further technological development followed, some of it known to be the fruit of the Mongols' interest. An improved, bronze armillary sphere built in Peking in 1275, for example, probably incorporated knowledge from a Persian astronomer, as did instruments made in succeeding years. Other developments may have owed something to foreign knowledge and something to the Mongols' support of the material and the practical, though we cannot be sure. In the course of the Yuan, for example, the very important discovery was made of how to transmit power mechanically by a system of crank, connecting rod, and piston rod. There were other notable advances in mathematics, medicine, ballistics, and architecture.

On balance, however, the Mongol legacy, despite what appeared to be a fruitful joining of scientific traditions, proved more important as a hated memory than as a scientific catalyst. As the Chinese drove the Mongols out, they drove out the foreign fellow travelers, too, or at least made it clear that they were not welcome. Nor, it seems, was much of what they did—whether in the practice of foreign religions or foreign sciences—welcome. Several centuries later, the astronomical instruments made in Peking still stood (they stand today) but no one remembered how to operate them. We shall never know whether the Chinese threw a baby science out with the Mongol bathwater, but living under a despised conqueror may well have inclined the Chinese gentleman to ignore the strange kinds of knowledge that conquest had introduced.

VII

The Third

Imperial Period

MING DYNASTY
1368-1644
CH'ING DYNASTY
1644-1912

Ming T'ai-tsu (Chu Yuan-chang)

The first Chinese to unify all China in four centuries was Chu Yuan-chang, founder of the Ming dynasty (Ming T'ai-tsu, r. 1368-98). Of his many unusual features, perhaps the most telling was that he was the first common peasant to found a dynasty in 1,500 years. There had been aristocratic officers, professional soldiers, and barbarian warriors, but no son of a simple family since Han Kao-tsu. As the child of poor peasants, Chu Yuan-chang received no formal education. Instead he learned a wealth of peasant lore, some of it probably superstitious, much of it practical and pragmatic, and some of it historical. His grandfather, who remembered the fall of the Sung dynasty and had traveled and seen much, told him stories that probably opened to him, as to many peasants, a surprising store of tradition. Yet his late start at book learning—he may have begun learning to read and write when he was about twenty, for he was preparing then to be ordained as a monk—set him apart forever from the literati. It must have been a keen native intelligence that told him to recruit to his organization, once he had turned to a life of rebellion, a few men of learning, whose advice on government helped him to avoid the fate of most peasant rebels and establish an effective administration of conquered territory. His use of capable advisers, reminiscent of one of the special virtues attributed to Han Kao-tsu, was the more remarkable for his ingrained scorn and distrust of intellectuals. It was distinguished as well by his absolute domination of whomever he used, for he was a great tyrant. After due weight is given to his other qualities—his unquenchable vitality, his intelligence, and his competence at organizing—this domineering force of his may be the primary factor in his rise in forty years from a poor farm boy to the emperor of China.

Establishment of Administration in the Third Imperial Period

In broad outline, the structure of government in the Third Imperial Period could be traced to Sung, T'ang, and even earlier antecedents; such distinctive features as there were appeared as changes within specific systems. Limited though they were, the changes nevertheless revealed something of the attitudes of the rulers, most obviously an interest in heightening their despotic power. To name only the most general instances of this, there were plans to insure the emperor more unimpeded powers of decision than ever before, to provide him with greater military security, and to reduce ever further potential opposition in the civil service and society.

THE SIMPLIFICATION OF AUTOCRACY

Ming T'ai-tsu introduced a plan for realizing his powers of decision more fully when he grew suspicious that his chief councilor, or prime minister, a companion of many years, was preparing a rebellion. T'ai-tsu eliminated the official, abolished the office of prime minister forever, and, with no more intervening councilors, dealt directly with the heads of the Six Ministries, theoretically gaining intimate control over the offices that carried out his will.

Actually, before long he found that the burden of work he had brought on himself made secretarial help necessary, even for a man of his enormous energies, and he established several grand secretaries, who read memorials and drafted suggested answers. Since they also had charge of instructing the heir apparent and carrying out other scholarly assignments, they amounted to "intellectuals in residence," a characterization emphasized later by the custom of drawing almost all of them from the ranks of *chin-shih* who had been sent for special advanced training to the Hanlin Academy. They were assigned to different positions in the palace administration, that is, the "inner court," and they were supposed to have no powers of decision or supervision over general affairs. In keeping with the limited responsibilities envisaged for them, they received at first relatively low rank— lower than that of a prefect.

In view of the long history of palace government, with its perennial contention for a share in power, it was almost natural that the grand secretaries should exceed their nominal role and influence the emperor. Despite their formal separateness they became known informally as the Cabinet. Eventually, as their authority made itself felt at every level, their ranks were raised and titles lengthened. Some grand secretaries, moreover, cultivated relations with the palace eunuchs, adding another element to the politics around the autocrat.

THE STANDING ARMY

The attempt to provide the emperor with greater military security followed the principle of the preceding northern invaders. Ming T'ai-tsu assigned his soldiers to a separate category in the registers of population, making military status hereditary, and established several hundred garrisons throughout the country, the garrisons in turn having charge of "chiliads," battalions of approximately one thousand men each. Each garrison was allotted land, and each soldier given a share of it. T'ai-tsu boasted of the economy of this arrangement, under which the soldiers could support themselves, but we have already seen, in the case of the T'ang militia, the inadequacy of such a system if the armies had to undertake long campaigns. What was striking about the Ming army was the extent to which it was conceived as a stationary force, and thus primarily defensive. The system, moreover, was submitted to a complicated and counterbalanced structure of command, in order to avoid insubordination and rebellion.

THE CIVIL SERVICE

To reduce tendencies toward opposition in society, T'ai-tsu began with the civil service, attempting, first, to draw officials from a broader segment of the people; second, to insure an ideological orthodoxy among them; and third, to symbolize clearly the actual servility of the civil servant before the throne.

The first goal, that of drawing from a broader segment of society than before, was embodied in T'ai-tsu's early establishment of schools in each district, subprefecture, and prefecture of the country. In them, men who aspired to pass the state examinations would register and in due course qualify, by local examination, for entering the national competition. Although in the long run the schools served primarily as registration and perhaps testing centers for students who learned their lessons elsewhere, they remained a nationwide network of offices at which would-be officials could make contact with the government.

The state's interest in schools reached its ultimate expression in T'ai-tsu's proclamation for the establishment of village schools everywhere. The purpose of tnis no doubt went beyond the simple recruiting of officials and implied a wish to extend the civilizing force of education to the whole rural population, an aim which revealed an impulse in T'ai-tsu, the man of the people, to affect all the people more profoundly than government had tried to do before. In this he overreached himself, as the idea of the schools languished in the absence of state money to support them. They persisted in name in many places, but there is no evidence of a revolution in popular education.

The interest in establishing an ideological orthodoxy bore fruit in the reign following T'ai-tsu's. The succeeding emperor put the whole examination system at the service of one school of thought, that of Chu Hsi, when he commissioned the publication of a new edition of the Classics with the commentaries of the Sung master. Questions of interpretation and scholarship in the examinations were to be based on the official edition. Thus the Neo-Confucian School of Principle became the learning that anyone ambitious to succeed must pursue. (A precedent for this state approval of Chu Hsi had been set late in the Yuan dynasty, during its brief revival of the examination system.)

By narrowing the learning to be tested in the examinations, the state simplified them. At the same time, it encouraged conformity in another way, by adopting a set style of essay, called colloquially the "Eight-legged Essay," which had originally been devised to make it easier both for the candidate to order and expose his thoughts and for the reader to grade the answer. The essay was expected to consist of four main parts, each having two "legs" or subsections written in an elaborately parallel style. A little more than a century after the founding of the dynasty, students seemed to be giving more attention to style than content, perhaps partly because the content had to be largely of a given nature, in a given form, leaving little freedom except in flourishes of rhetoric.

Among the measures that T'ai-tsu and his successors enforced to symbolize the servile relationship of official to emperor, the most obvious was the public beating of officials. In previous dynasties, men in office had not customarily suffered direct physical punishment. If charged with wrongdoing they might be fined, demoted, or even dismissed from officialdom, but they were beaten or otherwise physically punished, if the crime called for such measures, only after being deprived of their official standing. Ming T'ai-tsu dispensed with that kind of symbolical privilege and on occasion had officials stripped of their clothes and beaten before their colleagues.

T'ai-tsu's awareness of possible opposition among the people prompted him to follow the style of Han Kao-tsu and others in uprooting tens of thousands of rich families in the lower Yangtze valley and sending them to poorer regions or to his capital at Nanking, where he could keep an eye on them. More generally, he promoted conformity by attempting to indoctrinate the masses. He wrote six very general precepts, called the Six Maxims, which taught respect for superiors, the need of moral guidance of the young, and contentment with one's lot in life. The maxims were engraved in stone, and apparently rubbings were to be taken and distributed to every village household, and the maxims were to be read out by the village elders periodically. The effort, which was emulated by later emperors, aimed at indoctrinating the whole population with the virtues of order.

Extending Power Abroad

If T'ai-tsu had spent much of his prodigious energy giving his house a firm footing, his successor, whose reign was called Yung-lo, turned to more flamboyant displays of power. Some of his steps, of a boldness and aggressiveness not characteristic of Ming in the long run, were dictated in part by his originally shaky seat on the throne. The designated heir of T'ai-tsu had been a grandson, a nephew of the future Yung-lo, but the resentful uncle waited only a few years before seizing the throne from the legitimate successor and moving the capital to Peking, where he had his fief as a prince. There he built a whole new imperial city on the site of the old Mongol capital. The outlines of Peking today, including its walls, reflect the Ming plan. Meanwhile the magnificent Nanking was retained as a second capital which boasted its own array of ministries and offices, most having only local jurisdiction but providing positions for officials unneeded in the national administration.

Beginning in 1405, the emperor sent seven grandly equipped missions far into the South China Sea and Indian Ocean, the last returning in 1433. Most of the missions were directed by Cheng Ho, a eunuch of Muslim faith. The fleets were large, that of the first voyage, for example, including sixty-three ships and almost 28,000 men. The biggest ships of the fleet were over 400 feet long. They carried sailors, soldiers, buyers, and clerks. On one or another voyage, the ships, which were gone for two or three years at a time, reached India, Ceylon, Aden, Hormuz, and the African coast, not to mention nearer settlements.

Among the reasons for these missions, which were unprecedented in size and reach, the official history gave great weight to the emperor's obsession for hunting down the nephew whom he had forced off the throne and whose death had never been proven. That the missions were mostly in the charge of a eunuch suggests that the emperor considered the assignment an extraordinary and sensitive one. Another purpose surely was trade, as the missions brought back many luxurious and exotic goods, including zebras, ostriches, and giraffes; yet the sudden cessation of the voyages shortly after the emperor's death indicates that the commercial motive was not a sustaining one—nothing like that of the Portuguese who were probing down the west coast of Africa at the same time.

A further motive, specific yet characteristic of ambitious emperors, was probably the wish to spread the fame of the dynasty abroad and receive the satisfying acknowledgment of its power in the form of tribute. The Ming emperor felt this satisfaction, for not only tribute arrived in return missions but also a few foreign rulers, either as prisoners or as willing tributaries, and there was even a report that the voyagers had massacred 5,000 overseas Chinese who apparently failed to pay proper respects when one of the missions reached Sumatra. The extension of the dynasty's power in this way must have been particularly satisfying to an emperor whose love for power had led him to usurp the throne.

Other thrusts outward by the emperor had the more familiar purposes of securing pliant neighbors and taking new territory. To the northeast, campaigns into Manchuria allowed many garrisons to be established. The emperor himself led campaigns into the north and defeated the Mongols repeatedly, though not finally. Ming forces and colonists moved into what is now Yunnan. A campaign assured the subjection of Burma under native administration. Several expeditions in North Vietnam (Annam) resulted in the capture of hundreds of thousands of men and animals and the establishment of an uneasy Chinese or puppet administration there.

WITHDRAWALS AFTER YUNG-LO

The Yung-lo period saw Ming power at its height deployed abroad, and while this crescendo of activity did not include campaigns as brilliant as some of Han or T'ang it established the Ming as a major Asian power. In the long run, however, the Ming was not to be known for probing into the world abroad. Rather soon after the end of the Yung-lo reign Ming forces beyond the country proper began to be withdrawn. The maritime missions ceased. Ming foreign relations became more characteristically defensive, and Ming government more characteristically preoccupied with itself. Even earlier, the Yung-lo exuberance had led to internal strains.

THE ADVANCEMENT OF EUNUCHS

It had been a long time since eunuchs had held important assignments. Late in the T'ang dynasty, in the latter half of the ninth century, the roles of eunuchs in that harried court had even included that of kingmaker. The memory of their sordid complicity in the ruin of their dynasty apparently remained vivid in the minds of the Sung emperors, for eunuchs gained no great importance under them. Nor were they prominent in the conquest dynasties. The restrictions that had kept them in their place as household servants for five centuries were reaffirmed in the Ming dynasty, when the founder warned against using eunuchs as administrators. Yet in the Yung-lo reign they rose again, their usefulness apparently counting for more than their reputation, and served not only in the great expeditions abroad (other eunuchs besides Cheng Ho were involved) but also as military supervisors elsewhere. Their powerful supervisory assignments grew from then on, extending to industries and fiscal administration, until they constituted practically a whole supervisory administration by themselves and had become a large force in politics.

THE WEAKENED MILITARY SYSTEM

A second problem introduced by the Yung-lo activity appeared in the military system. The network of garrisons and stations was based partly on an assumption of limited movement in any event; the Mongol campaigns and other expeditions interfered with the assumed ability of the armed forces to support themselves and eroded the surplus of the state treasury. Apparently the forces in the field were weakened, for after the Yung-lo period reverses and withdrawals occurred on several fronts. Ming armies gradually gave up an outermost perimeter in northeast Manchuria, and some garrisons withdrew south of the Great Wall. In 1427 the unsatisfactory attempts to put Annam under a dependable vassal were abandoned and she was left independent. In other places Ming armies remained formidable, but to the record of defeats was added in 1449 one in which a combination of military ineptitude and eunuch interference figured: the T'u-mu incident. A young emperor, badly advised by a group of eunuchs, set out to chastise a Mongol leader only to be captured himself. The Mongols eventually returned the emperor, but the court did not quite return to its former ways. A whole new military component, standing bodyguard garrisons for the emperor, was called for, with correspondingly increased costs. The presence after the incident of two emperors in Peking, the old one and a new one who had been enthroned in the former's absence, precipitated a succession crisis that produced lasting hostility and contention in the court. If the crisis did not immediately cripple the government, it, and others that followed, turned the court toward a preoccupation with factional disputes, to the neglect of pressing issues of administration.

The Sixteenth Century: Inconstant Leadership and Constant Crisis

Through the sixteenth century the preoccupation with factional disputes seems to contrast sharply with the magnitude of the threats to the health of the state. There was a succession of foolish, headstrong, and derelict rulers. Eunuchs continued to work themselves forward. An observer of relations between them and the grand secretaries noted that, in the course of one reign covering the middle two quarters of the century, eunuchs at first bowed to the chief grand secretary, then treated him as an equal, and finally received salutations from him.

Besides a political give-and-take between eunuchs and grand secretaries, there were factions within the bureaucracy itself. A major debate over a question of imperial rites, this time centering on the titles appropriate to the emperor's forefathers, divided the court into hostile groups risking their fortunes on their arguments. The debate itself kept the court upset for four years, in the course of which many men lost their positions and were punished. Beyond that, the rites dispute generated habits of factional rivalry which persisted long afterwards and colored almost all major questions of government.

Meanwhile threats to the country increased. The troubles were not apparent, or similar, everywhere—indeed much of ordinary life followed a prosperous course, as will be noted shortly—and broke out only in certain parts of the social organism. Most remarkable, and more revealing of the limitations of the dynasty, were attacks on the borders by foreigners, especially two groups known as "northern plunderers and southern pirates."

The northern plunderers were the Mongols, to whom Ming had to relinquish the whole Ordos region. Of their repeated attacks in the northern provinces a particularly dangerous one in 1550 carried the horde through the Great Wall and down to the vicinity of Peking. Although the capital did not fall and the Mongol leader withdrew, he remained a power in the north.

The southern pirates were Japanese. From as early as the thirteenth century, small groups of Japanese boats had begun to appear along the coast of first Korea and then China itself. The Japanese apparently put out from home in quest of profitable cargoes, which they would acquire on occasion by trade but more often by raiding coastal communities. The raids diminished during the fifteenth century but increased again in the sixteenth, both in frequency and in scale, threatening the whole Chinese coast. Some raiders seized offshore islands as bases, and some attacked such great southern cities as Hangchow and Nanking. By the sixteenth century, moreover, the raiders were no longer only Japanese. Probably a majority of them were Chinese outlaws, whose recourse to this bold way of life suggested both the difficulties of livelihood facing some Chinese communities and the failure of the government to control the situation.

A very small proportion of the raiders was Portuguese. After Vasco da Gama had found his way around the Cape of Good Hope and into the Indian Ocean in 1498, explorers pushed eastward rapidly, a group arriving off the China coast in 1514. In bearing they were not much different from the other adventurers along the coast, and they were so few, among the thousands of seafarers of unknown business, that it is not surprising that the Ming court, after seeing a party of the newcomers who conducted a tribute mission in 1520-21, tended to relegate them mentally to the ranks of lesser barbarians. Perhaps the Portuguese ships, navigating skills, and firearms should have excited any minds sufficiently alive to their implications, but in the sixteenth century these were not so clearly superior to what the Chinese already knew.

THE INCREASE OF ECONOMIC AND FISCAL PRESSURES

Up to a point, the very durability of Ming China, as of old China generally, lay in the fact that the administration, society, and economy were not so closely knit that a tear in one place immediately unraveled the whole fabric. The court's frequent neglect of government in favor of its own political infighting demoralized regional administration, but only gradually. The Mongol and Japanese raids frightened and ruined border communities, but undermined the authority of the state only indirectly. Even as the effects of such damage were spreading, other sectors of the society seemed to follow an independent course. So it was with the economy. Basic production continued the slow growth that had been apparent from at least the tenth century. Early-ripening strains of rice, hardy kinds of wheat, and sorghum were grown more widely than before. Soon after the European explorers found their way to the New World, American food plants appeared in China. They included maize, the sweet potato, the Irish potato, and peanuts. It was still too early, in the sixteenth century, to observe the almost revolutionary potential of these crops in dry lands that had not previously produced much, but they later played an important part in maintaining a swelling population. That population had already begun its long growth, one modern scholar guessing that it may have increased from 65 million in the late fourteenth century to almost 150 million by 1600.

Many signs pointed to the liveliness of commerce. "Clubs" or "halls" were built in Peking and other big cities to serve merchants from out of town. At points along the southern coast, a rich and relatively influential class of men, the coastal equivalent of a "gentry," grew out of maritime trade. In the early seventeenth century, it has been estimated, more Chinese tonnage than any other was sailing Asian waters. Much of it was illegal, since private shipping had been banned early in the dynasty, though the law was irregularly enforced; and some merchants had bases abroad, in, for example, Japan. The commercial and industrial character of the lower Yangtze valley evoked from travelers comments like the following, by a Korean who passed the major city, Soochow, in 1488:

Learned men and gentry abound there; and all the treasures of the land and sea, such as thin silks, gauzes, gold, silver, jewels, crafts, arts, and rich and great merchants, are there .... Market quarters are scattered like stars .... The people live luxuriously. There are solid rows of towers and stands, and ... merchantmen and junks from Honan, Hopei, and Fukien gather like clouds.[1]

A particularly telling sign of economic development was the official use of silver as money. The Ming first began to accept silver as a regular part of the annual revenues on a large scale in 1436 with the commutation of assessments of grain from southeastern provinces to

1. John Meskill, trans. *Ch'oe Pu's Diary: A Record of Drifting Across the Sea* (Tucson, University of Arizona Press, 1965), pp. 93-94.

silver. Other commutations followed, until, in the sixteenth century, a new general method of making collections, called the Single Whip Tax, tended to make the major part of the revenues payable in silver.

THE SINGLE WHIP TAX

The method, which evolved more or less pragmatically in response to similar needs in several provinces, generally replaced the ancient Two Taxes. A bewildering variety of surcharges, incidental taxes, and new kinds of taxes had long burdened both taxpayers and record keepers. Aiming mainly to simplify collection—and so to reduce opportunities for evasion and obfuscation—the new procedure consisted of listing together on a bill a taxpayer's total obligations—of which the basic land tax and a *corvée* obligation were central—and converting them all into money values, the sum of which was the man's obligation for the year. The phrase "single whip" was an ironic pun on the term "amalgamation into one," by which the method was known, the single statement received by each taxpayer standing for the one crack of the whip he had to suffer for the year. (In fact, the tax was not so neat or uniform everywhere, and some taxes were never incorporated into it.) The Single Whip Tax marked a new fiscal era, in which taxes were collected mainly in silver. At the same time the administration was beginning to use silver instead of commodities for some of its payments, including the payment of its armed forces along the northern frontier.

As important as the penetration of silver into the official economy was, it did not open an era of general and purposeful reform in fiscal administration. To the contrary, the official handling of finances continued to suffer from enormous faults, if measured against a standard of efficient collection and use of funds. In practice, for example, there was little active central management of funds. Moreover, old habits persisted, including that of robbing Peter to pay Paul. It was once planned, for example, to make 80 percent of the salt produced under the official monopoly available for consumption, while reserving 20 percent against military crises. No sooner was the reserve established than it was made available at auction, and since it brought higher prices than the regular stock, selling the "reserve" became a standard practice. It can be inferred, from this and other actions, that in government there was little fiscal efficiency in any modern sense. The penetration of money resulted in a more complicated official economy, but there was neither a revolution in official outlook nor a new theory of the national wealth.

THE SIXTEENTH CENTURY: A MODERN TEMPER

In other ways, Chinese life in the sixteenth century displayed preoccupations and tensions that seem modern. The very growth of the material economy was partly responsible for this. There were more books, more publishers, and probably more schooling. One of the manifestations of the new temper was the spread of literate pastimes—writing verse, for example—among classes below the old literati in the city; poetry societies included shopkeepers and artisans. In favored places, like the lower Yangtze valley, wealth made possible a broad range of activities in life. The same practice that was noted in the Yuan dynasty—the renunciation or avoidance of an official career in favor of a private life—became a familiar choice in some educated circles, even though the government was no longer foreign. Life could be devoted to scholarship, teaching, art, the pleasures of the appetites, or local philanthropy; in any event service in government, though still a powerful ideal, seemed no longer wholly accepted as the way to the good life.

The Thinkers. Among original thinkers, the modern temper appeared in an emphasis on the individual mind's capacity to know, and even to contain in itself, the good. Typical of this emphasis was the Neo-Confucian School of the Mind, of which the great spokesman was Wang Yang-ming (1472-1529).

Wang Yang-ming's major points were concerned with the nature and function of the mind and its connection with the world. A man's original mind, he asserted, was nothing other than Principle, the ordering pattern or law of the universe. Thus every man had an innate knowledge of what was right and wrong. What was needed was a means of making this original knowledge the governor of all one's acts, that is, of "rectifying" the mind so that it followed its original, universal morality and not selfish, perverted ideas. Rectification began with establishing a firm will to follow the Way, progressed by means of meditation or "quiet sitting," and led to practicing righteous works—for right action was the proof of true knowledge; knowledge was inseparable from action.

Several implications of this position help to characterize Ming thought. First, the turning inward in search of the original mind implied a kind of individualism, as every man was a potential sage. Moreover, the inward quest opposed the comparatively outward emphasis of the Chu Hsi orthodoxy. Chu Hsi-ism had evolved, it was protested, into a superficial preoccupation with books, producing too many pedants and too few good men. The protest went further, by implication. Men were overly given to subordinate or hollow values—wealth and fame, for example—if not to actual corruption, at the expense of the cultivation of virtue. In the new thinking about the mind was implied a broad feeling of unease and protest. From such tensions came much of the nervous vitality of the Ming temper.

Academies. The outstanding form of intellectual organization was the academy. Known ever since Sung times as centers for the serious pursuit of wisdom, academies sprang up at a great rate in the sixteenth century, especially in the south. There were a dozen in Kiangsi alone. Wang Yang-ming and some of his immediate followers were prominent but not alone in establishing them. By implication, academies represented dissatisfaction with the standard education. While the state schools had become little more than registration centers, the academies actually brought master and disciples together in the time-honored way of human cultivation. The academies felt that they offered a life directed toward sagehood, as against the state schools and the examination system which too often led only to status, wealth, and moral vacuity.

However, the Confucian concern for government being what it was, it would have been surprising if social purpose had been completely absent from the academies. Wang Yang-ming, for example, insisted that knowledge required action. He himself was one of the most effective magistrates and soldiers of the dynasty. Almost inevitably, academies too began to be identified with political purposes, especially as high officials patronized them. Yet the anticonventional, reformist quality they suggested made them vulnerable to attack from a government that saw no good in an organized opposition. Becoming implicated in the factional disputes of the time, academies suffered a series of political repressions, which in the long run had the effect of bringing them under closer state control.

Radical Individualists. In the range of Ming experimentation and disaffection, a striking figure was the independent, and often deliberately outlandish, individualist—for example, Li Chih (1527-1602). Believing in his own potential for sagehood, Li Chih eventually disavowed all respect for tradition and convention. When he gave up official life after serving in a number of posts he neither retired quietly on some pretext nor entered an academy from which he might one day return to office a morally stronger man, but openly repudiated the Confucian official life. To emphasize his break with convention he wore Buddhist dress. Few who had found a place in a social "establishment," whether Buddhist or Confucianist, failed to be shocked by his wild spontaneity and his iconoclasm. The shock was the more powerful for his erudition and talent, which even his critics had to acknowledge. For many it must have been a revelation, not merely a shock, to see students flock to him when he urged "living in the present" and "spontaneity" and dismissed as artificial all references to loyalty, chastity, filial piety, and righteousness; for his popularity indicated a considerable disillusionment with the mouthed virtues of conformers and a thirst for new integrity.

The Arts. In literature the modern temper also appeared, not everywhere in poetry and prose, which remained for the most part bound by traditional forms and themes, but in certain especially lively works of fiction and drama. A love of spontaneity and action characterized the novels that were a conspicuous form of the time. *The Romance of the Three Kingdoms* (*San-kuo-chih yen-i*) and *The Water Margin* (*Shui-hu chuan*), both based on stories long in existence, the former telling of the struggles for power after the fall of Han and the latter of a robber band in Sung times, extolled heroes of action. So did *Hsi-yü chi* (A record of the western regions), translated by Arthur Waley as *Monkey,* which, derived from the pilgrimage of the T'ang monk Hsüan-tsang to India, made the hero of the journey a roguish monkey. Another strong element was sensuality. It permeated, for example, the novel *Golden Lotus* (*Chin p'ing mei*), the story of a rich man engrossed in beautiful women. Love became a major theme, especially of plays, such as *P'i-pa chi* (The story of the lute).

These arts also indicated a new level of popular culture. A "reading public" wider than ever before now existed, as may be gathered, for example, from the fame of commercial publishers, who fed and stimulated the taste for books. A "theater public" also became widespread, as indicated by the establishment of theaters in many places in the south, each offering distinctive drama of its own. In addition, below the level of fine art, there was what almost amounted to an industry of second-rate or hack painting, suggesting a wider "art public." It enjoyed, for example, pictures of beautiful women and the suggestions they conveyed of erotic pleasures.

The Christian Missionaries. It might seem that the desire for novelty so apparent at the time would have been favorable to the Christian missionaries, who arrived in the wake of the first Portuguese explorers and envoys. Portuguese commercial interests had made a start, though a modest one, in the region of Canton. In 1522 Peking forbade trade with the Portuguese, but in fact it continued, to the profit of all concerned. By 1557 the Portuguese had built a small depot on an uninhabited peninsula that they called Macao, in the Bay of Canton, and the local Chinese authorities proved willing to tolerate it, as long as the Portuguese did not disturb the peace too much to be officially ignored. At this settlement, too, the first significant order of missionaries, the Jesuits, established their center.

The Jesuits' efforts in China actually began with the famous "Apostle to the Indies," St. Francis Xavier. After working in India and Japan, Xavier went to an island near Canton and attempted to persuade Chinese shipowners to carry him to the mainland. After weeks of waiting, however, toward the end of the year 1552, he died there.

The Jesuits' interest in China was nevertheless fixed, and at a house established in Macao other missionaries prepared themselves for the day when they could move inland. The policy that was adopted has been called "accommodation." Briefly, it proposed that the missionaries not only acquire a maximum knowledge of the traditions and culture of China, beginning with the Chinese language, but also adopt Chinese ways to the fullest possible extent permitted by the Catholic faith. In practice the most successful of the Jesuits eventually spoke Chinese, dressed like Chinese literati, became conversant in the Classics, wrote in Chinese, and found many basic Chinese beliefs and practices compatible with Christianity. As intellectuals, they gravitated toward the literati, and as Europeans, they naturally (and theoretically in China correctly) associated the best in society with the ruling circles.

The real pioneer of the mission in China was Matteo Ricci (1552-1610). The year he arrived in Macao—1582—the long efforts of his colleagues to cultivate the friendship of Chinese officials were rewarded. Permission was granted to build a house in the capital of Kwangtung Province. In the following seventeen years the Jesuits pursued their mission with mixed results. They were able to establish houses in a few more cities, including Nanking, to make a number of conversions, and to interest many more Chinese, though for the time being inconclusively, by cultivating local officials, meeting with the local learned, and lecturing. The Jesuits became centers of curiosity wherever they went and engaged their many visitors and hosts on the broadest intellectual grounds possible, not only discussing the Chinese philosophy in which they had been steeping themselves and introducing their own religion and philosophy but also displaying the achievements of Europe in map making, astronomy, clocks (a favorite curiosity among the Chinese), and scientific instruments.

The cultivation of friends proved its worth in 1600, when Ricci was introduced to the court at Peking, where he spent the last ten years of his life. Late in the dynasty, his successors were appointed to the Bureau of Astronomy, which had customarily been in the hands of Muslims since the days of the Mongol rulers. The Chinese Muslims were not the scientists that their predecessors had been, and they misinterpreted or neglected the Arabic knowledge that had once been preeminent; they were no longer even sure how to use the great bronze instruments that had been cast in Yuan times. By comparison the Jesuits were more skilled, and they were assigned to compile a reformation of the imperial calendar, on which much religious and ordinary ritual depended. To be in the official world seemed a great step toward that success which Ricci had felt would slowly be achieved. By the beginning of the next dynasty, 150,000 Chinese had been received into the Church, and the harvest of previous efforts seemed to have begun.

Nevertheless, the missionaries' experiences both before and after Ricci's death indicated the difficulty of the way ahead. As foreigners they awakened not only curiosity but also sometimes fear and hostility among the people. These natural human reactions may have been stimulated and magnified by the Portuguese, for there had already been instances of Portuguese attacking Chinese villagers and kidnaping or buying young Chinese as slaves. Soon strange tales began to circulate about the big-nosed barbarians—how, for example, they liked to eat Chinese children. In Peking the more prominent the mission became the more inevitably was it caught up in the pattern, particularly labyrinthine at the time, of central factional politics. It was denounced to the throne as frequently as it was commended. When its opponents had the emperor's ear it sometimes was threatened by edicts of expulsion. Aside from such uncertainties, the Jesuits observed that regardless of the fact that relatively large numbers had accepted Christianity, the situation of the literati in general was not highly favorable. Success in life depended on passing the examinations, the preparations for which all but monopolized the intellectual life of the younger men. The Confucian conformity of the majority of literati was difficult to shake.

True, some were interested. The most receptive on the whole were the very ones mentioned earlier as being somehow disturbed by the drift of Chinese life. Academy men often welcomed the Jesuits, and showed a sustained interest in their knowledge. Ricci met Li Chih, the great apostle of disillusionment, whose comments on the missionary show his admiration. At the same time, his incomprehension of the Christian drive to convert the world shows the gulf that separated the Jesuits from Chinese of even extraordinary learning:

He is an extraordinarily impressive person. His mind is lucid and his appearance is simple. When a company of ten or a dozen people are involved in an argument, and each is defending his own view against the other, he stands at one side and does not allow himself to be provoked into intervening, and to become confused. Amongst all the men I have seen, none can compare to him . . . . But I do not know how it is that he came here. I have already been with him three times, and still do not know why he has come here. It would be more than foolish if it were perhaps his wish to alter our doctrine of the Duke of Chou and of Confucius on the basis of his doctrine. I believe that this is not [the reason why he is here].[2]

THE FAILURE OF LEADERSHIP

For all the liveliness of the sixteenth century, no new era of political effectiveness dawned. To the contrary, the disintegrating effects of factionalism, including eunuch power, seemed only to increase as time went on. For about fifteen years (1567-82) it seemed that some of the faults might be checked by the strong hand of a reforming grand secretary, Chang Chü-cheng (1525-82), who was somewhat reminiscent of Wang An-shih in his influence over a young emperor and his readiness to use his power to alter long-established arrangements. Chang set in motion projects to increase the state's income. He reformed, for example, the system of transporting tax payments. He adopted plans to reduce court expenditures. In the great reformist manner, he ordered a nation-wide resurvey of land tenure, bringing large areas of previously unrecorded land onto the tax registers in some places. However, the resurvey and other fiscal changes led to no lasting and significant improvements. Chang's approach, remarkable for its sweep, and the grip he was able to keep on government, aimed nevertheless to check rather than to come to terms with any new attitudes and conditions in society. That these might be signs of constructive change never occurred to him. He

2. As translated in Wolfgang Franke, *China and the West* (Columbia, University of South Carolina Press, 1967), p. 39.

seemed poorly equipped to harness new forces, and his lonely attempt to reinvigorate old ones stemmed only briefly the spreading ineffectiveness of government.

The last years of the sixteenth century and first decades of the seventeenth confronted a demoralized administration with pressing demands. Risings in satellite territories, such as Annam and Burma, successfully challenged Chinese power there. In a crisis in Korea, Chinese armies rose to the occasion but drained the treasury in doing so. In 1592 the great Japanese leader Toyotomi Hideyoshi (1536-98) set in motion his cherished plan of conquering the Chinese world, sending an army of perhaps 160,000 to invade Korea. Peking responded to the Koreans' call for help by sending troops, whose strength was enough, together with the heroic sea strikes of a Korean admiral and the harassment of Korean guerillas, to drive the Japanese back. A second Japanese offensive in 1597 had less success. Although the Chinese effort served the purpose, it cost millions of ounces of silver to support the soldiers, a heavy burden in any circumstances and a dangerous one when the administration seemed torn by conflict.

After Chang Chü-cheng died, factional competition resumed more intensely than ever. It was abetted by indifferent emperors, one of whom refused to meet with his ministers for years. Another much preferred carpentry to conferences. Eunuchs played an ever-expanding role in official business, their numbers reaching perhaps 100,000 and their organizations overshadowing much of the regular bureaucracy. The most infamous, Wei Chung-hsien, between 1624 and 1627 held dictatorial power, while the emperor attended to his carpentry. Wei used his power to build a loyal staff, which in the circumstances could only have been bootlickers. There was no lack of sycophants from which to choose; one compared Wei with Confucius. When a group of men associated with the Tung-lin Academy spoke out against Wei, he retaliated with a merciless purge. Hundreds of men were charged with offenses, and many were removed from the registers of officials, imprisoned, and even killed. The Tung-lin Academy was abolished, of course, as were others.

Although Wei Chung-hsien was soon gone, killing himself when his patron, the emperor, died, the dynasty had only a few years of life left, and they were marked by rebellions and then an invasion. Of the rebellions, the most destructive was led by Li Tzu-ch'eng (1605?-45), an unemployed porter who proved to be a natural leader, fierce of face, a lover of rough-and-tumble, and an excellent horseman and bowman. By 1644 he had proclaimed a dynasty, established a capital, and asserted control over the several provinces of North China. He then descended on Peking.

Meanwhile, the emperor had sought advice from his ministers in vain; even when they could be made to stop blaming each other for the disastrous turn of events, they had nothing effective to suggest. One powerful army that remained loyal and in position northeast of Peking, on guard against the Manchus, a militant people outside the Great Wall, was ordered to come to the capital, but too late. Li Tzu-ch'eng entered the city unopposed and took the throne. Most of the officials left in the capital reappeared and expressed to him their allegiance; indeed, they petitioned him to accept the title of emperor. They were confident that Heaven had transferred its Mandate.

They were wrong. The general of the northeastern army, Wu San-kuei, perhaps expecting a powerful role in the capital as the restorer of Ming, if not as a new emperor, decided that he should still defeat Li Tzu-ch'eng. However, to assure his victory he concluded an agreement with the Manchu leaders, whom he had previously been assigned to hold in check, to contribute some of their own troops to aid him in the assault. He assumed, perhaps, that once Peking was retaken the Manchus would accept a handsome payment and go home. Instead, once in Peking, the Manchus let it be known that, in view of the instability of the country, they would stay a while. They stayed for 268 years.

The Organization of the Manchus

Although the Manchus' conquest of China may have depended more on fortuitous opportunities than on long-laid plans, once in power the Manchus proved the most successful of China's foreign rulers. Their rise before the conquest had in some ways prepared them for success. They were Jürched people, living as hunters, fishers, and herders in the northern three quarters of Manchuria, much as their ancestors, the founders of the earlier Chin dynasty, had done. They had long experience of relations with the Chinese, their chieftains serving as Ming officers and making tributary visits to Peking, under cover of which the Chinese made them very handsome payments.

The transformation of these tribes on the margin of China into a state began with Nurhachi (1559-1626). With a love of power and talent for organization reminiscent of Chinggis Khan, Nurhachi brought the Jürched together under his command by means of warfare, negotiation, marriage, or alliance, whichever best served the purpose. At first he observed the proper respect for China, paying tribute and receiving fancy titles in return. He began the conversion of his federation of tribes into a centralized state by introducing the "banner" system. All the tribesmen were enrolled in newly formed military groups identified by colored banners. Eight Manchu banners were formed and later, when the state controlled large Mongol and Chinese populations, eight Mongol and eight Chinese banners. Centrally appointed officials, not the hereditary chieftains, came to administer the banners. At the center itself, a tendency grew, which continued under Nurhachi's successors, to subordinate the voice of tribal leaders to the monarch, who was served by an appointed council. Nurhachi also began the practice of drawing Chinese into his administration and reforming it in the light of their advice. Under him the Manchus' formula for success seems to have been discovered: the joining of Chinese techniques and staff to a new and vigorous ruling elite. It was essentially the "dualism" of earlier conquering peoples, but the Manchus were able to practice it for several decades on a much smaller population before going inside the Wall.

Nurhachi's strength grew until he was able to move against Ming forces in Liaotung, his armies occupying Mukden, which became his capital a few years later. His immediate successors extended Manchu power east, west, and north, subjugating Korea, Inner Mongolia, and the valley of the Amur. In 1636, with rule extended over a tripartite population of Manchus, Mongols, and Chinese, a ritual of imperial accession was performed and the state was named Ch'ing. In the same general period, Manchu armies repeatedly broke into North China, but over the Ming forces inside the Wall, even so late in the dynasty, the Manchus won no decisive victories. Only when invited through the pass by the general assigned to hold them in check did they demonstrate how much strength and skill in leadership they had developed.

THE RETENTION AND REINFORCEMENT OF MING INSTITUTIONS

At first the greatest demands on the Manchus in China were military strength and skill, since they defeated their last serious opposition only in 1683. Only their chief opponents can be mentioned here. They were several Ming princes in the south, the last of whom was pursued into Burma and killed in 1662; the "three feudatories"—

Wu San-kuei and two Chinese generals who had joined the Manchus in the early days at Mukden—who were given power over wide territories in the south and then revolted, to be put down finally in 1681; and Cheng Ch'eng-kung, known to the Dutch as Koxinga, a Ming loyalist whose last stronghold, on Formosa, held out until 1683. In that year a Ch'ing force landed, and formal Chinese administration of the island began for the first time.

On the administrative side of the young dynasty, which of course did not wait until all military action had ended to establish itself, a fortunate degree of stability was derived from the successive rule of three vigorous and diligent emperors, K'ang-hsi (r. 1661-1722), Yung-cheng (r. 1723-36), and Ch'ien-lung (r. 1736-95). Together they provided more than a century of strong leadership. It says much for the soundness of the machinery of government built by the Ming that the Ch'ing founders kept it on the whole intact, altering it only in certain details. Such changes as were introduced into the Ming system by the Manchus seem to have been been made chiefly for two purposes.

One was to tighten even further the autocracy of Ming. At the center of government, the Ch'ing first recognized the long-evolved importance of the grand secretaries by raising their rank from the middle level, to which Ming had assigned them, to the highest level, and giving formal existence to the cabinet which in Ming times had been only a customary term designating the grand secretaries as a group. Then, in 1729, a new body, a grand council, was established at the highest level. The cabinet would henceforth handle routine business, arranging it so that the emperor need merely approve or disapprove documents prepared in his name. The grand council would consider all urgent, crucial matters with the emperor in person, working informally and secretly. Thus the emperor sought once more a body to protect him from the coils of bureaucratic procedure and free him for attending to vital questions of state.

Connected with this was use of the palace memorial. The palace memorial grew from a convention by which officials sent letters congratulating the emperor on his birthday or a return to health or some other personal matter. The early Ch'ing emperors began to permit certain officials of whom they had formed a favorable opinion to include in these letters, which might be delivered by personal messengers, thus avoiding all channels of bureaucracy, reports on significant local conditions, evaluations of other officials, private

Sedan chair carrying a member of the K'ang-hsi Emperor's family through a city street.

179

accounts of events already related through more formal dispatches, and the like. The product, for the emperor, was private information on many matters, supplied by a high-level and secret network of informers. He seemed to use the system to try to frighten officials, but there is evidence that some of them, at least, were such masters at responding to an emperor without telling him anything he should not hear that the intended dictatorship was still far from perfect.

A second aim of changes introduced by the Manchus was to assure the supremacy of their own people in the state. They arranged their own form of "dualism," similar in several ways to that adopted by previous dynasties of conquest. As the most fundamental step, they reserved superior military power to themselves. Their banners were deployed in strategic portions: in a ring around Peking, at the intersection of the Grand Canal and the Yangtze, and in important southern cities. Bannermen received land and stipends, and were administered as a hereditary group separate from the mass of the population, much in the manner of the Ming garrisons. In the case of the Manchus, of course, distinctiveness of language and custom were added to that of occupation, and they were directed to maintain the differences. The high command of the banner forces consisted of Manchus. Probably there was also a military motive behind the planting of a "willow palisade" in a crescent across southern Manchuria, marking the northern limit of Chinese settlement and reserving the major part of the old homeland for tribesmen, who could carry on their spartan life.

In administration, in addition to the safeguarding of their interests by the alert emperors, the Manchus established a collegiate system which paired or balanced Manchu and Chinese officials. Of the major central offices, for example, the cabinet consisted of three Manchu grand secretaries and three Chinese grand secretaries. Each of the six ministries had a Manchu minister and a Chinese minister. In the provinces, most of the governors-general (men in charge of especially important single provinces or groups of two or three provinces) were Manchus at first, while most of the governors (men in charge of more ordinary single provinces) were Chinese. In all important offices, Manchus sat by the side of Chinese, although it was recognized that often the Manchus' task was only to watch the Chinese who did the real work. By such means a people no more than several million in number occupied a country of several hundred million and supervised an administration staffed largely by the defeated. The success of the

Manchus says much of the vulnerability of Chinese society to even a very small armed and close-knit organization.

THE MANCHUS AS CONFUCIAN RULERS

Another reason for Manchu success was that the great rulers, especially K'ang-hsi and Ch'ien-lung, followed the high Chinese traditions as few of the late Ming rulers had done. The examination system, the key to the advancement of literati, seems to have been taken for granted; examination schedules were published within a year of the Manchus' entry into Peking. Equally a matter of course was assent to the Chu Hsi orthodoxy on which the examinations were based. K'ang-hsi not only commissioned standard scholarly undertakings, such as the compiling of the Ming History, but also personally approved and patronized works that established new standards of their kind. One was the K'ang-hsi Dictionary, which defined over 45,000 different characters. Another was the *Ku-chin t'u-shu chi-ch'eng* (Synthesis of books and illustrations of ancient and modern times), an encyclopedia of 10,000 chapters. Ch'ien-lung's support of learning was even greater. In addition to numbers of reference works, he commissioned the greatest of all compilations, *Ssu-k'u ch'üan-shu* (The complete library of the four treasuries). The aim of this project was to review whichever books of the past had become rare and were thought to be of value, those judged worth preserving being copied whole, in meticulous characters, on pages of snowy white paper about half the size of a sheet of modern newsprint. When complete the Library comprised more than 36,000 manuscript volumes of uniform size and contained about 3,400 works. Six additional copies of it were made. As valuable to scholars as the works themselves was an annotated bibliography of about 10,000 titles that the editors had considered for the Library. It remained ever after the most complete index to the literature of its time, and the appraisals of the editors continued to be one of the primary resources of scholars.

Patronizing monuments of scholarship was but one of the ways in which the Manchu emperors established their government as the protector of Chinese civilization. K'ang-hsi and Ch'ien-lung also joined the literati. Each wrote volumes, and Ch'ien-lung, being both addicted to the brush and a voracious art collector, crowded inscriptions over many of the paintings of the Palace collection. While this particular habit displeased some connoisseurs then and later, the general effect of the emperor's behavior was to win the acquiescence of the literati.

This was the more remarkable for the considerable self-consciousness of the Manchus as conquerors, a feeling that was expressed sometimes bluntly and sometimes indirectly in policies. The leaders prohibited their people, for example, from marrying Chinese or adopting certain Chinese customs, such as foot-binding. Efforts were made, despite the pressure of social and political practicalities, to keep the Manchu language alive. As a reminder of Manchu domination, Chinese, who dressed their hair in a distinctive style to symbolize adulthood, were required to adopt the Manchu coiffure, shaving the sides of the head and braiding the rest into a queue that hung down the back. Even the great literary project, the compilation of Ch'ienlung's Treasury, was the occasion of a systematic suppression and destruction of works that were judged heterodox or seditious. In all about 23,000 whole works and parts of 350 more were proscribed, and hundreds of them were actually destroyed, although hundreds more survived. As an official attack on heterodoxy this "literary inquisition" was not new in principle, and some conservative literati supported it. As an attempt to eliminate from the record everything hostile to the Manchu people, it was another matter. It served notice on the literati that the Manchu dragon had claws.

THE BANNING OF CHRISTIANITY

The same sensitivity governed Manchu response when the Christian missionaries appeared to challenge imperial authority. The Jesuits weathered the change of dynasties well. Under the new Ch'ing administration they became directors of the Bureau of Astronomy. K'ang-hsi found several of them interesting and liked listening to them on science and other subjects as well as making use of their skills. A great map of the empire, presented in 1717, was one of their contributions. Several of the Manchu nobility were among their converts. With success in the capital, moreover, went increasing conversions in other places; in all of China there were over 200,000 Christians at the beginning of the eighteenth century.

Yet a disturbance that arose among the missionary Europeans illustrated the difficulties of accommodating cultural differences at the same time that it weakened the modest, if never smooth, progress of the missionary effort. At about the time of the change of rule from Ming to Ch'ing, missionaries of other orders, including Franciscans,

Dominicans and Augustinians, entered China. Although benefiting from the protection afforded by the Jesuit position in Peking, they disagreed with the prevalent Jesuit practices that had gained that position, feeling that to accommodate themselves to certain crucial elements of the Chinese cultural milieu would betray something essential to Christianity.

Because the debate concentrated on certain symbolic Chinese rites, even though the issues were broader, it was known to some Europeans as the Rites Controversy. One kind of rites questioned, for example, was the practice of sacrifices to ancestors. Did the Chinese place food and burn incense before the ancestral tablets in the belief that the souls of the dead dwelt, as a Jesuit sarcastically put it, "like so many worms in the pores of the wood"? The Jesuits thought not. They found no taint of idolatry and argued that, though the ceremonies could not with certainty be judged free of superstition, they were originally civil rites expressing the virtue of filial piety. The Jesuits' opponents, on the other hand, saw flagrant idolatry and superstition in the practice. Again, the Chinese obeisance, especially in its most extravagant form, the kowtow, a repeated kneeling and touching of the forehead to the ground, became a subject of dispute. When Chinese performed it before the ancestral tablets, the coffins of the dead, or the emperor, Jesuits saw a dignified and admirable expression of respect. Others suspected that such an elaborate gesture of abasement could only be directed towards objects of superstitious adoration. The dispute worked itself deeply into the councils of the papacy.

In China the arguments spilled out beyond the circle of priests into the lay Christian communities and, with more direct consequence, into the court itself. The Jesuits approached K'ang-hsi and obtained his endorsement of their position on the rites. In Rome, however, the opposition prevailed, and in 1704 the pope issued an edict against toleration in the Jesuit manner. Furthermore, he sent an envoy to inform and win the acquiescence of the Jesuits and the emperor. Far from acquiescing, K'ang-hsi resented what appeared to him to be an impudent interference with his sovereignty. He proclaimed that all missionaries who would obey the law, in which was implied acknowledgment of his interpretation of the rites, might remain in the country and propagate their doctrine. All who would not obey must leave the country. Many of the Jesuits, feeling that the last word in the argument had not been said, found themselves able to comply with the emperor and stayed. Many of the other orders retreated to Macao.

Soon afterwards, the whole Christian effort in China was all but wiped out. K'ang-hsi's successor, Yung-cheng, who had less taste than his father for European knowledge and was more suspicious of treachery, issued a sweeping ban on Christianity. His fear that missionaries were close to rival imperial princes may have played a part in his decision; he also may have had a more general feeling that Christianity might be seditious. In any event, in 1723 he ordered all missionaries working among the people to go to Macao or leave the country. Only those appointed to offices in the capital might remain and keep a church. The ban stopped the growth of the numbers of Christians and marked the beginning of a decline. The Jesuits, though remaining in Peking, suffered a final papal decision against them and, in 1774, an order dissolving their society. After about 1800 Christians were apt to be attacked as outlaws almost anywhere in China.

Although the suppression of Christianity meant the blocking of an important channel of communications, all connections between Europeans and Chinese did not end; trade continued and slowly grew more elaborate. In addition to the Portuguese, the Spanish early came into touch with Chinese, notably at Manila, the capital of the newly conquered Philippine Islands, where the Spanish bought silks from Chinese junks, paying in American silver. In the seventeenth century the Dutch and then the English became in turn the major traders in Asian waters, and they, and eventually other Europeans, built up trading relations with an officially designated group of Chinese merchants at Canton, in what became known as the Canton System.

WARNINGS TO THE INTELLECTUALS

It has been observed that the Ch'ing rulers used both carrot and stick on the literati, patronizing scholarship in the grand manner, while at the same time trying to eliminate books that offended them. How vigorously they would apply their repressive powers became quite clear in a series of famous cases during the early reigns.

There was, for example, the case of the History of Ming, in which a prosperous merchant and his son published, in 1660, a history revised from portions of a famous Ming scholar's work. The book alluded to the Manchus in terms current during Ming, for example, calling the early Manchu emperors by their personal names. Under the Ch'ing this was treason, and when the court was informed of the work it began an investigation and made an object lesson of the case. Some seventy of those implicated—the merchant's family, the families of scholars who had assisted in the compilation, the printers, and the known buyers of the book—were executed. Women and children became slaves of Manchu families. Other individuals were exiled.

An equally telling if less bloody case was that of the Southern Hills Collection. A famous writer whose pen name was Southern Hills published this collection of his essays in 1701. In it he expressed interest in preserving the historical records of the princely courts that had tried to carry on the Ming dynasty in the South in the days when the Manchus were pressing down from the north. He seems to have used the Southern Ming reign titles, whereas the Manchus required the use of their own. Furthermore, he compared the Southern Ming to the last loyal Southern Sung resisters of the Mongols. For this combination of explicit and implicit treason the Ministry of Law recommended putting the author to death or, if he was already dead, desecrating not only his remains but also those of his grandfather, father, brothers, sons, grandsons, uncles, and nephews. All other close relatives, including women, were to be enslaved or exiled. The families of other scholars associated with the author were also implicated, bringing the total recommended for heavy punishment to several hundred. Though the emperor mitigated the sentences so that only the author was put to death, others being exiled, the dynasty without doubt again made its point about political opposition.

These cases and others like them revealed how sensitive the Manchus were to aspersions cast on them. Dynastic houses had never taken kindly to hostile critics, but the Manchus seem to have affected the intellectual atmosphere more generally, turning the attention of men away from current affairs. At least, that is indicated by the contrast between Ming writing, which frequently was about contemporary or recent events, and that of the Ch'ing, which seldom was so.

SCHOLARSHIP AND THE VALUE OF HISTORICAL CRITICISM

The most vital scholarship of early Ch'ing had a positive impulse, which was the scholars' feeling that the fall of the Ming dynasty made necessary a thorough reexamination of the Classics and history. The cause of the defeat was sensed to be some failure in the Chinese themselves, especially a failure to understand or observe correctly the great classical principles. It was necessary therefore to go back to the books and look into questions of fundamentals. Whether by design or by coincidence, the questions were remote enough not to intrude into the dangerous zone of recent affairs.

One part of the new movement was dissatisfaction with the

interpretations of Neo-Confucianism in both the School of Principle, which remained orthodox and dominant, and the School of the Mind. The pedantry of the former and the empty speculations of the latter, in the view of some critics, were sufficient indication that the Sung and Ming philosophers had distorted the truths of the genuine old sages. To explore the scholarship that had preceded the Sung and Ming periods required the development of methods of studying early texts. One method, for example, was the study of the sounds of old characters by means of old dictionaries, for the sounds had changed in the course of centuries and knowing what the early pronunciation had been sometimes clarified the meaning and even threw light on the true age of the text. When words had taken on new meanings over the years, the old dictionaries also gave direct clues, of course, to a more precise meaning of ancient texts. Comparison of texts was another method;one dedicated scholar actually read through twenty-two dynastic histories from beginning to end, and left 100 chapters of notes on discrepancies he had found. Still another method was the broadening of the sources of historical knowledge, as seen in the attention some of the scholars gave to local "gazetteers," or regional records. From such efforts grew new standards of historical and textual criticism.

The giant of this scholarship was Ku Yen-wu (1613-82), who was interested in many subjects including the classics, phonology, history, and geography. His masterpiece was the *Jih-chih lu* (Record of knowledge gained day by day). It was a book of articles or essays that he kept revising until the end of his life, intending that each essay should express the essence of his thought on the subject as faithfully as possible. Behind his assiduousness was a special commitment. Ku was never able to renounce his loyalty to the Ming dynasty. In the days when the Manchu control of China was contested he had fought for the Ming, and later he avoided serving the foreign government. Instead he traveled and studied, seeking through experiences and books what was "useful" in scholarship, meaning that which contributed to an appraisal of the strengths and weaknesses of past periods. Ultimately, in short, he sought to understand what was right and what wrong in Chinese civilization.

The quest for the original teachings was strengthened by the work of one of Ku Yen-wu's younger friends, who worked thirty years applying the new analytical and historical techniques to the *Book of Documents (Shu ching)* and proved that a part of it that had been accepted since T'ang times was a forgery of the Period of Disunity.

The discovery added force to the idea that the true meaning of the Classics could best be approached through neither Sung nor T'ang interpretations, but rather through Han commentaries. The School of Han Learning became the name for the scholars, some of the most energetic of the day, who agreed on this emphasis.

OTHER SCHOLARS OF THE REASSESSMENT

The urge to reconsider Chinese civilization in the broadest terms appeared in several major figures in addition to Ku Yen-wu. Two of the most famous were, like Ku, "leftover" loyalists, who fought the Manchus and, when the cause became obviously hopeless, retired to a life of private scholarship rather than serve the new government. Each took an interest in a great variety of subjects but based his major conclusions on history.

Wang Fu-chih (1619-92) represented a small number of men who were brave or rash enough to commit their hostility to the conquerors to writing. Wang attacked Manchu rule as wrong, and even unnatural. He argued that it was the Way of Heaven that nations be segregated, each living apart and by itself. Though also a philosopher of originality, Wang remained relatively unknown in his time and has won his greatest fame only in more modern times as an apostle of Chinese patriotism.

Huang Tsung-hsi (1610-95) wrote in his treatise (*Ming-i tai-fang lu*) (A plan for the prince) a critique implying a need to reorient some of the longest established political attitudes and practices. For example, he maintained that the ruler ought to consider himself a guest of the people and ministers servants of the whole people, not of the prince alone. He also urged more consideration of good laws as no less necessary to government than good men. Like Ku Yen-wu, he seems to have been inspired by the desire to understand the causes of China's vulnerability to domination by a less accomplished people. This desire may also have been behind the second of his great works, an intellectual history of the Ming dynasty (*Ming-ju hsüeh-an*).

The vigor of Ch'ing scholarship in the seventeenth and eighteenth centuries has been only suggested here, and its quality is still to be adequately appreciated. Yet its effect on Chinese thinking was limited. While a great many volumes of the new criticism on the Classics were published, and some became important guides to the ancient meaning, no remarkable revival of spirit or crucial new ideas seized the scholars and impelled them to shake society. Although the histories were carefully reviewed, no new interpretation of the past resulted. In spite of the original impulse in historical criticism—the search for flaws to account for the weakness of the nation—not much new understanding was reached among the community of scholars, and no movement for reform grew among them. On the whole historical criticism tended to lose sight of its integrating goals and its purpose of coming to grips with the present. As the Manchu conquerors seemed ever more successful and tolerable as rulers, the once purposeful reexamination of the past detail by detail became more an entertainment for its own sake, a pastime of cultivated and comfortable gentlemen, enjoying what has been called "salon scholarship."

THE EIGHTEENTH CENTURY: PROSPERITY AND POWER

If it is possible to ignore the existence of an educated class that had abdicated its role as social critic, the eighteenth century was one of the most splendid of ages. Commerce and industry continued their long, slow growth. The luxury and elegance enjoyed by a rich family of the day were vividly pictured in the novel *Dream of the Red Chamber* (*Hung-lou meng*) by Ts'ao Hsüeh-ch'in. The book is also, however, a story of corruption, decline, and disillusionment, which no amount of richness and cultivation could overcome. Another novel of about the same time, *The Scholars* (*Ju-lin wai-shih*), satirized the shallow, opportunistic fortune hunters who passed for scholars and officials in the world. Nevertheless, in the more ordinary and conventional aspects of life, productivity and prosperity seemed to rule. European observers almost never failed to comment on the richness of the scene.

Concurrent with the internal prosperity went a display of power abroad. Even earlier, Manchu force had become a dominant factor in parts of Central Asia. Inner Mongolia had been defeated before the invasion of China proper, and Outer Mongolia submitted to Ch'ing armies before the end of the seventeenth century. The Ch'ing government intervened in Tibetan politics, at first indirectly, sometimes through Mongols, but by the 1720s directly, when Ch'ing armies installed a friendly government and two resident commissioners supported by an imperial garrison.

Ch'ien-lung's displays of imperial power were proudly called what may be translated as the Ten Total Triumphs. These included campaigns against a Western Mongol group called Dzungars, who controlled a great region centering on the Ili River. By defeating the

Dzungars, the Ch'ing dominated the northwest as far as the Pamir mountains. The last government of China to do so had been the foreign Mongols; no native dynasty since the T'ang had reached so far. Other campaigns of the ten were mounted against rebels in Szechuan and Taiwan, and insubordinate groups in Burma, Vietnam, and Nepal. The way to Nepal being through Himalayan passes, the military abilities illustrated in that campaign need not be stressed. Difficult military problems also faced Ch'ing forces in some of the other campaigns. The victories seemed to stand for the very heights of power of the dynasty. So manifest was its greatness that few considered the imperfections appearing by the end of the same century to be symptoms of deep decay.

VIII

The Breakdown of

the Traditional

Order

Despite the general picture of a powerful state and a stable society under the government of the Ch'ing, several faults in the structure had appeared by about 1800. Some of these seemed to be the familiar symptoms of an aging dynasty, others the products of new forces.

Weaknesses of Age: Lawlessness and Corruption

Lawlessness took the familiar forms of rebellion, secret societies, and piracy, and was not easily controlled. For instance, among a body of migrants who had moved from lowlands to the mountainous region where the provinces of Hupei, Szechwan, and Shensi meet, a rebellion (the White Lotus Rebellion, 1795-1804) broke out and grew to larger proportions than anything the administration had faced for a century. Staking out holdings in a poor land where the administration was still weak, the rebels were apparently goaded into action by overzealous tax collectors. In part, the spirit of rebellion came from the old White Lotus sect, which promised the advent of Buddha and salvation from present suffering. To that was added a new, anti-Manchu feeling and a call for the restoration of the Ming dynasty. Like other, earlier rebellions, however, it failed ultimately to build an organization to move beyond guerilla-like raids on imperial forces and attempts to control villages. Organization remained the strong point of the government, which concentrated the population in walled villages, left the open fields barren, and trained villagers as militiamen. Yet the final defeat of the rebels revealed that the regular banner forces were not the superior fighters they had once been. The real victors were the local militia men, an indication that the backbone of the Manchu defense system was no longer firm.

Another sign of weakness was in the rumored growth of secret societies. Typically a secret society was a symbolical brotherhood, often under a religious doctrine and observing special rites, such as the taking of oaths in blood, its members bound to defend and help each other in important activities. Strong secret societies were offensive to strong governments, yet several were prominent from the beginning of the nineteenth century. The Triad Society, for example, was famous in the south, and among its professed aims was the overthrow of the Ch'ing and the restoration of the Ming. There was more bark than bite to this, but it presumably expressed a thought that appealed to many.

Perhaps an even more brazen affront to Ch'ing authority, because more visible, were the pirate ships that seemed to multiply along the southern coast from about 1800. In addition to attacking merchant ships, pirate fleets sometimes raided coastal settlements as they had done during the Ming, while the coast guards proved ineffectual.

Another commonly cited sign of age was excessive corruption. In a state in which custom and local discretion were important, it was difficult to measure excess and dishonesty by any general rule. There is evidence, for example, that in the receiving of taxes officials frequently added handling charges and other surcharges, or demanded payments at exchange rates out of line with the market price, with the result that the cultivator parted with much more than the statutory tax. Sometimes the practices were condoned by custom, sometimes not. Yet by 1800 instances of irregularity came to light that were striking by any standards, suggesting that corruption might indeed have reached new heights. The charges for conservancy along the Yellow River, which had cost the government about three million taels a year in early Ch'ing, rose to 4.5 million by the early nineteenth century, and the greater part of the rise is assumed to have gone into officials' pockets. In 1843 the bullion in the vaults of the Ministry of Revenue was found short by ten million taels. Officials recently in charge were held responsible for the loss. Personal corruption seemed to be symbolized in the case of a privileged favorite of the Ch'ien-lung emperor. When this Manchu official was allowed to commit suicide in 1799 his ill-gotten fortune was said, no doubt with exaggeration, to amount to several times the annual income of the state. It included a gold table service of 4,288 pieces.

New Problems

Operating in a different way were changes that made social order increasingly difficult to maintain. First of all, the amount of arable land per capita was declining. Appearances were deceiving, for the absolute acreage of productive land had been increased and could be increased even more. Considerable portions of Manchuria and Taiwan, to name only peripheral regions, could absorb more people and produce more food. Moreover, new crops introduced from America, such as corn, sweet potatoes, and peanuts, were making hilly, sandy, and other lands previously little used more productive; and fast-ripening strains of rice continued to be introduced from Vietnam. Yet productivity could be increased by these means only slowly, within limits, and—of special significance to the question of social order—at the cost of economic and social strains on the farmers, for to grow more food often required poor farmers to migrate and even then to be content with only a secondrate livelihood.

The arable land per capita was declining because while total acreage was only slowly increasing, the population was growing enormously. It is estimated as 300 million in 1800, or about twice as large as it had been two centuries earlier. The growth could not have failed to affect the economy, probably in the form of greater inequities between rich and poor.

Rising Pressure from the West

By 1800 foreign trade at Canton had become sufficiently important to the leading trading country, Britain, that she was willing to exert considerable effort to bring about a change in China's established ways. The interests connected with the trade had grown. To the foreigners it was a trade of significant volume; more than twenty million pounds of tea, which was the product in greatest demand, were exported annually, as well as large amounts of silk and other goods. To the Chinese commercial world the trade was profitable, and an elaborate, if local, organization of merchants, boatmen, coolies, and others took part in it. Officials assigned to oversee trade at the port also profited from the assignment, which was full of opportunities for receiving special fees and gifts, as had been customary at the designated customs ports for centuries. Official utterances, however, in the traditional manner recognized no commercial advantage to the state, only the benevolent purpose of admitting the barbarians to the Chinese international family and permitting them incidentally to acquire the goods they so much wanted.

THE CANTON SYSTEM

During the eighteenth century a system grew that at first served these interests tolerably well. A guild of Chinese merchants, comprising a dozen or so houses, received official designation as *kung-hang* (approximated by the Western tongue as "Co-hong"), the guild authorized to deal with the foreigners. A supervisor appointed by Peking (*Hu pu*, English "Hoppo") held the Co-hong merchants responsible for the foreign ships and received fees. On the foreigners' side, representatives of the Canton committee of the East India Company, the English company that had been granted a monopoly of British trade in East Asia, acted as spokesmen for all the traders. From the Chinese point of view, the system kept the trade under sufficient control to prevent threats to security or irresponsible behavior. On the part of the Europeans it was accepted, perhaps because it seemed akin to mercantilist policies with which they were familiar but probably more because the profits outweighed the restraints.

Nevertheless the Westerners had complaints, and these were magnified by changing conditions until what had previously seemed tolerable in view of the rewards came to seem intolerable in view of what more could be had. Some complaints centered on frustrations in the trade itself, such as dissatisfaction with Co-hong monopolists, some of whom went into debt to the foreigners but could not be held responsible under any adequate commercial law; and numerous and irregular port charges. Others were broader, including anger over the Chinese treatment of prisoners and dissatisfaction over the lack of channels for communicating with the Chinese government. The complaints were aggravated by a more lively concern of the British government in trading the goods that its growing industrial economy was producing; the growth of the advocacy of free trade and pressure by private merchants to end the East India Company's monopoly; and the capture of some of the Canton trade by rivals, notably Americans.

THE MACARTNEY EMBASSY

Illustrative of the new mood were the goals assigned by the king of England to an embassy sent under the earl of Macartney to Peking in 1793. The embassy was carefully planned to make the most favorable impression. Macartney, who was experienced in foreign affairs, was accompanied by a large staff, including Chinese Catholic priests as interpreters, though, considering the standing of the church in the court's eyes, the priests probably did not greatly raise the prestige of the mission. The ambassador brought 600 packages of presents for the emperor. With these examples of British goods to smooth the way, he was instructed to seek three concessions: permission to trade at other ports in addition to Canton, the use of island depots near Canton and Shanghai to store goods and refit ships, and a fixed and printed tariff. Clearly the British were preoccupied with trade and the improvement of facilities for it. The emperor, on the other hand, looked upon the embassy solely as a tribute mission and commended George III for it as a sign of respectful submission. Apparently the court considered the occasion significant enough for a display of liberality, for Lord Macartney was not required to perform the kowtow, an elaborate prostration performed by those received in imperial audience (including Russian, Portuguese, Dutch, and papal envoys up to that time). Reflecting perhaps a burgeoning nationalism, Europeans increasingly found it insulting. When Macartney would agree only to go down on one knee, as he would before his own king, the Chinese masters of ceremonies apparently acquiesced, perhaps thinking they were making quite a conciliatory gesture. (This story of Macartney's refusal follows British sources: Chinese recorders were assiduous in getting into the record that he did kowtow.) In any event, not one matter of business was discussed. The best that could be said was that "the ambassador was received with the utmost politeness, treated with the utmost hospitality, watched with the utmost vigilance, and dismissed with the utmost civility." Other embassies had no more success.

THE CANTON SYSTEM BROKEN UP

Beyond the dissatisfactions and frustrations that beset the Westerners who participated in the Canton system, two developments in the early nineteenth century tended to make the system unworkable. One was the rise to dominance of private traders. As opportunities for making money beckoned, brokers, mainly British subjects, captured an increasing share of the trade (more than half of it by the 1830s), infringing on the company's monopoly and decreasing the authority of company spokesmen as leaders of the Western traders. The second development was the rapid expansion of the Chinese market for opium.

Although opium had long been known in China as a medicine, its use for pleasure had begun only recently. At first it was mixed with tobacco, which had been introduced from America in the seventeenth century. Smoking opium straight (actually, inhaling its vaporized essence through a pipe holding a small heated ball of it) increased notably from about 1800 on; most of the early smokers seem to have belonged to the upper classes, from which the habit spread especially among officials and soldiers, and at last to all kinds of people. By 1838 the sale of opium reached approximately 40,000 chests (a chest averaged perhaps 140 pounds) a year, most of it imported from India.

Since it was an illegal import, banned repeatedly by Chinese edicts, and a commodity for which there was increasing competition by importers, prices fluctuated drastically. On the whole, however, the profits to be made were great. Gross profits to the importers might reach $1,000 a chest, and Chinese distributors commonly imposed even greater markups.

Naturally the whole enterprise involved smuggling. An elaborate organization grew, foreign merchants bringing their cargo to the coast, sometimes transferring it to "receiving ships," Chinese brokers sending smuggling boats out to the ships to bring the chests ashore, after which they were moved over inland trade routes. Payments to officials helped to smooth the way, but when a determined official forced the receiving ships out of the Canton anchorage in 1821 the foreign traders only spread northward along the coast. The trade grew; of British imports valued at approximately 32 million Spanish dollars at Canton in 1835-36, opium accounted for about 17 million dollars.

Soon both sides adopted more rigid official positions that led to war. On the British side, the East India Company's monopoly of the China trade was ended in 1834, and the government appointed a superintendent of trade to assist the free traders at Canton. The superintendent soon had warships making shows of force to back up his demand to correspond with local Chinese officials as equals. Chinese officials reacted with their own forms of intimidation, cutting off supplies and providing other obstacles.

On the Chinese side, the emperor called for a radical attack on the opium problem in 1838. The spread of the habit, which it is estimated had been acquired by from two to ten million people, had left many signs of physical, psychological, and social damage. To that was added in the 1820s and 1830s a shift in the balance of trade at Canton, the larger imports of opium drawing payments in silver out of the country. After many discussions, the emperor appointed Lin Tse-hsü (1785-1850), a ranking regional official known for his competence, justice, and vigor, as well as his opposition to traffic in opium, to be commissioner at Canton with full powers to deal with the matter. Arriving in Canton in 1839, Lin attacked the commercial network in the city and forced the foreigners (by detaining them in their factories without servants) to turn over their stocks of opium, amounting to about 20,000 chests. Then as the people watched he had it all thrown into pits, mixed with quicklime, and (a prayer having been addressed to the God of the Sea, warning him what was about to happen), the poison was flushed into the river. The British superintendent backed later by his government, decided that he had reason to fight.

THE OPIUM WAR (1839-42)

The war introduced a new force, Western military power, to Chinese history. A British fleet organized around shallow-draft iron steamers and carrying a few thousand troops moved up and down the coast, raiding and occupying cities more or less at will, in an effort to bring the Ch'ing government to terms. After the blockade, occupation, or bombardment of such places at Canton, Amoy, Ningpo, and Shanghai, and finally a threat to Nanking, the Chinese agreed to negotiate. They had almost no strength on the basis of which to bargain. Nowhere had Chinese forces been able to hold back the British for long, although certain Banner forces and others had fought bravely and a force hastily put together as militia at Canton had briefly pressed back an outnumbered British unit. It now appears that the Manchu government, coping with a precarious social order internally, was little inclined to mobilize even as much power as seemed to be available, for military activity on a large scale might eventually threaten the dynasty more than the British.

THE TREATY SYSTEM

The treaties concluded as a direct result of the war and a second war (known as the "Arrow" War, the Anglo-French Expedition, and by other names: 1856-60) were mutually linked to one another and given the over-all designation of the treaty system. The system defined the legal relationships between China and the Western states for approximately a century. For convenience, a summary of the terms will be given here, although this will somewhat interrupt the order of other parts of the story. To begin with, the Chinese decided that once a treaty of the Western style demanded by the British had to be signed, similar treaties with other Western states should be accepted. An appearance of benevolence was preferable to one of grudging acquiescence in the face of possible coercion. Furthermore, it was probably safer to establish relations with several Western states rather than with only one—at least the old principle of using barbarians to control barbarians might be applied. Accordingly, the Treaty of Nanking with Britain (1842) was followed by treaties with the United States, France, Russia, and others.

Basically the treaties realized the aims of the Macartney embassy and went beyond them. The Co-hong was abolished, and Westerners could trade with anyone, thus upsetting the age-old practice of supervision by the state. Other ports in addition to Canton were opened to foreign trade and foreigners were permitted to reside and trade in these "treaty ports," to travel and trade on the Yangtze River, and to travel in the interior. The island of Hong Kong, ninety miles down the estuary from Canton, was ceded to Britain; later a bit of the adjacent mainland was added. The tariff was fixed at five percent of the value of the goods, not to be changed without the agreement of both sides. (Opium was eventually included in the tax schedule, showing how little the Chinese had made their point.)

Other terms expressed interests broader than the strictly commercial ones. The practice known as extraterritoriality was stipulated, according to which nationals of each party to the treaty should be tried in their own courts. Thus an American charged with a criminal act (or by extension involved in a civil suit) against a Chinese would be tried by American authorities, and vice versa. The agreement assured Western governments that their citizens would be treated according to Western law and protected from Chinese law, which they maintained did not acknowledge the rights of the defendant and punished the guilty excessively; the Chinese agreed readily enough at first because they assumed that the foreigners could be controlled most conveniently by their own leaders, as had other minorities under Chinese domination. The right of Christian missionaries to reside, lease or buy land, build houses, and practice in any of the provinces was granted. Permission was granted for foreign ministers to reside in Peking and to communicate with the Chinese government on terms of diplomatic equality. A "most-favored-nation" clause was included, assuring each Western government of the same privileges that China might grant to any other nation, and linking all the treaties together. Finally, for satisfaction and reparations, indemnities were imposed on China.

Even from the simple listing of the terms, it may be inferred that the treaty system could affect China's future significantly. The arrangement of extraterritoriality, though as noted not then a burning issue, meant in effect the loss of jurisdiction over certain questions. The fixed tariff, not seen at the time as a heavy economic blow, could seriously restrict the state's power to raise revenues and regulate foreign trade. Such terms, and the unqualified rights of residence, especially as they were backed up by threats of force, or "gunboat diplomacy," seemed to Chinese in later years, when they had accepted the Western notion of equality among states, to be so clearly an expression of the will of only one side that the system came to be called the "unequal treaties." Ironically, perhaps the most difficult terms for Chinese to accept at the time demanded equality in some sense, such as the agreement to treat foreign diplomats as representing equal, rather than tributary, states, and the acceptance of Christian missionaries, reversing a policy of the previous century. On the whole, however, the full implications of the system became apparent only slowly, and immediately following the Opium War remarkably little changed.

THE FIRST EFFECTS OF THE WARS

Very few of the literati responded seriously to the Opium War. Among them one of the first was Lin Tse-hsü himself, who began to see that danger of a new kind threatened the dynasty. At Canton he used a few Chinese who had studied English, mainly under missionaries, to translate for him sections of Western books and newspapers to provide more knowledge of the West. After observing the war (and being sent into exile, his punishment for the debacle at Canton), he wrote confidentially to friends of his conclusion that the state must acquire the two key devices of Western power, modern ships and guns. Another relatively farseeing man was a friend of Lin's, Wei Yüan (1794-1856), a scholar and official already known for his interest in military achievements. Using Lin's translations and other materials, Wei wrote *Hai-kuo t'u-chih* (Illustrated guide to countries overseas), his purpose being "to show how to use barbarians to fight barbarians, how to make the barbarians pacify one another [to our advantage] and how to employ the techniques of the barbarians in order to bring the barbarians under control." Wei's analysis of what was required—ships, guns, and the organization to use them—resembled Lin's, and his quest for knowledge of the West was a step forward apparently appreciated by others, for his book became widely known. A few other responses to the recent events came, mainly from men who had observed the Western technical capacity firsthand; on the whole, however, scholars and officials were perhaps more curious than perturbed.

The main reason for the scarcity of imaginative response must have been that the majority of thinking men failed to sense the magnitude of the problem. In a vast domain, the events on the coast, disturbing though they were, did not seem unprecedented. Even the most enlightened saw what was needed as only a few technical innovations. If greater needs occurred to anyone, a reluctance to entertain ideas that might weaken the established order would have discouraged the pursuit of such ends. In any event, larger challenges were arising within the society, and it was to be some time before external and internal issues fused into one general crisis.

The Disintegration of
Internal Order

By the middle of the nineteenth century such a combination of troubles disturbed China that it is difficult to know which to stress. What must have seemed the salient manifestations at the time were described in an analysis made in 1852 by an official, Tseng Kuo-fan (1811-72), who was to take an important part in attempts at reform. One major cause of distress among the people, he maintained, was that the price of silver was so high that it was difficult to pay taxes. Connected with this was an increase of pressure from tax collectors, who even sometimes collected in advance. All the signs pointed to a government that was in financial distress and seeking relief through heavier burdens on the people. Yet what Tseng called the higher price of silver was probably not set entirely at the will of officials, even though they did their part in squeezing more from the taxpayer. It may also have been affected by a loss of silver that left the country in considerable amounts, if much less than Chinese officials thought, to pay for opium. Even more, the price of silver was related to the value of copper cash, the only official coinage, which the mints had been progressively cheapening in recent decades by making the coins smaller. Where in the past one thousand "good" copper coins had been equivalent to one Chinese ounce of silver (called by Westerners a "tael"), by mid-century as many as two thousand of the cheap coins were required. Today the result would be called inflation and regarded not primarily as a disease in itself, however harmful its effects, but as a symptom of more basic economic difficulties.

Another of Tseng Kuo-fan's observations was that robbers and bandits were numerous. Too often either they were joined by soldiers and petty government workers in stealing from the people, or the threat of robbers was used as a pretext by the nominal officers of law and order to extort protection money. The breakdown of local safety as he described it not only resulted in distress to the people, but, more important in the long run, stimulated the formation of self-defense forces by a variety of groups, such as families of the literati or gentry class, and secret societies. Although the forces may at first have been meant to ward off outlaws, once formed, they were equally useful for pursuing other ends, such as fighting rival groups for land or even intimidating those who had been slower in preparing to protect themselves. Thus bandits not only harassed the people but also encouraged a proliferation of armed forces that tended to break the peace.

Finally in his memorial Tseng Kuo-fan mentioned the miscarriage of justice. It is curious that the machinery of the law should be ranked among great causes of distress when so little has previously been said of the law as an institution. Possibly the role of law in the later dynasties has been underestimated, for recent studies have seemed to show its importance during the Ch'ing. In any event, its failure to meet Tseng's standards here may be taken as implying increased corruption and inefficiency in the bureaucracy.

Tseng might also have considered other evidences of disorder that are accepted today. One, a favorite among those impressed with the theory of a dynastic cycle, was weakness of leadership. The two emperors to rule in the first half of the nineteenth century, following the splendid reign of Ch'ien-lung, displayed only moderate virtues in the face of gathering disasters. Both, for example, assented to the dog-eared Confucian theory that personal frugality on the part of the ruler would ameliorate the economic difficulties of the state. True, both at times showed an appreciation of the need of correcting major weaknesses, in favorable contrast to the third emperor of the century, who under the strain of continual calamities lost heart and gave himself over to excessive diversions away from the palace.

Yet a degree of good will and intelligence was hardly enough, for natural disasters occurred that would have tried much greater men. The Yellow River broke its dikes at least twenty times by mid-century, flooding out tens of thousands. The Grand Canal had become impassable, leaving tens of thousands of boatmen unemployed. The worst was yet to come; in the 1850s the Yellow River shifted its course to enter the sea north instead of south of the Shantung peninsula, flooding millions of acres of land and ruining thousands of communities. Almost every year there were floods or droughts elsewhere as well, including the lower Yangtze valley in 1849. Although bad weather must have contributed to the disasters, human failure was no less to blame, for the organizations formed to maintain the dikes and waterways were not doing their job. The great change in the course of the Yellow River, for example, was sufficiently foreseen but not vigorously resisted, money troubles and corruption having apparently undermined to will to act.

Finally, to a list of disorders at mid-century might be added some generated by the activity of Europeans on the south coast. That Tseng Kuo-fan did not dwell on them was a clue to the secondary position they seemed, to most Chinese officials, to hold among the great issues of the day. Yet they contributed to the more familiar disturbances. Canton, for example, remained after the Opium War a hotbed of resentment against the foreigners, with local militia groups as apt to turn rebellious as to fight foreigners. In view of the hostility in Canton, the opening of Shanghai and other ports provided new and attractive depots for tea and silk, leading to a shift of commercial routes and corresponding unemployment of people along the old routes. It is still difficult to be sure how directly such local conditions affected the great rebellion that followed, but easy to see that they helped to prepare the country for violence.

THE TAIPING REBELLION (1850-64)

In a country that was poorly governed and economically upset in general, the province of Kwangsi was a pocket of special disorder. Remote from the capital and with something of a frontier quality, it had long ranked low among the provinces in both population and revenues, and in the decades just prior to 1850 it had suffered from indifferent governors. In Kwangsi lived a volatile mixture of peoples—tribes of aborigines who had resentfully retreated into the hills of the southwest; a majority of Chinese settlers who had driven them there and styled themselves the "natives"; and a Chinese minority called the Hakka, immigrants from the north, distinct from the majority in dialect and other ways, whose quest for land brought them into conflict with the others. Among many of the Hakka who were discontented and frustrated, the spirit of rebellion smoldered close to the surface.

The revolutionary leader who set it aflame was Hung Hsiu-ch'üan (1813-64) who, though born not far from Canton, the capital of Kwangtung, achieved his first great success in Kwangsi. Hung was the son of a Hakka farmer. From the time he was six he had been sent to school to study in preparation for the state examinations, which as a young man he took, only to fail several times. After one of his failures he fell ill and in the course of forty days experienced visions that established his mission in life.

He found himself taken to heaven in a sedan chair and received by the Heavenly Mother, who called him "my son." After an operation to replace his old organs with new ones and a bath for purification, he was presented to the Heavenly Father, who was sitting on a throne. The Heavenly Father was tall and strongly built, and he had a golden beard that hung down to his belly. He was wearing a high-brimmed hat and a black dragon robe. In the course of the visit, Hung learned that the family included, in addition to the Heavenly Father and Mother and himself, a Heavenly Elder Brother and his wife and younger sisters. The Heavenly Father complained that the world he had created was infested with devils, who misled the people so that they worshiped false gods. He appointed Hung to be the Son of Heaven, with the mission of exterminating the devils, restoring the Kingdom of Heaven on earth, and ruling it according to the true Way of Heaven. As symbols of his authority, Hung received a seal and a devil-killing sword.

Several years later, Hung read carefully a pamphlet he had picked up in Canton prior to his vision. It was a brief exposition of the essentials of Christianity and, though it is not clear that he had given it much attention at first, he was later convinced that the Heavenly Father was God and the Heavenly Elder Brother Jesus. He soon applied to an American missionary in Canton for instruction and stayed with him a month or more, but the instruction did not culminate, as Hung hoped it would, in his being baptized, for the missionary apparently doubted Hung's grasp of Christianity. The incident represented Hung's special position—that of a man possessed by an original religious vision that at first interested Westerners because of its Christian features and revealed only gradually its strong native foundations.

There is not much doubt that Hung's message found its target in the hearts of many who heard him, and a brief description of it may help explain the movement that grew up around him. As Hung's glimpse of paradise showed, the keystone of the faith was the omnipotent Heavenly Father, God, who created heaven and earth and was the father of all men. Men's responsibilities were summed up in

Ten Heavenly Commandments, which bore a close resemblance to those of the Bible. (The Bible itself was repeatedly printed as the movement grew.) The influence of the Bible is obvious at many other points as well, and it may be, as has been said, that the the feeling that all human beings, as children of a universal Father, were moving together toward salvation provided the self-sacrificing fervor that many observers noted.

Yet even in the formal theology themes foreign to Christianity—and often familiar from the Chinese past—appeared. That the Heavenly Father was a family man, for example, has already been observed. Jesus, moreover, was married and, although the eldest of God's children and revered for his mission, was perhaps not fundamentally more divine than Hung. Even the fervor of the faithful reminds us of earlier rebellions, such as that of the Red Turbans at the end of the Mongol rule, when the promise of the Buddha to come and proclaim a Kingdom of Buddha on earth sustained believers against their oppressors.

Morality followed lines that, while often compatible with Christian teachings, on the whole seemed to draw most deeply on native ideas. Though, for example, love of others as brothers under God was very important, so too were filial piety and fine distinctions of social status. Perhaps the most important single precept was "reverence," that quality of mixed self-control and seriousness most familiar in Confucianism. Even more indebted to the dominant tradition, and suggesting particularly the influence of the Ming thinkers, was the doctrine that the original mind of man was good.

The programs that Hung and his followers conceived aimed at demolishing the established order. Politically, they set up their own government, which they expected to impose in place of Manchu rule. Economically, they published plans, apparently never widely put into effect, to redistribute the land, assigning equitable allotments to everyone and allowing all to share the produce, which was to be turned in to storehouses established for each group of twenty-five families and portioned out as needed. (The latter practice, the pooling of goods with common claim on them, seems to have been observed during the growth of the movement.) Socially, in addition to the communal organization, the movement more or less consistently promoted austere behavior, providing for segregation of the sexes among the rank and file and condemning such personal vices as prostitution, drinking wine, smoking opium or tobacco, and gambling.

Finally, the programs included, in addition to the pursuit of goals by military means, an element we may regard as in part nationalistic. That is, Hung and his followers saw their mission as the restoration in China of the Heavenly Kingdom, which was sometimes referred to as the "spiritual continent," specifically resisting the encroachment of the Manchus, who were devils and guilty of the foulest crimes, from the defilement of Chinese women to the wish to exterminate the Chinese people.

In many of the movement's features it is possible to see the Chinese past. The government it established used names of offices drawn from the Classics, was arranged in a most careful hierarchy, recruited officials by means of examinations, and served a ruler as theoretically autocratic as any previous head of state. Its fully regulated economic egalitarianism for the common people reflects Classical ideals and earlier historical experiments, either under governments like the T'ang or in rebellions like that of Huang Ch'ao. Its austerity seemed not to echo any major theme of the great tradition (although the ideas had been there, however neglected they have have been, since Mo Tzu), but had long been known, especially as a means of steeling men for combat. Similarly the hatred of barbarians and exhortation to attack them were familiar themes, frequently voiced in the later dynasties. It recalled the hatred of the Mongols by the founder of the Ming dynasty, among others, and it revealed that a residue of opposition from the earliest days of the Manchu occupation remained. One of its theorists, a man who joined the movement late, drew some of his arguments from the "leftover" Ming loyalist of the seventeenth century, Ku Yen-wu.

When the weight of influences is compared, it is not surprising that the ancestry of the rebellion proved to be Chinese rather than foreign, but its revolutionary and, in the narrow sense, nontraditional aspects should not be overlooked. It was, for instance, consciously anti-Confucian most of the time. Hung felt that the Four Books of Confucianism exerted a baneful influence; in his visions the Heavenly Father himself had traced the evil deeds of the devils back to the teachings of Confucius. True, the movement often followed concepts and practices that Confucianism had fixed in the Chinese mentality, but against the more or less unconscious acceptance of much Confucian substance should be weighed a conscious rejection of certain Confucian forms, notably ancestor worship and Confucian historical authority. The rejection of even that much helped to turn the literati against the movement. The movement's tone, or attitude, was also revolutionary in its militancy and exclusiveness. The battle against devils meant that all idols had to be smashed and all superstitions attacked head on. Little of the syncretic toleration that had reconciled popular Buddhism, Taoism, and other cults remained. There was a sense, too, of the involvement of culture in revolution, as the movement drew upon popular novels for some of its rhetoric and even its military strategy, and conversely made a virtue of plain style in writing, in opposition to the classical allusions and fanciful metaphors of the literati. Most striking of all, it developed an attitude that had been expressed earlier by, for example, the Ming iconoclast Li Chih, in opening to women opportunities for status and work on a level with men. Though inconsistent and unaware of how bound to the past it remained, the movement felt in some degree a need to work free of tradition in pursuit of its Utopia. It may not have been the first rebellion to do so, but as a great and recent one it became, despite its failure, something of a tradition itself for modern nationalist revolutionaries.

Its course, after the preliminary period in which Hung had his visions and formed with kinsmen and friends the Society of God, passed through a phase of military victories, followed by a period of internal dissension and military stalemate and ended in defeat. As the society grew to several thousand converts in Kwangsi it responded to a skirmish with a detachment of official troops (1850) with the capture of a town and the proclamation of a dynasty (1851). The state was named the Heavenly Kingdom of Great Peace (*T'ai-p'ing t'ien-kuo*) and Hung was entitled Heavenly King. From the Chinese name of the state, the rebels became known to Westerners as the Taipings. Their members, at first mainly Hakkas, included at one time or another members of secret societies, miners, boatmen, outlaws, peasants, and a few men of greater wealth and education. The next year they moved out of Kwangsi and made their way generally northeast through Hunan to Hupei and the Yangtze River, where they captured their first provincial capital. Their numbers were said to have grown to hundreds of thousands. From there, they moved down river in a great fleet, breaking into Nanking, once the capital of the last native dynasty, in 1853. From then on, they remained mainly in the vast region of the lower Yangtze valley. From first to last they touched sixteen provinces.

The period following the capture of Nanking, which was made the capital, included more important victories but significant defeats as well, both military and political. An expedition to the north, for example, after a long and tortuous march, was stopped short of the capital. In Nanking, a prominent lieutenant, who maintained that his tongue was guided by the Heavenly Father, became such a threat to Hung, the Heavenly King, that Hung had another leader kill him, together with about 20,000 of his followers. The loyal assassin in turn proved intolerable, and was put to death with two hundred of his associates. A third leader who had meanwhile gained in popularity left Nanking, embittered by the intrigues of the palace, and finally Hung was left with only untalented relatives as aides, and the discipline of the leadership notably deteriorated.

Yet another setback, though less definite, was the failure to win powerful allies. Of those who were conceivable, secret societies and other rebels came closest to a kind of partnership. One, for example, the Small Sword Society, seized the Chinese part of Shanghai and held it for seventeen months, issuing proclamations friendly to the old Ming dynasty and the Taipings, but Nanking, probably failing to see the importance of such aid, did not respond. Another conceivable source of aid was Europeans, some of whom looked favorably on what they thought was a Christian rebellion. True, the likelihood of aid from them was lessened by the force of another argument, put forward by a well-informed British official, that aid instead to the Manchus would elicit all sorts of commercial concessions. Yet the Taiping leaders did not carefully explore the possibilities, and even made it clear to European visitors that with God on their side, as it were, they needed no barbarians. In the end, the European powers moved from a formal neutrality to actions helpful in modest ways to the Manchus. A mixed French and Manchu force, for example, broke through the walls of Shanghai and slaughtered the Small Swords rebels. The consuls of Britain, France, and the United States agreed to manage the maritime customs at Shanghai for Peking, though this was related to concessions under which the Westerners gained a free hand in the administration of their resident quarters. A small force of Chinese mercenaries, trained and led by Westerners, won many small battles in the Yangtze delta, taking the name "Ever-Victorious Army." Most serious for the Taipings, however, was their failure to attract any important proportion of the educated class. Considering their religious doctrine and revolutionary aims, it is not clear how they could have done so, although halfway along they attempted to give

Confucian elements more room in their ideology. No matter, the literati on the whole were repelled by what they regarded as vulgar wreckers of their native civilization. It is characteristic of the spirit of the educated class of the time that they were moved less by the Taipings' appeal to national feeling than by their hostility to the Confucian tradition. The Manchus were more important as upholders of the tradition than as barbarous oppressors of the nation.

In the direct sense, it was not the Manchus but the Chinese scholar-officials who defeated the Taipings, for the end of the great rebellion came as talented organizers and administrators emerged and built forces to do what the imperial armies could not do. The chief figure was Tseng Kuo-fan (1811-72), whose rise to prominence was by the usual standards of bureaucratic life extraordinary and yet typical of several new leaders. He was born into an obscure family and was the first in recent generations to win the *chin-shih* degree. That he showed promise seems to be indicated by the fact that he was kept in the capital for the next decade, serving in the Hanlin Academy and various ministries. His reputation, however, rested less on brilliance than on moral seriousness and self-cultivation; he may never have become a towering figure in the elegant arguments at court, but he embodied Confucian ideals in action. To him the Taiping movement threatened the very soul of Chinese civilization.

In preparing for the counterattack, he relied upon techniques that were more Chinese than Manchu. In 1852, when Tseng was at home in Hunan mourning the death of his mother, he was asked to organize a militia army. Its core was to be local groups that had already fought well defending the capital city as the Taipings swept through, and for the organizing mechanism Tseng apparently exploited his acquaintance and prestige with other literati families who could contribute forces they had raised. Many of the officers of the new army were students who in their new positions became Tseng's protégés. To support the army, Tseng depended, with growing dissatisfaction, on contributions from the local literati, or gentry, families. To make soldiers of good quality, he insisted not only on ample military training before committing the men to more than local engagements but also on moral training, or indoctrination in Confucian standards of behavior. Further, to strengthen morale, Tseng adopted the policy, unusual in other armies, of paying the soldiers regularly. His methods eventually made of his "Hunan Braves," as they were called, a strong force, the officers tied by personal loyalty to Tseng, the men carefully trained, and all possessing *esprit de corps*. They first justified Tseng's idea of an army in 1854, when they stopped a Taiping force moving back into Hunan from Nanking and pushed it down the river. Yet many more battles were still to be won and lost.

Another scholar-statesman to rise to the military crisis was Tso Tsung-t'ang (1812-85). Although also born into a Hunan family, Tso's tastes and early experiences were different from Tseng's. Tso studied widely, taking special interest in agriculture, geography, and military strategy. He never won the highest academic degree, though he took the examinations three times, and he served no apprenticeship in Peking. Yet his talents impressed influential men who were concerned with the state of affairs in Hunan, including Tseng Kuo-fan, and he received appointments as assistant for military affairs in two provincial administrations. Finally, in 1860, he was ordered to raise and train a corps in Hunan. Within the year his army was attacking the rebels and by 1862 it had made Chekiang its field of battle, bringing pressure to bear from the south in support of the Hunan Braves' attacks from the west.

A third civil figure to provide military leadership was younger than the two just discussed and achieved his greatest fame later in other ways, but his early experience prepared him for times in which few questions lacked a military aspect. He was Li Hung-chang (1823-1901), the son of a classmate of Tseng Kuo-fan, who became his patron and friend for life. After studying under Tseng, winning his *chin-shih* degree, and serving in the Hanlin Academy, Li went home to Anhwei Province with his father in 1853 and organized local militia against the Taipings. From that time on he led forces the general success of which, together with the support of Tseng Kuo-fan, established him among the competent leaders of the day. By 1862 he had brought a force into Kiangsu, occupying the northern arc of the ring being tightened around the Taipings. In that position he chose to cooperate with the foreign-led Ever-Victorious Army in the vicinity of Shanghai, a decision that was justified by victories, despite disagreements and distrust on both sides of the alliance. His association with foreigners probably also gained him diplomatic insight, a quality that would serve him well in later years.

The building of new armies and the making of strategy that have been outlined here implied a much more complicated course of events to come than the suppression of a massive rebellion. True, one major result was the defeat of the Taipings. By the 1860s the loyalist forces had improved their organization and were winning more victories. The loyalty of some disputed territories was being regained by a lightening of taxes. On the other side, the Taiping discipline had degenerated. Although a field commander of great talent kept the fighting forces formidable, signs of corruption and disintegration were more numerous than before. In early summer, 1864, Hung Hsiu-ch'üan put an end to his life. A month later, loyalist forces fought their way into Nanking, and the Taiping rebels, but for scattered remnants, were destroyed.

Yet the emperor might well have said, "If we have such another victory we are undone." He would have meant an undoing not of his armies, in the Pyrrhic sense, but of the old strength of the dynasty, its monopoly of power. In 1860, when the Taipings inflicted a particularly humiliating defeat on imperial forces, the court reluctantly granted Tseng Kuo-fan the greater powers that he had long wanted to support his efforts. He was appointed governor-general of the lower Yangtze provinces and imperial commissioner with special powers to cope with the situation. The court accepted his nominations for important subordinate appointments, including those of Li Hung-chang and Tso Tsung-t'ang to be governors of the coastal provinces of his region. While better organization followed as a direct result, misgivings with regard to the future were appropriate, for the court was certainly aware of disastrous historical precedents in which combined military and civil authority, including that of levying taxes, had been given to regional officials. The most famous was probably the system of regional military governors in the T'ang dynasty, which had consequently disintegrated. Even at the start of the Ch'ing, the "enfeoffment" of renegade Chinese generals as a reward for their services had ultimately led to war. No such disaster followed immediately among the cultivated conquerors of the Taipings, for the main point of their efforts was to protect a social order with which they were essentially satisfied, and to which they thought political stability was the key. Yet their organizations of men remained somewhat apart from the normal bureaucracy, at least in feeling loyalty to their own leaders, and a degree of independence from other authorities, and later contributed to destructive militarist rivalries. Even aside from military matters, the organizations may be understood as factions, the unorthodox but characteristic feature of imperial politics, and their growth provoked rivalries at court, as might be expected, adding to the instability of government.

Seldom had there been a time when weakness of government was less tolerable. By the end of the rebellion the country had suffered an estimated 20 million to 40 million deaths, many towns were left in ruins, much of the richest farmland had gone neglected, and of course tax revenues were greatly reduced. In addition, other serious rebellions drained the dynasty's strength. North of the Taiping region, between the Huai and Yellow rivers, secret societies, some of them descended from the earlier White Lotus groups, had long exercised influence in villages, several hundred of which built earthen walls to defend themselves against rival groups and bandits. In the 1830s floods aggravated the social instability there, and fortified groups recognizing a single leader in 1853 drove out imperial officials, administered the region themselves, and conducted raids on neighboring regions. The Nien rebels, as they were called, remained out of control from 1853 to 1868 and at one time dominated the rural life of an area of 100,000 square miles. They yielded gradually to a strategy of blockade devised by Tseng Kuo-fan and continued by Li Hung-chang.

A much greater threat in terms of possible loss of territory, though far from the center of power, was that of Muslim rebellions that broke out in the southwest (Yunnan) and the northwest (Shensi, Kansu, and Chinese Turkestan), and required campaigns in one place or another between 1855 and 1878. Communal hostilities between the Muslim minority and ordinary Chinese in some instances and oppression by officials in others seemed to be among the conditions preceding the rebellions, which as a whole provided more evidence of the decline of Ch'ing control. Again locally recruited militia played a part in suppressing them. The most spectacular achievement was that of Tso Tsung-t'ang, who took an army, half of which were men from his native Hunan, to the arid northwest and by prodigies of logistics, self-sufficiency, and tactics brought the area under control. Furthermore, he confirmed his sense of a mission to rehabilitate the people (as did the other new leaders in their own pacified areas) by, for example, printing booklets on cotton weaving and bringing wasteland under cultivation as well as by killing as many rebels as possible.

Finally, to the major burden of rebellions against the government in mid-century was added the growing aggressiveness of the Western powers. The new treaty concessions of 1858 and 1860, following the Anglo-French campaigns, have already been mentioned. Sharing in these agreements was Russia, but her position differed from the others in that she showed a desire for territory as well as for trading privileges. In the seventeenth century the Russians had been the first Europeans to establish relations with China by treaty when, coming into the watershed of the Amur River in the course of the penetration eastward through Siberia, they intruded on what a youthful and strong Ch'ing government regarded as its territory. The result was the Treaty of Nerchinsk (1689), in accordance with which the Russians withdrew from the Amur watershed and recognized a boundary well to the north. In return they won agreement on trade relations. Four decades later (Treaty of Kiakhta, 1727), Russia also recognized a boundary farther west, according to which Outer Mongolia was Chinese. Again there was an agreement on trade. By the middle of the nineteenth century, however, the evidence provided by the Opium War that the Ch'ing dynasty was no longer the power that it had once been and the increased energy of Russian expansion into Central Asia led to new Russian probes and settlements in the Amur region. Mixing shows of force with suggestions of a common interest in holding the British and French in check, Russian officials won two new treaties (Aigun, 1858, and Peking, 1860), by which the territory north of the Amur River and that facing the Sea of Japan as far south as the Korean border became Russian. In fact, both treaties only confirmed Russia's possession of what had already been taken. In cutting away pieces of the empire, the Russians raised barbarian problems higher on the list of Ch'ing concerns. As a Chinese official put it to the emperor, the Taiping rebels menaced the heart of the nation, the Russians the trunk, and the British only the extremities.

中華文化大綱

IX

Acceleration

of the Pace of

Change

The major rebellions added to the growing demands of the foreigners made it unmistakably clear that the dynasty faced a critical period. The precedents of earlier great dynasties suggested that to pass the crisis successfully would require a restoration, that is, a rededication and reinvigoration of government. It was true, of course, that history also suggested that no dynasty as old as the Ch'ing had much chance of achieving any such restoration, but leaders could be forgiven for not dwelling on that idea. The debatable point was what kind of action was necessary.

In the arguments over this, the political splits that had already taken place exerted their own influence. To factions at court and those clustered around the great regional officials it seemed that their fortunes were bound up with one or another position on the question of change. In addition, palace government worked once more in favor of a powerful woman; in 1861 a woman who had originally entered the palace as a low-ranking concubine, having won the confidence of the late emperor and borne him his only son, acquired the rank of empress dowager (she was also known in the West by several other names, including Tz'u-hsi, which was part of her title, and "The Old Buddha," which was a popular Chinese term). From then until her death in 1908 she held virtually absolute power in the palace—as regent for child emperors or in some similar position—for a total of forty-eight years, an intelligent, energetic, and forceful but provincial, covetous, and conservative personality at the center of decisions in a fateful time.

Under regional and court officials, and eventually other men of less established authority, the last half century of the dynasty followed its course, a course that led from traditional restoration to modern revolution. The result, so contrary to the intentions of the protectors of the established order, may be considered generally as the product of three factors. One was the movement for reform and innovation, an attempt, widely supported in principle though controversial in method, to strengthen a regime still regarded as the legitimate guardian of civilization. A second was the growing pressure from foreigners, whose intrusions tended to raise practical questions of what should be done (for example, how were parts of China to be kept out of foreign hands?), causing the traditional spiritual values to seem less relevant. Consequently, the growth of the spirit of nationalism, at least among some, for whom the main concept shifted from saving the civilization to saving the country, became a third factor. In the following sections the role of each of these factors will be considered briefly. The period from approximately 1860 to 1895 reveals the slow exposure of the inadequacy of traditional methods and the erosion of traditional principles, while the period from 1895 to 1911 shows the rise to dominance of revolutionary fervor.

Efforts Toward Reform (1860-1895)

A good measure of the quality of the spirit of reform could be found at court, in which the new effort was called, after the reign-title of the new child emperor, the T'ung-chih Restoration (strictly speaking, the T'ung-chih period lasted from 1862 to 1874). A number of innovations appeared, perhaps most significantly a new responsiveness to what the situation of the dynasty required. The widened authority given Tseng Kuo-fan to lead the campaign to reduce the Taipings, which was mentioned earlier, was one example of the greater awareness of the chief ministers. On the whole they continued to support the more effective new regional leaders in their other pacification campaigns. At the capital itself they recognized the need of certain new organizations. In 1861, for example, a subcommittee of the Grand Council was appointed to conduct foreign affairs in Peking. Commonly called the Tsungli Yamen, the subcommittee supervised, in addition to diplomatic relations, a variety of experiments, such as a college of foreign languages, which eventually trained men in the new style of diplomacy; the acquiring of knowledge of the West through translations (soon leading to successes in arguing with Western diplomats on the basis of their own international law); the establishment of new industries under the more progressive regional governors; and the education of students in Western techniques, including sending the first group of students abroad.

The arrangement of that first mission abroad illustrated the motives behind the reform efforts. In 1871 it was agreed that 120 teenage Chinese boys would go in groups to America for fifteen years of education. At the headquarters established in Hartford, Connecticut, the two senior supervisors represented, it might be said, two poles of aspiration for the mission. One was the first Chinese graduate of an American college (Yale '54), a proponent of the rapid introduction of Western techniques to China. The other was a conservative official chosen to balance the Western enthusiasms of the former with his own devotion to classical learning. When the boys, lodged with

American families and attracted to new ways, neglected not only their Chinese studies but abandoned their Chinese dress, decorum, and attitudes as well, the Yale man was indulgent, the Confucian scholar troubled. Reports reaching Peking suggested that the boys were learning corrupt practices and ideas. After ten years the criticisms in Peking contributed to a decision to abolish the mission and bring the boys home. Back in China they were received with some suspicion of their characters and uncertainty of their usefulness, but a large proportion of them eventually came to be employed in technical and modernizing positions. The mission showed, however, the limits of the effective conception of Westernization. It was to be, as has been said, a coat of armor with which to protect the living core of Chinese civilization, that it might continue undisturbed. In this the reformers were at one with even the most rigid conservatives, who saw as the greatest need of the time the revitalization of native, mainly Confucian, virtues. The innovations discovered among the Westerners would improve only one feature of Chinese life, and that one of only rudimentary importance—the strength to defend the country physically. The nobler Chinese features, the humane values and customs of tradition, need only be revived to be at least the equal of anything to be found abroad.

While the recent history of industrializing countries suggests that Western techniques and products cannot be acquired independently of other, less tangible features, we need not condemn the Confucian reformers too harshly for regarding the West as superior only in ships and guns. Historians of Europe's expansion have frequently stressed the powerful effect of these inventions. In any event, the more progressive members of the court and regional officials saw innovation in much the same light throughout the T'ung-chih Restoration and beyond. Training in the use of European firearms began with a force stationed near Peking in 1862, for example, and a navy yard was opened in 1867. By 1894 Chinese forces had available a variety of modern arms and about sixty-five modern warships, either bought or built.

The most obvious signs of the reform regarded by the Chinese as fundamental—the rise of superior men—appeared in the provinces, which had been rescued from rebellion by the statesmen-generals mentioned earlier. The same men were the original proponents and direct executives of many of the programs supported by moderate officials at court. The leader in reform as in the pacification campaigns was Tseng Kuo-fan, who promoted (on the recommendation of the Yale graduate mentioned above) the establishment of what became the Kiangnan Arsenal at Shanghai. With characteristic clarity of purpose Tseng warned that for him, too, "self-strengthening," an old phrase again made current by the emergency, was not an end in itself but a means of protecting the traditional way of life. For the self-strengtheners in the provinces, then, innovation was, as for the progressives at court, an aspect of defense and foreign policy.

Yet the new industries almost inevitably drew more than ships and guns from Western technology. Arsenals and shipyards had been established in several cities by the 1870s, and with them machine shops and technical schools which increased the knowledge of Western techniques. From acquiring warships it was a reasonable step to operating cargo ships which, under the China Merchants' Steam Navigation Company (1872), promised to improve the transport of tribute rice from the south and safeguard Chinese dominance of the coasting trade. The use of steamships in turn encouraged the development of coal mines, using modern techniques, which included short railways. On the grounds of military defense the Imperial Telegraph Administration was justified.

Two special developments, possibly to be attributed to the pragmatism that distinguished the self-strengtheners from the most conservative officials, were the modern Imperial Maritime Customs and a modern postal service. The origin of the Customs lay in expediency. The disruption caused by the Taiping rebels in the 1850s had led the Ch'ing to employ foreigners to collect the revenue from foreign trade. The foreign staff proved honest and efficient, making customs the largest new source of government revenue in the period. The postal service developed as part of the Customs.

The idea of innovation as mainly a protective device was stretched very thin by the establishment of other enterprises. By the 1890s, for example, a textile mill under the patronage of Li Hung-chang, the most active of the great official entrepreneurs, was so successful that the aim of eventually monopolizing the China textile market, driving out foreign imports, grew. Such a concept of commercial competition seemed to anticipate a more general interest in modern production. Furthermore, in the later decades a small secondary group of what we might call Confucian entrepreneurs, some of them protégés of the great self-strengtheners, devoted themselves to modern experiments, including mills and other manufacturing enterprises as well as schools with technical subjects in the curriculum. These men, too, tended to conceive of their efforts in a largely traditional sense—if not as a strengthening of the dynasty, then as the obligation of a Confucian gentleman to promote the people's livelihood.

THE ACHIEVEMENTS AND LIMITS OF REFORMS (1860-95)

It is fundamentally true to say that the traditional reform effort failed, but to say only that may be unjust. It certainly failed to give the dynasty a long second life, such as the word "Restoration" implies when used of other dynasties. Even so, to use another possible standard, that of the prolongation of the life of an aged dynasty by half a century or so, as Wang An-shih may have done for the Northern Sung or Chang Chü-cheng for the Ming, the Ch'ing reformers may have accomplished as much as a small group of men could in the face of widespread degeneration. At least they put down rebellions that might well have spelled the end, and they came sufficiently to grips with a novel technical civilization to begin to modernize the most populous society of the world.

The beginning of modernization, however modest in comparison with the size of the project, deserves recognition even though overshadowed by the final political failure. The economic dimensions of the period are discussed in chapter XVI, where the reader will find described the production, characteristic organization, and material contribution of the new economic activities. Shortcomings and mismanagement, ambivalence of motive—from constructive enterprise to personal gain—and other faults diminished what even those enterprises undertaken might have contributed if properly handled. Nevertheless, the self-strengtheners introduced to China skills necessary to modernization. Thousands were trained, often at first by foreigners, in the use of Western machines, languages, and technical management, and the alien occupations and work places began slowly to become part of the Chinese scene, even though frequently resisted by farmer and literatus alike as long-established practices were supplanted by what seemed outlandish projects.

Yet the self-strengthening movement fell short in another sense, failing to generate a rapid, sustained, and cumulative technological and economic growth afterwards, as is concluded by modern students when they follow subsequent history and find, as it seems, no further striking material and technical progress until much later. Although that judgment overlooks a continual if slow growth of productivity and commerce, it is, nevertheless, generally true.

To account for the limitations of the reforms would add to an understanding of the old civilization as well as of its transformation. No answer has been universally accepted in scholarly circles, but several aspects which have been discussed may be listed here. Among the most general, the material condition of China is generally acknowledged as important. The vastness of the country made it difficult to mount any change that would quickly affect all regions. The size of the population likewise hindered change. Perhaps an even greater obstacle was the ratio of people to the available natural resources, for so heavily did the basic material needs of the people weigh upon the capacity of the land to provide them that surplus wealth to pay for modern innovations was hard to find; worse still, almost any technological change threatened to upset precarious economic balances and impose, at least for a time, intolerable hardship on the unfortunate.

Intellectual conditions have also been considered. The attitudes formed by Confucianism, it has been argued, prevented the innovator from accepting some of the essential features of modern life. The habit of glorifying the past blocked any new vision of the future. A long history of leadership and superiority in the world prevented any quick recognition of foreign values and any sustaining sense of nationalistic rivalry with competing peoples.

In addition, specific institutional conditions might be kept in mind, for the general factors above, important though they be, had not been so damaging in the past. Despite the difficulties that size, populousness, and poverty put in the way of ambitious undertakings, vigorous Chinese dynasties of the past had achieved wonders of construction and administration. Confucian conservatism did not always prevent innovations when they were needed, as is shown by the interest of the early Ch'ing in Western guns. A specific condition that limited the response to crisis was that of the aging of the dynasty, in which the pattern of factionalism often seen before largely prevented unified and consistent administration. What appeared to be the faults of conservatism, then, might more truly have been lack of direction, for the reformers were never more than a faction in the court, though at times the dominant faction, and the normal source of vigorous direction, the throne, had become in the old manner preoccupied with its own vanities, pleasures, and protection, the empress dowager leaning more and more on the assistance of eunuchs. In another reversion to earlier ways, the central administration had yielded some of its power to regional leaders. While such men as Li Hung-chang, unlike warlords, remained loyal and obedient to the throne, they also held in effect considerable personal power, based on their organization of loyal followers, the innovative enterprises they sponsored, and the strength of their voice in the court. Although they used their power on the whole in support of the dynasty, they were not always above profiting themselves and their followers and opposing rival self-strengtheners, so that a form of regional factionalism also weakened the general effort. It may be asked whether the movement might not have had different results if the dynasty had fallen earlier, and the self-strengthening had begun under the direction of a young, ambitious, and strong regime. Chinese history is silent on the question, but the experience of Japan, whose self-strengthening of the same era had begun desultorily under an old government and quickened remarkably under a new, invites comparison.

THE FOREIGN PRESENCE (1860-94)

Though it had been reasonable in 1860 to rank rebellion ahead of external aggression among the crises facing the dynasty, the following decades made the foreign presence take first place in the thoughts of many, from farmers to grand councilors. It had a strong psychological impact on at least some groups in the population, coloring their emotions and affecting their outlook so that they began to think of themselves as members of a nation challenged by other nations. The most tangible agents of the presence were missionaries, the foreign communities in the treaty ports, and foreign armed forces.

By the treaties of 1858 and 1860 Christian missionaries had acquired the right to travel, reside, and buy or lease land and buildings anywhere in China. As a result, missionaries and converts increased in number. It would be difficult to measure adequately the spiritual benefits the new teaching bestowed, although the tenacity with which some had kept the faith earlier—there were still about 150,000 Catholics in the country in 1800, after three quarters of a century of prohibition—suggests that true believers found deep satisfactions. In addition to imparting the gospel, some missionaries, especially Protestants, saw their work as the diffusion of Western civilization. They published journals and books and founded schools, which increasingly dealt with the secular aspects of Western life, strengthening the new currents of reform but by the same token identifying the missionary as an enemy of the tradition in some respects. The same suspicion and hostility that had met his foreign ways during the Ming dynasty reappeared in the nineteenth century, with greater justification. The Jesuit policy of accommodation had long since been abandoned (although Catholic missions were often well adjusted to Chinese ways and a few missionaries, both Catholic and Protestant, were serious students of Chinese civilization), and intemperate condemnation of native customs often took its place.

If insults gave offense to some Chinese, others were frightened by recent history or made resentful by scattered incidents. The Taipings had confirmed in the minds of many, especially literati and landlords, the conviction that Christianity fed rebellion. The rights given in the treaties seemed to some to place the missionaries in a privileged position. As missionaries took complaints directly to district magistrates, members of the gentry felt their own privileges encroached upon; and when missionaries summoned their country's gunboats to their support, as they occasionally did, local officials felt humiliated. Against the spiritual and secular improvements that the missionaries brought to many, therefore, must be placed the hostility and fear they roused in others. An antimissionary literature in the form of books, pamphlets, and posters appeared in the streets, some of it dwelling on the vile practices that the foreigners were said to relish, and hundreds of incidents of hostility occurred.

The most terrible, which revealed many typical attitudes, was the Tientsin Massacre of 1870. It arose from the indignation of local Chinese who believed that a Catholic establishment, in offering fees for orphans, was encouraging kidnapers to supply children, whose eyes and hearts were then taken out and used for magical purposes. Egged on by gentry, a mob gathered in front of the buildings. A choleric French consul, insisting that the mob disperse, first threatened the superintendent of trade with his pistol and then fired it at the district prefect, but missed and was killed himself, together with a score or more of other Christians, foreign and Chinese. As foreign gunboats gathered, threatening reprisals, the old Tseng Kuo-fan was assigned to investigate and settle the case. His combination of justice, conciliation, and temporizing avoided a major confrontation, but the product of this mixture of ignorant fear and malice on one hand, and insensitivity and arrogance on the other, was an embittered atmosphere. Certainly no similar tension surrounded most missionary establishments, but the element of hostility, though in milder form, appeared often.

The effect of the missions on any of the great movements in China, whether in terms of modernization or of chauvinism, was limited by the fact that in a country of some 400 million there were in 1870 only about 250 Catholic priests and 350 Protestant missionaries. By the 1890s the number had risen to about 750 priests and 1,300 Protestant missionaries, who reported (the figures vary) some 500,000 Catholic believers and 37,000 Protestants. A Christian community of little more than one one thousandth of the population was unlikely to exert much direct impact on the society as a whole. Tied to the foreign presence, however, it affected the intellectual and emotional landscape.

Probably more important, though in effect equally intangible, was the foreign presence in the treaty ports. These ports, of which there were fourteen in the 1860s and more later, aroused mixed feelings in some Chinese. The foreign concessions became, as mentioned earlier, examples of Western urban life, friendly to business and offering opportunities to Chinese merchants alert to the new Western ways as well as to Westerners themselves. Increasingly the concessions also attracted young Chinese intellectuals who were curious about the civilization that could assert itself so vigorously against their own. Yet the ambition, curiosity, and eventually the fascination with which some approached these outposts of the West were frequently qualified by indignation and resentment at the ubiquitous reminders of Western superiority. In the concessions the Westerners of course comprised the administrative, economic, and social elite, holding all the top positions in government and business, making the most money, and living the most luxurious and expensive life. It was not so much the gap between standards of living and status that disturbed some Chinese, however, as the implication of Chinese inferiority that went with it.

On closer look, the concessions were not in fact true replicas of Western cities. They lacked a Western working class, as all hard labor was done by Chinese, an arrangement that prompted some Chinese intellectuals to compare the Westerners with themselves as a corresponding elite. Yet the Westerners were not notably given to books or other familiar pursuits of cultivation (leaving aside such exceptions as some of those in missionaries' schools). They were overwhelmingly middle-class businessmen whose apparent preoccupation with money, dinner parties, and sports, and whose indifference to the concerns the Chinese intellectual would expect of a superior people, made them difficult to admire. When Westerners, moreover, expressed their sense of superiority or clannishness in social ways somehow reminiscent of old Chinese gestures—barring Chinese from Western clubs and remaining blissfully ignorant of the Chinese language, for example—some Chinese felt constrained to accept the achievements of the West while resenting the Westerners themselves, who represented the power that China lacked.

A third reminder of the foreign presence came in the form of armies invading the old tributary regions. Russia's seizure of territory the Ch'ing regarded as its own has been noted above. Through much of the 1870s territory that the Ch'ing had dominated in the far northwest was out of control, with Russian and British moves complicating the issues, especially the Russian occupation of the strategic Ili River region. While the combined efforts of Tso Tsung-t'ang's armies and Chinese negotiators were reducing the danger of loss in that direction, Japan raised another at the opposite end of the empire. In several unilateral steps she drew the Ryukyu Islands, from which previously tribute had been paid to both China and Japan, under her sole control, making them the prefecture of Okinawa. Under the pretext of punishing Formosan aboriginals who had murdered some shipwrecked Ryukyuans, she sent an expeditionary army into the eastern portion of Formosa for half of 1874. To these moves Peking responded only with belated protests over the Ryukyus and a mobilization of forces on the coast facing Formosa until the Japanese withdrew.

Shortly afterwards, a British diplomat, threatening a rupture of relations or worse if his demands were not met, won an agreement that the British government of India might mark the border between Burma and the province of Yunnan. The agreement meant in effect that China abandoned her hold on Burma as a tributary state, no other course seeming reasonable in the light of two previous British invasions, which had already resulted in the annexation of parts of Burma. After the third Anglo-Burmese War (1885-86), China recognized Burma as a British colony.

At about the same time she relinquished, but only after fighting, the much older and more kindred territory of Vietnam. Since the 1850s French forces had extended their control over south Vietnam and forced concessions by treaty in the north, despite resistance and rebellions. In the 1880s, when Chinese irregular forces were aiding the north Vietnamese rebels, French forces attacked Chinese border towns, leading to a Chinese declaration of war. The Chinese forces shattered the French army at the border, bringing down the French government, but they suffered defeats elsewhere, especially from the guns of French warships, which destroyed a small Chinese fleet in Foochow harbor and the shipyard that Tso Tsung-t'ang had built there. In 1885 China acknowledged by treaty a French protectorate over Vietnam.

Before that mark of acquiescence, however, signs of a new spirit had appeared, especially in Kwangtung, where during the war nationalistic anger, perhaps incited by the new, popular journalism, took such forms as attacks on foreign establishments. The aggression of the Europeans, although it had not yet been directed toward seizing any great territory of China proper, began to seem a threat not only to the ruling class and their concept of civilization but also to many who felt a common bond in being Chinese.

THE INTELLECTUALS' PERSPECTIVE (1860-94)

The crises of the period slowly but persistently brought to the fore the question whether or not the quality of life was faced with a profound change. Some of the major administrators took the position, as mentioned before, that a combination of moral regeneration and technical innovation, concentrating on the devices that gave the West its physical strength, should be used to protect the inner core of Chinese life as it was. Others were like the grand secretary who opposed all the new techniques and tactics on the grounds that the empire was better served by decorum and moral conduct; if, nevertheless, mathematics or the like had to be taught, it should be possible to find a master of the subject in the empire; there was no need to learn from barbarians. A third and new position was taken by a few men who argued that even greater changes of method were needed; according to some of them, these had been anticipated in China's own classical past. Most prominent in this group was Wang T'ao (1828-97?), who, never moving into bureaucratic circles by way of the examinations, became instead an editor of a foreign mission press and assistant to a major British sinologist (James Legge); traveled in Europe and Japan; and spread knowledge of modern affairs by founding newspapers and writing books. His ideas went beyond those of the self-strengtheners, even to advocating a parliament and such other fundamental changes as an improvement in the status of women. He based his views, he wrote, on the sanction for reform inherent in the Classics, with their recognition that the ages moved in cycles, each with its own institutional requirements. It seems obvious, nevertheless, that, although he was able to place his ideas in a traditional framework, his longstanding interest in foreign matters and association with foreigners had much to do with what he advocated. His ardent patriotism, evident for example, in his newspaper when the Japanese annexed the Ryukyus, seemed to express a more modern spirit than that which moved the government. The fact that he attracted many readers suggested a spreading interest in the new questions. Yet Wang T'ao was ahead of his time, for few in power admitted as great a need of change as he did.

THE REVELATION OF THE SINO-JAPANESE WAR (1894-95)

Eventually a more damaging blow than any previously inflicted by foreign hands exposed the inadequacy of the limited, grudging reforms. It was damaging psychologically as well as physically, for the opponent was Japan, hitherto belittled tributary; and the issue was the status of Korea, whose closeness to China in both the tributary and the strategic sense gave her importance. For over two decades, almost since the establishment of Japan's new, modernizing government, Japanese leaders had anticipated a new relationship with Korea. Some of them thought it essential for Japan's own safety that she help Korea and other East Asian states modernize to hold off the Western imperialists. Others considered Korea a fitting part of a new Japanese empire. Yet others saw Korea as a base that must be denied to a menacing Russia. A consensus for greater Japanese influence resulted; following the establishment of modern relations by treaty in 1876, Japanese aided those Koreans who were considered progressive and friendly. This involved Japanese officials (and eventually Japanese military units protecting the establishment in Seoul) in the factional disputes of Korean politics. Correspondingly the Chinese commissioner and his establishment, including troops, became more active in affairs at Seoul, advising and aiding in an effort to block the Japanese (and any others, like the Russians, who seemed interested in changing the traditional Korean orientation). The rivalry had grown so intense by 1885 that China and Japan agreed to withdraw their troops and to send no more without notifying each other. The agreement meant only that both sides wanted time to improve their positions. Nine years later, when the Chinese sent troops in answer to a Korean request for aid in putting down a rebellion, the Japanese sent more of their own, the increased tension culminating in the Japanese seizure of the palace in Seoul and a mutual declaration of war between China and Japan.

Although the treaty concluding the Sino-Japanese War (1894-95) was not signed until nine months later, the first two months of the fighting revealed China to be weaker than the world had imagined, and no match for Japan. Japanese columns advanced from the south, took P'yongyang, and entered Manchuria. When a Japanese fleet of a dozen ships engaged a comparable Chinese fleet off the mouth of the Yalu, the Japanese, with no losses, sank four of the enemy within four hours. The remainder of the Chinese fleet took refuge in a harbor and stayed there until attack left it useless a few months later. The hard terms of the Treaty of Shimonoseki (1895) reflected the magnitude of China's defeat: acknowledgment of the independence of Korea; the cession to Japan of Formosa and the Liaotung Peninsula of South Manchuria (the demand for the latter being given up when Russia, Germany, and France intervened diplomatically, concerned lest Japan put them at a disadvantage by her possession of that well-placed territory); the payment to Japan of an indemnity of two hundred million taels, plus thirty million in exchange for forgoing Liaotung (an amount apparently more than twice Peking's annual revenues); and extensive Japanese commercial and industrial privileges in China.

Beyond the treaty itself as a measure of the disaster, the manner of the defeat shocked observers. Before the war many had thought that China was the stronger of the two countries, a view based on both her larger number of ships and her enormous size. The war revealed critical faults in organization and leadership. Worse still, it exposed a frivolous misuse of huge funds. Because of a lack of coordination among the varied armed forces of the empire, as well as the pattern of regional commands that had become pronounced since the Taiping Rebellion (a pattern repeated in the growing navy, which was divided into four separate fleets), the total national power was never mobilized; the Northern Army and Northern Fleet, two of Li Hung-chang's projects of modernization, bore the brunt of the fighting while other units were not used. The admiral in command of the Chinese task force, which had been expected to tip the balance in favor of victory, had not learned his lesson in tactics as well as had his Japanese opponent, though both fleets had had British instructors. A former cavalry officer, the admiral brought his ships out abreast, like a line of horses charging, while the Japanese circled about, finding their targets without being found themselves. Worse still, the admiral's flagship carried very few shells to fire from its main guns, and when one of the precious few hit the admiral's own bridge he was wounded too seriously to continue directing even the stolid plan of battle he had been following. In the cities rumors circulated that funds labeled for the navy had really been used to furnish the summer palace, outside Peking, for the empress dowager on her retirement. It was later shown to be true; thirty-six million taels earmarked for the navy had gone instead into the summer palace and the purses of the empress dowager's favorites. Indeed, the court had virtually ignored the navy in the years just before the war. Doubt grew concerning the regime's will to reform.

QUICKENING IMPERIALISM

Japan's victory quickened the pace at which European imperial powers enlarged their interests in China. Until the war the very size of China, as well as her state organization and her past achievements, had seemed an image of latent strength that it was better not to provoke too far. The Japanese victory showed, however, that the Chinese administration was virtually helpless and suggested that a breakup of the country might be expected. At the same time the European rivalries that had been at play around the borders seized upon China herself as a prize or, in the famous metaphor of the Chinese, as a melon to be cut up.

The more aggressive policies took the form of a "scramble for concessions," which were so varied and involved with each other that we shall mention only a few as illustrations. One profitable undertaking was loans, of which those negotiated just after the war were most important. It was imperative that China quickly pay off the indemnity imposed on her by the Treaty of Shimonoseki, but only borrowing could make this possible. The size of the sum involved attracted European bankers, especially as they and their governments, which supported the investment, considered such sources as the future revenues of the Chinese Imperial Maritime Customs strong security. At least one government, moreover, the Russian, which had led in the intervention to prevent Japan's taking Liaotung, saw a loan as strengthening her role as China's friend, a role that should lead to further advantages. In the three years following Shimonoseki, three bankers' groups, one Franco-Russian and the others mainly Anglo-German, lent China a nominal £47.8 million at terms favorable to themselves. With prior discounts, China actually received only £43.2 million yet would have to repay, counting principal and interest, a total of £102.4 million. The revenues of the Maritime Customs and certain other internal taxes were used to pay the debts, thus restricting a significant proportion of the government's expected revenue to unproductive purposes.

Another type of undertaking was the construction of railroads. Soon after the Franco-Russian loan Russia asked to build a railway across Manchuria to Vladivostok, a proposal that was tied to a secret Sino-Russian treaty of alliance against further Japanese expansion on the continent. The railway company, which Russia controlled, received rights of administration in the railway zone, including the right to station guards along the railway.

Another form of enterprise, still more clearly leading toward something beyond economic penetration, was the acquisition of a leasehold. Shortly after the German emperor had revealed to his cousin, the Russian Tsar, that he would like a base in China, two German priests were killed by bandits in a raid on a town in Shantung Province. A German naval squadron entered the bay of Kiaochow and demanded compensation. As a result, Germany acquired Kiaochow for ninety-nine years and rights of railway building and mining in Shantung.

These and other kinds of concessions shaped by 1898, the year of greatest activity, several "spheres of influence," in each of which one imperial power considered itself entitled to a monopoly of concessions. Russia took Manchuria as her sphere; Germany, Shantung; Great Britain, the Yangtze valley; and France, the territory abutting Vietnam. It was generally inferred that the spheres would become colonies of the Europeans as political events moved China toward disintegration. Not all the trading states welcomed the idea. Great Britain probably preferred the equality of trading opportunities provided by the original treaty system. The United States proposed, in the "Open Door" notes of 1899 and 1900, that in effect no power act against equal opportunities of trade. From about 1902, moreover, the European powers drew back from a form of competition that threatened to involve them in a war that they did not want, and the most virulent phase of imperialism waned, except in the policies of Japan and Russia. Yet to Chinese in the 1890s the encroaching powers represented a life-or-death crisis, and to the present day they have remained at the center of the patriots' dark image of imperialism.

THE RISE OF RADICAL REFORMERS

More than ever, events were demanding fresh thought, and for the first time a distinctive cast of mind, iconoclastic, radical, and nationalistic, seemed to grip a definite group of men. They were young literati, notably those just coming up for the examinations or just past them. Their most famous spokesman was K'ang Yu-wei (1858-1927). As a young man K'ang visited and was impressed by the foreign settlements at Hong Kong and Shanghai. He delved enthusiastically into reform, reading whatever he could find in translation about the West, without neglecting to prepare himself in the orthodox curriculum for the examinations. On one of several trips he made to Peking to compete in the highest examinations he began writing memorials on China's state of affairs, especially on reform and national security. At home in Canton he also opened a school to teach Western history and philosophy in addition to Confucian learning. In 1895, when he was again in Peking for the examinations (he passed them that year), he gained further recognition by leading 1,200 fellow candidates in submitting a memorial proposing that the peace treaty with the Japanese be rejected, the war carried on from a new capital inland, and reforms undertaken. By 1898 K'ang had come to the attention of some of the ranking members of the court as a proponent of vigorous reform.

Possibly the officials were not fully aware how radical K'ang's ideas were. A book by him had already been published arguing (with great persuasiveness at the time, though not today) that parts of the Classics were forgeries of the Wang Mang era (A.D. 9-23), not the legacy of the sages, as tradition said. The impact had been sharp enough to cause the burning of the printing blocks by officials the year before K'ang passed the capital examinations, but even bolder ideas were taking shape in his mind. He was convinced that Confucius had really written the Classics, not merely edited them, as was believed, in order to show that the ancient sages sanctioned his own ideas of reform. In short, the spirit of Confucianism was reform, making it possible for one like K'ang to advocate almost any change, keeping sacrosanct only the figure of Confucius as presiding spirit of the nation. K'ang published *Confucius as a Reformer* in 1897. Even more shocking was his vision of the ultimate goal of change, as contained in a work that was not published until the empire had fallen. The book was called *The Grand Unity,* and in it K'ang presented his theory that the world was moving by stages toward one great commonwealth of man. Eventually all barriers separating men into exclusive groups—classes, races, nations, and the like—would come down, leaving a vast, open community of equals. The book stood out as a turning point in Chinese intellectual history, for underlying its many interesting utopian ideas was the revolutionary notion of a human pattern of progress. The old idea of recurrent cycles was challenged, and the possibility, even the inevitability, of a future of continual change accepted.

In 1898, when the scramble for concessions produced an atmosphere of crisis in the court, K'ang Yu-wei suddenly was given an opportunity to put his ideas to work. A young emperor was on the throne, nominally ruling since the empress dowager had retired from the regency a few years earlier. In fact, she continued to assert herself in matters of appointment and other political affairs, so that loyalties remained divided and actual political authority was in doubt. The young emperor, inclined toward reform, accepted the recommendation of advisers whose motives in promoting K'ang were partly factional, in that they wished to establish their own reform group in distinction to that of the empress dowager, who was thought to have Li Hung-chang in her pocket. Yet more than factional favor separated the younger reformer from the older. At a meeting in which some of the highest officials interviewed K'ang, a grand secretary and Li Hung-chang pointed to what they regarded as of highest value, the age-old institutions and systems, considering them the framework of the civilization itself, and asserted that they could not be changed. K'ang answered that institutions and systems that could not preserve China deserved only to be abandoned. For the younger man it was more important to preserve the nation than the civilization.

Accordingly, it was not wholly surprising (though the older ministers were apparently shocked) when K'ang recommended and the emperor ordered a sweeping list of reforms. In a period called the "Hundred Days," during the summer of 1898, edicts called for a new school and examination system, modernization of the armed forces, and official encouragement of a range of scientific, industrial, and commercial projects. The succession of imperial commands for change no doubt gave heart to many of the young, but it also disturbed or at least puzzled a number of officials, who felt their accustomed ways threatened and could not make out the shape of the future. Like some previous reformers, K'ang proved a fertile source of ideas but a poor judge of the organization he would need and the political opposition he would face. The empress dowager, seeing her hold on power and money about to be broken, rallied her followers, including military forces, and resumed the regency. The emperor was confined for the remaining years of his life. K'ang Yu-wei fled, with British help, to Hong Kong and a colleague, with Japanese help, to

Tokyo. Six others of those who had risen with K'ang were put to death. In retrospect, it seems unlikely that they could have unified and inspired a court long caught in a web of contending factions. Yet the Hundred Days brought to light a feeling for change revolutionary in its cultural implications.

PROGRESS AS THE LAST RESORT OF THE CH'ING

The Hundred Days jarred the dominant conservatives more by its extremism than by its advocacy of change, for change was more than ever in the air. The "self-strengthening" approach, though discredited in the eyes of the radicals by the debacle of the war, remained alive. Although Li Hung-chang might be eclipsed, other conservative reformers became prominent, chief among them Chang Chih-tung (1837-1909), who as governor of several regions introduced arsenals, railroads, mines, and new disciplines and techniques with such competence that he seemed yet another proof of the adequacy of Confucian leadership. Moreover, his erudition made him a spokesman for enlightened conservatism, which he summed up in the slogan, "Chinese learning for principles, Western learning for instruments," a balanced formulation that was elegant in theory even though it was a poor description of what actually happened. Besides Chang and other high officials, the proponents of reform seemed to be growing more numerous in certain provincial places, such as the capital of Hunan Province, where leading families cooperated with officials in forming study societies, patronizing modern journals, and contributing to city improvements.

While the central government generally supported or acquiesced in this, it did so with misgivings and, in the hearts of many of its members, hostility. When the reaction to the radical reformers of the Hundred Days strengthened some of the most conservative voices in the court, they urged one last violent defiance of the foreign enemies who had so interrupted the accustomed ways. The occasion was the rise of a rebellious movement among peasants, beginning with a society called the Boxers, an English approximation of "Boxing for Righteousness and Harmony," which was the name of a cult involving calisthenics for achieving oneness with the cosmic forces and thus becoming indomitable. The Boxers, an old organization, apparently provided the spiritual program and leadership to focus grievances that were by then widespread among a suffering and upset farming population, and armed actions were first reported in the northern provinces in 1898. The Boxers' targets at first were two: the dynasty, which was the usual target of important rebellions, and the Christian community, which was stigmatized as an alien element. Reactionary officials in some of the northern provinces encouraged the rebels, turning their anger away from the dynasty and against the foreigners. In other parts of the north and in the south more enlightened officials kept the rebels under control, knowing the futility of thinking that the foreigners could so easily be driven out. By 1900 the Boxers had seized Peking, where opinion was also divided, although dominated by reactionaries who thought the chance to throw out the foreigners had come. The court declared war on the foreigners and sent some of its forces to assist the Boxers in their siege of the legation quarter, while simultaneously officials in the provinces, cooler heads of the type of Li Hung-chang and Chang Chih-tung, tried to gloss over Peking's blunder and keep the crisis contained there. Late in the summer an international force including Japanese, Russian, British, American, German, and other troops reached Peking from the coast and lifted the siege. With the empress dowager and her entourage on a "western tour," as her flight inland was called, and the foreigners plundering Peking and other northern cities, the task of settlement was given to old Li Hung-chang, who saw an agreement signed in 1901, two months before he died. Among other things, it provided for foreign garrisons and fortifications in the legation quarter and along the way to Peking from the sea, the punishment of scores of officials, and another enormous indemnity.

When the desperate gamble on the Boxer movement failed, the Manchus seemed to realize at last how dangerous their position was, in relation to both foreign powers and the most competent Chinese officials,who saw no salvation but in reform. The empress dowager proclaimed that the government would adopt the features that gave strength to foreign countries, implying, as events later showed, extensive and radical changes. Ironically, the reforms resembled those with which a few years earlier K'ang Yu-wei had shocked many of their present proponents. Moreover, many specific measures, beginning with the empress dowager's statement, resembled what Japan, recently resented as an enemy, had done earlier, for Japan's victory in the war had not only angered the Chinese but had also impressed many of them as proof of her ability to domesticate the methods of the West. In the last decade of the dynasty the Ch'ing saw reform as the only way to retain the Mandate of Heaven.

In the broadest sense, all the innovations were intended to make the state stronger and wealthier. Some, such as those affecting administration, would work directly. Piecemeal changes began, for example, in the organization of offices, with new agencies created to take over gradually the functions of older ones and, presumably, perform them better, that is, carry out more effectively the policies laid down in the highest councils. Between 1901 and 1906 a number of new ministries were established, combining some of the traditional categories such as Rites, Civil Appointments, and War, with some new ones, such as Foreign Affairs, Internal Affairs, and Education. Experiments were conducted in fiscal administration and plans for furrher changes drawn up, chiefly to bring revenues more fully under central control. For years a bureau worked to write a new code of law in closer conformity with Western standards. (One argument for imposing the principle of extraterritoriality in the treaties had been the capriciousness of Chinese justice.)

To a remarkable degree, the reforms touched on themes that would be important in twentieth-century China long after the Manchus were gone. One such theme was constitutionalism and popular representation, for example; the empress dowager proclaimed in 1906 that the state would in due course adopt a constitution. At first glance it may not seem that a constitutional government, in which some form of representative assembly was implied, would strengthen the ruling house, which had always asserted its undivided political authority; but the times were so dangerous that to continue ruling at all required modifying the age-old pattern. More effective central control over the whole country was required, for instance, yet in moving in that direction, the court seemed to be overreaching and intruding on traditional local interests. The feeling was all the stronger in a time when many innovations, especially new economic enterprises, had been begun by regional officials and unofficial leaders, notably a growing class of entrepreneurs who in response to the times had devoted themselves to economic development. Moreover, patriotism was a growing force among some groups, as in 1905, when merchants and students in most of the treaty ports joined in a boycott of trade with the United States, in protest against an American policy excluding immigration of Chinese laborers. The Ch'ing councils recognized a need to wed these interests and feelings to the court and here as elsewhere took Japan as a model.

Japan's prestige as the pioneer of Asian modernization had just grown to heroic size as a result of the Russo-Japanese War (1904-05). The conflict was over a sphere of influence claimed by the two imperialist states, Japan insisting on exclusive rights in Korea and the development of her interests in Manchuria, Russia determined to expand her activities in Manchuria and even probing Korea. When Russia rejected a Japanese proposal to divide the zone, Japanese forces attacked Russian bases in Manchuria and in the following months won a victory that appeared comparable with that over China ten years earlier. The Russian navy, part of which had sailed halfway around the world from the Baltic Sea to reach the scene, was almost wholly destroyed. Russian armies retreated in Manchuria (while taking a toll of the Japanese, it is true). The peace treaty (Portsmouth, 1905) left no doubt that Japan had won. The Russians recognized the paramountcy of Japan in Korea (which she formally annexed five years later). Japan received the Russian rights (leaseholds and a railway) in South Manchuria and the southern half of the island of Sakhalin.

The impact of the Japanese victory was far greater in the East than in the West, which saw its importance as contained in the fact that a small, energetic nation had beaten a large, disunited one. To Asians it meant that an Oriental nation had beaten a European, a message that excited patriots everywhere, not least in China, despite the fact that the war had been fought in and for control of a part of China regardless of Chinese wishes. The aroused patriots in turn added to the anxiety of the Ch'ing governors, for of course the helplessness of the government during the war had not increased popular respect for it. Under the circumstances, the official mission that visited Japan in 1906 to inquire about constitutional government welcomed the message of Itō Hirobumi, the father of the Meiji Constitution. He told the visitors that a constitution and the wider discussion of state issues it implied could strengthen the state, assuming that sovereign power remained entirely with the emperor. Coming from one of the great figures of a state that had enjoyed triumphant success in modernization the message carried weight, the more so since it promised to strengthen, rather than weaken, the dynasty. The subsequent announcement by the empress dowager, promising a constitution, quickened one of the major movements of Chinese life in the twentieth century, the popularization of political issues.

Another development in the twentieth century stemming partly from the Ch'ing reforms was a greater political role for military leaders. We have already noted the growth of relatively self-sustained leaders with separate, loyal military organizations in the face of the Taiping threat. Those leaders, holding strong Confucian convictions, devoted themselves to the legitimate ruler, often contributing to the decisions he made, and occasionally finding loyalty no obstacle to personal profit. It was only in the light of the experience of previous weakened dynasties that the relinquishing of so much military and political authority seemed ominous. Japan's victory in 1894-95 stimulated a new effort to build modern armies, the most notable of which was a new imperial army, later called the Northern (Peiyang) Army. The Northern Army became important of itself in the period of the reforms, as it was built into the single strongest military force in China, including perhaps 60,000 men trained to modern standards. It was also important in the following years because of its leader and his officers.

The army was the instrument of one man, Yuan Shih-k'ai (1859-1916). Through his distinguished family and his own aggressive capacity for military organization, Yuan had risen in the esteem of Li Hung-chang and was put in charge of promoting the Chinese interest in Seoul in the decade before Japan settled the Korean issue by warfare. He then was appointed to build the new army and, always rising in honors and influence (it was widely believed that he betrayed the emperor at the end of the Hundred Days by siding with the empress dowager), he became, as his patron Li Hung-chang and other self-strengtheners of the preceding generation died, the most powerful executive of moderate reform—an executive, however, who understood military expansion better than other kinds of reform.

His officers supplied the cohesiveness that made his army powerful, for as protégés they were all loyal to him, much as the officers of the earlier self-strengtheners had been. Moreover, they stood to inherit some of his power when he had passed from the scene, so that he was to be known later as the "father of warlords." In a more general sense he furthered military vitality by establishing military schools. It was widely recognized that the ineffectiveness of Chinese armies against modern enemies could be blamed largely on incompetent officers. The academies founded by Yuan and others not only began to correct that fault, but did more: they became an avenue of advancement newly attractive to young men who were vigorous, ambitious, and patriotic. When some of these men went to Japan for additional training and imbibed the spirit of military patriotism there, they returned to make the soldier a greater force in Chinese life.

The Ch'ing reforms hastened the growth of another force in

modern Chinese life, the new intellectual. The leaders considered education to be the key to all their hopes, in the manner of the famous reformers of the past. It was decided to establish a system of schools at different administrative levels, from the district up, much as had been done in previous times and with the same primary aim of preparing students to be officials. There were important differences, however. The new schools would be centers of systematic teaching and learning, not merely ceremonial and registration centers; the curriculum would combine Chinese and Western subjects; and graduates would be qualified for office side by side with those who took the examinations, which would be continued in modified form for the time being. To begin with, the system could count on the Imperial University in Peking (later National Peking University), one of the surviving innovations of the Hundred Days, and a number of academies, which had been subsidized and could be converted to the the new use. Beyond these and the experimental schools founded by progressive governors, almost everything else necessary—teachers, books, and buildings—was lacking and could be acquired only slowly.

Despite energetic efforts along the new lines, learning in the old style and the familiar preparation for the examinations remained the more popular. The traditional education persisted for various reasons, from the elementary fact of its being deeply rooted as the true and good learning in the minds of the majority, which was not yet disillusioned with it, to its practical convenience, in its reliance on tutorial or independent study, in contrast to the rigid schedules of schools. Whatever the considerations that held the many to it, the reformers decided that the modern schools would not receive the students and public support they wanted unless the alternative of the examination system was abolished. They made known their decision to do so through an edict in 1905. So changeable had every system begun to seem, that the end of one more stirred no cry of outrage, but few others meant so much to the traditional order. For all its faults and the criticisms made of it, the examination system had been a channel for the ambitions and ideals of millions. Abandoning it removed an effective institution of unity.

At the same time that the government relinquished the ancient system many students were entering a new mental world. It was represented in the Western curriculum in the new schools but in an even broader sense was opened up through translations of Western books. Some of these were works of synthesis and theory, the most notable translator of which was Yen Fu (1853-1921), who gave Chinese readers the ideas of Herbert Spencer (*A Study of Sociology*), T. H. Huxley (*Evolution and Ethics*), Adam Smith (*Wealth of Nations*), and others. He also transmitted to his readers, through his interpretations and commentaries, his own understanding that the achievement of the great Western ideas had been to produce strong nations—that national wealth and power were the ends toward which Western values worked. Not all Western books becoming available to Chinese readers were so learned, but they probably played a part in establishing the imaginative and emotional qualities of the new intellectuals. Fiction, for example, became available notably through the translations of Lin Shu (1852-1924), a master of classical Chinese style who, knowing no language other than Chinese, listened to oral translations by assistants and produced polished written versions. These, it has been said, could not have been so elegant as they were had Lin Shu not taken great liberties with the originals; but probably they also would not have been so popular, and no doubt the story line got through. This was significant for the new taste, for of the 180 titles he published before his death, a large proportion was devoted to works of adventure and romance, two subjects that seemed to liberate the spirit of the rising generation.

A particularly fertile ground for stimulating new attitudes was Japan. Her proximity, the Western knowledge she had already acquired, and the connection of her written language and customs with China's, as well as the sympathy of many Japanese for the Chinese reformers' aims, made Japan a convenient place for training students. By 1907, between 8,000 and 10,000 young Chinese had gone there, with more to follow. These were all young men who in earlier days would have prepared for the classical examinations and now were thrown into a swiftly changing world. It is not likely that the major influences on them came through formal training, for only a minority of the students gained admission to the major Japanese universities; most of them took short courses or special programs at smaller institutions not known for impressive scholarship. Yet the atmosphere and examples of change were all around them.

THE RUNNING OF THE REVOLUTIONARY TIDE

In retrospect it is clear that a more extreme force than anything anticipated in the reforms had begun to grow. Hardly a step of the reformers failed to call forth condemnation by someone. The constitutional movement, for example, was criticized by provincial leaders for the delay in convening promised consultative provincial assemblies, and when at last these were established they in turn pressed for a parliament stronger than the Ch'ing had envisaged. The court, especially after the death of the empress dowager in 1908, seemed to invite doubt of its own good intentions, as when it named a cabinet so heavily weighted with Manchus that even moderate Chinese took offense.

The evidence of a feeling running beyond the control of the Ch'ing dynasty was clearest in Japan. There the commanding intellectual figure for a time was Liang Ch'i-ch'ao (1873-1929), the pupil and assistant of K'ang Yu-wei. After the failure of the Hundred Days, Liang had fled to Japan, where for the following decade he promoted his ideas through journals and political societies. Widely learned and an influential stylist, he spread ideas as revolutionary by implication as some of those in Yen Fu's work, among them the idea of history as a progress toward a better condition; the notion of Social Darwinism, that human society evolves through the struggles of nations and "the survival of the fittest"; and the idea that the Chinese people must renew themselves, dedicating themselves to the interests of the nation. Yet, for all the impact of his theories, Liang spoke too softly for some of his young readers, for he was not disposed to dwell on political revolution.

The radical but relatively reasoned and complicated reformism of a Liang Ch'i-ch'ao was challenged by a fervent and simple cry demanding that the Manchus be turned out. The primary obstacle to solving China's problems was, in the minds of the revolutionaries, the rule of what was described as an inherently evil and inferior people. As to what lay beyond the overthrow of the government, there was general agreement that a constitutional republic was to take its place, and possibly a sense that the young students would be the tutors of the new Chinese democracy. The more complicated issues in the achievement of these goals, though recognized in general terms, gave less pleasure for the moment than the thought of the revolutionary confrontation itself.

X

The Revolutionary

Period: The Contest

for Primacy

The Revolution of 1911

The history of China in the twentieth century has about it an air of special moment, or elemental consequence, as if the almost uninterrupted conflict that is its main theme signified something different from the similar turmoil suffered by the rest of the non-European world. The feeling partly reflects the image expressed by Napoleon when he called China a "sleeping giant": the giant in the twentieth century seemed to be stirring; in some unknown future day it might shake the world. It also reflects, at least in the minds of students of China, a recognition that one of the greatest civilizations of the world was beginning to change fundamentally, to change not simply by growing or evolving naturally but by being transformed under pressure from outside. The Chinese revolution—that is, the whole process that began at least as early as the first decade of the twentieth century and continues today—holds our attention through the extent of the change involved. Much of the remainder of our account will be devoted to the steps of the change. Yet we hope not to lose sight altogether of the native ground of tradition on which those steps were taken. It is difficult to do this, for the main actors in the drama are all revolutionaries, or say they are revolutionaries. Some of them, moreover, are fond of describing the Chinese as a "clean slate" on which the formulas of modernity can be readily inscribed. The Chinese, though, even if unmarked by the slogans of our day, bore the graffiti of centuries. They could be marked over, or additionally marked, but not marked for the first time. The revolution will come into truer perspective if it is seen as a compound of the old and the new.

THE REVOLUTIONARY SETTING

In the first major event of the revolutionary period, the overthrow of the Ch'ing dynasty in the Revolution of 1911, the element of the old was apparent in the setting, which resembled that in which earlier dynasties had met their ends. Rebellious groups proliferated, most of them, but not all, independent of one another. Not only in Japan, as discussed elsewhere, but in China itself, there were groups ready to take up arms, some of them secret societies, like the Triad Society, combining vague doctrinal opposition to the Manchus with concrete grievances or interests; others associations of literati engaged in propaganda for modern change. In schools, most openly in the treaty ports, students formed revolutionary societies. In garrisons there were revolutionary army officers, many of whom had developed their views in the course of a stay in Japan. While peasant rebellions, the classical symptom of decline, were for the moment inconspicuous, widespread riots, some involving tens of thousands of people who stormed granaries and attacked tax collectors, warned that popular rebellion was not far below the surface.

When the climax finally came, it had the appearance of that massive spontaneity that was supposed to accompany the withdrawal of the Mandate of Heaven. In October, 1911, fighting broke out between the military and groups of the population in Szechwan, where subscribers to a provincial railroad company bitterly opposed a decision of Peking to take over the nation's railroad projects. As the insurrection continued, an accidental explosion in a house far away in the Russian Concession in Wuhan, along the Yangtze in Hupei, disclosed the hiding place of an arsenal of guns and ammunition stored by a revolutionary society with headquarters in Japan. It also exposed a list of local members, many of whom were officers of the garrison. They quickly decided that only one course of action remained open, and they took it, occupying the provincial capital. The date of the hasty step was October 10, celebrated by Nationalists since then as the birthday of the revolution, the Double Tenth (the tenth day of the tenth month). Within two months similar revolts broke out in all but a few of the major provinces, young officers often taking the initiative and receiving the support of the provincial assembly.

The response of the Ch'ing court resembled that of other dynasties in similar circumstances. In several ways it faltered in enforcing its authority (hesitation in suppressing the Szechwanese uprising was only one instance), which gave confidence to the revolutionaries. One of them wrote in a moment of exhilaration, "Expelling the Manchus [will be] like killing chickens."[1] Also like other degenerate dynasties, the Ch'ing turned as a last resort to its strongest general, who was Yuan Shih-k'ai (1859-1916). Finding himself in a position like that of Ts'ao Ts'ao at the end of the Later Han, Yuan Shih-k'ai realized that his armies were stronger than his bonds of loyalty. He decided to replace the dynasty, rather than save it.

If hesitating to meet the challenge of would-be revolutionaries and then relying excessively on an overpowerful general resembled the

---

1. See Chün-tu Hsüeh, *Huang Hsing and the Chinese Revolution* (Stanford University Press, 1961), p. 19.

familiar steps of aging dynasties earlier, there were other elements that distinguished the situation from earlier revolutions. Among many groups, rich and poor, there was apparently a hatred of the Manchus, again seen as aliens despite their two and a half centuries of rule in Peking and, among some who were disturbed by the changes of modern times, a hatred of other foreigners. True, this was not wholly new. The Chinese had hated foreign rulers before, and the hostility against the Manchu invaders in the seventeenth century had only been driven deeply underground, never completely dispelled. Yet there was something new in the concept with which an important minority of Chinese—mainly young students, young officers, and Westernized Chinese in treaty ports and abroad—opposed the foreigners. That was pride in China as a nation, the feeling that membership in this nation rather than, as before, loyalty to the emperor, or participation in the traditional way of life, created a distinctive social solidarity. Patriotism in this sense was probably new, at least as a relatively intense feeling. It was symbolized by the growing currency of the term "the Han people" or "the Han race," meaning narrowly the Chinese as opposed to the Manchus, and connoting more broadly some special virtue that distinguished the Chinese from everyone else. Many actions were justified by the need to save the nation.

There were new ideas about the good life for this nation, all of them owing much to the West and requiring great changes in Chinese ways if they were to be realized. The most comprehensive slogan was perhaps expressed in the call for "wealth and power," an old formula put to new use. It had been associated with the Legalist Ch'in state in classical sources, the activist Wang An-shih in the period of Sung reforms, and the recent Japanese reformers—a list suggestive of the new direction Chinese envisaged for their country. The young revolutionaries, especially the students, also experimented intellectually with such new concepts or doctrines as democracy, socialism, and anarchism, all of which repudiated in theory the age-old Chinese despotism—even though the young advocates, being lovers of their country as well as revolutionaries, preferred to believe that some of their new ideas had been known in ancient China. In short, aims and ideals were expressed that would not be attained simply by replacing the Ch'ing with a fresh ruling house. Also new was the fact that groups professing these ideas were at work in many different places—in schools, the army, treaty ports, and abroad. Probably never before had revolutionary organizations spread so widely in their preliminary efforts to disrupt the state.

SUN YAT-SEN AND HIS ORGANIZATION

Eventually one man, Sun Yat-sen (1866-1925), rose above all others in these organizations as the leader of the revolution, the "Father of the Country." In his person and his methods he illustrated that mixture of the old and the new that so often appeared at this time. He was born in a village near Canton, where his father was a farmer, and spent his boyhood amidst relatives, one of whom, an uncle, taught him and other boys of the village a little reading and writing. This, moreover, was no ordinary uncle; he had fought for the Taipings. In stories that Sun heard from him, Hung Hsiu-ch'üan appeared as a great hero of action. In other stories, Sun learned of marvelous California and its gold, for the village, placed as it was between Canton and Macao, the old point of contact with Westerners, was in the region from which many Chinese emigrated overseas. Thus, an early sense of heroism, adventure, and opportunity in the outside world may have helped to shape his character.

Direct Western influences began to take effect when he was thirteen. He was sent off to his elder brother, who had gone earlier to Hawaii, perhaps among the indentured laborers sought for the sugar plantations in those days. Apparently successful enough to have his own piece of land and a small general store, the elder brother sent Sun to a school maintained by the Anglican church. Sun thrived in the atmosphere, which must have been largely one of confidence, order, and progress. He earned a place in the choir, developed a high regard for Christianity, and on graduation day took the second prize in English grammar. Eventually his native zeal carried him beyond his family's modest economic ambitions for him, as he revealed when he began admonishing his brother against keeping pagan idols and, shipped home, began breaking idols there. Measured against the career of his Taiping hero, he was already on the way to becoming a rebel. He studied further, in Hong Kong and Canton, and earned a medical degree from a British mission hospital. The practice of medicine was one of the more popular careers envisaged by young men who wanted to help China at that time. For Sun as for some others, however, the rescue of China meant more than healing the sick. He practiced for a few years, but his mind was already intent on revolution.

In 1895 Sun was twenty-nine. It was the year in which the weakness of the Manchu government was marked by the humiliating conclusion of the Sino-Japanese War and in which Sun struck his first blow. In several ways the first effort typified Sun's practice of revolution. The core of his organization was the *Hsing-Chung hui,* founded November 24, 1894, in part a secret society though less vulnerable to attack by the Ch'ing administration, as it had branches in such sanctuaries as Hong Kong and Hawaii. Its members swore loyalty to each other as brothers. Its strategy was to seize control of one spot in China and move on from there, reinforced by others who had been inspired by its example to take action. As its first target, the society chose the offices of the provincial government in Canton. Sun and his fellow revolutionaries organized a "Scientific Agricultural Association" in the city and opened a shop in Hong Kong, the former a front for the headquarters, the latter a center for purchasing arms and enlisting fighters. The preparations had to be abandoned prematurely, however, when the Maritime Customs at Canton discovered that a shipment of casks labeled cement contained in fact six hundred pistols. Sun and other leaders went into hiding shortly before authorities raided the headquarters, arresting dozens of men, of whom a few were put to death later. A price on his head, Sun fled via Macao and Hong Kong to Japan. The conspiracy at Canton was the first of ten famous attempts to foment revolution before the successful, if partly accidental, rising of the Double Tenth in 1911. In all of them, a small group of revolutionary plotters organized armed men (some acquired through secret societies, some hired for the occasion) to capture local offices of government, on the theory that this would set off more attacks or would provide a local base from which to expand the revolution.

Yet the relatively familiar methods of conspiracy and revolt were not the only elements of Sun's style. There were novelties as well, beginning with the nature of his following. Many of the leading members of his society were young, partly westernized nationalists like himself. Most opinion and money supporting his society's actions came from groups touched by Western values—the new Chinese businessmen in the treaty ports, for example, and even more the communities of Chinese overseas. Sun spent much of his time before the revolution in Honolulu, Singapore, San Francisco, and London, "everywhere preaching that to save our mother-country from threatening destruction we must overthrow the [Ch'ing] dynasty, and that the duty of every Chinese citizen was to help to reconstruct China on a new democratic basis."[2] From more complicated motives Japanese patriots and behind them sometimes the Japanese government also supported Sun, reasoning that a progressive revolution in China would help keep back the white imperial powers.

Effective support did not come readily at first, partly because the ineptness and failure of one rising after another eroded confidence, and partly because Sun was only one among many promising to save the country. Among the others the most important was Liang Ch'i-ch'ao, for his writings in favor of reform were accepted as authoritative by a large number of Chinese students in Japan as well as Chinese overseas elsewhere. Further innovations in Sun's movement followed from attempts to overcome this rivalry. First, one of the Japanese patriots who had befriended Sun brought him together with other leaders of revolutionary societies in Tokyo. The Chinese agreed in 1905 to combine their forces into a new League of Common Alliance (*T'ung-meng hui*), with Sun as its head and an initial membership of about a thousand men, the largest revolutionary group yet. Revolutionary planning and coordination were begun in China itself, where agents of the League enlisted support among many groups and sought ways to disrupt the administration.

Second, Sun and his associates developed an ideology and a program in response to the growing revolutionary fervor among students. The immediate impact of these theoretical statements may be better understood by remembering their context, which was the bitter rivalry between the reformers, whose champion was Liang Ch'i-ch'ao, and the revolutionaries. Liang argued generally, perhaps out of a remainder of Confucian loyalty and ecumenism as well as a belief in necessary evolution which he had acquired from reading Western theorists, that the Manchu dynasty need not and ought not be brought down. Sun and the revolutionaries answered that the Manchus were an evil race whose rule was incompatible with Chinese independence and salvation. Liang proposed a constitutional monarchy as suitable for China's stage of political development. Sun answered that, rather, a constitutional republic was appropriate, as China already had a democratic spirit. Liang felt that the laws of evolution demanded that all change come gradually; Sun answered with the idea of a great leap forward. However weak the reason of some of the answers may seem

2. Sun Yat-sen, *Memoirs of a Chinese Revolutionary* (Taipei, China Cultural Service, 1953), p. 147.

today, their apparent success in their time indicated that a spirit of revolutionary faith had seized many students.

THE THREE PRINCIPLES OF THE PEOPLE (*San min chu-i*)

In 1905 and 1906 some of these attitudes were put in the form of declarations of the League of Common Alliance. They became known as the Three Principles of the People and, after revisions in a later decade, were widely promoted as the doctrine of the revolution. The first principle, Nationalism, required the overthrow of the Manchu government to relieve a subjugation that was painful to the Chinese. The new nationalism thus demanded government by Chinese, not merely by a sinified ruling house, as had been accepted in the form of the Manchus for two and a half centuries. The second principle, Republicanism, aimed at the establishment of a constitutional democracy. The entire discussion of this principle turned on Western political terms, such as autocracy, republicanism, aristocracy, and democracy; but China was considered prepared for democracy, once the Manchus had been overthrown, as among her own people she had no distinctions of class. The third principle, the People's Livelihood, seems to have been meant to show the concern of the League for an equitable material welfare for all. Specifically it stressed, in the statement of 1905, an "Equalization of Land Rights," which was an adaptation of an idea, then popular in the West, of the appropriation by the state of future increases in the value of land, the revenue to be used for the common welfare. This "single tax" proposal, drawn from the ideas of the American economist Henry George, was inspired by the rise of urban land values in the industrializing West and the concurrent abuses of speculators. Since the proposal could have only marginal relevance to the Chinese economy, the major issue of which was the condition of farmers, not the plight of the cities, the incongruity showed that Sun had not arrived at any revolutionary economic program, even though he was tending toward thoughts of state control or socialism. The statement of 1906, which was written by a colleague and endorsed by Sun, presented a much more radical proposal for state control of land, but the true position of the League remained vague. The point on which there was unanimous agreement was that China must be made a wealthy and powerful nation. If the leaders spoke more of state control than of private enterprise, the Chinese tradition that equated the former with the public interest and the latter with selfish aggrandizement probably influenced their thinking. On the whole, however, the Three Principles of the People reflected the language and ideas of the West.

THE THREE STAGES OF REVOLUTION

Attacking further the argument that only gradual change could strengthen China, Sun also presented in 1905 a program for moving rapidly to political democracy. He divided the revolution into three stages, of which the first was to be a period of martial law, under which the evil old systems and customs would be destroyed, and the third was to be the period of constitutional government, marking the success of the revolution. The middle period was the key to the program, for it met the argument of Liang Ch'i-ch'ao that China was not ready for democracy. It provided for a phase of provisional constitutionalism under which the people would be trained locally in self-government. The period of political tutelage, as Sun called it later, was to last for the successful districts only six years. By training, Sun was saying, the patterns set by millennia of absolutism could be quickly erased and the slow evolution described by Liang Ch'i-ch'ao, with his call for an "enlightened despotism," made unnecessary.

The ardor and visionary optimism represented by this were apparently more attractive to many students than the more controlled proposals of Liang Ch'i-ch'ao, for the League of Common Alliance grew, even though it remained a secret society in form. Military students were important among its new members. One young cadet who joined in Tokyo in 1908 was Chiang Kai-shek. A new revolutionary energy also seemed to be generated, in the form of more recruitment in China proper and at least one relatively new disruptive technique, that of political assassination.

Another young man who would figure later in the revolution, Wang Ching-wei, tried to assassinate the prince regent in Peking in 1910. He failed and was put in jail. Indeed the heightened activity of the League was signalized by its failures. Plot after plot collapsed from contradictory orders, premature exposure, or futility. Financial backers overseas cut their donations, and the leaders argued over tactics. On the Double Tenth, as the exposed revolutionary officers rose in Wuhan, Sun himself was literally out of touch with the action. He was traveling again in western America in search of funds and first learned of the rising in a Denver newspaper. Well may he have wondered then whether in promoting the revolution he had not mounted a wayward tiger.

THE REVOLUTION AND YUAN SHIH-K'AI

As accumulated grievances and frustrations burst out in rebellion against Ch'ing authority across the country, two new centers of power appeared. They cooperated on the immediate purpose, the overthrow of the Manchus, but split on everything after that, leading China into its deepest trough of disunity in centuries. One of the new centers of power was in Nanking, where the League of Common Alliance and other leaders of the provincial rebellions established a provisional government. Almost from the first, the leaders sparred for status, even while the future of the movement was imperiled by a lack of agreement on plans, a shortage of funds, and doubts about its strength in the face of still-formidable imperial armies. Yet the symbols of unity and success were established. Sun Yat-sen returned and was elected provisional president of the Chinese Republic, taking office formally on New Year's Day, 1912. At the same time, the government adopted the 365-day Western calendar, a symbolic step away from the past, but retained the old system of counting years from the start of a reign-era, calling 1912 "Year One of the Republic." In the summer of the same year the League of Common Alliance, under the influence of Sung Chiao-jen, the firmest advocate of parliamentarianism among Sun's associates, was reorganized to be less a secret society and more an open political party appealing to public opinion. It took the name Kuomintang, or Nationalist Party. By that time the Manchus were out of the way, but the new Republic was proving less effective and more violent.

The second new center of power at the height of the rebellions was the Garden for Cultivating Longevity, a villa at which Yuan Shih-k'ai was spending a few years of ostensible retirement. His protégés, who continued to hold important offices in government, kept in touch with him, the more easily as his villa was on a railway line to Peking. The Northern Army, the most powerful army in the country, remained under officers loyal to him. Yuan might appear the model of the recluse, sipping wine with visitors and writing bucolic poetry, but everyone in the court and among the revolutionaries knew that the outcome of the national crisis would depend very much on how and when Yuan used his power.

Yuan knew it as well, and temporized until conditions should favor him. To one of his generals, commanded by the court to march against the rebels, he said only, "Go slowly and wait and see." To the first messengers from the court, ordering him back into office, he replied that his foot was ailing—an ancient pretext for avoiding service. To agents of the revolutionaries, who sought him out as soon as the risings began, he expressed interest in cooperating, if the terms were right, but promised nothing. Sun Yat-sen made the revolutionaries' hopes clear when he offered to resign the provisional presidency if Yuan would take his place as head of the Republic. In the meantime Yuan had returned to office under the Manchus, as premier and commander of the armies. From that position he negotiated with both sides, allowing his armies to occupy some favorable new position or to appear to be checked, whichever reinforced his argument of the moment. In the end he had his way in everything. The boy-emperor abdicated (1912), having been promised a comfortable stipend, and empowered Yuan Shih-k'ai to organize a provisional republican government. Sun Yat-sen resigned as provisional president and Yuan took his place. (Sun, though he was, like many republicans, too ready to believe that principles could be quickly realized, was aware of the danger that Yuan might manipulate events to suit himself. This is evident in his complaint against the Edict of Abdication, which gave full powers to Yuan and did not recognize the Nanking government. Yet no one else gave this great weight. The fall of the Manchus had so inflated the republicans' hopes that their telegram to Peking hailed Yuan as "the Washington of the Republic.") The inauguration awaited only his going to the revolutionaries' capital, Nanking, a journey that would symbolize his embrace of republicanism.

Yet Yuan, far from dreaming of a new age of the people, assumed that leadership meant sovereignty. He demonstrated the limits of his understanding of the new political currents when he said, "The only possible difference [between a president and an emperor] lies in the succession." As events required him to shape his government, he moved toward the form most congenial to him by reason of experience and belief—a monarchy to succeed the one whose mandate he had inherited, modified by the products of self-strengthening and the outward forms of constitutionalism, and based squarely on armed force. In the process he applied his power so ruthlessly that he embittered all the revolutionaries and strengthened a trend towards strong-arm methods in politics.

THE ROUT OF THE REVOLUTIONARIES

Hardly had Yuan been elected provisional president before he began to weaken those who had elected him. He wired that it was difficult to go to Nanking for the inauguration because the restlessness of the north required his firm hand, and a mutiny among the troops—

all commanded by loyal followers of Yuan—broke out as if to emphasize his point. The revolutionary leaders agreed that Peking should be the capital. Yuan in turn agreed to uphold the constitution that the revolutionary senate was preparing, but swore allegiance to it without knowing what was in it, an act that did not say much for the weight of the document. He appointed as premier a protégé who formed a cabinet in which a majority, those whose posts were closest to power and money, consisted of men Yuan could control. The revolutionary minority, including the premier, feeling themselves continually thwarted, resigned within four months. Even so, Yuan was not prepared to move too openly against the revolutionaries. He entertained Sun Yat-sen lavishly during a month of conferences. Since Yuan had become president, Sun seemed to feel that the first two of his People's Principles, Nationalism and Republicanism, had been effected. He quixotically emphasized that his remaining mission was the third principle, the People's Livelihood, and apparently was delighted when Yuan appointed him head of railway development, with the task not only of making plans for a national system but also of finding the money to build it. As Sun left he said that he found himself in almost complete accord with the president's views.

It was an optimistic judgment, to say the least. On every practical level, Yuan moved to weaken the Kuomintang. Soon after Sun left Peking, Yuan, aiming at harassment of the Kuomintang, banned local secret organizations. He began to appoint to each province in which he had support a military governor, loyal of course to him, as chief official. When a potentially troublesome opposition appeared in the form of a Kuomintang majority in a new parliament, elected early in 1913 on a very narrow franchise, Yuan permitted more direct methods of assault. Sung Chiao-jen, the parliamentarian who led the Kuomintang campaign in the successful election and demanded a party cabinet, was shot to death in a railroad station by a hoodlum. Police investigations revealed that the assassin had extraordinary connections with the very top level of government. The Kuomintang members of the new parliament were bribed or threatened, and numbers of them left the party. At last, in the summer of 1913, as Yuan attempted to replace military governors supporting the Kuomintang in the south and central provinces, seven provincial governments took up arms in what they called a Second Revolution. Poorly planned and led, and lacking any such wide support as the revolution against the Manchus, it collapsed in two months. Sun and his comrades fled to Japan, Sun embittered and demoralized. Once again the Kuomintang was without an effective base or organization in China. By early 1914 Yuan had suspended the parliament and begun to rule openly as an autocrat.

INTIMATIONS OF THE PROBLEMS OF THE REVOLUTION

These events illustrated some of the inherent dilemmas of the revolution. On one hand there were the revolutionary ideals, which implied some form of conflict between progressive and conservative groups. On the other there was the requirement, if the revolutionary promise of an improved way of life was to be kept, of a leadership able to limit conflict. The embodiments of these two forces, one preoccupied with change and the other with control, were the revolutionary party in Nanking and Yuan Shih-k'ai in Peking. Perhaps the real difficulty of the revolution was obscured by a tendency to view the two sides as symbolic opposites; the democratic revolutionaries versus the dictator. No doubt the outcome would have been different if the revolutionaries had been more practical and the dictator less vicious, but nothing, not even the revolutionary party's coming to power in Peking, could have reconciled quickly the conflicting demands of change and order.

Similarly, the revolution intensified conflicting demands in the conduct of foreign relations. Here two elements appeared which were to affect China's modern political life profoundly. One was the inevitability of China's involvement in international relations under disadvantageous conditions. Manifestly the foreign powers were so active and China so weak that she was not at liberty to solve her problems in isolation, much less to order her foreign relations along the lines of her old imperial greatness. The second factor was the growing power of nationalistic feeling among Chinese, which made every concession to foreign powers seem an exploitation of China's weakness. Like the tension between revolutionary ideals and administrative necessities, the opposition between being a supplicant among the powers on one hand and feeling the modern pride of nationhood on the other often showed events in a light that damaged the reputation of Yuan more than that of the revolutionaries. Yet giving power to the latter would not of itself have removed either China's basic weakness or the sensitive pride of her patriots.

To give an example of the clash between technical backwardness and nationalistic pride, one of Yuan's first problems arose when he found that his new government had inherited an empty treasury. Furthermore, he could count on little from the provinces, where most of the military governors kept whatever they collected to support their armies. As a solution, one that had become familiar from late Ch'ing examples, Yuan opened negotiations for an enormous Reorganization Loan, a figure of sixty million pounds being mentioned at first. A consortium of banks of six powers (Great Britain, France, Germany, Japan, Russia, and the United States), willing to provide not sixty million pounds, but twenty-five million, called for stringent conditions, including the pledging of particular taxes as security and the appointment of foreigners to administer some of the taxes and supervise expenditures. Despite the fact that the new parliament rejected the conditions and the American government forced its bankers to withdraw in objection to them, Yuan's representatives signed the contract (1913). The loan excited so much patriotic indignation that the minister of finance took refuge in the foreign concession in Tientsin, and the signers met late at night, to escape the attention of the outraged parliament. However necessary the loan seemed to be, it offended patriotic feelings. It also increased suspicion of the motives of foreign powers, who appeared willing to back a "strong man" who would protect their interests, even against the wishes of politicians claiming to speak for the people.

That Yuan Shih-k'ai was far from being a pliant tool of the foreign powers became clear during events arising from World War I; yet again what China's weakness seemed to make unavoidable cast him as leader in an unfavorable light. As the war began China declared her neutrality, considering that no interest of hers would be served by engaging in that distant contest. (By 1917 conditions had so changed that a Chinese declaration of war against Germany seemed prudent.) Japan, on the other hand, saw an advantage in coming to the aid of her ally, Great Britain, and, after declaring war on Germany, landed troops in the province of Shantung and claimed the German leasehold and other rights there. The Chinese government judged it futile to resist.

Half a year later, in 1915, the Japanese minister presented to Yuan Shih-k'ai a document that became known as the Twenty-one Demands, stressing as he did so that they must be kept secret. They included stipulations that China recognize Japan's new position in Shantung; rights of property, industry, commerce, and residence for Japanese in South Manchuria and Eastern Inner Mongolia, including the extension to ninety-nine years of leases Japan already had; and a special Japanese interest in the Hanyehp'ing Company, the major coal and steel works in central China. Finally, the Demands included a group that would place Japanese in the Chinese administration as advisers in political, financial, and military affairs, as joint administrators in Chinese police departments, and as cooperators and technicians in armament programs. To have kept the Demands secret would have deprived Yuan of the one defense that seemed possible, the objections of the other powers, and his officials quickly leaked the terms to foreign diplomats and correspondents. By discussing the Demands article by article with the Japanese negotiators, the Chinese managed to delay a final accord for several months. The strategy helped, if only a little: the publicity generated some hostile opinion, though among the powers only the United States formally remonstrated. The Japanese government conceded that the final group of articles, those that would have put the Chinese administration virtually under Japanese direction, could be shelved; but by an ultimatum forced the rest to be accepted. Yuan Shih-k'ai said that he was sad and humiliated but could see no alternative to yielding.

To Yuan as ruler, yielding was the better part of valor. To the new patriots, who did not have that responsibility, yielding could not compare with resisting. The new spirit was expressed in an outpouring of protest and indignation as the two sides carried on their discussions. Liang Ch'i-ch'ao mounted a campaign in the press. There were boycotts of Japanese goods and mass rallies in opposition to the Demands. Nineteen of Yuan's own generals declared their willingness to fight rather than yield, a statement that made clear what the alternative was but would have carried more weight if the generals had been better known for patriotism than for calculating their own advantage. By the time the Demands were met, Japan had become an object of patriotic anger that was nurtured by an annual "National Humiliation Day."

Yet the conflict between hard political necessity and patriotism was apparent in a curious sidelight on Sun Yat-sen. The leader of the revolution was in Japan, having fled after the failure to unseat Yuan Shih-k'ai, and desperate to find means to take up again his mission to build a new China. So compelling was his need that in 1914, and again during the period in which the Twenty-one Demands were outstanding, Sun offered Japanese officials concessions even more sweeping than those demanded from Yuan Shih-k'ai. Sun promised to let Japan dominate China commercially, to employ Japanese military advisers and specialists, to give priority to Japanese capital and assistance in economic development, and many other advantages—in exchange for Japanese help against Yuan Shih-k'ai. The most famous patriot's compromises with political wheeling and dealing gave the Japanese a telling argument to use with Yuan Shih-k'ai. The Japanese might support the revolutionaries if Yuan did not cooperate. The revolutionaries themselves, unfortunately, found their loyalties seriously strained. Many of those who had fled with Sun to Japan returned to China.

THE PORTENTS OF A NEW DYNASTY

In the meantime Yuan prepared to clothe his political power in the greatest dignity he could imagine, that of the founder of a new dynasty. A story circulating in 1915, while meant to ridicule Yuan's old-fashioned faith in portents, pointed in the direction of his ambition. It was said that when Yuan woke up from his customary afternoon nap one day he saw that his tea was in a different cup, not his favorite one of jade. He summoned the cup-boy and asked what had happened. The boy, who had dropped the cup upon entering the bedroom and seeing a great toad on the couch where his master should be, knew that he could not tell the truth. The toad stood for the vulgar upstart, distantly related to the Occidental swine, as in the Irish saying, "Don't bring a pig into a parlor." The boy lied, changing the apparition. When he entered, he said, he had dropped the jade cup in surprise, for he had seen on the couch not his master but a five-clawed golden dragon. The five-clawed dragon symbolized imperial power. When Yuan heard this, he snorted in derision but pressed a one hundred dollar bill into the boy's hand and warned him not to say a word to anyone else. Significantly, the mocking story was popular among Yuan's officers, whose feelings of independence grew as their leader devoted less of his time to them and more to questions of state and his position.

There were many signs of what was in the making. In 1914, for instance, officials were classified into nine ranks, as of old, and Yuan sacrificed at the Altar of Heaven, arriving in an armored car, which was not quite as the old emperors had done, but wearing a robe and headgear much like those of his predecessors. In 1915 Yuan quickened the pace. An American adviser on constitutional law, Dr. F. J. Goodnow, submitted an opinion favoring monarchy over republicanism for China at the time, provided that neither the people nor foreign powers objected strongly and that a constitution be developed. The opinion was published and cited repeatedly. One group especially impressed with it was a new Planning for Peace Society, which on August 14 published its plan to hold a national conference on political systems and on August 23 passed a resolution in favor of monarchy. In November a National Congress of Representatives, consisting of delegates chosen by provincial generals and governors, voted on the question whether to adopt a monarchical system. The vote was, Ayes: 1,993; Nays: 0. To each vote, curiously enough, was attached an identical message, urging Yuan Shih-k'ai to assume the title of Emperor and pass it on to his sons and grandsons. Yuan demurred until December, when he gave it out that the following year, 1916, would be the first of the reign-title "Grand Constitutional Era."

To the mass of the people, Yuan's stage-setting, of which the hustle and bustle of the delegations and conferences were conspicuous parts, seemed only what was to be expected of a man in his position; like him, they were monarchists by birth. To others of strong political views, however, his plans seemed utterly opposed to what the times required. Some of his own generals avoided identifying themselves vigorously with his cause. Among the foreign powers Japan disliked the prospect of Yuan as emperor and persuaded several others to join her in advising the Chinese government against the move. Most articulate in expressing his offense, however, was Liang Ch'i-ch'ao, who had accepted the events of recent years as a form of progress and participated in government despite his earlier opposition to the Revolution. To annul the Revolution would be to interrupt progress, he thought, and from the sanctuary of the Japanese concession in Tientsin he wrote an attack on the monarchists. Furthermore he conferred with disaffected generals, most notably a protégé of his, who then made his way to Yunnan and used his influence there to precipitate a declaration of independence by the governor. Other military governors in the south and west gradually made clear their opposition to Yuan.

The crisis should have been a golden opportunity for Sun Yat-sen's revolutionaries as well, but the party had been so reduced by failures and defections that the best it could do was in the old style of plot and prayer. A company of raiders, including a few Japanese adventurers and young Chinese patriots like Chiang Kai-shek, boarded several warships in the harbor of Shanghai while the officers were ashore and forced the crewmen to open fire. The idea was to take Shanghai and prepare for the triumphal return of Sun Yat-sen. After a few rounds had been shot in the direction of the target, however, the raiders hesitated over what to do next and at last took to their boats and disappeared.

Yuan fell with surprising speed. As the rebellious generals won a few battles and the extent of opposition to Yuan's plans became clear to him, he was stunned and tried to retreat from his position. First he put off the inauguration of the monarchy. When that seemed not enough he abolished the plan altogether, but the generals sensed that a bigger victory was possible and pressed their demands further. In the spring of 1916 Yuan fell ill, apparently of nervous fatigue. As generals whom he once had trusted began to declare their independence he offered to resign, but the matter was beyond his control. He died in June without knowing what the shape of the future might be. It should at least have been clear that an emperor was no longer the sole idea of authority.

POLITICAL DISINTEGRATION UNDER THE WARLORDS

Yuan's death brought China to the extremity of political disintegration. As in the period of anarchy between the T'ang and Sung, its major figures were generals. The number of generals, or "warlords," as opponents called them, was very large if we count everyone who commanded an independent army, for in many regions the only authority was that of a self-proclaimed army, often no different from a bandit gang. The most prominent warlords, however, were the dozen or two who imposed themselves on areas as great as a province or even larger, often as leaders of a faction of generals, each with an armed force of his own. In the north several of these were Yuan Shih-k'ai's protégés, who split into cliques. Elsewhere, in addition to Yuan's men, there were some who had risen more or less independently. Peking retained a trace of its old authority in that some of the generals justified their position in the provinces by using titles, such as Military Governor, to suggest that they served the central government. More concretely, whoever held Peking received the diplomatic recognition of foreign states; a Chinese government, even if only a nominal one, was needed to deal with the many international affairs in which China was involved. Peking also provided whoever controlled her with certain special sources of revenue, including loans from abroad and the proceeds from the customs and postal services, which had been kept in operation and were centered there. For the rest, nothing but the ideal of unity remained. By the early 1920s there were almost as many military governments as provinces.

All the strongest warlords probably allowed themselves to think of ruling all China, but few were unmannered enough to say so openly. They spent much of their time from 1916 to at least 1928 trying to build up their armies, concluding alliances and counteralliances, denouncing, threatening, bribing, or flattering their rivals, feinting with their armies, and fighting. The whole period could be described as an uninterrupted time of war, with the qualification that the consummation of war, the battle, was avoided whenever possible. Not that there was no fighting; and there was even more death and destruction than the fighting alone accounted for, owing to the rapacity of most warlord armies against the civilian population. Yet the short-range aim of most warlords was to enhance their territory and thus increase their revenue, both for immediate pleasure and the better to pursue the longer range goal of political power. Fighting often seemed the riskiest course, for the outcome was seldom certain, and the side effects, such as the involvement of other rivals watching nearby, incalculable. In short, the warfare of the period was governed as much by a political outlook as by a martial one. While the political tactics employed were elaborate and complicated, the political purpose was usually simply the enlargement of the warlord's power. Since maneuver followed maneuver inconclusively until the revived Kuomintang entered the field with new tactics, no significant pattern of political development is apparent, at least in the scope of our present knowledge. Yet the revolution, considered in a broad sense, went on. Chapter XVI indicates that the modern sector of the economy tended to grow despite the political chaos, while the traditional sector may have deteriorated. There were crucial developments in intellectual centers, as described below.

Despite the chaos of the political scene, it is possible to see, in what is known about several of the generals, a few relatively common tendencies, which tell us a little more about the large theme of the century, the interplay of modern and traditional forces. The generals themselves acted out of a variety of experience and character. Some, perhaps many, came from the relatively well-to-do classes from which most candidates for the examinations had come in earlier times. Some had received a standard classical education and thought of themselves in terms of the benevolent and cultivated ruler. Others were from poorer families, knew only the books that had attracted them in the course of an erratic and independent interest in learning, and thought of themselves more as great military heroes. Some exerted themselves in many different fields, from education to manufacturing; others attended exclusively to the size of their troops. Some had long experience as officials in relatively legitimate administrations. Others were no more than bandits.

Yet some generals, especially the most powerful ones, had much in common. Several were products of the Northern Army and the patronage of Yuan Shih-k'ai, making them the distant heirs in that dispersal of governing power that had begun with the transfer of authority to the self-strengtheners during the Taiping Rebellion. Many had studied in military schools in Japan, or under graduates of those schools. Though self-serving by nature, most of them were patriots, at least under some circumstances. Against the Manchus and Japanese especially, warlords spoke and may have felt like champions of China, though they were not such purists that they always disdained arrangements with foreigners at the expense of other Chinese. Finally, although all of them had chosen the gun as their means of pursuing their ends, the fact that many of them recognized the inadequacy of the gun alone and even preferred what may be regarded as diplomatic arts shows their common awareness of the value of politics.

The several sides that the warlords were required to display, as well as the variety of their character, gave rise to different opinions of them. One judgment emphasizes their native competence and vigor. Pearl S. Buck, the author who spent much of her life in China, wrote,

Without exception, the warlords I have known have been men of unusual native ability, gifted with peculiar personal charm, with imagination and strength, and often with a rude poetic quality . . . . The warlord sees himself great—and great in the traditional manner of heroes of ancient fiction and history . . . .[3]

Another opinion, much more common among Chinese intellectuals, noticed less the superior qualities and more a shocking ruthlessness, as in the sarcastic obituary of Chang Tsung-ch'ang (1881-1932), a particularly brutish general, by the writer Lin Yutang:

So one more of the colorful, legendary figures of medieval China has

3. "Chinese War Lords," *The Saturday Evening Post,* CCV, No. 43 (April 22, 1933), p. 77.

passed into eternity. And yet Dog-Meat General's death has a special significance for me, because he was the most colorful, legendary, medieval, and unashamed ruler of modern China.

He was a born ruler such as modern China wants. He was six feet tall, a towering giant, with a pair of squint eyes and a pair of abnormally massive hands. He was direct, forceful, terribly efficient at times; obstinate and gifted with moderate intelligence.[4]

In part the generals attracted or repelled their observers according to the importance the observers attached to the changing of Chinese ways. The present evidence indicates that many warlords were indeed caught up in the currents of change; to what extent they promoted change remains a question. Their stated aims, for example, used the most powerful modern terms. "Revolution" was on everyone's lips, and warlords frequently described themselves as revolutionary generals. Many spoke well of republicanism or democracy. Almost all expressed love of China, some even embroidering their comments with fashionable Western references to the "survival of the fittest."

When it was possible to see what lay behind these modern terms, however, they appeared to have meanings different from their usual Western ones. Revolution, for example, though of course it had many different connotations, might take on in a warlord's mind the primary sense of an organizing mandate—to "save" the country and the people—rather than a mandate to change the whole political or social structure. Republicanism stood not for a system based on the sovereignty of the people—a concept that seemed the very opposite of sound government—but for a system that, in the words of one warlord, "makes use of the people." Even the patriotism of some warlords had a special sense, stressing respect for the military as a mark of the patriot.

The administration of warlords also showed a mixture of progressive and conservative tendencies. Several promoted social reforms, including the suppression of narcotics, prostitution, and gambling. Some established programs of public works, repairing roads and walls, planting trees, and providing assistance to farmers. Some sponsored vocational schools and looked favorably on manufacturing that was profitable or useful otherwise. Arsenals, for example, were usually prized.

Yet it would seem that much of the motivation behind the reforms

4. *With Love and Irony* (New York: John Day, 1940), p. 196.

was closer to that of the T'ung-chih Restoration and the old self-strengtheners than to the modern revolutionaries. Social reforms were important because they restored the frayed moral fibre of society, public works programs because they reestablished the farmers' livelihood. Both aimed at the rehabilitation of the old order, not the introduction of a new one. Such innovations as vocational schools and modern industry, modest as they were, evoked the image of the self-strengtheners seeking Western devices to protect the Chinese Way, although in the new circumstances they too often seemed subordinated to the warlords' personal ambitions.

In another way, the warlords had the sanction of a strong tradition, in that their organizations were built on personal loyalties. Warlords in following this customary approach showed one of their most conservative aspects and one of those most clearly distinguishing them from modern ideas. In modern life, at least in the theories entertained by some of the revolutionary intellectuals of the day, loyalty should go to ideals or concepts, like democracy, which bore equally on everyone and usually implied reversing the established privileges and burdens of superior and inferior classes. The organization of warlords had nothing of this revolutionary style. A warlord's officer corps was founded on personal relationships and reinforced by all the familiar forms of connection, including kinship, marriage, regional ties, and school ties. In civil administration the old Ch'ing pattern of local and district government was left alone and simply supervised by commissioners of the warlord.

Taken together with such conservative characteristics, one further feature common to most warlords, their insatiable appetite for money, tended to confirm the opinion of the times that they served only chaos, and to obscure the improvements that some promoted. Warlords sought revenue by any means. They collected the land tax, of course, and added surcharges to it. They imposed transit taxes on goods in commerce. They seized income from utilities, such as railroads and customs, normally earmarked for the repayment of foreign debts, while the debts went unpaid. At the same time they borrowed money, pledging future revenues in repayment. They demanded sums from the merchants in cities, threatening to loose their troops on the city if not paid. Some of the offices established nominally to control the sale or production of opium operated in fact as agencies to tap the profit in the opium trade. Controlling their own mints, warlords frequently sought profit in altering currency—reducing the amount of silver in a new issue of dollars, for example, and using the whole issue quickly before the word spread.

Partly as a result of such policies, the warlord period became known as a time of increased hardship for the people. They were required to pay heavy and arbitrarily imposed taxes. Weakened currency provoked inflation of prices. In some places the production and use of opium increased. There were droughts and famines, natural disasters whose effects were made worse, as often in the past, by the neglect of precautions and relief that stronger governments could have administered. By the early 1920s, fighting, famine, and oppression had either uprooted from their farms or left at the edge of destitution tens of millions of people.

THE REVOLUTIONARY ENCLAVES: THE CITIES AND UNIVERSITIES

Amidst the political anarchy of the period 1916-28 there remained centers in which forces of change were growing rapidly. These were the major cities, especially those along the coast. For several reasons they were left relatively free of interference by warlords, even when actually governed by them, as was Peking. Several of the cities had important foreign concessions, the immunity of which could be tampered with only at the risk of war. Warlords, usually preoccupied with questions of their own political and military rivalries, were not inclined to give great attention to developments in the cities. Besides, the cities were often sources of money; hence even the narrowest self-interest dictated that they be treated with restraint. As a result the cities were the incubators of modern revolution more radical, in both its broad social and narrow political senses, than anything the warlords encouraged.

In the broad sense, the cities, where much of the "modern sector" of the economy was growing, gave rise to new classes of people and new organizations that encouraged change. As has been noted, a class of merchants and manufacturers based on the "Westernized" sector of the economy had already been growing for half a century. With the establishment of more factories, both foreign and Chinese, a hired working class in the "Westernized" sector also formed, many of its members drawn at first from the impoverished countryside. It is estimated that by 1919 over one million people were working in factories. Moreover, the interests of both the business class and the workers disposed them favorably to new organizations and aims. By 1914 more than 200,000 business men belonged to over one thousand

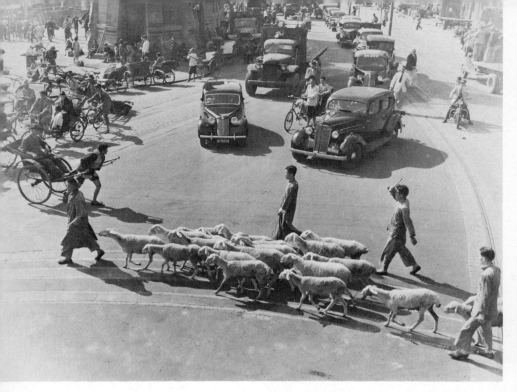

East and West meet in Shanghai traffic in 1947.

local chambers of commerce, the aims of which were of course the promotion of prosperous trade, manufacture, banking, and related conditions. That these conditions inevitably included a cooperative attitude on the part of government was indicated in the rising interest of Chinese businessmen in being represented, for example, in the government of foreign concessions. Among the new class of workers, on the other hand, a symptomatic new organization was the labor union. It represented a considerable break with the past, in which trade or regional guilds had taken the traditional attitude that all in an enterprise were united by a common loyalty to the group. Labor unions, assuming instead the attitude that the workers' interests often were opposed to those of the managers, grew slowly but under energetic organizers notably from about 1920 onwards. The unions, more deliberately than the chambers of commerce, came to regard their interests as inseparable from political issues. Of the new classes and their organizations it need hardly be said that they comprised an extremely small proportion of the Chinese people, certainly less than one percent. Yet they proved a not insignificant group. They were concentrated in the coastal cities; they were relatively influenced by the world beyond China (the children of prosperous businessmen were usually sent to modern schools, often those maintained by foreigners); and the ideas of the vague revolutionary ideology of the day were more significant to them than to the majority of the people. In political action, however, their receptivity was more important than their leadership. For revolutionary leadership, the fertile ground was the schools.

Despite the turbulent times, the system of schools that the Ch'ing government had begun in its last years had never wholly been abandoned. The rivalries of warlords made it difficult to speak of a true system, in the sense of an organization well directed from one center, and the quality of instruction, much of it in Western subjects, may well have declined from earlier levels, but schools continued to exist in every province. In simple numbers, they may even have increased. Although the deep-rooted concern of the Chinese for education must have had much to do with this, the schools themselves were noteworthy evidence of the acceptance by many Chinese of a Western system. One feature of the system, a variation chosen by the Ch'ing government partly from economic necessity, was the charging of tuition, in general beginning at the secondary level. These fees also must have helped to maintain schools despite the unreliability of the political administration.

As the collecting of fees suggests, the students of the new schools, especially from the secondary level upwards, came mainly from families of means. Although the fees were as nothing compared to modern charges—and in general much less than those of the higher mission schools—only rarely could the son of a poor farmer find the money to go to a secondary school. A survey taken slightly after the warlord period proper (1916-28) implied that fewer than one percent of the agricultural population could afford the fees. Other factors increased the difficulty. Most middle schools were established in district seats or higher administrative cities, following an old hierarchical pattern for state offices, and the student from the distant village had to find the means to travel and live away from home. The higher the schools, the less accessible. About one half the colleges and two thirds of the college students were in two provinces, those containing Peking and Shanghai, in 1922. In short, the majority of Chinese who received the new education above the primary level came from families that would have been called gentry in the old days, though in recent times they may have acquired new sources of income in addition to land, or that belonged to the modern business and professional classes. Moreover, the number of such students was low in relation to the population, probably smaller than one percent.

The tendencies restricting and concentrating the new education were strongest at the very highest level. In the early 1920s only about 37,000 students were enrolled in fewer than 150 colleges. Many of the colleges were specialized schools, such as teachers' colleges, colleges of law and political science, and industrial colleges. There were a handful of more comprehensive universities, of which the acknowledged leader was the National University of Peking, with about 2,500 students and 200 faculty members.

The beneficiaries of the higher education felt most intimately and self-consciously the tensions between Chinese life as it actually was and as it might be. They were keen patriots, and they saw a Chinese people unable to act as a nation, hobbled as the students thought by selfish leaders and aggressive foreigners. They were visionaries, who could imagine a future society of harmony, justice, and plenty but could only see the present fighting, corruption, and poverty. Not least, as the educated elite they inherited the attitude that they were the proper leaders of the society, but they could not discover the means by which to lead. More immediately, some of them did not find employment that they thought suited to their capacity. While a considerable proportion turned to teaching, others found that the Western curriculum, though it might be a preparation for a useful life in the West, was not useful to Chinese life in its present state. This was especially so of students returning from study abroad, where, in Japan, as we have seen, and also in European countries and the United States, training for a modern society was combined with heady draughts of alien political theories and ideals. Consequently a feeling of separation from the established ways of Chinese life and apparent despair of changing them were often combined with a compelling if diffuse urge to bring about such change.

THE NEW CULTURE MOVEMENT

Nowhere were the elements of change more obvious than in the academic circles of Peking, whose smallness as a component of Chinese society little suggested their prestige and power in the intellectual life of the country. Something has already been said of the students there. It is also helpful to know something of the teachers, especially at Peking University, who still retained much of the old aura as embodiments and examples of wisdom. The most prominent among them promoted radical changes in cultural standards, their dedication to the new and the western carrying all the more weight in that most of them had been educated in the old, classical way. The chancellor, Ts'ai Yuan-p'ei (1867-1940), for example, had been appointed when he was young to the Hanlin Academy, the office of scholars of the old Ch'ing government, but he had supported the Hundred Days Reform and turned revolutionary when it failed. He studied in Europe and helped to promote work-and-study plans by which several thousand Chinese students went to France, an experience notable for contributing more to their revolutionary ardor than to their professional skills. As chancellor he injected new vitality into the university from 1917 on by increasing its budget—to six times (and more) what the average national college received—and laying it down as policy that the purpose of the university was academic research, its aim a new civilization; that students should not regard the university as simply a means of obtaining office; and that the university would permit all rationally maintained points of view to be expressed freely. Most vital of all, however, he assembled a faculty to express strong points of view, particularly in support of the secular Western values that he himself favored. The primary interests of the day included an attack on Confucianism; a call for a more lively and popular literary style; and an espousal of various Western ideals, such as democracy, the victory of reason through science (and the application of that attitude to social issues as "positivism"), and Communism.

When Ts'ai Yuan-p'ei became chancellor he appointed as dean of letters a revolutionary journalist, Ch'en Tu-hsiu (1879-1942). Ch'en had been brought up in a wealthy family and educated in the Classics. Inspired also by the radical reformers of the Hundred Days, he studied Western subjects, going to Japan and France in the last decade of the Ch'ing dynasty. After the revolution, he worked mainly as an editor of magazines. The most famous was *Hsin ch'ing-nien*, or *La Jeunesse*, (New youth; the title being given in both Chinese and French), which he began to publish in 1915. It became the most widely read of the many intellectual journals of the time. One of the articles appearing there established Ch'en as a leading critic who attacked broadside what he considered the guiding spirit of Chinese life, the Confucian way. Stressing the restraints that Confucian ethics imposed on social behavior, especially that of the young and of women, he concluded that what Confucius taught had nothing to do with the happiness of the majority of individuals in modern times. In another article he expanded on his alternative to the Confucian way, the creation and enjoyment of happiness by individuals and the storing up of happiness for individuals of the future. When Ch'en moved to the University of Peking, *Hsin ch'ing-nien* went with him and became the medium for other members of the faculty.

Of these, one was Hu Shih (1891-1962), who began to teach philosophy in the university in 1917. Hu was also the son of an official and had been trained in the Classics before exploring the "new" education. He, too, continued his education abroad, but in the United States, where he studied at Cornell and Columbia (Ph.D. 1917). The pragmatism of John Dewey, his teacher at Columbia, contributed to his outlook in many ways, including perhaps the first article he wrote for *Hsin ch'ing-nien,* at Ch'en Tu-hsiu's invitation. Called "A Preliminary Discussion of Literary Reform," it proposed that the transparent artificialities and clichés of the literary style, epitomized in the Eight-legged Essay, be avoided and a more vernacular, flexible style adopted. (The changes are discussed more fully in chapter XIX.) Hu Shih was convinced that a style of writing closer to the living language would encourage a new flowering of literature, a "renaissance" that he assumed would contribute to the improvement of life. Ch'en Tu-hsiu supported Hu, and discussed a reformed literature more explicitly as a tool of political reform. *Hsin ch'ing-nien* soon came to be written in the vernacular, and in 1920 even the Ministry of Education in Peking ruled that this should be the style taught in elementary schools. As to the powerful literature that the new style was meant to encourage, it is still too early to judge its merits. The new style was widely accepted at the same time as enthusiastic literary societies were established, which discussed theories and forms of literature and were much inspired by the achievements of famous Western writers. New novels and short stories caught the quality of life for a fervid young readership. If their great strength was social criticism, and their art and perception less certain when measured by broader standards, they nevertheless must have made revolutionary change seem all the more attractive as they emphasized the chasm that separated Chinese realities from the visions of the intellectuals.

The intellectuals were indeed concerned with visions, in the sense that they characteristically tried to see, however dimly, some new totality, spiritual and social, on the far side of the cultural crisis through which they were passing. Perhaps the integrated universal order implicit in the old concept of the Way encouraged this. In any event, certain vital issues clustered around those questions that had been at the heart of much of the thinking of the past: What principles ought to govern society? What knowledge leads toward the fulfillment of a man's potential? For a while, the issues were summed up in the watchwords "Democracy" and "Science."

"Democracy" stood for more than the system of lodging ultimate authority in a free people voting by secret ballot. Indeed, the very question of how to put political democracy into effect turned many intellectuals away in despair. "Democracy" stood rather for a generally liberal atmosphere, especially one in which the familial and social pressures of the old society had given way to individualism, an individualism in which the accumulation of happiness, as noted above in the discussion of Ch'en Tu-hsiu, was stressed more than rugged independence of belief. It also stood for rejection of the cynical maneuvering and brutality of warlords and connoted instead public spiritedness and benevolent administration.

"Science" was also a watchword that meant both more and less than ordinarily. It did not mean that all those who invoked it worked in the sciences. They were more typically men who had been introduced to the current theories and conclusions of scientific knowledge and, impressed by the material achievements of the West, were ready to believe that its science not only spoke more truly about the world than any other previous kind of knowledge but also that it could eventually explain the role of human life in the universal scheme and provide guides to moral behavior. "Science" would free the modern man from metaphysics, superstition, and religion.

Another element to enter the New Culture movement, and to alter the connotations of the watchwords "Democracy" and "Science," was Communism. One of those who promoted it was another member of the Peking faculty, Li Ta-chao (1888-1927). Li differed from the other men mentioned above in being a northerner and the son of a farmer. Yet he was raised in a relatively comfortable and old-fashioned style, his grandfather, who was a small landlord, taking him in when he was orphaned as a baby. He studied the Classics until he was an adolescent and first tasted Western subjects when he enrolled in a prefectural secondary school. After attending a college in Peking he went to Japan and studied at a university, at the same time beginning to write political journalism, which he continued when he returned to China. By 1918, at the age of thirty, he was invited by Ts'ai Yuan-p'ei to become chief librarian in Peking University. Within two years he also became professor of history, political science, economics, and law. He was known for being especially friendly to the young, helping among others one Mao Tse-tung, whom he employed as a library assistant. The professions of humanitarianism of the Bolsheviks caught his imagination, and in *Hsin ch'ing-nien* in 1918 he celebrated the first anniversary of the October Revolution in the tones of one inspired by a revelation.

> They will unite the proletariat of the world, and create global freedom with their greatest, strongest power of resistance: first they will create a federation of European democracies, to serve as the foundation of a world federation. This is the ideology of the Bolsheviki. This is the new doctrine of the twentieth-century revolution.
>
> . . .
>
> Henceforth, all that one sees around him will be the triumphant banner of Bolshevism, and all that one hears around him will be Bolshevism's song of victory. The bell is rung for humanitarianism! The dawn of freedom has arrived! See the world of tomorrow; it assuredly will belong to the red flag! . . . [5]

The appeal of this vision owed something to what young intellectuals thought, however incorrectly, to have happened in a Russia whose modern writers seemed similarly tormented about their society. It probably owed even more to other features—that it was based, for example, on a doctrine, Marxism, which claimed to be true as science is true; that it purported to be ultimately egalitarian or democratic in a more complete sense than that of a merely political democracy, and to be a key to everything in the world, especially history and human events, like the Way that so many young men had been seeking. It was supported, moreover, by a repertory of techniques of organizing and acting in ways to give political power to even a small elite. No doubt these aspects had an effect on the small Marxist study groups that were formed by Li Ta-chao and others.

At the same time a much larger proportion of students had been caught up in a nationalistic fervor which was more intense than the

---

5. As translated in Wm. Theodore de Bary, Wing-tsit Chan, and Burton Watson, comps., *Sources of Chinese Tradition* (New York: Columbia University Press, 1960), pp. 864-65.

enthusiasm for Marxism but less sure of the direction it should follow. Events in 1919 made one thing clear: that the feelings of students had grown strong enough to drive them to physical action.

THE MAY FOURTH MOVEMENT

The patriotic frustrations that had found a target in Japan, against which students vented their anger in the period of the Twenty-one Demands, turned, intensified, against the Peking government in 1919. At the beginning of World War I Japan had joined the side of the Allies and demanded that Germany turn over her leased rights in the province of Shantung, soon enforcing the demand with troops. (The Peking government declared war on Germany only later, in 1917, partly out of a desire to have a voice in the peace settlement.) Chinese patriots deplored the Japanese seizure of the territory that had nurtured the Duke of Chou, Confucius, and Mencius—who remained symbols of national greatness even if no longer intellectually respectable—and anticipated the righting of this wrong at the peace conference. In the minds of many of the new intellectuals the conference was to open a new era in international relations, guided by such principles as those outlined by Woodrow Wilson, including open covenants openly arrived at, adjustments of territory with weight given to the interests of the population, and a League of Nations to assure political independence and territorial integrity to all nations. Students and teachers joined a great victory parade in Peking at the end of the war.

As the Peace Conference at Versailles progressed, however, the news brought disillusionment. The Japanese delegate made it known that Great Britain, France, and Italy had signed secret agreements with Japan two years earlier, promising to support Japan's claims to the old German rights in Shantung. Moreover, less than a month before the war ended the Peking government had secretly obtained a large loan from Japan and in connection with it had agreed that Japanese troops, police officers, and railroad workers should be stationed in Shantung. Against this combination of political interests and legal acquiescence, even the American delegation, which had been inclined to support China, gave way, and Japan's claim was incorporated in the text of the Peace Treaty.

The wave of emotion created by this defeat came to a crest among intellectuals at the end of April, 1919, during preparations to commemorate National Humiliation Day, the anniversary of the Twenty-one Demands. What was regarded as a betrayal of the highest ideals could be met only with some kind of action. In the statement of one angry patriot,

When the news of the Paris Peace Conference finally reached us we were greatly shocked. We at once awoke to the fact that foreign nations were still selfish and militaristic and that they were all great liars ... ... We had nothing to do with our Government, that we knew very well, and at the same time we could no longer depend upon the principles of any so-called great leader like Woodrow Wilson, for example. Looking at our people and at the pitiful ignorant masses, we couldn't help but feel that we must struggle![6]

Student organizers in Peking planned a mass parade for the anniversary. Some of the more radical groups apparently went further, secretly deciding to capitalize upon the heated atmosphere of the demonstration by attacking three high officials who were thought to be friendly to the Japanese.

On May 4, upwards of three thousand students from thirteen colleges and universities in Peking assembled in front of the great Gate of Heavenly Peace to make their demonstration, ignoring the advice of officials to disperse. After hearing speeches and acclaiming manifestos of opposition to the Great Powers abroad and the "traitors" at home, they paraded through the streets. As they failed to find the foreign ministers they wished to confront and the police began to force them back from their planned route through the Legation Quarter, tension grew, and shouts went up against the traitors. Moving to the home of the minister of communications, they were enraged by the attempts of police to block them and broke into the house, smashing furniture and setting part of the building afire. Of the three officials who were the special targets of their fury they found only the Chinese minister to Japan, in the home of the minister of communications. They beat him unconscious. Fighting continued until the police were reinforced and dispersed the remaining students, arresting about thirty of them.

The May Fourth demonstration showed that the new nationalism had become a political force to be reckoned with, and made political action attractive to many students. Even on the day of the demonstration, apparently, they wakened in onlookers a sense of sympathy and admiration for what was judged a successful defiance of a disliked

6. As quoted in Chow Tse-tung, *The May Fourth Movement* (Cambridge, Harvard University Press, 1960), p. 93.

authority. In subsequent weeks their cause grew stronger. A student union was organized in Peking, and delegates went to other cities to promote similar organizations there. The activities of the unions were characteristically political, including further demonstrations, the organizing of groups to make street-corner speeches, and the addressing of demands to the government. The most powerful weapons, however, were discovered about the middle of May. The student unions called a general strike against the schools in all major cities and promoted a boycott of Japanese goods, using street-corner agitators and representatives who dealt with merchants' associations. The threats to order presented by the groups of students in the streets and the economic and even international implications of the boycott goaded the government into using more force than before. Over one thousand students were arrested, and parts of Peking University were used as a jail. The main effect, however, was only more sympathy for the students. The press, professional intellectuals (some organizing on the student model), politicians, and even warlords seeing a chance to undermine the Peking government on the issue of patriotism—all made known their sympathy. Most effectively, the jailing of the students was followed in Shanghai by a week-long closing of shops of almost all Chinese merchants and strikes of workers in some forty factories. The government retreated, releasing the students, and then came to terms, accepting the resignation of the cabinet and refusing to sign the Versailles Treaty. The students seemed the masters of a new triumphant force.

In the long run the effects of the May Fourth movement were more complicated, though there is little doubt that they furthered revolution in the broad sense. They included, for example, a proliferation of discussion societies and little magazines, all promoting new perspectives and attacking tradition. On the other hand, a style of political action had been established, to persist through subsequent decades, in which students expressed objections to national or local conditions by means of strikes, demonstrations, and occasionally attacks on offending authorities or groups. Although the complaints were often justified, the action taken in protest frequently interrupted schooling. The philosopher John Dewey, who was lecturing in China at the time and sympathetic to the students' eagerness for change, remarked, "At present the zeal for ideas outruns persistence in getting knowledge with which to back up the ideas." The tendency of the students' action was also generally coercive rather than democratic. If a more rational society was meant by the watchwords "Democracy" and "Science," the students were not obviously bringing it closer. A resulting sense of the inconclusive effects of isolated actions by students probably impelled some in the direction that became clearer in subsequent years, cooperation with political parties, especially as they seemed to offer a master plan to solve China's problems.

The heightened urgency given politics by the May Fourth movement also posed a dilemma that painfully divided the leaders of the New Culture movement. The question was one of ends and means. Could a more humane, enlightened, and progressive China be realized only after the people had themselves become so, by education and personal experience? Or could such a China be realized only after the ruling establishment had been destroyed by a revolutionary party determined ro direct such improvements? Among the intellectual leaders already mentioned, for example, Ts'ai Yüan-p'ei took an ambivalent position in the demonstration, attempting to win the release of the arrested students and then resigning, leaving no clear explanation but later saying that he had been exhausted by the situation and needed a rest. Afterwards he was associated with a political position that favored constitutional, elected government committed to both social welfare and individual freedom; but he continued to give most of his attention to education, not politics. Hu Shih made clearer the fundamental temperamental divergence between the liberals, for whom he became spokesman, and the zealots when he published his article, "More Study of Problems, Less Talk of 'Isms,'" in which he argued that the doctrines which appealed to so many of his fellow intellectuals were no substitute for solving actual problems. He himself saw the primary problems as being in education. A single-minded absorption in politics seemed to him likely to lead to perverted ends in view of China's cultural state, and he spoke out only because "the slaves of Confucius and Chu Hsi have decreased in number, [but] the slaves of Marx and Kropotkin have appeared."

The Establishment of the Chinese Communist Party

Li Ta-chao and Ch'en Tu-hsiu went a different way. Both had vigorously supported the actions of students following May Fourth, and Ch'en had followed Li into one of the small societies studying socialism. Probably, like many of their fellow intellectuals, they had been deeply impressed a few months later by a Soviet declaration (the Karakhan Manifesto, July, 1919), which stated, "The Soviet Government returns to the Chinese people without any kind of compensation the Chinese Eastern Railway, and all mining, gold, and forestry concessions which were seized from them by the government of Tsars." Many Chinese idealists felt jubilation, contrasting this selfless diplomacy with the cynical actions of the European powers at Versailles. That the Soviet government would deny or obscure the statement later, as in fact it did, and in actual negotiations insist on a much more conventional Russian influence in the northeast would have been expected only by much more skeptical men than the incipient revolutionaries. Li and Ch'en were well disposed to this new kind of man, the Communist, at once humanitarian idealist and practical planner.

In such favorable circumstances an agent of the Third Communist International, or Comintern, an organization founded in Moscow to set policy and coordinate the revolutionary efforts of Communists throughout the world, arrived in Peking early in 1920. He was introduced to Li Ta-chao and others and later sent by Li to Shanghai to meet Ch'en Tu-hsiu. Apparently the agent explained to the Chinese that he could assist them with the organizing experience at his disposal and with money. Ch'en brought together a small group of revolutionaries of varied socialist and anarchist sympathies and founded a Chinese Communist Party. A subsidiary organization, the Socialist Youth Corps, was established soon afterwards. Under the guidance of the Comintern agent, his aides, and Chinese revolutionaries, branches of the Party, the Youth Corps, and affiliated organizations were soon established in several other cities, such as Peking (under Li Ta-chao), Changsha (under Mao Tse-tung), Wuhan, and Canton. At about the same time, a Young China Communist Party was established by some Chinese worker-students in Paris, a group in which one of the principal figures was Chou En-lai. The Chinese Communist Party convened its first National Congress in Shanghai the next summer, 1921, which is the official date of its founding. The twelve Chinese who attended, together with one or two Comintern agents, represented the perhaps sixty or seventy Chinese who were members of the party or its affiliates at the time. Almost all were intellectuals. They elected Ch'en Tu-hsiu secretary of the Central Committee (the top post) and adopted his view that, while the seizure of political power was their ultimate aim, this must be in the future, and for the present it was preparatory work which was required. They established only two departments, Organization and Propaganda, and committed themselves to increasing their own membership and organizing workers, the industrial proletariat which was supposed to be the prime revolutionary class. Among its many implications for the spirit of Chinese revolution, the founding of the Chinese Communist Party introduced quickly three features that distinguished it from the previously generally liberal range of thought of the revolutionary intellectuals. It introduced the ideas of a modern dictatorship in contrast to political democracy, class warfare in contrast to individualism, and doctrinal orthodoxy in contrast to liberalism. It was reported that the representatives resolved to guard their secrecy and purity. In this the conspiratorial nature of the Communist movement must have seemed familiar to those used to the ways of secret societies. Yet some who had been willing to join the party withdrew when they began to understand its demands. Still others—by far the larger proportion of modern-minded men—distrusted the radical and doctrinaire tone of the party and preferred the reawakened Kuomintang of Sun Yat-sen.

THE BEGINNINGS OF ORDER: THE NATIONALIST REVIVAL

The revival of Sun Yat-sen's party depended on two main factors, the development of Sun's own attitudes and the enforcement of a new revolutionary strategy by the Comintern. Since its moment of glory early in the Revolution, the Kuomintang had declined—intimidated, bribed, and outlawed by Yuan Shih-k'ai and successive warlords in Peking, split internally by quarrels over policy and rivalry among leaders—until in effect it was little more than a band of secret revolutionaries. In the course of nine unsettled years, from 1913 to 1922, Sun Yat-sen, based now in Tokyo, now in the foreign concessions of Shanghai, now in Canton in alliance with a local warlord, grew firmer in the conviction that his movement suffered from an excess of independence, resulting in factional disputes and insubordination. To succeed ultimately would require a much more tightly knit and controlled organization. He stressed from time to time various means of tightening it, including a turning back from the open political party to the secret society, requiring the members to take an oath of obedience to himself as leader, and developing the idea that the party, once in power, would move the country toward republicanism by means of a period of "tutelage," that is, the party would teach democratic procedures to the people, who had no experience in such ways. Republicanism, to which Sun remained theoretically committed, would be reached, he seemed to be suggesting, by means of dictatorship.

As his preference for strong leadership grew, his hope of being helped by the Western countries or Japan diminished. He had promised Japan economic privileges dwarfing anything the Western countries had asked for if she would help him against Yuan Shih-k'ai, but in vain. He had approached Britons and Americans, apparently feeling that China's future and his own would flourish only with massive foreign investments, but had been turned away.

The frustrations of the party were relieved to some extent by the May Fourth incident. Quick to feel the pull of the patriotic tide, the party established new periodicals that brought the names of Sun and other famous figures to the attention of the reading public once again, and showed them to be concerned with the further development of the revolution and sympathetic with the May Fourth spirit. Sun urged students to become revolutionaries and made speeches arguing that the first requirement of the times was the destruction by a revolutionary party of the established political order. As a result, many who had taken part in the May Fourth movement gravitated toward the Nationalist Party. Sun's new optimism was marked by a reorganization of the party and a restatement of its platform in 1920. According to this, the party aimed to implement in China the Three Principles of the People and a five-power constitution (Sun thought of combining the three divisions of American Government—executive, legislative, and judicial—with two he regarded as uniquely Chinese—a censorial division and an examination division). The achievement of that end was to be reached through three stages. The first would be a period of rule by military government, a stage in which the revolutionary army would destroy the old political forces and also stamp out social evils such as opium-smoking and superstition. The second, which could overlap the first, would be a period of political tutelage, in which the party would control all political and military affairs and guide the people in local self-government. When local self-government became sufficiently effective, a National Assembly would be elected and eventually the third stage, that of constitutional government, would be declared in existence. At times Sun envisaged the transitional period of political tutelage—the means by which the Chinese people "learned" democracy—lasting six years, but later he said less of its limits. These and other steps showed the renewed vitality of the party.

Yet when Sun tried to establish a new base of operations by collaborating with a warlord in Canton, the two allies fairly soon had a falling out, and the one who had to flee was Sun. The new vitality had still to be embodied in a strong organization.

THE COMMUNIST COLLABORATION

The new growth of the party largely coincided with a policy of assistance adopted by the Comintern, the final aims of which were different from Sun Yat-sen's. The major impetus in this came from V. I. Lenin, the Bolshevik leader, who saw that revolutionary feelings were stirring China, as well as other countries of Asia, and was determined to channel this fervor in ways that would aid the Communist movements of the West, where the major progress toward workers' revolutions was theoretically bound to occur. For that purpose he put forward several arguments or "theses" that elaborated on—some say distorted—the nineteenth-century Marxist view of Asia. One was his thesis of Imperialism. As suggested in the title of his book, *Imperialism, the Highest Stage of Capitalism,* he maintained that as capitalists in the industrial Western countries exhausted the opportunities for further investment and increased profits at home they turned to undeveloped regions, where their capital could buy cheap land, cheap labor, and abundant raw materials, resulting in "super-profits." Accordingly a race began among capitalist powers for regions to exploit, reducing backward countries to either colonies or semicolonies (e.g., countries like China, whose independence was a fiction hiding the real power of the foreign concessions and other economic rights). The race gradually became desperate and could be resolved in no way but war, the imperialists struggling among themselves, to the advantage of worker-revolutionaries in Europe. Although Lenin saw this affecting Europe more concretely than Asia, he noted also that the idea of exploitation by greedy Western capitalists could stimulate great hatred among Asians. It is apparent today that the thesis of Imperialism, so widely accepted, touched in passing on a psychological force much more explosive than the economic one it stressed.

Another thesis, advanced by Lenin in 1920 at the Second Congress of the Comintern in what is now Leningrad, was that backward countries could under certain circumstances be helped to speed up their evolution toward Communism. In the ordinary Marxist interpretation of history, societies passed inevitably from feudalism into capitalism before moving on to socialism. (We ignore here a school of Marxian thought that accepted a distinct and separate Asian form of society, for it was not used by any Communist organization.) Lenin, however, perhaps too excited by the vision of millions of restless Asians to let theory stand in the way, insisted that the backward countries could, if aided by the strong proletarian organizations in other parts of the world, leap over the capitalist stage of development. To do so would require Communists to form a temporary alliance with the nationalist revolutionaries of those countries in the common task of fighting the imperialist interlopers and the native ruling class. The alliance was never to become a merger, for at the same time the Communists were to preserve their organization intact and independent, ultimately dedicated to the special task of fighting even their allies when the revolution had progressed further. The idea was given some plausibility in theory by the fact that the major nationalistic revolutionary force was identified as the "bourgeois-democratic," which was struggling against the "feudal" ruling classes and, according to the established Marxian categories of progress, would inevitably give way to the "proletarian" revolution led by the Communist Party. Yet Lenin's argument met opposition, especially from the Asian delegates to the Congress on the grounds that cooperation with the bourgeoisie would betray Communistic principles. Lenin's proposal seems indeed to have been more a strategy than a "thesis." It appeared (at least to the Europeans predominant at the Congress) to be realistic and it was adopted, but the lingering uneasiness over the "united front" tactic, as it was later called, carried over into its enactment in China.

In the three or four years following the Comintern meeting the alliance called for in China was gradually formed. The Comintern came to the view that the most promising "bourgeois-democratic" party was the Kuomintang and sent agents to speak with Sun, both to discover more about him and to suggest to him the advantages that would follow from a partnership. Sun was more receptive the more his fortunes declined. He seemed impressed by what he considered parallels between the Russian experience and China's, including the efficacy of rule by a single party; he found the Soviet economic policy (at the time the New Economic Policy, an expedient retreat from full socialism) similar to his own economic ideas; and he felt himself and his party strong enough not to be exploited by any small number of international and Chinese Communists, whose help might, nevertheless, be useful. A statement he issued jointly with a Soviet representative in 1923, saying that the conditions for the introduction of the Soviet system of Communism into China did not exist and suggesting that the Soviet Union wished nothing more for China than national unity and independence, signaled in fact Sun's acceptance of Comintern aid. Soon afterward, when local armies friendly to Sun had retaken Canton he established his headquarters there and began to receive Comintern advisers.

The Chinese Communist Party issued in 1922 declarations asserting the need of a "democratic united front" and naming the Kuomintang as the democratic organization most likely to succeed. There is evidence that some members of the party, including Ch'en Tu-hsiu, opposed the tactic and that the Comintern agent who proposed it had to invoke loyalty to the Comintern to make the members agree. The argument of practicality that had apparently influenced Lenin may also have carried weight, for the Communist Party and Youth Corps had only a few hundred members at the time, while the Kuomintang counted some 150,000. In any event, the alliance was realized when Sun accepted first Li Ta-chao and Ch'en Tu-hsiu, and then others, into the Kuomintang while they remained members of the Communist Party.

As a factor of the future, the alliance drew together the two parties most prominent in their insistence on change. Under the partnership, revolution became a palpably growing political force, as it had not obviously been for a decade or more. At the same time, certain characteristics of the reorganization that followed suggested that revolution had not entirely broken free from the past. Rather, the past seemed a force like gravity, which was only weakened, but not destroyed, as the revolutionary rocket climbed higher. The main features of the reorganization were three: the strengthening of the structure and work of the Nationalist Party, the publicizing of a party ideology, and the building of "mass" organizations and a party army. A look at each of these will reveal the persistent influence of the past. It will also help to explain the antagonisms that soon arose in the uneasy partnership.

The new strength of the structure of the party came from the model of the Bolshevik party, the same model followed in the main by the Chinese Communist Party. Its pyramid of committees and congresses, descending from the national level to regional levels and widespread local "party cells" is described in chapter XVIII, as is its principle of discipline and participation from top to bottom, called "democratic centralism." Combining the idea of a disciplined hierarchy, the establishment of detailed rules for the behavior of members and the conduct of business, and the scheme of disseminating units of the party widely in the population, the party prepared to pursue its purposes more powerfully, that is to say in a still familiar authoritarian style, but more thoroughly than old-fashioned Chinese revolutionary movements.

Yet the party was far from being a slavish copy of the Bolshevik model, and some of the differences evoked the Chinese past. Especially was this so in the concentration of authority in the hands of Sun Yat-sen. In the party's new constitution Sun was named chairman of the two highest bodies, the National Congress and the Central Executive Committee. Moreover, he organized a Political Council beyond the constitution, gave it powers of initiative greater than those of the Central Executive Committee, appointed himself chairman of it, and gave himself the power to decide all political and diplomatic policies. All this corresponded to Sun's own developing firmness about authority, of course, but beyond that it suggested the old pattern of loyalty to one man, the emperor, as the core of political order. True, the Bolshevik system also lent itself to one-man rule in time, but never with the candor of Sun when he explained (in 1920) the inseparability of a national order from its leader. The Three Principles of the People, he asserted, were his own, and to subscribe to them and to the revolution of which they were the slogan necessarily implied obedience to him.

That this strong sense of rulership was considerably adjusted to Communist tactics of revolution was owing in good measure to the chief Soviet adviser, Michael Borodin. Having done his best to further revolution and Comintern policies in such different places as the United States, Mexico, and Turkey, Borodin arrived in Canton in 1923, a man impressive and experienced enough to win Sun Yat-sen's confidence quickly. The reorganization of the party was in the main Borodin's work, and he had a hand in much else, including the military strengthening and the framing of the party's ideology.

The central statement of the ideology came in the form of a series of lectures Sun Yat-sen gave in Canton in 1923 and 1924 on the Three Principles of the People. In this last elaboration of his doctrine, he suggested somewhat revised meanings of his principles, which now acknowledged the necessity of certain kinds of change but saw error in other kinds. The principle of Nationalism, for example, was obviously colored by the ideas of Lenin, purveyed by the new Communist allies. Where hostility to the Manchus had once been the central theme, foreign imperialism now stood as the threat that made national solidarity imperative. China was reduced to the status of a "hypo-colony," as she was subject to the oppression of all the imperialist powers, not just one. Yet, in discovering "imperialism" to be the enemy, Sun did not accept the Marxist-Leninist theories of what had caused imperialism. He still seemed to think that the primary cause was political aggressiveness, not economic greed. The defense against imperialism was correspondingly not the Marxist brotherhood of the world's oppressed, it was a strengthened China. And a stronger China would grow not only through the application of new knowledge but also through the recovery of her ancient morality. What the Chinese needed, Sun said, was renewed self-cultivation in such virtues as Loyalty, Filial Piety, Harmony, and Peace—all of them long known to the philosophers. Thus the virtues of the past pulled at his revolutionary movement, no doubt to the discomfiture of many of those whom he disdainfully called "intoxicated" with the new culture.

On his second principle, Democracy, he placed another new yet familiar emphasis. The struggle in China was not for liberty as it had been in many Western revolutions, for the Chinese people had not suffered a lack of liberty, he said. If anything, the Chinese people had too much liberty, to the detriment of national unity. The liberty needed was the liberty of the nation. To be free, the nation needed a competent and effective government. In order to assure strong government, Sun introduced what he regarded as an important theoretical distinction, that between sovereignty, which rested in the people, and the ability to rule, of which some men had more than others. Without pursuing the implications of the distinction, it is apparent that Sun was thinking of his Democracy more in terms of a strongly led and unified nation than of a country of free individuals.

The principle of People's Livelihood remained, in the lectures that Sun devoted to it, mainly concerned with economic developments of the future, rather than problems of the present, except poverty, which Sun regarded as the dominant characteristic of all Chinese economic life. It was not the oppression of one class by another that hurt China. Sun held forth at length on the fallacy of the Marxist theory of class warfare, calling it a "disease" incidental to progress, not the cause of progress. China had no classes, only differences in the degree of poverty. What was needed, he seemed to be saying, was simply more wealth, and he went on to suggest that it would be produced in large part by state-controlled enterprises. His tendency to think of state domination of the economy could be explained as well by Chinese experience as by foreign. Similarly, his concern for fixing land values and reserving subsequent increases of value for the state—a borrowed idea appropriate to conditions in industrializing countries—was compatible with old Chinese ideas of justice and political economy.

Sun's own life having been only marginally Chinese, it was not surprising that, when it came to economic theories, those he put forward were culled from Western writings. Perhaps for the same reason, he mentioned only briefly the greatest single failing of the Chinese economy (or what now by hindsight seems that): the precarious hold on life of much of the peasantry. He acknowledged that the farmer should not suffer, as for centuries past, uncertainties regarding his right to the land and its yield, but Sun did not suggest what steps might be taken to improve these conditions. Rather he dwelt on the promises of science—the increase of yields that might be expected from using better seeds, applying fertilizer, and adopting other modern techniques. His ideas of revolution extended therefore to the ready acceptance of many improvements, but they were far from insisting that the whole Chinese past must be repudiated.

Nevertheless, farmers and certain other groups did receive the attention of the party. What was done, however, signified the working of another ideology, or at least a strategy, that seemed quite foreign to Sun's way of thinking. This was the stress laid on "mass" organizations which, properly integrated with the party hierarchy, could be used for political purposes. In particular, according to party statements, peasants and workers should be recognized as strong forces for revolution, since they felt, it was asserted, special hatred of the imperialists and other oppressors. The party established a workers' department and a peasant department to further the organization of these classes. The leadership in these efforts—either Chinese Communists or members of the Kuomintang "Left"—was a clue to the special impulse behind the movement. It was, largely, the impulse given by the theory of class conflict that brought Communists to the fore in efforts to organize masses, especially in a spirit of militant hostility, which was never far beneath the surface and would in theory help to bring a revolution against those described as oppressors. Well aware that differences of opinion on this divided the Kuomintang, the

Communists always gave their support to what they called the Left Wing, namely those who approved the alliance with Russia, the alliance with the Communists, and the organizing of workers and peasants. The opposition was called the Right Wing.

An example of the power of mass organization to disrupt established society was provided in 1925, when an incident took place (the May Thirtieth incident) in which nationalist feeling burst out in the form of massive action. After a Communist labor organizer had been killed in a dispute with Japanese in a Japanese-owned cotton mill in Shanghai, students organized a demonstration in protest in the International Concession. The demonstration led to arrests, the arrests to the gathering of an angry mob outside the police station, and the threat of the mob to a round of fire by the police, under orders of a British officer. Several demonstrators were killed. Communist-Nationalist organizers soon arranged further protests, demonstrations, and strikes in many cities. In Canton a demonstration against the foreign concessions brought on another shooting, killing more Chinese. A highly effective strike and boycott of goods from Hong Kong began and continued for fifteen months. Recognizing that the patriotic and antiforeign fervor of the young had reached a new peak, Communist organizers worked hard to channel emotions into their own programs. According to one set of figures, membership in the Communist Party and Youth Corps multiplied several times over, until it reached about 20,000 in late 1925.

Although the Kuomintang supported such efforts during the alliance with the Communists, many members found the spirit wrong and the motives suspect. A movement that encouraged violent confrontations in the guise of economic demands, interrupted the economic life of the great cities, and brought the foreign imperialists together in increasingly belligerent distrust of the revolution seemed not an unmixed blessing. Furthermore, many followed Sun Yat-sen in thinking of the Chinese as a largely classless nation with common, not fundamentally conflicting, interests—a way of thinking perhaps descended from the old ideal of social harmony. On the whole the party seems to have pursued the organizing of the masses less diligently than, for example, its military program.

For many in the Kuomintang, including, it seems, Sun Yat-sen, the building of a party army was the most promising aspect of the reorganization. Several dozen military advisers arrived in Canton with Borodin, and the first shipment of Russian equipment, several thousand rifles, arrived a year later. The major effort was concentrated in the new Whampoa Military Academy near Canton, cadets being selected and trained by a Chinese staff, many of whom owed their own training to Japanese. The Russians gave advice. Naturally, great stress was laid on discipline and obedience.

Naturally, too, all who took part in administering the academy were keenly interested in directing the loyalties of the cadets, who would lead the party's armed force. By various means there was a contest for influence, mainly between Communists and members of the Kuomintang. Chinese Communists generally sought and obtained assignments as political officers attached to various units to organize courses of indoctrination and supervise political attitudes. The deputy head of the political education department was Chou En-lai (1898-). The work did not go well, apparently, for the Russian advisers were known to complain of the slowness of the growth of "political consciousness," meaning Communist attitudes. Furthermore, some parts of the military organization, such as higher general staff appointments, included no Communists.

Representative of the kind of opposition that the Communists met, and eventually the leader of it, was the superintendent of the academy, Chiang Kai-shek (1887-). Like so many other young men in the tottering years of the Ch'ing regime, Chiang had felt impelled to help his country and had trained to be a soldier, arriving at a Japanese military school and joining Sun Yat-sen's revolutionary group in Tokyo shortly before the Revolution of 1911. In subsequent years Chiang won Sun's respect, apparently for both his ability and his loyalty, and was sent as head of a mission of inspection to the Soviet Union when the alliance was formed. The few months abroad seem to have impressed upon him both the ability of the Soviet leaders and the deceit with which they professed sympathy with the Kuomintang. As superintendent of the academy, however, he accepted Soviet advisers, expressing dissatisfaction with them only now and then, and behaving with sufficient ambivalence toward the left-wing components of the revolution that his basic position remained something of a mystery. Later events would suggest that his makeup resembled that combination we have seen in some of the warlords—ambitious soldier, patriot, and Confucian moralist.

One other characteristic of the Nationalist military effort continued an old but vigorous tradition. That was the habit of warlords of pursuing their larger aims by means of expedient alliances rather than pitched battles. The Kuomintang counted among its forces a number that were really "guest armies" of independent origin. Their generals were warlords who typically cooperated in consideration of some reward, whether money or territory or some future benefit, without surrendering their own ultimate independence. The Soviet advisers were known to complain that army commanders undermined plans to centralize finances and could not be counted on always to carry out orders from the center. The commanders, or some of them, were by earlier standards warlords, and their existence reminds us that great areas of China remained politically untouched by the reorganization in Canton.

It becomes apparent also that the Kuomintang military system was much more a patchwork than the idea of a Party army suggested. This composite quality existed in other Kuomintang organizations as well. Neither the Party nor the institutions it created approached the unity of its Communist associates; and the very involvement of Communists in Nationalist affairs was itself a major source of strain. Little wonder that a contest for direction and leadership grew in intensity after 1925, when Sun Yat-sen, who had made himself so central, died of cancer.

THE NORTHERN EXPEDITION

While the tensions in the movement grew so did its strength, and in 1926 its armies opened a Northern Expedition, the campaign Sun Yat-sen had long dreamed of to bring China under unified control. By 1928 Chiang Kai-shek, the commander in chief, could announce before his old leader's coffin in Peking that the campaigns had succeeded. This was true in the sense that the revolutionary armies had defeated or uprooted several warlords; had made possible the establishment of a national capital at Nanking in the Yangtze valley; had taken Peking, the site of the Chinese governments internationally recognized until then; and had persuaded most foreign governments to recognize the Nationalists as the rulers of China. It was not true, however, that China was quite unified. The campaigns northward had employed the familiar combination of attack and accommodation. A few hostile warlords had been destroyed, others enlisted—swelling the revolutionary army, on paper, to many times its original size. In fact, there were several military forces or coalitions in effect autonomous in, for example, Kwangtung (the province from which the revolutionary army had set out), much of west and southwest China, parts of the north, and Manchuria. The Nationalist government could be confident of controlling only the provinces of the middle and lower Yangtze valley. These limits affected fundamentally the political and military future of the government.

Yet another kind of political disunity was confirmed in the course of the Northern Expedition, in the spring of 1927, when the Kuomintang expelled the Communists. Chiang's growing dissatisfaction with the Communists had been obvious for some time. The success of his military campaign probably gave him confidence in his own strength and his appeal to others in the party. The combined Left Kuomintang and Communists seemed to be increasing their efforts to curb him. Whatever the combination of circumstances may have been, as his forces arrived outside Shanghai, Chiang had apparently made up his mind to act. Communist leaders inside the city were preparing to seize power when local anticommunist groups, supported or at least unopposed by Chiang, attacked them and the labor organizations they controlled, hunting down and killing many. Chiang soon declared that the seat of the government was at Nanking, not Wuhan (the complex of cities which the Left Wing and the Communists had established as the capital farther up the river). Supported by most of the Kuomintang Central Executive Committee, he accused the Chinese Communists of trying to dominate the party, and he set out to destroy the Communists and the labor unions led by them in the regions he controlled. The Wuhan government attempted to face him down, but the members of the Left Wing of the Kuomintang felt uncomfortable. They could see that they had been separated from the party's major military power and had little of their own to depend on. Many of them doubted the wisdom of the insurrectionary tactics that their Communist associates encouraged, and they were uncertain whether they preferred Communist allies to members of their own party. The breaking point came when a Comintern agent revealed to members of the Kuomintang a telegram from Stalin, who was by then in charge in Moscow, ordering the Communists to deal with the crisis by arming party members, workers, and peasants and punishing insubordinate army officers. As ignorant and impractical as the orders were, they completed the disillusionment of the Kuomintang members, who realized finally that the Communists would take over the revolution if they could. The Left Wing, after expelling the Communists, went to Nanking—all except a handful, including the widow of Sun Yat-sen, who chose exile. The Communist advisers, led by

Borodin, left for the Soviet Union. The Chinese Communists dispersed, some hiding in cities, others disappearing into the countryside. A few attempted local risings or putsches later in the year, including an "Autumn Harvest" rising directed by Mao Tse-tung in Hunan, but were quickly put down. The Communist movement had not died, of course, but it had been disorganized and rejected by the dominant force of the revolution at the time. In the process the Kuomintang had defined its own revolutionary character somewhat more clearly: it was a movement for national unity, promising a constitutional future but dictatorial for the present, vague on plans for social and economic change but opposed to revolutionary or radical tactics. Needless to say, it condemned the Chinese Communists.

One more factor in the future of the revolution was introduced in the course of the northward campaigns: the Japanese Army. In the spring of 1928, as the revolutionary forces moved forward to take Peking, they entered the city of Tsinan, the capital of Shantung Province, which stood astride the railway leading north. Japanese troops had recently arrived there, sent to protect Japanese lives and property during the period of tension raised by the Northern Expedition. Almost immediately the two sides clashed, and after a few days of serious fighting the Japanese drove the Chinese out of the city. Although the Tsinan incident was settled later by negotiation, the Japanese pointed to one of their larger interests when they warned that if the prevalent disorder threatened to spread to Manchuria they might take appropriate steps, by which they meant war. About a month after the Tsinan incident the Japanese motive of expansion appeared again. Chang Tso-lin, the Chinese warlord who was in charge of Peking at the time, noting that the city was about to fall, took a train bound for his home base in Manchuria. As the train approached Mukden it was blown up, the warlord with it, by arrangement of officers of the Japanese army in Manchuria. The officers apparently wanted in his territory a puppet more pliable than the old warlord had been. The combination of events drew attention to an aggressive quality in China's most powerful neighbor, a tendency that later took the form of an invasion and profoundly affected the Chinese revolution.

XI

The Revolutionary

Period: The Quest

for Unity

The Nationalists in Power

After 1928 the Kuomintang, working as the government of the Republic of China, came closer to exerting unified power than any organization since the days of Yuan Shih-k'ai. (The Kuomintang was not formally identical with the National Government, but the differences did not matter much: see chapter X.) We may follow the direction of the revolution by noting briefly a few of the features of the government in the decade from 1928 to 1937 when a large Japanese invasion overwhelmed all domestic plans.

At first the style of government seemed to resemble the old imperial style. The Kuomintang never conformed to the tight, disciplined hierarchy on the modern Leninist model that its Comintern advisers recommended. The government it established worked as an elaborate combination of offices and divisions given whatever cohesion they had not by a constitution but by their common acceptance of the authority of the leader. At first Chiang Kai-shek had to compete for that authority with others whose ties to the Kuomintang and Sun Yat-sen were older than his, but gradually he established, probably mainly because of his indispensable military power as commander in chief and his native political intelligence, a preeminence most in the party acknowledged with loyalty. Though Chiang never took on the air of sanctity that had been a source of strength to emperors, who could assert their possession of the Mandate of Heaven, his political ability to hold different factions in balance by means of loyalty may have been like that of founding emperors. The relative modesty of his major concerns—he was much more interested in building a strong army and promoting moral behavior than in, for example, industrialization or agrarian cooperatives—also seemed to make him more like a traditional ruler than a modern, protean leader.

Yet the men and factions Chiang dominated were, like him, far too obviously products of modern times to be merely the old imperial court in business suits. Any sample of important names would suggest something of the conglomeration of aims and interests. There was, for instance, Ch'en Li-fu (1900-), whose uncle was a revolutionary patron of Chiang Kai-shek when the Manchus still held the throne. Ch'en became director of the investigation division of the Kuomintang, the office concerned with the internal security of the party, including the ferreting out of suspected Communists and others of questionable loyalty. He acquired great influence in staffing the party and government and with his brother was known as a leader of the "Organization Clique" or "CC Clique," which was a conservative group regarded by its critics as anything from reactionary to diabolical. Yet Ch'en Li-fu had earned the degree of Master of Science in mining engineering at the University of Pittsburgh, had worked as a coal miner and joined the United Mine Workers. He described his ambitions as being to awaken the youth of China to the past glories of their civilization and imbue them with new self-confidence; to bring China abreast of the West in science; and to encourage the study of the doctrines of Sun Yat-sen. The stance seems very close to Sun's: the acknowledgment of Western superiority in science (and perhaps only in that), the pride in the Chinese past (and perhaps, like Sun, disapproval of the "New Culture" and its iconoclasm).

A different interest was represented in Ho Ying-ch'in (1890-). Following much the same career as Chiang, he studied in Japanese military academies, joined Sun Yat-sen's revolutionary organization, and at the time of the Revolution of 1911 became attached to the headquarters of Ch'en Li-fu's uncle. He began a long and close association with Chiang when he became director of the training department of the Whampoa Academy. He was one of the chief field commanders of the Northern Expedition and became minister of war in the government in 1930. Ho represented an important group of soldiers, many of them students or associates of Chiang at the Whampoa Academy, who spoke for the primacy of military requirements in the national program, a primacy toward which Chiang leaned temperamentally and favored increasingly as time passed. Yet many of the generals like Ho, trained in an earlier day for old-fashioned warfare and experienced mainly in the half-militant, half-political art of warlord maneuvering, proved foresighted neither in the administrative duties of building a modern army nor the inventive tactics needed against modern guerrilla insurgents. Their loyalty was appreciated by Chiang, but their faults could not always be hidden even from the public.

Representative of what might be called a group of patriotic civil servants of a high level was Chu Chia-hua (1893-1963). Educated at first in German-sponsored medical and engineering courses, he showed his sympathy for the revolution early but did not immediately devote his life to it. Instead he studied in Europe, earning a doctorate in geology, and joined the faculty of the University of Peking as professor of geology and head of the department of German. As the

Nationalist movement gained momentum in 1927 he entered the government and reached the ministerial level by 1932, when he was appointed both minister of education and minister of communications. Although he left no ringing statements of purpose, he and many men like him, of modern learning and cosmopolitan tastes, indicated their hope for the National Government by joining it.

Also important were two men who suggested both new and old patterns. The new was apparent in the very Westernized forms they preferred for their names, T. V. Soong (1894-1971) and H. H. Kung (1881-1967). Soong was a graduate of Harvard, had taken postgraduate courses in economics at Columbia, worked in a banking corporation in New York, and became minister of finance in the National Government in 1926. H. H. Kung went to college at Oberlin, took a master's degree in economics at Yale, and was appointed minister of industry and commerce in 1928. The two men led in introducing modern financial procedures in the government.

What their prominence suggested of the old pattern was nepotism, for they were both relatives of the leader's wife. (H. H. Kung also was considered a direct descendant of Confucius, but it is not clear what benefits this brought, if any, beyond a general social respectability.) The ancestor of this group of kinsmen was Charles Jones Soong, a runaway from a South China village who was given an American education and returned to Shanghai to make money and become a supporter of Sun Yat-sen in the early days when Sun was making plans against the Manchus. Sun married one of Charles Jones Soong's daughters, Chiang Kai-shek married another, and H. H. Kung married a third. T. V. Soong was their brother. The two financiers established certain effective modern procedures in the National Government, but their position as relatives led to suspicions, expressed in sardonic references to the "Soong dynasty," that government was still in some measure a family affair.

A longer listing of the administrators would show an even greater variety of interests that were held in some kind of balance, but it would also show one strong tendency already suggested, that of an orientation toward urban, Western, "modern" life. Accordingly, the major efforts and achievements of the civil administration were concentrated on the urban parts of Chinese society, mainly on the coast. For example, much work went into progressive legal codes. No fewer than seven constitutional codes—draft constitutions, organic laws, and the like—were published between 1925 and 1936; they embodied such principles as legal checks on the executive, the vesting of certain powers in an elected legislature, and the legal definition of rights and duties of citizens. Certain social standards, such as a preference for monogamy and equal rights of inheritance for males and females, and economic standards, such as maximum rents on farm land, were proclaimed as law. In many respects, the legal codes looked to standards that were derived from Western values and meant most to urban Chinese who were familiar with the world's modern currents. As to their effects, the laws remained on the whole only paper proposals, for the government did not perfect an administration comprehensive enough to compel their observance, even if it had wished to, and the documents themselves reflected little sense of how offensive some of the new standards would be to conventional Chinese.

In the economy a similar emphasis on the modern sector was apparent, with more tangible results (see chapter XVI). The National Government won recognition from most Western states and Japan as Chiang curbed the aspects of the revolution that most menaced foreign lives and property and indicated that he meant to respect the treaty rights of foreigners. From this followed one of the earliest achievements of the government, the revision of treaties to restore China's autonomy over tariffs. Customs were increased and became an important source of revenue. (Foreign states also proved willing to relinquish twenty of the thirty-three quarters they held in cities as concessions under the old treaties; they gave way more slowly on another sensitive feature of the "unequal treaties," the right of extraterritoriality, which was not given up until the 1940s.) In the sphere of capital, which the administration might seek to direct into the building of a modern economy, great efforts were made to establish a strong financial system. Government banks were established, and through them a nationalized, unified paper currency issued. That the financial reforms were successful in at least one important respect is clear from the fact that prices remained stable until war with Japan began.

Yet the pattern common to most countries that have imposed a modern industrial economy on a pre-industrial agrarian base in the last century—the extraction of surplus capital from the old economy and its investment in enterprises of the new—seems not to have been followed. Some kinds of production increased, and the foundations of a self-sustaining modern economy may be revealed as stronger when the period has been more thoroughly analyzed. At present, however, it seems that in the time when the National Government enjoyed relative, though precarious, peace, it did not guide investment into enterprises aiding over-all development. There were, it is true, promising achievements, especially in communications, with some 1,400 miles of railways and several tens of thousands of miles of motor roads. On the whole, however, the government seemed able neither to capitalize sufficiently on the resources within its domain nor to spend productively what it had.

The most apparent failure to exploit resources, remarkable in comparison both to what other industrializing countries have done and to the past history of Chinese administration itself, was the forgoing of a land tax. The central government relinquished its claim in deference to the provincial governments, apparently giving up what had been the major source of revenue since the beginning of Chinese history. In fact, the decision was part of the price the government paid for the kind of unity it achieved. The government in effect compensated warlord-generals and provincial authorities for their conditional cooperation by leaving the land tax to them. In this sense, the arrangement was a political necessity, not the result of free decision.

Yet more is needed to explain how the government could tolerate an arrangement that, by all the signs of history, could only weaken the central authority. It is suggestive that not only the land tax but almost all matters concerning the Chinese countryside received only secondary attention from the goverment. The British historian R. H. Tawney[1] suggested in 1931 that the improvement of the economy of China (he had in mind the amelioration of hardship and want in the intermediate future, not a utopian state) would be bound up with rural conditions. These he discussed under three general categories of possible improvement: cheap transport (to free the farmer from local market conditions that often worked against him), science and education (to produce higher yields and more progressive farmers), and cooperation (among farmers, to make available low-interest credit and other arrangements that would assist farmers to free themselves from debt and other impoverishing obligations). He also warned that land tenure, specifically the condition of tenant farmers paying exorbitant rents, needed attention, though this was less critical than

1. *Land and Labour in China* (London, George Allen & Unwin, 1932; reprint, Beacon Paperback, 1966).

the need for credit. We have noticed Nationalist programs addressed to some of these issues, such as the road building and the law limiting land rents. There were also plans to provide cheap credit through a Farmer's Bank, agricultural experiment stations, and other related measures.

Yet Tawney observed what distinguished the government's efforts in this field, a divergence between programs and performance. A visitor, he says,

is interested in some particular problem or line of policy. He is shown a scheme of reform more complete than any which will be applied in his own country in the next quarter of a century. He pricks up his ears, and inquires what is being done to carry it out. He learns that nothing is being done, that there is little of the finance or trained administrative *personnel* required to do it, that the last official concerned in the business was not wholly above suspicion in the matter of money, and that his successor cannot visit the areas which most need attention for fear of being kidnapped.[2]

Although Tawney did not say so, others have added that the government also was disinclined to press for change in the countryside and stir up landowners, especially as they were an important constituency of the Kuomintang. No doubt the Kuomintang furthered the interests of landowners if they appeared to coincide with rural stability, as they might, for example, when a newly organized peasant association gave voice to demands never before so strongly made. Yet the Party's failures in the countryside could not wholly be explained in terms of a conspiracy of landlords. It is necessary also to keep in mind, in addition to the working of selfish economic interests, the very Westernized urban cast of mind of much of the new bureaucracy, which was not stirred by a sense of the urgency of rural problems. Sometimes it did not even acknowledge their existence. The new China would rise along the coast, in what Tawney called the "modern fringe ... stitched along the hem of the ancient garment." Though serious and valuable rural studies and experiments were made by the few who saw the needs, the Party as a whole remained indifferent. The divergence between ideas and action of which Tawney warned was revealed sharply here, for the government never devised a modern administrative system that would reach effectively into the villages. It relied on a local administration not essentially different from that of the Ch'ing dynasty, one that had hardly any

2. *Ibid.,* pp. 166-67.

offices below the level of a county seat. Accordingly, the revolution seemed far away from the villages.

As remarkable as the neglect of the countryside, and the consequent restriction of sources of revenue mainly to maritime customs, the salt monopoly, and excise taxes on consumers' staples, was the National Government's pattern of spending, specifically the favor shown the armed forces. This, too, was partly inevitable and partly deliberate. The warlords remaining on the outskirts of the National territory could hardly be trusted to resign themselves to peaceful coexistence. Chiang's armies engaged in several campaigns against them and many more maneuvers and feints between 1928 and 1937.

Japanese actions were also beyond the control of the National Government, yet they created unavoidable military demands. The new vigor of the Nationalists ruling in Nanking was felt in Manchuria in several ways displeasing to the Japanese army in South Manchuria. The new Chinese warlord, Chang Hsüeh-liang, successor of his unruly father who had come to such an unfortunate end in his railroad car, proved no more pliable to the Japanese; on the contrary, he declared himself loyal to Nanking, to which he referred questions of foreign affairs, rather than handle them himself. Equally disturbing to those Japanese who saw themselves as the developers of Manchuria was the growing immigration of Chinese settlers and the building of new Chinese railways. The Chinese challenge in Manchuria especially disturbed certain army officers who cherished the vision of a Japan superior in East Asia, and in 1931 a few of them planned to precipitate an incident that would provide an excuse for the army to occupy Manchuria. On September 18, 1931, a bomb exploded on the Japanese railway. Within days of this event, known as the Mukden Incident, the Japanese army was spreading out through the country. (The Japanese government, which had not been informed of the officers' plot, at first tried to stop the army's advance, but finding itself disobeyed became gradually an apologist for the action. The League of Nations condemned Japan, but no great power was willing to resist the aggressors with force.) Within a year the Japanese set up and recognized a state called Manchukuo, under Pu-yi, the boy-emperor of the last years of the Ch'ing dynasty, who was assigned a carefully chosen corps of Japanese advisers. Still there was no end to the aggressive spirit. In Chinese cities, the "Manchuria Incident" touched off a great wave of angry demonstrations, in the course of which Japanese subjects were attacked in Shanghai. In retaliation the

Japanese struck at parts of the city and the vicinity with sea, air, and land forces, later agreeing to a settlement. In less than a year (1933) they were moving again, occupying Jehol and probing territory to the west and south, penetrating the Great Wall, on the pretext of repressing "bandits," until it seemed that to take Peking only the decision was needed. At that point Nanking and the Japanese agreed to a truce, involving the establishment of a demilitarized zone of some five thousand square miles south of the Wall. Nanking officials had little confidence in the stability of the agreement.

Thus the National Government found itself in a situation in which the need to strengthen its armed forces was beyond question. Chiang employed a group of German officers to help improve the training and organization of the forces and the production of arms and certain other equipment, and to prepare war plans and fortifications.

The attention given to military matters also suggested that the government preferred a strong role for the military. Chiang made the armed forces separate from the civil government, so that though they were answerable to him they were not subordinate to any other branch or office—not to the legislature, for example, or even to the minister of war. Under his command the autonomous commission directing the armed forces even tended to set up offices that went beyond strictly military concerns, with political and economic functions superseding civil offices. Some of the projects for economic development—in transport and communication especially, it has been argued—served hypothetical military purposes more reasonably than economic ones. The funds allotted to the armed forces were not included in the official budget of the government and the expenditures were not audited. It is not clear how much the armed forces received and how they spent it, but few would doubt that the major portion of the national revenue went to the military.

As the Japanese grew more menacing, some critics of the National Government professed to see one more sign of the affection in which Chiang held his army: that he refused to use it. It was charged that the failure to contest the Japanese occupation of Manchuria, or to back up individual units that fought well at Shanghai or in the north, cast doubt on the qualifications of Chiang's government to represent the Chinese; the thought of some ulterior advantage, it was suggested, had taken precedence in Chiang's mind over patriotic duty. It is impossible to say whether this contained any shred of truth. Those who made the charge usually had ulterior motives of their own. Yet

Chiang's basic position was clear. He well knew that his forces were no match for the Japanese. The alternative of building an army of civilians to defend their country by any means possible, even guerilla warfare, seemed foreign to his thinking. He saw nothing to do but buy time to grow stronger.

In the meantime he assigned a high military priority to eliminating what he knew to be a potential source of great internal disunity, the remnant bases of the Chinese Communists.

The New Bases of the Communist Movement

After being expelled from the Kuomintang, the Chinese Communist leaders found their movement in pieces. Comintern headquarters in Moscow, seeking a scapegoat for the disaster, demanded a change of leadership, and Ch'en Tu-hsiu was removed (and later expelled from the party) and replaced by a man trained in Moscow, the first of several Russian-educated appointments to the Central Committee. The Central Committee established itself underground in Shanghai, but it was probably a sign of the uncertainty of the leaders that the first Congress of the Party after the split was held in Moscow (1928). In its resolutions the Congress called upon the Party to prepare for armed insurrections, to be launched on an inevitable "new revolutionary rising tide," and tended to reaffirm the orthodox emphasis on the urban workers, the "proletariat," as the leading revolutionary class, although an agrarian revolution was acknowledged to be a major task. During the next year or two several armed attacks on cities, sometimes coordinated with risings or strikes inside, were launched, only to fail. The series of failures damaged the spirit of the rank and file and raised dissension within the leadership itself.

After the split other leaders had gone into the countryside. Some had kept control over troops from the revolutionary armies which they led away to remote refuges. Others brought together remnants of peasant associations organized before the split, or uprooted city workers, and organized them into fighting bands, not much different from the familiar bandits of the countryside, except for the ideas of their leaders. Several of these groups established themselves in places where they might consolidate their strength relatively unmolested. Typically, the bases were inaccessible, often along a border between two provinces, the authorities of either of which would try to shift to the other the difficult task of ferreting out the fugitives. The bases enveloped a local population which could feed the group and support it in other ways.

One of these bases, the one that came to mean most in the development of the movement, was a fastness along the border of Kiangsi and Hunan provinces, in steep mountains called Ching-kang-shan. Much of the country was wild, with forests and preying animals, but in an area about 150 miles in circumference there were also five villages, with about 2,000 people.

In 1927, Mao Tse-tung arrived there, in flight yet confident that he saw a way to revolution which had been overlooked by the Central Committee. Mao's work in the period of collaboration with the Kuomintang had included organizing peasant associations. In 1927, before the split, he wrote a report on efforts to organize peasants in Hunan, a document revealing his impassioned conviction that the peasantry, especially the poor peasants, could be led to become an irresistible revolutionary force. "Within a short time," he wrote with typical hyperbole, "hundreds of millions of peasants will rise in Central, South, and North China, with the fury of a hurricane; no power, however strong, can restrain them." Then he added, underlining the question so that the Central Committee would not miss his implied criticism, *"Are we to get in front of them and lead them or criticize them behind their backs or fight them from the opposite camp?"* Without a word for the urban workers, the proletariat toward which the Central Committee had been directing its major efforts with so little success, he spelled out corollaries of his faith in the latent peasant power: that peasants could be organized into peasant associations; that the peasant associations would attack their enemies and take total authority in villages; that the so-called excesses of the peasant associations—denying the landlords the right to speak, parading them in the streets in tall paper hats, and creating an atmosphere of terror in villages—were right and necessary, as only by violence could one class overthrow another.

Of course Mao was not saying that the peasants themselves realized all this. It was their response to a path opened before them that he counted on, the path that would be pointed out by the Communist Party. When he arrived in Ching-kang-shan, his immediate problem was not to raise any such general questions but to make himself reasonably secure. In this he was in a position not much different from that of any old-fashioned rebel leader, taking command of aggrieved peasants by a combination of coercion and promises. He reached the mountains with about one thousand men, the remnants of a combination of deserters from Kuomintang units, armed peasants, and miners, whom he had recently used nearby in the Autumn Harvest Uprising. In addition, two bandit chiefs who had regarded the Ching-kang-shan territory as their own before Mao arrived allied their bands with his, probably because both sides found it expedient. The combined force took the defenseless villages late in 1927.

Within a few months the base received new strength through the arrival of Chu Teh (1886-). Chu Teh was an experienced soldier who had charge of cadet training and security in the Kuomintang administration of the city of Nanchang at the time of the split. He was also a covert Communist, and he joined a military insurrection that meant to seize the city. When the Nanchang Uprising also failed, Chu went south with part of the fleeing forces, falling on towns here and there in attempts to seize a base, only to be driven on by the pursuing enemy. In the spring of 1928 he brought his soldiers to Mao's mountain stronghold. The new force, the fledgling Red Army, now numbered perhaps 30,000 men with 4,000 rifles (to choose the mean among widely varying estimates). Chu Teh was its commander, Mao Tse-tung its party representative. The attention given the armed forces at this time and later—their organization, discipline, morale, and training—indicated, though it was put into words only later, that a professional army was a crucial component of the emerging technique of the revolution. Ideally dependent on two other components, an acquiescent or cooperative peasantry and a territorial base, the professional army was nevertheless the tool by which the Party actually took power.

In the next few years (until 1934), a time of, first, expansion of territory and then, under attack, attempted consolidation, the leaders of the base developed tactics in the light of experience. As the army grew and found itself able to defend the mountain base against a few tentative assaults by government forces, it mounted its own campaigns, generally in the direction of southern Kiangsi. In the new territories that came under control, the leaders established political organizations called "soviets," culminating in the proclamation in 1931 of a "Chinese Soviet Republic," with its capital at Juichin, Kiangsi. The rhetoric of the Kiangsi Soviet, for example in the terms "republic" and "democratic dictatorship of the proletariat and peasantry," by which it was described, was rich in Western concepts as transmitted through the Russian Communists. Its actual operation no doubt diverged sharply from the meanings of "republic," "democratic," and even "dictatorship of the proletariat and peasantry," for everything known—which is not much—points to a dictatorship of the Communist Party. Yet significant of the Communist political style was a kind of parallelism: on one hand, nominal participation in government by favored classes and on the other functional power kept by the Party elite.

As to social and economic action, the scanty evidence suggests that the leadership—in these fields no doubt mainly Mao—was learning politics, which has been called the art of the possible. In theory, agrarian reforms, which were a distinctive part of the program, were to be very radical, according to the statutes of the Kiangsi Soviet, which called for confiscation without compensation of all lands belonging to "feudal landlords, village bosses, gentry, militarists, and other big private landowners," and redistributing what was confiscated among poor and middle peasants. The "middle" peasants were a crucial group between the poor peasants, whom Mao championed, and the rich peasants, whom he attacked. In fact, the earliest confiscations of the band, as it sallied forth from its mountain, may well have been indistinguishable from what others would call looting, the theft of goods from the rich for consumption, which could perhaps be done with the assurance that many peasants would approve, as the victims were the classical targets of peasant rebellions. Yet it became clear to the politically astute leaders that for continued growth care must be taken not to disaffect a dangerously large proportion of the rural population. Compromises with the communistic principles of the revolution became apparent. The statutes did not mention collectivization or communization, for example, presumably because Mao had learned that peasants would be repelled by the idea. The middle peasants were exempted from the redistribution program if a majority of them desired it. Other expedient tactics, presumably born of trial and error in the field, apparently brought criticism of Mao from the Central Committee in Shanghai, which from that distance thought the practices not radical enough.

In a sense, the relations between Mao and the Central Committee pointed toward the new direction that the movement was taking. The Central Committee had not been entirely satisfied with Mao's behavior for some time. It had criticized him and even removed him from the Politburo, an executive subcommittee of the Central Committee, for various instances of insubordination and deviation from set policy. Mao rebutted the criticisms, and in the course of replying to one argument summarized the views he had developed on tactics. The statement has become famous, perhaps more famous than it deserves in consideration of how elliptical it is and how early in Mao's experience (1929). Yet it combines succinctly Mao's sense of his own originality and confidence; his three-part formula of "the masses," a mobile armed force, and a territorial base; and above all his sense of his group as the masters of the action.

The tactics we have worked out during the last three years in the course of the struggle are indeed different from any employed in ancient or modern times, in China or elsewhere. With our tactics, the struggles of the masses are daily expanding and no enemy, however powerful, can cope with us. Ours are guerrilla tactics. They consist mainly of the following points:

Disperse the forces among the masses to arouse them, and concentrate the forces to deal with the enemy.

The enemy advances, we retreat; the enemy halts, we harass; the enemy tires, we attack; the enemy retreats, we pursue.

In an independent regime with stabilized territory, we adopt the policy of advancing in a series of waves. When pursued by a powerful enemy, we adopt the policy of circling around in a whirling motion.

Arouse the largest numbers of the masses in the shortest possible time and by the best possible methods.

These tactics are just like casting a net; we should be able to cast the net wide or draw it in at any moment. We cast it wide to win over the masses and draw it in to deal with the enemy. Such are the tactics we have applied in the past three years.[3]

Critical though the Central Committee might be, Mao's base could not be denied as the major center of Communist strength. The transfer of the Central Committee from Shanghai to Kiangsi in 1932 foreshadowed the growth of the Party under Mao's domination.

The Government's Offensives and the Communists' Long March

Probably the surviving Communists were never long out of Chiang Kai-shek's mind. It was late in 1930 before other challenges to his government were sufficiently under control to allow him to try to wipe

3. Mao Tse-tung, *Selected Works* (4 vols.; New York, International Publishers, 1952-56), 1:124.

them out. The first and second "encirclement" campaigns made it startlingly clear that the Communists had a formidable style of warfare. They outmaneuvered and seriously weakened much larger enemy forces, taking perhaps 30,000 prisoners, some of whom were induced to change sides, and many thousands of rifles. The third campaign (1931) went differently. Chiang took personal command, used better troops, and moved them much more rapidly and aggressively. His main forces were threatening the Communist capital at Juichin when news of the Manchuria Incident arrived and created such military and political uncertainties that the campaign was stopped short. The Japanese threat required the National Government's full attention until well into 1932. In the meantime, the Communists spread into new southern territories, necessitating in the fourth encirclement campaign (1932-33) the deployment of half a million Nationalist troops. In the first battles the Nationalist forces drove large Communist units into flight, but later the Communists stiffened and counterattacked. The fighting was then suspended, as both sides planned the next blow. Shortly the Nationalists began preparations more thorough than before, establishing a line of blockhouses along the Communist periphery, and, in a manner reminiscent of tactics of the self-strengtheners' days, sapped the rebels' vitality by blockade. When the next offensive began (1933) Chiang had mobilized perhaps a million men. The Nationalist forces moved forward slowly at first, and sometimes lost battles, but by spring of 1934 they were closing the trap. As Communist armies began trying to break through, some were cut off and put to flight. In the fall Mao joined in the decision to abandon the base. Leaving behind thousands of guerrillas to slow down the enemy, the main Communist force of 100,000 slipped out of the ring.

The flight that followed, known as the Long March, became a legend among Communists. It ran twisting and turning far to the west and then north, across mountains, rivers, and grasslands, until it ended (1935) in the dry and poor province of Shensi, where the last sizable Communist base area survived, its leaders literally underground in the loess caves that were the common dwelling of the region. The refugees had marched more than 5,000 miles and had taken a year to do it. Mao called it a victory, an unprecedented march that succeeded despite ceaseless attacks and natural obstacles, a march proclaiming that the Red Army was manned by heroes, whose enemies were perfect nonentities. Further, he said, the march had brought news of the Red ideas to millions who would not otherwise have heard so quickly and had left seeds of revolution in its wake to sprout later.

It appears that the march was indeed remarkable, though not for the reasons given by Mao. The two major favorable effects of the march were the consolidation of Mao's leadership and the growth of a strong spirit of solidarity. The march had begun under joint direction, the group including members of the transferred Central Committee. It was joined along the way by the leader of another southern base area that had been broken up. Two important conferences were held en route, both drawing out sharp differences of opinion. As to the first, the issues are not clear, but they seem to have included a thorough airing of recent tactical errors, to the detriment of Mao's opponents in the Central Committee. The main result of the conference was Mao's gaining control of the central machinery of the Party (as chairman of the Politburo). The second conference involved a difference of opinion over the destination of the march, and consequently a contest between Mao and the other base leader for command of the military power. Eventually Mao prevailed in this, too. The growth of solidarity was linked to these events, but even more to the camaraderie generated by the great dangers and hardships that all who survived shared in memory. The long cohesion of the core of the Party probably owed something to that memory; certainly the veterans of the Long March were surrounded by a special aura in the Party.

Yet in other respects, which Mao could hardly be expected to emphasize, the Long March was a disaster. A large base area near the economic center of the country had been lost. A force that numbered 100,000 at the beginning of the march was scarcely more than 20,000 at the end (though the leadership suffered hardly any losses, in contrast to the rank and file). Even when joined by the forces already in the Shensi base, the Red Army had shrunk to about 50,000 men. As the passing Communist force threatened regions of the west, local authorities had welcomed pursuing Kuomintang armies or cooperated with them as never before, leading to an extension of the influence of the National Government. It was conceivable that the next campaigns the National armies mounted, now that the Communists were holed up and surrounded in Shensi, would destroy them as a military threat. That conjecture left out of account, however, the growing crisis in the east.

The War Against the Japanese

While the National armies pursued Chiang's policy of internal unification, the Japanese forces in North China extended their influence by steps short of open warfare. They moved troops forward on the pretext of extirpating communists or bandits, for example, collected taxes in territories they controlled, established monopoly markets, permitted the growth of a large commerce in narcotics, and loosened the National Government's grip on the administration of Hopei Province. In 1935 a puppet regime was proclaimed under the name of the East Hopei Anti-Communist Autonomous Government.

Such steps, eliciting as they did from Nanking only responses that were almost conciliatory in their effort not to force an open war, raised the pressure that patriotic feeling exerted on the National Government. Intellectuals, and especially idealistic students, more and more expressed their eagerness to see the country fight the foreign enemy instead of seeing brother fighting brother. The Communists quickly made a point of agreeing. Their own position could only be improved as they showed themselves patriots, and they could do so conveniently. The Kiangsi Soviet declared war on Japan, a wholly symbolic act, since hundreds of miles and the National Armies stood in the way of their coming to grips with the enemy. As the Long March began, it was declared that the Red Army would go north to resist the Japanese. Towards the end of the march, in 1935, the theme of the "United Front" was first heard; the Red Army sent an open telegram to the National Government appealing in the name of patriotism for an end to the civil war and a common defense against the enemy. It probably took a special effort of self-discipline for all the Communist leaders to support this tactic, considering the beating they had suffered from National armies, but the appeal justified itself by inspiring one of the turning points of the civil war.

In the government's front line, facing the Communist territory in Shensi, were battalions of Manchurian troops, those of the warlord Chang Hsüeh-liang, whose father had been killed by the Japanese and who now himself had retreated from the expanding Japanese army. It was expected that the Manchurians would play an important part in the final offensive against the Communists. Having lost their home-land to the Japanese, however, the Manchurians proved especially susceptible to the Communist call for an end to fighting among Chinese. Chang Hsüeh-liang met with the high-ranking Communist

Chou En-lai, who argued the benefits of cooperation so effectively that the two sides secretly agreed to stop fighting and to stay regularly in touch with each other.

As word reached Nanking that the Manchurian troops were not thirsting for Communist blood, Chiang Kai-shek decided to go to the ancient city of Sian in Shensi to discuss the coming offensive with Chang Hsüeh-liang and the officers of his staff at their headquarters. Chiang's intention of insuring the officers' obedience by his presence was not unreasonable, for at the time he was becoming a national hero, the leader acknowledged by the great majority of those Chinese who followed national affairs. Yet he did not know how far the insubordination had gone among the Manchurians. In the course of the conference he was arrested and presented with the demand that the war against the Communists be stopped and a national united front formed against the Japanese. Leaders from a shocked Nanking, including T. V. Soong and Madame Chiang Kai-shek, flew to Sian to support the imprisoned leader in his discussions with the mutineers. A Communist delegation headed by Chou En-lai arrived. After almost two weeks Chiang accepted the rebels' essential demands and was released (December, 1936). When he returned to Nanking, throngs of people celebrated there and in other cities, testifying to his power to unite national sentiment, as even the Communists acknowledged. Soon the National Government approved the truce and the united front, which placed the Red territory and armies nominally under its direction. Although Mao Tse-tung made it abundantly clear to his party that no essential independence would in fact be surrendered, and the united front soon proved to be little more than an uneasy and imperfect truce, some of the more ebullient spokesmen of the Kuomintang described the new arrangement as a victory. Surely Chiang Kai-shek had no such illusions. The Sian Incident freed the Communists from mortal peril and turned national policy toward a resistance that could succeed, if at all, only after a long and destructive struggle up and down the land.

The war was not long in coming and altering the distribution of power in China. In July, 1937, Japanese troops on maneuver just outside Peking, near Marco Polo Bridge, clashed briefly with Nationalist troops. After only a few shots had been fired, negotiations began. Ordinarily a settlement would have been expected, owing to the Nationalists' policy of avoiding war and the various forces of restraint operating on the Japanese army. The sequel to the Marco Polo Bridge

Incident was different, though the immediate reasons remain undetermined. At the end of the month the Japanese attacked in force and drove the Chinese from Peking and Tientsin. The next month the navy attacked Shanghai, as it became clear that what the Japanese called the "China Incident" was growing into an unlimited invasion. Nanking, the capital, fell late the same year. The National Government established a war capital at Chungking, far up the Yangtze River in Szechwan, which became the goal of a remarkable migration of students, teachers, and others from the east coast, many bringing with them the tools of their trade, so that temporary universities, factories and even arsenals were set up around the new capital, as signs of the determination to continue the fight. By the end of the following year (1938) Japanese forces had established the basic geographical shape of their occupation. They dominated most of the eastern plains, reaching inland in the north approximately as far as the eastern leg of the great bend of the Yellow River and in the center to the Wuhan urban complex on the Yangtze. Beyond the south bank of the Yangtze, in the hilly southeastern provinces, they confined themselves through most of the war to enclaves centering on the ports of Canton, Swatow, and Amoy. Within these regions they kept their strongest hold on the cities and lines of communications. In parts of the countryside Japanese soldiers appeared only occasionally, and there National troops or, increasingly, guerrillas under Communist control might exercise a rudimentary governing power.

The war affected the rival Chinese parties in profoundly opposite ways. For the Kuomintang it meant, in the terms we have been using, suspending the revolution. The end of progress, and even a step backward, was symbolized in the move of the capital from Nanking, the lower Yangtze city in the midst of some of the major modernizing projects and only two hundred miles from Shanghai, China's modern cosmopolis, to Chungking. Chungking was a town of some 200,000 before the war, a commercial center of the old sort, with its site above the great gorges of the Yangtze safely inaccessible and the caves of its rock cliffs proof against Japanese bombers. Yet everything from the narrowness of its streets to the languor of its citizens spoke of past ages and provincial unawareness, and it was oppressive to the Eastern refugees who soon swelled its population to almost one million.

All the varying layers of Chinese society in all their stages of development blended together in a city whose essential personality was compounded in equal parts of exasperation, madness, and charm. The Shanghai and Hong-kong women sneaked away to get bootleg permanent waves, which the government declared illegal; the native boatmen and carriers sneaked away to get bootleg opium, which the government likewise declared illegal. The few automobiles of the rich, screeching through the streets, dodged trussed pigs, squeaking barrows, battered rickshas. Parades adorned with green leaves besought the gods for rain in time of drought; traditional marriage processions merrily paraded behind red-draped bridal chairs under archways and banners that called on the public to celebrate National Aviation Day. The city was full of drifting odors, both nauseous and fragrant. Chestnuts roasted over charcoal and gravel, and the winds drew faint, sweet scents out of herb shops. In summer the overpowering stench of human filth in the open gutters blended with the intoxicating aroma of Chinese foods frying in deep fat with spices.[4]

The "charm" felt by these American observers was little appreciated by the Chinese refugees, who saw in its place only the old-fashioned ways they disowned in their modern view of civilization. They were drawn to Chungking by their will to be part of the new China, and their brave spirit under enemy air raids and the privations of war impressed many visitors. Yet in the long run the native atmosphere of Chungking, torpid and dark to modern Chinese, took its toll. A mood of disgust, discouragement, fatigue, and cynicism descended on many who were with the National Government in exile.

Feeding that mood were harder material circumstances. The stability of prices enjoyed until 1936 broke with the war. Inflation began and grew until a civil servant's salary in 1943 was worth (it is estimated) only 10 percent of what it would have been in 1937, a teacher's salary only 17 percent, and a soldier's only 57 percent. The situation deteriorated even more drastically after 1943. The hardship and discouragement that this brought to individuals could conceivably have been outweighed by the promise of achievement gained by sacrifice, but the government's considered plans had been undermined. It had lost the very region—the advanced east coast—on which its revenues and its projects of modernization had depended. Fifty percent of its revenues, for example, had come from maritime customs now denied it. New sources had to be found, and a land tax became at last one of them, but it provided no surplus above what was required by the war for building the new China—and no doubt could not have done so even if administered according to modern standards

4. Theodore H. White and Annalee Jacoby, *Thunder Out of China* (New York, 1946), p. 10.

of efficiency and fairness. In fact the tax collection, according to some observers, resembled closely the exigent and bullying style of imperial times at their worst.

The object of the government's major attention was the army, whose crucial importance had ambivalent effects. On one hand, the future of the whole program depended on the army. Chiang's strategy centered on a prolonged resistance, in which territory would be slowly sacrificed or a stalemate achieved until time began to weaken Japan in her gargantuan task. The first part of his plan was achieved when the front was more or less fixed along the lines described above. It was necessary to keep a huge army, said to be between four and five million men, to defend strategic points along the front and—as the United Front became little more than a slogan—to watch and blockade Communist regions. The maintenance and deployment of such a force were of themselves remarkable achievements. That the second part of the plan, a general counteroffensive against a weakened enemy, might still be effected, seemed at least imaginable in 1941, when Japan multiplied her enemies by attacking the Americans in Hawaii and the Philippines, the British in Malaya, and the Dutch in the East Indies (the Pacific War, 1941-45, the Eastern theater of World War II). An American program of military aid began almost immediately, promising improvements in the supply and training of at least some of the Chinese forces.

On the other hand, there were signs that the sacrifice of so much else did not necessarily develop a highly efficient military machine. Over the several million troops was an outsized corps of half a million officers, whose contribution to fighting efficiency was probably often difficult to demonstrate. The compound nature of the contest—the need felt by the National Government to counter both Chinese Communists and Japanese—made it difficult to commit large forces to major campaigns, even when the Japanese seemed vulnerable, and the resulting war of waiting, in which National armies undertook no major offensives, probably weakened their discipline and morale. Possibly more ominous in general was the fact that a large proportion of the armies remained under the command of generals whose loyalty to the Kuomintang, and renunciation of the warlord type of independence, was doubtful.

A less immediate concern but in the long run, in the light of the past, as important to the effectiveness of government as the armies was the attitude of intellectuals. During the war many of them tended to become estranged from the National Government. For some, the cause was apparently a combination of frustration over political defeats within the Kuomintang and the temptation of mediating between a victorious Japanese government and the Chinese population. They joined in one or another of the puppet states organized under Japanese auspices in the occupied territory. For others, mainly writers, the May Fourth movement had left as one of its legacies the idea that the purpose of art was to promote a better society. In the Chinese circumstances, that meant emphasizing injustice, immorality, and ignorance in contemporary society and advocating a revolution in social practices, often vague as to means but making Marxist assumptions, such as the identification of "feudal" and "capitalist" exploiters as the enemies of progress. Well before the war, such intellectuals had become frequent critics and increasingly opponents of the government. In 1930 a League of Left-Wing Writers was organized, including many of the most prominent of them. It had close connections with Communist organizations and was probably subsidized by the Comintern. As the war with Japan and an increased hostility of the government towards dissenters made a change of stance advisable, the Chinese Writers' Anti-aggression Association was formed in 1938. It, in turn, lost vitality as the Japanese occupation was completed, depriving writers of any single center such as Shanghai had been. Most of the prominent writers, including those of the left wing, spent the war in government territory, where their work, though emphasizing patriotic themes, was still occasionally marked by social protest. That they continued to be published at all, despite censorship and various degrees of persecution, illustrated not the benevolence but the clumsiness of the National Government. Significant numbers of young students, the specially sensitive audience of writers of fiction, made their way from government territory to the Communist base in Shensi, where they expected to help bring about that better world their mentors had imagined.

For a third group of intellectuals, including professional scholars and scientists who wanted a new China yet were suspicious of the means of the extreme revolutionaries, estrangement from the government came more gradually, as a slow loss of confidence. It would be difficult to describe the process analytically. In concrete terms there were the unstemmed inflation, the hardships of exile that fell with disproportionate harshness on those without good political connections, the lack of progress in the war, and other sources of disappointment. In the sphere of ideas, the government's pronouncements became trite and admonitory. Literary organizations promoted by the government to counter left-wing propagandists sounded as incredible in their conservatism as their opponents did in their radicalism. The leader of the government, Chiang Kai-shek, before the war fostered a New Life movement, which based a campaign for better social conduct on Confucian principles. In *China's Destiny,* a book published in 1943, he named, among other requirements for China's reconstruction (the leadership of the Kuomintang being primary), an appreciation of what was immutable in Chinese culture and a return to the Confucian virtues; and he attacked, as among the obstacles, the "superficialities and nonessentials" of Western culture that Chinese academic circles had adopted and taught, not only "class-struggle communism" but also "ultra-individualistic liberalism." Although other parts of his thesis, especially an attack on Western imperialism, which he blamed for demoralizing the nation, may well have struck a responsive chord in his readers, his attacks on the new culture must have offended the many intellectuals who thought the revolution was committed to new and liberal attitudes.

The Communists of Yenan

For the Communist Party, established in its headquarters at Yenan in Shensi, the effects of the war were in no way so disastrous. Partly that was because the Party was a simpler organization with more rudimentary immediate aims. As primarily an insurrectionary movement determined to build an army supported by peasants, it was accustomed to a rural and poor environment. It had no ties to an industrial or commercial base, such as the East had promised to be in Nationalist planning, and lost little to the Japanese invaders. Its immediate plans required no important effort toward industrialization, the development of commercial facilities, the provision of national services, or any similar enterprise of modernization in the full sense. It could count itself successful for the time being if it preserved and expanded its membership, its fighting forces, and its control over peasants.

The Party pursued these tasks avidly. For membership, the major resources were the peasant population in the regions the Party controlled. Relieved first by the United Front and then by the Japanese invasion from the Nationalist pressure that would have made rural organization more difficult, the Party apparently sought out promising members from among the peasantry to lead peasant associations and village committees of one kind or another. The war may have favored organizing efforts by disrupting ordinary social patterns, uprooting people, and weakening the customary ways that would have resisted the Communist appeal to latent discontents. The presence of Japanese (Communist organizers and eventually fighting forces penetrated the occupied areas) also made it possible to introduce patriotic arguments for organizing. A significant proportion of the claimed growth of Party membership (from 40,000 in 1937 to 1,200,000 in 1945) was said to be peasants.

However true that may be, more prominent was the other major kind of recruit, students. Peasants, like workers, never rose in any number in the Party. Students were the current representatives of the educated group which had been basic in Chinese government for centuries, and they probably supplied a large proportion of the more versatile "cadres," the Party workers who carried out policy in a variety of social settings. To prepare them, the Party established several training institutions in Yenan, one called a university. In fact the schools, unlike some of those in government territory, did not aim at the pursuit of learning and knowledge in any sense as broad as "university" implies. The Yenan institutes were meant to train cadres—party operatives—in the tactics and techniques that would advance the revolution. Thousands of students made their way to these schools from the territory occupied by the Japanese. Others came from the government's territory.

Probably the swelling of the Party by open-minded intellectuals was one of the reasons for another strengthening step, the rectification movement, which was especially notable in 1942. This was an effort to establish uniformity of style and outlook more systematically than had been conceived by the Kuomintang. Mao Tse-tung made several speeches laying down the correct line. He discoursed, for example, on the need to combine the generalities of Marxism-Leninism (theoretical knowledge) with the practical experience of the Chinese revolution (empirical knowledge); the need to subordinate one's individual interests and work to the decisions of the leadership; and the superiority of the values of politics to those of literature and art. Regarding documents of this kind almost as scripture, small "study groups" discussed the performance of their members and others, leading to criticism and self-criticism and, for more serious cases, larger assemblies to level charges and hear public confessions and vows of repentance. All these components—the written line, discussion, exposure (and of course the threat of other punishment, such as expulsion from the Party)—helped to tighten the organization.

The members of the Party also benefited in their relations with outsiders by being provided with political propositions that had been carefully prepared as the tactics appropriate to the moment. One proposition, for example, was directed mainly at the educated and urban. It was expounded in Mao's essay *On the New Democracy* (1940). Mao carefully points out that the revolution is not communistic—not at its present stage. It is, rather, new-democratic, the New Democracy being a Chinese type of democracy, a joint dictatorship of all revolutionary classes (headed by the proletariat) operating through a complex of elected people's congresses (subject to the system of democratic centralism). Economically it is also new-democratic, owning large-scale industrial and commercial enterprises but allowing other capitalist production to develop privately and, while making certain necessary confiscations from landlords, leaving peasants, including rich peasants, their private property—until the time comes for "socialist agriculture." Culturally, the New Democracy is national, not blindly foreign; scientific, not superstitious; and of the masses, not feudal. In these assurances, Mao gave the Party something with which to appeal to almost all its intellectual friends, except convinced democrats, and moved the harsher prospects of the Communist revolution discreetly into the background. Other propositions were contrived with equal care; addressing peasants, for example, Party cadres presented no such elaborate and confusing notions as those of the New Democracy—much less the ominous suggestions of socialized agriculture, which farmers would distrust immediately. Among farmers the opportune tactics could be summed up in such concrete slogans as: "Down with landlords," "Reduce taxes," "Fight the Japanese."

To strengthen its armies, the Party adopted many methods, for nothing was more vital. Morale, for example, was given great weight. Enlisted men were assured a piece of land and the income from it even while in service. Ostentatious material privileges of officers were few. A considerable amount of time went into lectures and other forms of instruction on standards of conduct and political values. Pride in the Red Army was one of the chief lessons to be learned. Technical training and experience were as industriously sought as morale, through programs ranging from competitive military drill and war games to actual engagements, often in guerrilla style, against Japanese, Kuomintang, or a warlord's forces. One aspect of the training of particularly great consequence in the effort to make a modern army was the drive for literacy. Apparently almost all companies included in their daily schedules a period for learning how to read. A comparatively literate army could be expected not only to do its job better but also to absorb more fully the political attitudes that the leadership wished to teach. Along with morale and training, tactical and strategic skills grew, benefiting from lessons learned by many different commanders in the field. The greatest strategist of all, according to the Party's present version,was Mao Tse-tung. He wrote several essays on war and strategy in the Yenan period, proposing, among other ideas, that three styles of fighting should be recognized and assigned different values at different stages of the war. Guerrilla warfare (hit-and-run tactics by local forces) was appropriate in some circumstances; mobile warfare (strikes by the main forces—the Red Army—when a victory was certain) appropriate in others; and positional warfare (defense of territory) in still others. Attention to warfare was indeed vital for more than mere survival; the very means of making revolution was to have command of guns. As Mao wrote, "Every Communist must grasp the truth: 'Political power grows out of the barrel of a gun.' . . . Everything in Yenan has been built up by means of the gun. Anything can grow out of the barrel of a gun."

By 1945 the Red Army probably numbered about one million men.

Although the men with the guns came first, the society of the countryside in which they lived was not neglected, for it was largely in the name of the peasants that the revolution justified itself. Once again, however, tactics dictated that the policies adopted should not create too much opposition for the Party to control. As mobile and guerrilla forces brought under control communities in the Japanese zone in North China—the principal region of Communist expansion—the political cadres adopted "moderate" measures of political and economic reform. Instead of filling governing bodies with Communists, they confined themselves to one third of the available positions, reserving another third for representatives of "progressive" left-wing groups and the remaining third for "independents." This gave an appearance of a broadly representative government, excluding only right-wing "reactionaries," consonant with the New Democracy. It probably reduced active hostility to the new bodies, although in fact the non-Communist members had been carefully screened for compatability with Communist aims.

One way in which this was done was through mass associations, enlisting large numbers of people with something in common, such as peasants in the peasants' associations, and women in women's associations. Formed under the leadership of Communist cadres and organized in ways that assured Communist control, the mass associations gave the Party extremely useful lines to almost the entire population in their territory and made it possible to disseminate doctrine and mobilize large numbers for a great variety of activities. Conversely, the associations promoted among their members a sense of being included in a political process. It was far from democracy, but it was closer to the machinery of power than most of them had ever been before. More tangibly, many of the associations promoted social improvements, the most striking of which was a widespread effort to teach the uneducated to read. Such satisfactions probably balanced or outweighed at the time the interference of the associations in the members' lives, for some farming communities seemed to cooperate readily—more so than fear or coercion alone could have led them to do—with Communist forces.

Economically, a similar calculation of advantages made it expedient to adopt moderate tactics. It has already been noted that socialistic land tenure was put off, and that the economic activities of even rich peasants were tolerated. Going even further, the Party abandoned at times its seizing of landlords' property, which in the early days it had used as a major source of income, and instead limited rents to 37.5 percent of the crop (an old Nationalist law never much enforced) while guaranteeing the landlords their rents. In short, the need of an environment friendly enough to permit survival and growth commended to the Party tactics that fell far short of its ultimate revolutionary ideals. Yet the concessions, which gave its programs some resemblance to social projects that the Kuomintang had abandoned, made it more popular and stronger, not less so.

The Civil War, 1946-49

The Japanese, whose invasion had meant so much to both Chinese parties, brought on the final crisis by their withdrawal. In 1945 the great Japanese armies, obeying the terms of the surrender to the Allied Powers though undefeated by either Chinese party, began to relinquish their control and move coastward to be carried home. The National armies sprang to the great cities and provincial capitals, speeded by American planes and ships. The Americans, continuing to aid and advise the National Government as a potentially stabilizing and friendly power in postwar Asia, had attempted to prevent civil war by mediating a political settlement, a coalition government of Nationalists and Communists under Chiang, but it became apparent that neither side wanted anything less than absolute domination, and each was confident of being able to win it in a fight. The Red armies raced into the North China countryside and then into Manchuria. There, they no doubt came in touch with the forces of the Soviet Union, which had sped into Manchuria a few days before Japan surrendered. The Soviet approach to the two Chinese parties was a complicated one, but in general the Russian dictator Stalin had seen the Kuomintang as the dominant power in China and had felt relations with it to be more in Russia's national interest than openly partisan support of the Communists. Yet a certain benignity was to be expected in Manchuria, where the Russians procrastinated in turning over control of the cities to Nationalists, partly, it seems, in order to give themselves time to dismantle and take away huge Japanese industrial works, and allowed large numbers of Japanese arms to be seized by the Chinese Communists. Eventually the Nationalists established themselves in the major Manchurian cities, but then a decision by Chiang to commit some of his best forces there, apparently in the confidence that he could strike a crippling blow against the Chinese Communists, proved to be a major strategic error. The Nationalists found their lines of communication constantly imperiled and the Communist armies sufficiently strong in the countryside to strike time and again without allowing themselves to be trapped. To the contrary, the Nationalists themselves were trapped, and in 1948 surrendered. In the meantime the desperate situation of the National Government was becoming apparent in many other ways. Inflation, for example, fed on the shattered economy and grew wildly. In many instances a demoralized bureaucracy failed to take needed action or showed itself corrupt. The military leadership became highly unstable, assignments and tactics being shifted rapidly and unsuccessfully. Whole armies began to defect to the other side. By 1948 the Communists were also winning decisive battles in North China. In 1949 great cities fell— Tientsin, Peking, and then, across the Yangtze, Nanking, Shanghai, and Canton. As the Communist armies pursued and pinned down remnants of opposition in the south and west, Chiang Kai-shek retreated with much of the National Government and several thousand troops to Taiwan, the island known in the West by its Portuguese name of Formosa.

The Kuomintang Government
on Taiwan

The move to Taiwan, until comparatively recent times a remote frontier of Chinese civilization and, lying as it does across the Straits of Formosa, the only province physically detached from the others, must have brought home to every Nationalist a realization of defeat. The appointment of committees to reform the structure of the party, the disappearance from central positions of many of the leading figures of the past, the gradual disbanding of remnants of warlord armies that had made the crossing with more dependable forces— these acts as well as attempts by members of the party to analyze or explain the defeat in print pointed to the impact of the disaster. Perhaps the psychology of defeat is also illustrated in the harsh treatment accorded the Taiwanese. They were mostly (apart from a few aboriginal tribes of Polynesian stock, long since driven into mountain settlements or reservations) the descendants of immigrants who came from Kwangtung and Fukien beginning in the seventeenth century. Their rough-and-ready society had seemed to mainland observers different from the more settled mother country even before the twentieth century, and the Japanese administration from 1895 to 1945 contributed other differences. The demoralized Nationalist newcomers treated Taiwan almost like an alien land when they took over from the Japanese, beginning with a military administration that apparently (though exactly what happened is disputed) conducted a program of intimidation, killing a number of Taiwanese who were labeled subversives, without much regard for the justice of each case. Even when the administration was reformed on higher authority, the Nationalists maintained their supremacy over the Taiwanese so carefully that the distinction between the two groups flowed as a subcurrent in the subsequent history of the island. The main point, for our purposes, was that the Kuomintang, far from disintegrating under defeat, remained, or became once again, an effective political organization. It resumed its program of revolution, though modified by recent history and a drastic change of territory. Again the interplay between revolution and tradition sometimes became apparent.

To take, for the sake of convenience, the basic program of the Three Principles of the People, the first principle of Nationalism, since it could not be fulfilled in its primary sense of the unity of the Chinese nation, tended to be upheld in secondary and sometimes curious ways by the Kuomintang administration. The general idea had been to put a high value on a sense of solidarity among the Chinese people and to promote loyalty to a national government. Although members of the Kuomintang unquestionably felt an identity of interest with the nation, and maintained that theirs was the only legitimate government of China, the Straits of Formosa separated them all too obviously from the main territory of their concern. Nationalism took the form of a great project, that of the reconquest of the mainland. As unlikely as it might seem, the policy was argued along lines remarkably similar to those once used by Sun Yat-sen and other revolutionaries, that the people on the mainland were seething with discontent and would rise up against their masters, if a liberating force struck at the right time. Many administrative decisions, such as those concerning the armed forces, were justified in terms of this policy. Although as years passed the right time did not come, to question the policy publicly was dangerous. When the editor of a journal did so, also questioning the one-party rule of the Kuomintang and helping to organize an opposition party, he was charged with sedition and sentenced by a court-martial in 1960 to ten years in prison. Yet he probably only expressed what many intellectuals privately felt, that the recovery of the mainland was an illusion. The thought of battle receded even further owing to the relative security of Taiwan. In 1950 the American government, committing its forces to the defense of South Korea against the invading North Koreans, decided that conflict over Taiwan should be prevented if possible and ordered a fleet to stop any attempt at invasion from either side of the Formosa Straits. The following year, it began large-scale military and economic assistance to the Kuomintang administration.

A corollary of the principle of Nationalism as it appeared in Sun Yat-sen's lectures was the glory of the Chinese past. On Taiwan the Kuomintang presented itself more consistently than ever before as the defender of tradition. Courses on Confucianism were required of high school and university students, and the government subsidized Confucian ceremonies. When opportunities arose for an expression of official preferences in the arts, such as a choice of plans for a new building or an award for painting, works in traditional style almost invariably won. Not that this expressed the consensus of the intellectual and artistic community; to the contrary a considerable proportion of the intellectuals who accompanied the party to Taiwan in 1949 or arrived later were those of the May Fourth generation or others whose preoccupations were modern and experimental. Painters, sculptors, and musicians made use of modern forms. The freedom of such groups to work testified to the relative tolerance of the administration, in sharp contrast to the totalitarian strictures on the mainland. Yet the Kuomintang threw its weight in these matters, and in more broadly cultural matters as well (it pictured itself as a great champion of the family and the familial virtues, for example, in contrast to the Communists), on the side of conservatism. In some respects that weight was effective, as in literature. Regarding the May Fourth movement as the seedbed of Communism, the Kuomintang arranged that almost nothing written by the major authors between 1919 and 1949 was available on Taiwan. Young writers on the island either were ignorant of the major modern wave of Chinese social realism or found it prudent not to reveal its influence; almost no serious fiction was written about contemporary Taiwanese society or the era of the defeat on the mainland.

In another respect the principle of Nationalism may be said to have been modified, not by design, perhaps, but by the force of older habits. That was the failure on the whole of the refugees from the mainland to accept Taiwan as their nation. For most, however slight their expectation of returning home, Taiwan remained a place of exile, somewhat like the worst assignment conceivable to an official of the old days. Mainlanders tended not to mix with Taiwanese of a comparable cultural level. Intellectual Taiwanese felt distant in return, aggravating the sense of grievance bred by the mainlanders' dominance in government and politically controlled enterprises.

Under the second principle, Democracy, an arrangement emerged that followed Sun's vision in some measure, though it differed essentially from Western ideals of representative government. In 1947, in the hectic days of the civil war, a constitution was promulgated, and afterwards national elections were held, obviously under questionable conditions, and a National Assembly and Legislature convened. The country nominally moved from the Kuomintang's period of Party Tutelage into the period of Constitutional Government.

Soon, however, the war dictated the declaration of a state of martial law, which remained in force thereafter, vitiating certain features of the Constitution, such as the legal protection of civil liberties. The move to Taiwan, moreover, made it impossible to animate the national bodies by periodic elections, since only the citizens of one province, Taiwan, would be able to vote. Since the maintenance of a constitutional apparatus was regarded as an important symbol of national authority, the National Assembly and the Legislature continued to sit in the "temporary" capital, Taipei, though much diminished in numbers as the original members died with no one to replace them. The Constitutional government was both a luxury, since a provincial government also existed, and a convenience, which provided positions for the faithful. In short, despite an increased acknowledgment of constitutional procedures, the government remained in matters of greatest consequence a party dictatorship, at the center of which, apparently never surer of his power, remained Chiang Kai-shek. The powerful executive, compatible with much of Sun Yat-sen's own view of government, inevitably invited comparison with the old imperial system.

Nevertheless, at lower levels, true democratic elections began to be held. The provincial assembly was elected (though the provincial governor was appointed by the national government) and county and city elections became common. The Kuomintang tried to keep a firm grip on positions of major importance, but it was not especially prominent in local offices, which usually went to non-Party candidates. At that level Taiwanese democracy gave power to the ballot. Real issues, though local, divided candidates, and the practice of political choice may have begun to be rooted among the people.

The most notable achievements were related to the third of Sun Yat-sen's principles, that of the People's Livelihood, or Socialism, though it was the one least clarified in theory and most controversial in practice in earlier days. Contrary to those times, the Kuomintang set itself to a serious agricultural program soon after settling down on Taiwan. The impetus may have come from a reappraisal of its policies of the past or from the urgings of American advisers and their Chinese colleagues on a Joint Commission on Rural Reconstruction, an organization begun in the last year on the mainland. It has been observed that the political obstacles to a reform of land tenure were minor compared to those on the mainland, where the Kuomintang was said to hesitate to disturb the vested interests of its own membership. On Taiwan, to the contrary, land reform would hurt only Taiwanese gentry, who, as the native elite, happened to be most resentful of the Kuomintang intrusion. In any event, programs including limitations on rent and long-term financing of the farmers to enable them to buy land the landlords were required to sell resulted by 1964 in a high proportion of small proprietors. Arrangements for credit, cooperative buying and marketing, and technical information through farmers' associations contributed to a generally more prosperous and highly productive farming population. Sun Yat-sen's idea of "land to the tillers" was realized, and by a means as compatible with traditional Chinese precedents as with modern developmental practices—the initiative of the state.

In the sphere of modern industry the Taiwanese economy grew as did few other newly developing regions in the same period. One factor was the foundation laid by the Japanese, who had increased literacy in the population, accustomed it to technological change, established good systems of communication and transportation, and introduced a few industrial facilities. When the Japanese managers and technicians withdrew, Chinese of comparable skills were available among the mainland refugees, whose generally high competence was a second aid to growth. A third factor was American aid, which provided an important surplus for investment until 1964, when economic growth became self-sustaining. The varieties of industry are named in chapter XVII.

However uncertain was the total effect of the revolutionary forces on Taiwanese life, the change in Taiwan's material conditions was unmistakable, for the growth of productivity was followed closely by a rise in per capita consumption and an extension of such social facilities as universal education and public health services. No doubt Sun Yat-sen would have been amazed to find Taiwan the most prosperous of Chinese provinces half a century after his Republic was declared, but on the whole he would probably have recognized the cardinal features, though in miniature, of the future he had once imagined.

The People's Republic of China
(1949-)

As the National Government in flight moved from ruling a nation to ruling a province, the Communist Party in victory moved from ruling a province or two to ruling a nation. Its responsibilities, as the power behind the new People's Republic of China, proclaimed from the capital, Peking, in 1949, exceeded those it had had before not only in scale but in kind. It had to extend, of course, its special revolutionary characteristics, such as its elaborate political organization reaching every part of the population and its doctrine of elevating the old lower classes at the expense of the upper. It also had to attempt much that it had not done before: to plan and build industry, to increase greatly the productivity of agriculture, to establish on the foundation of what had already been done a universal school system, to defend the country and serve its interests internationally—in general to improve the quality of life as commonly desired in modern times regardless of political doctrine. Many aspects of the undertaking appear in the topical chapters in the second part of the book. Even so, with a subject so vast, we are still too close to the trees to be able to say much about the wood. What follows here is an essay, a tentative contribution to our theme, the significance of the past to the revolutionary present.

THE SOCIAL ORIGINS OF THE LEADERSHIP

The administration of the country after 1949 was comprised in its upper levels mainly of men who had been born to privilege. Within the Communist Party the largest single category of members was that of peasants, but the peasant members, and the workers who made up a smaller portion of the Party, usually occupied local positions on a low level, such as membership in farmers' associations, the ranks of the army, and factory committees. Though there were millions of such positions in the Party, which was said to have 17,000,000 members in 1961, and their functions important to the efficiency of the organization as a whole, they had little to do with making policy and setting the style of administration. The higher positions that did so—those in central ministries and central committees of mass organizations, regional administrations, special commissions, and the like—were filled in large proportion by men classified as intellectuals. Though the term remained a bit vague, it generally connoted a higher education and employment at mental, not physical work, characteristics which in turn pointed almost certainly to a background the Party classifiers might call "feudal," that is, supported by land rents, or "bourgeois," engaged in some modern enterprise in the city. The highest or most crucial positions went to old Party men, who had spent so much of their lives as professional revolutionaries that the class to which their families belonged hardly counted ordinarily, yet even they were often the sons of landlords and had come to the Party by way of a higher education. At intermediate levels, which had to expand rapidly as the Party won control of the country, "intellectuals" were the most likely qualified recruits. Moreover, governing the country required more men than the Party, with its standards of loyalty and obedience, was willing quickly to enroll. As a result a large number of non-Party intellectuals entered positions of importance, the coalition of "progressive" groups that had been embodied in the New Democracy remaining a practical necessity. In crude terms, the leadership of the People's Republic, on the basis of social origin alone, was not more deeply rooted in the people than had been some of the great imperial dynasties—the Han or the Ming, for example. This is not to say that the aim of social upheaval and its apparent achievement in the countryside were not revolutionary, only that those who conceived and directed the upheaval had been born and bred to regard themselves as the leaders of the people, an elitist attitude not far from that of the old scholar and official. The manner in which the leaders saw the problem revealed that they were sensitive to the formal, if not the psychological, drawbacks of an elitist tradition in a populist age. They frequently warned against "commandism" and other symptoms of arrogance. Yet what they considered the greater issue was not the existence of the elite, but its quality, as exemplified by the perennial debate over the relative importance of being "Red" and "expert." Being "Red," mastering Marxism-Leninism and the thought of Mao Tse-tung, took priority over merely technical knowledge and skills, evoking the old standard of the Confucian gentleman, whose devotion to a moral vision made him a man better qualified to govern than one who only thought about getting things done.

THE OVERTURNING OF THE ESTABLISHMENT

Despite signs that the new elite owed something to the old, its view of its primary task distinguished it from victorious dynasties of old and even from the Kuomintang. The old dynasties generally contented themselves with establishing control of the administration of the country, leaving alone the social structures by which most small communities regulated themselves, unless special circumstances, such as the growth of rebelliousness or other faults, recommended a display of force. It might be said that the Kuomintang had aimed for a similar stability and self-regulation in the countryside, while concentrating on changing national administration and beginning to modernize the economy. The Communist Party, as its early rural policies sometimes suggested, regarded as essential to its very concept of revolution the breaking down of the customary social structure. Mao Tse-tung dwelt on it, asserting that force was the necessary means, as early as 1927, in his report on efforts to organize peasants in Hunan.

A revolution is an uprising, an act of violence whereby one class overthrows another. A rural revolution is a revolution by which the peasantry overthrows the authority of the feudal landlord class. If the peasants do not use the maximum of their strength, they can never overthrow the authority of the landlords which has been deeply rooted for thousands of years. In the rural areas, there must be a great fervent revolutionary upsurge, which alone can arouse hundreds and thousands of the people to form a great force. All the actions ... labeled as "going too far," are caused by the power of the peasants, generated by a great, fervent, revolutionary upsurge in the countryside. Such actions were quite necessary in the second period of the peasant movement (the period of revolutionary action). In this period, it was necessary to stop malicious criticisms against the peasant association. It was necessary to overthrow all the authority of the gentry, to knock them down and even trample them underfoot. All actions labeled as "going too far" had a revolutionary significance in the second period. To put it bluntly, it was necessary to bring about a brief reign of terror in every rural area; otherwise one could never suppress the activities of the counter-revolutionaries in the countryside or overthrow the authority of the gentry.[5]

The steps that Party representatives took as they appeared in thousands of villages following the end of the fighting clarified what Mao meant. The occasion was an economic project—a massive reform of land tenure, carried out, according to official statements, almost everywhere between 1950 and the end of 1952. As gigantic as the economic reordering was, it was only one aim of the project, an aim that even proved transitory when the countryside was later reorganized again. A more important aim was to reorder local political authority and social status. The means of doing so consisted of a carefully worked-out procedure, commonly including the following steps: the dispatch of armed units to confiscate all firearms from the villagers; the dispatch of land reform cadres, often quickly trained organizers from the city; the cadres' selection of "active" or "positive" villagers, preferably poor peasants but in any event relatively aggressive and cooperative ones, to lead the peasant association and people's militia; the cadres' agitation of "active elements" by organ-

5. *Selected Works,* 1:27.

izing discussions around leading questions, such as, "Who has supported whom?" and "Who has made whom rich?", and the encouragement of the aggrieved to "spit out their bitterness"; the inauguration of "class struggle," with the more militant peasants confronting and making demands of landlords; the creation of terror by the conspicuous beating or killing of offending villagers, whether landlords or not; and the confiscation and redistribution of land. In this last step, the land was generally taken from landlords and "rich peasants" and given to "poor peasants" and landless workers. Many landlords were tried in kangaroo courts and killed (estimates vary from several hundred thousand to twenty million), and deeds of possession were issued to the new landholders.

Simultaneously campaigns in cities promised to affect similarly the structure of authority in urban society. For example, the "Three-anti" and "Five-anti" campaigns of 1951-52 were aimed at officials and businessmen respectively. By means of official statements, articles in newspapers, meetings, and in other ways, the three vices of corruption, waste, and "bureaucratism" came under fire in the bureaucracy, and the five of bribery, tax evasion, stealing state assets, cheating on material or labor, and stealing state economic intelligence in the business community. Cadres were specially assigned to arrange open meetings in all kinds of organizations to hear charges and confessions, and to man offices to receive letters of accusation, which it seems could be anonymous. In spirit, moral indignation became nobler than respect for facts. It was given out that the mayor of Shanghai, a ranking Party man, said, referring to the "Three-anti" drive, "charges need only be five percent correct." With virtue so triumphant, evil things could be expected to happen. In addition to many open confessions and apologies there were secret proceedings, ending in the imprisonment, forced labor, or execution of the accused. Incidentally, the "Five-anti" campaign also showed those big businessmen who had eyes to see that their days of free enterprise were numbered. By 1956 all large enterprises had been expropriated.

Several of the steps taken to reorganize the countryside corresponded in part with one or another element of the past, as did the companion campaigns in the cities. The disarming of the population, for example, had been a policy of imperial dynasties, though perhaps never so effectively enacted, and the quick action of the new government affirmed that it felt at least as strongly as its predecessors about monopolizing arms. When the farmers were induced to "spit bitterness" they also reanimated something of the past, perhaps from two sources. A litany of grievances was an ancient rite, before combat between rival camps, for example; and the farmer no doubt had long known a ritual style of complaining before he rebelled. However, the Communists' exploitation of grievances was probably more systematic than anything in the past. Another element familiar from the past was the resort to terror; what gave it special significance was its indiscriminate quality, for despite the theory of the Party that it represented the exploited classes against the exploiters, the beaten and the dead came from no one class, and the sight of them could frighten high and low alike, with only membership in the Party promising a degree of safety. Even then a resemblance to older practices remained, for the purge of officials in the Three-anti campaign carried into the modern bureaucracy the kind of fear that the emperors had often found useful. Finally, the confiscation of property, that of both landlords and entrepreneurs, also recalled an ideal of some of the greatest peasant rebellions. The distinctive aspect, that the redistribution was only the first step toward communization, the Party did not choose then to stress to the fortunate farmers.

In general, it was the distinctiveness of the new programs rather than their resemblance to ancient ways that stood out. The Party, although bound necessarily by certain Chinese styles of behavior (surely even more than we have been able to note), saw itself creating a new China. The sense of novelty, of all steps, no matter how familiar, as part of a monumental effort to remold the civilization, dominated the picture of what was happening. Not all was simply Communist, to be sure, but almost all owed something, at least, to the modern West. The totalitarian aim of the Party, although compatible with the authoritarian claims of old Chinese governments, was much more ambitious than anything in the past had been. The administrative hierarchy, for example, reached more directly into basic social groupings—the village in the countryside, the ward or street in the city. Government began to touch regularly more people in more ways, an extension of scope that is generally associated with modern Western political trends. One of these ways seemed fundamentally Marxist: the encouragement of class struggle, for which the land reform and the Five-anti campaign, for example, gave opportunity. In other ways policies were defined not so much in class terms as in terms of "the people," an approach suggesting a looser kind of populism. The people not only were the justified makers of the revolution, so this view implied, but also the bearers of innate virtues. Thus poetry written by the people was published, the art of the people extolled, and the wisdom of the people commended—not only, it appeared, to hold the acquiescence of the people, though that motive no doubt played a part, but to influence the behavior of the cadres in their relations with those they governed.

Of all the factors giving a sense of profound revolution, the strongest, after that of the ubiquity of government, was the mobilization of the masses. There were national campaigns, drives in which the various mass organizations cooperated, toward certain goals or to publicize great issues—to kill the grain-thieving sparrows and rats, for example, or the germ-laden flies, or to fill moments of rest in the daily routine with practice in reading. With an ability to direct the activities of hundreds of millions of people, the government seemed capable of working miracles. It apparently had a sure sense of the sources of unity, as when the power of patriotic feeling was invoked in support of the Chinese intervention in the Korean War (1950). Advantage was taken of the opportunity both to encourage public hostility to the United States and to expose "counter-revolutionaries" at home.

RADICALIZATION AND RESISTANCE

In a few years, the image of a nation plunging boldly but deliberately and smoothly into revolution was blurred. Opposition and obstacles appeared, while the leadership seemed to press for more radical positions. It is impossible to date this changing atmosphere exactly. There were reports of farmers dragging their feet from about 1952, as the regime moved quickly from the pattern of individual farms that it had seemed to support by its land reform to progressively more comprehensive and compulsory forms of farmers' cooperatives. In industry, certain problems of development appeared more stubborn than they had seemed at first. Two events of 1957, the "Hundred Flowers" episode and the *hsia-fang* (manual labor movement), illustrate changed conditions involving the elite.

The "Hundred Flowers" episode revealed serious dissatisfaction with the regime among intellectuals. In 1956 spokesmen of the Party expressed support for open debate and criticism in scientific and literary work, including even criticism of the bureaucracy. The slogan put out to describe the policy went, "Let a hundred flowers bloom, let a hundred schools of thought contend." It has been suggested that the leadership wished to foster a healthy atmosphere for intellectual work, assuming that vigor and loyalty could be best assured by relatively free conditions. There were limits, generally connected with the doctrine and role of the Party, which could not be exceeded, but Mao Tse-tung, it has been proposed, was confident that the vast majority of people, including intellectuals, shared his basic satisfaction with China's course. The popular revolt against the Communist regime in Hungary in the fall of 1956 apparently also reinforced the feeling that channels of communication must be kept open. It has been suggested, too, in view of what happened later, that open expression was considered a means of disclosing any poisonous weeds that might be lurking among the flowers. The proportional weight of these motives remains uncertain.

At any event, in 1957 Mao made a speech, published later, that established the policy and served to bring the campaign to an intense pitch. Called "On the Correct Handling of Contradictions among the People," the speech had wider theoretical implications than the question of freedom of expression alone, but on that it suggested that differences between the people (the friendly classes, of course, not the enemy reactionaries, etc.) and the government were not basic. They required discussion and persuasion, not force. After some delay, presumably owing to the suspiciousness of the intellectuals, and possibly some priming of the movement by letters planted in the press, a tide of criticism rose up in statements to newspapers, on the walls of universities, and at meetings. Many exceeded by far the limits the Party could tolerate. There were accounts of individuals long held in prison without trial, of scientists who could not do scientific work because of endless political and planning meetings. There were more general charges: that the Party gave preference to those who were loyal over those who were able, that it intruded on disciplined scholarship in many ways, that it showed contempt for the past and for the people and adopted the imperious attitude that "the world belongs to the Party." Some charges came close to the most vital matters, asking whether Marxism had not stagnated, taking exception to one-party rule, and even condemning the entire "system." We cannot discuss here all the suppressed attitudes revealed during the period. Many of the liberal viewpoints familiar from the days of the New Culture movement were obvious, as well as cases of special-interest pleading. What mattered more generally was the evidence of disaffection of significant numbers of intellectuals, who had often prided themselves in the past, justifiably, on their own effect on the condition of the Chinese state.

After about six weeks, notices began to be issued closing the "Hundred Flowers." An "Anti-rightist" campaign followed, directed against the many who had revealed "bourgeois democratic," "individualistic," and other counterrevolutionary tendencies. So widespread was the need of correction, however, that the Anti-rightist campaign was expanded into the manual labor campaign. With it was also merged a "Rectification" campaign designed to correct abuses among the swollen and young bureaucracy, including "commandism," "dogmatism," and "opportunism." Under the manual labor campaign, called *hsia-fang* (literally "downward transfer"), as many as several million students, teachers, and urban bureaucrats were sent to collective farms for various periods. This was meant to accomplish several things: punishing offenders, providing assistance in the harvest, and freeing the young elite of their disadvantageous "separation from the masses." In theory it had far-reaching implications, especially as it became a regular practice thereafter, for it suggested the willingness of the Party to interrupt the education normally considered essential for the techniques of modernization in favor of a quite different kind of education, which might be called psychological education. While the idea itself brings to mind the traditional view of education as primarily a moral, transforming endeavor, we cannot say what of that kind, if anything, actually happened. Nevertheless, the plan acknowledged by its scope how strong the Party thought the latent cultural opposition to be.

At approximately the same time that these evidences of dissidence appeared, the Party began adopting policies and positions that made it seem an instrument of ever more radical revolution. In its relations with the world outside, the Party moved toward presenting itself as the one true heir of Marxism-Leninism. The first visible signs may have been in the Chinese response to the speech of the Russian leader Khrushchev in 1956. Khrushchev attacked the dead Stalin as a ruthless conqueror of the Party, the fomenter and beneficiary of a "cult of personality," that is, the glorification of himself. The Chinese responded to this "news" (widely known earlier outside Communist circles but never admitted within them) in measured terms, never carrying "de-Stalinization" as far as other Communist parties. In fact, the Chinese Communist Party had reason not to admire Stalin uncritically, but it appears that Mao Tse-tung doubted the wisdom of dwelling overmuch on the dangers of a cult of personality. He was the object of a cult himself, a fact that probably affected his judgment, but, beyond that, it may be suspected that the old Chinese idea of

individual leadership still carried weight. De-Stalinization nevertheless had consequences of another kind, for Chinese statements began
to point out the need for real consultation among the world's
Communist parties, in implicit contrast to the dictatorship under
Stalin. With his passing, the Chinese apparently began to have a sense
of autonomy like that of other parties at the same time. Among the
Chinese, however, that feeling grew until the true Marxist succession
seemed to have passed to Mao Tse-tung.

Intimations of this attitude no doubt contributed, with other
factors, to the split with the Soviet Union, the most visible mark of
the radicalism of the Chinese Party. When the Russians tested an
intercontinental ballistic missile and launched the first and second
earth satellites in 1957, Mao Tse-tung summed up the enormous
strategic significance of the events, as he saw it, in the slogan, "The
east wind prevails over the west wind," and pressed for more
aggressive Communist policies against the West. To that the Russians
must have answered cautiously, for with their different assessment of
the cost of challenging the West they tended to prefer peaceful
coexistence. Other differences may have included matters of such
specific concern to the Chinese as Russian cautiousness over Taiwan
when the Chinese considered taking the initiative there in 1958 and a
Russian refusal to supply nuclear weapons. In general the two sides
found themselves increasingly at odds on global strategy, China's own
internal development (as mentioned below), and even points of
relevant doctrine, with the Chinese taking the more revolutionary,
more aggressive, "tougher" position. In addition, issues of direct
national rivalry, such as border disputes, increased the tension
between the two. In 1960 the Russians withdrew the technical advisers
who had been assisting Chinese industrial projects and reduced other
forms of aid and trade. By 1963 the central committees of the two
parties were issuing long attacks on each other, the Chinese charging
the Russians with, among many other faults, "revisionism," that is,
abandonment of the revolution, and asserting the fidelity of the
Chinese leadership to the true doctrine. The Russians answered with
equally long lists of Chinese faults, including warmongering.

While presenting themselves as the true revolutionaries of Communism, the Chinese resembled their dynastic predecessors in the way in
which they sought hegemony in bordering regions. As the most
notable example, in 1950 Chinese forces entered Tibet, whose own

theocracy had asserted the country's independence shortly after the fall of the Manchus. Without acknowledging that independence, the Chinese Communists signed a treaty assuring the Tibetans of autonomy and religious freedom. In 1956, however, the Party began organizing in Tibet revolutionary changes similar to those carried out in China, which would draw Tibetan life under the firmest control. Tibetans rebelled, but the Chinese continued their reorganization, although it led to the killing of tens of thousands of Tibetans; the flight of the ruler, the Dalai Lama, and thousands of followers to India in 1959; and sporadic fighting for years afterwards. Another border region to be secured lay along the Himalayas adjoining India in several places. In 1962 Chinese forces drove Indians out of disputed territories and absorbed them, although the campaign cost China the good will of India, whose support in international bodies had been a diplomatic asset. China's assertiveness on her borders was also animated by a strong dose of modern nationalism, as her adamancy over the return of Taiwan showed. Where the Ch'ing government had maintained relations with a Japan that had taken the island as a prize of war, the People's Republic insisted that she could contemplate no sovereignty there but her own.

Although the Party would have abhorred any suggestion that it had embraced attitudes of the "feudal" past, traces of what seemed to be the old habit of making Chinese experience a model for humanity appeared even in some of its most radical statements. In 1965, for example, one of Mao's ranking lieutenants wrote an article on the nature and prospects of "people's wars," that is, Communist-led revolutions. He asserted that the key to success—not only of individual revolutions but of the world revolution—lay in the Chinese example.

It must be emphasized that Comrade Mao Tse-tung's theory of the establishment of rural revolutionary base areas and the encirclement of the cities from the countryside is of outstanding and universal practical importance for the present revolutionary struggles of all the oppressed nations and peoples, and particularly for the revolutionary struggles of the oppressed nations and peoples in Asia, Africa and Latin America against imperialism and its lackeys. . . .

Taking the entire globe, if North America and Western Europe can be called "the cities of the world," then Asia, Africa and Latin America constitute "the rural areas of the world." . . . In a sense, the contemporary world revolution also presents a picture of the encirclement of the cities by the rural areas. . . . [6]

Although the Chinese have not been the only people to think of themselves as being at the center of the stage, the official reassertion of the trait in the modern world had an archaic and dogmatic ring to it.

The Party also adopted more radical policies at home, most dramatically the Great Leap Forward, which was launched in 1958. At the center of the plan were two main ideas that might seem contradictory, though both were revolutionary. On one hand, there was to be an enormous increase of production, to which the "Great Leap" most directly referred. On the other, the society, beginning with the rural population, was to be reorganized into communes, highly organized units at once politically, agriculturally, and industrially integrated—an undertaking which might have been expected to require in every aspect of life so many readjustments that production would fall, not rise. In retrospect, close observers have thought they detected in the plan for communes signs of differences within the Party over the direction of the revolution. Whether this was so or not, the Great Leap Forward was promoted as a distinctive and unprecedented advance. Millions of Chinese hands were to perform miracles without waiting for machines. The energy liberated among the people, inspired by the great step toward communism, would be apparent in the production figures. In some of this, such as the pride in the constructive power of organized millions and even, in part, the idea of communes, there seemed to be a debt to the Chinese past, but the essential goal was the creation of a radically new way of life. The revolution—the world revolution as well as the Chinese—was on the threshold of a new phase.

Within little more than a year, however, it became clear that the leaders' visions had so exceeded the practical that, far from approaching utopia, they must struggle to maintain the existing standard of living. In practical terms, the advantages that were supposed to follow from the establishment of communes were not realized. It had been thought that communities averaging between 20,000 and 30,000 people, highly organized in order to benefit from large-scale cooperation and efficient division of labor, and using systematically certain

6. Lin Piao, "Long Live the Victory of People's War!," *Peking Review*, Sept. 3, 1965, p. 24.

Peking street scene in 1971: power lines, motor vehicles, and students in formation.

favored techniques, such as deep plowing, would produce striking increases in the production of food. Instead, the Party reduced by 100 million tons the figures it had originally published for grain produced in 1958. Zealous officials, it was explained, had exaggerated their production figures (an action reminiscent of the old practice of padding figures to impress those higher on the ladder), but the revised figures still claimed an increase of about 74 percent over 1957. Nevertheless, in the following years the communal organization was greatly loosened, where it continued to function at all, suggesting that the results had been more harmful than beneficial. From 1961 to 1963 China bought grain from Canada, Australia, and other countries, to make up in some measure for a shortage of food that apparently resulted in widespread hunger. The Party blamed the weather, but there is evidence that the practical and emotional turmoil brought by the Great Leap had played a part. The industrial leap also fell short. Symbolic of the new plans had been small furnaces built in the thousands by neighborhood groups for the manufacture of iron and steel. It was hoped that in this way local needs for simple metal implements could be met more adequately, over-all production increased, and the ideal of communal self-sufficiency advanced. Actually, production did not advance as much as had been predicted, and the metal produced in the small furnaces proved next to useless, leading to the abandonment of the scheme. By the early 1960s the Great Leap Forward was seldom mentioned.

A CRISIS IN LEADERSHIP

The Party was able to weather its miscalculations of productivity and set new and more modest goals of economic growth. Nevertheless, a sense grew that the revolution was approaching a crisis. Significantly, the emerging issues centered not on production quotas but on attitudes. The core of the revolution, it seemed, consisted of ways of thinking (and the behavior following from them), particularly the ways of officials and intellectuals. The perennial interest in "correctness" of thought, and in the moral transformation of man, remained as relevant to Communism as it had to Confucianism. Equally familiarly, the crisis exposed factional disputes and led to accusations that the opposition was guilty of heterodoxy and wickedness.

The first sign of the new preoccupation of the Party came in 1962, the year of the beginning of a Socialist Education Movement. At first, the movement resembled a "rectification" campaign, directed principally toward lower-level cadres and farmers, to correct "unhealthy tendencies" that had appeared in the lean years following the Great Leap Forward. The tendencies included, for example, a "spontaneous inclination towards capitalism" among certain peasants and instances of corruption among cadres, but the first statements about the movement suggested that the faults were not widespread or deep and would yield to more intensive propaganda and education on the subject of class struggle and, for the cadres, more systematic "going downwards" into the masses. By 1965, however, the tone and implications of the movement were sterner. The *Jen-min jih-pao* (People's daily), a mouthpiece of the leadership, stated, "The principal contradiction in China today is the contradiction between socialism and capitalism." Surprising though that might seem, years after the establishment of collectives and communes and state control of major industries, a confidential Party document explained,

In our cities and villages alike, there exists serious, acute class struggle. After the socialist reform of the ownership system was basically completed, the class enemies who oppose socialism attempted to use the form of "peaceful evolution" to restore capitalism. This situation of class struggle is necessarily reflected within the Party ... [7]

7. "Some Problems Currently Arising in the Course of the Rural Socialist Education Movement," in R. Baum and F. C. Teiwes, *Ssu-Ch'ing: The Socialist Education Movement of 1962-1966,* China Research Monographs, No. 2 (Berkeley, 1968), p. 119.

There were some, it would seem, who at least mentally opposed the true way. Furthermore,

The key point of this movement is to rectify those people in positions of authority within the Party who take the capitalist road . . . .
Of those people in positions of authority who take the capitalist road, some are out in the open and some are concealed. Of the people who support them, some are at lower levels and some are at higher levels . . . .
Among those at higher levels, there are some people in the communes, districts, hsien, special districts, and even in the work of provincial and Central Committee departments, who oppose socialism . . . .[8]

However few the opponents were, they were to be found at every level of the system.

As a guide to correct views and a safeguard against the degenerate ways that seemed to remain everywhere, propaganda and all kinds of educational activities began in 1966 to stress fanatically the thought of Mao Tse-tung. Illuminated by that thought, according to authoritative reports, Chinese found almost anything possible. Cadres overcame their separation from the masses, factory workers discovered better techniques of galvanizing, farmers learned to judge exactly the right amounts of manure, and the manager of a group of food stores increased his sales of watermelons by seventy-nine percent. Even the successful firing of a guided missile armed with a nuclear warhead in 1966 was called a great victory for Mao's thought. The apotheosis of the leader, who began to acquire epithets such as "our great teacher, great leader, great supreme commander, and great helmsman," and "the red sun in the hearts of the people of the world," drew forth a number of explanations from outside observers. The existence of an opposition, as asserted in the Socialist Education Movement, for example, demanded that Mao make every effort to mobilize the country to his side. Beyond that, Mao had grown old and would soon die. Everything must be done to fire the Party and country with loyalty to his ideas of revolution. The references to those who believed in "peaceful evolution" and "capitalism," it was speculated, suggested that the Party included leaders who would prefer a rate of change more moderate than the radical policies Mao had pursued, sometimes with harmful results. These explanations were credible, yet to them might be added two old and strong motives of the great movers of China, to win a firm and high place in history and, as a founding father, to leave a legacy to ages to come. Mao may have felt something of that sort when the campaign was begun to enshrine his

8. *Ibid.,* p. 120.

"thought." His writings were published in enormous numbers; 150 million sets of his *Selected Works* were distributed between 1966 and 1968, for example, and 96 million copies of his poems. Most astonishing of all, 740 million copies of a little book, *Quotations from Chairman Mao Tse-tung*, came out between 1966 and 1968, theoretically assuring every Chinese of one for himself, with some left over for the rest of the world. In its form—brief passages on a variety of subjects—its sententiousness of tone, and even its exhortations to the reader to rectify himself, the *Quotations* seemed intended to be a revolutionary *Analects*. It was conceivable that Mao meant to be a revolutionary sage.

THE GREAT PROLETARIAN CULTURAL REVOLUTION

In the spring of 1966 the educational movement entered into a more strident and turbulent phase, a Great Proletarian Cultural Revolution, which exposed to attack almost all who were well educated and middle-aged or older. They were the carriers of the old exploiters' culture, which still survived in the form of ideas, even though exploitative rule had been overthrown. Even within the Party, as it was put later, a "handful of persons in authority were taking the capitalist road," presumably also in the form of ideas opposing those of the chairman. The *Jen-min jih-pao* set the new, extravagant tone:

For the last few months, in response to the militant call of the Central Committee of the Chinese Communist Party and Chairman Mao, hundreds of millions of workers, peasants, and soldiers, and vast numbers of revolutionary cadres and intellectuals, all armed with Mao Tse-tung's thought, have been sweeping away a horde of monsters that have entrenched themselves in ideological and cultural positions. With the tremendous and impetuous force of a raging storm, they have smashed the shackles imposed on their minds by the exploiting classes for so long in the past, routing the bourgeois "specialists" "scholars," "authorities," and "venerable masters," and sweeping every bit of their prestige into the dust.[9]

The immediate occasion of the launching of the Great Proletarian Cultural Revolution, or more likely the immediate excuse for launching it, indicated that indeed a cultural opposition was making itself known, and by curiously traditional means. Early in the 1960s a group of intellectuals holding positions of some influence in the municipal

9. Translated from the issue of June 1, 1966, in Asia Research Centre, comp. and ed., *The Great Cultural Revolution* (Rutland, Vermont, and Tokyo: Charles E. Tuttle Co., 1968), p. 210.

government and Party in Peking wrote and published a series of pieces that were political critiques disguised in various ways traditional to that dangerous genre. One, for example, was ostensibly a play about a Ming emperor and a remonstrating official, who really stood for Mao Tse-tung and a general who had been so unfortunate as to find himself in disagreement on a question of policy. Another referred to a political satire of the Ming in which a victim of amnesia (understood as the Party) absent-mindedly stepped in his own dung. When the deeds of this "black gang," who had found in the literary tradition the means of criticizing tyranny, were exposed, other "monsters" and "demons" began to be smoked out, attacked, and dismissed. Many were prominent in universities and institutes; others were in the Party and government. Of the latter group it became apparent that a chief target was the President of the People's Republic, Liu Shao-ch'i, long the comrade of Mao and his successor when Mao had relinquished the presidency of the government in 1958, ostensibly to give all his attention to his vital role as head of the Party. As the campaign gained momentum, there were conjectures that Liu's position and the charges of "revisionism" against him identified him as the leader of the "evolutionists" whom Mao saw as the mortal enemies of his revolution. The Party had been shaken, it seemed, by the question whether revolution meant the making of a new man or, more conventionally, the building of a modern society, the "Red and expert" question in its largest sense. The Great Proletarian Cultural Revolution was Mao's effort to take the more radical, "Red" way and purge the system of its opponents, even though it meant risking the capacity of the Party to rule.

In the summer of 1966 the shock forces Mao would depend on appeared in the form of the Red Guards. Mostly young students, the Red Guards grew quickly from a few bands in Peking to troops of thousands in all the major cities. It was thought that the Minister of Defense, Lin Piao, who had advanced rapidly to a position just below Mao in the Party's hierarchy, had taken a major part in organizing the Red Guards, for they were urged from the beginning to emulate the revolutionary experiences of the Red Army and thus imbue themselves with revolutionary spirit. This some did, for example, by taking long marches across the country, but more characteristically their work was to disrupt, unsettle, and destroy habits, patterns, and symbols of the past. They "occupied" schools, for example, and forced changes in procedure, making "Redness" and a humble social class much more important qualifications for admission than scholastic ability; perhaps more immediately to the point, they disrupted classes entirely in many schools, so that much of formal education apparently stopped for almost two years. They roamed the streets, changing or destroying symbols of less enlightened times. People with Western styles of haircut or dress were humiliated, offices and houses suspected of unwholesome influences were entered and offending objects destroyed or removed. Red Guards in Hangchow renamed everything that had been named after Su Tung-p'o, the Sung dynasty poet who was too feudal to be tolerated. In Shanghai the name of the Wing On (eternal peace) department store was criticized and the substitution of "Yong Hong" (red forever) proposed. In some places it was decided that red lights should mean "go," not "stop." More serious interventions followed, in factories and local administrations, for example, and in 1967 armed clashes occurred, apparently between Red Guards and local authorities not willing to submit to the induced revolution. Increasingly the Army entered critical confrontations as a stabilizing force, and in place after place "revolutionary committees," comprising some combination of groups, such as the army, the Party, and the "workers," took over the administration at least temporarily. In 1968 Liu Shao-ch'i was at last attacked by name. A typical headline referred to him as a renegade, traitor, and scab. The political contest seemed to have been decided, at least for the moment. The Red Guards went home, what to do was not certain. Whether they had made themselves revolutionaries to the bone, justifying in Mao's mind whatever the cost had been to such conventional undertakings as formal education, only the future would tell. It seemed likely that other kinds of men, who would not let the past go so lightly, were holding their peace until another day.

PART TWO

Aspects of Chinese

Civilization

XII

China: An

Anthropological

Overview

BY
MORTON H. FRIED

This essay attempts within a restricted compass to present a picture of the anthropological approach to an understanding of China. First let me clarify what is meant by anthropology, which by nature and development is a congeries of fields and approaches rather than a tightly focused discipline. At its core, anthropology is marked by a basic division between interest in man as a biological organism, product of long physical evolution, an animal still subject to processes of mutation, selection, and adaptation, and interest in man the actor, whose activity is to an unparalleled extent determined by the organized pressures of his previous behavior. Because almost all of it is learned and transmitted through complex systems of arbitrary symbols, divorced from both specific genetic components and situations, we refer to the prime context of human behavior as culture. In the present case we are interested in a particular local variant of culture, the Chinese. To make an anthropological analysis of that culture forces us to cross disciplinary boundaries. To begin with, all of Chinese history is grist for the mill of anthropological (e.g., "culturological") analysis. So, for that matter, are the data of economics, political science, social psychology, not to mention philosophy, art and archaeology, literature, linguistics, and every other field that contributes in any way to our understanding of Chinese culture. Not yet mentioned, but standing in especially close relationship to the cultural anthropological approach to China, is sociology. It is hardly profitable to distinguish between anthropology and sociology in their sinological phases; certainly most of the people who do the research pay little attention to the question of whether they are acting as sociologists or anthropologists. For those who would persistently seek to distinguish these two disciplines, however, it may be suggested that anthropology takes a much wider view of its subject matter. Including almost all of the usual content of sociology, anthropology also adds specialized interests in human biology, cultural evolution, linguistics, and a concern for the entire range of cultural things, food habits as well as social structure, details of architecture as well as social stratification, and the minutiae of daily life as well as elaborate ceremonies and major crisis rites.

Obviously, this brief treatment of the anthropological approach to China cannot consider all of the topics mentioned or implied. To do so would not only violate space allocations, but would constitute a case of disciplinary imperialism; fortunately, much that might otherwise be touched upon is discussed in the other chapters by more specialized colleagues. I shall therefore concentrate on certain problem areas because they are of particular theoretical concern and likely to be in the area of primary anthropological research.

One more introductory thought. The problem of defining "China" is also somewhat complex from the anthropological viewpoint. We know, for example, that the boundaries of the area designated as China have changed considerably; although they have rarely been so widely flung as at present, there have been times when those boundaries were much tighter and there has been considerable fluctuation in detail. More complicated than the problem of defining China as a geographical area is the problem of distinguishing China as a cultural area. The Chinese people themselves deal with this problem on what amounts to a daily basis when they call themselves "Han" and distinguish themselves, essentially on behavioral grounds, from those who are not Han, such as the Manchus or Mongols of the north, the Chiang and Tibetans of the west, the Lolo, Miao, or Yao of the southwest, or the Li or Yi of the southeast. The folk-anthropological distinctions thus made are not necessarily consistent with historical and cultural reality. Thus some populations, such as the Chuang of Kwangsi or the Minchia of Yunnan, are indistinguishable, as far as laymen are concerned, from their Han Chinese neighbors, but no Chinese to my knowledge would think of identifying them as Han. On the other hand, considered Han are large populations in Fukien and Kwangtung, not to mention other provinces, whose ancestry is undoubtedly traceable to ancient non-Han peoples who were completely submerged in two thousand and more years of penetration by populations originating in northern China. Much of the regional character of Chinese culture can be attributed to different mixtures of aboriginal and Han Chinese cultural elements that occurred in different areas. It is also appropriate, while on this topic, to note that regionalism has been and continues to be a major force in Chinese cultural life. Regionalism has many aspects but two may be mentioned in this preliminary consideration of what it means to be Chinese. There is a fairly simple geographical regionalism which was produced in part by the variable ethnic history previously alluded to, and by ecological pressures which operated on the productive economies and through these on social structure and ideology in the broadest sense. Thus China has long tended to decentralize into large regions characterized by a certain geomorphological uniformity, the largest such areas being on the order of magnitude of "the southeast," "the northwest," "the southwest," etc., and the smaller units being essentially of provincial size. Crosscutting such regionalism, however, are variations of language, diet, and subtle aspects of daily life and general orientation which produce fairly well defined and discrete populations with distinct self-identification. The people known as the Hakka are quickly recognizable on sociocultural grounds, as are the Tanka (the "Boat People" of the southeast), and various other ethnic variations *within* the Han designation. Leaving further discussion of this matter to a later section of this article, let us briefly turn our attention to an anthropological appreciation of the population of China in certain of its biological aspects.

Physical Anthropology and the Study of China

There is no scientifically recognized entity known as "the Chinese race." Although many Chinese, and also a good many foreigners, believe that they can distinguish Chinese on the basis of physical characteristics, there is ample reason for skepticism. Of greatest importance is the fact that the population of the national space known as China fades off and blends into the populations of all surrounding spaces. Thus, the people in the northeast are difficult to distinguish, on purely physical grounds, from neighboring Koreans, encysted Manchus, Goldi, or Tungus. In the northwest physical similarities between people identified as Han Chinese and others who are recognized as Mongols overwhelm the differences, as is also the case in southern China where the overlap is great with the Thai and other Southeast Asian peoples. Furthermore, throughout China there are great numbers of individuals who, on purely physical grounds, cannot be distinguished from Japanese or Koreans. The consequence of all this is that most physical anthropologists refuse to describe a Chinese physical type as such, but recognize that the Chinese area is inhabited by several races, variously identified and labeled. Thus, the Chinese are usually distributed among several more general categories such as "Mongoloid" and "Malaysian."

The fact that professional taxonomists do not group even a majority of Chinese into a single discrete category has considerable significance. It reinforces the belief that the population of China is genetically heterogeneous, which further implies that, while different portions of the Chinese area knew isolation in varying degrees throughout history, the Chinese area at large was time and again penetrated by different populations with resultant genetic exchange. The process is still going on. For example, quite apart from the genetic reshuffling that has accompanied the mating of relatively recent migrants from the mainland to Taiwan and the descendants of those who migrated as long as 400 years ago, there is continuous intermarriage between these populations and the aborigines. Detailed information relating to the current situation on the mainland is lacking, but it seems reasonable to presume that, if anything, the rate of intermarriage between Han Chinese and non-Han populations has risen because of increased mutual exposure and a number of favoring conditions, such as government approval for such unions. (Probably more accurate is the suggestion that the important factor is the general governmental policy of de-emphasizing the influence of family on marital choices.) Despite their heterogeneity the Chinese have long considered themselves a population. In part the perception was based on physical appearance as can be gathered from such a common self indicator as *li min* (the black-haired people), which can be used as a synonym of "the people" or "the masses." It is also clear from ancient books that cultural rather than physical differences provided the main basis upon which the Chinese made distinctions. To the present day, the more common terms which Chinese use to designate themselves as a population reveal this cultural bias.

Although the most general and common Chinese designation for China, *Chung-kuo,* has existed for a long time, neither it nor its derivative meaning "Chinese," *Chung-kuo-jen,* has been particularly common in usage until fairly modern times. Even today most Chinese seem to prefer to designate themselves by terms of narrower meaning, sometimes referring to regional and linguistic identity, such as *Min,* a term for people from Fukien based on an ancient name. Some segments of the population have themselves developed vague terms of reference, like the frequently encountered Cantonese *punti,* meaning "local [people]," while others have designations bestowed upon them, like the Hakka or "Guest People," because they are known to have migrated to Fukien and Kwangtung many centuries ago and were considered strangers by those already in that area.

Having strayed from physical anthropology into the cultural problem of ethnic names, let me return briefly to the former topic to note that the Chinese area has been a major site of human evolution for at least half a million years. At this time of writing it is generally held that the Chinese area was not the scene of emergence of our genus, that distinction falling on the basis of available evidence to eastern and southern Africa. The same evidence seems to indicate that the earliest men in the Chinese area, *Sinanthropus pekinensis,* were of the species *Homo erectus.*

Although occasional finds of fossil man have been made in China in recent years, there is not enough physical evidence to enable us to make a clear reconstruction of the biological course of human history in that part of the world. Some distinguished physical anthropologists have declared that the Chinese *Homo erectus* possessed many features resembling those of modern inhabitants of the same region. On the other hand, there is also evidence from the same general region of later fossils of our own species, *Homo sapiens,* some of which, at least skeletally, are indistinguishable from present inhabitants of north China, while others in what seems to have been one and the same population display much more variation. The archaeologically recovered remains of people who lived in China during the neolithic period and in the earliest historic times tend to fall, however, well within the range of the present population, although there is an interesting suggestion, which I cannot present here in detail, that the later neolithic inhabitants have greater resemblance to Mongoloid populations found in Southeast Asia and the adjacent Pacific than to the Mongoloids of Central and Northern Asia.

I cannot take too much additional space for remarks about the physical anthropology of China, but I would like to give a few examples of the sorts of things that are involved, apart from race and human evolution in paleontological terms. There is, to begin with, the remarkable success of the Chinese as a population—they are more numerous than any other. Why are the Chinese so prolific? If there is a genetic basis, it has yet to be scientifically demonstrated. We know, for example, that the historical census records suggest that the population of China, for more than 1500 years prior to the sixteenth century, fluctuated between rather divergent highs and lows but bracketing a norm that seems to have increased from perhaps 40 million in Han to about twice that in Yuan. Then, in Ming, population began to soar, continuing to enlarge, and threatening to reach a billion by the close of the twentieth century. Although the main reasons for this increase are thought to be cultural, in the sense that they involve such things as developments in food production and large-scale medical measures, physical anthropologists are interested in seeking broader ecological explanations which will integrate biological as well as cultural data. Such inquiries will also raise questions about performance and adaptation under stress, how Chinese have surmounted difficult health conditions, marginal diets, crowded dwelling patterns, and a variety of virulent and endemic parasitic diseases.

Cultural Anthropology and the Study of China

As can be seen from the foregoing, the transition between problems faced by physical anthropologists and those studied by cultural anthropologists does not involve a sharp line of demarcation, but traverses areas of mutual concern. Indeed, such subjects as demography, stress biology, and health and medicine require the combined efforts of specialists from many disciplines and there is little doubt that coordinated studies will have to develop in the future. As yet, unfortunately, the government of the Chinese People's Republic either does not believe it has the means to encourage serious research ventures of this kind or fails to see their utility under present circumstances. Even in the Republic of China (Taiwan), where problems are simpler if only because the population is so much smaller and more available, little in the nature of such research has been carried out. Instead, most cultural anthropological research in China has been limited to individual or very small group efforts, with most of its empirical content derived from social surveys and community studies.

Until recently a certain aspect of the anthropological approach to China seemed anthropology's own. There was a handful of studies that had been carried out by anthropologists in the Chinese countryside and these spoke in detail of actual structures and events in certain living small communities. In the past decade, however, at least with regard to the study of Chinese society as represented in Taiwan and Hong Kong, it is no longer the anthropologist alone who goes to the people for his data. Many social scientists now conduct field research to test hypotheses or to seek additional information that cannot be discovered in libraries or archives, but may be reclaimed from the overlapping memories of informants, or scattered primary documents.

In the pages that follow I will take up the problem of bounding Chinese culture and society in place and time, discussing its essence and varieties, and some of the factors that seem to have gone into its production, as well as the things which seem to be impinging upon it today and may help determine its shape in the future. Without being explicit about sources, this will dip into the information amassed by community study and social survey, but it will also draw upon the materials of the contingent disciplines already mentioned.

"TRADITIONAL CHINA"

One of the most frequently encountered notions in the literature on Chinese culture and society contrasts contemporary configurations with something usually called "traditional China." The latter term amounts to an attempt to specify a regular set of institutions which has distinguished China from some early historical period until the recent dawn of a modern age. Such an idea is suspect and misleading to the extent that it implies that China has been relatively immune from the processes of social and cultural change. Despite common opinion to the contrary, Chinese culture and society have not remained stagnant through the centuries, but have gone through many periods of alteration. Because of this variation the model of "traditional China" is usually drawn in terms of huge generalizations that neglect major variables of time, location and social class. An alternative has been to select a particular historical epoch and make it stand for traditional China. Late Ming and middle or late Ch'ing have been presented in this way. Of course, in using such a model, certain aspects of change and variation are completely ignored, although the model does a better job of dealing with synchronic heterogeneity in Chinese society and culture.

To illuminate the temporal difficulties that may be encountered in setting up a generalized concept of traditional China, consider the question of Confucianism. The thought of traditional China without Confucianism will probably be ludicrous, even to people with small knowledge of the country. Yet it is possible to question whether China was ever truly Confucianist, if we mean by this that Confucianism permeated all social class levels. More to the point regarding time, it can be readily demonstrated that "Confucianism" is not a simple, unitary philosophy or ethical code, but a complex body of values and ideological concepts that has altered through time. Indeed, there is only a distant relationship between sometimes popular folk-Confucianism, which ironically treats Confucius as a divinity and mingles doctrine with Taoist and even shamanistic beliefs, and the state cult of Confucius; meanwhile both of these differ from philosophical

Confucianism and Neo-Confucianism. Which of these is the basic form which should be included in a model of "traditional China?" A similar problem is encountered if we take up the question of Buddhism in China, or alleged Chinese aversion to militarism, or alleged Chinese toleration of alien religions, or non-Han ethnic groups. In each of these cases, as in many others, China's long history has seen great variation and sometimes one thing has been in favor or vogue, sometimes another, quite different. To the degree that the concept of traditional China has suppressed awareness of this aspect of the vitality of Chinese culture, it is dangerous and to be avoided or at least treated with suspicion.

Nor does it resolve the question to permit a particular period to furnish the model for traditional China. The second half of the nineteenth century has often been used in this way. Actually, in a number of respects this is a particularly poor choice.

Its greatest strength is the amount of information we have about it: less than we enjoy about the present (although the selective screen employed by the Communist government means that certain areas of late Ch'ing life are better known than comparable sectors of modern mainland Chinese life), but greater than for any preceding epoch. On the other hand, it is clear that the Ch'ing period involves a non-Han top ruling group, an unusual undercutting of the strictly Chinese situation, particularly in the nineteenth century when European influence began to predominate in government. What is more, the long-range Chinese cycle of revolution was in its maximum phase in the nineteenth century and decades were dominated not by the politics of centralization but by the intrigues of local rebellion.

As to large-scale theories of Chinese society, one of the most impressive, the hydraulic theory, places such extensive emphasis on the feature of tight central political control, that it is sometimes called the theory of Oriental Despotism. Undoubtedly there have been longer and shorter periods of Chinese history when such central control was an actuality, although some historians believe that, far from being an old and constant factor, it reached full development only as recently as Ming. In any event, it is clear that the hydraulic theory is based to a considerable degree upon consideration of the centripetal forces in Chinese history and concomitant neglect of equally impressive centrifugal forces. There have been long stretches when China was not under any form of central political rule, or when effective government was confined to relatively small areas beyond which lay guerrillas, bandits, and seething unrest. Such was certainly the case during much of the period between the decline of Han and the emergence of Sui (i.e. the Period of Disunity). There are even times during tightly organized dynastic periods, such as nineteenth-century Ch'ing, when central control was something between myth and propaganda, a tenuous reality asserted by a fading power. If the sociopolitical climate of China varied so drastically, how can proper understanding be conveyed by a simplistic "traditional" model?

AREAL CONSIDERATIONS

In the light of things said in the earlier pages of this essay, it is not necessary to belabor the areal limitations on the concept of a "traditional China." We have already seen, albeit in sweepingly broad statements, that Chinese ("Han") culture-bearers expanded into regions inhabited by peoples whose culture contrasted with that of the Han, with the result that a variety of local cultures formed, most in the end being recognized as Chinese. The differences, however, are significant and manifest themselves in numerous ways, the following being among the most important. To begin with, members of the populations bearing regional cultures tend to associate primarily among themselves. Not only are they largely endogamous, but their daily interactions take place almost exclusively among individuals of like subculture. This, of course, tends to reinforce the situation even more, producing further and further involution.

Southeast China, a rather clear-cut region with a distinctive character of its own, is almost the limiting case. Actually, it comprises not a single homogeneous region, but a congeries of varied subcultures associated with fairly sharply marked language differences of the type laymen attribute to "dialect." Perhaps best known outside of China, certainly in the United States, is the subculture of the Cantonese, who make up the greatest portion of the Chinese in the United States. But the Cantonese, although they can identify themselves in a variety of ways as a "we-group," for example, as *t'ong-yen* (people of T'ang) or *punti* ("natives"), more commonly do *not* regard themselves in such terms, but prefer to identify with counties or even villages, which have some correlation with linguistic subgroupings. Thus someone is likely to identify himself as *Toi-san* (*T'ai-shan*) on the basis of his county of origin, or he might call himself *Sze-yap* (*Sze-i*), "four districts,' because Toi-san is considered linked with *Yan-p'ing*, *Hoi-p'ing* and *Sun-wi,* all sharing a distinctive variety of the Cantonese language and considering it superior to the dialect of a neighboring unit, *Sam-yap* (*San-yi*). This kind of differentiation, pronounced in the southeastern parts of China, departs from the situation elsewhere primarily in scale.

Related to the existence of sharply defined regional differences is a widespread Chinese belief in what may be called a folk-theory of subnational character. That is to say each locality is believed to be associated with a rather definite set of personality characteristics. In broad strokes the Chinese reverse the folk anthropological views common in the United States by portraying their northerners as slow of speech and wit, uninventive, and placid, contrasted with southerners who are seen as quick, sharp, innovating, and smart. Sometimes the characterization applies to much smaller areas, such as specific cities. People from Tientsin, for example, are said to be ferocious traders, this tied to the role Tientsin people played for centuries in the trade with Turks and Mongols of northwest China and adjacent Central Asia. For that matter, Shanghai people are thought to be naturally gifted in finance, despite the evidence of great poverty in that city.

Returning to the theme of centrifugal forces in Chinese history we note that formal political structures in China, especially those emanating from the central government have long coped with divisive tendencies based upon regionalism. One of the main instruments that was developed to cope with this problem is sometimes known as "the law of avoidance." In effect, this was a policy which saw to it that officials served in localities other than that in which they were natives. Conversely, regionalism was so pronounced and so clearly recognized by government, that most legal proscriptions were accompanied by provisions enabling troublesome cases to be settled, at least in part, on the basis of local custom. Precisely such mechanisms continue to exist in China, even under the present Communist government, although available evidence is not sufficient for us to draw firm conclusions about the utility of such exceptions in daily life.

Given the strictures against officials serving in their native districts, we begin to see some of the basis on which students of Chinese society identify the literati as the connective tissue of that society. As is indicated elsewhere, the administrative structure of the Chinese state for perhaps two thousand years has involved a pyramid of official statuses, most of which were achieved primarily through success in a long process of formal education and examination. In a real sense the national ideology of China was the ideology of the class that had primary access to education, hence to the examinations. Thoroughly Confucian, it would be difficult to synthesize another ideology that would better represent the interests of that ruling class. On the other hand, not all men who possessed the financial means to seek official careers did so, nor did all those who tried succeed. As a consequence, some students of Chinese society describe a ruling class which includes more than office holders, adding a variety of nonofficial persons of substantial means, large landowners and prosperous merchants in particular. Such people usually formed informal alliances with the officials posted in their localities, obviating much of the desired effect of the principle of avoidance.

In other ways local interests tended to overwhelm national interests. For example, successful degree holders and officials were not distributed as to origins in anything like random fashion. Certain provinces, certain localities placed inordinate numbers of their sons in the bureaucracy, while others were virtually unrepresented year after year. Of course, to some extent this was a product of many factors; remote and backwoodsy places are as characteristic of China as of other metropolitan civilizations, and hicks and hayseeds as poorly regarded in the games of social mobility. Nevertheless, the distribution of official positions can leave no doubt that forces of nepotism and cronyism were very strong, with consequent reinforcement of localism. It is not surprising that symptoms of these phenomena can be detected in Communist China, despite great efforts to suppress them. Thus, developments in the southeastern part of China, Kwangtung in particular, during the decade 1955-65, display marked regional character as the head of the local Communist Party, T'ao Chu, is said to have slighted national policy for local benefit, the accusations against him being recorded in Red Guard newspapers and wall posters after his fall from grace.

In sum, it can be seen that China, which looks quite homogeneous to the lay observer from a distance, is actually a mosaic of differentiated local cultures. The amazing thing is not that China has frequently been divided, but that it has so often and for so long achieved a high degree of unification. Chinese commentators regard this matter somewhat ironically and have pointed out that Europe exclusive of Russia, comparable in area to China, has never achieved a comparable degree of integration.

CONSIDERATIONS OF SOCIOECONOMIC CLASS

A final axis along which it is difficult to articulate a completely valid model of "traditional China" has to do with the cultural variety that is associated with the systems of ranking and stratification that have existed in China since neolithic times. The society of pre-Shang China, as represented in what Chang Kwang-chih calls the "Lungshanoid" culture, may have already known socioeconomic classes. The evidence, as Chang has pointed out, includes the spread of the culture, which probably occurred as the result of, hence indicates, population pressure on the permanent agricultural settlements; fortification of those settlements is further indication of population pressure. Increased frequency of burials associated with different amounts of grave wealth and concentration of jade artifacts in certain graves and localities supports the notion of ranking and perhaps stratification. In any case, it is academic for the purposes of the present article to establish the temporal point at which early Chinese society became stratified; there is no doubt that by the time of Shang, traditionally dated from 1766 B.C., such stratification existed. The question for us is rather to determine the extent to which class differences comprised a scale of variation worthy of being called subcultural.

The problem is akin to that which faced us in the discussion of regional variation in Chinese culture. Despite such differences, there is a widely spread "national culture" manifest in the stratum of literati-gentry-bureaucrats, previously described as a kind of social connective tissue. It is a relevant fact, for example, that local, upwardly mobile status-achievers, whether they are ethnically Minchia, Miao, or Goldi, attempt, sometimes with success, to break into the gentry class and do so by substantially adopting Han culture. Similarly, ethnically Han persons who are upwardly mobile regard various aspects of gentry life style as the milestones of achievement. When they can wear certain clothes, speak and write Chinese, have large families organized in a certain way, and eat in certain style, they can, in fact, regard themselves as members of the gentry and can begin to be looked upon by others as members of that status group. That this is so, however, frequently complicates rather than simplifies the picture. Many analysts of Chinese society accept a certain degree of *de facto* variability in Chinese culture and associate this with class, but go on to argue that underneath these differences are economic disabilities that preclude living in gentry style. In other words, such authorities argue, there is a very extensive and very pervasive set of national values that can be detected in every class in China. On the basis of values, they assert, China must be judged homogeneous, a single, highly integrated culture with tightly knit social fabric.

The contrary proposition asserts greater independence of the life style of different classes. Accepting as a truism that upwardly moving individuals and families will adopt gentry patterns in "bettering themselves," it argues that a different set of values operates in lower classes so that Confucianism is absent or exists only in attenuated forms, that filial piety is also anemic if present, that the kinds of interpersonal associations that are formed are different from those which occur among the gentry, and that even tastes in art and decoration are regularly divergent from those characterizing the gentry.

A moment's reflection will reveal the importance of this theme. If the statement is valid that class is accompanied by subcultural variation, then some interpretations of events in contemporary China will be drastically affected. Specifically, with the advent of the Communist government many phenomena have been declared to be new to the Chinese social scene, such as the intergenerational conflict revealed by the Cultural Revolution, the hostility to intellectuals, the tendency to convert surplus not into savings but into consumer goods, and the like. But, if the thesis of class as subculture is correct, these tendencies may not be new at all. Rather than being attributable to the impact of the West, the influence of communism, or the genius of Mao, they could be traits of long standing in the culture of the Chinese masses—the peasants—more directly expressed in the new social structure than ever before.

Major Institutional Aspects of Chinese Society

The remainder of this essay is divided into two parts. The present section will consider a sequence of institutions that are usually identified as the most important in the social organizational repertory of China. Of course, I will proceed with awareness of the message given just above and shall take pains to point out where the view of a "traditional China" must yield to a more complex model comprised of significant alternative forms. In the final section an attempt will be made to illuminate some of the sociological phenomena associated with the revolutionary events in the mainland and with the smaller scale but sometimes almost equally interesting developments in Taiwan.

FAMILY

The popular view of the Chinese family involves a fecund domestic unit composed of many conjugal unions and abundant children layered in numerous interacting generations. Actually, the popular view is a murky one for, when questioned, laymen tend to be unclear whether the family is large because couples have a great many children, or because relatives stick together in a unified family long after reaching what is assumed to be a breaking point in Western society. There is, of course, some truth in these popular images but they are partial and, as expressed, more likely to mislead than to inform.

No matter how Chinese census figures are evaluated, and there is some controversy about them, everyone is prepared to agree that China is the most populous country in the world. Associated with the acceptance of current population size that may be as large as 700,000,000 or more is the belief that Chinese families are also very large. In the United States in 1965, according to the *Statistical Abstract of the United States 1967,* total population stood at 194,592,000, and the number of families was given as 47,836,000. While it is not altogether accurate to seek to determine average family size by dividing the larger of these figures by the smaller, there is no better way of crudely approximating the value we are seeking. The division offers the figure of 4.07, indicating that the average American family is a small unit composed of parents and two children. Indeed, statistics I will not place in evidence show that, in 1966, 78.3 percent of American families had two or fewer children [61.5 percent had one or fewer and 44.3 percent had no children at all].

It would be wonderful if we could take this information about the United States and compare it with the situation in China, but that is not possible. The most recent census of China seems to have been carried out in 1957, but as far as I have been able to discover none of its details have been released. The major census that preceded this one was by far the greatest ever attempted in China and took place in 1953-54. While portions of the data have become available, nothing so far released throws any light on the problem of the number of either families or households. To delve too deeply into this problem, however important it is, would overburden the generality of this essay. Let me, however, give a few interesting bits of information which will help the reader form his own picture of the situation.

Classical Chinese census data were usually presented in terms of the statistical abstractions *ting* and *hu*. The former related to males between the ages of sixteen and sixty (in Ming times) from whom *corvée* or tax was extractable. Sometimes totals for women were also reported, at other times all were lumped under the designation *k'ou* (mouth). In any event, it is thought that these figures present far from accurate totals. Furthermore, the concept of *hu* normally is more closely associated with the concept of household, as usually defined (implying shared residence without requiring kinship), rather than family.

If we now attempt to perform an operation similar to that executed above, dividing a figure presumed to represent total population by a smaller figure presumed to represent the number of households or families applying to that population at the same time, we get an interesting result. One historian has done this with data obtained for the period A.D. 2-742 and discovered that family/household size seemed to oscillate but averaged about 5.5 members. Another historian analyzed materials relating to households and population of fourteen provinces in 1812, discovering that each household on the average held 5.33 "mouths." A Chinese demographer analyzed data pertaining to ten different regions of China collected between 1932 and 1942. This material is of exceptional interest despite the relative smallness of the sample, because it was carried out under unusually favorable conditions, with fairly rigorous modern methods. The lowest average family size, 4.18, was found in Kunming (City), Yunnan. Urban areas apart, the lowest average, 4.41, was found in Cheng Kung County, Yunnan. When the entire sample, covering several regions of China, was averaged, the result was 4.84. The highest average, 6.17, was obtained in Kunyang County, Yunnan (1942), which may be compared with the subcounty region of Pu Yen in Taiwan where, in 1958, the average household size was 5.83. I give this last datum because it is frequently said, by experts, that Taiwan in recent decades has had high fertility and tends to have larger families than much of the mainland.

It is interesting to compare the deflated reality of Chinese family size with Chinese concepts of ideal family size as manifested in desire for children. While there is very little information of this sophisticated social questionnaire sort from mainland China, either pre- or post-Communist, data collected in the United States reveal that in 1945 women between the ages of twenty-one and thirty-four indicated desire for three children as their average ideal (marking an increase over immediately pre-World War II norms which were closer to two). In Taiwan, about 1955, urban women indicated a preference for four children and rural women for five. Older women in fishing villages indicated a preference for six or more children as their ideal.

As earlier indicated, the size of a family is only in part determined by the number of children born to the household head; we are also concerned with manipulations of family form. The form of the family is extremely variable, as anthropologists so well know: the extreme case they frequently cite came from India, where in Kerala the Nayar were said to have had families (*taravads*) in which no husbands/fathers could be found, but only mother's brothers/(maternal) "uncles." Nonetheless, despite its obvious ethnocentric taint, the conjugally based unit of husband, wife, and offspring (natural or adopted) is conventionally regarded as the "nuclear" or "elementary" family. The statistical evidence already presented seems to indicate that this form of the family is the predominant one in China, but we must be cautious for reasons that will be spelled out below. Before offering qualifications, however, let us note that all forms of the family more expansive than the model just presented are varieties of what is usually called the "extended family." The simplest kind of extended family is that which develops when one or more relatives of one of the basic conjugal pair joins the unit, for example, the wife's mother, or the husband's brother. This form exists in China, certainly, but it is not particularly important as a structural type under normal conditions. Much more important is a certain recurring form of extension that sees a three-generation spread among its members such as that in which an old couple (or the survivor of that couple) lives with one married son and his wife and the children of that married son and wife. It is possible, indeed often likely, that other children of the old couple will also be found in such families, but the crucial thing is that they will not marry and stay in the original family. Only one married couple can exist in that family per generation. Others can and should get married, but when they do they must move out. The form of the family that develops from these processes is known as "stem" and stem families are highly characteristic of the Chinese social landscape.

Like other social phenomena, families comprise part of the cultural means by which people, organized into groups, face diversified challenges and hazards in order to maintain individual and group life. It is, in other words, an adaptive phenomenon which must be understood, like all such phenomena, in broad ecological context. The fact that he is interested in certain manifestations of this institution in a complex and ancient civilization does not relieve the anthropologist of this broad perspective. Since he views family forms as part of adaptation, the anthropologist seeks to understand, for any given society, what forms of the family occur, in what frequencies, in what circumstances and situations. In the course of doing so the anthropologist usually learns that the society in question has not one form of the family but several. What is more, the forms are often related to each other in such a way that some members of the society experience different portions of their life in the context of different forms of the family. Conversely, taking a particular group of persons as the subject, it can be determined that there are regularly recurring sequences of family forms, sometimes referred to as the "family cycle." This is very much a part of social life in China, but before we go into it more deeply, let us take a look at one more archetype of Chinese family organization, the joint family, which is "the Chinese family" in the mind of much of the world, despite the fact, already seen, that it comprises a small minority of all Chinese families.

The easiest way to present the joint family is to diagram it, and while I am doing that, I might as well toss in basic diagrams of the nuclear and stem family models. (See Figure 1.)

A joint family is comprised at the moment two or more siblings maintain common residence with their spouses and children. In diagram it appears that a joint family is composed of a number of overlapping nuclear families and the impression is correct—with certain reservations. In a tightly knit joint family the component nuclear family may lack certain functions which are present in autonomous nuclear units, for example, in a tightly structured Chinese joint family there is only limited fiscal authority in a nuclear unit as most of the resources of the household are controlled by the household head, who is usually the eldest male in the active generation.

Chinese society is formally quite rigid about male dominance. As Mao Tse-tung noted in his "Report on an Investigation into the Peasant Movement in Hunan" (1927): "A man in China is usually subjected to the domination of three systems of authority [political

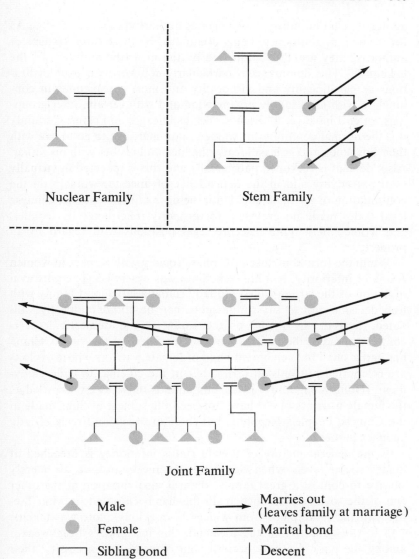

Nuclear Family

Stem Family

Joint Family

	Male		Marries out (leaves family at marriage)
	Female		Marital bond
	Sibling bond		Descent

Figure 1. Joint, nuclear, stem families.

authority, clan authority, and religious authority] ... ... As
for women, in addition to being dominated by these three systems of
authority, they are also dominated by the men (the authority of the
husband)." This dominance is particularly noteworthy in such institutions as patrilineality and virilocality and most conspicuous in conjunction with joint family organization and with certain other groupings which I have yet to discuss, such as lineages and clans. Certainly
it is the normal condition for women upon marriage to go to live with
their husbands and at least ideally the husband resides with his father.
Also, descent is reckoned patrilineally and this is reflected in virtually
total patronymy and in the dependence of ancestor worship on the
continuation of the male line. Until the days of the Republic, Chinese
legal codes made no provision for property inheritance by females,
and women held quite insecure legal positions with regard to all
property.

While the formal picture of Chinese society with respect to women
is one of inferiority, real life sometimes was otherwise. The portrayal
in fiction of the strong-willed old lady ruling a large joint family with
firm decision, not to say ruthlessness, can be ethnographically vali-
dated. Indeed, the theme of the shrew at the domestic level is
complemented at the national level by the figure of the virago. China
has had a small but celebrated band of female warriors whose exploits
are celebrated not only in opera, but in the cinema, to wide enjoyment. [Hong Kong and Taiwan film studios only; to my knowledge,
the female warriors of old have not been the subject of films made in
the Chinese People's Republic, but there are reels and reels of lady
people's heroes.]

If the general picture of female status inferiority is breached at
higher social levels when dowagers become empresses, or merely
survive to control a great family, there is also variation at the other
end of the social scale. Once again this has been noted by Mao Tse-
tung (in the same piece from which the previous quote was taken):
"As to the authority of the husband, this has always been weaker
among the poor peasants because, out of economic necessity, their
womenfolk have to do more manual labor than the women of the
richer classes and therefore have more say and greater power of
decision in family matters." While this bald statement is perhaps
somewhat more optimistic than facts may warrant, it contains essential truth. The joint family can be viewed in its light. As a corporate
entity of some complexity, such a family faced a personnel problem,

and experience dictated a policy of personnel selection. On the male side this policy was founded in the concept of *hsiao* (filial piety), strongly integrated with Confucian ideology. It is in this sector of Chinese society that Confucianism was deeply rooted and to some extent the Western belief in the universality of Confucianism in that society is coupled with the erroneous belief that the joint family is typical for China. On the distaff side, concern for personnel selection was manifest in a variety of widespread customs. Marriage, for example, was treated as the primary concern of the senior members of the household; to some extent the desires of bride and groom were taken into account, but only insofar as these desires could be satisfied without disturbance to the corporate family. The elders wanted a girl likely to bear a number of strong and healthy children; one who was capable of performing whatever functions were assigned to her, meaning, in well-to-do families, some minor domestic tasks (servants did most of the more arduous work), but mainly being submissive to elders and attentive of their needs and comfort. One of the less important things to be considered was the attractiveness of the girl, although ugliness and deformity were to be avoided. High on the list was the social and economic status of the girl's family, and marriage alliances were of considerable importance in both rural and urban social structure.

For the most part negotiations leading to marriage would be carried on by intermediaries, usually third parties not directly related to either contracting family. Although bargaining might be sharp, it was frequently covert, often handled through mutually shared symbols and circumlocutions. Crucial was a comparison of horoscopes (*pa-tzu,* the "eight characters" based on date and hour of birth) that gave a face-saving device for retreating from partially completed negotiations, for it could be decided that the marriage was doomed by the heavens.

Although provisions for divorce existed, it was a rare occurrence. In theory men might rid themselves of wives who were barren, diseased, or even too talkative; on the other hand, a man might not divorce the wife who had mourned his parents, nor the one he had married when he was poor if he later became wealthy and successful. Although such was the theory, much of this was beside the point in terms of the realities of Chinese social structure. A woman's children were considered primary members of her husband's kin group and only more remotely related to her own kin; the woman involved in divorce would effectively relinquish her children, possibly never to see them again. On the man's side, marriage was not necessarily congruent with sexual activity, since depending on wealth he had access to an elaborate system of prostitution, to the possibility of taking one or more concubines, or to affairs with female servants in the household. It may be assumed that the existence of such alternatives reduced the motivation for seeking to terminate marriage, particularly since its occurrence would certainly produce a rupture between the wife's family and that of the husband, strife that could develop into feud, including possibilities for violence.

The foregoing applies, of course, to sectors of the society deeply involved in joint family organization. For China as a whole this pertained primarily to the gentry. However, it is important to note that the distribution of the joint family seems to have oscillated through time, certain periods witnessing a great efflorescence of this particular institution (as in the Six Kingdoms of the fifth and sixth centuries A.D.), while at other times joint families were less common. Also, as briefly remarked earlier, certain areas of China in recent and contemporary times have been noted for greater frequency of joint families, Southeast China being conspicuous.

As for the great masses of Chinese, they usually got on with much less elaborate family structure. For untold numbers of adults marriage was not an economic possibility and for vast numbers the *de facto* family form was nuclear. For a very large segment of the population, including most of the people that the present Communist government refers to as lower and middle peasants, and for some tenants with relatively secure leaseholds, the preferred family form was stem. Here we have something of a paradox. For about two thousand years, going back to the Han Dynasty, Chinese society has included a strong prescription of equal inheritance for all male offspring. Indeed, we know how this customary rule has led to intense fragmentation of the agrarian space of the country as a patrimony was parceled out among numerous heirs. Over the generations fields were divided so often as to almost vanish. Sun Yat-sen in dealing with the theme of "People's Livelihood," for example, liked to tell the story of a weary farmer who cultivated nine minuscule plots. Once, when he put his hat down to wipe his brow, the farmer paused and checked his holdings. Counting again and again, his anxiety rose to panic as he discovered only eight plots. In desperation he picked up his hat, and the ninth plot was uncovered.

Under such circumstances, with the most rigorous desire to do the culturally accepted thing, a peasant frequently found that equal division would produce plots so tiny that none of his sons would be able to live on their yield. The most common solution of this problem was the stem family, which assured at least one son of sufficient means to keep a family going, thereby and very significantly permitting the continuation of at least minimal rites of ancestor worship. The father also attempted to pool whatever liquid assets he had and divided this among the other sons, hoping that the pittance might provide a basis for a new start in life for the dispossessed.

The study of the Chinese family as an adaptive mechanism in the face of monumental population pressure on scarce resources has produced a rich literature that cannot be adequately summarized here. Reluctantly, we must move on to consider some other institutions of kinship, turning first to lineages and clans.

LINEAGES AND CLANS

Distinguishing lineages from clans need not be a difficult task if certain criteria of identification are kept in mind. I believe that the most essential difference lies in the way these two kinds of kinship group treat the problems of relationship, that is, the basis on which it is determined whether one is a kinsman, hence eligible for membership in the concerned kin group. I suggest that we can distinguish on the basis of empirical evidence between demonstrated and stipulated kinship. The former exists when one traces and specifies all connecting links in a genealogical web. The latter involves an agreement that kinship exists without specifying exactly how the parties to the relationship are in fact connected. Thus in China a member of a lineage of, let us say, the surname Chang can exactly specify how he is related to each and every other member of the lineage. On the other hand, if the same person is also a member of a Chang clan he cannot say how he is related to each and every member, although he may be able to precisely specify how he is related to *some* of his fellow members. This is the result of the basic process of recruitment in clans which assumes that all who have a tangible claim to common descent are potential members, the tangible in the Chinese case being common possession of a patrilineally acquired surname. At this moment there are clans in Taiwan, for example, whose membership comprises people from Taiwan, from many provinces of mainland China, and even some of recent aboriginal extraction (i.e., those whose ancestry is known to stem from one or another group of Taiwan aboriginals). In any case, all members of the clan bear a common surname.

Since the matter of surname has been raised, a few words may be added about this very important institution in Chinese culture and society. China is certainly among the places where the institution of a definite surname arose most early, the use of such names disappearing into the mists of history in earliest dynastic (Shang) times. It is a commonplace in China to be told that there are some 400 family names in total, but this is simply not true. It seems that the maximum number of names may have existed in Sung times, with as many as 5,000 said to have been recorded. In our recent study of the 1956 census in Taiwan, however, Chen Shao-hsing and I found some 1,195 names in current use. Surname (*hsing* in Chinese) provides a certain minimal potential basis for privileged interaction in Chinese culture. Two Chinese who are utter strangers to each other but who bear a common *hsing,* may, upon meeting, feel some slight common bond, sufficient to provide a basis for mutual dependency where none at all would otherwise exist. Related to this is a widespread but not universal custom of surname exogamy; even today Chinese bearing the same surname will usually not marry although they may derive from families which have been located a thousand miles apart for a thousand years. When one delves more deeply into the nature of Chinese surname groups many other interesting phenomena are encountered, for example, the grouping of two or more names into larger exogamic aggregates common in some areas. Unfortunately, this is not the place to penetrate more deeply into such matters.

Returning briefly to lineages and clans, we note first that there is a strong functional difference that helps to explain why they diverge on the matter of recruitment of membership, why Chinese society simultaneously includes both kinds of groups, and why the portion of contemporary Chinese society in Taiwan is experiencing a boom in clan organization and what amounts to a collapse of the lineages. The crux of the matter is economic, although the primary manifest functions of both lineages and clans are ideological and ritual since they provide a major vehicle for proper conduct of ancestor veneration. Beyond this, however, lineages are based on capital accumulations, usually in the form of real estate, farm land in the countryside and commercially useful space and buildings in the city. In most cases the property is in the lineage as a patrimony inherited from an ancestor now generations dead. The property is rented out and the return is parceled out in minutely prescribed shares to all members. The more members, other things being constant, the smaller the return to any individual member, hence the ready conclusion that such organizations tend to be restrictive with regard to membership. The most effective way of accomplishing restraint with respect to size of membership is to require that all members be able to detail exactly how they are related to the founding ancestor, always a definite, historical person; from this necessarily comes the fact that any given member of a lineage can exactly specify how he is related to every other member. In China (and, of course, Taiwan), this is reinforced by the keeping of fully documented genealogies, the *tsu-p'u*. Conversely, clans may also have a property base but it is usually of a different kind, treated in a different way. The clan property most often consists primarily of a particular edifice, a temple. If it also has some additional property, land and buildings, the return from this goes entirely to the clan as a corporation for support of the temple and its rituals, and does not revert in shares to individual members. A clan's property was acquired as the result of its own corporate activities and is not inherited from a particular founding progenitor, but from an original board of directors who gathered, incorporated, raised funds, and purchased a site. Since the clan gains strength by attracting a large membership it is less concerned to restrict the qualifications for joining and in many cases it is sufficient to be *t'ung-hsing* (of the same surname). It is completely congruent with the foregoing that the original ancestor of most clans is a mythical or legendary figure, such as the God of Literature, or the promethean Shen Nung, inventor of agriculture. Clan genealogies forsake the attempt to gather all members into a single coherent structure but show how the remote and often divine ancestor actually bore the surname of the clan, and some segments of genealogy are published either to celebrate great men of history who carried the clan name, or active and heavily donating contemporaries.

As a result of the Communist revolution, both lineages and clans have been at least temporarily swept away in mainland China as institutions subversive of the Communist state. (Actually, while clans seem to have been obliterated, there is a little evidence to indicate that informal lineages continue to function in the mainland countryside, although often either covertly or with implicit rather than explicit structure.) In Taiwan land reform is one of several factors that seem to have produced a crisis for the lineages. Stripped of much of their property, they have become very poor and tax assessments threaten to deprive them of what remains. Under these circumstances the members bicker and demand the sale of whatever can bring cash; year after year more lineages sell out, distribute the money and go noisily out of existence. Meanwhile, in Taiwan and to some extent among overseas Chinese, people see the need of maintaining larger webs of kinship than families provide, especially under the changes of modern life which make nuclear families increasingly prevalent. Many of these people band together to establish new clans, or seek to join existing ones. Simultaneously, the Nationalist government encourages the clans, hoping to strengthen a mechanism for achieving pan-Chinese solidarity in Taiwan.

Before leaving the topic of kinship in China, I wish to say a few things about certain ancillary matters of considerable importance. First, the kin terminology itself. Figure 2 shows the essential terms of the system of reference, which comprises the formal terms used to designate relatives in their absence, as contrasted with terms used in direct address. Certain principles appear quite consistently in the system of terms used in China. There is sharp distinction between generations, and the concern for seniority is strongly reinforced by additional designations of age differences, particularly among siblings. Thus, where English has only the word "brother," which it modulates by use of additional words such as "older," or "youngest," the Chinese has two distinct morphemes, *koko,* (elder brother) and *titi* (younger brother). It is quite usual for a string of siblings to be identified by their order of birth, *"ta-ko, erh ko, hsiao ssu,"* a third brother might say, meaning, "big older brother, second older brother, and little number four." (Note that girls don't count and are not included in the numbering, although sisters may be separately numbered in their own series.) The Chinese system of kin nomenclature also takes clear account of the various descent lines and distinguishes father's relatives from mother's. These distinctions have been given extensive formal and functional significance in the system of *wu fu,* or "five grades of mourners (literally: mourning clothes)," dating back to Sung times.

The subject of kinship in China, fascinating to the anthropologist, may hold less interest for others. Before leaving it, however, we must note that Chinese place much emphasis on *ch'in-ch'i* (relatives in general). Although the term *ch'in-ch'i* can be applied to all agnatic kin, it usually includes other kin as well, particularly the *nei-ch'in,* which

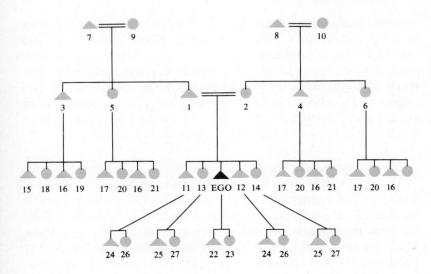

COMMON REFERENCE TERMS—

1. Father	fuch'in	15. Cousin (O)*	tanghsiung
2. Mother	much'in	16. Cousin (Y)*	piaoti
3. Uncle	pofu	17. Cousin (O)*	piaoke
4. Uncle	chiufu	18. Cousin (O)*	tangfang chiehchieh
5. Aunt	kumu	19. Cousin (Y)*	tangfang meimei
6. Aunt	i	20. Cousin (O)*	piaochieh
7. Grandfather	tsufu	21. Cousin (Y)*	piaomei
8. Grandfather	waitsufu	22. Son	erhtzu
9. Grandmother	tsumu	23. Daughter	nutzu
10. Grandmother	waitsumu	24. Nephew	chih
11. Elder brother	koko	25. Nephew	sheng
12. Younger brother	titi	26. Niece	chihnu
13. Elder sister	chiehchieh	27. Niece	shengnu
14. Younger sister	meimei		

*(O) Older than ego; (Y) Younger than ego

Figure 2. Common reference terms.

comprise one's maternal kin and one's wife's relatives. It has been shown in community studies that *nei-ch'in,* affinals in most cases, are very important in rural areas, where they often supply a farmer with many of his exchange labor partners. In earlier days, it is known, over much of China a special role pertained to mother's brother with respect to his sister's children, especially her sons. In many regions among gentry families, for example, the mother's brother was supposed to take his young nephew to school on the very first day.

NON-KIN ASSOCIATIONS

The great weight given kinship in Chinese society and the idealized and sometimes romantic treatment accorded it has tended to obscure the fact that a great state-organized civilization, such as the Chinese has been for thousands of years, cannot function on kinship alone. True, nepotism and other kin-based particularistic (as opposed to universalistic) mechanisms have pervaded the organization and operation of Chinese government as long as has been known. Indeed, such mechanisms continue to be very important not only in the Republic of China (Taiwan), but perhaps more surprisingly in the Chinese People's Republic as well. During the Red Guard phase of the Great Proletarian Cultural Revolution, Liu Shao-ch'i and other ranking Communist officials were excoriated for having swollen state payrolls with their relatives; Mao Tse-tung himself is known to have provided positions for many of his kin. On the other hand, the basic workings of Chinese economy and political organization have for more than two thousand years depended on sociological principles ramifying far beyond kinship.

We have already seen a bit of this in our previous discussion of the Chinese bureaucracy and its literati functionaries who were forced to work in a basically non-kin milieu by the action of the "law of avoidance." At the other end of the social continuum rural life ran its course in an ambient non-kin environment of which local manifestations of government were a ubiquitous part. The peasants tried in various ways to insulate themselves from the direct affects of government even including taxes, labor drafts, and military conscription, and they avoided the law courts in the magisterial *yamen.* Probably most successful were those who lived in single surname villages, where all inhabitants shared unilineal descent and might comprise a lineage as well as a village. Even in such cases, however, though government might usually be held at a distance by quiet and proper behavior, its impact could not always be completely avoided, for its rapacious demands sometimes exceeded what even the most compliant community could anticipate. Most of China's villages, in fact, seem not to have been of the single surname type, hence villagers usually lived to some extent among non-relatives. This is expressed in common phrases, examples of which are *ch'in-lin* (relatives and neighbors) or *ch'in-yu* (relatives and friends). There are also many relevant proverbs and folk sayings, such as "friendly neighbors are worth more than distant relatives."

Organizationally, there were numerous widespread responses to the need to go beyond kinship. I shall mention only five which are especially common and functionally very strong. Although, as previously noted, farmers sometimes preferred to develop mutual labor exchange with affinal relatives, it is a commonplace that such groups are primarily localized, hence may include many members who are not related. Such groups are usually informal, lacking charters or written rules, but persisting for many years and sometimes generations, with sons replacing their fathers. Rather like the labor exchanges but usually distinct, albeit with more or less overlapping membership, was the irrigation society. More irregularly distributed than any of the other kinds of association I am mentioning, such groups might also be long lived and undertook more the task of regulating the flow of irrigation water from one member's field to another, and the mediation or other settlement of disputes relating to such water, than the actual building or maintenance of dikes and ditches. A third type of association existed for purposes of mutual defense, often against similarly organized neighboring villages (sometimes eager to avenge an earlier wrong, a violation of water rights, an act of expropriation, or the abuse of one of its women), but more frequently as protection against marauding bandits. Sometimes closely associated with the self-defense association was a crop-watchers' society that patrolled fields as harvest approached. A fourth common association was the credit club. This generally was an ad hoc organization that endured for a set period and then went out of existence to be replaced by another club, perhaps of largely different membership. Such a club frequently was begun by a particular individual needing capital and wanting to avoid usurers, heavy interest, and demands for collateral. Gathering ten participants from relatives, friends, and neighbors, and assuming he has immediate need of, say, $500, he is likely to set the donation at $60, which he collects from each of the others, giving him $600. Thereafter he must pay each of the others in turn, at generally semiannual meetings which coincide with the harvests. At each meeting the organizer usually provides a modest banquet, the costs of which are tantamount to his interest payments, and he also has the responsibility of calling the meetings, notifying the participants, and ensuring that none default on obligations. The others bid at the meetings, the maximum usually being the amount of the original donation (i.e., $60 in the previous example). But one may bid less, and if he has a pressing need for cash, he may bid much less (say $35 or $37.50 in the example), hoping to get the pot right away, although it will cost him rather dearly if he pays others up to the amount of the original donation. Nonetheless, the payment of such increments, regarded as legitimate interest, represents great savings in an economy in which credit terms have a history of rapacity. Conversely, richer members not only pocket substantial profits, by waiting until the last meetings and bidding at the maximum, but enjoy the feasting and company as well.

The fifth and final example of non-kin association I offer is the temple or religious cult. This may well be associated with a major local structure which represents a country-wide religion, such as a Buddhist or Taoist establishment. Especially in conjunction with a Buddhist temple, the lay association is largely if not exclusively comprised of gentry and rich merchants. The peasants have their own religious groupings of non-kin membership, often connected with shrines housing a tutelary divinity or *genius loci*. Such groups may be cultlike in some parts of China, particularly the southeast, when they are associated with practices of healing and divination. In any case, the association counts among its main functions the provision of one or more special occasions of worship which provide a situation for extensive economic exchanges, especially of food in the form of a banquet. Perhaps the major development of this custom is to be found in present-day Taiwan where, despite official government disapproval (an ancient conflict theme in the relation between Chinese government and the people), food and goods to the valuation of tens of thousands of dollars (U.S.) are expended at neighborhood celebrations or *pai-pai*, and hundreds of thousands at the many great pan-Taiwan *pai-pai*.

As important as non-kin associations are in the countryside, they are even more significant in towns and cities. Thus, with only partial exception of such things as crop-watching, irrigation and self-defense societies, Chinese towns and cities have had all the associations found in the countryside and many others that are much more specific to city life. Those I shall mention will be of the non-kin variety, but I wish to state emphatically that Chinese towns, and cities in particular, have been a fertile habitat for kin associations. (My fieldwork for the past decade has concentrated on the study of clans and lineages in Taipei, a city of over a million population.)

Associations found in Chinese cities can be classified in various ways: most common is grouping on the basis of recruitment, in terms of the main interests served. It will be seen, however, that this conventional approach, adopted here for convenience, is quite imprecise since the actual function served by any given association is likely to overlap several other categories, if not all. Let us keep this warning in mind as we look into five kinds of urban associations: religious, occupational, common origin, governmental, and common interest.

Religious groups need not detain us; urban groups resemble in fine detail their country cousins already discussed. Let us note merely that this applies not only to the elegantly organized lay memberships of Buddhist or Confucian temples, but to the same scatter of religious associations and cult groups we located in rural areas. One can still find shamanistic mediums in Taipei and other Formosan cities and I suspect that they also exist, albeit in tight secrecy, in mainland cities, and that many such mediums are at the center of organized associations.

Occupational groupings are well known in urban China and have a long history, at least as far back as T'ang; probably they are even older. The outstanding form of such grouping until modern times has been the guild, similar in many respects to the phenomenon of the same name known in Europe. The guilds served many functions, including responsibility for proper worship of one or more tutelary divinities, hence most to some extent were also religious societies. More to the point, guilds served major economic purposes, helping to standardize and control prices and quality of goods and services, to control and regulate competition, to administer the recruitment and flow of labor, to set and administer standards of craftsmanship and training, and to provide a collective means of relating to and dealing with government. While guilds were capable of interurban activity, they were primarily adjusted to dealing with problems in a particular city or town and their organization was assisted by the customary close physical grouping of enterprises of a given kind. Peking still carries the impress of this system in such of its street names as Gold, Silver, and Brass, along which, at least as recently as 1948 in the personal experience of the author, the shops were mostly of the type specified by the street name. The organization of guilds is a complex matter which has been the subject of various books and scholarly papers. Suffice it to say here that most were quite formally structured with officers, boards of directors, and written by-laws. Needless to say, the power structure of such organizations was representative of and responsive to the needs of the masters and not the rank and file.

Starting in the last decades of the nineteenth century, China saw the development of a genuine worker-oriented labor movement. The most successful unions tended to spring up in connection with service industries, particularly transportation, hence did best among seamen, railroad workers, longshoremen, and even ricksha pullers. Such degrees of success (measured in terms of settlements received after strikes) as were achieved can be associated with workers whose principal employers were foreign or capitalized by foreigners. To some extent this success was based on the combination of strike and boycott against foreign concerns which were competing with what the Communists refer to as "national capitalists," self-capitalized Chinese in modern industrial and commercial ventures. These capitalists often assisted the Chinese labor movement, although it may be surmised that they did so less out of compassion or patriotism than self-interest, as their enterprises continued to produce and market goods when foreign-dominated concerns were closed down by strikes and boycotts. Moreover, the Chinese labor movement was inhibited and placed under a difficult handicap by the extent to which the industrial labor force comprised women and children who were difficult to organize for various social and cultural reasons. It was probably partly because of this that the transport unions proved relatively strong as their attraction was to essentially male adult workers. Finally, the Chinese labor movement seems to have benefited at strike times by the fact that many workers had not originated in the cities where they worked, but came from the countryside. As strikes continued beyond the ability of union treasuries to support them, and in the absence of any other source of funds for individual strikers, many workers returned to their places of origin. Although their reappearance must have created hard times and sometimes economic crisis for the stem families in the countryside, it is empirically clear that survival was achieved for thousands by this means and the strikes could continue until some kind of favorable settlement was obtained.

Until 1927 the Nationalist government and the Kuomintang in particular, played a role that, if not directly supportive of the labor movement, did not particularly seek to crush it. When Chiang Kai-shek changed the policy and cracked down, partly because of the alleged association of the labor movement with Chinese and Soviet Communism, a new chapter was written in the history of the Chinese labor movement. From 1927 on, that movement was basically weak and fragmented. The time of change, significant to say, also coincides with the decision of Mao and the Chinese Communist Party (although the two were not the same nor quite simultaneous) to pursue revolution not among urban workers but in the countryside, among the harried and disaffected peasants.

Associations based on common origin have long been of great importance in urban China. To some extent city-based clans are a special form of such groups, especially if, in contrast to some of the things mentioned previously in my discussion of clans, certain additional restrictions are placed on membership, as that all who present themselves must speak a common first language (e.g., Amoy or Sei-yap) or be known to have originated in a particular part of China. Urban-based clans show many of the features of other kinds of common-interest groups: they provide possibilities for easy term credit, job introductions, cheap legal advice from fellow members who may be lawyers, some political leverage, and a host of other potentially valuable services.

The major non-kin form of common origin association is the *t'ung-hsiang hui* (same-*hsiang* club). A *hsiang,* as already noted, is a geographical and administrative subdivision of a *hsien* or county. (The *hsien* in imperial times was known as *chou,* but the *hsiang* designation continues unchanged, even in the Communist administration, although the ideally stipulated unit of *kung-she,* People's Commune, might have replaced the *hsiang* if it had succeeded). In imperial times the people of several *hsiang,* among the thousands existing in China at the time, were involved in activities which caused them to relocate elsewhere in China. For the most part these people were engaged in trade, although some participated in the bureaucracy at various levels. They began to formalize their situation and ultimately constructed in various cities a number of buildings which served as domiciles for their young men seeking their fortunes, transients conducting some specific bit of business, and a meeting place for sojourners from the native *hsiang* who were, to all intents and purposes, residents of the city, perhaps two or more generations removed from ancestors who had come from the "native place" in question. There may be a direct connection between the establishment of such *t'ung-hsiang hui* and the quite ancient custom whereby affluent and successful degree holders and bureaucrats from certain areas established houses in the provincial and national capital where people from their native districts who wished to take the official examinations could temporarily reside and perhaps also receive tutorial assistance and advice.

The typical *t'ung-hsiang hui* provided a domicile for some and a social center for others, mainly people involved in commerce. It tended to be located in an entrepot, later in those designated as treaty-ports. In the past century, some of the best-known associations of this type have been found outside of China in various cities where there are numbers of overseas Chinese. In the United States, *t'ung-hsiang hui* can be most readily located in San Francisco and New York, although there are some in a few other cities.

At various times over the centuries the government of China has constituted *de facto* groups as a means of social control, although in the long run every such attempt was ultimately subverted. The present Communist government has experimented with a variety of groupings in both rural and urban settings. With respect to the latter we are familiar with the failure of the grandiose plans for urban communes which were to have organized tens of thousands of people into units for the purpose of controlling production, distribution, and consumption, plus social and political activity. On a much less ambitious scale and with evidently greater success the Communists also have experimented with neighborhood groups, usually street by street associations. Used primarily for political indoctrination and control, these groupings are new only in the precise details of their structure and functioning; in principle such organization has long existed, for example, as the well-known *pao-chia* system. Somewhat more novel, but not entirely without foreshadowing is the "study group," which brings together a relatively permanent small assemblage for the study of key materials, in recent years more and more exclusively the works of Chairman Mao. The *hsueh-hsi* groups, as they are called, also provide a primary but not exclusive locus for the activities of self-analysis and confession.

The *pao-chia* system, which some of the organizational attempts of both the Nationalists and the Communists at times resemble, is said by the noted scholar Ch'ü T'ung-tsu to date from the founding of the Ch'ing dynasty in 1644, but the *Tz'u Yuan,* a Chinese encyclopedia, describes the system initiated by Wang An-shih in Sung times. The two systems are clearly related, both being essentially decimal. The Sung system grouped ten households into a *pao,* and five of these units comprised a *ta pao* (great *pao*) with ten of these units making a *tu pao* (metropolitan *pao*), each with an appropriate headman. In the typical version of the Ch'ing system, ten households formed a *p'ai,* ten *p'ai* a *chia,* ten *chia* a *pao,* each unit headed by a chief who was appointed by the magistrate. A basic component of the system is expressed in the character *pao,* which means "to guarantee." Theoretically each person in a unit stood as guarantor to all others, especially if someone traveled away from the unit or committed a crime. But the authority of *pao-chia* leaders, who were unpaid, was often poorly defined. The *pao-chia* system extended over rural and urban areas and its effectiveness is widely considered to have been limited. To increase this effectiveness, from time to time attempts were made to have the lowest level groupings cohere more closely to natural divisions among the people. The rigid decimal system would be loosened to permit the aggregation of greater or fewer households already having some basis for interaction such as kinship or a tradition of neighborly cooperation. The process of adjusting *pao-chia* to natural social conditions is most interesting because a similar tendency is clearly visible in Chinese Communist efforts which have seen retreat from such units as communes to labor brigades and labor teams which tend to represent the organized labor power of the old natural villages.

Chinese society, both rural and urban, is marked by extensive development of non-kin groups, and in addition to those already mentioned there are several kinds of common interest associations. The Chinese word *t'ung* has several related meanings: "all," "together," "to share," "alike," etc. *T'ung* appears in scores of combinations, for example, *t'ung-chih* (literally "common objective") means "comrade." The word also designates potential membership of kinship groups as *t'ung-hsing* (of common surname), or *t'ung-tsung* (of common patrilineal descent), or it designates the kinds of groups we have already considered, as in *t'ung-hsiang hui* (common subdistrict club). Among common interest groups not yet mentioned one of the most important is *t'ung-hsueh* (study together), graduates of the same school, usually further specified, as in other countries, by their class year (*t'ung-pang;* actually this is an old expression which was formerly applied to people who passed the Imperial examinations at the same time and such ties were of very great significance in the later careers of officials).

Before leaving the subject of non-kin associations one additional type of particular importance must be mentioned, although its description and analysis would take volumes. I refer to the secret societies which have existed in China for many centuries. Such societies have tended to crosscut most other divisions in Chinese society, rural-urban, kinship and non-kinship, regional, class, and other. Central authority in China, at least as far back as Han, has been plagued and sometimes toppled by the action of secret societies, from the Red Eyebrows two thousand years ago, through the Yellow Turbans who, indeed, are credited with a major role in bringing an end to the Han dynasty, to the San Ho Hui or Triad Society, which shook the Ch'ing, and the many others that participated in and survived its downfall, such as the Ko Lao Hui, Red Spears, Bastards, and Big Sword. It has been estimated that by 1928 secret society members north of the Yangtze alone ran to three quarters of a million.

Secret societies have many fascinating aspects. For one thing, internal organization was commonly on the basis of fictive kinship. Members regarded their sponsor as "father" and his cohorts were regarded avuncularly; fellow members of similar vintage regarded themselves as brothers, and use of such "relationships" often violated principles of chronological age or preexisting genealogical kinship ties. Secret societies invariably had religious aspects and sometimes involved special cults with extensive ritual; often the express religious purpose was reformative, some societies adhered to strict puritanical behavioral codes. There is also an interesting problem in the relationship between secret societies and crime. By definition, such groups were explicitly illegal and membership itself was a crime to be severely punished. In the same vein, the primary activity of such societies was usually direct or indirect assault on the government. Logistical support of such efforts was not infrequently obtained by raiding towns and villages. Such activity confirmed the government propaganda identifying the members as antisocial bandits and outlaws. Beyond this, there is little doubt that truly criminal secret societies have existed. Pre-Communist Shanghai was infamous for its organized criminal gangs some of which, like the Green Gang, are reputed to have participated in the highest levels of government.

CHINESE SOCIETY: PAST, PRESENT, AND FUTURE

The intricate complexities of Chinese society have scarcely been broached in this introductory excursion. I hope, however, that some of the major features of the society are now clearly visible, as well as some idea of the way in which anthropologists and sociologists have contributed to the general understanding of that society and culture. Let me conclude by turning briefly to certain problems that have already been fleetingly mentioned, problems having to do with continuity and change, the relation of the past to the present, and what may be discerned of the future.

Some commentators view modern China in such a way as to emphasize novelty, attributing her extensive changes to foreign contacts and linking these, in turn, with a variety of causes among which influences from Western countries and Japan play a prominent role. A polar analysis is made by those who regard every detail of contemporary China as a restructuring of some older pattern or elements. In many instances, of course, the truth in the final analysis will probably be found between these extremes: some of China is new, much is old, a great deal is the result of the reworking of old parts to adapt to new pressures and demands.

It is fascinating to compare and contrast the "two Chinas," Taiwan and the mainland, for, despite marked differences in political and economic structure, and despite even more marked differences in ideology, there are a number of parallel processes taking place. Among the most fascinating for the social scientist to observe are those involved in the alteration of family structure and kinship. The Chinese Communists, with a Marriage Law enacted in 1950, claim to have broken with the "feudal" past and assert a new breakthrough in domestic affairs. Only a few years ago, however, they waged a major campaign in such journals as *China Youth* and *Women of China,* again and again striking at what are labeled "feudal remnants." It would be foolish to expect a major civilization such as the Chinese to respond to such colossal overtures toward change in but a few years and it is only the strident and endlessly repeated assertions of tremendous success that makes some "China-watchers" react by overemphasizing the evidence of counterrevolutionary tendencies and slowdowns. Conversely, with much less fanfare, the Republic of China is witnessing many of the same changes, albeit at a slower rate. In both parts of the culture the drift is against the joint family, and with the growing importance of the nuclear family, in the context not of economic deprivation but of increasingly diversified employment possibilities, changes are also occurring in the relations between men and women, between the generations, and toward universalistic institutions.

Similarly, albeit with regard to totally different units, we must note the tendency to stability and recrudescence of certain basic forms of organization. The recent attempt in mainland China to replace natural villages with synthetic social units seems to have failed. Similar efforts to reorganize higher levels, culminating in the attempt to transmute *hsiang* into large-scale People's Communes, also proved abortive for most purposes. Behind this it is possible to show, following G. William Skinner, how villages fit into a network of economic structures providing a hierarchy of locations of exchange, growing more complex from level to level, through local market towns, to intermediate centers, and finally to provincial capitals and great entrepots. Despite massive efforts, the main outlines of this network continue to show through the social and economic structure of the People's Republic of China.

What the future will bring is certainly not clear. It is unlikely that China will return to customary patterns no matter what government ultimately emerges. Conversely, as we have already seen, much that will come to pass will no doubt be found strongly foreshadowed in the past and in the present. It is hoped that some of the clues given here will help you come to your own understanding of this tremendous process.

XIII

Chinese

Archaeology

BY
KWANG-CHIH CHANG

Archaeology is the discipline that studies past human life and history by means of physical and cultural remains. The study of man and his works takes these remains, since the first man emerged some two million years ago, as primary sources of information; written records are available only for the last five thousand years and even then only for restricted areas of the world. Because of the nature of his material and the scope of his inquiry, the archaeologist has several distinctive characteristics. His material is tangible and visual, and thus his interpretations of human life and history are based above all upon physical variations; his time spans ten million years and his space stretches over the globe, and thus his studies are consistently comparative; having to deal with variations in vast time and vast space, he tends to take a dynamic rather than a static viewpoint toward his material; and his variations must be classified to reveal their significance, and thus his books deal with cultural and social groups, traditions, and horizons, instead of individual heroes and villains.

Written records began in China during the middle part of the second millennium B.C., and the earliest historical China is known through writings from the two earliest dynasties of the Middle Kingdom, Shang and Chou. Archaeology essentially supplements written records in providing data about the Shang and Chou civilizations, but archaeology alone gives back to China the history of its first million or so years. Having begun less than fifty years ago, modern scientific archaeology in China is still in its infancy, and China's temporal and spatial expanse is vast. The panorama of human life and history in China shown by archaeological remains is only beginning to unfold (see Table).

Early Man in China

Some one or two million years ago (the exact date is still under dispute) a series of geological events—tectonic movements, climatic changes, and the emergence of new biological forms—ushered in on earth the epoch known as the Ice Age or Pleistocene, and the true story of human evolution, both physical and cultural, begins with this period. Climatic fluctuations, the resultant alternations of glacial and interglacial stages, and the development of animal and plant forms enable us to make a subdivision of this prolonged time interval, according to which the scattered human and cultural remains and archaeological sites are usually arranged in ordered interrelationship,

Location of Important Archaeological Sites

Chronological Subdivisions of Chinese Culture History

Period	Human Fossils and Culture-Industries
Early Pleistocene	*Hemanthropus peii,* Hsi-hou-te implements
Middle Pleistocene	Lan-t'ien Man and Fen-hoian Industry
	Peking Man and Chou-k'ou-tienian Industry
Late Pleistocene	Ting-ts'un Man
	Ordos Man and Ordosian Industry
Early Postglacial	*Homo sapiens*
	"Mesolithic"
	Shen-wen Horizon (?)
	Painted Pottery Horizon
	Lungshanoid Horizon
	Lungshan Culture
ca. 1700 B.C.	Shang
	Early Chou
ca. 600 B.C.	Late Chou
221 B.C.	Ch'in Empire
206 B.C.	Han
A.D. 220-	Historic Dynasties after Han

so that it is possible for the archaeologist to place them both according to time and as parts of a process. Thus the Chinese Pleistocene is divided, according to a series of glaciers that occurred in the Himalayas and different forms of animals and plants that succeeded one another, into three time periods: Early, Middle, and Late. Early Pleistocene in China includes the First Glacial and First Interglacial; Middle Pleistocene, Second Glacial and Second Interglacial; and Late Pleistocene, Third Glacial, Third Interglacial, and Fourth Glacial. These subdivisions permit the placement in time of fossils and archaeological sites in China as well as their comparison with remains throughout the world. Generally speaking, climatic conditions are severe during glacial stages and mild during interglacial periods; thus, the chronological placement of archaeological sites gives further indication of the environmental conditions under which Early Man lived and to which he must have adapted both bodily and culturally. Minor fluctuations in climate and geological conditions are also in evidence during each of the broad glacial or interglacial stages, and variations resulting from differences in altitude and latitude sometimes must also be taken into account.

EARLY PLEISTOCENE

Abundant human fossils from Early Pleistocene deposits, which have been found in many parts of the Old World, amply demonstrate that during this period the earliest hominid forms emerged and became widely distributed. Man's existence in China at this time cannot be doubted. G. H. R. von Koenigswald, the Dutch palaeontologist, has discovered in druggists' shops in Hong Kong (see below for the connection between these and fossils) a number of hominid teeth believed to have come originally from the limestone caves in Southwest China, that show unmistakable similarities to the teeth of *Paranthropus,* an Early Pleistocene African primate closely related to our human ancestors. Koenigswald, who has given to these teeth the Latin name *Hemanthropus peii,* is convinced that they indicate the australopithecine occupation of South China.

Crudely chipped implements of quartzite pebbles were found during 1959-61 at a Palaeolithic locality close to the village of Hsi-hou-tu, near Jui-ch'eng Hsien, in southwestern Shansi, North China. They are believed to derive from pre-Middle Pleistocene deposits associated with an Early Pleistocene fauna.

These findings are notable evidence of human occupation of China during this early geological period, and future explorations of China in this time horizon are certain to characterize more specifically Early Pleistocene Man in China and to throw light on the earliest history of mankind in general.

MIDDLE PLEISTOCENE

Early man in China is now very well known for the Middle Pleistocene period, and the sites at Chou-k'ou-tien, a village some twenty-six miles southwest of Peking, in a region called the Western Hills, played a leading role in this study. There was found Peking Man, the story of whose discovery must begin any account of Chinese archaeology.

Ever since the Late Chou period (*ca.* 600-200 B.C.) the mythological dragon has played manifold roles in Chinese life—an animal with "a camel-like head, deerlike horns, rabbit-like eyes, cattle-like ears, a snake-like neck, a sea-serpent-like abdomen, carp-like scales, eagle-like claws, and tiger-like paws." One of the roles the dragon has played is therapeutic; its bones (*lung ku*) are an important Chinese medicine. According to *Pen-ts'ao kang-mu,* the classical Chinese pharmacopaeia compiled during the Ming dynasty, dragon bones cured a variety of digestive, reproductive, and skin ailments.

For two thousand years Chinese patients meekly consumed the bones of the dragon, prescribed by doctors. If it occurred to the pharmacists and doctors that these bones were of a remarkable variety of shapes and substances, this must have seemed rather natural, since the dragon resembled a variety of different animals. To a modern scientist of the Western persuasion, however, who is used to calling a spade a spade, bones must be classified taxonomically rather than mythologically. In 1899 a man of some scientific training, K. S. Haberer, who was at Peking with the German Ministry, collected a large number of dragon bones from the druggists' stores in many cities in China and sent the collection to Professor Max Schlosser of the University of Munich for examination. In 1903 Professor Schlosser published his report, establishing for the first time that the so-called dragon bones were in fact fossils of various ancient extinct mammals. He further reported that in the collection he studied there was a single tooth undoubtedly from a primate. China was rich in the material paleontologists eagerly seek, available no farther away than the corner drugstore. Great scientific interest inevitably was stimulated, all the more since primates, and possibly even hominids, awaited discovery. So scientists enthusiastically began collecting dragon bones throughout China.

Dr. J. Gunner Andersson, Swedish mineralogical consultant to the Chinese government, quickly found many fossiliferous localities in many regions of North China, and in 1918 he traced some of the dragon bones to their source near the village of Chou-k'ou-tien. There, in 1921-22, the first hominid teeth were found. The discovery led to the extensive excavation of the Chou-k'ou-tien sites in 1927-37 by an international team of scientists (prominent among whom were O. Zdanski, B. Bohlen, W. C. P'ei, C. C. Young, Pierre Teilhard de Chardin, Davidson Black, and Franz Weidenreich), and the discovery of a large number of teeth and bones of Peking Man, known scientifically as *Sinanthropus pekinensis, Pithecanthropus pekinensis,* among other designations.

Over twenty fossiliferous localities have been found in the limestone caves in the Chou-k'ou-tien region, in the so-called Western Hills area at the eastern extremity of the great T'ai-hang Range bordering the Shansi plateau, and evidence of human occupation is manifest at several localities. The evidence consists of human fossils and cultural relics (stone implements, fragmented bones, hackberry seeds, and hearths), which make this the richest Early Man site of its period in the world. The fissure deposits in these caves, from which

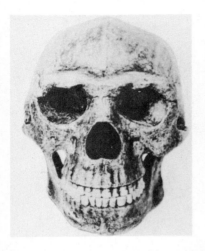

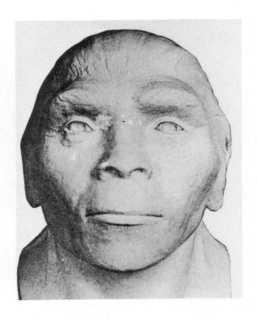

Figure 1. Skull and reconstruction
of head of Peking Man.

the Peking Man relics were derived, have yielded a large quantity of
such characteristic Middle Pleistocene mammalian fossils as a thick-
skulled deer and ancient elephants that are found widely in the
reddish clay deposits of comparable age throughout North China. The
relative positions of the deposits in the ground and analyses of the
pollen found with them further correlate the Peking Man occupations
with the Second Glacial, Second Interglacial, and Third Glacial stages
of the Himalayas.

The bony remains of Peking Man all came from a single limestone
cave at Chou-k'ou-tien. The bones consist of fifteen crania, six facial
bones, twelve mandibles, a miscellaneous collection of postcranial
bones, and 147 teeth. Studies of the physical characters of these bones
by Davidson Black and Franz Weidenreich disclose that Peking Man
was still in an early stage of human development, comparable to the
Homo erectus of Java. The limbs were highly developed and quite
modern, indicating that he stood upright and walked on two feet, but
the cranium is characterized by low vault, heavy bony features, thick
wall, and small cranial capacity (914-1,225 cc., with an average of
1,043 cc., as against Java Man's 860 cc. and modern man's 1,350 cc.)
(Fig. 1). On the basis of a sequence of development proposed by some
paleontologists, such as Sir Wilfred Le Gros Clark, Peking Man
belongs with *Homo erectus* of Java and its African and European

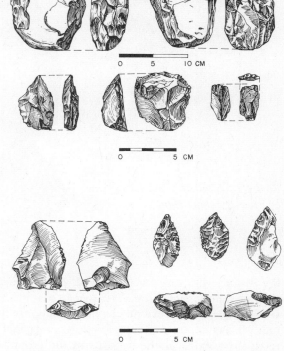

Figure 2.   Chou-k'ou-tienian implement types.

affinities, later than the earliest "men" (*Australopithecus*) and earlier than the latest (*Homo sapiens*).

Despite the distance Peking Man still had to travel before the modern stage of human development was reached, he was a fully cultural creature capable of using fire for cooking and making stone implements for hunting game and for daily use in connection with domestic activities and sustenance. The implements were largely made of quartz and quartzite pebbles. Although the techniques were of the crudest kind, standardized types of implements were already in existence and included scrapers, awls, and points. The basic processes of implement-making can be described under two major industrial traditions, *flake* and *pebble*. The former involves the production of crude flakes struck from coarsely prepared cores, and the latter has to do with the rough shaping (by striking off a small number of flakes) of natural pebbles and pebblelike stone nodules into what Hallam L. Movius has referred to as choppers and chopping-tools (Fig. 2). The bifacially flaked handaxes and the so-called Levallois flakes struck off carefully prepared cores, that are characteristic of contemporary stone industries in much of Africa, western Asia, and Europe, are conspicuously absent at Chou-k'ou-tien. This had led many prehistorians to postulate a Middle Pleistocene beginning for the division of the Old World into western and eastern spheres.

There is no archaeological evidence of artistic activities or house construction. These cave dwellers near Peking apparently subsisted mainly on deer meat, for deer bones are abundant. The fact that the Peking Man skulls are invariably broken and that the skull base is particularly fragmentary has led scholars to believe that Peking Man fell victim to his own kind.

Scattered remains of Early Man contemporary with Peking Man have been discovered in several areas in China, but the one important center is on the lower Fen-ho River in southwestern Shansi and the adjacent Huangho Valley in central-eastern Shensi and northwestern Honan. A fossil mandible of man was discovered near Lan-t'ien in central-eastern Shensi in 1963, and a cranium was found in 1964 in deposits considered to be Early Middle Pleistocene in age, in association with faunal elements suggesting a warm climate. The skull of Lan-t'ien Man (also known as *Sinanthropus lantienensis*) exhibits features comparable to Peking Man, but the skull wall is thicker, the vault even lower, and the cranial capacity apparently smaller (estimated at 780 cc.). These features have led Dr. Woo Ju-kang to conclude that Lan-t'ien Man (Fig. 3) is more primitive than Peking Man.

From the same time horizon as Lan-t'ien Man, and in the same general area, Palaeolithic implements have been brought to light in large numbers. Prominent among the sites is a series of Palaeolithic localities near the village of Ko-ho, in Jui-ch'eng Hsien, southwestern Shansi; and other sites of similar time periods and contents are found along the lower courses of the Fen-ho River. The implements are comparable to those at Chou-k'ou-tien in basic techniques and general typology, but several tool types, such as stone balls, prismatic picks, and discoidal scrapers, are distinctive of this area. These assemblages are thus sometimes referred to as Fen-hoian, in contrast to the Chou-k'ou-tienian assemblage of Peking Man. Both are without question part of a larger eastern Asian chopper-chopping-tool tradi-

Figure 3.   Skull of Lan-t'ien Man.

tion of Lower Palaeolithic industries, but the Chou-k'ou-tienian and the Fen-hoian are apparently two somewhat different local manifestations due to geographical and perhaps other variables.

Implements identical with the Chou-k'ou-tienian and the Fenhoian in time and similar in type have been located in several other areas in both North and South China in reddish clay or comparable deposits. A *"Pithecanthropus"* tooth was collected by G. H. R. von Koenigswald in Hong Kong and believed to have come originally from South China, which during early Middle Pleistocene times presumably served as a link between Peking and Lan-t'ien Man of North China and Java Man in Southeast Asia. Further investigations there of Early Man remains are awaited with eager anticipation.

LATE PLEISTOCENE

Geologists believe that at the close of the reddish clay deposition a major erosion took place with an interglacial climate (probably Third Interglacial), and after this aeolian loess, a wind-driven, powdery, yellow soil, began to accumulate over a large area of North China under dry and cold conditions of the Fourth Glacial. The Fen-hoian tradition of stone industries continued into the erosional stage, and the best-documented Palaeolithic localities of this period are the assemblages near Ting-ts'un, in Hsiang-fen Hsien, southern Shansi, in the Fen-ho Valley. Stone implements discovered here show continuation of the older Fen-hoian flake and pebble types and techniques, but more elaborate preparations and retouches are apparent, showing a transitional tendency toward the next phase of Palaeolithic development. Three human teeth, establishing the existence of Ting-ts'un Man, came to light together with stone implements. In shape, the teeth resembled those of Neanderthal Man of Europe. Bones of ancient men of similar morphological character have been found near Ch'ang-yang, in Hupei of Central China, and near Ma-pa, in northern Kwangtung of South China. The distribution of neanderthaloid human fossils is apparently widespread in China from Third Interglacial and early Fourth Glacial deposits.

During the Fourth Glacial period, in which considerable loess had accumulated in North China, a new, Upper Paleolithic industrial stage was reached. It is called Ordosian, after the Ordos region of North China, where the Jesuit priests Emile Licent and Pierre Teilhard de Chardin discovered the first Palaeolithic implements in China in the 1920s. The characteristic elements of this new culture are tools made of blades—narrow, parallel-sided, and elongated flakes struck from well-prepared blade-cores. Regular types of blade implements include points, scrapers, and burins (Fig. 4), some of which resemble their western European counterparts so closely that the European term "Aurignacian" has been sometimes given these Upper Palaeolithic tools. Often associated with the tools are bones of mammoths and wooly rhinoceroses, presumably game animals Ordos Man hunted. Skeletal remains of Ordos Man include some skull bones, a tooth, and some long bones. Preliminary studies of these bones disclose strikingly neanderthaloid features. Two skulls from South China deposits of a comparable period—Tzu-yang Man of Szechwan and Liu-chiang Man of Kwangsi—however, are described by Woo Ju-kang as unmistakably *Homo sapiens*. There is a strong likelihood that modern man appeared in China, as he did elsewhere, during the Fourth Glacial Period.

Weidenreich observed that a number of morphological traits often

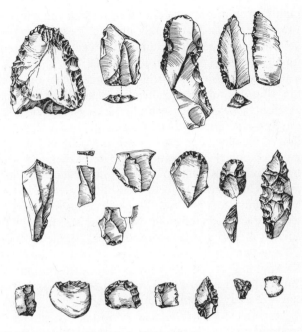

Figure 4.   Ordosian implements.

found among the modern mongoloid peoples occurred among the Peking Man population, such as the sagittal crest and the shovel-shaped incisors. Skulls from both Tzu-yang and Liu-chiang Man also exhibit features that are mongoloid, but Woo Ju-kang believes that some of their other features are ancestral to some nonmongoloid inhabitants of the Pacific area at the present time. It is probable that the ancestry of both races can be traced, at least in part, to the earliest *Homo sapiens* of the China area.

POSTGLACIAL PERIOD

The retreat of glaciers and ice sheets from the mountainous areas of China and the gradual climatic amelioration in North China began approximately ten to twelve thousand years ago. For a time—about 8000-4000 B.C. in southeast China, according to recently analyzed pollen data—there was a period of "climatic optimum," during which at least a large part of China had a higher average temperature than it has today. Moisture and forest cover characterized some of the areas previously barren or sparsely vegetated. The cold fauna of the Fourth Glacial disappeared from the scene.

Archaeological sites that fall chronologically into this period are widely scattered in the area of China. In the north, the Upper Cave of Chou-k'ou-tien and the sites in the sand-dune area (Sha-yüan) in central-eastern Shensi are the best known. The former site has yielded a large number of bone and antler implements and ornaments, and the latter a predominance of microblades. Some archaeologists in other areas of the world have thought that during the early postglacial period the Upper Palaeolithic cultures often had to readapt to changed environments, so that their remains exhibit characteristics of forest-hunting and fishing subsistence patterns. The Mesolithic cultures of North China appear to fall within this category also.

Formation of the Chinese Culture

The late Henri Frankfort, noted archaeologist and historian of the ancient Near East, saw two major aspects of the study of the ancient civilizations: *identity* and *change*. "What constitutes the individuality of a civilization, its recognizable character, its identity which is maintained throughout the successive stages of its existence? What, on the other hand, are the changes differentiating one stage from the next?" He went on to propose calling the identity of a civilization its "form," and the totality of its changes its "dynamics."[1]

The identity of the Chinese civilization demonstrably predates the emergence of its writing. The emergence of historic civilization in China is in itself a manifestation of change. The origin of the Chinese civilizational form and the initial phases of its dynamics are problems that are archaeologically pertinent. To answer the questions when, where, how, and why the Chinese civilizational form began and changed, archaeological data must be employed, sometimes exclusively and sometimes as a supplement.

It can be said that the following characteristics of the earliest Chinese culture are identifiable as definitely "Chinese":

1. The cultivation of millet and rice.
2. The domestication of pig, dog, chicken, horse, cattle, and sheep, the so-called six domestic animals.

1. *The Birth of Civilization in the Near East* (Bloomington: Indiana University Press, 1951), p. 16.

3. *Hang-t'u,* or compressed earth structures.
4. Silkworm and hemp.
5. Tailored garments.
6. Pottery impressed with cord, basket, or mat patterns.
7. Characteristic cuisine style and kitchen utensils.
8. Stone reaping knives.
9. Ceremonial vessels of characteristic forms.
10. A distinctive art style.
11. Scapulimancy, or divination by animal bones (especially shoulderblades).

All these components of culture are recognizable in the earliest available archaeological remains of China, and all of them continued into the historical period. Although they did not all originate in China, together they serve to identify the distinctive form from its beginning of a major culture of the world. Where did it begin? When did it begin? How did it come about? What were the steps that led to its flowering into a historical civilization? Archaeological evidence has suggested the following tentative answers.

EMERGENCE OF VILLAGE FARMERS

The Upper Cave and the Sha-yüan inhabitants were the last of the food gatherers in North China; their age is perhaps nearly ten thousand years before the present. Archaeological remains of the next phase are those of village farmers—food producers (plant cultivators and animal raisers) living in villages—contributing to the identity defined above as "Chinese." Their age is unknown, since such modern dating techniques as the radiocarbon method have yet to be applied to Northern Chinese data. By the principle of simple accumulation from the beginning of historic records (*ca.* 1500 B.C.) we may tentatively arrive at a date of six or seven millennia before Christ and use this figure as a background for discussion.

The transition from a hunting-fishing way of life to that of village farming probably took place in North China in a region that has been called the "North China nuclear area," that is, the region around the confluence of the three great rivers of North China, Huang-ho (Yellow River), Fen-ho, and Wei-shui, or where the three provinces Honan, Shansi, and Shensi meet. It is in fact a small basin encircled on the north, west, and south by plateaus and mountains, but open to the eastern plains. During the climatic optimum that probably occurred, the nuclear area was on the border between the western highlands and the swampy eastern lowlands, a type of environment where potentially cultivable plants found a natural habitat, and a relatively sedentary life was feasible so that prolonged experimentation with cultivation and domestication could be carried out. Archaeological evidence for an initial, incipient agricultural stage is unfortunately lacking, and it is as yet impossible to define the precise forms in which the significant transition took place. Whether or not a prepottery horizon of agricultural life occurred here, as it did in other known nuclear areas of the world, remains in the sphere of conjecture. That the earliest ceramic phases in North China were probably characterized by the cord-mat-basket-impressed wares (a *Sheng-wen*, or cord-marked pottery, horizon) has been speculated upon, on the ground of geographic distribution, and is substantiated by some stratigraphical evidence. But of the general cultural configuration of the earliest ceramic phases we know next to nothing.

More than a thousand prehistoric sites, probably only slightly later than the initial phase, have been found in that small part of North China, with the nuclear area as a center, including northern and western Honan, southern and central Shansi, southwestern Hopei, central Shensi, and eastern Kansu. These sites can be grouped together according to their similar stratigraphic position and by the presence of a number of common distinctive horizon markers— painted pottery, some pottery forms (pointed-bottomed jars, flat- and round-based cups and bowls, thin-necked and big-bellied jars), and some characteristic stone forms (rectangular reaping knives and round axes, most with symmetrical edges and partially polished). Since painted pottery is a diagnostic feature of this cultural horizon, the term has been used generally to describe it.

Archaeological remains of the Painted Pottery horizon indicate the appearance of moderate-sized villages, each comprised of a dozen or so round or rectangular semisubterranean or ground dwellings (Fig. 5), or sometimes a few long, partitioned communal houses. Millets (*Setaria italica* and *Panicum miliaceum*) were the sole staples, and dogs and pigs the principal domestic animals. Chipped or polished stone hoes and spades are commonly discovered, and stone knives were made, probably for weeding and reaping. According to the shifting and repetitive pattern of settlement—shown by the multiple components of the sites, the brevity of occupation of each component, and the vegetational changes indicated by pollens from one of the sites—

*Figure 5. Reconstructed house at Miao-ti-kou,
Painted Pottery stratum.*

it seems reasonable to assume that these early farmers engaged in slash-and-burn cultivation. Stone axes were made, presumably for clearing fields in the woods.

Hunting and fishing were practiced along with farming, and they were locally of continued great importance. Bows and arrows, harpoons, spears, and fishhooks were among the principal implements, and painted fish and animal figures sometimes occur on bowls (Fig. 6). Possibly silkworms were raised, and hemp may have been cultivated; fabrics were spun, woven, and sewn.

A variety of pottery characterizes the sites of this horizon. It was made by hand (often coiled) or with the aid of a mold. Most of the wares were of a domestic nature: cooking pots, water jars, storage jars, serving dishes, bowls, and cups. Many were impressed with cord-mat-basket patterns, and others were beautifully painted in monochromic or bichromic decorations. There is a large variety of painted designs (Fig. 7), and their variations afford an important clue for the chronological ordering of the sites.

Each village of these early farmers was apparently a self-contained "little community," consisting of a dwelling area, an incorporated or separate work area with kilns, and a village cemetery. It is not easy to differentiate the villagers according to kind of work or status. Little of the evidence suggests warfare.

EXPANSION OF THE VILLAGE FARMERS

Archaeological sites of the next time level, often from a higher stratigraphical position than the remains of the Painted Pottery

394

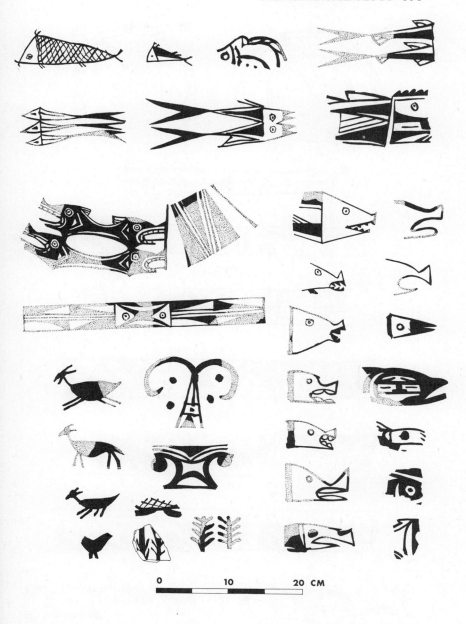

Figure 6. Painted fish and animal figures on bowls, Pan-p'o.

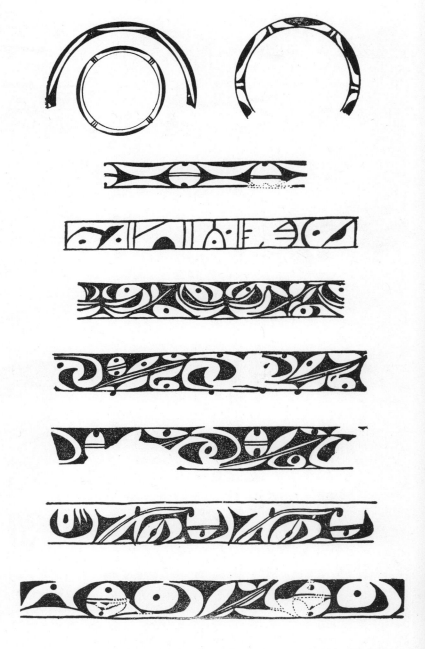

Figure 7.   Some decorative patterns on painted pottery.

horizon, show considerable change in character and are distributed much more widely. The first indication of the emergence of this new cultural horizon—the Lungshanoid—is the diminished number of painted pottery sherds and a growing amount of coarser plain grayish-blackish pottery, often decorated with impressed cord and basket patterns. Sites are larger in many instances, and many show a more permanent occupancy. There is a growing number of harvesting knives and woodworking adzes.

Lungshanoid sites occur over a wide area—mainly in the eastern parts of the nuclear area but also in the eastern plains of North China and along the entire eastern coastal area, as far north as the Bay of Pohai and as far south as Taiwan and the delta of the Pearl River. Archaeological remains from this vast space show a remarkable homogeneity, apparently indicating that the expansion of this new culture from the nuclear area into the eastern low and coastal countries was explosively rapid. The remains indicate that this was the time when northern Chinese farmers extended their influence into Southeast Asia, an area hitherto occupied by a rather different culture, a hunting-fishing people in the main, with perhaps an incipient kind of plant cultivation.

The factors responsible for this presumably rapid expansion of Chinese culture from the nuclear area can only be conjectured at the present time. Well-documented studies of the history of early farmers in the Near East have shown that the village farmers often descended from hilly areas into the fertile river plains and alluvia after the initial experimental stage of plant cultivation and when the cultigens had been adequately conditioned to be planted outside their natural habitats. This could have happened in China also. Exhaustion of arable land in the nuclear area, and the pressure of a growing population supported by agriculture instead of hunting and fishing, can also reasonably be assumed to have prompted the Lungshanoid inhabitants to seek land elsewhere.

Whatever the reason, the Lungshanoid farmers populated eastern and southeastern China. Inasmuch as this was a new environment, it is not surprising that changes in culture occurred that can be described as adaptive in nature. Rice (*Oryza sativa*) was cultivated alongside millet, and many varieties of fruits, vegetables, and water plants are in evidence in the archaeological remains. The wattle-and-daub structures on semisubterranean floors gave way to timber structures built on stilts. Shell implements and utensils supplemented those of bone and antler.

FORMATION OF LATE PREHISTORIC LOCAL TRADITIONS

Soon after the Lungshanoid horizon in the archaeological record of China came a series of local culture traditions that immediately antedate the historical civilizations. The sites in Shensi and southern Shansi are characterized by gray pottery, often cord-impressed, often in the shape of a jar with three hollow feet. The area of Honan is distinguished by gray and black beakers, tripods with hollow feet, and small pots impressed with basket designs. Thin, lustrous, wheelmade, jet-black pottery, mostly plain but occasionally incised and engraved with decorations, appeared in Shantung (Fig. 8), and here the stone implements are characteristically rectangular and highly polished. Finally, tripods with solid feet, dishes on high and perforated pedestals, and special varieties of stone adzes and knives characterize the entire eastern coast. Since this stage of cultural development was first recognized in 1928 with the excavation of the Ch'eng-tzu-yai site near Lung-shan in central Shantung, these cultures are often referred to as the Lungshan cultures.

That there should be local cultures at this stage is not difficult to explain. Instead of being confined to a relatively small and culturally homogeneous nuclear area, the Lungshan cultures were widely scattered. The area spanned approximately twenty degrees of latitude, with broad differences of climate, vegetation, and topography. The widely separated communities could not possibly be in constant touch with one another to any significant degree, and their isolation, together with adaptive changes, tended to push these cultures of common descent farther and farther apart. Of probably equal importance were the pre-Lungshanoid cultures on the Chinese periphery. They varied notably north to south and contributed demonstrably to the new forms in which the immigrant Lungshanoid people molded themselves.

The time span of the Lungshan cultures varies greatly. Broadly speaking, they began with the end of the Lungshanoid horizon, which has been said to be comparatively homogeneous in both time and substance. They ended, on the other hand, at the emergence of historical civilizations that took place in different times in different areas of China. The Lungshan culture of Honan gave way to the Shang civilization around 1750 B.C., but those in Shansi-Shensi and in western Shantung did not give way to historical civilizations until the late Shang or early Western Chou period, toward the end of the second millenium before Christ. The Lungshan cultures in Southeast

China are shown to have persisted until the middle of the first millennium when the Eastern Chou civilizations arose south of the Yangtze Valley.

The Beginnings of Civilization

The word civilization is used by the British archaeologist Stuart Piggott to mean a

society which has worked out a solution to the problem of living in a relatively large permanent community, at a level of technological and social development above that of the hunting band, the family farmstead, the rustic, self-sufficient village or the pastoral tribe. Civilization is something artificial and man-made, the result of making tools of increasing complexity in response to the enlarging concepts of community life evolving in men's minds.[2]

Archaeological sites and remains in China beyond the threshold of civilization are not difficult to recognize, for the society they reflect and indicate is clearly of a qualitatively more complex order than that

2. *The Dawn of Civilization* (London: Thames and Hudson, 1962), p. 11.

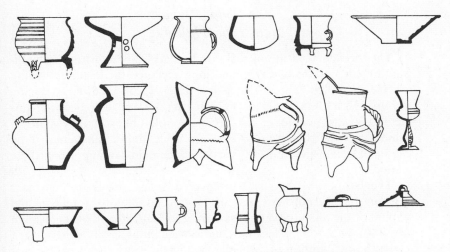

Figure 8. Pottery and Stone implements, Shantung Lungshan Culture.

of the Lungshan farming villages. Each locus in which archaeological remains are concentrated is no longer a microcosmic version of the cultural whole, for different loci have distinct functions; some are more complex than others, some are apparently seats of political power, some are quarters of particular industries. Many different sites combine to form a network that assumes the characters of an urban-rural continuum and contrast.

The society indicated by the settlement patterns is a highly stratified and differentiated one, and stratification and differentiation are most sharply shown by remains of a highly developed bronze industry. Some sites produced bronzes, while others used them. Bronzes were primarily ceremonial vessels and weapons; the agricultural and domestic implements continued to be made of stone, bone, or antler.

The emergence of writing is both indication and result of the high level of social complexity. Although the full story of the civilizational origins remains to be told by archaeologists, the Chinese began at this point to put down some events of their daily life in writing. Prehistoric anonymity now gives way to specific and individual names for peoples and dynasties, and the Shangs and the Chous are known to belong to the initial stages of Chinese civilization.

The Shang Dynasty
(ca. 1766-1122 B.C.)

The legendary nature of early traditional Chinese history notwithstanding, historians of China had long accepted the historical reality of the so-called Three Dynasties, Hsia (2205-1766 B.C.), Shang (1766-1122 B.C.), and Chou (1122-221 B.C.). Archaeological remains definitely attributable to the Hsia are still unknown anywhere in China, but the Shang and Chou are both amply substantiated by archaeological sites and by written documents dating from these periods.

The best-known and first discovered Shang site is the one near Anyang, in the northern part of Honan, definitely the relic of the capital of the Shang royal house during its last 280-odd years of reign (ca. 1401-1122 B.C.). The first clue to such ruins in the general area came to the attention of a scholar of ancient history who paid a visit to a sick friend and noticed that the medicines his friend was taking contained some dragon bones that were *inscribed*. Efforts were made

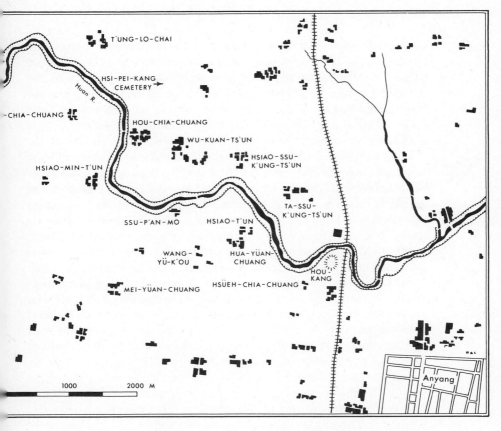

Figure 9. Shang Sites at An-yang.

to trace their origins, and it was learned in the year 1899 that the inscribed bones had come from Anyang. It was not until 1928, however, that the Institute of History and Philology, Academia Sinica, brought modern archaeologists to explore the site. From 1928 through 1937 fifteen seasons of large-scale excavations were carried out here under the direction of Dr. Li Chi. The Anyang excavations are comparable in magnitude and importance with the work at Chou-k'ou-tien, but unfortunately, because of the outbreak of war in 1937, full publication of the results has been much delayed.

There are about a dozen localities of Shang remains in the Anyang area, believed to have been occupied at approximately the same time (Fig. 9). Most were residential hamlets of the farmers, but many

401

workshops were also found. Two sites are of particular interest—Hsiao-t'un and Hsi-pei-kang. The former is the site of over twenty large house floors, arranged in three clusters and believed to be the ruins of a palace-temple complex used during the Shang period by the royal house and the priests. The houses were of considerable size (the largest floor being over 70 meters long), and the pole-bases of stone and bronze give some indication of the size and elaboration of the pillars; but the walls were constructed of wattle-and-daub, and the architecture of the Shangs was apparently less than spectacular. Their accomplishments, shown by remains at Hsiao-t'un, lie mainly in the many elaborately made and decorated ceremonial vessels and weapons of bronze (Fig. 10) and the inscribed shoulder blades and turtle shells (Fig. 11). The bones and shells were scraped, polished, grooved, and burned for divination purposes; questions and answers were often inscribed and incised on these oracle bones. The chiakuologists (*chia:* turtle shell; *ku:* bone) have been able to obtain a variety of information on customs and manners, genealogical background, and religious beliefs and practices from the inscriptions, thus gaining much material that can properly be called historical. It is known, for instance, that the genealogical record of the Shang royal house in the *Records of the Historian,* by the great Ssu-ma Ch'ien of the Han Dynasty, is essentially in agreement with the oracle inscriptions; that the major area of the Shang activities was confined to the eastern part of Honan and the adjacent regions to the southeast; that communication and contact reached as far south as the southeastern coast; that ancestor worship rites were performed by the royal family according to a well-organized schedule; and that major conquests and military expeditions took place toward the end of the dynasty, and were thought to be a major factor in the dynasty's downfall.

Hsi-pei-kang, a flat, high ground north of Hou-chia-chuang village and about three kilometers northwest of Hsiao-t'un, is perhaps the most spectacular relic of the Shang Dynasty, for here some eleven tombs, referred to as "royal tombs," were brought to light. All the tombs are basically rectangular pits, some fifteen meters to a side and over ten meters deep; the bottom is invariably smaller than the opening because of the sloping walls. A wooden chamber was constructed at the center of the pit, and the coffin was placed inside the chamber. Two or four ramps connect the pit and the ground above in two (north and south) or four directions, the longest being over thirty meters (Fig. 12). Human retainers, guardians, and chariot-

TING LI YEN (HSIEN) TUI TOU

KUI FU

CHÜEH CHIAO CHIA HO TSUN

KU CHIH YU HSI-KUANG YI

NIAO-TSUN HU LEI P'AN CHIEN YI YÜ

Figure 10.   Some Shang and Chou bronzes.

403

warriors were killed and buried in various places in the tomb, and clusters of ceremonial and decorative articles and whole chariots and horses were placed inside before the pit was filled with dirt. In these tombs were found bronze vessels and weapons of the most excellent workmanship; elaborately carved white pottery; carved and engraved bone objects (Fig. 13); remains of wooden structures and articles inlaid with turquoise, marble, and bronze; and stone carvings in the round (Fig. 14)—providing the most elaborate testimonial to the artistic achievements of the Shang. Shang art is frequently characterized as an animal style, for bronze and bone objects were often adorned with a variety of mythologically rendered motifs of animal origin, such as the *t'ao-t'ieh* or split-faced animals, the serpent, and the mythical bird *feng* (Fig. 15).

Other Shang sites have been found in a wide area of North China, the most important being those at and near the modern city of Cheng-chou, also in North Honan. Here a stamped earth wall encircled the area, comparable with Hsiao-t'un of Anyang in importance and function, and this is among the earliest known city enclosures in Chinese history. Scattered around the city enclosure are some two

Figure 11. Inscribed oracle bone.

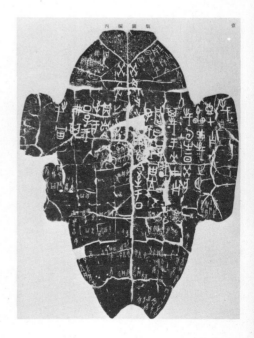

Figure 12. Hsi-pei-kang royal tomb, HPKN-1001.

dozen small hamlets and burial areas; many of the hamlets appear to have specialized functions: bronze foundries, pottery kilns, bone workshops, and so on. The urban-rural network pattern is even better defined in Cheng-chou than in Anyang, although only a few pieces of inscribed oracle bones have come to light, and few art pieces are found that match the Anyang masterpieces in excellence and workmanship. The Cheng-chou sites are particularly significant for remains that are demonstrably earlier in time than the earliest Shang remains at Anyang and, further, for the fact that these early Cheng-chou remains serve as an important link between the full-fledged Shang civilizational manifestations and the Honan Lungshan culture.

This link is highly relevant to the question of the origin of the Shang civilization. Many elements of the Shang civilization are without prehistoric antecedents in China—their sociopolitical form, bronze foundries, horse chariots, and writing. There is no reason why the Shangs could not have invented any of these things themselves, especially new sociopolitical patterns, but the fact that bronze tech-

405

Figure 13. Bone carvings, Shang Dynasty.

Figure 14. Stone sculpture, Shang Dynasty.

406

nology, writing, and horse chariots appeared some thousand years earlier in the Near East very much complicates matters. Whatever the origin or origins of these and other isolated items, the *form* of the Chinese civilization of the Shang period without any question is descended from the Chinese culture of the Neolithic period, because the over-all character of the stone, pottery, and bone artifacts, the houses constructed, and the plants and animals domesticated show the same identity for both periods. The question of origin is essentially one of *dynamics:* why and how the Shang civilization arose when, where, and the way it did. Was this an outcome of indigenous growth of the Lungshan culture, while the emergence of the bronze industry, chariot warfare, and writing were incidental consequences? Or was it because of the emergence of these skills that the civilizational growth was given momentum and incentives? Current available archaeologi-

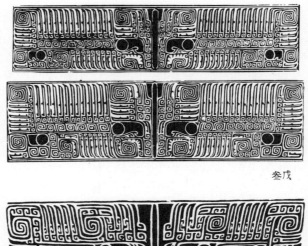

叄戊

叄戊

Figure 15. Shang animal motifs.

肆乙

408

cal data do not answer these questions, and different historians hold different views in accordance with their interpretation of the historical process.

A study of the distribution of Shang remains and sites reveals Shang spheres of dominance and influence. The Shang dominated northeastern Honan, southern Hopei, western Shantung, and perhaps northern Anhwei and Kiangsu, as shown in sites characteristically Shang in pattern of settlement, technological complexity, and stratification. They influenced a much larger sphere—almost all of North China east of the Wei-shui valley, north to the edge of the Mongolian steppes, and south to the Yangtze valley, as indicated by remains of apparent Shang derivation or inspiration in basically prehistoric culture contexts. The predominant culture pattern in the sphere of Shang influence must be characterized essentially as surviving Neolithic.

Chou Culture Changes
(1122-221 B.C.)

The third of the Three Dynasties, Chou, is the best documented by written records, although such records are still scarce from the beginning of the period. It is usually divided into a western Chou (1122-722 B.C.) and an eastern Chou period (722-221 B.C.), and the latter is further subdivided into the Spring-Autumn (722-481 B.C.) and Warring States periods (481-221 B.C.). Such divisions are based mainly on political events, and in archaeological remains the dividing line within the Chou period must be made around 600 B.C. Before this date, Chou was essentially a continuation and propagation of the Shang civilization; after that, a series of related changes transformed the Chinese cultural scene and paved the way for the political unification of the land by the Ch'in Empire in 221 B.C. Although historians use their own data to characterize the manifestations of this developmental sequence, the archaeologist uses another set of data. The most important of the latter are the following:

1. If the level of complexity and elaboration of archaeological remains and sites is any gauge of sociopolitical power or at least of sociopolitical sophistication, then Chou archaeology shows an unmistakable trend in this direction, bespeaking a diffusion of the seat of power. In the beginning of the Chou period the sphere of dominance was confined to the old territory of the Shang in addition to the Chou

homeland of southern Shansi and eastern-central Shensi. Areas surrounding the Chous were still occupied by primarily Neolithic village farmers, even though the Chous enjoyed a somewhat expanded sphere of influence, reaching farther south than the Yangtze valley. After approximately 600 B.C., however, there was no longer a single center of civilization but a series of them over all of China. Sophisticated and numerous bronze assemblages and city ruins are seen in Central and South China as well as in the north, a phenomenon in essential agreement with the historical fact that the early Chou despotism gave way in later Chou times to a proliferation of local powers throughout the area.

2. Throughout the period that can be referred to as the Bronze Age—between approximately 1600 and 600 B.C.—tools and implements (for cultivation, manufacture, and other utilitarian and domestic use) continued to be made of stone, bone, wood, and antler. Archaeological relics of tools and implements of bronze are extremely rare, for bronze was used exclusively for ceremonial and military objects. The ancient Chinese maintained that the two paramount functions of the state were rituals and conquest, and it was with these—that is, with the seat of sociopolitical power—that bronze objects were associated. Beginning in the sixth century before Christ, however, iron came to be widely adopted for tools and implements and, to some extent, weapons (Fig. 16). Iron in China was both cast and wrought, and quickly came to be used as an effective and inexpensive material for implements. The wide-ranging consequences of such a change are immediately obvious.

3. Archaeological knowledge of Chou cities is rather limited, but enough is known to demonstrate that the basic components of the Chinese cities during the ancient period remain constant throughout: an enclosure of stamped earth; a square or rectangular shape oriented according to the four cardinal directions; the construction of politically or ceremonially significant buildings on earth platforms; important buildings facing south and arranged within the city with appreciable regularity. Changes, on the other hand, did occur; some were minor, having principally to do with details of construction, but others were major. The early Chou cities followed the blueprint of Anyang and Cheng-chou, having a locus of aristocratic power and scattered farming and industrial hamlets around it. After approximately 600 B.C., as shown by such Eastern Chou cities as Lin-tzu of Shantung, Hsin-t'ien of Shansi, and Han-tan of Hopei (Fig. 17), the city

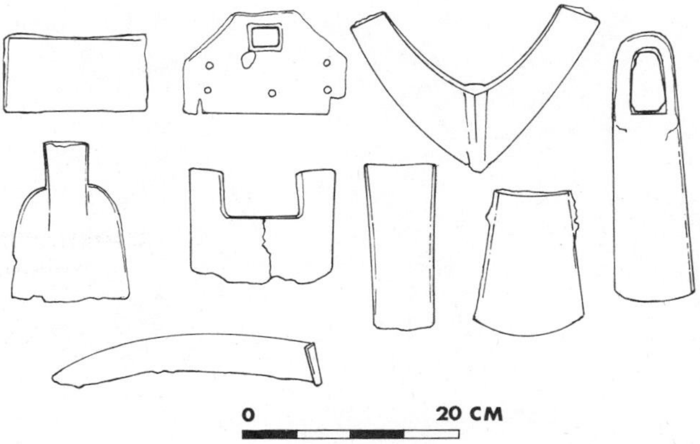

Figure 16.
Iron implements,
late Chou.

enclosures were enlarged to include not only the seat of political power but also industrial and commercial quarters. Many cities had two enclosures, an inner one containing palaces and temples, and an outer one sheltering workshops and markets. Such changes in urban planning apparently suggest the emergence of a new status for industry, dominated by iron, and for an expanded commerce linking the widely distributed and equally prosperous local states.

4. Archaeologically, perhaps the most expressive change that took place during the Chou period was in decorative art, especially bronze art, which is shown to be related to changes in Chou mythology, philosophy, and general outlook on life and the world. The Swedish sinologue Bernhard Karlgren distinguishes three major styles of art of Shang and Chou: Archaic, Middle Chou, and Huai. The development of these styles bespeaks a major change from an outlook essentially mythologically oriented to one essentially humanistically oriented (Fig. 18). The present writer has been able to demonstrate, in a study of Shang and Chou myths, art, and society, that such changes of art styles are related to technological and sociopolitical innovations toward the second half of the Chou period.

These archaeological evidences of cultural change during the Chou period must be considered together with the teachings of traditional history to gain a fuller picture of the civilizational development of ancient China. Archaeology by itself is sufficient to indicate that the latter part of Chou was essentially a transitional period from ancient

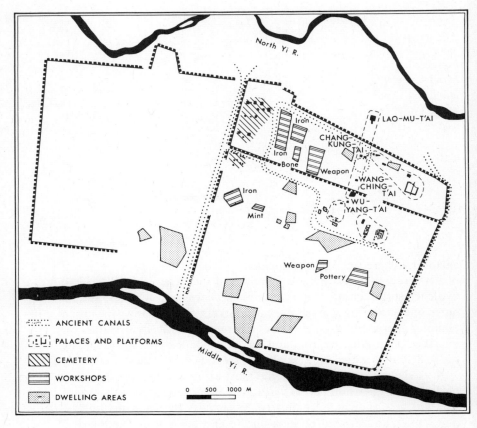

Figure 17.   Plan of the city of Hsia-tu, state of Yen.

China to the Imperial China first represented by the Ch'in dynasty. The nucleated total power of the Shang and early Chou royal houses who ruled restricted areas gave way during this period to a large number of local states and local traditions in a much expanded area, essentially Chinese in form but diffuse in geography, such as the Warring States of North China and Ch'u, Yüeh, and other kingdoms of South China. A political consolidation of these local states and traditions of essentially Chinese identity that took place in 221 B.C. gave rise to the Ch'in empire and marks the end of archaeology as the primary instrument for the study of Chinese history.

Figure 18. Animal and human figures on late Chou bronze.

Archaeology After Chou

By the end of the Chou period, written records became adequate for historians. The writing style, which had several local varieties, became almost uniform as a result of extensive communications throughout the land. Paper was soon invented, and most of the states maintained official scribes to keep archives. The unfortunate episode of book-burning allegedly undertaken as an official policy under the first Ch'in emperor destroyed much of the late Chou literatures, but by the beginning of the Han dynasty, in the first two centuries before

413

Christ, systematized history came into existence and the earliest written histories survive to this day. Archaeology is the sole instrument for the study of China before the Shang dynasty, and it is the principal tool for the full description of Shang and Chou cultures. After the Chou period, it becomes supplementary as a rule and remains indispensable only for certain aspects of culture.

The principal aim of the traditional antiquarianism in China—*chin shih hsüeh,* or the study of bronzes and stone monuments—has been the discovery and interpretation of ancient historical texts that were not a part of the traditional repertoire of written documents, and this must remain a singularly significant area of continued archaeological investigation. Many archaeological artifacts bear inscriptions, and long texts were often carved onto stone monuments; any new discovery of inscribed pieces means an addition to the pool of historical literature. Some recent discoveries of this kind are even of first importance, such as the many T'ang texts discovered in Chinese Turkestan, which in most cases are the sole documents concerning the ancient states in this region; the numerous handwritten copies of ancient texts found in the caves of Tun-huang, in western Kansu, dated between the Northern Dynasties and the Five Dynasties; and the many wooden tablets of the Chinese classics found in tombs of the Han dynasty.

It is obvious that archaeologists will have to continue to study directly in the field those aspects of culture that are not likely to have been adequately described and recorded in historic documents, no matter how abundant the latter might be. A study of the rubbish-dumping habits—which are indications of many aspects of manners and customs—of even a modern metropolis, for instance, can best be undertaken by an archaeologist. Such uses for archaeology increase as one moves back in time and as the amount of historic literature diminishes.

One aspect of culture to which archaeological research is essential is the pattern of settlement. Excavations of the imperial capitals of many dynasties (especially the T'ang capital at Ch'ang-an, in central-eastern Shensi) and of ruins of ancient towns and villages have brought to light information throughout Chinese history concerning planning, urban ecology, and urban-rural spheres of interaction.

The study of material culture and art requires the study of the visual characters and the physical properties of the objects, for which writing rarely suffices. Implements, utensils, mortuary models, and coins provide information on technology, economy, and architecture, and sites of kilns and foundries are the most useful means for the study of industrial and technological details. Any book on art history, no matter of what period, must be illustrated with archaeological relics rather than historical texts.

And, finally, archaeology furnishes direct evidence for the study of cultural contacts both within China and between China and her neighbors. Ruins and relics along the Silk Route have supplied invaluable information on communications between China and the West, and southeastern archaeology has brought to light evidence on the oversea routes used by China in trade with Southeast Asia and beyond.

中華文化大綱

XIV

Chinese Art

BY
CHU-TSING LI

One of the best means of understanding the breadth and profundity of Chinese civilization is through its artistic expression. In many aspects, Chinese art is almost unique among the great arts of the world's cultures. First, it is the fountainhead of the art of East Asia. Second, there is a continuity in its development from the primitive to the most sophisticated in craftsmanship, form, style, and expression. Third, the strong tradition of antiquarianism in China has helped to preserve a large amount of documentation and related materials, thus enabling us to appreciate deeply the theories, ideas, and historical meaning of the various aspects of Chinese art. Fourth, an understanding of its full range has become possible only in recent years, as more and more new material has been brought to light. Even discounting what has perished, the amount of surviving pottery, jade, bronze, lacquer, textiles, sculpture, calligraphy, painting, architecture, and much else, from the long history of China and from its numerous regions, is simply staggering. Moreover, nowadays, on the mainland, thousands of objects are being unearthed every month, and hundreds of paintings and works of calligraphy are being published every year. What appeared to be missing links and gaps in our knowledge of Chinese art have rapidly been found and filled. As a result, Chinese art has become one of the most exciting and challenging fields of study in recent years.

The limited amount of space available will not permit an extensive history of Chinese art. I shall limit myself to a small number of media, namely bronze, sculpture, and painting, as examples of this great tradition. This means that very little will be said about such interesting subjects as Chinese architecture and ceramics. In the case of the former, my justification is that, in spite of the long history of China, very few major architectural monuments have come down to the present day. Except for underground tombs, no major palace, temple, or other public structure predates the Ming dynasty. In the case of ceramics, materials are so abundant that the topic deserves separate treatment. I can only refer my readers to the specific studies of this subject.

Bronze Art

The bronze age began rather late in China as compared to the Near East and Europe, but its development is perhaps the most brilliant among the world's bronze cultures. From the middle of the second millennium B.C., the Chinese quickly developed a sophisticated bronze-casting technique and turned out an exceptionally large quantity of bronze objects. Despite attrition during the course of history, hundreds of pieces have been found in recent archaeological excavations.

Bronze seems to have always had a very strong appeal for the Chinese. In addition to its use for weapons, ornaments, and cooking utensils that characterized its beginning in Chinese society, bronze vessels were made for sacrificial rites and other important occasions and as symbols of the power and authority of kings and dukes. Their subtle, dark color, their greenish patina, their imaginative shapes, and their intricate decor all were much to the taste of the antiquarian Chinese of later periods.

Since bronze development in China is later than in the West by more than 1,000 years, it has generally been assumed, especially by Western scholars, that the bronze technique was an importation from the Near East. Although no absolutely conclusive solution to this problem can be established, recent finds have given convincing support to the indigenous origin and development of bronze-making in China. At a site called Erh-li-t'ou, near the town of Yen-shih, not far east of Loyang, archaeological excavations during the period 1959-64 have turned up a large number of objects, mostly ceramics but also some lumps of bronze and a few bronze weapons such as arrowheads, knives, fishhooks, and bells in a very impressive complex that Chinese scholars have come to identify as the first capital of the Shang dynasty, predating Anyang by two centuries. This is a missing link, giving substance to the idea that bronze-making in China did have a humble but logical beginning, at a time when the Chinese first came to recognize the potential of this metal but had not yet mastered the complex technique of casting vessels. Still, this discovery cannot prove whether the technique was an indigenous invention or an importation from the West. It is quite possible that the Chinese learned about this metal from some of the migrating tribes that came into contact with China in the middle of the second millennium B.C.

However, even if the Chinese did borrow this technique from outside, they seem to have quickly turned it into something entirely their own. For many decades, Western scholars have followed the theory that the Chinese adopted the Western *cire-perdue* method of casting. Recently, a convincing theory has been established showing that the Chinese developed a very elaborate piece-mold casting

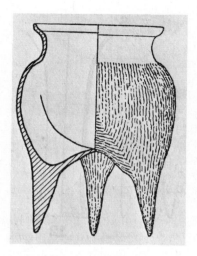 

Figure 1. Li *from Erh-li-t'ou, Yeh-shih, Honan province, Early Shang Dynasty.*

Figure 2. Li *from Liu-li-ko, Hui-hsien, Honan Province, Middle Shang Dynasty.*

method used throughout the Shang and Chou periods, and only many centuries later borrowed the *cire-perdue*. Moreover, a large group of ceramic pots was unearthed at Yen-shih and elsewhere as prototypes to the earliest bronze shapes. Two varieties, called *li* and *ting,* of a characteristic three-legged vessel, which was originally ceramic, will show the development of bronze style in the two early dynasties. A few objects of other shapes will be brought in to supplement the discussion.

A *li* (Fig. 1) from Yen-shih shows a shape so well developed that it comes very close to the bronze shapes, such as the *li* from Liu-li-ko at Hui-hsien, in Honan Province, which is located halfway between Yen-shih and Anyang. This site, together with Erh-li-kang of Cheng-chou, has been identified as belonging to the Middle Shang period, just preceding the establishment of the last capital of that dynasty at Anyang. In this bronze *li* from Hui-hsien (Fig. 2), the general shape of the ceramic pot is retained, with a few elaborations. Two handles have been added, and the lip extends horizontally. The neck has been considerably lengthened, and decorated with a band of abstract lines

420

Figure 3. Ting, *bronze, Nelson Gallery, Kansas City, Missouri. Late Shang Dynasty.*

punctuated with two "eyes" in the center. The main body of the *li* is largely undecorated, like the ceramic prototype, except for two parallel lines that start from the legs and form an angle just below the eyes. In this transition from ceramic to bronze vessels, there is a definite change of technique. While the pot shape gives an impression of an object done in one piece, with each part flowing into the next, and without much separation between them, the bronze vessel is treated part by part, each distinguishable from the others. The pot has a profile of curves, but the bronze has more angles and sharp transitions. There is in the middle Shang bronze a firmer, more solid and stable look and a sense of mystery and power suggested by its imposing appearance and strange decor. Perhaps this development in style came about because the bronze was used for ceremonial purposes rather than simple utilitarian ones.

The style of late Shang, with its capital at Anyang, is represented by a large number of bronzes not only from that famous site but from many related ones in Honan. Many vessels, though not scientifically established to be from these sites, can be related to this style. One of

421

Figure 4. Fang-i, *bronze, Freer Gallery of Art, Washington, Late Shang Dynasty.*

Figure 5. Yü, *bronze, Sumitomo Collection, Kyoto. Late Shang or Early Chou Dynasty.*

them is a *ting,* now in the Nelson Gallery of Art, Kansas City (Fig. 3), which is closely related to the *li.* But the *ting* differs from the *li* in having solid rather than hollow legs. Thus, in this *ting* there are three round and strong legs instead of the hollow ones of the *li* that taper to a point at the end and a round body with no breastlike divisions of volume as in the *li.* As a result, the *ting* looks even more stable and solid than the bronze *li,* more imposing and dignified. At the same time, the sense of mystery is greatly enhanced by further elaboration of the decor. The whole body is almost totally covered with graphic incisions, which can be clearly discerned as a *t'ao-t'ieh* mask, made up of two confronting zoomorphs in profile with a ridge in between that resembles the nose of an animal face and with a round eye on each side. In spite of the fact that the whole mask is very stylized, it has a very formidable look and a powerful expression.

A *fang-i* (Fig. 4) shows in both shape and decor a very elaborate culmination of earlier developments. The *fang-i* is a square vessel for wine. Its large size (height 13-3/16 in.) and imposing appearance seem appropriate to a sacrificial ritual function. Its bold, plastic decor and protruding and hooked flanges place it toward the end of the Shang dynasty. Its flat bottom gives it a firm and solid stability of form, and the design of the main body shows a great deal of subtlety. A slight concave recess on the base prepares for the bulging of the main body, while another slight concave area just above the main body echoes the base. The shape and decor of the main body are repeated, though in an upward manner, by the lid, which terminates in a knob that repeats its shape. The decor of the main body, repeated but inverted on the lid, is a *t'ao-t'ieh* image, formed by two confronting dragons with the same stylized and hooked flanges as the vessel's, thus achieving a sense of unity. Set against the finely incised cloud patterns, it stands out very clearly and plastically, achieving a kind of almost violent power. Just above it, on the small band, is a more natural image of an animal, with big eyes and huge ears or horns, that protrude in high relief like the flanges. It ends in two serpentlike bodies, one to the left and the other to the right. In the band below the *t'ao-t'ieh,* there are four birds, two on each side, facing each other. In technique, shape, and decor, the piece represents the achievement of several centuries of development toward aggressive forms and forceful expression in symbolic meaning.

The most unusual of all the vessels of this period seems to be a *yü* (Fig. 5), representing rather naturalistically a man in the mouth of a tiger. The *yü* is a zoomorphic wine container which usually takes on the appearance of a bird, though sometimes that of an elephant or buffalo. The tiger of this *yü* is represented as standing, supported by the two hind legs and the tail, while holding the man with the two front legs. This rather humanlike position is typical of some of the Shang stone or jade sculptures. The head, though less stylized, is somewhat reminiscent of the *t'ao-t'ieh,* especially in the appearance of hornlike objects above the brows, the big round eyes, and the absence of the lower jaw. Although it opens its mouth, as though about to devour the man, it does not show any ferocity or greed. At the same time, the man with his head in the tiger's mouth displays no sign of fear or struggle, but returns the embrace of the animal. This image, together with the first account of the *t'ao-t'ieh* in Chinese writing, datable to the third century B.C., that it is a monster with a head but no body and, being gluttonous, takes men into its mouth to devour them but, before it has swallowed them, itself disintegrates, has given rise to a whole range of speculations on the meaning of the *t'ao-t'ieh* and many other images on these bronze vessels. However interesting as this image on the vessel appears to be, its meaning is lost to us, although we can be quite positive that the image is not ordinary or accidental, but had some special meaning to its own time, more or less as an objectification of the fears and yearnings of the Shang people.

The conquest of Shang by the Chou people from the west late in the eleventh century did not put a stop to the development of bronze. In fact, the late Shang style seems to have persisted for another century into the early Chou, although some changes can be discerned. This can best be represented by a four-legged square *ting* (Fig. 6) which has a short inscription indicating that it is "King Ch'eng's vessel," thus putting it toward the end of the eleventh century. In contrast to the Anyang type which is more graphic in approach, this is entirely plastic, giving one a disquieting feeling. The whole vessel is distinguished by an extravagant style, with spikes, hooked flanges, horns, and vertical ribs. This harsh, hard, and angular quality is perhaps typical of a people more martial and vigorous. The absence of the *t'ao-t'ieh* may indicate a change in the belief of the Chou people. Departing from the primitive elements as reflected in the Shang objects, Chou was beginning to move toward a more abstract set of beliefs that led to the formation of many schools of thought, including Confucianism and Taoism, after 600 B.C.

A radical change in style and a deterioration in technique appeared during the Middle Chou period, from the ninth century to the seventh century B.C. A *ting* from around the eighth century (Fig. 7) is a typical work of the period. The vessel looks very massive and heavy. Its legs begin to take on a curve, creating a rather squat effect. The decor, while retaining some general features of earlier times, has become much simpler, bigger, and bolder, and has dropped any suggestion of those masks and animals, becoming abstract in a rather monotonous and meaningless way. Gone are the *t'ao-t'ieh* and many other animal images, together with their fearful and powerful expression. Aesthetically the vessel is awkward and unrefined, and iconographically it lacks meaning and purpose. There are, however, more frequent and longer inscriptions. In general, it seems to be transitional work.

The situation during the Spring and Autumn period (771-480 B.C.) and the Warring States period (480-221 B.C.) seems to have stimulated new developments in bronzes, done in various centers and in various

Figure 6. Fang-ting, *bronze, Nelson Gallery,*
Kansas City, Missouri, Early Chou Dynasty.

Figure 7. Ting, *bronze,*
Fujii Yurinkan, Kyoto,
Late Western Chou.

Figure 8. Ting, *bronze with gold*
and silver inlay, Minneapolis
Institute of Arts, Late Chou
Dynasty.

styles. Recent excavations have found many important sites, giving us an idea of the broad artistic activities and the great diversity of styles during the period. These sites include Hsin-cheng, Hui-hsien, and Chin-ts'un in Honan Province, Li-yü in Shensi, Shou-hsien in Anhwei, and Ch'ang-sha in Hunan, with objects ranging in date from about the seventh century B.C. to the end of the Chou period (third century B.C.).

During the period of the Warring States, the *ting* (Fig. 8) underwent a radical development in both technique and style. Technically, inlay was introduced. Gold and silver brighten up the dark surface, the colors providing contrasts which were earlier given by incisions and projections. The smooth surface gives a new splendor to the vessel. The shape is now changed to a covered type, with big round body and curving legs. It is elegant and decorative. In spite of the inlaid representations of serpents and plastic animals on the cover, the symbolic function seems to be no longer very strong. The piece lacks the power and mystery of the Shang objects; it seems to be purely decorative.

This short survey with an emphasis on the *li-ting* development serves the purpose of showing the stylistic evolution during the bronze age in China. The significant point here is that there is a marked difference between the earlier vessels, including those of Shang and early Chou, and later vessels, mainly of late Chou, a difference that is generally interpreted to represent a change in the cultural make-up and in the beliefs held by these two peoples. The *t'ao-t'ieh,* together with a host of dragons, birds, serpents, fish, cicadas, and other creatures, seems to be part of the world of the Shang people, related to their beliefs. Shang bronzes, then, seem to be the crystallization of the Chinese creative impulse and religious beliefs during that period. On the other hand, the Chou interest seems to be different. Though their beliefs are known through literary writings, they are not necessarily reflected in the abstract decor of the bronzes. In the late Chou period the artisans strove more for technical refinement, for exquisite craftsmanship, and for pure aesthetic appeal. The pieces seem to be the products of a more art-conscious, more materialistically oriented, and more fragmented culture. The conquest by Ch'in of all of China during the later part of the third century B.C. must have diminished much of the diversity of the Chinese culture during the late Chou period. This centralization of authority and the strict measures adopted by the First Emperor of Ch'in, especially in his control of the

Figure 9. Bronze mirror, TLV type, Metropolitan Museum of Art, N.Y., Han Dynasty.

use of metal by the common people, also closed the most brilliant era of Chinese bronze work, though many bronzes, such as mirrors and Buddhist statues, were to be made in later periods.

Art of a New Order

The First Emperor of Ch'in unified all of China into one empire, laying the foundation for a political, economic, and social organization that was to be the model for all the later dynasties. However, in art, his dynasty was too short to leave any long-lasting effect. It was during the Han dynasty that the whole country was stabilized into an apparently permanent unit. A new art resulted from this new order.

The new order can be seen in some of the Han bronze mirrors, which are the best bronze objects in a period when bronze vessels were poorer than those of Shang and Chou. One type of mirror, nicknamed the TLV type (Fig. 9) because of some details in the pattern that resemble those letters, belongs to middle Han and according to many inscriptions suggests a unified view of the cosmos at that time. In the center of the back is a knob, symbol of the world-axis, surrounded by a square, symbol of the earth, or China itself. The TLVs are details adopted from a sundial design, making the mirror symbolical of a source of light like the sun. Likewise, the round shape of the mirror and the radiating pattern on the outer ring of the decoration are all part of this symbolism. Thus, the whole design of the mirror back gives one an idea of how the Chinese saw their world and the universe at that time—a unified land located in the center of the world.

Within the empire the Confucian school was adopted as the guiding light of society, especially in the court and upper levels of China. Wall reliefs from the Wu family and related shrines in Chia-hsiang, Shantung Province (Fig. 10), have given us some basic idea of the whole Confucian approach. The reliefs center on such moral subjects as virtuous kings and ministers of the past, paragons of filial piety, lessons from history, ancestor worship, and a family feast. Executed with very shallow carving on flat slabs of stone, the reliefs look like painting in incised lines. Figures are shown in silhouette, all on one plane, with little overlapping or indication of depth. A register system is used to take care of all the details, one above another. Like the mirror design, the composition is very schematized, the representations orderly, and the feeling restrained, reflecting the conceptual

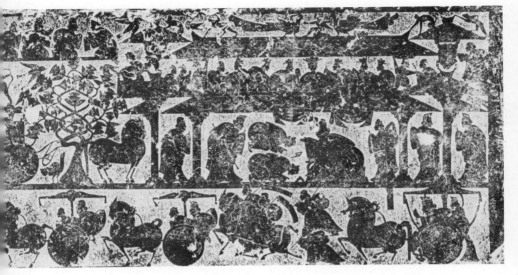

Figure 10.   Rubbing of stone relief, from Wu Liang Shrine, Chia-hsiang, Shantung Province, Late Han Dynasty.

Confucian approach to art. If the TLV mirror is a symbol of the cosmological view of Han China, the Wu shrine reliefs present an encyclopaedia of human life and history from the Confucian point of view. Both are products of the attempt of Han China to search for an underlying order in this newly unified country.

In its emphasis on human relationships, the family system, and ancestor worship, this Confucian approach can also be seen in a

Figure 11.   Rubbing of Tomb Tile, from Cheng-tu, Szechuan, Han Dynasty.

variety of objects done in the Han period. Most typical are the large number of figurines, made of clay, that have been found in tombs. They represent figures from all walks of life, and are intended to serve the deceased in the after life. Among human figures, the higher their status in life, the more formally and statically are they represented. Musicians, guardians, and shamans, being less exalted, are usually more actively portrayed. But the most active poses and expressions belong to the animals—dogs, horses, and bears. The convention shows a kind of hierarchy connected with the Confucian approach to art, indicating more self-control and more refinement among those of higher social status.

Some of the liveliest activities of man can be seen in the tomb tiles of Szechuan, on which are depicted people working in salt wells, farming in the field, or hunting by a lake. A rubbing of a tile (Fig. 11) represents the two latter scenes in two registers. In contrast to the scenes of the Wu shrines, figures are here shown more naturally, engaged in various activities, and set against a landscape. Although the scale of the figures, animals, and trees is not entirely correct in the Western sense, it does show an intuitive grasp of the realistic scene that creates an illusion of figures in landscape. This shows the less official, more naturalistic style of the western part of China, in contrast to the more formal, restrained, and abstract approach of the east, as in the Shantung reliefs. In the tilemakers' interest in men and their activities within their social status, part of the broad Confucian order of the world is still revealed.

Buddhist Art

If the more primitive people of Shang dynasty made the *t'ao-t'ieh* images and all the other zoomorphic creatures on their bronze vessels as a crystallization of their beliefs, and the Han Chinese expressed a new order of a unified empire in bronze mirrors and Confucian shrine reliefs, the Six Dynasties, Sui, and T'ang seem to have adopted an Indian image, the Buddha, as a symbol that unifies man and the universe; past, present, and future; and the inner feeling and outer experience.

The coming of Buddhism from India to China brought along not only a new religious and philosophical outlook but also a new artistic expression that attracted for many centuries the creative geniuses of China. Although this expression can be found in architecture, paint-

Figure 12. Colossal Buddha, from Cave XX, Yün-kang, Shansi Province, second half of 5th century.

431

ing, and a number of the so-called minor arts, it is in the extant works of sculpture that we can see most clearly its development and its florescence. As mentioned above, there are only a few scattered remains of sculpture of animals and figures, in marble, wood, and ceramics, from the Shang through the Han dynasties. Buddhism brought along the strong influence of Indian sculpture, which was itself influenced by Persian, Hellenistic, and Roman art, and gave China the necessary foundation to develop a sculptural tradition of its own. With the Buddhist, especially Mahayana, demand for images in sculpture and painting as objects of worship and signs of piety, Chinese artists for five or six centuries built a glorious tradition of their own.

Most representative of this early archaic phase of Chinese Buddhist sculpture are the colossal Buddhas in the imperial caves of Yün-kang (Fig. 12) near Ta-t'ung, first capital of the T'o-pa dynasty of Northern

Figure 13. Bodhisattva Maitreya, from Lung-men, Honan Province, Museum Rietberg, Zurich, first half of 6th century.

Figure 14. Monk, from Southe Hsiang-t'ang-shan, University M seum, Philadelphia, Northern Ch'i Dynasty, A.D. 550–77.

Wei. Built between 460 and 494, the undertaking was inspired by the Indian idea of cave temples and monasteries that had spread across Central Asia to China. The Buddha of Cave XX, measuring 45 feet high, is an attempt to use sheer size to symbolize the superhuman status and the great spiritual power of the Buddha. Although such archaic features as the sharp-cut planes, the arching brow, the slight smile, and the flat bands of the robe are quite evident, the strong sense of volume, full round face, raised chest, and broad shoulders reveal sufficient mastery of these early techniques of sculpture to express the inner power of the figure.

In this early representation of the Buddha in China, an indebtedness to Indian sculpture in both iconography and style is quite evident. Such special details as the topknot, the long ear lobe, the "third eye" between the brows, among many others, are symbolic indications of the unusual quality of the Buddha in the Indian

Figure 15. Seated Bodhisattva, Limestone, Freer Gallery of Art, Washington, Sui Dynasty.

Figure 16. Seated Bodhisattva with one leg pendant, from Cave XIV, T'ien-lung-shan, sandstone, Tokyo National Museum, T'ang Dynasty.

tradition. The strong mass of the figure, the sense of vigor in the face, and the clinging drapery on the body, are characteristics of the Indian sculptural style with traces of Hellenistic and Roman naturalism. However, in their lack of interest in sculpture in the round, the Chinese have turned some of these details, such as the drapery folds, into flat, abstract patterns that have nothing to do with revealing the body structure underneath. Yet both the archaism and schematism, together with the colossal size, seem to have imbued the statue with an otherworldly, spiritual power befitting the Buddha.

With the moving of the Northern Wei capital from Ta-t'ung to Loyang in 494, the Buddhist style, like the T'o-pa people, went through a period of Sinification. The figure of Maitreya, originally from one of the niches of the Lung-men Caves near Loyang (Fig. 13), is typical of this new style. The figure is represented as a smiling youth, with an elongated face and a high headdress. His garment covers both shoulders. His right hand is in a fear-not gesture while the other hand touches the head of the guardian lion. His legs are crossed, as in the typical Maitreya figure. The figure, though carved in a considerable amount of depth, seems light and immaterial, and even ethereal. The drapery folds form rhythmic patterns, creating a sense of elegance and refinement. Gone are the archaic qualities of the Yün-kang style and the vigor and massiveness of the Indian approach. The figure is one of the best embodiments of the Buddhist ideal of renunciation of the material world and of attainment of serenity of spirit.

During the second half of the sixth century various foreign elements, such as the Hsien-pi and Turkic peoples, and the Chinese developed great rivalries, resulting in further divisions and decentralization of China. Among the many dynasties that changed in succession, the Northern Ch'i seems to have produced the most interesting and novel Buddhist art. Most characteristic of this style are the stone sculptures of a temple of Southern Hsiang-t'ang-shan, some of which are now in the University Museum, Philadelphia (Fig. 14). The oversized statue of a monk, whose hands are holding a lotus in a devotional gesture, differs from the earlier styles in the new sense of volume and roundness. The interest in surface pattern, especially in the monk's robe, is still there, but the body underneath shows through. The elongation and severity of the Northern Wei have given way to subtle proportions, rhythmic curves, and a serene expression. This interest in an organic and rhythmic treatment of the body form

Figure 17. Western Paradise of Amitabha, wallpainting at Cave 139A, Tung-huang, Kansu Province, second half of the eighth century.

is partly the result of some new Indian influence. Most important, following the Indian examples, all these elements are subordinate to the main goal, a spiritual power.

When China was reunited again under one empire during the Sui dynasty, late in the sixth century, all this diversity of style was gradually brought into a single unified approach. The seated bodhisattva, in limestone, at the Freer Gallery (Fig. 15), shows the same roundness and massiveness as the Northern Ch'i example, but here the elaboration of surface ornaments is carried to a great extreme. The halo, the headdress, the jewelry, the beads, and the folds of the garment all receive a considerable amount of attention. Again, it is the

Indian influence that is responsible, but the floral motifs and surface decoration are more Near Eastern in origin. All these are blended together in this statue of Chinese Buddhism.

The Sui emperors were devout Buddhists and during their reigns Buddhism flourished as never before. Under the first emperors of T'ang, the faith reached its most exciting development in China. A series of Chinese monks such as Hsüan-tsang brought back from India sacred texts and images that stimulated lively interest in the religion. The statue of a bodhisattva from Cave XIV of T'ien-lung-shan, in Shansi, now in the Tokyo National Museum (Fig. 16), is one of the best examples of early T'ang style. While the facial features remain Chinese, the rest of the figure is treated very differently. Not only is there a strong sense of volume and mass, as in the Sui statue, but also a very frank treatment of the body never seen before in Chinese art. The torso is almost entirely bare, except for a few ornaments and part of the drapery. The body is either exposed or shown under a wet, clinging garment, revealing some of the anatomical features. The relaxed, curved movement of the body, and the different positions of the arms and legs, are all part of the new approach. This style undoubtedly is the result of some new Indian influence, emphasizing the sensuous as a reflection of the spiritual. It helped to bring about a synthesis of the Indian and Chinese approaches in a style that combines naturalism and idealism.

Throughout these periods, a change in Buddhist iconography in sculpture can also be seen. Up to the fifth century, the Buddhism that came to China seems to have been a blend of Mahayana and Hinayana. The Hinayana, which emphasizes salvation through individual effort in the footsteps of the founder, Sakyamuni, the historical Buddha, is best embodied in the statues of this figure. At Yün-kang, he seems to be the most common figure among the numerous statues. After A.D. 500, Maitreya, the Buddha of the future, a Mahayana concept which sees him as the next savior, became quite popular, perhaps due to a general belief that a thousand years after the last Buddha, Maitreya would come to save mankind from suffering. But after the middle of the sixth century, Amitabha, who had promised to save all who called on him, became the focus of worship in China. With him, many bodhisattvas, especially Kuan-yin (Avalokitesvara), who worked to bring mankind to enlightenment, were also often objects of devotion.

In painting as in sculpture, Buddhism introduced subjects and styles unknown before. Among the many wall-paintings decorating the interiors of four-hundred-odd caves of Tun-huang, in Kansu, which had been traditionally the gateway to the West, the Western Paradise (Fig. 17), where Amitabha rules, is often the subject. The painting, one of the most complex up to this time in Chinese painting, depicts paradise in terms of a sumptuous palatial complex in combination with Buddhist iconography. A huge, elaborate platform rises over a pond where the reborn souls are emerging from the hearts of floating lotuses. Amitabha, represented on the largest scale, is seated in the center of the painting where all the architectural lines seem to converge. On both sides of this Buddha are bodhisattvas in their hieratic positions. On the platform in the foreground, musicians and dancers perform their acts of ceremonial worship. Instead of the earlier abstract treatment, T'ang artists employed the most worldly and naturalistic means to glorify the spirituality of the Buddha. This is a type of painting which reflects the taste for gorgeous beauty at the height of T'ang culture, the culmination of Buddhism in China, and the synthesis of Chinese Buddhist art after several centuries of assimilation and development. It was the most encompassing Chinese artistic expression up to this time.

What is most interesting in Buddhist art in China is the ability of the Chinese to absorb a foreign religion and art and eventually transform it into something of their own. The success of Buddhism in China is partly due to the temporary eclipse of the Confucian school after the breakdown of the Han empire, and partly due to its absorption of certain Taoist ideas and local cults which made it adaptable to the Chinese. In the same way Buddhist art in China, though indebted to Indian and Central Asian sources, essentially developed along the line of adapting foreign forms to the Chinese tradition. Eventually, as reflected in the T'ang period, a happy synthesis was achieved between the two traditions. This synthesized Chinese Buddhist art also laid the foundation stones for Buddhist art in Korea and Japan.

The contribution of Buddhist art cannot be overestimated. It was the great art of the Six Dynasties and T'ang dynasty. Some of the most important names in Chinese art, such as the "divine" Wu Tao-tzu, were primarily Buddhist painters. Aside from the creation of a great sculptural tradition in China, as mentioned above, the most important result of Buddhist art was the deepening of religious sentiment in Chinese artistic expression. Chinese art, as far as we

Figure 19. Lady with Bird and Dragon, silk painting from Ch'ang-sha, Hunan Province, Chou Dynasty.

Figure 18. Monkey with Her Baby on a Pine Branch, by Mu-ch'i, late 13th century, Daitokuji, Kyoto.

know, was basically symbolic or narrative up to the arrival of Buddhist art. With the demand of Buddhism for spiritual content, Chinese art gradually came to express some of the most profound religious and spiritual feelings in sculpture and painting. Formally, it brought to China a sense of hieratic arrangement, such as the symmetrical order of Buddha surrounded by disciples and bodhisattvas on two sides, as a new organizational principle in Chinese art. In addition, from Indian and Central Asian art, some elements of representation, such as shading, volume, and space as means to depict nature, and the organic depiction of the human figure, were also introduced into China. Yet all these were used by Chinese artists to serve the Chinese tradition. Most important of all, it brought Chinese art to a new high plateau in its exploration of the possibilities of

438

Figure 20. Admonitions of the Instructress to Court Ladies, *by Ku K'ai-chih (ca. 344-406), British Museum. Detail of Lady Fang.*

embracing all human experience and yearning in a single religious image in human form.

Buddhist art in China, like the religion itself, received its greatest blow during the mass persecution of 845. The destruction of thousands of temples and monasteries all over China eliminated the majority of great paintings and many sculptural monuments. The secularization of a quarter of a million monks and nuns and the weakening of the Buddhist church eventually deprived Buddhist art of its patronage and support. With the resurgence of Confucianism to attract the best minds of China from that time on, Buddhism went into a decline and became more associated with superstition and local cults. In consequence, Buddhist art, though it continued, also lost its appeal to the artistic geniuses of China.

439

Only one sect of Buddhism survived this heavy blow with a new vigor, Ch'an Buddhism. This meditative sect was a purely Chinese development of Buddhism, although it claimed Indian origin. Its subordination of scriptural studies and intellectual effort and its emphasis on the idea of "sudden enlightenment" made it essentially different from all other sects of Buddhism. Because of its reliance on individual effort rather than an organized church, it did not suffer a fatal blow from the great persecution. In art, its idea of self-cultivation through introspection and meditation as a means of reaching enlightenment, and its intuitive and spontaneous approach had a great appeal to later Chinese artists. It is in this connection that we can understand a painting such as *The Monkey* by Mu-ch'i (Fig. 18), a Ch'an monk of the thirteenth century who lived in one of the monasteries around the beautiful West Lake outside of Hangchow. Its subject, a monkey holding its young in a tree, is totally unlike the standard Buddhist subjects. Compared with the images of Buddhas and bodhisattvas, this is small, humble, and insignificant. However, while the treatment of the former is so often dignified and solemn that it inspires awe and respect, that of the monkeys is intimate, sympathetic, and understanding, as if the artist had been able to penetrate into their minds, lifting the subject up to a level of Buddhist seriousness and making possible a spiritual identity between the observer and the object. Furthermore, the quickness of the execution, the use of ink rather than colors, and the elimination of details all give evidence of the Ch'an demand for concentration and intuition, in order to achieve the goal of seeing a whole world in what is generally considered a trivial object as a means of reaching sudden enlightenment, the discovery of Buddhahood inside oneself.

That such an approach to painting in Ch'an was possible in the thirteenth century indicates the sophistication of Chinese art during the Sung period. With the mastery of technical means, the deepening of spiritual feeling, and the opening up of any subject in nature as worthy of serious depiction, Chinese art reached a flowering in the development of painting.

Figure Painting

The people who made the bronzes, sculptures, and other objects discussed above are no longer known today. In their own day, they were regarded as artisans whose job was to make useful or beautiful objects. Few of them had any individuality in their artistic practice. The works that they achieved represent a persistent technical refinement and formal beauty as aspirations of the group, but not private thoughts and dreams. Hence they remain anonymous. None of the objects came to be recognized by later Chinese as the greatest works of the Chinese artistic expression.

In Chinese eyes, the truly great forms of art are painting and calligraphy. Although most of the early works have disappeared, there are still records of famous painters and their activities as far back as the Han dynasty. Painting and calligraphy, like essays and poetry, came to be recognized as among the achievements proper to the literati. Painters became accepted as members of the Chinese cultural elite, who, since the Six Dynasties, but especially since Sung, have dominated the Chinese political, economic, and cultural life until today.

In the days when Buddhist painting was done extensively, wall-painting was commonly practiced in temples and monasteries as well as in palaces. Because of the large-scale destruction following the collapse of each dynasty or a religious persecution, very few early wall-paintings have survived. The largest group of wall-paintings, ranging from the Six Dynasties to the Sung period, are those found in Tun-huang, as mentioned above. However, since the early days the Chinese have also painted on silk and paper, neither of which is a very durable ground. As a result, one of the typical practices in China to try to preserve old paintings has been the making of copies. Although this practice has helped to preserve images of many famous paintings, it has also created many problems of connoisseurship, especially the problem of attribution of old paintings.

The earliest known Chinese painting on silk is the one excavated not too long ago from a tomb in Ch'ang-sha (Fig. 19) from the late Chou period. It is a painting executed with a brush and depicts a woman in profile with a dragon and a phoenix in front of her. While the symbolic meaning is not known, it shows that in early Chinese painting the human figure was the dominant subject, with little accompanying background to provide a setting. The reason is obvious. Painting in early China served a definite purpose, whether magical or didactic. Although the actual date of this silk painting is not known, it is a work from the Warring States period in the state of Ch'u, an area in late Chou with very different beliefs from those of the north.

Figure 21. Portraits of
Thirteen Emperors,
*attributed to Yen Li-pen
(d. 673), Boston Museum
of Fine Arts. Detail of
Emperor Wu of Late Chou
Dynasty.*

*Figure 22. Same scroll. Detail of
Emperor Wen of Ch'en Dynasty.*

From the Han dynasty on, when an eclectic Confucianism became
the guiding philosophy in Chinese political and social life, many
important works seem to have served the purpose of its doctrines. A
painting attributed to Ku K'ai-chih (*ca.* 344-406), *The Admonitions of
the Instructress to Court Ladies,* now in the British Museum (Fig. 20),
is typical of this kind of work. It is a handscroll showing a series of
scenes, each illustrating a passage from a text with Confucian or
Taoist overtones. The scene shown here represents Lady Fang, the
concubine of a Han emperor, in a courageous act. When a bear
breaks loose from its cage and is rushing toward the emperor, she
moves forward to stop the animal even though she puts herself in
danger. The high moral tone of this episode as a lesson for court ladies
is characteristic of the Confucian ethical system at that time. In style,
figures are the chief means of expression, for there is no indication of
background. All are depicted by a fine, even-width line that creates a

442

sense of rhythm throughout the painting. The large scale of the emperor, the flying bands of Lady Fang's dress, the convex and concave quality of the draperies, the inverted perspective, and the various facial expressions of the characters all show the power of frozen pictorial representation in this archaic style. It seems that the Confucian sense of restraint is at work here in the figure depiction, so that subtle linear portrayal is used even in as dramatic a scene as this.

A new sense of realism in portraiture is seen in the scroll *Portraits of Thirteen Emperors,* attributed to Yen Li-pen (d. 673), in the Boston Museum. Undoubtedly these portraits are meant for didactic purposes in the Confucian tradition. In an arrangement similar to that of the last scroll, the thirteen rulers are depicted in succession, each flanked by two or more attendants, and each marked by an identifying inscription. The two represented here, Emperor Wu of the Later Chou dynasty (Fig. 21) and Emperor Wen of the Ch'en dynasty (Fig. 22), form an interesting contrast. Realism can be seen in the power of the artist in depicting the different personality of the two emperors. While the Later Chou emperor is portrayed as a robust and powerful figure, with large mass and volume, a symbol of strong military power and centralized administration, the Ch'en ruler is shown seated, reserved and serene, deeply absorbed in Taoist meditation. Emperor Wu, of barbarian origin, is an imposing figure of expansive volume and convex lines, while Emperor Wen, of Chinese background, is dreamy and impractical, and is rendered by concave lines and given a self-contained expression. This ability of characterization is the new power of T'ang artists, although these portraits in all likelihood are only reconstructions from historical references.

With another famous painting, *The Night Entertainment of Han Hsi-tsai,* attributed to Ku Hung-chung (mid-10th century), now in the Peking Palace Museum (Fig. 23), figure painting reached a fully developed stage. Han Hsi-tsai, a man of great learning and ability living in the twilight of the Southern T'ang court, was reported to have spent his nights in lavish parties at his home when the emperor was considering appointing him to a high position. Disturbed, the ruler was said to have sent the artist Ku Hung-chung to attend one of these parties and paint a picture of the activities. The result was this painting, or its original version. The scroll unfolds one scene after another, with the main characters appearing again and again, without the interruption of texts in between. As shown in the beginning scene, each episode has its focus and its drama. Han Hsi-tsai, the host,

Figure 23. Night Entertainment of Han Hsi-tsai, *attributed to Ku Hung-chung, 10th century, Palace Museum, Peking. Detail of first episode.*

depicted in slightly larger scale than the other figures, is seated on a dais at the right and facing a group of friends. The focus is a lady playing the *p'i-p'a,* a Chinese lute, shown at the extreme left of the first scene. The ability to depict a group of people seated indoors in a circle, with proper sense of depth and with details of beds, dais, tables, chairs, paintings on the walls and screens, and food and drink on the tables, all clearly painted, shows a new mastery of pictorial representation.

The high point in the figure-narrative painting tradition in China is the *Spring Festival on the River,* a scroll attributed to an early twelfth-century artist, Chang Tse-tuan. The painting must have caught the popular imagination for many centuries, for there are several dozens of paintings bearing the same title in existence. The oldest extant version, probably of the twelfth century, is now in the Palace Museum, Peking (Fig. 24). Another long handscroll, it starts from a scene of fields outside the capital city of Sung, Pien-ching (now K'ai-feng), gradually moves into the city along the river, showing boats, bridges, wineshops, streets, and mansions in a grand panorama, with thousands of people around, and eventually leads into the Imperial

444

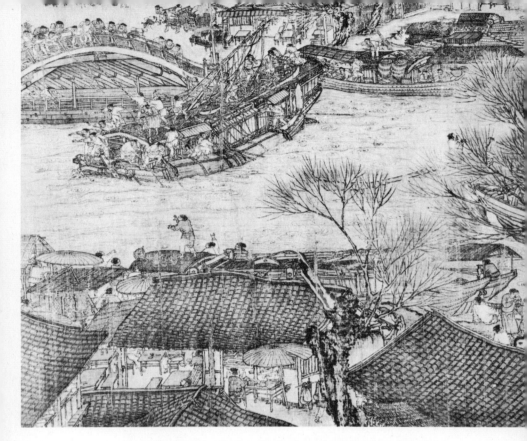

Figure 24. Spring Festival on the River, *attributed to Chang Tse-tuan, 12th century, Palace Museum, Peking. Detail of the bridge scene.*

Palace. Here, in this famous scene of the bridge, one can see an almost photographic image of twelfth-century life in the capital city. A large crowd on the bridge and the banks watches the exciting scene of a big boat lowering its mast in order to pass under the bridge. It is a panoramic view of life as observed by the artist. (For another detail from the same scroll see Part One, Fig. 6.)

It is important to note that these four paintings (all of which may be copies) are handscrolls, which seems to have been the most widely used format for earlier Chinese paintings of small scale, and are all painted on silk, a characteristically early medium. They are all obviously painted for very specific purposes, either the illustration of certain didactic Confucian and Taoist ideas, such as the Ku K'ai-chih and Yen Li-pen scrolls, a criticism of someone failing to display

445

proper social behavior, such as the Han Hsi-tsai, or a picture of peace and prosperity, the goal of the Confucian society, as reflected in the Spring Festival scroll. There is, then, a strong social overtone in these works. Appropriately, figures are the prominent pictorial elements, for it is through them that an artist can directly display standard social behavior or unacceptable aberrations. Whether there is background depiction or not is of only secondary importance. The development of Chinese painting is seen in a gradual elaboration of the background, which reached its climax in the Sung period. Similarly, in order to convey the ideas as directly as possible, the style tends to move in the direction of greater realism.

Yet as representational problems were gradually mastered by Chinese artists, there was among the creative artists an urge toward deeper meaning in content and greater individual freedom in expression. As early as the Six Dynasties, Hsieh Ho, in his Six Canons of Painting, places "animation through spirit consonance" as the first and most important canon, over the others which are mostly techni-

Figure 25. Travellers among Mountains and Streams, *by Fan K'uan, early 11th century, Palace Museum, Taipei.*

cal. This is an emphasis upon essence, or the ultimate source of life, rather than superficial resemblance. Later, Yen Li-pen was said to have advised his sons not to be painters because he felt great humiliation in being ordered by the emperor to paint a water bird during an outing while others enjoyed the scenery. This could only happen to an artist who was himself a learned man, a high official, and a creative artist who was not satisfied with the role of an artisan. But paintings serving the Confucian doctrines or Buddhist religion did lay many restrictions, both iconographic and stylistic, on the Chinese artist. The Confucian approach tended to restrain artistic expression by its insistence on propriety and decorum, the Buddhist treatment by its strict requirements of iconography and symbolism. Eventually, Chinese painters turned to something else to express themselves.

Landscape Painting

This new medium for self-expression was landscape painting, a logical alternative for Chinese painters. Landscape has always played a part in the Chinese consciousness, probably from the days of primitive worship. Then, in divination, in omens, in the significance of the four directions, five elements, and twelve zodiac signs, and in Taoist philosophy, nature commanded attention. However, when Confucianism became the dominant political and social philosophy of Han, its didactic figural art also had a great appeal to the Chinese. Not until the collapse of Han, when China was beset by chaos and turmoil, as a result of internal struggles and external invasions, did Chinese nature poetry begin to reach a new high. Yet from this period, the Six Dynasties, not much about landscape painting has been known, except for a few backgrounds in figure paintings, and a number of literary references indicating the artists' awareness of nature. During the T'ang period, when Buddhism was in full swing in China, most of the great painters, such as Wu Tao-tzu and Lu Leng-chia, were attracted to the services of that faith, painting on the walls of the temples and monasteries. Others, such as Yen Li-pen and Han Kan, performed the official function of painters, doing ancient figures, contemporary leaders, and famous horses. Although landscape had already become an independent genre, and artists such as Li Ssu-hsun and Wang Wei had formulated new styles, it was still ranked lower than paintings of Taoist-Buddhist subjects or figure painting.

Again it was partly the great persecution of Buddhism in 845 and partly the collapse of the T'ang empire that drove Chinese artists away from those favored subjects. With another chaotic period during the early part of the tenth century, when China was again broken up into many kingdoms and short-lived dynasties, Chinese artists began to concentrate their most creative effort on landscape. Now without the restrictions of the religious and Confucian approaches, but with a new freedom gained through Ch'an Buddhism in the choice of subjects for serious expression, they found landscape the best answer to their quest for order. The tenth century has been regarded by later Chinese artists as the age of giants in landscape painting. Such masters as Ching Hao, Kuan T'ung, Tung Yüan, Chü-jan, and Li Ch'eng have come to be revered as originators of the great landscape painting tradition. From that time until today, landscape has been the chief means of Chinese artistic expression.

The early ideal in landscape painting seems to have been best summarized by the Northern Sung artist Kuo Hsi (*ca.* 1070), who wrote this passage in the opening paragraph of his treatise on landscape painting:

Why does a virtuous man take delight in landscapes? It is for these reasons: that in a rustic retreat he may nourish his nature; that amid the carefree play of streams and rocks, he may take delight; that he may constantly meet the country fishermen, woodcutters, and hermits, and see the soaring of the cranes, and hear the crying of the monkeys. The din of the dusty world and the locked-in-ness of human habitations are what human nature habitually abhors; while on the contrary, haze, mist, and the haunting spirits of the mountains are what human nature seeks, and yet can rarely find.[1]

In this attitude, there is a definite Taoist overtone in the yearning for nature to set free the human spirit. However, there is also a strong Buddhist reference in its statement: "the din of the dusty world." Furthermore, the "virtuous man" (*chün-tzu*) is a typical Confucian term. Throughout the text, there is this same kind of blending together of ideas of all three major religions into one single stream of thought, which seems to be reflected in many paintings of this period.

Travelers Among Mountains and Streams, a hanging scroll by Fan K'uan (active first quarter of 11th century), now in the Palace Museum, Taipei (Fig. 25), shows well what Kuo Hsi's statement

1. Kuo Hsi, *An Essay on Landscape Painting,* translated by Shio Sakanishi (London: John Murray, 1935), p. 30.

means and also offers some hints concerning the achievements of all those tenth-century masters. The painting depicts a scene of high mountain cliffs rising above streams and rocks where a human trace in the forms of several buildings and a group of travelers with donkeys carrying their goods can be seen. Compositionally, it is handled with masterful skill. The foreground rocks serve as our stepping stones into the picture. In the middle ground, which occupies twice the surface space of the foreground, the scene breaks into two parts, separated by a cascade with a bridge in the center. In the final movement, occupying the top three fifths of the surface space, a high mountain peak rises vertically and centrally, until it almost reaches the upper edge of the picture. Thus both the fore and middle grounds are mere preparation for the movement of the high mountain, which starts from the mist, but quickly grows into a soaring shape, until it reaches a powerful, ultimate culmination at the top, the end of a long spiritual journey. In this painting, the grandeur of nature and the smallness and insignificance of man are revealed in sharp contrast, and the image of the mountain has assumed the same capabilities of aesthetic and spiritual expression as those of the human figure and the Buddha image.

Behind the Taoist love of nature manifested in this painting of Fan K'uan is the insistent hieratic arrangement of the mountains. So orderly is their placement that they immediately remind one of a Buddhist Western Paradise, such as the one at Tun-huang shown above, with a large Amitabha in the center flanked by many bodhisattvas and surrounded by musicians and saved souls. Yet the fact that the scheme has been transferred to a landscape painting indicates the artist's search for more freedom in expression. What he tries to show here is perhaps not so much an expression of his own self but one of his own perception of nature. In other words, he seems to be searching for an underlying principle, or a cosmic order, in nature, an aim which corresponds to ideas of Neo-Confucianism, the new synthesis of Chinese thought in the Sung period. The artist starts with all the details of rocks, water, trees, buildings, figures, and animals, and eventually ends up with an ideal order resulting from the rational approach. In this, Fan K'uan's painting can be seen as an aesthetic as well as a philosophical synthesis of Confucian, Taoist, and Buddhist traditions of expression, a far cry from the schematic objectification of a cosmic order in the Han mirror.

After the fall of Northern Sung and the transfer of the court to

Figure 26. Sailboat in the Rain, *by Hsia Kuei, early 13th century, Boston Museum.*

Hangchow in the south, both the rational and the monumental approaches to landscape as reflected in Fan K'uan's painting were gradually given up. Under court patronage, a new type of landscape, usually in small format, or the album leaf, done in quicker brushwork, was developed. A number of artists, particularly Li T'ang, Ma Yüan, and Hsia Kuei, were masters of this approach. Although the *Sailboat*

450

in the Rain by Hsia Kuei, now in the Boston Museum (Fig. 26), still shows the logical three-step progression into space, the high mountains are almost entirely covered by mist and seen only in silhouette; and the middle ground is cleverly indicated by the sailboat while the foreground is amplified into great prominence, with tall trees and houses standing out clearly. However, in total, all the painted elements seem to be only pointers toward something that is not represented. It is perhaps an indication that the cosmic order, or the ultimate reality, is too profound to be reached by the rational approach as before, but rather must be sought by the intuitive or even mystical one being cultivated in Southern Sung, among both some Neo-Confucianists and Ch'an Buddhists.

The Mongol domination of China from 1280 to 1368 was a great change not only in political and social development, but also in art, especially in painting. While many intellectuals declined to serve under the new rulers, Chao Meng-fu (1254-1322) was one of the very few who rose to high position in the new court in Peking. Through his artistic effort and influence, he helped to give a new direction to Chinese painting. His short handscroll, *The Autumn Colors on the Ch'iao and Hua Mountains,* now in the Palace Museum, Taipei (Fig. 27), was executed after he had spent about ten years traveling all over the newly reunited China absorbing the various traditions he had seen and studied in the north. As an attempt to search into the remote past for the essence of the Chinese tradition, the painting is based not so much on Southern Sung or Northern Sung as on the archaic landscape style of the T'ang dynasty. It is a new synthesis, fusing together the classicizing approach with continuing realism and anticipating the expressionism of the future. Based on an actual site in Tsi-nan, Shantung Province, where Chao served for a few years as a high official, this realistic scene has been given a treatment that is reminiscent of T'ang poet-painter Wang Wei's country villa near Ch'ang-an in the eighth century. At the same time, the whole scene is depicted with a masterful handling of form which resembles that of a symphony. Typically, the transformation of actual scenes into paintings of formal beauty shows that Yüan artists were not so much concerned with cosmic order as with personal feeling and expression and a new aestheticism.

As a great scholar, poet, calligrapher, and painter, Chao Meng-fu was able to study all the traditions of the past and point in a new direction. In particular, he drew on the theories of a group of

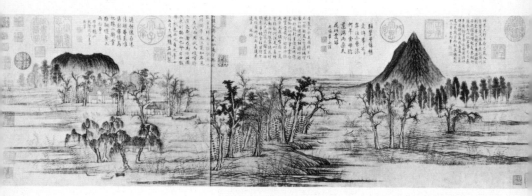

Figure 27. The Autumn Colors on the Ch'iao and Hua Mountains, *by Chao Meng-fu (1254-1322), Palace Museum, Taipei.*

eleventh-century literati, who had extolled the expressive quality and personal approach of painting. Departing from rich colors, naturalistic details, and limited subject matter as used in the Academy of Emperor Hui-tsung, they reasserted spirit consonance rather than resemblance to nature as the primary consideration of painting, in an amateurish and playful approach that reflects their sophistication and individuality. To the Yüan artists, disillusioned by the social disintegration of the period and by the lack of opportunity to show their administrative talents, this new direction was especially welcome. The Yüan period is the time when such artists as Huang Kung-wang, Wu Chen, Ni Tsan, and Wang Meng, all natives of the region of the Yangtze River delta, achieved their very distinctive and influential personal styles.

One of the youngest of these late Yüan masters, Ni Tsan, developed a personal style that was to be one of the most revered in Ming and Ch'ing. Known for his eccentric taste for cleanliness, he evolved a style so simple and "pure" that it has since been identified with him. *Yung-hsi Studio,* in the Palace Museum, Taipei (Fig. 28), was done in 1372, at the age of seventy-two. Although it depicts a lake view in his home district, a great number of details seem to have been left out. Rocks, hills, and islands seem to be all barren, except for a few moss-dots. Five trees, with a great variation of species and growth, rise above the foreground. A single pavilion suggests some-

Figure 28. The Yung-hsi Studio, *by Ni Tsan (1301-1374), Palace Museum, Taipei.*

Figure 29. Landscape in the Style of Ni Tsan, *by Shen Chou (1427-1509), Nelson Gallery of Art, Kansas City.*

thing human, but lonely, out in the open landscape. Everything is done with the greatest economy, so much so that later writers described him as "treasuring ink like gold." Following the ideas of Chao Meng-fu, Ni Tsan feels free to manipulate the formal elements either by accentuation or simplification to transform the painting into a symbol of the personality, taste, and spirit of the artist, reflecting his classical education, his experience in nature, and his yearning to be free from all the troubles of the world.

With the country back under Chinese rule, the Ming dynasty attempted to recapture the grandeur of T'ang and Sung, but fell far short of it. In a similar way, Ming artists under court patronage

453

during the fifteenth century tried to revive the Southern Sung style, but became more imitative than creative. Their works appear grandiose and affected, lacking the spirit of Sung painting.

The more creative school of the Ming period is the Wu school, named for the prosperous city of Soochow, once called Wu, in Kiangsu Province. Inheriting the approaches of the Yüan masters, a group of artists made Soochow the great stronghold of literati painting, which reaches its height in the sixteenth century. The founder of this school is Shen Chou (1427-1509), who came from a line of prominent scholars and painters, and who developed his own personal style out of the traditions of Ni Tsan and other Yüan painters. In his *Landscape in the Style of Ni Tsan,* in the Nelson Gallery, Kansas City (Fig. 29), dated 1484, his indebtedness to that late Yüan master is quite obvious. However, one cannot mistake Shen's style for Ni's, for somehow the former's approach is not so "pure" as the latter's, but stronger and more masculine. What is more noticeable is that in the Ming work, following the development of formal emphasis, the whole surface structure is more complex and a strong narrative interest is evident. Trees are more elongated and mountains become more contrived. There is greater interest in brushwork for its own sake. In this connection, the Ming artist seems to be concerned less with nature, more with the study of past masters. Somewhat similar to the Ming gardens in Soochow, which are filled with artificially constructed landscapes, Ming paintings are the literati's extended dreams of the past.

Shen Chou was followed by a host of Soochow artists during the sixteenth century, led by his pupil Wen Cheng-ming, who in turn became the master of several generations of literati artists. But in the city of Soochow, which became the unchallenged artistic center of China during the sixteenth century, there were also other artists usually not associated with the literati group. Many of them were professionals who painted for their livelihood. The most famous of this group is Ch'iu Ying, whose true image is almost totally submerged by the large number of his mediocre imitators. One of his finest works, *A Lady in a Pavilion Overlooking a Lake,* now in the Boston Museum (Fig. 30), shows a sharp contrast between his approach and that of Shen Chou, although both paintings seem to have been derived from Ni Tsan. While Shen is robust and strong, Ch'iu is delicate and feminine. His composition is very much in the same category as that of Ni Tsan, but the foreground is entirely different. Instead of being a lonely pavilion, his architectural structure is depicted with elaborate details and exquisite colors and filled with beautiful ladies and decorations. No longer is it like a scholar's retreat. It has the sumptuous quality of the houses of the rich and powerful, who patronized Ch'iu Ying and other professional painters of that period. It is, in a sense, a typical Ming professional work, using the literati interest to serve more mundane taste. In style, its emphasis on representational elements seems to put it out of step with the formal interest in literati painting of its own time.

Toward the end of the Ming period, all the literati traditions in art seem to have flowed together into one main current. The great personality who summarized all these was Tung Ch'i-ch'ang (1555-1636), who was a highly influential official, a first-rate calligrapher, and an interesting painter. Above all, he was the most respected critic and connoisseur of his own time, and greatly conditioned the artistic taste of the Ch'ing period. In his *Ch'ing-pien Mountains* (Fig. 31), in the H. C. Weng Collection, New York, dated 1617, he claims to follow a tenth-century artist of the same monumental landscape tradition as Fan K'uan. However, Tung Ch'i-ch'ang's imitation is extremely free. No longer interested in the outer appearance, he only makes use of certain major motifs from the past, and distorts some of them and rearranges others, in order to achieve greater pictorial unity and expression. The result is quite a departure from Fan K'uan's realistic depiction of nature, something like what Cézanne did to modern art.

The importance of Tung Ch'i-ch'ang lies chiefly in his theoretical discussions, which consist of a large number of short comments that he put on his own and other artists' works as colophons, and which were later collected into a number of books. From these the main body of his theories can be reconstructed. Summarizing the literati theory from the eleventh century down to his own time, he strongly emphasizes that painting, especially landscape, is a vehicle for expression for the cultivated man, the literatus. As such, he must free himself from the vulgar and the conventional, and have an individuality of his own. To prepare for his paintings, he must "walk ten thousand miles and read ten thousand books." By this Tung means also the intense study of the techniques of former masters, especially their use of brush and ink. Thus equipped, he can proceed to paint his landscapes, such as the *Ch'ing-pien Mountains,* using the brush and ink technique of the tenth-century artist. Yet, while the early artist must have captured the likeness of nature, the seventeenth-century artist seems to be much more concerned with spirit consonance achieved through purely formal elements, such as brush and ink, as an expression of the inner worth of the artist.

In this development, form itself, independent of its representational value, has been elevated to the same importance held previously by the *t'ao-t'ieh* image, the cosmic mirror, the Confucian shrine reliefs,

Figure 31. Ch'ing-pien Mountains, *by Tung Ch'i-ch'ang (1555-1636), H. C. Weng Collection, N. Y.*

Figure 30. A Lady in a Pavilion Overlooking a Lake, *by Ch'iu Ying, mid-16th century, Boston Museum.*

the Buddhist image, and the monumental mountain formation in the history of Chinese art. In other words, in Tung's view, painting should be appreciated in the same way as calligraphy, which must be enjoyed for its purely abstract, formal elements.

Another aspect of late Ming painting, not affected by the theories of Tung Ch'i-ch'ang, is exemplified by the works of another artist. Wu Pin enjoyed great fame early in the seventeenth century. In spite of

Figure 33. Landscape, *by Wang Yüan-ch'i (1642-1715), Cleveland Museum of Art.*

Figure 32. Landscape, *by Wu Pin (early 17th century, Chai Yüan Chai Collection, Berkeley.*

Figure 34. Landscape in the Style of Ni
Tsan, *by Shih-t'ao (1641-before 1720)
dated 1697, Princeton Art Museum.*

being a court artist, he was a truly creative man. Also deriving from
Northern Sung masters, his landscapes, such as the one in the Ching
Yüan Chai Collection (Fig. 32), have a strange, weird, fantastic
quality. It is a turning of the classical landscape into an expression of
mannerism, of inner tensions and emotional strains, of free distortions
and strange associations. Like the painting by Tung Ch'i-ch'ang, it
draws its inspiration from the past to express something new. But a
major difference between the two artists lies in the direction each one
of them takes. Wu Pin, in technique and detail, is imitative and
conservative, but in conception and expression is inventive and
ingenious. This impulse to turn something classical in the Chinese
tradition into an anti-classical expression is perhaps a reflection of the
stress and tension of the late Ming period.

Painting of the early Ch'ing period was almost entirely dominated
by the influence of Tung Ch'i-ch'ang, both in theory and style, which
can be seen in two main trends. A number of artists deriving directly

Figure 35. Landscape, *by Kung Hsien (1617/8-1689), Charles Drenowatz Collection, Zürich.*

from Tung's own style became associated with the Manchu court late in the seventeenth century. Favored by the emperors K'ang-hsi and Ch'ien-lung, who, each with a sixty-year-long reign, ruled until almost the end of the eighteenth century, this approach developed into the "academic" style of the Ch'ing, in the sense that it was the court-sponsored style.

The landscape by Wang Yüan-ch'i, now in the Cleveland Museum of Art (Fig. 33), shows clearly the approach of this school. Following the Tung Ch'i-ch'ang tradition, the painting is based on certain past masters rather than on nature itself. Apparently derived from a combined influence of Huang Kung-wang and Ni Tsan, it shows a new departure from the tradition of the latter. Like the others of his group, Wang Yüan-ch'i spent long years practicing the basic forms of rocks, trees, land masses, mountains, and compositions of Sung and Yüan artists. In his own paintings, he usually takes one master's style as his point of departure and builds his compositions with various elements derived from that artist. Thus, in this painting, he captures some of Ni's feeling for lake views of the Yangtze delta, with simple and "pure" brushwork. However, while Ni Tsan still

459

shows a strong feeling for the lake views in the Yangtze delta, though with more individual brushwork, the Ch'ing artist is not so much interested in nature itself as in the brushwork as a pure aesthetic element. Spirit consonance is achieved through the arrangement of objects and patterns of brushwork on the picture surface. In other words, Wang Yüan-ch'i's painting represents a synthesis, blending together a new aestheticism and a dream of the past by way of Ni Tsan.

In contrast to this group of "academic" literati, there is another group in which orthodox theories are outweighed by more individual tendencies and even eccentricities. One member of the group is Shih-t'ao, a descendant of the Ming royal line who became a Ch'an Buddhist monk when the Manchus conquered China in the middle of the seventeenth century. Although in his treatises he tends to reject the imitation of the past and to emphasize originality, creativity, and direct contact with nature, he is not entirely unaffected by tradition. The *Landscape After Ni Tsan,* in the Princeton Museum (Fig. 34), draws the motifs of the pavilion and trees from the Yüan eccentric, but has an entirely new composition, leaving out the lake view and bringing all details, including the mountain, close to the picture plane. Again it is the great boldness of the brushwork that marks his individualism and personal vitality. The subservience to the past is turned into an expression of a very strong personality.

One of the most interesting of all the individualists in the seventeenth century is Kung Hsien, who, after the collapse of Ming, retired from the world as a hermit, living on a small farm near Nanking. His paintings have a kind of hypnotic power in conveying to the fullest extent the feeling of loneliness and desolation by means of landscape. Developing a style of rich dark ink and powerful mountain formations in almost abstract structures, he achieves both formal excellence and profound expression. The landscape in the Charles Drenowatz collection (Fig. 35) is an example of how far the Chinese artist has explored landscape painting to convey the inner feeling of his own life and the world in which he lives.

Summary

In this short survey of the long and continuous development of Chinese art, several major characteristics are quite evident. First, from the Shang bronzes to Ch'ing painting, there is a persistent search among Chinese artists for a form of expression that can best embrace the largest body of their ideas and experiences. Second, traditionalism plays an important role in Chinese art. Constant imitation of earlier examples brings to a work of art a greater historical awareness and a deeper spiritual meaning. While the more imitative artists often remain very close to past models, the more creative ones always attempt to transform them into something of their own, expressive of their inner feelings through the tradition developed by earlier masters. This is particularly strong in the development of painting. Third, Chinese artists, in the evolution from mythological, religious, metaphysical to aesthetic expression, have gained their status as the foremost literati of society. In this process they gradually command more and more freedom to express their own feeling and ideas. Fourth, because of this long emphasis on the spiritual, the Chinese artist has always attempted to achieve, through his works, an identification between his inner self and the object depicted, as the highest goal of his artistic expression, and the main source of the "spirit consonance."

Since the eighteenth century some impact of Western art has been felt in China. The introduction of Western naturalism by the Jesuit painter Giuseppe Castiglione to the Chinese court of Emperor Ch'ienlung created a new taste in art, but it was never strong enough to challenge the predominance of literati painting. Even during the twentieth century, with the weakening of the Chinese confidence after a century of foreign intrusions and the establishment of a Western-oriented republic, the traditional approach retains its hold in spite of the fact that Western practices of art have attracted more and more younger artists. Only in recent years, especially since 1949, when social realism was laid down as the guiding approach to art in mainland China, has the pace of Westernization been quickened. At the same time, since the beginning of this century, with the development of new aesthetics in the West, Chinese painting has found an enthusiastic response among Western artists. It is only recently that a number of younger artists, trained in the traditional styles but attracted to Western approaches, have discovered the similarities between the ideals of literati painting and those of modern Western art and attempted to achieve a new synthesis.

XV

Economic Structure

of Traditional

China

BY

NAI-RUENN CHEN

Introduction

The history of China may be broadly classified into four periods according to the stages of her economic development. The first period covers the formative centuries from the beginning of Chinese history to the unification of China by Ch'in, during which the Chinese people developed the basic patterns of an agricultural life. Then comes a period, covering approximately two thousand years and ending with the Opium War of 1840, which was characterized by the overwhelming preponderance of traditional agricultural pursuits and the subsidiary role of nonagricultural activities.

The agrarian economy of China began to undergo significant changes after the Opium War as a result of the introduction of foreign capital into the country, which in turn stimulated the formation of Chinese-owned capital in modern manufacturing industries. But revolutionary changes in the Chinese economic structure have taken place only since 1949 when the Communists took over the mainland. These developments are treated elsewhere in this volume. The present essay will be devoted exclusively to a survey of the Chinese economy before 1840 with emphasis on fundamental changes in economic structure. Structural changes of the Chinese economy during this prolonged period of history were so extensive and diversified that only the highlights can be covered in a short essay like this.

The Pre-Ch'in Economy

Little is known about the Chinese economic structure before the Chou dynasty. Available evidence seems to indicate that the Shang dynasty was already an agrarian civilization with towns, some of which have been discovered by excavation. However, the agricultural implements of the Shang people were extremely primitive. Artisans already existed probably as dependents of the ruling class.

Relatively more information is available on the economic activities of the Chou people. After the conquest of the Shang territory in the closing years of the twelfth century B.C., the Chou kings (known as Sons of Heaven) established a feudal system by creating a number of

The author wishes to express his gratitude to Professor Knight Biggerstaff for reading the manuscript and making many useful suggestions. He is also indebted to Professor John C. H. Fei, with whom he spent many evenings discussing interesting issues of Chinese economic history, particularly in the pre-Ch'in period.

fiefs to be governed by relatives and those who had aided in the conquest. They in turn enfeoffed their subordinates, although in theory every square inch of land belonged personally to the king. Each fief-holder obtained tribute from below and submitted part of it to his superior. The actual tiller of the land was the *shu jen*, a peasant attached to the land as a serf and obliged to work for his lord.

Not much is known about the administration of the farm land. According to the classical tradition, land was laid out in squares, three plots to a side, making a tick-tack-toe pattern, which was called the well-field (*ching-t'ien*) system. Of the nine plots in the square, peasant families were said to work the eight on the outside and raise their own food and the one in the middle to raise in common their payment to their lord. Such a system seems too idealized to have been practiced exactly, and historians have conjectured about the actual system. Little is certain beyond the knowledge that the lord possessed the land and the peasant worked it, the produce being divided somehow between them.

In addition to providing his lord with food, the peasant was required to perform regularly labor services such as repairing houses, building new walls, growing vegetables in gardens, and raising sheep in pastures. There was little commercial activity except for very small-scale barter trade. Occupational specialization was not significant; only royal crafts existed, serving the nobility.

Therefore, in the early Chou period (probably in Shang as well) Chinese economic life was centered in domains like manors or fiefs. The manor, or the fief, was as a rule self-sufficient. Such an economic structure may be illustrated in Figure 1. The ruling class allocated land to the peasants, who provided goods and services for self-consumption as well as for the consumption of the ruling class. Royal crafts, not being independent producers, were fed by the ruling class and submitted their products to the nobility in return.

The economic structure of the domain broke down during Ch'un-ch'iu and Chan-kuo times, which represented a most important turning point in Chinese economic history. The breakdown was caused by many factors, the most important one probably being technological advances in agriculture.

A number of remarkable innovations took place in agricultural technology. The most revolutionary one was probably the adoption of iron implements in the Chan-kuo period. The harnessing of animals to plows made greater yields possible. The evidence of longer settle-

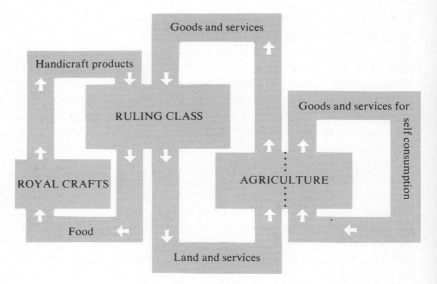

Figure 1. Pre-Ch'in economic structure.

ment in one place suggests that a fallow system may have been introduced. Manuring of fields was already known in Shang times, but available evidence seems to indicate that in the Ch'un-ch'iu and Chan-kuo periods the use of fertilizers was more widespread and different kinds of fertilizers were applied to different soils. Irrigation facilities were known to have been expanded considerably. All of these evidences of technological advance suggest that there was in all probability a substantial increase in agricultural productivity, which in turn through increased agricultural surplus may have raised the income of both the aristocrats and the peasants.

A substantial increase in agricultural productivity and output contributed to a number of important economic changes in Ch'un-ch'iu and Chan-kuo China including (1) the emergence of private ownership of land; (2) occupational specialization and the rise of industry; and (3) development of commercial activities and the rise of the merchant class. Although the enlargement of agricultural surplus may have been the fundamental cause of these new developments, there were some other factors, as will be shown below, helping to shape a new economic structure in Ch'un-ch'iu and Chan-kuo times.

EMERGENCE OF PRIVATE LAND OWNERSHIP

As noted above, the Chou king in theory possessed all the land. In practice, especially as the central power grew weaker, his vassals hardly respected his ownership, and the idea of possession of land by others than the king could be conceived, at least among the aristocracy. Probably, too, minor lords who found themselves in financial difficulties took to disposing of some of their land, in effect selling it, perhaps to merchants. Among the lords, it may also have happened that the produce they received from the peasants could come to be regarded as the important thing, not so much the stationary peasant himself, so that some exchange of possessions even among peasants is conceivable, so long as the produce, viewed more as rent than service, was paid. We also know that new land was being opened up, and gifts of land being given to the meritorious by the lords. About the middle of the fourth century B.C. Shang Yang, minister in the state of Ch'in, initiated a series of reforms among which is usually counted the acknowledgment of private land ownership. This may well have been no more than an official recognition of an existing situation, but it was still important, as the idea of private ownership is valid, after all, only so long as powerful parts of the society accept it. The acknowledgment of private ownership by the state, which in doing so by no means ruled out its own preeminent domain, introduced new possibilities of land tenure and promised new problems.

OCCUPATIONAL SPECIALIZATION AND THE RISE OF INDUSTRY

Since the economy of the domain was basically self-sufficient, there was little division of labor. The farmer in a manor had to perform practically all kinds of tasks for his family and for his lord. The emergence of a large agricultural surplus in Ch'un-ch'iu and Chan-kuo times promoted occupational specialization. With an agricultural surplus farmers sought to exchange it for manufactured products and the nobles demanded more luxuries. In Chan-kuo times, for example, the farmer frequently exchanged grain for cloth, cooking pots, or implements. Artisans who had accumulated technical experience for centuries as dependents of the ruling class prior to the Ch'un-ch'iu period had gradually become independent producers, manufacturing articles and selling them to the aristocrats and the peasants.

In Chan-kuo times, therefore, there was quite a large number of specialized occupations such as smithery, carpentry, the weaving of reed curtains, the washing of silk refuse, and the making of shoes, bows, and chariots. Recent excavationary discoveries in mainland China reveal that certain Chan-kuo industries were engaged in large-scale production of one line of goods such as iron implements, bronze vessels, or pottery. There is little doubt that some handicraft industry was gradually becoming an independent, though small, sector of the economy toward the end of the Chan-kuo period.

DEVELOPMENT OF COMMERCE AND THE EMERGENCE OF THE MERCHANT CLASS

Merchants already existed in Shang and early Chou China. These merchants, however, did not form an independent professional class but were a group of people retained within the domain to perform certain minor services for the feudal lords. Included in the functions of the merchants were purchasing for the lords a few items, such as jewelry and salt, from other areas, distributing food for the lords to the *shu jen,* and supervising the work of the artisans.

The specialization and differentiation in occupations and in the production of commodities in different areas in Chan-kuo times stimulated trade activities both within and between regions, giving rise to a new class, the merchant class. The development of trade in turn created a demand for a higher degree of specialization of industry. Thus industrial specialization and trade development were both cause and effect of each other, and of the economic prosperity of late Ch'un-ch'iu and Chan-kuo China. Commercial progress at that time was furthered by the political unity of large areas, the relative security of travel within these areas, the improvement of transportation, and the appearance of metallic money.

The development of local and interregional trade created a new prosperous class of people who carried on this trade and who did not have to till the land but nevertheless accumulated more wealth and more grain than the toiling peasants. Many of these *nouveaux riches* became large landowners by buying up the land that farmers were forced to sell because of high taxes, usury, and other economic pressures.

Chinese Economic Structure
from Ch'in to Early Ch'ing

A MODEL FOR THE TRADITIONAL ECONOMIC STRUCTURE IN CHINA

By the time China was unified under Ch'in, an economic structure which was basically different from that of the ancient period emerged. The new economic structure may be conveniently classified into four sectors: government, agriculture, industry, and trade. This classification parallels the traditional four-part division of Chinese society (i.e., *shih* [officials], *nung* [farmers], *kung* [artisans], and *shang* [merchants]). These four economic sectors are by no means completely independent of each other. For example, both the state and the merchant sometimes owned industries and the peasant often engaged in handicraft work. The classification made here is based on the main economic activities or functions of each sector.

Unfortunately, no estimates are available on the shares of the total output of goods and services produced by each of these four economic sectors in traditional China. If national income estimates for China in the early 1930s can be used as a guide for gauging orders of magnitude, it may be conjectured that in earlier times, say the Ch'ing period, agriculture was by far the most important sector of the traditional economy, producing probably at least 70 percent of the national output, followed by industry, trade, and government in that order.

The interrelationships between these four sectors may be shown in a highly simplified form in Figure 2, which presents thirteen inter- and intra-sectoral flows of goods and services, or resources. An explanation of each of these thirteen flows follows:

Flow 1. This flow moves from government to agriculture, representing the right granted the peasants to the use of land and technology-enhancing services generated by governmental efforts, such as agricultural encouragement programs and government investment in agricultural infrastructure including roads, irrigation facilities, water-control projects, and granaries.

Flow 2. This is a flow of goods and services moving from agriculture to government for the payment of taxes, and rents. It takes the form of farm products, products of farm crafts, and labor services.

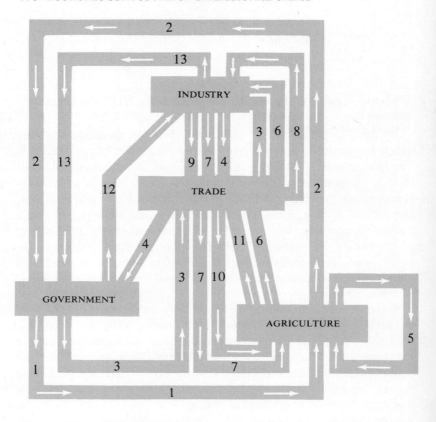

1. Land and technology-enhancing services
2. Goods and services
3. Agricultural products
4. Industrial products
5. Goods and services (for self-consumption)
6. Agricultural products
7. Industrial products
8. Capital investment (merchant investment in industry)
9. Industrial products (income from investment)
10. Capital investment (merchant investment in agriculture)
11. Agricultural products (income from investment)
12. Capital investment (state investment in industry)
13. Industrial products (income from investment)

Figure 2.   Economic structure from the Ch'in to the Ch'ing

Flow 3. Government uses part of the income obtained from the agricultural sector to purchase industrial products. A flow of agricultural products moves from government through the trade sector to industry in exchange for industrial products.

Flow 4. These industrial products move through the trade sector to government, which may either consume them or use them as materials for constructing buildings, roads, irrigation projects, granaries, and the like.

Flow 5. This is an intrasectoral flow within agriculture, indicating that portion of the output of farming and subsidiary occupations to be retained by the peasants for self-consumption.

Flow 6. This flow indicates that the peasants exchange their surplus through the market for industrial goods.

Flow 7. These goods move from industry through the trade sector to agriculture.

Flow 8. This is a flow indicating that the merchants in the trade sector either invest in industry or lend capital to the craftsmen.

Flow 9. In consequence, the merchants own part of the industrial output.

Flow 10. The merchants also invest in agriculture or lend money to the peasants.

Flow 11. The merchants, therefore, also own part of the agricultural output.

Flow 12. This flow indicates state investment in industry.

Flow 13. The government receives industrial products as returns on its investment.

This highly simplified model explains to a large extent the fundamental relationships between the four sectors of the Chinese economy during the two thousand years from the Ch'in dynasty to the early Ch'ing period. Needless to say, there were many significant changes in the Chinese economy throughout this prolonged period of history; but these changes took place largely within the confine of the traditional structure as shown in the above model. An attempt will be made in the following sections to describe each sector in the model, and to present the highlights of significant development in each sector.

GOVERNMENT

The main economic functions of the government in traditional China were severalfold. First of all, the government raised revenues. For example, it collected taxes as the ruler of the society, and rents as an owner of the land. It also provided resources and services, including land and state investment in infrastructure, for the other three sectors of the economy. It sometimes adopted measures to stimulate agricultural production, such as the various agricultural encouragement programs sponsored by different dynastic regimes. Frequently the government also owned factories and supervised industrial production. In addition, the government played administrative roles in matters related to commerce, such as money, foreign trade, and customs and market supervision.

In spite of participating in the economy in these important respects, the government in traditional China failed immensely to promote economic growth. This was probably due to the conservative attitudes of government officials. Prior to the T'ang dynasty, government officials were largely a class of aristocrats, most of whom had risen to office through hereditary privilege. They were oriented primarily to the idea of power holding, and not to production and distribution.

In T'ang times the state examination system was established for the purpose of recruiting a professional bureaucracy on the basis of personal merit. The system gradually developed, and by the eleventh century the graduates began to provide a majority of the official cadres. Although the new ruling elite benefited from new blood more or less throughout the centuries that followed, essentially the same kind of people, versed in classical learning and on the whole with a stake in the economic structure as it was, ruled China until modern times. The dominant patterns of thought of this official-gentry class were heavily influenced by Confucian teachings. Confucianism conceived of economic welfare not in terms of economic growth but in terms of subsistence, of satisfaction of basic minimum needs. The dominant economic concern of the Chinese ruling class was maintenance rather than development: maintenance of bare subsistence for the masses and maintenance of a cultural life for the official-gentry class. The emphasis was on stability rather than on growth. Moreover, the attitude of the official-gentry was one of great caution, avoiding any action not consistent with tradition and any undertaking without clearly foreseeable consequences. Such conservatism was inadaptable to the risk-taking, decision-making, and innovating entrepreneurial activity which was required in any successful modernization effort.

AGRICULTURE

Land Tenure. It may be recalled that before the Ch'in dynasty land was possessed and controlled by an aristocratic elite and that private land ownership had not been officially recognized until the Shang Yang reform. With the emergence of private land ownership, land tenure had gradually become a matter of governmental concern. Before the ninth century attempts were made at times and in different degrees at state control of tenure. Among the various controlled systems of land, the best known was probably the equal field (*chün-t'ien*) system which was first adopted in A.D. 485 by the Northern Wei dynasty and later developed under the Sui and the T'ang. Under the system the state granted lands on more or less limited tenures to the peasants, who in turn accepted various fiscal responsibilities.

The latter part of the eighth century witnessed a complete revolution in the state's relationship with the land, when private *de facto* rights both of possession and of disposal of landed property were acknowledged in practice. The new system of free tenure of land, which was in sharp contrast with land allotment systems characteristic of the period of division in the third to sixth centuries, was symbolized by the tax reform of 780. As a result of that reform, the system of fixed head taxes imposed during the period of division was replaced by one of progressive taxation based on assessment of property on one hand, and of land levies based on the area under cultivation on the other. The free land tenure and the acknowledgment of a large degree of private ownership resulted in the accumulation of estates and growth of tenancy which characterized the Chinese economy from the ninth century to the Communist takeover in 1949.

Agricultural Production. Generally speaking, Chinese agriculture consisted of three principal activities—crop growing, animal raising, and farm subsidiary production. Crops constituted by far the major part of total agricultural output. Wheat, millet, and rice were traditionally the key crops in China with wheat and millet largely grown in the north and rice in the south and the southwest. Between the thirteenth and seventeenth centuries China had acquired from the outside world improved strains of rice and supplementary crops such as sorghum, maize, sweet potatoes, Irish potatoes, peanuts, and tobacco. Cotton, which was first commonly grown in the Sung period later became the most important cash crop in the country.

From the long-term point of view, Chinese agriculture made important progress, although such progress was painfully slow. There were several sources of agricultural progress in China. One of them was technological improvement due to governmental efforts which generally took two forms. First, very often in the course of Chinese history special programs were introduced by the government to encourage and improve farming. As early as the Former Han dynasty, for example, a special administrative apparatus was set up for the encouragement of agriculture, and officials were appointed on both the central and the local levels to teach the peasants to use improved farming methods and new implements.

A second, and perhaps more important, form of governmental effort was public investment in social overhead, such as the building of roads, the digging of canals, and the construction of irrigation facilities, water-control works, and granaries. All of these undoubtedly yielded favorable effects on agricultural production. But the effects of both state encouragement programs and public investment should not be overemphasized since these measures mostly did not represent a continuous, concerted national effort to promote growth, but were *ad hoc* and localized in nature, designed to increase agricultural production for the purpose of raising government tax revenue.

Another important source of agricultural growth in China was the gradual accumulation of technical experience and knowledge on the part of Chinese farmers over the centuries. The use of iron implements became more and more widespread; new techniques of cultivation were introduced; the utilization of animal power in farming was increased. Also, as already noted above, a number of important crops were introduced.

Although current investments in Chinese agriculture were very small, there was a large accumulation of man-made capital structures which represented an extensive and long-continued investment of labor over the centuries. The accumulation of direct investments in various irrigation facilities, farmstead buildings, and the like, in turn made possible a more efficient application of labor to soil. Moreover, the Chinese farmer was known for his thriftiness and industry. Although in all probability he did not receive even a rudimentary education, year after year he sowed the same crops on the same land and brought them to maturity in the same way, by methods that time had proven. Few significant inefficiencies could be found in the allocation of the limited resources at his disposal. A crude optimality was evident in Chinese agriculture, making possible relatively high yields per unit area from the overcrowded soils.

A third source of Chinese agricultural growth stemmed from the expansion of cultivated acreage. The farming area in China was concentrated along the Yellow River in ancient times, and had been expanded into the Yangtze valley by the Han period. After T'ang and Sung times lands in the south including present-day Fukien and Kwangtung were extensively cultivated. By the time of the Ch'ing dynasty areas such as Kwangsi, Yunnan, and Kweichow in the southwest and Liaoning and Heilungkiang in the northeast became important agricultural regions. There is no question that the growth of the aggregate production of Chinese agriculture was partly a result of the increase in the area brought under cultivation. But in per capita terms the picture was not so clear. Available evidence suggests that for the whole period of Chinese history under survey the growth of population had outpaced the expansion in cultivated acreage, resulting over time in a declining magnitude of cultivated area per capita.

Finally, commercialization of crop production represented another significant development in Chinese agriculture. Agricultural commercialization, which began as early as T'ang, reached a significant stage after the late Ming period largely due to the development of handicraft industry at that time. In Ming and Ch'ing times there emerged a large number of handicraft workshops manufacturing or processing products such as cotton textiles, sugar, tobacco, and tea, all of which required industrial crops as raw materials. The increase in the demand for these crops in turn stimulated specialization in crop production. Previously, Chinese farmers mostly aimed at self-sufficiency, producing food grains as their main occupation while planting industrial crops as subsidiary activities. After the late Ming period, however, a large number of farmers specialized in the growing of particular industrial crops. Thus the development of handicraft industry had resulted in the growth of industrial crop production. On the other hand, the production of food grains may have been adversely affected, since resources including cultivated land and farm labor were diverted from the production of food grains to that of industrial crops. In the absence of authentic data, it is not possible to gauge the net effect of handicraft development on agricultural output as a whole in Ming and Ch'ing times.

INDUSTRY

Although industry had begun to appear toward the end of the Chan-kuo period, it was primarily localized in the sense that both the purchase of raw materials and the marketing of products were carried out within a given locality. At that time the implements employed were still very crude, and methods of production very primitive. Industry began to make wide advances after Ch'in both geographically and technologically. As the Chinese came in contact with the peoples to the west and south they put their own ingenuity to the solution of new problems. As a result, the number of products increased; the level of skills improved; and the division of labor became more specialized.

During the period under review, Chinese handicraft production may be divided broadly into three groups. The first one was farm crafts, which existed partly because output from the land was usually so small that the farmer could not depend solely on it for subsistence. Moreover, the seasonal character of farm operations resulted in an uneven distribution of labor power during the year. Handicrafts provided the Chinese farmer an occupation supplementing agriculture when there was no work for him either at home or outside during the off-seasons. This type of handicraft production was usually performed in the farmer's home with his own labor and with the help of his family. The techniques of production were primitive, and only simple and crude tools were used. The products were generally not marketed, and their quality was very low. The number and variety of handicrafts were large, and most frequently pursued among them were hand-weaving, shoe- and ropemaking, charcoal and paper manufacturing, pottery, carpentry, and tailoring.

Strictly speaking, farm crafts were not a part of industry, but merely subsidiary activities within agriculture. Industry in traditional China comprised primarily two groups: individual craftsmen and handicraft factories. Some of the craftsmen could be found in rural areas where they were engaged primarily in subsistence industries such as smithery, carpentry, weaving, pottery, and tanning. Sometimes they also manufactured relatively luxurious products such as silk cloth, metal utensils, and furniture. These craftsmen catered to the needs of the peasants and contributed significantly to the economic life of Chinese villages.

By far the largest number of individual craftsmen worked in cities. Chinese urban craftsmen obtained a high degree of skill and artistic excellence, and their products were highly prized in distant markets.

Even before the Opium War there were a large number of Chinese handicraft products well known to Westerners such as silver, jade, ivory ornaments, embroidery, silk, and porcelain. The characteristic form of organization in the urban industry was some variety of the master craftsman system, with its journeymen and apprentices, usually related by family and neighborhood ties. Three major categories may be distinguished, frequently overlapping with each other. First is the craftsman who dealt directly with the customer and worked with his own materials and equipment. Second is the craftsman who, while dealing directly with the customer, was provided with materials and was paid for his work in processing them. Last is the craftsman who was supplied with credit and raw materials from a middleman who marketed the finished products.

Handicraft factories represented a higher stage of development in Chinese traditional industry, and normally had a greater size of employment, a larger amount of capital, a higher level of skill, and greater specialization than individual handicrafts. The master craftsman system remained as the main form of organization, but an employer-employee contract system also emerged.

Large-scale handicraft factories appeared as early as the Former Han dynasty when some workshops owned by the rich merchants producing iron implements employed as many as one thousand men each. There was a rapid expansion of iron and other metallic industries stimulated by an increase in demand for various metallic products during Northern Sung, which in turn brought about increased use of coal. Such development in the use of iron and coal was quite comparable to an early industrialization of England from 1540 to 1640, but failed to lead to an industrial revolution in China. The internal disunity of the Sung and the Jurchen and later Mongol invasions and conquests may have accounted partly for the failure.

Large-scale handicraft factories made great strides in Ming and Ch'ing times when noted technical progress was achieved in the iron-smelting, pottery, textile, printing, and shipbuilding industries. Some factories were operated or supervised by the state such as those producing salt, certain kinds of pottery, and textile products. In addition, a number of industrial centers began to appear, including the "porcelain town" of Ching-te-chen in Kiangsi, the silk industry in Southern Kiangsu, the cotton textile industry in Kiangsu and Chekiang, the ironware-manufacturing center of Fushan in Kwangtung, and the mining industry of Yunnan.

TRADE

As noted above, the emergence of trade activities and of the merchant class in Ch'un-ch'iu and Chan-kuo China led to the expansion of industry, which in turn stimulated trade. These mutually stimulating effects between industry and trade developed further in the period after Ch'in and Han.

One characteristic of trade development in traditional China was that a small group of rich merchants accumulated a large amount of commercial capital, while the great majority of the merchant class scraped out a bare subsistence as small traders. The rich merchant accumulated wealth in a number of ways. Since the peasant producers in general could not effect exchange in large volume and over a wide region, the merchants were able to realize substantial profits by taking advantage of local variations in market price to purchase grains where they were cheap and sell them dearly where they were in great demand and could bring higher prices. Moreover, a considerable amount of capital was accumulated by those merchants who were granted by the government monopoly or monopsony rights, or both, in trading specific commodities. In the late Ming and Ch'ing periods, for example, a number of merchants monopsonized the purchase of salt from manufacturers and monopolized its sale to distributors.

In addition, Chinese merchants frequently accumulated capital through not only trading activities but also through landowning, manufacturing, and moneylending. Many merchants used their surplus commercial capital to purchase lands, thus becoming absentee landlords and owning part of agricultural production. They also operated factories managed by hired personnel. This may be seen from the fact that a number of salt merchants in eighteenth-century China became also owners of the whole or substantial parts of the salt factories and were, therefore, large-scale producers. As the merchants accumulated more and more capital, they together with rural landlords provided a principal source of credit from which small, needy peasants and craftsmen borrowed funds often at usurious rates.

Despite the accumulation of commercial capital, a full-fledged capitalistic system failed to develop in China. This may be explained in part by the dominant intellectual attitudes and traditional patterns of thought in Chinese society. By the most respectable standards, merchants bore a social stigma. They were seen as essentially parasites on the other classes of the traditional ranking system, and thus were assigned the lowest status in the system. The ideal pattern for a man was to exempt himself from mercantile activity and to be identified with the gentry-official who commanded high social prestige in traditional China. A study of the salt merchants of Yang-chou in the eighteenth century indicates that affluent salt merchant families habitually entertained and subsidized scholars on a lavish scale, and that "almost as soon as the family became well-to-do, its youthful members were encouraged to embark upon a scholarly, and ultimately an official, career, with the result that the merchant element in the family became less and less predominant."[1] Thus the mode of life and social mobility of Chinese merchants frequently diverted the bulk of their wealth to nonproductive uses. The amount of commercial capital so diverted may have resulted in splendid cultural and intellectual progress but not in economic development.

Although rich merchants were able to accumulate a considerable amount of commercial capital, the majority of the merchant class consisted of persons who depended solely on trading activities for a living. Like individual peasants and craftsmen, these small traders remained at the very margin of subsistence. They possessed only a meager amount of capital, operated a small shop, a stand, or stall, or traveled while peddling their wares. They were widely dispersed in town and countryside, and provided services of purchasing, retailing, and transporting commodities over short distances. Unlike the rich merchants who with large commercial capital were able to affect to a certain extent agricultural and industrial production, the small businessmen were dependent on agriculture and industry for subsistence.

Concluding Remarks

According to a modern theory of economic development, for a predominantly agricultural country with an abundant supply of labor there exist at least two basic preconditions for economic growth. First, agricultural productivity should be raised to such an extent that a sufficient amount of agricultural surplus can be created to finance industrial development; and second, certain means should be found to convert such surplus into industrial capital. In the China of pre-treaty-port days, neither of these preconditions existed.

1. Ping-ti Ho, "The Salt Merchants of Yang Chou: A Study of Commercial Capitalism in Eighteenth-Century China," *Harvard Journal of Asiatic Studies,* 17 (Nos. 1 and 2, June, 1954), 130-68; quotation on p. 165.

The productivity of Chinese agriculture had remained at a very low level primarily due to the small scale of farming and the abundance of farm labor, both of which tended to limit the possibilities of technological development. The small size of landholdings was mainly a result of the traditional framework of Chinese agriculture, characterized by the growing degree of tenancy particularly after T'ang times and by the traditional inheritance system of dividing land more or less equally among surviving heirs. Moreover, according to China's age-old practice there was frequently a further subdivision of fields within these small farms for the purpose of enabling peasants to pool the risk of flood and drought.

The minute scale of farming, coupled with the abundant supply of farm hands, meant that cultivation involved an intensive application of labor. The methods of cultivation employed in China were very primitive and unscientific. Farm work was performed almost entirely by human labor equipped with simple and crude implements. Irrigation work was largely carried out through laborious means. Fertility was conserved primarily by the use of night soil and other forms of organic matter. The use of these labor-intensive methods of farming inevitably resulted in low output per farmer.

Low labor productivity had kept the small farmer in traditional China at a very low level of income, which in turn made it difficult for him to abstain from consumption as would be necessary for savings and capital accumulation. Among those who did save, there was the problem of economic incentive for channeling their savings into productive uses. As land became scarce and labor abundant, the farmer had little interest in introducing labor-saving improvements. This was especially true for the tenant, because whatever improvements he made on the land through investment of either labor or capital would belong to the landlord and not to him.

In consequence, any impetus toward enhancing agricultural productivity in China had to come from the landlord. But the landlord in general was not interested in improving the land. The most parasitic and oppressive of the landlords were the absentee owners, including official-gentry and merchants, who often took no interest in the land other than to count their income. In view of the social value attached to the owning of land, they often spent a great deal of their savings in augmenting land holdings, which sometimes resulted in higher land values but not in real capital creation. While they tried to squeeze as much as they could from the output of their tenants, the landlords put very little into the land in return.

The chronic lack of productive investment and of technological improvement had resulted in low agricultural productivity in China. The low productivity of Chinese agriculture, while not capable of yielding sufficient surplus, does not imply that agricultural savings did not exist in traditional China. In fact, the huge amount of government expenditures on indemnities, servicing foreign loans, and military activities in the late Ch'ing and Republican periods suggests that a certain amount of savings potential in agricultural China could have been mobilized to finance economic development. But such efforts had never been made in pre-1840 China. There did not exist in China a special class of people willing and able to perform entrepreneurial functions, like the one in Meiji Japan. Very few people in the official-gentry, landlord, and merchant classes were willing to invest appreciable proportions of their income in industry. No significant portion of state revenues had been devoted to industrial development as in the case of early Meiji Japan, in which the proceeds of taxation on agriculture were utilized to create certain key industrial projects, or as in the case of post-1949 China, in which industrialization was financed by means of forced savings in agriculture. All in all, in traditional China no concerted, all-out efforts were attempted to effectively mobilize existing savings for development.

In the absence of preconditions for economic growth, the traditional economic structure continued to dominate until the Opium War, after which the monolithic character of the agrarian economy of China began to change as a result of foreign participation in the Chinese economy. But more drastic and revolutionary changes have taken place only since 1949, when the Communist government has taken a series of measures to reorganize the Chinese economy.

XVI

Economic

Trends in Modern

China

BY

CHI-MING HOU

Introduction

This essay deals with the major economic trends in China since 1840. The selection of this date is, of course, highly arbitrary; I simply follow the common practice of regarding the Opium War as the starting point of modern China. For my purpose this might be justified on the grounds that whatever economic change China has had after 1840 may be regarded as a step toward or identified as modern economic growth. Economic growth is commonly defined as sustained rise in per capita income, and modern economic growth may be considered that epoch of economic growth which is primarily based on the extended application of science to problems of economic production.[1] This is the type of economic growth which the West has experienced in modern times—a type China has followed.

In this sense, the economy of modern China differs from that of traditional China. In traditional China, that is before 1840, there were undoubtedly economic changes—for example, the commercial growth and urbanization on the lower Yangtze in the sixteenth and seventeenth centuries, the introduction and widespread dissemination of cotton in early Ch'ing—but these changes were not patterned after the West. It is doubtful that in traditional China there was any epoch when there was a continuous or regular flow into the economy of new technology and a prolonged rise in per capita income.

But has modern economic growth really taken place in China? Obviously, there have been economic changes in modern China and these have been after the Western pattern. But is it true that there has been a substantial rise in per capita income or even product per worker?

In the following pages, I will first describe the nature of economic change which took place in modern China until 1949 and discuss the underlying forces which brought about such a change. I will then describe and discuss the economic developments under the Communist regime.

The Western Challenge

Some thirty years ago, Dennis Robertson spoke of trade as an engine of growth. He was, of course, talking about the role of

1. Simon Kuznets, *Modern Economic Growth: Rate, Structure, and Spread* (New Haven: Yale University Press, 1966), p. 9.

international trade in economic development: trade opens up markets, permits greater division of labor and hence efficiency, serves as a means and vehicle for the dissemination of technical knowledge and the transmission of ideas, and induces movement of capital and enterprise. Many would agree to the view that this "engine" led to, or at least accelerated, the rapid economic development of the newer countries (such as United States, Canada, New Zealand) in the nineteenth century.

China was by no means a new country, but she, too, was affected by this engine. Indeed, much of the economic change which took place in China after 1840 could be traced to international trade. It was trade which drove the West to open China's door by force and led to foreign investment in China. It was foreign trade and investment which set off a chain of reactions that were responsible for whatever industrial development or economic modernization China had before 1937.

Trade relations between China and the West had existed for centuries before the Opium War. In fact, there had been a sharp increase in China's external trade since the latter part of the eighteenth century. Trade with England and India, her principal partners, increased more than ten times from the 1760s to the 1830s.[2] But Chinese external trade, except for Spanish trade at Amoy, was carried on only at Canton, the one port open to foreign trade since 1757. Even in Canton, foreign merchants were not allowed to deal with Chinese directly: they could deal only with a government-authorized organization known as the Co-hong, a group nominally consisting of thirteen merchants. Furthermore, foreign merchants were confined to a limited area with very stringent restrictions; for instance, no women, guns, spears, or arms of any kind were permitted.[3] To the English merchants who saw China as a huge potential market, this restrictive system was intolerable. But to the Chinese who never saw much need for Western products, who now were outraged by the harmful effects of the most important item of imports, opium, and who never deemed contact with foreigners desirable anyway, there was little reason to relax the trade restrictions. This was the fundamental cause of the Opium War in 1839.

2. Chi-ming Hou, *Foreign Investment and Economic Development in China, 1840-1937* (Cambridge, Mass.: Harvard University Press, 1965), p. 7.

3. Yu-kwei Cheng, *Foreign Trade and Industrial Development of China* (Seattle: University of Washington Press, 1956), p. 4.

China lost and was forced by the Treaty of Nanking to relax her trade restrictions. Thus, five ports were opened where foreign merchants could trade directly with their Chinese customers (these ports have been known as treaty ports) and "treaty tariff" was imposed to assure that tariff could not be used as a weapon to restrict trade (the tariff rates were fixed at five percent ad valorem for all imported and exported articles, and China did not regain her tariff autonomy until 1928). Foreign merchants, now under the protection of extraterritorial rights, learned more about China, made more profit on trade, and began to expand their economic activities. By taking advantage of Chinese material and labor they established factories to manufacture in the treaty ports and the nearby interior. Quite naturally their manufactures were in fields related to trade, such as ship repairing, shipbuilding, processing for exports (especially tea) and import-substituting products (matches, paper, soap, etc.). But all this was done illegally, for foreigners were not allowed to establish factories in treaty ports until 1895 when China was defeated by Japan and the Treaty of Shimonoseki was concluded. (Then, all powers received this privilege by virtue of the most favored nation clause.)

But treaty ports were no place to build railroads and open mining. Railroads were necessary to promote trade and extend political influence, and mining was desirable to supply coal for steamers or for export (especially iron to Japan). The right to build railroads and open up mines had to be obtained from the Chinese government. Thus, the "scramble for concessions" for these rights (or *sphere of interest*") reached its height in the decade after 1895. The Chinese Eastern Railway (Russia), South Manchuria Railway (Japan), Yunnan Railway (France), Kiaochou-Tsinan Railway (Germany), and Canton-Kowloon Railway (British Section) were all built around this time primarily for political and military reasons. In mining, France, Russia, Japan, Germany, and Great Britain all obtained important concessions.[4]

In the meantime, more unequal treaties were concluded between China and Western powers—all served the purpose of protecting or extending the latter's economic privileges in China. Quite understandably, many Chinese were outraged by the growing foreign economic activity which was imposed upon the nation against her will. The presence of foreign businessmen was regarded as a symbol of invasion

4. Hou, *Foreign Investment . . . in China*, ch. 3.

and foreign domination, and their success was feared as a drain of wealth from the Chinese economy and a threat to Chinese-owned industries, both modern and traditional.

It was under these circumstances that China began to develop modern industries. First, fearful of foreign domination, the Manchu government began to build in the 1860s arsenals and dockyards to manufacture military weapons and ammunition in support of the "self-strengthening" (*tzu-chiang*) movement which was initiated for the purpose of defending the country. In the 1870s it began to adopt economic measures to counterbalance foreign economic penetration: by establishing state enterprises and, more important, by adopting the formula of "official supervising and merchant undertaking" (*kuan-tu shang-pan*), according to which the government was to exercise initiative and supervision while the private individuals supplied capital, skill, and management.

Shocked by the fast expansion of foreign enterprises in China since 1895 and the fierce economic rivalry among the Powers in search for spheres of interest, the Ch'ing government was now joined by the populace in the movement of Recovering Economic Interests. From 1903 to 1908, no fewer than 265 corporations were founded by private individuals. The by-laws of many corporations explicitly stated that they were founded for the purpose of resisting foreign economic influence in China.

Thus, foreign economic activity in China, which was regarded as a symbol of foreign invasion, provoked the spirit of nationalism and provided the will to develop modern industries. When this was aided by its positive effects such as demonstrating that investment in industrial undertakings was profitable, introducing new kinds of industry, providing a training ground for Chinese to acquire modern techniques, and establishing a framework of social overhead (banking, public utilities, railroads, etc.), the basis of a modern sector eventually emerged in the Chinese economy.

This is not to say that any substantial industrial growth took place in China: in the 1860s only ten arsenals and dockyards were built; between 1870 and 1900 only a dozen or so enterprises were formed under the arrangement of *kuan-tu shang-pan*. From 1903 to 1908, the total capital of private enterprises is estimated to have been less than Chinese $130 million.[5] The total expenditure of official funds for all

5. *Ibid.*, p. 134. See also Albert Feuerwerker, *China's Early Industrialization* (Cambridge, Mass.: Harvard University Press, 1958).

government-owned and private enterprises (in the form of loans) was only a few million taels a year in the 1860s and 1870s and probably close to 10 million in the 1890s. As a proportion of total government revenues, which probably amounted to 60-70 million taels in the 1860s-1870s and to 80-90 million taels in the 1890s for the central government, and perhaps twice as much for the provincial governments, an expenditure of as much as 10 million taels represented a large sum. In relation to the total population or total national income, however, it was surely pitifully small.

But the performance must be evaluated in terms of the historical background. After all, as late as 1867 a powerful government official (Wo-jen) was still arguing that the fundamental effort to establish a nation would lie in the minds of people, propriety, and righteousness, not in techniques, and that astronomy and mathematics would be of very little use.[6] And as late as 1880 there was still a lively debate among Chinese officials over whether railroads should be built.[7] Thus, to change the traditional environment into one in which modern development was possible was by no means a small achievement. Development in China was basically a matter of change in the attitude of the goverment and the people toward economic affairs, in the ways savings were employed, and in the level of technology and inventiveness. It is this change of attitude and habit of doing things which is often difficult to make and requires a long time. In the case of China, foreign economic activity in China surely played an important role in initiating and accelerating such changes.

The Modern Sector
(1840-1937)

The development of the modern sector in the Chinese economy displayed certain characteristics which are quite different from many other countries (both developed and underdeveloped) and are often inaccurately understood. Let us examine these characteristics more carefully.

6. Ssu-yü Teng and John K. Fairbank, *China's Response to the West: A Documentary Survey, 1839-1923* (Cambridge, Mass.: Harvard University Press, 1954), p. 76.
7. Hou, *Foreign Investment . . . in China*, pp. 242-43.

FOREIGN TRADE

In physical terms, China's foreign trade grew continuously at about 2.5 percent a year (compound) from 1867 to 1932. The total volume at its peak in 1928-29 was about U.S. $1,500 million. It dropped to U.S. $724 million in 1933 and U.S. $809 million in 1936 (Manchuria included)[8] partly because of upward tariff revision and partly because of world-wide depression. For the year 1933, for which national income estimate is available, the trade-income ratio was about 9 percent.[9] Since there was as almost always in previous years (except 1864 and 1872-76) an unfavorable trade balance (total imports of merchandise being greater than total exports of merchandise), total merchandise exports formed about 3 percent of national income for that year.[10] The trade-income ratios were, of course, higher when trade volume was at its peak levels in 1929-31 (assuming national income was roughly the same as in 1933). Total trade was about 12 percent and total merchandise exports about 5 percent of total national income.[11] These ratios were probably smaller in the earlier year than in the 1930s (the rate of growth of foreign trade can be assumed to be larger than that of national income). As compared with other countries, China was among those with the lowest trade-income ratios. This may be explained partly by the low level of income per capita, partly by the size of the country (as measured by total product),[12] and partly by the lack of "export development," which will be explained below.

An important feature of China's external trade was the increasing tendency toward diversification. In the early years imports consisted chiefly of opium and textiles. In the 1860s these items accounted for nearly 80 percent of total imports. By the 1930s no single item formed more than 10 percent of total imports (with the exception of raw cotton in 1930 and 1931). Exports showed the same tendency. In the

8. Teng and Fairbank, *China's Response to the West,* p. 189.

9. The national income estimate was made by Ta-chung Liu and Kung-chia Yeh, *The Economy of the Chinese Mainland: National Income and Economic Development, 1933-1959* (Princeton: Princeton University Press, 1965), p. 66. Their estimate was actually for net domestic product, which may be regarded as roughly the same as national income.

10. Hou, *Foreign Investment . . . in China,* p. 189.

11. *Ibid.*

12. Kuznets, *Modern Economic Growth,* p. 430, suggests that there is an adverse relationship between foreign trade proportions (that is, foreign trade as a proportion of national income) and the size of a country as measured by national income.

1840s tea and silk constituted more than 90 percent of total exports. By 1931, silk accounted for no more than 14 percent, and tea for only 4 percent of total exports. The only commodity which accounted for more than 20 percent in the 1930s was beans and bean cakes (22 percent in 1936). Aside from silk, and tea (before 1915), no other commodity constituted more than 10 percent of China's total exports in the twentieth century (up to 1937). This figure may be contrasted with that of other underdeveloped countries, many of which in 1938, for example, had 50 percent or more of their exports concentrated in one primary commodity. As a result, the Chinese economy was subject to much less instability due to fluctuations of exports than many other countries.

Rates of Growth of the Modern Section of the Chinese Economy Before 1949*

Indicator	Period	Annual Rates in Percent
Physical quantity of imports	1867-1932	2.5
Physical quantity of exports	1867-1932	2.4
Railroad mileage	1894-1911	22.1
	1911-1935	2.2
	1894-1937	10.3
Tonnage of Chinese-owned foreign steamers	1882-1910	5.1
	1910-1924	11.2
	1928-1935	12.8
Pig iron production of modern mines	1900-1937	9.8
Coal production of modern mines	1912-1936	8.2
Cotton yarn spindles	1890-1936	11.6
Loans of Chinese modern banks	1921-1936	12.3
Industrial production	1912-1949	5.5
	1912-1936	13.8
	1931-1936	9.3

*Includes Manchuria.

Sources:
   For industrial production, see John K. Chang, "Industrial Development Mainland China," 1912-1949, in *Journal of Economic History*, 1 (March, 1967) 68.
   For all other indicators, see Chi-meng Hou, *Foreign Investment and Economics*.

A major reason for the lack of concentration on a few commodities for export was probably the fact that only a small amount of foreign investment in China was employed for export development. Total foreign investment in mining was U.S. $59 million in 1914 and U.S. $123 million in 1931, forming 3.7 percent and 4.0 percent of total foreign investment in China in the respective years. Foreign investment in agriculture was virtually nonexistent. The fact that foreigners had to negotiate with the Chinese government in order to obtain the right to invest outside of the treaty ports, the restrictive nature of Chinese mining regulations, and the expected difficulty of organizing Chinese farmers for large-scale production must have been important reasons why foreign capital was small in primary production.[13]

INDUSTRIAL DEVELOPMENT

Available statistical data are not adequate to construct a comprehensive index of industrial growth in China before 1949. But they are sufficient to justify the belief that modern industrial growth did take place, perhaps at a rather rapid rate. The various indicators as given in the table testify to this point. All these indicators (except railroads) display a linear trend when plotted in a semilogarithmic scale, showing, in the long run, a constant rate of growth. There are, of course, fluctuations in the growth rates, but the general upward trend is clear. (For instance, Chang's index of industrial production shows that the average annual rate of growth was 13.8 percent for 1912-20; 8.4 percent for 1928-36; and 4.5 percent for 1936-42.)

That foreign capital played a significant role in industrial development is beyond doubt. Foreign enterprises not only performed the pioneering entrepreneurial function of introducing modern technology in many fields of production, but also accounted for a large share of the modern sector of the Chinese economy. China's railroads were in the main either foreign-owned (foreign direct investment) or built with foreign loans. Foreign share in total shipping (steamers) accounted for about 80 percent of the total from the 1890s to 1930. Nearly all the pig iron and iron ore that were produced by modern mines before 1937 came from mines which were financed wholly or in part by foreign capital. More than half of the total output of coal in China from 1912 to 1937 was produced by mines that were either

13. For other issues related to foreign trade, such as the unfavorable movement of the terms of trade and the balance of payments problem, see Hou, *Foreign Investment . . . in China*, ch. 8.

foreign-owned or controlled by means of large loans. For a number of manufacturing industries, foreign-owned enterprises accounted for more than 50 percent of total output in 1933, although for the manufacturing industries as a whole the ratio was 35 percent. The largest part (perhaps as high as 90 percent as late as the 1930s) of China's external trade and other international transactions was handled by foreign banks and trading firms in China. Thus, there can be no doubt that foreign capital was dominant in the modern sector of the Chinese economy.

The dominance of foreign capital did not mean, however, that there was no room for Chinese-owned modern enterprises. As a matter of fact, the Chinese share in the modern sector remained remarkably stable in the long run, suggesting that Chinese firms as a group could grow as fast as foreign firms. The growth records of some of the large Chinese firms (especially in cotton textiles and coal mining) are quite impressive, indicative of the strength of Chinese firms in the face of foreign competition. Thus, the evidence does not seem to support the fear expressed by Chang Chih-tung (in protest against the Treaty of Shimonoseki) and later by many others that the Chinese firms could not grow in the presence of foreign enterprise.

It is not easy to explain how it was possible for Chinese and foreign enterprises to coexist. It may be that the often-mentioned advantages enjoyed by foreign firms as compared with Chinese firms (such as strong financial background, better technical and managerial skill, and immunity from Chinese laws, taxes, and official abuse) has been exaggerated. It may be that the Chinese firms enjoyed certain advantages which were denied to foreign firms such as nationalism, boycotts, the "buy-Chinese" appeal, labor relations, local knowledge, and location. Or it may be that in many fields of production the market was divided between Chinese and foreign firms with the latter concentrating on finer products in the case of textiles and cigarettes, serving a different region in the case of mining, specializing in international transactions in the case of banking, or eliminating price competition by agreement in the case of shipping. Probably all the above factors were at work, though with varying degrees of importance.

The dominance of foreign capital was probably also responsible for the location of industrial development in China. Since foreign investment (except railroads and mining) was confined to treaty ports, it was natural that China's modern industries should be founded mainly in the coastal areas and along the navigable rivers where treaty or open ports were found. It was in these places that Chinese-owned enterprises also clustered at least in part because of the advantages created by foreign firms (banking facilities, public utilities, labor force, law and order in foreign concessions, etc.).

Probably the same may be said of the pattern of industrial development before 1937, which was heavily consumers' goods-oriented (textiles, food, drinks, tobacco, and utilities in particular). For foreign direct investments in China were made largely in fields associated with foreign trade—shipping, banking, ship repairing, coal for steamers as well as for export, and public utilities to serve foreign residents. The increase of imports established a market for many articles which were then produced in China, taking advantage of cheap local labor and raw material. This explains why, in manufacturing, foreign investment was most active in textile, tobacco, chemicals, water, gas, and electricity. The same pattern prevailed for Chinese capital.

The Traditional Sector, 1840-1937

It is sometimes maintained that the "traditional" or "indigenous" sector of the Chinese economy, such as handicrafts, small mines, native banks, junks, and coolie carriers, was helplessly hampered or even ruined because of competition from the modern sector of the economy. How true is this assessment? Available evidence indicates that as late as in the 1930s the Chinese economy remained traditional. In mining, aside from coal and iron where modern mines scored tremendous progress and became predominant in the 1930s small native mines remained important for other minerals before 1937, although their exact shares in total production cannot be determined. In manufacturing, handicrafts accounted for no less than 72 to 76 percent of the total production in 1933. In shipping, traditional means accounted for no less than 86 percent of the total output in 1933. Native banks were active in all commercial centers of the country and were engaged in all types of financing. (In Shanghai, where modern banks grew most rapidly, the financial strength of native banks was estimated to be equal to one third of that of Chinese modern banks in the 1930s.)

The emergence of the modern sector, of course, means there must have been a decline of the relative share of the traditional sector.

There are no statistics to suggest, however, that the latter suffered any absolute decline. On the contrary, in cases such as coal mining, shipping, and cotton weaving, it may even have grown, although at a low rate.[14] An important explanation for the ability of the traditional sector to survive is that traditional technology employed more labor relative to capital, as compared with the modern sector, where more capital intensive technology was used. Since labor was cheap and capital expensive, it was entirely possible that the unit cost of production by traditional technology was the same or even lower than that of production by modern technology. As a result, modern technology could do no more than concentrate on products which were beyond the reach of traditional technology. Since these products were expensive, they were also beyond the purchasing power of the masses. This seemed to be the case in many fields of production. The above analysis does not exclude other factors that may have helped the traditional sector to survive: high transportation costs, consumption habits, etc.

It is almost impossible to assess in quantitative terms the nature or direction of agricultural development in modern China. We have little reliable data on the trends of land-population ratio, total food production, yield per unit of land, labor productivity, agricultural organization, and agricultural technology. After regarding the official Chinese population data for 1851-1949 as most defective, Ping-ti Ho[15] suggests or "guesses" (this is his own word) that the Chinese population may have reached 430 million in 1850. Liu and Yeh[16] estimate that in 1933 the total Chinese population was roughly 500 million. If we take these two estimates, the increase was about 16 percent over a period of eighty-two years. (The rate of increase of agricultural population would be slightly smaller than this because of urbanization.) But it is not possible to make even such rough estimates for total cultivated area.

If it is not possible to make quantitative statements on the historical development of important indicators of agricultural development, we do have some quantitative knowledge about Chinese agriculture in the 1930s thanks primarily to the monumental work of John Lossing Buck.[17]

14. *Ibid.*, ch. 7.
15. *Studies on the Population of China, 1368-1953* (Cambridge, Mass.: Harvard University Press, 1959), p. 97.
16. Liu and Yeh, *The Economy of the Chinese Mainland*, p. 171.
17. *Land Utilization in China* (3 vols., Shanghai: The Commercial Press, 1937).

Buck's survey was a study of 16,786 farms in 168 localities and 38,256 farm families in twenty-two provinces in China, 1929-33. According to this study, the average size of farms was 4.22 acres for owners, 4.25 for part owners (owned and rented), and 3.56 for tenants, with the average of 4.17 for all farmers. (The mean size of family was as follows: total families, 5.21 persons; landlord, 5.14; owner, 5.38; part owner, 5.68; tenant, 4.76.) But the farm land of a family was scattered in different localities. The average area per parcel (in acres) ranged from 0.52 for small farms to 1.75 for very large farms. This parceling system, evidently a product of equal inheritance, resulted in waste in boundaries and in operation.

There were enormous amounts of underutilization of labor on a year-round basis. According to Buck, idleness averaged 1.7 months per able-bodied man (over fifteen and under sixty years of age). The winter months, however, accounted for 80 percent of the idle time. This does not mean that there was disguised unemployment in the sense that, other things being equal, farm labor can be reduced without lowering total output. For many farms reported a labor shortage during busy seasons. It may have been possible that with some modification of farm practices (changing the cropping system, for instance) or some modest amount of investment in farm imple-ments, considerable amounts of labor could be removed without reducing output.

The small amount of land per head of farming population resulted in a low level of output per person. According to Buck, the average production of grain-equivalent per man-equivalent for all localities was only 1,400 kilograms. (The corresponding figure for the United States was 20,000 kilograms.) Despite intensive farming, the unit yields (output per acre of various crops), though better than those of India or Russia, were not as high as those of Japan or many other countries, such as Italy, Germany, Great Britain, and the United States.

The low level of output per person was of course the fundamental reason for low standards of living.

The lot of the peasants, especially the poor peasants, was further worsened by high interest rates (averaging 32 percent per year) which often kept them perpetually in debt following an extraordinary event such as a funeral or a wedding. These rates also made it extremely difficult to borrow for investment purposes. On the other hand, the peasants' lot was improved to some extent by the favorable movement of the terms of trade (prices received by farmers for products they sold in relation to prices paid by them for products they bought) from 1906 to 1930. (For the next three years, the reverse was true.)[18] Also, farm taxes, an important burden to the peasant, did not rise as fast as farm prices from 1906 to 1933.[19]

Farm land was mostly privately owned (93 percent). Nearly three fourths of the farm land was owned by the farmer himself and a little over one fourth was rented.[20] Over one half of the farmers were owners, less than one third part owners, and 17 percent were tenants.[21] In North China (wheat region, to use Buck's terminology), tenancy was less, over three fourths of the farmers were owners, while in the south (rice region) less than two fifths were owners. Thus, on the basis of Buck's data, the problem of land tenancy was not quite as serious as is generally believed.

As in other underdeveloped countries, rentals were high. The actual levels differed, according to the type of renting systems. In the case of share rent, the most common rate was from 40 to 50 percent of the total crop, depending upon the amount of assistance (seeds, implements, etc.) given by the landlord. In the case of cash rent, the rent averaged 46 percent of the gross product. These rates were obviously extremely high from the viewpoint of the tenant.[22] But in terms of the value of land, the average cash rent was only 11 percent and the average share rent 14 percent.[23] They were by no means out of order as compared with the returns of other forms of investment.

A Dualistic Economy, 1840-1937

The above analysis suggests that in pre-1937 China a modern sector and a traditional sector coexisted. The modern sector was largely confined to the coastal areas and grew at a fairly rapid rate. But its share in the total economy was rather small. It was, in Tawney's phrase, merely a modern fringe that was stitched along the

18. *Ibid.* I: 319.
19. *Ibid.,* I: 316, 330.
20. *Ibid.,* I: 194.
21. *Ibid.*
22. Whether this would make the tenants resentful of the landlords, thus creating a feeling of class antagonism, is hard to say. R. H. Tawney, in *Land and Labour in China* (London: George Allen and Unwin Ltd., 1932), observed that it did not.
23. Hou, *Foreign Investment . . . in China,* p. 26.

hem of an ancient garment.[24] Although there was some change in the garment, it remained basically ancient in the 1930s.

It is estimated that in 1933 modern nonagricultural sectors contributed (in 1933 prices) only 12.6 percent to the net domestic product,[25] and gross domestic investment (in 1933 prices) was only 5 percent of gross domestic expenditure.[26] Thus, even allowing for a large margin of error, these figures make it clear that the Chinese economy in the 1930s displayed the characteristics of an underdeveloped country.

There were, of course, changes in the traditional sector. As noted earlier, there was growth in certain areas. There was also improvement in technology. For example, the yarn consumed on the hand looms in many areas was largely supplied first by imports, and subsequently furnished by textile factories established in China. Also, the replacement of the age-old wooden hand looms by iron looms (first made available by import from Japan and then produced at home) made hand weaving much more efficient. Improvement in technology may also be found in other handicraft industries.

The fact remains, however, that the traditional sector witnessed no fundamental change. This is particularly true for agriculture. The various attempts by the government to raise agricultural output (beginning in the 1860s) evidently had no significant effect. The establishment of modern industries had some effects on farming (for example, the manufacture of cigarettes induced the growing of American tobacco by some Chinese farmers), but again they were limited.

War and Inflation, 1937–1949

The Sino-Japanese War of 1937 played an important role in the recent history of China both economically and politically. The war ended the momentum of the modernization programs under the Nationalist government and eventually brought about economic collapse and the downfall of the government. Progress toward modernization had been made in the early 1930s on a broad front:

24. Tawney, *Land and Labour in China*, p. 13.
25. Liu and Yeh, *The Economy of the Chinese Mainland*, p. 89.
26. *Ibid.*, p. 80.

industrial development, education, public health, banking, the monetary system, agricultural experiment stations, rural credit, etc. But these changes needed time to affect the total picture. Then the war changed the picture completely.[27]

The immediate result of the war was a sharp increase in government expenditures. This could not be met by government revenues, which actually declined, principally because of the loss of the rich coastal regions. (By the end of 1938, Japan had occupied regions producing about 40 percent of the agricultural output and possessing virtually all the modern industrial capacity.) The only resort available to the government was printing money. This inevitably resulted in inflation which, once started, accelerated at an increasing rate. Thus, the increase in the general price level was 40-50 percent a year from 1937 to 1939 but jumped to 300 percent a year in 1941-45.

There was a pause (in fact a drop for a few months) in price increases right after the war in 1945. But, as the political situation became tense and civil war broke out, there was little recovery in domestic production and little decline in government expenditures. The expected foreign aid was also very slow in coming. As a result, inflation resumed its upward course at an even faster rate. (From the middle of 1946 to the middle of 1948 the general price level increased 600 times.) After some unsuccessful attempts to remedy the situation in late 1948 and early 1949, the monetary system completely collapsed.

As is well known, inflation always nas an effect on income distribution. In the Chinese case, the losers were principally civil servants, soldiers, teachers, and other salaried employees whose living standards were lowered sharply. These were the groups, or the modern successors of the groups who had an important role in Chinese political and social change.

It should be noted that during the war with Japan there was considerable industrial development as well as inflation in the occupied areas. In Shanghai the index of industrial production went up from 75 in 1937 (1936=100) to 138 in 1941. In North China it went up from 100 in 1939 to 148 in 1942.[28] In Manchuria, which had been

27. The following discussion relies heavily on Kia-ngau Chang, *The Inflationary Spiral: The Experience of China, 1939-1950* (New York: Massachusetts Institute of Technology and John Wiley, 1963); Shun-hsin Chou, *The Chinese Inflation, 1937-1949* (New York: Columbia University Press, 1963); and Arthur N. Young, *China's Wartime Finance and Inflation, 1937-1945* (Cambridge, Mass.: Harvard University Press, 1965).

28. Cheng, *Foreign Trade and Industrial Development of China*, p. 116.

occupied by Japan since 1932, substantial industrial development took place. Industrial and mining production increased 5.5 times from 1931-32 to 1944-45, or at an annual rate of 14 percent, although the tempo was not accelerated until after 1937.[29] Unfortunately, much of the industrial development in Manchuria during the war was disrupted by the massive dismantling of plants by Russia in 1945.

After 1945 the civil war did tremendous damage to the economy. According to Chang's index of industrial production it was 101 in 1948 and 119 in 1949, as compared with 135 in 1936, 177 in 1942 (the peak), and 141 in 1944.[30] For a number of key commodities, the level of production in 1949 was substantially lower than in previous respective peak years.[31]

Goals of the First Five-Year Plan

The initial task of the Communist regime was, of course, to rehabilitate the economy, a task which was officially announced to have been completed by the end of 1952. Official statistics claim that national income increased 70 percent from 1949 to 1952. While it is not possible to say how reliable such statistics are, it is interesting to note that according to one estimate the total and per capita products in 1952 exceeded those in 1933 by about 20 percent and 6 percent respectively.[32] The First Five-Year Plan (FFYP) began in 1953, although the actual details of the Plan were not made public until August, 1955.

The primary long-range goal of the FFYP was to establish a socialist society through "socialist industrialization." "Socialist" means the socialization or state ownership of trade and industry, while industrialization means the development of heavy industry at such a speed that in fifteen years the foundation of a self-sufficient industrial state and a modernized national defense will be laid. To the Communist planners, all these goals were, of course, consistent.

29. *Ibid.*, chs. 9 and 14.
30. John K. Chang, "Industrial Development of Mainland China 1912-1949," in *The Journal of Economic History,* I (March, 1967) 56-81 (p. 66).
31. Alexander Eckstein, "The Econmic Heritage," in *Economic Trends in Communist China,* ed. by Alexander Eckstein, *et al.* (Chicago: Aldine Publishing Company, 1968), pp. 33-85.
32. Ta-chung Liu, "The Tempo of Economic Development of the Chinese Mainland, 1949-65," in Joint Economic Committee, Congress of the United States, *An Economic Profile of Mainland China* (2 vols., Washington, Government Printing Office, 1967), I, 45-75.

National defense requires economic self-sufficiency, and the development of heavy industry is necessary for these purposes. Agricultural development was expected at a much slower pace, but the planned mechanization of agriculture would also require the development of heavy industry to produce necessary tools, machines, and other things formerly imported (chemical fertilizer, for instance).

The inherited economic base and the expected speed of development would necessarily imply a slow rise in living standards. A large proportion of the national income would have to be saved in order to finance the vast investment programs necessary for the rapid development of heavy industry. Thus, it was a part of the Plan that the rate of increase of real wages would fall substantially behind the rate of increase of labor productivity.

The socialization of trade and industry was probably regarded both as an end, in that state ownership was believed equivalent to the elimination of exploitation, and as means, in the sense that only state control could advance society toward the goals the state set. But this was to be done gradually. Early in 1950, the state had already set up a control apparatus in such a way that private commercial and industrial concerns were reduced to no more than the agents of the state trading firms, which controlled daily necessities and strategic raw materials. Then the formula of state-private joint operation was adopted, which by the fall of 1955 included virtually all except the very small private firms. In 1956, only 3 percent of retail sales and 1.3 percent of gross industrial products were by the private sector.[33] The term "joint operation" is actually misleading, for the previous private owners had virtually nothing to say about the fundamental policies under which their enterprises were operated. They were merely paid a certain fixed rate of interest for their capital and salaries for their services (if they were retained).

For agriculture, socialization did not mean state ownership of land and other means of production. According to the First Five-Year Plan, it called for no more than the transformation of one third of farming households into elementary producers' cooperatives by the end of 1957. In fact, even this was done on a gradual basis. After land reform (redistribution of land from the rich to the poor) was completed by 1952, efforts were made to induce peasants to join mutual-aid teams, a time-honored institution in Chinese farming. By the end

33. Choh-ming Li, *Economic Development of Communist China* (Berkeley, Calif.: University of California Press, 1959), p. 16.

of 1954, 60 percent of the farm households had joined these teams. This was the first step toward group or collective farming.

Elementary producers' cooperatives aimed at a larger unit of operation containing about 30 or 40 households each. Land, draft animals, and farm tools were still privately owned but were utilized under central management. Each household was allowed to retain a small private plot (not in excess of five percent of the per capita land acreage of the cooperative). Rent was paid for land by the cooperative, and labor was rewarded according to its contribution to production. By the end of 1954, only 11 percent of farm households belonged to these cooperatives; the ratio rose to 60 percent by the end of 1955.[34] This increase was greater than the FFYP had planned, evidently due to the insistence of Mao Tse-tung.

The advanced producers' cooperatives (or collectives) were not even mentioned in the FFYP, but in one year's time (by 1956) nearly 90 percent of farm households joined the collectives. The size of such collectives varied, the government-recommended size being from 100 to 300 households. Probably for most collectives they comprised the households of a village. Under the collectives, land and other major means of production were collectively owned. Land was collectivized without compensation, whereas other means of production (draft animals, for example) were bought by the collective from their owners at fixed prices. Private plots continued as under the cooperatives. For income distribution, labor was paid according to its contribution, but rent was no longer paid for the use of land or other resources.

Pattern of Development
1952-1957

The Chinese Communists scored a very impressive record of industrial growth in 1952-57. Estimates vary. The average annual rate of growth of factory production was 14 percent according to Kang Chao,[35] and 19 percent according to Liu and Yeh.[36] As planned, the growth of heavy industry (producers' goods) was much faster than that of light industry (consumers' goods). According to the Commu-

---

34. Kenneth R. Walker, *Planning in Chinese Agriculture: Socialization and the Private Sector, 1956-1962* (Chicago: Aldine Publishing Company, 1965), p. 16.

35. *The Rate and Pattern of Industrial Growth in Communist China* (Ann Arbor, Mich.: University of Michigan Press, 1965), p. 92.

36. Liu and Yeh, *The Economy of the Chinese Mainland,* p. 66.

nist estimate, the gross value of producers' goods increased at an annual growth rate of 29 percent in 1952-57. For individual industries, it is estimated that the annual growth rate in these five years was nearly 30 percent for petroleum and ferrous and nonferrous metal. More than 20 percent of the annual growth rate was in electricity, machine building, and chemicals. But for consumer goods, the picture was quite different, the annual rate of growth being only 6.5 percent for textiles and 9.3 percent for the food industry.[37]

Much smaller rates of growth were achieved for other than industrial sectors. This is particularly true of agricultural production. The official claim that agricultural production increased by 4.5 percent a year in 1952-57 is generally not accepted on grounds of statistical underestimation for earlier years of the period. The Liu and Yeh estimate gives an annual growth rate of no more than 1.7 percent a year for these five years.[38]

Taking all sectors together, the Chinese Communist economy (as measured by gross domestic product in 1952 prices) grew at 9 percent a year according to the Communist estimate and 6.2 percent a year by the Liu and Yeh estimate for the period 1952-57.[39] This was no small achievement by any historical standard.

How was it achieved? A reasonably adequate answer would require a close examination of a number of factors, political, social, and psychological; and this cannot be attempted here. But economic development means the production of more goods and services. To the Chinese Communists, the way to achieve this was first to increase the capacity to produce, that is to produce those goods which are capable of producing more goods. This is, of course, precisely what happened as noted above.[40] In economic analysis, this meant a high proportion of national income devoted to savings and capital formation. Total gross investment (goods not consumed but used for further production) constituted on the average about 24 percent of domestic

---

37. Chao, *Rate and Pattern of Industrial Growth,* p. 97.

38. Liu and Yeh, *Economy of the Chinese Mainland,* p. 87.

39. Liu, "The Tempo of Economic Development of the Chinese Mainland, 1949-65," in *An Economic Profile of Mainland China,* I: 62.

40. The pattern of development may also be reflected by the allocation of investment. In 1952-57, nearly half of the total public capital investment was for industry and 15 percent for transportation and communications. Only 13 percent was devoted to agriculture, while the remaining 23 percent went to all the other sectors. This pattern was very close to the Soviet pattern for 1928-29 to 1932. See K. C. Yeh, "Soviet and Communist Chinese Industrialization Strategies," Rand Paper 3150 (Santa Monica, Calif.: The Rand Corporation, May, 1965), p. 10.

product (in 1952 prices) in 1952-57 both by the Communist and the Liu and Yeh estimates. In net terms (total investment minus depreciation), the ratio is about 20 percent.[41]

Such high capital formation rates would necessarily impose serious restraints on consumption. In fact, the average annual rate of increase of household consumption was no more than 5.2 percent in 1952-57 by the Communist estimate and 1.98 percent by the Liu and Yeh estimate.[42] On a per capita basis it was much less, for population increased at an annual rate of about 2.2 percent during the same period. As compared with the 1930s, the per capita consumption level was only 90 in 1957 (1933-100) by the Liu and Yeh estimate and 140 in 1956 (1936-100) by the Communist estimate.[43] The fact remains that rationing has been required for most daily necessities.

The impressive economic achievements in 1952-57 could not be attributed entirely to internal efforts. External (basically Russian) help also played an important role. The backbone of the FFYP industrial program was the 156 large, modern projects designed and built with the help of the Russians. It has been reported that 10,800 Soviet and 1,500 East European specialists and technicians were sent to Communist China between 1950 and 1960. A vast variety of technical blueprints was given by Russia to Communist China in accordance with a Sino-Soviet agreement in 1954.[44] The fact that the Chinese Communists had to pay for technical assistance (except blueprints, licenses, etc.) does not negate the important role Russia played.

Another form of Soviet assistance was the credits advanced to Communist China. In the years from 1950 to 1955 these credits financed more than a quarter of Communist China's imports from Russia. Russian exports to Communist China consisted primarily of machinery, equipment, and plants which were essential to the success of the FFYP.

Thus it seems justified to suggest that Soviet technical assistance, loans, and commodity exports to Communist China made a decisive contribution to the latter's industrialization during the 1950s. In view of the U. S. and allied trade embargoes, and the general unfavorable international climate, it is doubtful that Communist China could have

41. Liu, "The Tempo of Economic Development," in *An Economic Profile of Mainland China*, I: 62.

42. *Ibid.*

43. Liu and Yeh, *Economy of the Chinese Mainland*, p. 120.

44. Alexander Eckstein, *Communist China's Economic Growth and Foreign Trade* (New York: McGraw Hill, 1966), p. 169.

obtained all this help (especially technical assistance) from other sources.[45]

The Great Leap Forward

Despite the substantial economic gains achieved during the First Five Year Plan period, there were signs that serious economic difficultues developed toward the end of the period. The production of food grains in 1957 was virtually the same as in 1956 (by official estimates). Urban unemployment and rural underemployment were considerable.[46] Russian economic aid (in the form of credits) virtually came to an end after 1955. (Mao Tse-tung was in Moscow in late 1957 only to return home empty-handed.) The Great Leap Forward which was launched toward the end of 1957 was basically an attempt to speed up economic development by relying upon China's own resources, especially labor. The basic strategy is contained in the slogan of "walking on two legs." By "two legs" was meant simultaneous development in industry and agriculture; in heavy and light industries; in centrally and locally managed enterprises; in large, medium, and small enterprises; in modern and traditional technologies; in centralized leadership and mass participation. Simultaneous development did not mean development at the same rate, however, for industry was still given priority over agriculture, heavy over light industries, large over medium and small enterprises, modern over traditional techniques, central over local enterprises.

There was, of course, not enough capital to do all this. The scarce capital was to be used, as previously, primarily for the development of heavy industry, while labor was to be the main input for other developments. In a nutshell, the strategy was one of large-scale substitution of labor for capital, a massive utilization of the underutilized manpower. Thus, in industry, the establishment of small, highly labor-intensive indigenous plants was an outstanding feature of the Leap, while in agriculture intensive farming (close planting, deep ploughing, etc.) and multiple operations (forestry, animal-raising,

45. *Ibid.,* p. 168.

46. Urban unemployment was largely a result of the demand-supply relationship of the nonagricultural labor force. The large capital-intensive projects limited the demand for labor force. The unexpectedly high rate of growth of the urban population greatly increased the supply of labor force. As a result, there was increasing unemployment. For evidence, see Chi-ming Hou, "Manpower, Employment and Unemployment," in *Economic Trends in Communist China,* edited by Alexander Eckstein, *et al.*

irrigation projects, subsidiary work, etc.) were followed. All this had been attempted before, but the grand scale and manner in which the Leap was launched made it unique.

Unfortunately, the Great Leap years also saw the downgrading of technical expertise, as the party cadres gained control of production in the name of mass participation and "politics takes command" and pushed the campaign so ambitiously and fanatically that many basic technical constraints were neglected. The result was a gross misuse and misallocation of resources. The fanatic adventure of building backyard furnaces that produced steel of little worth, the ill-designed irrigation programs that hindered the regular function of rivers and resulted in alkalinization of soil, and the large-scale application of untested farming techniques that wasted much farm labor (such as deep ploughing) are all cases in point. Moreover, the use of rural labor force for nonfarming activity resulted in a serious labor shortage for farming.

The Great Leap was at its peak in 1958. Early in 1959 it was realized that more labor should be used in farming, fertilizer-accumulation, and subsidiary production and less labor in water conservation, deep-ploughing, and backyard furnaces. The Leap programs began to be modified in 1959, and by the end of 1960 they were brought to an end.

The Rural Communes

The rural communes began to be organized in April, 1958, at least partly for the purpose of facilitating the efforts to mobilize rural labor to carry out the Great Leap programs. The organization of the communes varied from region to region, but in general the commune was the amalgamation of a number of the collectives (advanced producers' cooperatives) with each commune comprising four or five thousand householders (in 1958 and 1959). All means of production (land, draught animals, and farm implements) were put under communal ownership, including private plots.

For management the basic principle was centralized leadership with management organs at various levels. The commune was divided into a number of production brigades, which in turn were divided into a number of production teams. The production brigades were the basic units organizing and directing production, whereas the production teams were the basic units of organizing labor. Large factories, mines, lumberyards, and livestock farms were run directly by the commune, while the smaller ones were left under the care of production brigades. Small machines and equipment were entrusted to production teams.

For distribution purposes, the production brigades were called the basic accounting units, but their profits or losses were to be pooled at the commune level under a unified system, implying that all the production brigades, rich or poor, would be treated alike for income distribution purposes. The payment system was a combination of wages and free supply of food. Members of the commune were all entitled to a certain amount of food, free of charge, regardless of how far they participated in production.

By the end of August, 1958, about 30 percent of the total farm householders were organized into communes. The percentage went up to 99 percent by the end of the year. Evidently, there was much resentment on the part of peasants, especially over the tendency toward "egalitarianism." The Wuchang Resolution of December 10, 1958, was in part intended to meet this criticism. A basic retreat in the commune system took place in February, 1959, the beginning of a rectification or "tidying up" of the communes. The basic points of the rectification were the establishment of three-level ownership and the principle of distribution according to work. Now the production brigade became the basic unit, possessing all important means of production, including land. These means of production, together with labor, were then assigned to the production teams on a more or less permanent basis. The basic decisions on what and how to produce were to be made jointly by production brigades and production teams. Thus the commune level was left with little control over farm production; its main function was to be in charge of commune industry, forests, basic construction, and communal activities.

As for income distribution, the production brigade became the accounting and distribution unit. (Members of different production brigades would not have the same level of income and consumption if they differed in production resources and productivity.) The payment system was still one of combining wages and free supply, but the free supply part became less important. (In 1959 it was to be about 30 percent of total distributable income.) In the meantime, private plots were restored under the 5 percent rule (as in cooperatives described earlier).

The system of three-level ownership lasted from February, 1959, to November, 1961. It was essentially the same as the advanced producers' cooperatives.

The commune system underwent another drastic change in November, 1961, when the production team was changed into the basic unit of ownership and accounting. (The production team was roughly the same as that of the elementary producers' cooperative.) In some communes, the production brigades remained the basic unit of accounting and ownership; in others, the means of production were to be owned by the commune and income was distributed on the basis of the whole commune. But, in general, the commune system since the end of 1961 has virtually embodied the same principles as under the system of elementary producers' cooperatives.

The New Economic Policy

The Chinese Communist leaders must have been as confused as shocked by the deepening economic crisis since 1959. The Great Leap and the rural communes were supposed to bring wonders—they were supposed to enable the country to be completely modernized in both industry and agriculture in no more than fifteen to twenty years. What happened instead was a sharp decline first in agriculture, and then in industry. It is not possible to ascertain in quantitative terms the exact magnitude of the decline of the economy, since the Communist statistical system virtually collapsed as party cadres gained control of the statistical apparatus during the Great Leap. Probably food production was higher in 1958 than in 1957, then began to decline in 1959. The lowest point was probably reached in 1960. After a visit to Communist China, Lord Montgomery reported that the production of food grains in 1960 was only 150 million metric tons, as compared with 185 million metric tons in 1957. As for industrial production, it probably continued to grow until 1960 (by utilizing inventories accumulated before) and then began to decline in 1961, with the lowest point being reached in 1962.

There seems little doubt that bad weather contributed in part to this economic decline. According to official estimates, nearly 40 percent of cultivated areas were affected in 1959 and nearly 54 percent in 1960 and 1961. Even allowing for deliberate official exaggeration to minimize policy blunders and a wide margin of statistical errors, the adverse effect of bad weather must have been significant. The fantasy of the Great Leap and the radical phase of the communes undoubtedly also played an important role in the slump of the economy. The withdrawal of Soviet technical personnel in mid-1960 certainly caused heavy losses and dislocation in industry.

Probably out of the sheer necessity of survival, a new economic policy evolved. While the Great Leap programs were abandoned, and the radical features of the communes were eliminated or modified, the entire strategy of development came under revision. The new economic policy called for a new scale of priority of development: agriculture, light industry, and heavy industry, in descending order. Industry was to serve agricultural development because it was recognized that modern inputs were essential for further agricultural improvement. Investment in industry was to be curtailed in order to concentrate on strengthening the agricultural front.[47] It also called for a policy to stabilize urban population to assure an adequate supply of labor for agriculture and presumably to minimize urban unemployment.

The idea of regarding agriculture as the foundation, with industry taking the lead in economic development, was advanced in early 1960 in Li Fu-ch'un's report on the draft economic plans for 1960. It gained momentum in the autumn of the year when another poor harvest was reported. This policy was further reaffirmed in December, 1961, when a secret document (known as the Seventy Articles of Industrial Policy) was reportedly issued to the cadres of the Communist Party, and on March 27, 1962, when Chou En-lai set forth "the ten tasks" for national economy. Later official statements suggest that this policy as formulated in 1960-62 has continued to prevail until today (the summer of 1967).

No data are available to assess in quantitative terms the effects of the new economic policy. (For that matter, there are no data even to describe the new policy in quantitative terms such as saving-consumption ratio or the percentage distribution of investment and output in various sectors of the economy.) But there is no doubt that the Chinese Communists have been serious in implementing the new policy. There have been concentrated efforts to aid agriculture, especially in what is called "four transformations" in agriculture: namely, mechanization, electrification, irrigation, and chemical fertilizers. The particular emphasis has been on the use of chemical fertilizers, the 1957 supply of which was more than trebled by the state in 1964.[48]

Despite these modernization efforts, which admittedly are still in the initial stage, the fact remains that the level of agricultural

47. Chi-ming Hou, "Communist China's Economy Since the Leap," *Communist Affairs*, V (January-February, 1967) 10-15; p. 11.
48. *Ibid.*

production has remained low. According to a report by Chou En-lai, the level of food grain production in 1957 was not "surpassed" until 1964. (This has generally been interpreted as saying that the level of food grain production in 1964 was about the same as in 1957.) For 1965 the official figure is 200 million metric tons (as compared with 185 million metric tons in 1957). No official figure is available for 1966 except the report that it is the highest in history. But Western observers in Hong Kong suggest a decline of about 3 percent a year in 1965 and 1966 because of adverse weather conditions.[49]

All this should be read in relation to population data. Chou En-lai has reported an annual population growth of 2 percent for 1960-62 and nearly 2.5 percent for 1963 and 1964. Another official report put the rate of population increase in 1963 at 1.8-2.0 percent.[50] If these figures reflect the real situation, the per capita output of food grains obviously declined.

Statistics of industrial production since the Great Leap are extremely confusing. It has been officially reported that: (1) the gross value of industrial output increased by 66.2 percent in 1958 and 39.3 percent in 1959; (2) the gross value of industrial output increased by 18.4 percent in 1960; (3) the output of light industry in 1962 surpassed the level achieved in 1957; (4) the gross value of total industrial output increased by 15 percent in 1964 and was well above the 1957 level; (5) the gross value of total industrial output in 1965 was expected to be 11 percent higher than in 1964.[51]

The reliability of all these statistics is open to serious question. For instance, it is almost inconceivable that the output of light industry in 1962 could surpass the 1957 level when food grain and cotton production in 1961 and 1962 were substantially below the 1957 level. But it is difficult to ascertain quantitatively what the real picture has been except to say that there has been an important industrial recovery probably since 1962.

Conclusion

From the above discussions, it is clear that the Chinese economy began to undergo change toward modernization in the mid-nineteenth century after military and economic confrontation with the West.

49. *Current Scene,* XX (November 10, 1966), 12.
50. Hou, "Communist China's Economy Since the Leap," in *Communist Affairs,* p. 12.
51. *Ibid.*

From the 1840s to the 1930s a small but rapidly-growing modern sector had been developed, mainly along the coastal areas, while the vast hinterland remained traditional. Modern nonagricultural sectors contributed no more than 13 percent to national income (in 1933 prices) in 1933. The real importance of the development of this sector cannot, of course, be fully appreciated by such quantitative measurement. The change of attitude on the part of the government and the people toward economic affairs which made the development of the modern sector possible would certainly be essential for any further modernization efforts.

It is not easy to explain why the modern sector was so small and exerted so little influence on the traditional sector. It might be that the Chinese economy had already reached in the 1840s an economic situation which is often described as a vicious circle of poverty—a situation which would be difficult to break for any country. This difficulty was further strengthened by a well-integrated cultural tradition and technology that were formidable to any modernization attempts and the frequently fought external and internal wars were certainly not conducive to speedy development. An exceptionally strong government might have overcome some of these difficulties, but the Chinese government was never strong both financially and politically except perhaps in the 1930s during the Nationalist period, when the situation became better. A large and properly used dose of foreign investment might have helped but such investment was never large in relation to total population.[52] Much of the foreign investment in China in the 1930s was really not a product of flow of capital from abroad; much of it started in China "on a shoe string" or was "built up from nothing,"[53] and much of it was employed in fields associated with foreign trade.

Whatever reasons there may have been, and this certainly requires further research, the fact remains that in the 1930s the Chinese economy was basically underdeveloped in the usual sense of the term. There are no data to indicate the direction of movement of per capita income in the century before the 1930s.

The Communist regime undoubtedly scored impressive progress toward industrialization and the Chinese economy was certainly more modernized in the 1950s than in the 1930s. The contribution of the modern nonagricultural sectors to net domestic product (as measured

52. Hou, *Foreign Investment . . . in China,* ch. 5.
53. *Ibid.,* p. 120.

in both 1933 and 1952 prices) doubled from 1933 to 1957.[54] And, in terms of location, the "industrialized area" was extended beyond the coastal provinces.

A persistent feature in the modern period of Chinese economy, however, has been, and still is, the lack of important progress in agriculture. In the 1950s, the Communist strategy was to increase agricultural production through institutional reorganization; and it was rather successful. Whatever increase of agricultural output there was in the 1950s (there is still no agreement among experts as to exactly how much increase there was), it was primarily due to more intensive and efficient use of labor. Very few modern inputs were used to improve agriculture. An avowed purpose of the institutional changes was more efficient use of labor. Communist data on agricultural inputs and output seem to support this claim.

But there may be limits to this strategy. The fact that in 1964 and, according to Western observers, in 1965 and 1966 as well, the level of food grain output was about the same as that in 1957 despite the increase in labor force strongly suggests that no significant increase of agricultural output can be effected simply by relying upon more intensive use of labor. The argument that the present low level of production is a result of the adverse effects of the Great Leap and the radical features of the communes does not seem very persuasive in view of the fact that the Great Leap was abandoned by 1960 and the radical phase of the commune was largely eliminated by early 1959. It seems plausible to hypothesize that no significant increase of output may be expected unless modern inputs are used. Perhaps this is why the Chinese Communists have recently emphasized the "four transformations," as noted earlier.

Thus, until now the agricultural problem is basically unsolved. How long it will take to find the solution remains a question, given the Communist ambitions for industrial development and national defense. Rapid industrial growth requires agricultural growth (in that the latter provides food, raw materials, foreign exchange, etc.). But if agricultural growth must rely upon industry for its modern inputs (chemical fertilizer, for instance), an important decision the communist authorities have to face is how to allocate the limited resources among various competing demands. Surely, it would require enormous amounts of investment in order to effect an "agricultural

54. Liu and Yeh, *Economy of the Chinese Mainland,* p. 90.

revolution" technically. Meanwhile, population growth shows no signs of slowing down in any significant way despite government efforts to reduce birth rates in recent years (as well as in the late 1950s). If the current level of per capita income is just about the same as in 1957,[55] it means that there has been no economic growth whatsoever in the past decade, and it is anybody's guess whether per capita income will go up appreciably in the near future. It is not possible to assess how the current movement of the Proletarian Cultural Revolution has affected or will affect the economy. It is equally hard to predict how long the absence of foreign assistance will continue.

Thus, to answer the question first posed at the beginning of this paper, one would have to say that the Chinese economy has undergone fundamental changes in the direction of modernization or Westernization. But if economic growth means a sustained rise in per capita income, it is doubtful that such growth has taken place. To use Rostow's phrase, it remains to be seen whether the Chinese economy has really taken off into sustained growth. Evidently economic development is tough business whether you are a Confucianist, Nationalist, or Communist![56]

55. Liu, "The Tempo of Economic Development," in *An Economic Profile of Mainland China,* I: 50.

56. It might be noted here that the Nationalists have seen in Taiwan what they doubtless would have liked to see on the mainland while they were there. From 1951 to 1965 the average annual compound rate of increase in real GNP (gross national product) in Taiwan was 7.6 percent. On a per capita basis, the rate was 4.2 percent a year (despite the high rate of growth of population which was about 3.3 percent a year). From 1951 to 1963, agricultural output increased at 5 percent a year while industry registered an annual growth rate of 13 percent during the same period. Eor an analysis of Taiwan's economy, see Neil H. Jacoby, *U. S. Aid to Taiwan* (New York: Frederick A. Praeger, 1966).

POSTSCRIPT: Since this essay was written (summer of 1967) some further purportedly official data on grains production have become available. They were reportedly given by Chinese officials in Peking privately to a visiting Pakistani agricultural delegation in 1965. According to this report, the output of all food grains was 215.2 million metric tons in 1958, 192.7 in 1959, 161.3 in 1960, 189.2 in 1961, 203.8 in 1962, 218.9 in 1963, 237.8 in 1964, and 258.0 in 1965. (S. Swamy and S. J. Burki, "Foodgrains Output in the People's Republic of China, 1958-1965," *The China Quarterly,* No. 41, January—March, 1970, pp. 58-63.)

It has also been reported that Chou En-lai told Edgar Snow in Peking in late 1970 that grain production for that year would be 240 million metric tons—just about the same as in 1964, as reported by the Pakistani delegation. For 1971, the first year of the fourth five-year plan, the grain output was 2.5 per cent higher than in 1970, according to Chinese Communist official announcement (New York *Times,* January 2, 1972). But

"Specialists" in Hong Kong according to a New York *Times* report (January 24, 1972) believed that grains output for 1971 probably did not increase much over the estimated 1970 production of 210 million to 220 million metric tons, an all-time record.

Thus, for a period of 14 years from 1957 to 1971, there was an increase of 33 percent or about 2.36 percent per year (simple average) even if official estimates are used. Such a growth rate, after adjusted to population growth, does not seem to suggest that any "agricultural revolution" or "green revolution" has taken place.

Also, since the essay was written, an important study has been made on Chinese agriculture by Dwight H. Perkins (*Agricultural Development in China 1368-1968,* Chicago: Aldine Publishing Company, 1969). The reader is referred to this study for further information not covered in this essay.

XVII

A Geographical

View of China

BY

RHOADS MURPHEY

China in Geographic Context

Chinese culture and the Chinese state arose largely in isolation at the extreme eastern end of the continental land mass of Eurasia. Traditional Japanese and Korean civilizations may be considered primarily as offshoots of China's, and both are in fact often lumped with China under the heading of the "Sinic" world. The other major center of traditional Asian civilization, India, was far away and difficult to reach, and its interchange with China was minimal. The area now known as Southeast Asia, from Burma east through Indonesia and north to Vietnam and the Philippines, owed nearly all of its civilized tradition to China (especially in the eastern half) or to India (in the western half). North and west from China stretched a vast, relatively empty area of boreal, desert, and mountain country which produced no major civilized tradition and which tended to insulate China from more distant contact westward. Beyond Japan, its own culture an echo of China's, ranged an enormous and forbidding ocean. These were not a set of geographical circumstances conducive to extensive contact with other cultures, and in fact most of what historical contact took place was one-way: from China to Korea, Japan, and Southeast Asia, and from India to China in the form of Buddhism; Chinese civilization seems to have made little or no impact on India, nor does China seem to have been significantly affected by influences from less fully developed Southeast Asia or Japan. There was relatively extensive trade with the latter two (though very little with India), but it did not for the most part act as a cultural vehicle bringing new ideas or techniques into China.

China was also surrounded by a formidable set of physical barriers which tended further to insulate it from external contact to a greater extent than has been true of any major civilization. A high and rugged mountain wall almost encloses the western limits of the Chinese State. The Himalayas and the related Tibetan plateau, and the Pamirs, Kun Lun, and T'ien Shan ranges are not only among the highest in the world, but present a barrier-in-depth which was only infrequently crossed and which helps to account for the very small scale of what trade did take place between China and areas to the west and southwest, including India. Beyond these mountains (and also on the Chinese side in the Tarim Basin of Sinkiang) lies the hundreds or even thousands of miles of steppe-desert which has been called "the dead heart of Asia," an additional and perhaps even more effective barrier-in-depth. To the south and southwest, external contact was in practice restricted at least as much by the spectacular gorge and rain forest country of western Yunnan and northern Burma, whose barrier qualities were further reinforced by endemic diseases, such as malaria. This alternative route to India was used even less than the arduous trails across the Himalayas and through Sinkiang. The one relatively easy avenue southward from China was the nevertheless restricted one down the gorge and valley of the Red River to Tonking (modern North Vietnam) and along the narrow and interrupted coastal plain; Chinese settlement and culture spread early and effectively into Tonking, but further penetration and contact southward and eastward were greatly slowed or arrested by the rugged and heavily forested landscape which covers most of the peninsula, as it blocked contact along a southwesterly route with India. China's northern frontiers appear more open, but although the mountain chain of the Altai, Yablonovi, and Khingan ranges is far from continuous and leaves many wide gaps, steppe-desert (including the Gobi and the Ordos) and subarctic climate operated in practice as an effective limit north of the Great Wall. This area was traditionally not attractive to the Chinese; it presented obvious difficulties, and few rewards; in terms of significant culture contact, the northern sector was also largely barren, and that direction seemed to the Chinese little more enticing an avenue than that offered by the barren and frightening ocean which lay to the east.

The two greatest poles of world civilization, Europe and China, thus took form and reached maturity largely in ignorance of one another and without benefit of any significant contact. The simple friction of distance between them, at opposite ends of a great land mass whose center was both physically forbidding and relatively empty, also ensured that contact would be minimized. The journeys of the few overland travelers from Europe who reached China, including Marco Polo and a number of his less well-known contemporaries, and the less successful and earlier Chinese efforts to discover what lay westward beyond their mountain-desert wall never produced at either end a real awareness of the scale or nature of the other. It was not until Europeans perfected their ability to use the sea, beginning with the age of da Gama, that these two great traditions began to meet face to face, as a result of European circumnavigation of the barriers which had separated them. Europe's previous experience may be said to have led understandably to such an outcome. From classical Greek times, and again with increased weight after the end of the Middle Ages, Europe had been accustomed to seeking and to benefiting from varied cultural and trade contacts, both internally among the congeries of separate-but-related cultural traditions of which Europe was composed, each in its own distinctive geographic or peninsular base, and externally along the ancient Mediterranean routes to the Near East, eventually to flower in the active search for a sea route to Cathay and the consequent European discovery of the rest of the world. Europeans were long aware of other civilized traditions as accomplished as their own, and eagerly sought exchange.

The Chinese experience was different, and geography helped to make it so. Chinese attention tended in the long run not so much toward the exploration of the unknown world as toward the development of the peerless Chinese geographic base. High rewards could be won from it, but in return for relatively high effort, especially in irrigation. The over-all physical advantages of climate, soils, and plains were great enough to repay handsomely the heavy investment of labor and capital in a variety of forms which came to characterize Chinese agriculture as a model of intensiveness and productivity. As the level of intensiveness rose, especially from Han times on with the increasing cheapness and availability of iron tools and the increasing use of manures, there seems little question that the area we may refer to as "agricultural China," where Chinese agrarian settlement was concentrated, became by a considerable margin the most productive in the world, in terms both of total output and of yields per acre. Such a development weakened still further any incentives to increase contact with other areas; effort and capital were more fruitfully employed in domestic development. Within the very large area of China, and given its generally high productivity, there were also ample opportunities for trade, and for a level of manufacturing which compared favorably even with Europe until perhaps as late as the eighteenth century. The Chinese provinces were on the scale of the larger European states, in area, population, and production, and intraprovincial trade was very large. External trade, especially with Southeast Asia, varied from period to period but never approached the levels of domestic trade. The Chinese saw themselves quite rationally as prosperously self-sufficient. These developments further reinforced the Chinese image of themselves as the Middle Kingdom, compared to which all other areas were inferior. China was not referred to as a state—that term was reserved for lesser political entities such as Japan or Burma—but as *the* Empire, encompassing in its literal sense of *t'ien-hsia* (everything under heaven) not merely the dominant but the only imperium.

This cumulative experience was to prove a singularly unfortunate preparation for China's eventual confrontation with the real nature and dimensions of the world beyond her traditional ken. The idea that Western states could in any sphere rival China, or that Western knowlegde, culture, or products should have anything of value for China, was resisted. Despite the collapse of traditional dynastic rule in 1911 and the eventual coming to power of the Communists in 1949, elements of the old attitudes about China as the center and pinnacle of the world remain. The experience of two millennia cannot so easily or quickly be forgotten or set aside; neither the humiliations, pressures, and self-questionings which have racked China during the past century nor the Communist success in reestablishing a strong government have entirely displaced the idea of China as the Middle Kingdom. The Communist government continues to foster an often generally unreceptive attitude toward the rest of the world, including its erstwhile friends in the Soviet Union. China is still seen as ideally self-sufficient, and for the present as taking pride in its self-reliance. The Chinese state still attempts to play in some respects the kind of role which the old Empire played, as the great power and arbiter of Asia. The West is seen for the most part as a rival, but as a corrupt and fragile system, which the China model will ultimately outdistance once more. In brief, the world is still seen through Sinocentric glasses, a view developed with good reason out of China's premodern experience, but in the world of the twentieth century no longer in full accord with the bases of and needs for global and mutual understanding. This is necessarily a two-way street, and Western perspectives too are faulty, based just as much on outmoded and potentially destructive ethnocentric assumptions of superiority; in particular, the West has yet to understand and to accept the new China. The problems which this poses are greatly augmented by China's size: something over a fifth of the world is at odds with most of the rest, in the absence of mutual knowledge and acceptance. Both sides must recognize that the world has changed.

Geographic Foundations of Chinese Society

The nature of Chinese society also bears a close relationship to its geographic base. China has always been a predominantly agricultural country, as it still is despite the recent rapid growth of industrialization, and most of the Chinese people are still village-based farmers. The system of agrarian land use developed over the past two millennia put a premium on intensive cultivation, whereby very high yields were obtained from relatively small fields. Farmers typically lived as they still do in nucleated village settlements rather than in the dispersed farmhouses more common in most of the West, and the fields which they tilled were grouped around the village; the distance between house and field was minimized by the small size of the latter. People thus lived and worked very closely together, and the high yields from agriculture also furthered the growth of population, which was especially dense in the most productive agricultural areas. Under such circumstances, the proper ordering of society was seen to depend on the adherence to strict rules of individual and group behavior to minimize conflict as well as to insure necessary cooperation. Agriculturists, as the Chinese have preeminently been, must also, however, be sensitive to natural conditions; land will yield well only if it is conscientiously cared for in accordance with a proven method, adjusting to the vagaries of climate, the seasons, and the physical limits and advantages of a particular site. The Chinese farmer has probably modified his landscape, through terracing, irrigation, deforestation, and other techniques, to a greater extent than agricultural man has done elsewhere, but he has also tended his fields with greater care, seeing himself as a steward or even a servant of nature, and with an eye for the welfare of future generations. Man and nature were seen ideally as cooperating in harmony, because man adjusted to natural conditions, as any agriculturist must, rather than attempting to conquer or ignore them. Harmony through adjustment and through the acknowledgment of limits was thus a familiar theme common to both Chinese society and Chinese land use, and in both a connection may be traced to the agrarian base of Chinese civilization. Communist China has inherited this tradition, and has further stressed the need for subordination of individual desires to the greater good of the whole.

The Spread of Chinese
Civilization

The origins of the dominant Chinese civilization on the North China plain are discussed in Chapter XIII, "Archaeology," but the south was physically a very different area, and settlement of the Yangtze valley in particular required the drainage of large areas and their protection from flooding, while in other large parts of the south upland areas or those on slopes could be made fully productive only by bringing irrigation water to them, and by terracing. The long period of the development of water control and the manipulation of the environment in the north, together with the spread of iron tools which could be used in particular to clear forested land, were necessary preparation for full-scale Chinese occupation of the south, as was the development of techniques of fertilization and wet-rice growing. The southward spread took place gradually over several centuries, beginning at least as early as middle Chou, and concentrating at first on the potentially highly productive Yangtze basin with its fertile alluvial soils, normally adequate rainfall, and long growing season. Farther penetration followed the several valleys which lead south from the Yangtze, particularly those of the Kan, Hsiang, and Yuan Rivers, and reached the lower valley and delta of the West River in the Canton region, agriculturally the most attractive and productive of all southern areas, relatively early. As production and trade increased, navigability on the Yangtze and its several tributaries, and on smaller streams in the farther south, was an additional southern advantage, for the silted and fluctuating Yellow River system was at best indifferently navigable. But level land is not plentiful south of the Yangtze or west of modern Hunan, and this greatly retarded Chinese occupation of the south as a whole, where non-Han[1] groups remained in occupation of much upland area, unsuited to intensive Chinese agriculture, in the southwest (Yunnan and Kweichow) and even in the mountainous areas on the margins of the lower West River valley. Along the southeast coastal zone as well, broken hill and mountain country helped to preserve traces of a variety of originally non-Han groups; in these parts of Kwangtung,

---

1. Since the time of the Han dynasty, the Chinese have referred to themselves as the Han people, an ethnic term in this sense, distinguishing them from the variety of "non-Han" groups such as the Tibetans, Mongols, or originally tribal groups in the south.

Fukien, and Chekiang linguistic and other cultural differences from the main body of China still survive.

By the time of the T'ang dynasty (618-907), the south probably had a larger population and production than the north, and thereafter continued to enhance its primacy as more area was brought under cultivation and as agricultural techniques were further improved and adjusted to the far more favorable southern conditions. Although no longer the center of economic gravity, the north remained the site of the national capital, with few and brief exceptions, until the present. This was partly the inertia of tradition, but partly also the desire to keep the politico-military center of the empire close to what was consistently regarded as the exposed frontier. Until the nineteenth- and twentieth-century pressures by Europeans and the final Japanese attack, external military threats to the Chinese state came invariably from the north and northwest, in the person of steppe or nomadic groups like the Mongols who harried the Chinese frontiers and periodically attempted invasion or conquest. The chief sector of active threat remained largely in the northwest until the end of the T'ang dynasty, and for most of this period the imperial capital was at Ch'ang-an (modern Sian) in Shensi. With the shift of the main external threat eastward and the rise of the Mongol power, the capital also migrated, to Kaifeng on the great bend of the Yellow River, and then to Peking, whose position enables it to guard against invasions both from Mongolia and from Manchuria, the original base of the Manchu conquerors as well as the base from which the Japanese ultimately launched their attack.

Outer China

Since the time of the Han dynasty, over half of the area controlled by China during most periods of political power has never been occupied in significant numbers by Han Chinese, primarily because aridity, cold, or mountains ruled out agriculture. But as the power of the empire grew, its authority was extended over the mainly nomadic peoples who surrounded it to landward. This was done partly for imperial prestige, but also for security: nomadic raids and invasion threats were a chronic problem. No dynasty was ever fully successful in the peaceful control of its borders, but the Han first established a Chinese position of supremacy and sovereignty not only over south China (plus most of Annam [Vietnam] and Korea) but also over

Sinkiang, Inner Mongolia, and southern Manchuria. The political frontier retreated and expanded again in succeeding centuries as China's power waned and waxed, but the Han established and later dynasties reaffirmed most of the outlines of the present Chinese frontiers. Tibet was included later and, until the 1950s, less effectively; it too was periodically a base for raids and incursions into Chinese-settled territory. Part of the motive for the control of Sinkiang was the protection of trade routes which ran through it and which were for many centuries China's chief link with the rest of the world via the Kansu Corridor. Whenever China was weak, these outer areas tended to break away, but only twice, under the Mongols and under the Manchus, did outer groups unite to conquer the whole of China, although there were several smaller scale conquests of the north.

The Great Wall was built in successive stages during the first millennium B.C. not only as a military defense against the mounted nomad, but also as a line to separate non-Chinese nomad from Chinese farmer, the steppe from sown land, "barbarism" from civilization. The wall largely follows the line between traditional agricultural and nonagricultural areas in cultural terms, and in physical terms reflects the limit of farming on the basis of traditional techniques. During the past century and with the help of new techniques, especially in irrigation, Chinese settlers have spread particularly into Inner Mongolia (in general, the area south of the Gobi Desert, which lies between Inner and Outer Mongolia), where they are now a strong majority of the population. New irrigation is still increasing the cultivated area, and Chinese industrialization and railway building have also penetrated this formerly nomadic region, which is now firmly incorporated into the Chinese state, although under the label of the Inner Mongolian Autonomous Region. Outer Mongolia was established in the 1920s as an independent state, the Mongolian People's Republic, and past Chinese claims to this area have been withdrawn.

Chinese settlement in Sinkiang, now the Uighur Autonomous Region, has remained on a very much smaller scale. This huge area offers relatively little basis for agriculture, or for a more than modest increase in irrigation. Its inhabitants are still predominantly non-Han, the largest single group being the Turkic Uighurs, who are concentrated in the string of small oasis-based towns along the old trade routes through Sinkiang following the base of the Kun Lun and T'ien Shan ranges which mark the edges of the arid Tarim Basin. North of the T'ien Shan, in the part of Sinkiang known as Dzungaria, rainfall is somewhat more plentiful and most of the land is steppe rather than desert; it supports nomadic pastoral groups, principally Kazakhs and Mongols. There are, however, some significant mineral resources in Sinkiang, most of them recently discovered as part of the Chinese Communist drive for resource development, and these are now beginning to be exploited by Chinese technicians and workers on a rapidly growing scale. There are extensive petroleum wells in production at Karamai and elsewhere in Dzungaria, and a booming industrial center at Urumchi, the capital of Sinkiang, where iron and steel are being made from nearby ores and fuel. A rail line has been built to connect these new developments with China Proper, and efforts have been made to induce more Chinese to settle in Sinkiang, both to develop new resources and to strengthen the Chinese political position in this border area adjoining the USSR where Han Chinese are still a minority. The industrial and transport development will no doubt continue to bring in Chinese workers and technicians, but the possibilities for extending the cultivated area as a basis for Chinese agricultural settlement appear to be relatively limited, since most expansion must depend on new irrigation. Sources of water for irrigation in most of this desert or semi-arid country are not plentiful, although there are the beginnings of an ambitious development to dam and make use of water from the Ili River in Dzungaria; elsewhere increases in workable farm land, especially in the Tarim Basin, may have to be more modest.

Tibet had largely broken away from Chinese control in the declining years of the Ch'ing (Manchu) dynasty, but the present government has reasserted its sovereignty, against Tibetan resistance. Remoteness, mountains, cold, and aridity leave little attractive basis for any extensive Chinese settlement or investment. Even for the Tibetans, the total resource base is small, and remoteness plus costs of extraction and transport handicap whatever mineral-based development might occur, although the mineral resources of Tibet are poorly known. A precarious agriculture is the main support of the economy, but most of Tibet's area cannot be cultivated and over large areas the land is not even suitable for grazing, although pastoralism based on the yak is the only other major economic activity. The Chinese government has built three motor roads into Tibet, in the interest of better control and to accelerate the Sinification of what is nevertheless called the Tibetan Autonomous Region. One indirect result of the Tibetan revolt of the middle and late 1950s was the border dispute between China and India, which erupted into brief fighting in the autumn of 1962. China built a road from Sinkiang into western Tibet, to improve its military position there, through territory claimed by both China and India, the Aksai Chin, which India contested. The dispute remains unsettled, and in this snow-and-ice-covered waste of the high Himalayas it has been impossible to demarcate a boundary and difficult even to be sure of exact locations. But the Chinese government, newly conscious of prestige and power, made use of this opportunity to assert both its territorial claims and China's renewed status as the great power of Asia. The Indian case was weakened by intransigence, and the Chinese claim and actions easy to defend.

Manchuria was sparsely peopled until the beginning of the twentieth century, and had largely been avoided by Chinese settlers; in traditional agricultural terms, it was merely an inferior version of North China. But as North China became increasingly overcrowded and a series of floods and famines produced drastic economic distress, large streams of impoverished migrants began to pour into southern Manchuria and the plain of the Liao River, in numbers reaching at their height a million a year. This movement coincided in time with a period of intense international rivalry over the control of Manchuria, especially between Russia and Japan, both of whom were eager to develop the impressive mineral and forest resources and the potentially productive agricultural land. The Japanese defeat of Russia in the war of 1904-5 left Japan in *de facto* control of Manchuria, given China's weakness, and the military conquest of 1931 allowed Japan to formalize her absorption of Manchuria. Japanese investments in railways, mines, manufacturing, and commercial agriculture largely built Manchuria's modern economy. Wheat and soybeans were moved along the rail lines and out for export, and one of the largest heavy manufacturing centers in Asia was established, centered on the Mukden area. Commercial agriculture was concentrated in the Liao valley, where climate and soils are more favorable than in the dry, cold, and hilly margins of Manchuria on the west, east, and north. Most of Manchuria's large deposits of coal and iron ore are also in or near the Liao valley, including the famous coal mines at Fu-shun, some thirty miles east of Mukden, another large coal deposit a hundred miles to the west at Fou-hsin, and a large reserve of iron ore at Anshan, fifty miles to the south. Anshan became the major iron and steel center under the Japanese, and still is so; the ore there is relatively low grade, and is hence expensive to move to the coal; coal accordingly moves to it from Fu-shun, Fou-hsin, and from high quality coking-coal deposits in the Pen-ch'i area in southeastern Manchuria. With these major developments in its immediate hinterland, Mukden (now called Shen-yang) became the largest Manchurian city, and is still one of China's four largest, but other heavy and light manufacturing centers also arose north of Mukden at Ch'ang-ch'un (now the leading Chinese producer of motor vehicles) and Ch'i-lin (Kirin), at Fu-shun and Anshan, and in the southeast at Pen-ch'i and An-tung. Dairen (Ta-lien) was developed, largely by the Japanese, as the principal port of Manchuria, with its new highly commercialized and industrialized economy.

Manchurian industrial and agricultural production was fed largely into the Japanese economy, but the Japanese investment in Manchurian economic development, including a major rail network, was inherited by China after 1945; Manchuria still contains China's largest single heavy industrial complex and biggest source of agricultural surpluses. Repossession of Manchuria has made a critically important contribution to Communist China's economic growth. The Chinese claim to Manchuria was immeasurably strengthened by mass immigration, and the area's population since 1900 has been overwhelmingly Chinese. The present government refers to it simply as "the northeast" and is anxious to consolidate its incorporation as an integral part of China, after the history of foreign rivalry and investment of the past century, and with the growth of Manchurian regionalism on the part of Chinese settlers who had never been effectively controlled by a Chinese government before 1949.

Formosa (Taiwan) is another area settled in significant numbers by Chinese surprisingly late, beginning only in the early seventeenth century, about the same time as the first English settlements in America. Since the island is only some hundred miles from the mainland and its existence was well known to the Chinese for two thousand years, this belated settlement may, like that of Manchuria, further suggest the Chinese reluctance to emigrate or to leave one's ancestral place of origin. The ultimate occupation of Formosa (so named by the Portuguese, in whose language the name means "beautiful") was related to the conquest of China by the Manchus and the consequent retreat of many who remained loyal to the Ming, as well as to mounting population pressure on the mainland, especially in the crowded and mountainous southeast, which was already becoming serious in Fukien and Kwangtung by the seventeenth century. Until 1950 nearly all of the Chinese on Taiwan (referred to now as the Taiwanese) were descendants of settlers who migrated originally from Fukien, Kwangtung, and southern Chekiang. In the course of the seventeenth, eighteenth, and nineteenth centuries their settlement spread from early nuclei close to the western coast, at both the southern and northern ends of the island, over all of the lowland areas and into most of the hill and mountain region as well, killing off or dispossessing most of the comparatively primitive peoples who had previously been the sole inhabitants; these "aborigines" (recent research suggests in fact that they themselves were not the original inhabitants) now survive only on a few protected reservations, rather as the American Indians do. Taiwan is dominated physically by a high mountain chain running north-south nearly the whole length of the island and extending for most of this distance right to the east coast, where it meets the sea in rugged cliffs. The western slopes are more gradual, and give way to the broad alluvial plain which covers approximately the western half of the island and where nearly all of the population is concentrated. Taiwan as a whole has a subtropical climate, and the surrounding sea further helps to prevent extremes of temperature, although the south is somewhat wetter as well as warmer than the north, as on the mainland.

Like Manchuria, Taiwan's modern development was due largely to the Japanese, who took the island over as part of the Japanese Empire in 1895; it was they who built most of Taiwan's present rail and road network, planned and built most of the modern cities of Taipei (the present capital), Chi-lung (Keelung—the port of Taipei), Kao-hsiung (the leading southern port), Tainan, and Taichung, and transformed the agricultural system into the highly productive commercialized structure which is still the mainstay of the economy. Sugar, tea, and later pineapples, mushrooms, and other horticultural specialties became large staple exports, rice production was greatly increased, and the island's population and its urban commercial centers boomed. With the defeat of Japan in 1945, Taiwan returned to Chinese sovereignty, and in 1949-50 the island became the major base remaining to the defeated Nationalist Government. Some two million Nationalist refugees from the mainland, including troops and officials of the Nationalist Government, retreated to Taiwan; with the help of extensive American economic and technical assistance, the island became economically self-supporting by 1964 despite the continued increase in population, which by 1970 had reached about 15 million. Industrial development, begun on a small scale under the Japanese but until the 1950s largely limited to agricultural processing and service industries such as fertilizer production, has increased very rapidly and the economy was by 1965 no longer predominantly agricultural, although the majority of the labor force remained in farming. Food processing and canning, textiles, chemicals (including fertilizers and refining), shipbuilding and ship repair, metal and machine industries, power generation, and a variety of consumer goods production dominate the still rapidly growing industrial structure. Taiwan's relatively small deposits of coal near Taipei, the island's only mineral resource of major significance (apart from natural gas wells in the same area), were first mined extensively by the Japanese and are now used mainly to produce power, but are not at present a leading factor in Taiwan's industrialization. The agricultural system is still benefiting from new investment in irrigation (especially in the somewhat drier north), improved seeds and cultivation techniques, and increasing use of chemical fertilizers; per-acre yields, already high, are still rising. Taiwan's physical advantages of a warm, humid climate, large areas of alluvial soil, and sizable hydro power potential, given its mountain spine and heavy rainfall, are being put to use more and more fully. Adequate representation for the Taiwanese under Nationalist rule and ultimate political sovereignty over the island remain unresolved questions.

Physical Patterns: Rivers and People

China Proper, still the home of the great majority of the Chinese people as of the roots and body of Chinese civilization, is in essence grouped around three great river systems, each rising in the mountainous west and flowing eastward across the widest extent of the country. The Yellow River (Huang) system, which drains approximately the northern quarter of China Proper, is a typical dry-climate stream plagued by excessive fluctuation and flooding and carrying a heavy load of silt. Its watershed, which includes Kansu and the Ordos Desert, is poorly covered by vegetation and the loess soils of this area are in any case highly susceptible to erosion—hence the yellowish silt which gives the river its name. Frequent and disastrous floods have been made worse by increased siltation of the river's bed, aggravated as cultivation spread within the watershed. Natural and artificial dykes along the lower course have also prevented the regular release of silt, and the river's bed is thus in many places above the level of the surrounding country. Silt progressively chokes normal channels and may lead directly to floods as pent-up water finds its former outlets blocked or breaks out through the dykes. The flood plain of the river is densely populated, as one of China's major cereal-producing areas, and the damage caused by floods is thus magnified.

Major changes of the Yellow River's course have also taken place more or less in every century as floodwaters have sought an entirely new outlet; changes of this sort have taken the river both north and south of the rocky Shantung peninsula in its course to the sea, so that its delta and flood plain are very widespread; the soil fertility of the north China plain is of course in large part attributable to the periodic flooding of the river and its tributaries, but the destruction caused exacts too high a price. The present government is engaged on an ambitious project to control the Yellow River by a series of dams along its upper and middle course which are designed to extract silt, even out the seasonal flow of water to prevent or minimize floods, increase navigability, store and distribute water for irrigation, and produce hydroelectric power. This is accompanied by a mass program of afforestation in the watershed, which is the only long-term solution; meanwhile new irrigation water, so desperately needed in North China, and new electric power are available, as well as increased protection against floods. Similar flood control, irrigation, and power development schemes are remaking nearly all of the other rivers of the north, which traditionally generated similar problems.

The Yangtze valley dominates all of central China, and includes in its basin about half the total population of China Proper. Major navigable tributaries enter it alternately from the north and from the south, greatly enhancing the transport usefulness of the system as a whole and also helping to reduce floods, since northern and southern tributaries peak at different times. They include, as one ascends the master stream, the Kan from the south, the Han from the north (entering the Yangtze at Hankow), the Hsiang from the south, emptying into Tung Ting Lake, a natural spill reservoir for the Yangtze which also helps to restrict flooding, and the Chialing and Min entering the Yangtze from northern Szechuan. The master stream is navigable for smaller ocean vessels as far as Hankow, 630 miles from the sea, but smaller ships and junks use altogether over 20,000 miles of waterways in the basin as a whole. Ichang, at the downstream end of the famous Yangtze gorges where the river has cut through the mountain mass of central China, is at present the physical limit for deep-draft shipping, but is surrounded by mountains and cannot rival Hankow, at a major confluence in a productive lowland area, as the dominant center of the middle basin. The Yangtze system has helped to draw a large part of China's trade to the great river, and down it to Shanghai, which by the early 1900s became the country's largest city, as it still is. This is a reflection of the productivity of the Yangtze basin as well as of Shanghai's unrivaled transport connections with it. Low transport costs and nearness to the major block of China's population and production also contributed to Shanghai's early industrial development, and it is still the largest single industrial center in China Proper. The Yangtze basin combines in greater amount than any other part of China level or near-level land, adequate moisture, and a long growing season, plus the important advantage of cheap transport; by T'ang times it was already the country's dominant economic area, and so it seems likely to remain as industrialization progresses.

The West River (Hsi or Si) is a much lesser stream, and its watershed is restricted by the mountainous landscape of south and southwest China. River shipping uses it extensively, but the main river lacks major navigable tributaries on the scale of the Yangtze and its basin is far less productive: level land is scarce. The lower river and its delta, in the Canton area, comprise, however, the largest lowland in the south, and the river's basin as a whole is the obvious core of South China.

Rivers and their basins are significant in the Chinese context for two main reasons. First, although China outside the north is not on the whole well supplied with fertile soils or with extensive lowlands, alluvium is concentrated in the river flood plains, where the easy availability of supplemental irrigation water is a further asset. The country's population is as a result sharply concentrated in river valleys and flood plains, reaching its highest densities in the level and productive deltas. Second, water is the cheapest and often, except in the arid north, the only available means of transport for bulk goods moving beyond local markets. Railway development is growing fast but is still relatively small in comparison with the area and population to be served, and will remain more expensive than water haulage in most cases. Most of North China is in effect the flood plain and delta of the Yellow River. West of the north China plain, in Shansi, Shensi, and Kansu, settlement is concentrated in smaller river valleys where some irrigation is also available. Railways were built first in the north and are still more prominent there than in the south; waterways are much fewer, and coal mining sites in the north attracted railways relatively early. But even so, northern settlement remains densest in association with valleys or flood plains. In the south, settlement is coincident with river basins to a greater degree, since level land, naturally fertile soils, and easy transport are found for the most part only there.

Patterns of Topography

In topographic terms, China has often been schematically divided into the mountainous south and the more level north, but such a distinction ignores the similar difference between the western uplands and the eastern plains. The western two thirds of north China, more or less, are covered with rugged uplands; the loess cover is quickly dissected by rainfall, and the northwestern landscape is highly carved. Streams are deeply entrenched and, although cultivation has spread up the hillsides, the irrigation necessary for security in this arid climate is concentrated in the valleys. The great plain to the east presents a sharp contrast; its level and fertile expanse supports China's largest area of dense population, spread over the plain with considerable uniformity but with major urban nodes at Tientsin and Tsinan, in addition to Peking. A narrow coastal corridor between the sea and the mountains north of Tientsin joins north China with Manchuria, and here the Great Wall meets the sea at Shanhaikuan ("mountain-sea gate"), through which rail lines now provide a link with the industrial northeast. In the south, as well, although the pattern is less clear, lowlands are concentrated in the eastern half while the western half contains only few and small breaks in the jumbled mountains and uplands which dominate the landscape. The lowland basin of the Yangtze extends to Tung Ting Lake, some 700 miles from the sea, and farther south the West River duplicates this pattern on a smaller scale. It is, however, true that south China as a whole is predominantly hilly or mountainous and that the north contains very much larger areas of level terrain.

There are few clearly defined mountain ranges within China

Proper, but these include the sharp front of the Tsinling range from southeastern Kansu to central Honan, which marks a pronounced physical and cultural line, between the arid plain of the north and the green hills of the south. The Hwai Yang Shan (*shan* "mountain") between Hunan and Hupei in central China carry this north-south line less sharply farther east, but beyond Nanking the delta and coastal plain open out and north and south merge unhindered between the lower Yangtze, lower Huai, and lower Yellow Rivers. South of the Tsinling in Szechuan lies the extensive and productive Red Basin, sheltered by surrounding mountains and with low enough relief to make it one of the three largest areas of dense settlement and agricultural production, together with the north China plain and the lower Yangtze valley. South of the Yangtze basin, the only major gaps in an otherwise rugged landscape are the delta of the West River and the series of smaller river flood plains north of Canton along the coast. Difficult highland country, including the ill-defined Wu Kung, Ta Yü, and Yün Ling ranges, extends for at least a hundred miles inland from the coast between the Canton delta and Hangchow, forming a barrier which has tended to isolate southeast coastal China from the main body of the country. The highly indented coastline does include a great many excellent harbors, but the general poverty of the mountainous hinterland has prevented the growth of a major port. Trade and emigration to Southeast Asia, and piracy, however, became characteristic of this coastal region, and offer some indication of its physical handicaps.

The southwest, sometimes mislabeled a plateau, is actually heavily dissected, and level land is as scarce as in the southeast. Non-Han groups still occupy most of the land, although they are a minority of the total southwestern population. This country, in effect the foothills of the Tibetan mountain mass, continues northward through western Szechuan and into Kansu; high relief combined with remoteness has retarded Chinese penetration, although the present government is promoting the industrial and urban growth of these previously neglected areas, especially in the Kunming region of Yunnan.

Overland connection between north and south was easiest along three routes. One was the partly man-made Grand Canal, which from the seventh century on joined the political center of the northern plain with the lower Yangtze basin. The other two led from central China to Canton, following Yangtze tributaries, the Hsiang and Kan rivers, to their headwaters, and, after short portages across low saddles, the

Cheling and Meiling passes, joining one of the West River's tributaries, the Pei, leading to the Canton delta. These routeways have helped to keep the Canton area more intimately related with the rest of China than has been true for most of the rest of the south, and also helped make possible Canton's role until the mid-nineteenth century as the chief center of foreign trade for the whole country. Although this primacy has been lost to Shanghai and Tientsin, and the growth of Canton also overshadowed by the nearness of Hong Kong, it is still by far the largest city in mainland south China, the dominant service center for the West River valley, and the chief terminus of modern China's primary north-south rail line from Peking via Hankow, through the Cheling pass.

The Coastline

The geographic distinction between north and south as a whole is repeated in the coastline. The northern half, north of Hangchow Bay, is a long, low, sandy shore with shallow water and shoals near the coast and almost no naturally good harbors, except for the rocky peninsula of Shantung, where the lack of easy transport connections with the hinterland, especially by river, has reduced the usefulness of the harbors at Tsingtao and Chefoo. Tsingtao's greater proximity to the Shantung coal fields and the larger North China market by rail have, however, made it second only to Tientsin as a northern port. Talien (Dairen) and Lüshun (Port Arthur) at the rocky tip of the Liaotung Peninsula, now often referred to as the single conurbation of Lüta, do a still larger shipping business as the dominant ports for the highly commercialized industrialized economy of the Northeast, and profit from the excellent harbor of Talienwan (*wan* "bay"); inland connections with Manchuria are primarily by rail, since the Liao River is navigable only for small craft. Tientsin is the largest port of north China Proper, but only by virtue of shifting its actual shipping business successively to a series of outports. The city itself lies some forty miles from the sea on the shallow and silting Hai Ho (*ho* is one of several Chinese words meaning "river"), now navigable for the most part only by barges. A huge bar has formed off the river's mouth at Taku, so that the late nineteenth-century outports at Taku and Tangku became increasingly awkward even for coastal shipping, which often had to load and unload by lighter off the coast. The present government has built a new artificial harbor just north of

Tangku which serves as the port of Tientsin. All of the harbors along the featureless sandy coast of north China are chronically threatened by silt brought down by the Yellow River and several lesser streams, and, in the case of Shanghai, by the Yangtze. Apart from Tientsin and the Shantung ports, the only others of importance are Chinwangtao, maritime outlet for the large coal mines at Kaiping north of Tientsin, and Lienyün (Haichow) in northernmost Kiangsu, the terminus of a major east-west railway, but they also have had to depend on artificial harbors and on continual dredging.

Shanghai remains China's largest port, as it has been for the past century, despite the shortcomings of its harbor. Dredging can barely keep pace with the growth of the offshore bar at the mouth of the Yangtze, and the channel to the port itself is narrow and plagued with silting. The city and most of its port facilities are not on the Yangtze but on a small tidal tributary, the Whangpoo (Huang-P'u), where the strong currents and silt loads of the master stream are avoided but where both depth and moorage area are inadequate. In larger terms, Shanghai's unparalleled commercial access via the Yangtze system to the most productive part of China has been enough to offset the difficulties of the city's site, much as Tientsin has grown to become the dominant commercial center and port for the north China plain despite its inadequate harbor facilities.

South of Hangchow Bay, almost exactly the reverse conditions obtain, along a coast which has in effect been drowned so that the sea laps over the eastern edge of south China's mountainous terrain. Hangchow Bay represents the fulcrum, with the coast north of it having risen relative to sea level and that to the south having sunk. The highly indented southern coast is thus provided with innumerable good harbors, but not with major ports, since the mountainous hinterland is both relatively poor and difficult of access. The West River and its delta and basin make Canton a qualified exception, although its deltaic harbor is poor. The present government has constructed a new port for south China at Tsamkong (Chan-chiang) south of Canton on the excellent natural harbor provided by Kwangchow Bay, linked to the rest of the south by rail. But, despite its small and shallow harbor, Canton is likely to remain dominant, if only because of its proximity to the most productive part of south China. Ports north of Canton—Swatow, Amoy, Foochow, Wenchow, Ningpo—although still used, were relatively more important in the past when trade was dominated by tea and silk and by a few other high-value goods for which overland transport costs were less of a barrier. Tea and silk were produced primarily in south-central China, and tea in particular, as a crop grown on slopes, was centered in the hill and mountain country which forms the divide between Yangtze and West River drainage. As Chinese tea lost its position in the world market with the rise of plantation production in India and elsewhere, and as the export market for silk was largely lost to Japanese competition, these coastal ports declined and others with better hinterland transport connections increasingly dominated a more diversified trade.

Hong Kong, since 1842 a British leasehold and hence not part of China, became, nevertheless, the leading port for the south and to some extent an offshore entrepôt for the whole country. Its large and deep island-sheltered harbor just off the estuary of the West River made it accessible to the largest shipping, as Canton was not, and in many respects it acted as Canton's outport, although as a free port it was an attractive transshipment center for the whole coast. Since 1949 Hong Kong's trade with China has been reduced and its population swollen by refugees from the mainland, but the colony has successfully shifted its main economic base from trade to light manufacturing, taking advantage of the large labor pool and of cheap water transport. Kowloon and the New Territories, part of the Chinese mainland added to Hong Kong's area in the latter half of the nineteenth century, have become a rapidly growing industrial zone, although much of the total food supply must be imported, mainly from the Canton area.

Climate

Even China Proper alone is an area big enough to include gross climatic variety, stretching as it does over 20 degrees of latitude and broken up internally in many sectors by mountain masses. North China and Manchuria have a markedly continental climate of short, hot summers and long, cold winters, becoming more extreme farther from the sea, and dominated alternately by cold, dry air masses from Siberia and Central Asia and by warm, humid air from the sea. Although the classical monsoonal pattern is not as strong or clear as in India or in South China, nearly all of north China's rainfall occurs with the warm maritime air masses of summer, while the winter is normally dry as well as cold, and characterized by strong westerly winds. The uplands of the northwest tend to hamper the penetration of moist maritime air in summer, but do not prevent the intrusion of cold, dry air in winter, while on the north China plain summers are generally moister and winters milder. The same pattern may be observed in Manchuria, where the northern half is far from the sea and is exposed to extremes of both drought and cold; the climate of the Liao valley in southern Manchuria differs relatively little from that of eastern north China.

The great climatic problem of all north China and Manchuria is drought, not only as the result of an over-all insufficiency of average rainfall but also because of gross variability, from year to year and in the seasonal timing of its occurrence. Average annual rainfall variability in north China as a whole is about 30 percent; in the northwest and in northern Manchuria it reaches 40 percent. This is a precarious situation, especially when the annual rainfall average even for the north China plain is only some 25 inches. Seasonable variability may be equally disastrous; rain often comes too late to save a crop, or too early, or is too concentrated, so that destructive flooding results. The population of north China has increased to the maximum which traditional agriculture could support under optimum conditions, and in at least one year out of every three conditions are far from optimum. As population density mounted, famine became increasingly frequent, periodically worsened by flooding. Winter precipitation is too little to build up much moisture in the soil for spring crops, when temperatures have risen, and spring rains are thus essential, but far from dependable. The north depends primarily on drought-resistant crops: wheat, soybeans, and cotton in the moister and more level areas, millets and sorghums on the drier margins and on poor soils. Extensive new irrigation projects, large and small, have greatly reduced the risk of loss in this agriculturally hazardous climate. The leading sorghum is kaoliang, introduced from central Asia about the seventeenth century, whose marked ability to withstand drought made possible the settlement of drier areas neglected earlier.

The line of 40 inches average annual rainfall, coinciding fairly closely with the Huai River and Hwai Yang Shan and Tsin Ling ranges, makes an appropriate division between north and south, not only climatically but in terms of human adjustment. South of it rainfall is generally both adequate and reliable, and seasonal distribution also favorable. There is a monsoonal peak in June, July, and August, when rain is most needed for agriculture, but no month is generally without significant rainfall, and there is also substantial winter and early spring precipitation from air masses moving slowly down the Yangtze valley and over south China. With the additional advantage of relatively mild winter temperatures, most of the south can produce two or three crops a year. Rice dominates southern agriculture and commands the best land, but is accompanied by winter crops such as beans and wheat, which are raised without irrigation during the period between rice crops. Parts of tropical and subtropical Kwangtung, with their unbroken growing season, have long raised three crops a year (two of rice), and the present government has promoted the northward spread of double-cropping of rice, making use of specially developed early-ripening varieties. Rice is also increasingly grown in the north, under new irrigation.

The widespread upland areas in the south may support fruit, nut, or tea crops, or may less appropriately be pressed into use for unirrigated cereals like maize, where they cannot be terraced for irrigated rice. Much of the land in slope has however been neglected, or used only as a source of cutting for fuel; under traditional conditions, the Chinese farmer could not afford to cultivate slope land unless it could be made to produce relatively high yields, although as population pressure mounted, deforestation and terracing spread increasingly onto even the steeper slopes in the south. Most of the originally dense forest cover of south China has been removed, although a few stands remain in less accessible places such as the mountains of Fukien and southern Anhwei. The scrub growth which succeeds forest has continually been cut over for fuel, animal fodder, and building materials, and offers inadequate protection against erosion in the heavy rainfall characteristic of south China. Reforestation has been pressed since 1949.

The few lowland areas of the south, however, especially the lower river valleys and deltas, are uniquely densely populated. Alluvial soil, adequate moisture, and long or unbroken growing seasons are optimally combined only here, and the Canton delta, for example, may support more people per square mile than any agrarian area in the world. The southwest is a distinct region climatically as well as in other respects. Lying on the fringe of the monsoonal influence, Yunnan in particular suffers periodically from drought, and the scarcity of level land plus the area's remoteness combine with climatic disadvantages to explain why this is the most sparsely settled part of China Proper.

The Agricultural System

Agriculture, which will long remain the major sector of the Chinese economy, plays a critically important part in Chinese economic growth. But it confronts serious physical disadvantages, in relation to the enormous size of the population. Only about 30 percent of the total area even of China Proper is under cultivation; about one seventh of this figure represents land newly brought into use since 1949. New agricultural land is still being added, both within China Proper (although at a slow and decreasing rate) and in Manchuria, Inner Mongolia, and Sinkiang. But this is for the most part marginal land whose productivity per acre is likely to be low in proportion to the high cost of bringing it into production, except where highly fertile soils and a long growing season can be combined with low-cost irrigation. China's total area is slightly larger than that of the United States, but it is physically less well endowed for agriculture and about 70 percent of the country as a whole (as compared with about 50 percent for the U.S.) cannot be used for crops on any rational basis, because of unfavorable climate, slope, or soils. Most of the existing cultivated land is highly productive, but it must be worked hard to produce large surpluses. Since the total population and the total amount of cultivated land are not known precisely, one can use figures only with caution, but it is clear that on a per capita basis China has a limited amount of agricultural land—certainly less than one acre per head of its population, as against over six in the United States—and yet is at the same time already making use of a larger proportion of marginal land with relatively low yields and high costs. There is also still proportionally little managed range or pasture land which can add to gross food supply as in the American and other Western agricultural systems.

Understandably the dominant feature of Chinese agriculture is its intensiveness; much labor and capital are expended per acre of cultivated land. Although capital remains limited, the total investment of manures, irrigation facilities, tools, and work animals is very great, and the long-term investment of both labor and capital in the construction of paddy dykes, irrigation systems, and terraces at least equally so. This level of investment is best repaid by the growing in each area of the crop which under local physical conditions can produce the highest yields—rice in the south wherever possible, and mainly wheat, beans, millets, and sorghums in the north. As grain yields rise and commercialization and transport facilities spread, more diversification is becoming possible, but for the most part the farming system rests on the growing of cereals (and potatoes in poorer soil areas), which return a greater food yield per acre than any alternative, including the raising of animals.

China has sometimes accordingly been labeled "the vegetable civilization," but its heavy dependence on cereal and tuber crops is rational, given limited good land and high population densities. Animals fit into this system for the most part only where their draft labor is essential, or where they can be maintained at least to some extent on a scavenger basis. In the south, where the rice paddies are commonly ploughed wet and soils ideally contain considerable clay to hold the water, ploughing is commonly done with water buffalo, but the net gain, after considering the food and shelter for such large animals, is calculated to include also the buffalo manure. The lighter and drier soils of the north can be ploughed with the help of horses, mules, cows or oxen, but when necessary are also turned by unaided human labor, although tractors are now becoming more widely available. Draft animals are not kept for meat, and are eaten with a show of reluctance when they die. Pigs and poultry, and to a much smaller extent sheep, can however be maintained on crop residues, grass cuttings from nearby slopes, or leavings. Pigs and chickens are widespread, as are ducks (which graze in effect in paddies and ponds), although where there is reasonable access to a market the animals' diet may be improved to well above the scavenger level and some land may even be alloted to the growing of fodder crops. Generally speaking, however, animals are less efficient sources of food than cereal crops, per unit of land, and the Chinese agricultural system is conspicuous for the very small amount of land given to fodder crops or to pasturage, except in the outer areas of steppe where commercial grazing is rapidly replacing traditional nomadism. Transport by pack animal or animal-drawn cart remains important, especially in the more level north, but, as with ploughing, the animal must earn its food by its labor, not as a source of meat. The Chinese diet is heavily dominated by cereals, tubers, and beans, plus the vegetables which may be grown in small kitchen gardens or along field borders, although the growing commercialization of the economy is accompanied by the beginnings of larger vegetable, fruit, egg, and meat production for sale.

The intensiveness which characterizes Chinese agriculture is apparent in what is expended on the growing of rice, the leading cereal. Rice is a demanding crop, but one which amply repays additional effort and capital investment. While in many parts of China it could be grown with little or no controlled irrigation, and with minimal fertilization or weeding, it is, in fact, almost universally irrigated with great care throughout the crop season, and heavily fertilized with human and animal manures plus increasingly available chemical fertilizers. The water level in the paddies is periodically altered for optimum crop growth, and the irrigation system designed so as to enable the alternate draining and flooding of the fields at different times. New dams, canals, aqueducts, and pumps have more than doubled the amount of irrigation over the country as a whole since 1949 and are important also in the south. Weeding is carried out almost continously, and enormous effort invested in transplanting the crop from the small beds where the seed is planted to the larger field in which it will mature, a back-breaking process (now beginning to be mechanized) which has long been known to raise yields materially. Animal and human wastes (night soil) are carefully saved, aged in pits, and applied with studied precision to the crop at proper intervals. Ashes, bones, and other wastes may also be used as fertilizer, but chemical fertilizers are only beginning to be available in the amounts required. It is understandable that rice production by such methods and dense population go together, each both stimulating and supporting the other, and that Chinese agriculture has long produced high yields per acre. Although rice is treated with particular care, most other crops, including those in the north, are grown under similarly intensive conditions.

With all its shortcomings, traditional Chinese agriculture was, nevertheless, an admirably productive system, particularly in terms of its per-acre yields, and still stands as a model of efficient intensiveness in sharp contrast to most other premodern agricultural systems except for those, like Japan's, which followed the Chinese model. Agricultural yield figures for most preindustrial economies are notoriously unreliable, but it seems likely that in the 1930s, for example, average Chinese yields for most crops were about as high as for the same crops anywhere else outside Japan (overlooking unrepresentative situations such as small rice-growing areas in specially favored parts of Italy, Spain, and the United States). This presumably means that, until the great increases in Western yields during the eighteenth and nineteenth centuries, Chinese yields were perhaps twice or even three times as great as those elsewhere. Yields per worker were, however, relatively low, and still are, so that there is a pressing need for the kind of technologically based rationalization including selective mechanization which the Japanese have so successfully applied and which the present Chinese government is pursuing. As population continues to increase (at what rate is not precisely known), the critical question is whether agricultural production can go on increasing fast enough and far enough to maintain and widen the gap between the number of people and the supply of goods and still leave surpluses for investment. The record of agricultural production since 1949 has only recently appeared to be very encouraging; although Chinese agricultural statistics are incomplete, it does not seem that up to the mid-1960s total production had increased significantly faster than population, although it may then have begun to do so as the variety of labor and technological inputs began to take effect, and as the Chinese planners after 1961 apparently began to divert somewhat more capital into the previously capital-starved agricultural sector. Nature is no longer to be accepted, but challenged and transformed by collective labor in the new conviction that "It is *man* that counts."

Population

There are population records for China over a period longer by far than for any other part of the world. But the dynastic compilations which begin with the Han were not intended as complete censuses and can offer only a gross approximation of population totals, which are differently interpreted by different scholars. These records are concerned variously with the number of households, or of adult males, or of taxpayers, and commonly omitted non-Han groups, women, or young children. The records and their systems of tabulation are also not consistent from period to period, and even within any one dynasty reflect varying levels of efficiency or administrative control, as well as changes in the territory under Chinese authority. Nevertheless it is possible to derive a reasonably consistent pattern of over-all demographic stability between the early Han and approximately the sixteenth century, including perhaps a slight net growth but marked even more by the decreases and increases correlated with periods of political-administrative and economic weakness and strength in the traditional dynastic cycle. With reasonable interpolation, one may regard the height of population under the Han and within the maximum of Han-controlled areas as probably not less than 60 or 70 millions, a figure which seems likely to have been reached, more or less, at the peak of each subsequent dynasty which ruled the whole country until the Ming. For reasons which are far from clear, the population apparently began to grow much more rapidly about the sixteenth century, and its rate of increase seems to have accelerated during the two following centuries; it may have slowed somewhat after 1850, but continued to grow so that the first attempt at a complete census in 1953 showed a total of 583 millions (plus some ten or eleven millions in Taiwan), a figure which has generally been accepted as approximately correct, although perhaps with as much as a seven or eight percent margin of error. The introduction of new crops, beginning in the late sixteenth century, especially kaoliang, early-ripening rice, and, from the New World, potatoes, maize, and peanuts, helped to make possible this very great population rise, and may have been also a contributory cause. But the increase took place without any fundamental change in the economic system, and in particular without significant industrialization, so that population pressure became a mounting problem which an already overburdened agricultural system was less and less able to cope with.

The Communist response to what in Western terms appears to be a Malthusian dilemma has not been entirely consistent, but seems since 1961 to have been more appropriate to the nature of the problem, and to its seriousness, if only as a powerful threat to per capita welfare. The government has released only fragmentary demographic figures since the time of the 1953 census, but given the internal power of the Chinese state and social organization, and despite the markedly youthful structure of its population, it seems probable that the birth rate is being significantly reduced by a variety of inducements and sanctions, although there seems little question that the death rate is being brought down at least as rapidly, with the help of the efficient public health service and the progressive eradication of epidemic diseases and malaria. Any attempts to project the growth of the Chinese population into the future must be highly speculative, in the absence of sufficient data, but it does appear likely that well before the end of the present century the total will have reached one billion, a prospect which may well alarm the Chinese planners. Most demographers estimate the total as of 1972 between 800 and 850 million.

This enormous mass of people is concentrated almost entirely in the eastern quarter of the country as a whole, or the eastern half of China Proper, as shown on map 1 in the Appendix, which also demonstrates the continued importance of plains and river valleys as China's major resources for the support of her people. Relatively little of the population, by Western standards, lives in cities (as distinct from villages or agricultural market towns)—probably less than 20 percent, and a much smaller proportion is engaged primarily in industrial occupations, although both categories are growing very rapidly in both absolute and relative size.

Resources for Industrialization

The Communist government has set as its major economic purpose the industrialization of China, and has made an impressive beginning toward this goal with the help of the Manchurian industrial structure which it inherited and with the great advantage of a mobilized labor force under planned direction. The collectivization of agriculture and state control of the entire economy place all resources at the disposal of the central government, for it to allocate as it judges best in the pursuit of rapid industrialization. It is unwise to be dogmatic about how far or how fast industrialization can progress, given the revolutionary drive, central control, mobilization of human energies, and sense of mission which are such prominent features of contemporary China. Natural resources constitute only one of the many factors in any industrialization process, and not necessarily one of the most important, as the example of a highly industrialized but resource-poor Japan suggests. China's natural resource base is, however, on the whole rich, and should exercise for the most part a strongly positive influence. The problem in the past has been how to put these resources to work, in the face of an overburdened agrarian base producing few surpluses for investment, a limited and expensive transport system which imposed prohibitive costs on the movement of bulky raw materials or goods except in the areas served by rail or water routes, an acute shortage of skilled labor and technicians, the shortage and high cost of capital, and the absence of a well-developed national market. The present government aims to double or treble agricultural production (a not unreasonable long-term goal), construct a national rail and highway network (already far advanced), continue its mass program of technical training, extract capital especially from agricultural surpluses, and further promote the already intensive search for new mineral resources.

China's resource inventory has been poorly known until recently, and estimates have had to be continually revised upward as a result of discoveries made since 1949. It remains difficult, however, to use precise figures; official announcements of new discoveries and revised estimates of total reserves are often made in very general terms, both as to amount and in terms of grade or quality. Remembering this, and remembering also that in the future important new discoveries in this huge and still imperfectly surveyed country are almost certain to be made which could conceivably alter the whole pattern, it does, nevertheless, seem clear that China is richly supplied with coal, and perhaps with iron ore, but may be less well off in petroleum, sulphur, and copper, at least in proportion to the population and to the levels of future demand. Coal, iron ore, and oil form a trilogy of heavily used raw materials which are therefore of primary importance to industrialization; sulphur and copper are used in somewhat smaller amounts, but the presence or absence of most other mineral raw materials (except for water), which are used in much smaller quantities, does not under present technological conditions matter very much, since they can more easily and cheaply be imported, if necessary over great distances, without greatly affecting total production costs. Hydroelectric power is treated separately below.

China is so well provided with coal that the precise total of the reserves is not important, although it probably places China third in the world, after the United States and the USSR. Enough of the coal is of sufficient quality (including coking coal), and occurs in large enough, easily worked deposits close to present or potential industrial and market centers, that industrialization need not be limited by any prospective domestic shortages. This wealth in coal, on the whole at relatively low cost, can be a powerful stimulus to industrialization, especially since coal has such a great variety of industrial uses, including the production of electric power and of synthetics. Coal is the major resource factor in the industrial pattern of Manchuria and in the rapidly growing industrial areas of eastern North China. The similar but smaller industrial developments centered on Chungking in Szechuan, at Lanchow in Kansu, and at Kunming in Yunnan are related to local coal and iron ores but are also part of the government's efforts to spread industrial development into previously neglected regions, as is the big new steel plant at Paotow in Inner

Mongolia, using nearby ores and coal from the huge fields in Shansi. Older industrial centers in eastern North China, notably Tientsin and Tsinan, depend on major coal mines in eastern Hopei and Shantung. The other two principal industrial bases, at Wuhan (Hankow, Wuchang, and Hanyang) and Shanghai, use cheap water transport as well as railways to bring coal to them at low cost from both the Yangtze valley and the north. China's coal resources may also be important in the future as exports to nearby coal-poor industrial areas such as Japan or Southeast Asia.

Wealth in coal is not apparently matched in any of the other major minerals, although as indicated above, caution should be observed in making any such assessment. However, presently known reserves of cheaply usable high grade iron ore, while extensive and much augmented by recent discoveries, may not be plentiful in relation to population and future demand levels. As with most mineral resources, national totals alone can be misleading, and in China's case some of the ore deposits appear to be too small and scattered to be optimally useful under modern industrial conditions where large scale often means low cost. Much of the iron reserve may also consist of low grade deposits which are expensive to concentrate or refine, as is characteristic especially of the Manchurian ores. Recent discoveries of what is said to be higher grade ore in Szechuan, Sinkiang, Inner Mongolia, the central Yangtze valley, and elsewhere may significantly alter the total inventory. In short-run terms, in any case, the total reserve is more than adequate and is on the whole not unfavorably situated.

It is more difficult still to make a firm assessment of China's petroleum resources, in the absence of complete or accurate data and in the probability of important discoveries in the near future as geological survey work progresses at an increasing rate. It was believed until fairly recently that China was very poorly supplied with petroleum but major finds have been made since 1950, especially in Sinkiang, the northwest, Szechuan, and Manchuria; exactly how large these finds are or what the attendant costs may be is hard to discover. There are extensive oil shales, especially in Manchuria, which are also being worked as a source of petroleum, but at a much higher cost than for petroleum from natural pools. This may suggest that the total reserve is still seen as relatively modest even for present demand levels, which though still quite small are barely met by domestic production, let alone future demand levels, as industrialization gathers momentum. The main bottleneck at present is probably the shortage of refinery capacity and of transport. Petroleum in Sinkiang and the northwest, which together probably account for at least half of the national total of reserves, is, moreover, awkwardly located; oil can be moved, by pipeline and by tank car, much more cheaply than most other bulk raw materials, but Sinkiang and the far northwest are remote from most present and potential markets. The geographical center of demand for industrial raw materials seems unlikely ever to migrate farther west than Wuhan, and any heavy dependence on Sinkiang as a source must impose additional costs. Petroleum shortages, if they should develop, can, however, readily be filled by imports at low cost, as has been done in industrial Europe, and need not constitute a significant bar to industrialization.

China appears to be abundantly supplied with aluminum, antimony, and tungsten, and has plenty of tin. Over half of the known world reserves of antimony and tungsten are in China, and exports of these ores can help earn foreign exchange to pay for whatever must be imported. As indicated above, there may be shortages of sulphur, copper, and some naturally occurring mineral fertilizers, but while this might impose additional costs it cannot be considered a major handicap. Shortage or abundance of other nonferrous minerals or alloys (China has ample nickel, for example, but may be inadequately supplied with manganese) is unlikely to have any significant effect on industrialization, since such materials represent only a very small part of total production costs and can readily be imported where necessary, assuming reasonably free international trade. For obvious reasons of secrecy and security, very little is known about China's resources of fissionable ores, but it seems clear that they must be considerable, not only because of geological probabilities and the immense size of the country but also because of the series of largely independent Chinese successes in the field of nuclear weapons. Such resources may, of course, become of overriding importance to industrialization in the future; if so, it would appear that China will at least not be disadvantaged in terms of its actual deposits of fissionable materials. But in that field, as in so many other aspects of industrialization, mineral resources play a largely passive and relatively minor role by comparison with a host of other factors, including technology and organization, which influence the process of development.

China is relatively rich in hydroelectric power potential, but this is a resource whose exploitation depends far more on economic and technological factors than on the physical requisites. It is, however, also one which both Russian and Chinese Communist planners have picked out for particular development, as an orthodox part of Leninism and in keeping with the ambitious ideas about the transformation of nature and the creation of new resources. The Yangtze alone has a power potential greater than the total developed hydroelectric power of the United States in 1960, and there is a wide variety of other sources, in humid and mountainous South China, in the Yellow River system where an enormous multi-dam control project will produce huge amounts of power, and in Manchuria. But hydroelectric power production requires very heavy capital investment, not easily obtainable in China for some time to come, and since power cannot economically be stored or moved over great distances, its profitability or feasibility depends also on the existence of a nearby market with large and constant demands for power, a condition which is only beginning to be fulfilled in most of the country. Nevertheless, China's water power potential must be seen as a strong resource asset, and its growing development is already helping to stimulate the growth of the industrial-commercial economy on which its own feasibility will rest.

All in all, while China may not have the same balanced and compelling resource advantages which helped to accelerate industrialization in western Europe or the United States, and must also confront inherited shortages of skilled labor, technicians, capital surpluses, and transport, it does possess a spread of natural resources which is more than adequate to permit extensive industrialization, in most cases even on the scale suggested by the size of the population. Whether or not and at what rate this may occur seems unlikely to be affected negatively by China's resource base, and may in some important respects such as coal be strongly affected positively. One aspect of Chinese industrial planning may be mentioned briefly here, since it has clear geographical relevance. This is the decision to locate new industry as much as possible in the previously undeveloped parts of the country, such as Paotow, Lanchow, Kunming, Urumchi, and elsewhere in the remote west and northwest. Local raw materials are often given as the basis for such decisions, but in fact it would appear that the decisions are more influenced by an ideological and noneconomic commitment to the notion of regional development and local self-sufficiency per se, primarily of previously backward regions. From an economic point of view, there seems little question that industrial investment would bring a higher and faster return in the established industrial areas, which arose there in the first place because of clear geographic advantages of cheap access to raw materials and markets, and low-cost transport. Steel production in Urumchi, for example, for either the relatively tiny provincial or the national market, must be at significantly greater cost than in Anshan or Wuhan, and must also face high transport costs for serving any aspect of the national market. Manchurian and east coastal industrial centers are of course still associated with the foreigners who were largely responsible for their original growth, but the pre-1949 industrial distribution pattern was far more a result of economic and geographic realities than of imperialist designs.

Part of the purpose of the commune system established in the late 1950s was to provide an organizational unit which could manage both agriculture and manufacturing, as well as mining, forestry, and all other production and services (including health and education) on the basis of local self-sufficiency and drawing on local resources. A large part of China's industrial output, especially light manufacturing, now comes from small-scale local factories in the communes. This includes not only the rapidly increasing production of farm machinery and chemical fertilizer (well over half the country's fertilizer output) but also local metallurgical and other basic processes in addition to a great variety of consumer goods. Such a pattern does of course save transport costs and accelerates a more evenly balanced regional development. Short-run production costs may be higher than those in major urban centers in some cases, but may come down over time, and are in any case accompanied by other benefits. Gross national product is seen as less important than local welfare, including its non-economic aspects. China also recognizes the problems of pollution and of overcrowding implicit in any large industrial city and is anxious to minimize these problems by controlled dispersal. Over-concentration is to be avoided, and most of the big cities are not being permitted to grow bigger.

Urbanization

The older established industrial centers are not, however, being neglected, and will probably maintain their dominance, if in a decreasing proportion. Manchuria, eastern North China, and the lower and central Yangtze valley remain by far the most highly industrialized and urbanized areas, and most of the largest cities are there. Apart from Peking, most of these cities owe the bulk of their modern growth, since about 1850, to Western-inspired trade and manufacturing, and all of them were part of the treaty port system, which helps to explain many aspects of the Communist response, including their efforts to build new industry elsewhere. Shanghai, a relatively small city when it became a treaty port in 1842, is now by far the largest, with a 1970 population variously estimated between 7 and 10 millions. Peking (approximately 4.2 million in 1970) has grown rapidly as the administrative and cultural center of a huge bureaucratic system. Tientsin (about 3.2 million in 1970), also a treaty port, with its industrialization originally sparked by foreigners, comes after Peking as the third largest city, followed by Shenyang (Mukden—some 3 million in 1970), an even more foreign city in its modern origins under Japanese control. All of the other million-class cities were treaty ports, and among them Wuhan, Chungking, Harbin (northern Manchuria), and Lüta owed a large part of their commercial/industrial growth to originally foreign enterprise, while Canton and Nanking grew in significant part in response to the same developments. The dominance of these ten largest cities, most of them on the eastern fringe of the country as a whole, is reflected in the fact that according to the 1953 census they contained about a quarter of the total population classified as urban (defined by the census as those living in settlements of 20,000 and above). The total urban population was, however, given as only about 13 percent of the population as a whole, although both the total and the proportion have undoubtedly risen since then.

The present government has attempted, with considerable success, to control rural in-migration which in the early Communist years became a problem as some urban populations were awkwardly swollen by migrants in search of greater economic benefits. The state also periodically reallocates workers from urban to rural employment, and from overcrowded urban areas in east China to the newly developing west and northwest. In more general terms, the present urban pattern contrasts sharply with its traditional outlines before the nineteenth-century beginnings of Western pressures. Before about 1850 most cities were dominantly administrative in function rather than commercial or industrial, and the only one of major size on the coast was Canton. The imperial capital dominated the urban structure, and the provincial capitals occupied most of the rest of the urban hierarchy. Trade, as well as manufacturing, took place through urban bases, but the city was less an economic than a political vehicle, for the control, taxation, and administration of the agrarian base on which the economy and the state so largely rested. The dominantly industrial/commercial cities on a model originally Western,and their emergence as the chief growing points of the Chinese economy provide a telling illustration of the scope and nature of the changes through which China is now passing.

XVIII

Political

Institutions

BY

CHARLES O. HUCKER

Among the arts in which the Chinese are habitually considered to have had eminent success, government has always ranked very high. To be sure, China's troubles during the past century—the degeneration and collapse of the old imperial regime under pressure from the modern West, its subsequent lapse into chaotic warlordism, the failure of the Nationalist Government under Chiang Kai-shek to withstand challenges from Japan and from domestic rebels, and the emergence of a harsh and truculent Communist regime—have weakened the awed admiration with which outsiders were once accustomed to regard the Chinese state. And modern students, skimming through historical accounts in which bloody rebellions, assassinations, palace coups, and other sorts of dynastic upheavals receive dramatic emphasis, may be inclined to see more of instability than of stability even in the traditional governmental system. But it might be forcefully argued that no other state system extant in the twentieth century has for so long, and with fewer significant disruptions, maintained a great nation in unity, in material prosperity, in cultural florescence, and in domestic and international peace. That is to say, on balance, in the long perspective of history, Chinese government has served China's national needs remarkably well.

One important aspect of government in China is implicit in what has already been said. No one would dare to generalize about a European state system or even a Western state system enduring from pre-Christian times to the present. But generalizing about a long-enduring Chinese state system comes relatively easy. Because the Chinese conceive of their national needs in distinctive ways, government in China has a distinctive style of its own. And because Chinese expectations of what government ought to do, how this ought to be done, and by whom it ought to be done have changed remarkably little in historic times, certain basic governmental principles and practices have persisted from high antiquity down to the present.

The Formation of Political Institutions in Ancient China

The earliest Chinese state that we know anything definite about was that of the Shang dynasty (1766?-1122? B.C.) centered in the north China plain. Small cities, the chariot, writing, and high-level bronze technology were already in existence. The kings considered themselves subordinate to many gods and ancestral spirits, to whom human and other sacrifices were offered, and from whom guidance, approval, forgiveness, and help were constantly sought. Other dignitaries of the realm were apparently a mixture of appointed agents of the king and independently powerful hereditary chieftains who recognized the overlordship of the king.

The Shang state was eventually overrun by a coalition of related but semibarbarous tribesmen from the western frontier, led by chiefs who established the Chou dynasty (1122?-256 B.C.). The postconquest regent Chou Kung (the Duke of Chou) is considered the principal architect of the governmental system that consolidated, perpetuated, and gradually extended the Chou rule. The system, commonly compared to medieval European feudalism, had many familiar elements. The Chou kings retained their original homeland in modern Shensi Province for their own support and parceled out the regions formerly ruled by the Shang kings to their kinsmen and to allied chieftains, all of whom accepted a form of vassalage to the Chou king and were granted titles of nobility that are rendered into English as duke, marquis, earl, viscount, and baron. These ensconced themselves in walled fortresses and undertook to pacify and govern the peoples and lands granted them. Theoretically, every feudal lord's status and powers were legitimated by royal decree and had to be renewed every generation, but in practice they soon became hereditary. As centuries passed, the lord's fiefs became distinctive regional states, varying greatly in size, military power, cultural traditions, and economic patterns.

Within the royal Chou domain, and in each of the regional fiefs, attendants at the ruler's court were given responsibility for different realms of activity, as chamberlains in the household, as stewards of the ruler's treasury and personal property, as collectors of revenue, as dispensers of punishments, as masters of ceremonies, as military officers and aides, and so on. Some were sent out to be overseers of settlements or subregional areas. Though nominally appointed to serve at the pleasure of the ruler, these so-called ministers and great officers in their turn, like the feudal lords themselves, soon came to hold their offices hereditarily. In lieu of salaries, they were generally assigned certain lands within the domain, together with the farming families resident there.

In the beginning, the feudal fiefs of Chou times were military occupations of potentially hostile territories, and the warriors who comprised the occupying forces became a hereditary knightly class supported by and available for service to the local ruler, for his domestic policelike needs or for the fulfillment of his military obligations to the king. It was from this knightly class that posts as "ministers and great officers" were filled as need arose.

The kings, the feudal lords, the ministers and great officers, and the warrior knights, though conscious of differences in ranks and privileges among themselves, constituted a large nationwide body of nonlaboring aristocrats who lived off the peasants, patronized the craftsmen, were catered to by merchants, governed in the limited ways that were necessary, and devoted themselves to practicing the knightly skills of archery and charioteering and pursuing a wide variety of amusements. Once the conquest stage was past and the empire became pacified and stabilized, this elite group was increasingly drawn to more peaceful and genteel pursuits—fine arts, music, literature, learning, ceremonial ritual—and should be considered more a group of "gentlemen" than a corps of warrior knights.

In sum, the political system devised by Chou Kung and other Chou founders was a loosely centralized, feudal-like division of China among its aristocratic leaders, who drew material support for themselves and their knightly followers from the peasant commoners. The aristocracy conducted the business of government in a highly personal and paternalistic manner, and, although there was considerable specialization of functions, professional attitudes about governmental work were very slow to develop.

The lordly fiefs of early Chou times eventually developed into almost independent regional states, and rivalries among them could not be suppressed indefinitely. The grand alliance eventually broke up into competing leagues, in which one group of states allied itself against another, and even lip service to the king was eventually neglected. Showing their contempt for the last shreds of religious sanctions that legitimated the Chou rulers, feudal lords began to call themselves kings; by diplomatic intrigues and finally by imperialistic and increasingly rapacious wars they set about to win the whole of China for themselves. This process was well under way in the fifth century B.C. By the end of the fourth century B.C. China was immersed in endemic civil wars. Smaller states were swallowed up by bigger ones. The Chou royal house and domain were exterminated in 256 B.C. Finally, in 221 B.C., the western state of Ch'in established the political order that we know as the Chinese empire.

The chaotic multi-state competition that characterized the last half of the Chou era produced intellectual as well as social ferment, and out of this ferment gradually evolved the schools or modes of thought that were to provide an eclectic ideological foundation for the long-lived imperial system that succeeded the Chou feudal system. There were three principal schools: Confucianism, Taoism, and Legalism. Each was, in its own way, a response to the political and social disorder of late Chou times.

It was under the influence of Legalist advisers that the efficiently organized state of Ch'in in 221 B.C. subjugated the last of its rivals, united the whole of China under centralized rule, and expected that its dynasty would endure for endless generations.

Government in the
Imperial Age

Although its expectations of indefinite perpetuation proved unrealistic, when the state of Ch'in unified China it brought into existence a form of government whose basic characteristics persisted until A.D. 1912. During these two millennia, successive dynasties appeared and disappeared. At times China was again politically fragmented as in the late Chou era. Frequently nomadic barbarians from the north occupied and ruled substantial parts of the empire, and the Mongols and Manchus in turn even brought the whole of the empire under their rule. Significant socio-economic changes occurred: China slowly grew from a predominantly rural society into one with large urban components, and what had been a thoroughly agrarian economy slowly changed into one with large commercial and small industrial components. Religious and philosophical attitudes were transformed, primarily in response to the introduction of Buddhism from India. The Chinese homeland was enlarged, and the population grew and shifted. As all these and other changes appeared, the government necessarily had to be adapted to new circumstances. It grew in size and complexity, and its procedural techniques became increasingly sophisticated. Particular policies were successively adopted, modified, and discarded. But there was a continuing tradition in government that sets the imperial age apart from both the feudal age that preceded it and the republican age that followed it.

Some of the chief characteristics of this tradition might be briefly described as follows: 1. Sovereignty was vested entirely in a hereditary absolute monarch whose direct rule normally, and ideally, encompassed all of the Chinese people. 2. The ruler's government was structured as a three-faced pyramid comprising a civil administration, a military establishment, and a censorial system; and each of these was a hierarchy of agencies or units extending from the central government down to regional and local levels. 3. The government was staffed on bureaucratic rather than feudal principles, with officials who were appointed by and answerable to the ruler and whose powers were authorized by the ruler. 4. The government not only undertook to provide for the national defense, to maintain domestic peace, to dispense justice, and to levy and collect sufficient revenues to maintain itself; it assumed regulatory powers over, and accepted responsibility for, all aspects of the life of the Chinese people—their moral standards, their intellectual and aesthetic activities and development, their social customs and behavior, their religious attitudes and activities, their property, their physical and material welfare, in short, everything that the government at any time chose to become concerned about. 5. The government was totalitarian in the sense that neither individual citizens nor any organized group of people had any private status or rights that they could legitimately defend against the power of the ruler and his government. 6. The ruler assumed that his absolute authority properly extended over all people, not the Chinese alone; but as a matter of policy he did not interfere in the lives and activities of other peoples known to the Chinese so long as they did not threaten Chinese interests and did acknowledge his overlordship, even in token fashion.

THE SON OF HEAVEN

From Chou times onward, Chinese rulers were popularly called "Son of Heaven." They were not considered divine in any sense: the term implied that the ruler enjoyed Heaven's fatherlike favor and owed Heaven sonlike obedience. The familistic conception of the universe and the empire was also apparent in another term commonly applied to rulers, "Father and Mother of the People." In a broad extension of the familiar family pattern, the ruler was the intermediary between Heaven and mankind, playing one role as filial dependent to Heaven and another role as paternal exemplar to the people.

Chinese dynasties were founded in various ways. Most commonly, dynastic founders were former ministers or generals or, rarely, plain subjects who turned against incumbent emperors and wrested control of China from them by successful rebellions. In some instances, however, they were the leaders of relatively bloodless palace coups. In a few instances, also, men founded new dynasties with apparent reluctance, in response to "popular demand" at court.

By whichever of these varied means he might come to power, the founder of a new dynasty was ordinarily, and of necessity, a vigorous and capable man who had learned how to succeed in the world of reality. Also, he had a relatively free hand in focusing governmental attention on current problems; he was normally able to reduce government expenditures and the people's tax burdens, since it was expected that he would cut away sinecures and obsolete institutions accumulated during the prior dynasty; and he could exploit and benefit from the high morale and the sense of dedication among his supporters that normally made his initial success possible. Founding emperors, therefore, usually presided over eras of stability, prosperity, and expansion following eras of discontent and trouble; and their policies and achievements were almost always glorified and emulated by their successors. Whatever their personal idiosyncrasies might have been, dynastic founders generally received flattering treatment at the hands of Chinese historians as "good first emperors."

The emperors who followed founding emperors were molded by a different environment and were confronted with different problems and expectations. The family of a reigning emperor lived a secluded life in an elaborate palace complex, and his sons grew up in the care of palace women and eunuchs, their every whim being catered to immediately and their knowledge of the outside world being second-hand at best. They were educated in the classical literature by specially assigned officials noted for their erudition and deportment. Especially by the time a family had held the throne through several generations, new emperors characteristically came to the throne poorly equipped for bearing their responsibilities. Those of strong personal character were often tyrannical, and those who were weak were easily duped and exploited by self-seeking officials, relatives by marriage, or eunuchs. Moreover, the traditional institutions and policies handed down from the ancestors were not easily upset, and routine administration was securely dominated by prestigious and conservative officials. Consequently, later emperors in a dynasty seldom provided the sort of creative leadership that was required to make the government flexibly responsive to changing conditions and needs. After early deterioration, it was not uncommon for a "mid-dynasty revival" to come about under an able emperor; but eventually deterioration in state effectiveness reached a point where the government was overwhelmed by problems of domestic unrest or foreign threats. Then some strong man would emerge to found a new dynasty, and the so-called dynastic cycle would begin again. Because of the implications of the Mandate of Heaven idea, the final ruler in any dynastic line was inevitably blamed for what had happened and went down in history as a typical "bad last emperor."

THE INSTITUTIONAL APPARATUS

The state structure over which Chinese emperors presided had the continuing characteristic, from Ch'in times onward, of being organized into three functionally differentiated hierarchies, each comprising agencies extending from the central government down to regional and local levels. But the state institutions evolved in complex ways. Not only did the number and kinds of agencies in the structure multiply as the nation's area, population, and economy grew. Government also experienced a marked difference in character as it changed from a ruler-oriented sort of imperial household administration into a state-oriented national administrative organ. It experienced, too, a transition that found the status of the military rather steadily losing ground to the growing status of the civil aspects of government.

Of the three hierarchies of government, the one that might be called the general-administration hierarchy was always the most complicated and elaborate. It managed the ritual, fiscal, judicial, educational, personnel, diplomatic, and other general aspects of state administration. The military hierarchy included all the armed forces, which normally greatly outnumbered other governmental personnel, although their structural organization was simpler. The censorial hierarchy was a group of agencies that characteristically had no direct administrative responsibilities but were charged with maintaining surveillance over all governmental activities, civil or military, and in consequence impeached wayward officials and proposed changes in state policies and operations, sometimes through dramatic remonstrances about the personal conduct of the emperor himself.

The central government of Ch'in and Han times was dominated by a triumvirate representing these three facets of government: 1) a Grand Counsellor who was the emperor's chief agent or prime minister in dealing with general administration, 2) a Grand Marshal who was the emperor's chief agent in control of the armed forces, and 3) a Censor-in-Chief who was the emperor's chief surveillance agent. In these early times the central government otherwise consisted largely of organs whose names and functions suggest their primary concern with caring for needs of the imperial household: Court of Imperial Sacrifices, Court of Imperial Entertainments, Court of the Imperial Stud, Court of State Ceremonial, and so on. By T'ang (618-907) and Sung (960-1179) times the central government had greatly expanded and had become more institutionalized. The military establishment was coordinated under a Bureau of Military Affairs. The censorial system included two autonomous top-level agencies, a Censorate specializing in surveillance and impeachment and a Bureau of Remonstrance specializing in counseling and admonishing the emperor about his policies and personal conduct. For general administrative purposes there was now a coordinated cluster of top-level agencies—a Chancellery, a Secretariat, and a Department of State Affairs—whose ranking officials served as a state council, which made policy decisions under the chairmanship of the emperor. And the Department of State Affairs incorporated a group of six functionally differentiated ministries that had routine control over administration and were becoming the solid core of central government operations. These were the Ministry of Personnel, Ministry of Revenue, Ministry of Rites, Ministry of War, Ministry of Justice, and Ministry of Works. All governmental matters except tactical military operations and censorial activities now fell increasingly under the domination of these ministries. The Ming emperors (1368-1644) tried to do without the old executive superstructures entirely, leaving the six uncoordinated ministries as the highest level general administrative agencies and five uncoordinated Chief Military Commands as the highest level military agencies. But even in Ming times the obvious need for coordination produced a new, more informal executive body called a Grand Secretariat; and the succeeding Manchu emperors of the Ch'ing dynasty additionally created an even more prestigious and powerful policy-making body called a Grand Council of State. Meanwhile, there had developed through the centuries a vast assortment of lesser, more specialized organs. There were service agencies, some directly descended from the ancient Courts of Ch'in and Han times, that provided for the practical needs of the greatly expanded imperial household establishment. There were educational and literary agencies, culminating in a National University, which helped prepare men for the civil service, and a Hanlin Academy, which consisted of various erudites engaged in drafting and polishing imperial pronouncements of different sorts and in the compilation of imperially sponsored works, including dynastic histories. There was also a relatively autonomous judicial agency, the Grand Court of Revision, which served as a court of review when severe penal sentences were rendered by the line administrative agencies.

At the local level, the abolition of feudalism by the Ch'in dynasty, despite subsequent resurgences of feudalistic tendencies in times of disorder and disunity, eventually brought about a focusing of all the emperor's responsibilities and powers on his lowest level appointee, the magistrate of a county (*hsien*). He was the agent through whom the central government dealt ultimately with the people at large. He was assisted by locally recruited functionaries and by government-sponsored private groupings of community elders and others, who assumed responsibility for keeping order, settling litigations, fostering education, and in general carrying out all government policies at the grass roots level. But the county magistrate was answerable to the emperor for everything that transpired within his jurisdiction, which might encompass as few as fifty thousand or as many as one million residents. He assessed and collected taxes, dispensed justice, organized and at times commanded local militia, sponsored and patronized local schools, participated in religious ceremonies of local importance, regulated local business and industry, and above all by his own conduct set a good example for his people. If within his jurisdiction there existed a military garrison under the control of the military arm of the central government, he usually exercised at least indirect control over its use for any needed police or local defense work.

Between the county magistrate and the central government there gradually developed a complicated ladder of intermediate, supervisory agencies. The first step, historically, was to consolidate several counties under the control of a prefect, whose prefecture (*fu*) might be divided into several subprefectures (*chou*) for even closer supervision of counties. Then various kinds of supervisory agencies were imposed upon the prefectures, originally in the form of traveling commissioners sent out from the central government but by the thirteenth century taking the form of permanently established provincial (*sheng*) governments. Under the Ming and Ch'ing dynasties these were tripartite, as was the central government, comprising a provincial military command, a provincial general-administration agency, and a provincial censorial-judicial agency. These in turn sprouted subordinate circuit intendants (*tao-t'ai*), who gave closer supervision over regions comprising several prefectures. Beginning in the fifteenth century the provincial agencies in their turn were made subordinate to grand coordinators delegated from the central government, serving as provincial governors; and groups of provinces were further coordinated for military purposes under supreme commanders or viceroys, similarly delegated. Thus, by the last years of the empire, the line of general-administration responsibility ran from county to subprefecture to prefecture to circuit to provincial agencies to provincial governor (perhaps then to viceroy) to the six ministries to the Grand Secretariat to the Grand Council of State and then to the emperor, and the line of authority ran from the emperor back down the hierarchy in reverse order. The military and censorial hierarchies were not equally extended but were represented below the provincial level.

From an early time it was recognized that too much centralization and too much decentralization were both harmful; centralization made government too unresponsive to problems and needs at the regional and local levels, whereas decentralization undermined the central authority and permitted the rise of regional separatist movements. Attaining a sound balance between the two extremes was a continuing challenge to the Chinese, and fluctuations between the extremes account for the recurrence of despotism on one hand and of warlordism on the other.

THE CIVIL SERVICE

Both the general-administration and the censorial agencies of the traditional government were staffed chiefly with men originally selected for state service on the basis of their individual merits as demonstrated in competitive, public, written examinations, which tested their grasp of classical and historical literature and especially of Confucian philosophical principles, and their ability to apply the precepts and precedents of the past to either timely or timeless political and ethical problems, and to do so in good literary style. Having once entered state service with such a background, they were regularly shifted from one post to another, rated on their performances, and cautiously promoted step by step into steadily more responsible and prestigious echelons of government. They were classical scholars, historians, moralists, poets, essayists, and calligraphers. They were not professional specialists in any particular branch of administration, except as they gained on-the-job experience; and they were not expected to think of themselves as professional bureaucrats. They were genteel, right-minded men, proven so in examinations and in service; and their principal responsibility was to conserve and exemplify the religiophilosophical principles on which Chinese civilization was based. The longevity and the general conservatism of the traditional state system are due primarily to its domination by such men.

The abolition of feudalism in the third century B.C. set the stage for the emergence of this civil service system in Chinese government but did not automatically bring it to full flower. Through the Han era and for some centuries thereafter, the men who dominated the government were in large part direct or indirect representatives of powerful, wealthy "great families" which maintained aristocratic traditions and privileges. Newcomers to the state service were generally appointed on the basis of recommendations submitted by existing officials. But such nominees began to be subjected to qualifying written examinations in the second century B.C., and the notion gradually developed that educational achievement was a better basis for appointment than social status and contacts. In T'ang times, in the eighth century, the full transition from aristocracy to "meritocracy" finally came about, and from then on the typical successful civil servant was the examination graduate.

In its fullest development the civil service examination system functioned as follows. Every year educational intendants representing the provincial governments traveled about their jurisdictions giving examinations to the students in state-supported schools and to private scholars who presented themselves. Those who came up to the educational intendants' standards were given titles certifying them as state-recognized men of talents, or literati. They were thus entitled to wear distinctive costumes, their families were granted certain tax exemptions, they were honored as local heroes, they became confidants and social equals of local officials, their views on private and public matters were heard with respect, and they were sought after as tutors of the next generation.

Passing the local examination qualified a man to participate in provincial-level examinations in competition with candidates from all over the province, often numbering several thousand. These examinations were prepared, proctored, and graded by high-ranking scholar-officials sent out from the central government. The candidates faced a grueling ordeal: three full days of writing examinations, spaced over a week. Those who passed were very few, perhaps one in twenty; and the passers became provincial heroes overnight. They were given new titles, new costumes, and new privileges. They could be considered for low-ranking governmental appointments, and their new status need not be renewed at intervals. They were assured of social and economic success.

To be certain of a fully successful career in government, one more hurdle had to be surmounted. This was an empire-wide metropolitan examination conducted at the national capital several months after the various provincial examinations every third year. It also stretched out over a week, but was even more difficult, and those who passed were still relatively few, totaling two or three or perhaps four hundred. The graduates (generally called *chin-shih*) had a final ordeal, a palace examination presided over by the emperor himself; but this was a brief examination for the sole purpose of ranking all of the *chin-shih* in order of their excellence, and no one failed.

All new *chin-shih,* and especially those who ranked first, second, and third in the final list, were lionized both at court and in their home towns to a degree that even all-American athletes of our time would envy. They had been accepted into the fraternity of supreme literati to whom the state looked for leadership, with prestige and access to power and wealth that no other group in society could aspire to. Winning such status was the ideal goal of every filial son, and having a son or a grandson win such status was the dream of every father.

For all its glory, becoming a *chin-shih* merely opened the door to a civil service career. Graduates became part of the pool of literati from which the Ministry of Personnel called men to fill official vacancies when they occurred. All posts in the officialdom were ranked on a scale of eighteen degrees, ranging from 9b at the bottom to 1a at the top; and all qualified civil servants were comparably ranked, new graduates naturally falling low in the scale. When a 6b post fell vacant, an unassigned 6b official was assigned to it. His performance was evaluated by his administrative superiors at the end of three, then of six, and finally of nine years on the job; and he was also evaluated irregularly by touring censorial officials. All these evaluations went into the records of the Ministry of Personnel, which retained a man in one post and in one rank up to a maximum of nine years or demoted or promoted him as circumstances warranted. Progress up the ladder of ranks, through a succession of varied posts, was normally slow and erratic, so that those few officials who ultimately emerged into the top echelon of highest ranking officials who were the executive advisers to the throne ordinarily attained such distinction when they were full of years and experience, widely acclaimed for their erudition and probity, and sufficiently awesome to deserve respect and deference from even the most arrogant emperor.

The great prestige of the civil officialdom throughout the last millenium of the empire was based in considerable part on the traditional Chinese respect for learning, but it also derived from very real power exercised by the officialdom. The civil service was largely self-regulating. It conducted its own recruitment examinations. Although all appointments within the service were made by the emperor, he was customarily bound to accept nominations from the Ministry of Personnel or, in the case of very high-ranking posts, to choose one of two or three qualified men nominated by the Ministry. Moreover, although the emperor established state policies, the size of the empire and the complexity of its affairs made him almost totally dependent on the factual information and recommendations provided by the officialdom, which thus tended to limit the alternatives among which the emperor could choose in his policy decisions. The fact that the emperor, as Son of Heaven, had unchallengeable power to punish any official on any pretext in any way was, to be sure, a restraint on the officialdom's sense of independence. But, on the other hand, emperors of the most despotic inclinations had to realize that there were clear limits beyond which they dared not antagonize the officialdom or any substantial segment of it. The civil service, in short, had become a relatively autonomous and self-perpetuating power bloc in the state system. The emperor had no choice but to share his power with it and to accept the principles on which it insisted the state must function.

THE MILITARY TRADITION

So great has been the prestige of Confucian philosophy and the civil service system, and so poorly has China fared in military competition with the modern West, that students have long deemphasized the military aspect of traditional Chinese government. But the contemporary rise of Chinese militarism is not to be wondered at, since the authority of every imperial dynasty rested in the last resort on military force, and traditional China had a long history of military development and strength.

To be sure, one of the great themes of traditional Chinese history is the gradual evolution of a warrior elite into a literati elite. The ancient Shang and early Chou societies were highly militaristic. The knightly aristocrats inevitably became more genteel as the arts of civilization flourished, and the early Confucians transformed the knightly ideal into a gentlemanly scholar and moralist. The devastating civil wars of the late Chou era, combined with common beliefs about cosmic harmony, made war an abomination to mankind and Heaven alike, and the subsequent stabilization and growth of a huge and complex empire accentuated the importance of trustworthy administrators dedicated to peace and order. As an adviser told the founding emperor of the Han dynasty, "You might have won the empire on horseback, but you cannot govern it on horseback." The powerful families that dominated society through Han and into T'ang times were fond of the old aristocratic ways and devoted their leisure to archery and hunting. But a corollary of the growing dominance of a civil service bureaucracy in T'ang and Sung times was a corresponding loss of status among the old military elite, and the civil service gradually incorporated military affairs into its realm of control. In the last dynasties, therefore, what we in the West think of as civilian supremacy over the military was solidly established in China. Military planning, equipment, and personnel matters were all in the hands of the civil service Ministry of War, and control over military matters on a regional basis throughout the interior and along the frontiers was vested in supreme commanders or viceroys who were also of the civil service. The military service had become a corps of technicians subordinate to civil service directors, and military status and prestige had declined accordingly. In the last centuries of the empire it was taken for granted that soldiering was to be avoided at all costs by respectable people, and communities dreaded the coming of rowdy, undisciplined troops, friendly or otherwise, about as much as a swarm of locusts.

The Chinese had long experience of war, partly among themselves but most of all with the nomadic non-Chinese who were always present along the northern and northwestern frontiers—the Hunnish Hsiung-nu in Ch'in and Han times; the Hsien-pi, T'o-pa, T'u-chüeh, and other Turkic peoples in post-Han and T'ang times; the proto-Mongol Ch'i-tan and proto-Manchu Jurchen tribes in Sung times; the Mongols proper in the thirteenth and following centuries; and the Manchus proper in the seventeenth century. The Chinese consequently developed highly sophisticated and systematized techniques for waging war. As early as the fourth century B.C. specialists began producing treatises on warfare that dealt in persuasive common-sense terms with the complexities of military strategy, training, weapons, logistics, psychological warfare, espionage, fifth-column subversion of the enemy, and so on. The most noted of the ancient military classics is *The Art of War* by Sun Tzu, which has been translated into several modern Western languages and has been studied by Mao Tse-tung and his admirers in and outside China.

The military establishment never attained organizational permanency comparable to that of the civil service. Once the era of knightly charioteering had passed and warfare had evolved into mass action involving large numbers of infantrymen and cavalrymen, the Chinese vacillated between relying on "temporary" armies based on compulsory universal military service, "permanent" armies made up of hereditary soldiers, and either "permanent" or "temporary" armies consisting of men lured or coerced into service for pay. All efforts to create a standing army sufficient for ordinary needs, backed up with reserves adequate to meet emergencies, and to do all this without undue strains on the national treasury, deteriorated in time, so that major challenges had to be met at all times with drafts or impressments of poorly trained civilians supported at great cost to the nation. Non-Chinese fighting forces were readily utilized when available.

The military establishment normally had a hierarchical structure parallel to that of the civilian government, including local garrisons throughout the empire, regional and provincial-level supervisory commands, and a principal headquarters in the national capital. Along the frontiers and in other strategic places there were always special concentrations of garrisons. The settled garrisons provided routine guard and patrol service in their localities. When large-scale hostilities began, whether in the interior or at the frontiers, troops from all over the empire were assigned to campaign duty in armies created on an *ad hoc* basis and often commanded by dignitaries dispatched from the capital rather than by the regular local or regional officers. In the vicinity of the capital there was always a strong additional force, relatively independent of the line military units, of capital guards and imperial guards. These were the elite forces of the empire, but they were seldom committed to battle except in major undertakings, and they consequently had somewhat more a ceremonial character than a tactical character.

The Chinese faced severe logistical problems in their intermittent struggles with the nomads of the north and west. Since the frontier regions were deserts merging into steppes, grain-eating Chinese armies penetrating beyond the frontier could not live off the land but had to carry their supplies with them. They were, therefore, at a substantial disadvantage against nomadic herders who drove their herds with them on campaign, and who consequently had greater endurance and mobility. To offset this disadvantage, the Chinese often developed strings of self-supporting garrisons or military colonies in the oases dotting the Central Asian wastelands, which served as sturdy fortresses guarding the caravan routes to the west and bases from which small-scale campaigns could be mounted against the nomads. But such oasis garrisons were always dependent upon friendly support from local tribal chieftains, and they were highly vulnerable whenever widely organized nomadic empires developed in Central Asia.

On the other hand, China was always highly vulnerable to raiding assaults from beyond the northern and western frontiers. The sedentary Chinese farmers and city dwellers were tied down by their lands and property, on which their livelihood depended; and defenses had to be spread thinly across the whole frontier area. The nomadic peoples of the steppes, being totally mobile, could when well organized mass for a concentrated attack on any one point on the long defense line and, having broken through the defenses, ravage the exposed towns and countryside before Chinese reinforcements could be assembled. To help prevent, or at least to slow down, such assaults, feudal lords in Chou times began building frontier walls. One of the great achievements of the totalitarian Ch'in regime in the third century B.C. was to consolidate these local walls into a continuous wall stretching across the whole of North China. Rebuilt and repaired many times thereafter, this Great Wall of China did have significant effect in reducing nomadic raids. It remains today, largely as rebuilt in the Ming dynasty, as a monumental rampart some fifteen hundred miles long winding along the crests of mountains and hills between the Yellow Sea north of Peking and the Sinkiang desert. When in active defense use, the wall was studded with watchtowers within sight of one another, all manned by troops rotating on and off duty from nearby garrisons and equipped with signal flags and torches that allowed quick communication along the wall, and connected to garrisons in the rear by lines of signal stations. It was occasionally broken through, but in general the wall served its purpose.

The technology of warfare changed markedly through Chinese history, though not so dramatically as in the West. The knightly charioteers and archers of Shang and early Chou times gradually became obsolete as interstate competition became more intense and massed national armies came into being. Introduction of equestrian techniques from Central Asia in mid-Chou times revolutionized warfare by making the cavalry the main striking force of any Chinese army. Cavalry remained the core of military strength throughout imperial history, even into the nineteenth century. Since China has few extensive pasture lands and the Chinese for centuries have not engaged in animal husbandry except to keep such scavengers as pigs, chickens, and ducks, maintaining a supply of horses for military use was always a serious matter for the Chinese government. It usually managed to supplement the domestic supply with horses purchased from friendly steppe nomads, who developed a great taste for Chinese tea and were always willing to barter for it. Mounted archers of the cavalry were supported in battle, and were always greatly outnumbered, by massed infantry archers and lancers.

As early as Shang times, the Chinese used extraordinarily powerful composite bows of the general type known today as Turkish bows, made of laminated wood reinforced with horn and sinew. Such bows have been known to shoot more than 800 yards; their pull and power far exceed those of the bows traditionally used in the West. Bows of this sort remained standard equipment in Chinese armies into the modern era. Beginning in Han times they were supplemented with even more powerful trigger-released crossbows, which were the Han "secret weapons" against the Hsiung-nu and gave rise to the boast that one Chinese crossbowman was a match for ten nomads. By T'ang times the Chinese had invented gunpowder and used it for fireworks, but it was not until the long-drawn-out Sung defensive war against the Mongols that gunpowder was put to much military use. Then a variety of bombs, grenades, and bazooka-like rifles were developed. But thereafter the Chinese did not assiduously develop more and better firearms, as did Westerners. In early Ming times special army units seem to have been regularly equipped with primitive firearms, but, when modern Europeans appeared in China in the sixteenth century, Chinese forces were still committed predominantly to the use of ancient weapons. The Ming government borrowed cannons and cannoneers from Portuguese Macao to defend its capital from the Manchus, and both late Ming and early Manchu rulers commissioned

Jesuit missionaries to cast cannons for their use. Thereafter, the Chinese slowly introduced Western firearms or imitations of them into their armies, but in so cautious and conservative a way that China lagged even farther behind the West in weaponry.

Strangely enough for a continental nation traditionally at war with steppe nomads on its inland frontiers, China from an early time became quite adept at naval warfare. Inland waterways had been important travel and trade routes from the dawn of history, especially in the humid southern half of China; and domestic wars caused the military exploitation of rivers and lakes at least as early as late Han times. Great inland naval battles time and again were decisive in major wars, as in the extinguishing of the Sung dynasty and the founding of the Ming dynasty. Even the nomadic Mongols themselves developed naval forces for the conquest of South China and, later, for expeditions against Java and Japan. In the early fifteenth century Ming emperors sent a series of great fleets out to roam the Indian Ocean—large multitiered junks each capable of carrying several hundred men, which dominated the southern seas and coasts a century before the Portuguese rounded Africa. Although Chinese trading junks followed in their wake, and coastal Chinese migrated throughout Southeast Asia in an endless stream, the Chinese government's attention was quickly turned landward again, so that naval strength and traditions waned. In this regard, too, late imperial China was no match for the modern European powers.

LAW AND JUSTICE

In ancient China, especially during the chaotic centuries when the Chou kings had lost real power and feudal lords were contending for leadership and dominance, arguments for rule by law competed openly with arguments for rule by men. Legalists and the efficiency-minded ministers who were their forerunners insisted upon governing states systematically in accordance with well publicized and strictly enforced codes of administrative and penal law, and they decried as sentimental foolishness the Confucian notions about benevolent government conducted by moral gentlemen. The success of Ch'in in utilizing Legalist principles to conquer the whole of China, followed by its quick collapse into new civil war, led to the development of ambivalent attitudes toward the principles Ch'in espoused. Popular hatred of Ch'in's harshness made it impolitic for anyone thereafter to advocate Legalism openly. But Ch'in had accomplished much and had established a governmental pattern that showed the way in which China must subsequently be organized. The Han dynasty that followed therefore renounced Legalism officially while organizing a long-lived empire on essentially Legalist principles, merely moderating the harshness with which Ch'in had applied them. The imperial state system that emerged consequently had a Legalist form suffused with a Confucian spirit. The concept of rule by men triumphed over that of rule by law, and the system was perpetuated century after century because it provided a successful way of obtaining the right men to rule—conscientious, trustworthy, generally admired Confucian scholars. But Legalist forms persisted because in actual fact the administration of a large, populous, and complex empire required some measure of systematization and standardization.

The mixing of Legalist and Confucian elements is especially evident in the Chinese traditions concerning law and justice. The early Confucians emphasized setting a proper example and distrusted law codes, which Confucius himself felt must inevitably have loopholes that scoundrels could exploit. However, once Confucians found themselves responsible for governing the empire, they became assiduous codifiers of laws and regulations, and the codes they produced became the models that other East Asian peoples adopted for themselves. Yet they were strangely un-Legalistic in character, and recognizably Confucian. That is to say, the laws were not conceived of as absolute commandments to be enforced to the letter without fear or favor. Rather, they were intended to be general normative guides for conduct that must be interpreted and applied by wise magistrates in a flexible manner, depending upon the people and the circumstances confronting them. Justice was not an abstract thing, and men were not equal before the law.

What has been called "the Confucianization of law" in China meant that justice was administered in a very relativistic way. Who did what? To whom? Under what circumstances? With what effect on the community at large? All these questions bothered a Confucian magistrate. It was of course a serious matter if one man took another's life, for example. But there was no absolute rule that the penalty for murder is death. A father who killed his son for disobedience might not even be investigated, let alone punished. But a son who killed his father might be put to death as a most heinous murderer, even if the killing were so unintentional that had the victim been a stranger it would not have called for punishment at all. Thus, what society expected of anyone depended on his role in any given relationship and on his general social status; and law existed to bulwark and enforce these expectations, for the well-being of society as a whole.

Justice was administered at the lowest official level by the county magistrate. He served all at once as investigator, prosecutor, defender, and jury. His sentences were subject to automatic review by his administrative superiors and by censorial visitors, and death sentences usually required ratification at all levels up the administrative hierarchy to the throne itself. Provisions were also made that sentences could be appealed by the victims, in some cases directly to the throne. These review and appeal procedures no doubt ameliorated the harshness of judicial administration, but the system clearly functioned in such a way that innocent persons were often punished. In traditional China it was clearly understood that the social order and its values, rather than individual rights of any sort, were to be protected above all else.

Some modern writers of fiction have created the impression that the Chinese were traditionally masters of ingenious, sadistic punishments. The historical record suggests that the Chinese could indeed be cruel on occasion but that they were no more sadistic than their contemporaries in the traditional West, and probably less so. At least, they were not generally inclined to punish people for their religious beliefs, and they tended to be notably more cautious in imposing the death penalty than Westerners have been. Early modern Westerners who visited China generally wrote of China's judicial system quite favorably in comparison with their own.

The commonest official punishment in traditional China was beating on the haunches with a bamboo rod—from ten to a hundred blows. This was, of course, no light punishment, since the first blow sometimes drew blood and more extended beatings sometimes caused death. For more serious offenses, persons were normally beaten and then banished to live far from their homes and families in specified places under official surveillance, either for a designated span of years or permanently. To be banished to live in the "malarious districts" of China's far southwest was especially dreaded and often quickly fatal. Death penalties were normally carried out by decapitation, but strangulation could be substituted as a sign of special imperial mercy. In some periods, for especially heinous offenses, men were sentenced to more brutal executions, such as being drawn and quartered, or being cut in half at the waist.

FOREIGN RELATIONS

The notions that a Chinese emperor ruled by Mandate of Heaven and consequently was Son of Heaven and Father and Mother of the People coincided in traditional times with distinctive Chinese ideas and practices concerning non-Chinese peoples. It seemed obvious that Heaven's Mandate applied to "all under Heaven" (the Chinese term for what we call the Chinese empire) and that the Son of Heaven was the only legitimate intermediary between Heaven and mankind. Therefore, it was natural for the Chinese to assume that chiefs of other peoples exercised authority by grace of the Chinese emperor whether they realized it or not, and that anyone who failed to acknowledge the sole supremacy of the Chinese emperor was a "barbarian" who denied the will of Heaven, whether deliberately or in ignorance.

China considered itself the giver of civilization, and its defender. Some neighboring peoples—notably the Vietnamese, the Koreans, even the Japanese—rather eagerly adopted the Chinese way of life as their own. Although an aggressive leader on one side or the other disrupted friendly relations occasionally, these peoples did not question the superiority of Chinese culture. Other peoples, such as the southwestern aborigines within China proper, were not so admiring of Chinese civilization and repeatedly rebelled against Chinese dominance. The Chinese dealt with them firmly and tried to educate them, though they did not try very aggressively, so that the aboriginal tribesmen played a role in China's life and history quite similar to that of the American Indians in the United States. The nomadic peoples inhabiting the steppes and deserts of Mongolia and Central Asia were almost always hostile to the Chinese, or potentially so, and the Chinese way of life was not exportable to their nonagrarian homelands. In dealing with them the Chinese had to have a warily defensive posture, and open warfare regularly recurred. Even when Chinese rulers took the initiative in campaigning against the nomads, it was usually in the conviction that the best defense is a strong offense. In diplomatic ways, also, the Chinese tried to overawe or to divide the nomads. When possible, China kept princely hostages at its court under the guise of educating them. When necessary, the Chinese did not hesitate to bribe the nomads to keep the peace. At times, China even sent huge annual tribute payments to powerful nomad leaders.

In theory, however—and generally in practice—China was the

recipient of tribute payments from neighboring peoples. Making gifts of distinctive local products to the Chinese emperor at intervals was one symbolic way in which foreign rulers showed their submissiveness. In exchange for these tokens of submission, tributary rulers were promised protection from both domestic and foreign enemies; they benefited at home from the prestige that China's recognition gave them; and they profited handsomely in material goods, since the Chinese emperor, upon accepting the gifts of a tribute mission, paternalistically showered upon it gifts of Chinese goods having much greater value.

In sum, it might be said that, whereas inside China feudalism early gave way to a centralized bureaucratic organization, China's relations with other peoples were always conducted on a feudalistic basis reminiscent of the Chou dynasty's principles of organization. There was no conception of equality among nations. The Son of Heaven was everyone's overlord in what has been called "the Sino-centric world order."

EVENTUAL COLLAPSE OF THE IMPERIAL ORDER

The decline and final disintegration of the old imperial regime in China can be accounted for in many ways, not all of which are related to the governmental system that was the core of the old order. But the political aspects of China's inability to meet the challenge of the modern West in the nineteenth century are of major import, and two kinds of considerations require exploration. On one hand, it is clear that many of the basic principles and characteristics of traditional government—the very things that had served so well for centuries to stabilize, perpetuate, and defend Chinese civilization—now created an unfavorable environment for the sort of change that circumstances required of China. On the other hand, it is clear that by the nineteenth century the traditional state system had gravely corrupted its own principles and was operating with far less effectiveness than must previously have been the norm.

The traditional Chinese ideology was a significant handicap as China encountered the modern West. Not only did China's inclination to think of harmonizing with Heaven's Way dispose the Chinese against the industrial technology that gave the modern West its great military strength; Chinese concepts about the Mandate of Heaven and the Son of Heaven made it impossible for China and the Western nations to meet without one side or the other suffering humiliation and frustration. China could not engage in international relations on a basis of equality without undermining its whole ideological system, and the power-proud West could not tolerate playing even a nominally submissive role toward China. Many decades had to pass, and China had to endure many humiliations, before government-to-government discussions of useful and promising sorts could even begin. And China's conservatism, of course, was diametrically opposed to the dynamic expansionism of the nineteenth-century West. China exuded contentment with the *status quo* and did not wish to compete with the West, whereas change and competition were vital forces shaping the Western powers and thrusting their impact upon the rest of the world. The Chinese wanted peace and security and clung to the precedents that had for so long guaranteed them, whereas Westerners longed for the unprecedented and willingly courted danger and undertook risks in striving for it. Thus, in all Sino-Western relations, neither side could accept or appreciate the point of view of the other, and the initiative was always with the West.

The fact that China was dominated by a single homogeneous elite group of bookish, moralistic scholar-officials, who of all groups in Chinese society were most committed to traditional ways, put China at a particular disadvantage in its dealing with the soldiers, businessmen, and churchmen who spoke for the nineteenth-century West, often in discordant voices. The Chinese leaders never found Western equivalents with whom they could discuss problems in terms that were not offensive to them; and when China, nevertheless, finally undertook to learn from the West for the sake of its own survival it had great difficulty in deciding where the multifaceted West's strength really lay—in its military power, its industrial production, its commercial shrewdness, its political institutions, or its ideology. The Chinese literati were the last persons who could be expected to realize that the West's strength might derive precisely from the decentralized, multi-centered character of Western society that so confused and appalled them. Since the literati had the most to lose from any comparable development in China, they were highly unlikely champions of Westernization.

Even considering these and other aspects of the traditional order that inevitably handicapped China in its confrontation with the modern West, one might argue that the Confucian state system should, nevertheless, have been flexible and responsive enough to survive this new challenge as it had survived other challenges over the centuries. But in the nineteenth century special conditions existed that seriously weakened the traditional system, to the point where it could not respond even with minimal effectiveness. Prominent among these are the following:

1. During the last dynasty China was ruled by aliens, the Manchus. Some modern Chinese have no doubt gone too far in blaming the Manchus for China's decay. But it cannot be overlooked that, from the very beginning of the dynasty, there was always a strong element of nationalist, anti-Manchu feeling among the Chinese, reflected largely in patriotic secret societies, so that when China faced the challenge of the West it was not united in loyalty to its existing government. Moreover, in seeking to win Chinese loyalty, the Manchus for generations had zealously championed the traditional orthodoxy, perhaps to the point of being more rigidly defensive about it and more antagonistic to change than might have been the case with a native dynasty.

2. By the nineteenth century China's military establishment was stagnant. The Manchus had entered China in the seventeenth century as military conquerors and had segregated themselves from the Chinese population at large in "banner" encampments as the permanent, hereditary military service of the empire. The Manchus' policy of cultivating Chinese ways jeopardized their military effectiveness from the start, although domestic and foreign wars kept them militarily alert through the eighteenth century. But supplementary Chinese militia forces gradually took over some of their military duties, and decades of peace sapped their vigor. By the middle of the nineteenth century the bannermen had become indolent parasites, unfit and untrained for war service and barred by law from any other vocation. Manchus could no longer even give effective leadership to Chinese militia units, upon which the defense of the empire now rested.

3. The civil service had meanwhile been corrupted and demoralized, and its prestige was at one of its historic low points. The very fact that civil servants now served an alien ruler tended to discredit the officialdom in some measure, so that the people became willing to look for leadership in other directions—for example, secret societies. What was perhaps worse was that China's population had grown enormously while the officialdom had not grown, so that the officialdom seemed much more remote from the common man than ever

before. Moreover, in the nineteenth century no one could pretend that the civil service was a meritocracy, obviously deserving admiration and obedience. For one thing, it accommodated large numbers of Manchus, who monopolized certain key posts and who generally shared in all major responsibilities, although they were not judged for admission to the service in open, fair competition with Chinese examination candidates. Also, the examinations became steadily more bookish and impractical. By the nineteenth century the examinations actively discouraged thought and emphasized rhetoric and even calligraphy, which were easier to grade. By the nineteenth century, too, fiscal pressures had caused the government to put examination degrees and appointments up for public sale in ever larger numbers. All these factors contributed to a widespread feeling, by no means unjustified, that the civil service was dominated by Manchus, the wealthy, and the most conformist and uncreative kinds of academic drudges. There were talented and capable officials as before, to be sure; but the civil service as a whole was no longer the admired elite it had been in Sung and Ming times.

4. Instead of being centralized as prescribed by the tradition, political authority was steadily being fragmented. Until the nineteenth century the Manchu emperors jealously monopolized power, but the Taiping Rebellion, which ravaged large portions of China between 1850 and 1865, forced the central government to yield control over large regions to field commanders of the imperial armies such as Tseng Kuo-fan, who personally rallied Chinese forces for defense against the rebels, gathered the revenues that supported such forces, and saved the throne for the Manchus. Although Tseng and his lieutenants and successors remained loyal supporters of the Manchu rulers, they had such personal followings and personal resources that the late nineteenth-century Manchu court was more dependent on them than they were on it. Political power gradually shifted away from the court into the hands of provincial governors, who had military forces at their disposal. China was obviously on the verge of separatist warlordism.

As both domestic discontents and foreign pressures grew, China's political order deteriorated very rapidly. When the Manchu dynasty finally expired in 1911-12, the traditional state structure identified with it disappeared also.

Government in Nationalist China

The Manchu empire was overthrown primarily on the initiative of a small group of idealistic republican revolutionaries under the leadership of a Western-educated political exile, Dr. Sun Yat-sen, which eventually took the name Kuomintang, or Nationalist Party. On January 1, 1912, they established a government at Nanking and proclaimed the existence of the Republic of China, with Dr. Sun as its first president. Their uprising won such popular support that the Manchus soon abdicated, but they left in charge at Peking a general controlling the most modern army in China, Yüan Shih-k'ai, and Yüan had ambitions of his own. The Nationalists, finding that they were popular heroes but that real power was in the hands of Yüan and of provincial warlords who now looked to him for leadership, agreed to unite with Yüan's supporters in a republican government at Peking, with Yüan as its president. From 1912 to 1928 this Peking government was the Republic of China recognized by foreign powers. It theoretically was dominated by an elected parliament, but the first parliament was dominated by the only organized political group, the Nationalists; and they got on so badly with Yüan that he outlawed their party, banned them from Peking, and finally dissolved the parliament entirely in favor of dictatorial presidential rule. He even planned to found a new imperial dynasty of his own, but unfavorable reactions to this were so strong even among his own supporters that he had to abandon his plans, and in 1916 he died broken-hearted. From that time on, the Peking government maintained essential national services such as the postal system and the educational system, and it conducted diplomatic relations with other nations, to which it regularly gave mining, industrial, and commercial concessions in exchange for loans. But it had little control over the whole of China; real power was in the hands of provincial warlords who cooperated in shifting cliques to maintain the central government's facade and who occasionally warred on one another. The nation had little unity and little reason for pride, and it made very little progress.

When the Nationalist Party was outlawed, Dr. Sun and his followers found refuge in Canton in the south, where they were tolerated and sometimes even befriended by local warlords. They found no support among the Western powers, and World War I disillusioned them about the worthiness of Western political institutions and ideals. The successful Russian revolution seemed to offer more relevant and transferable experience, and they set out to reorganize themselves into a militant revolutionary group after the Russian Communist model. The Chinese Communist Party was organized in 1921, and on orders from Moscow it joined with the willing Nationalists in an effort to prepare for overthrowing warlordism and bringing to fulfillment the revolution begun in 1911. A Kuomintang army was organized. After Sun Yat-sen's death in 1925 the army chief, Chiang Kai-shek, successfully led the uneasy coalition of Nationalists and Communists northward, and in 1928 the warlord-dominated Peking government was dissolved. A new Nationalist-dominated Republic of China came into being with its capital at Nanking. Almost immediately, though recognized and befriended by the Western powers, it alienated Japan, which had developed strong imperialistic interests in North China since the 1890s. In 1931 Sino-Japanese hostilities broke out, and these gradually led to full-scale war lasting from 1937 to 1945. The war ultimately engaged the United States and other Western powers on China's side and ended in the defeat of Japan, but it left the Republic of China exhausted, demoralized, and divided.

Long before this—beginning in 1927 during the march to the north that established the Nationalist Government—Chiang Kai-shek had turned on the Communist members of his coalition, had outlawed their party, and had mounted campaign after campaign in efforts to exterminate the state-within-a-state that the Communist Party then set up in China's interior. The Nationalists and Communists were forced into a second, and even more uneasy, coalition by the need for common defense against Japan. But the Communists expanded their strength and control greatly during the war by guerrilla tactics behind Japanese lines in the north, and when the war ended the two sides confronted one another in contention for national control. Efforts to achieve a negotiated settlement failed, and civil war resulted. In 1949 the Nationalists retreated in defeat to the island refuge of Taiwan (Formosa), where they have continued to carry on the semblance of a national government. The Communists, in 1949, established a People's Republic of China on the mainland with its capital at Peking under the leadership of Mao Tse-tung, one of the original founders of the party.

The Nationalist Government is based on principles enunciated by

Sun Yat-sen in a series of lectures in 1924. These so-called Three Principles of the People are the Principle of the People's Nationalism, the Principle of the People's Democracy, and the Principle of the People's Livelihood. Under the topic People's Nationalism, Dr. Sun blamed the Manchus and foreign imperialists for most of China's modern troubles and tried to arouse a rather racist patriotism so as to restore unity and dignity to the nation. As for People's Democracy, he spelled out the form of government he wished to see emerge in China and the stages in which he foresaw that full multiparty democracy might be achieved. He never completed his lectures on People's Livelihood, but what he did say in this realm set guidelines for national efforts at industrialization and other forms of economic development, for patterns of taxation, and for a range of state-sponsored welfare activities and efforts to curb the worst excesses of private capitalism. These lectures in their entirety, which serve as the ideological foundation for the Nationalist Government, suggest a conscientious effort to strike a balance between authoritarianism and democracy and between capitalism and communism, conserving the many elements of the Chinese tradition that Dr. Sun considered good.

The changing shape of the Nationalist Government has been spelled out in three basic documents: an Organic Law promulgated in 1928, a Provisional Constitution of 1931, and a final Constitution of 1947. Much Nationalist effort went into constitution-making, in the conviction that setting things right on paper was a big step toward setting them right in reality. The form of government prescribed in these documents has remained fundamentally the same. There is a president under whom national affairs are supervised by five coordinate organs called *Yüan*. The Executive Yüan, incorporating many specialized ministries and commissions, carries on the general administrative business of government. Its president is often referred to as the premier. The Legislative Yüan drafts and enacts laws. The Judicial Yüan supervises the administration of justice and interprets the law. The Examination Yüan, whose existence reflects Sun Yat-sen's respect for old civil service principles, qualifies men for appointive offices. The Control Yüan, suggestive of the old censorial system, exercises powers of impeachment and audit. Until the end of World War II the military establishment was controlled by a Military Affairs Commission having autonomous status, but the Constitution of 1947 placed the military under a Ministry of National Defense subordinate to the Executive Yüan.

The Nationalists divided China into twenty-eight provinces and made provisions for elective governments with variations according to local customs at the provincial level and at the more basic county level. But the Nationalists never had effective control over all these provinces, because of Japanese conquests, Communist occupations, and concessions made to regional warlords. While on the mainland, they controlled such areas as they could through appointed governors and military commanders, and they never had much opportunity to develop governmental machinery at the county level, where affairs languished under traditional local leadership. After the Nationalists retreated in 1949 to Taiwan, one of the smallest and least populous provinces, they gradually allowed the development of free, multiparty elections of provincial governors and councils and of county councils. But they retained all the superstructure of the national government in exile, skeletonized and waiting to resume its theoretical control over the twenty-seven mainland provinces.

Throughout its history, the Nationalist-dominated Republic of China has been a façadelike institutional apparatus through which the Nationalist Party has tried to control China. Since the coalition years of the 1920s, the party has been organized along the lines of the Russian Communist Party, in local cells that elect representatives to county executive committees, which in turn send representatives to provincial congresses, which in their turn send representatives to a national congress. The party's national congress meets rarely, delegating its powers to a central executive committee, the standing committee of which, like a communist politburo, is actually the policy-making body for the party and the nation. Since the 1920s the party and the nation alike have been dominated by Chiang Kai-shek. Men he trusts have been chief officers of the party and, simultaneously, chief officials in the government. Personal loyalty to him has been the key to success in party and government, and both have been affected by the rise and fall of cliques in his favor. Unlike Sun Yat-sen, Chiang has not been particularly interested in or adept at political theorizing; but in his later years he has become a moralist of conservative and rather Confucianist mien. He has been a remote figure much in the tradition of Chinese emperors. His power has derived from his control over Nationalist military forces and the support of China's business community, and his popular image is a blend of the stanch defender against Japan, the tragic hero who refused to compromise with communism, and the somewhat ascetic exemplar of personal incorruptibility.

History confronted Chiang Kai-shek and the Nationalists with very complex and difficult problems. Sun Yat-sen had foreseen that nothing could be achieved in China without political unification and that unification could be achieved only by military means. The first phase in his plan, consequently, was military conquest. This was to be followed by an era of political tutelage, during which the Nationalist Party in paternalistic fashion would prepare the people for full multiparty democracy, the third and final phase of Sun's plan. But the Nationalists never wholly unified China. Immediately after their first successes, Japanese attacks and communist threats forced them to carry on the processes of military conquest and political tutelage indefinitely, while more and more Chinese, weary of war and despairing at economic disintegration, blamed the party for the inflation, the corruption, and the dictatorial militarism that developed, and demanded immediate implementation of full democracy, which they believed would end their troubles. As critics became more insistent, the Nationalists became more suspicious, more conservative, more intolerant, and more convinced that China could not be abandoned to chaotic democracy. The Nationalists lost the mainland in 1949 because the Chinese people at large would no longer tolerate existing pressures and had lost faith in the possibility that the Nationalists, with their demands for patience and sacrifices and moral self-cultivation, could alter the situation for the better. The relatively successful Nationalist administration of Taiwan after 1949 did much to restore the party's morale and its reputation in the outside world, but did not prevent the ousting of Nationalists and seating of Communists by the United Nations in 1971.

Government in Communist China

The Chinese Communist Party, organized in 1921, won control of mainland China in 1949 by its own efforts, with very little help from the Soviet Union. On orders from Moscow, it had collaborated with Sun Yat-sen and Chiang Kai-shek in the 1920s; but it had then been driven underground, and almost exterminated, by Chiang's armies in the early 1930s. Reorganized and reoriented by Mao Tse-tung, it survived by taking advantage of popular clamor for a united front against Japan, then grew by taking advantage of Japanese vulnerability to behind-the-lines guerrilla activity, and finally conquered by taking advantage of the Nationalists' deterioration in wartime conditions and especially of their lack of sympathy for economic distress at the grass roots level and for the complaints of idealistic intellectuals. The Communists came to power in 1949 with a dedicated, experienced, toughened corps of leaders ready to grapple with real problems, and they were welcomed with relief by a people tired of war and disillusioned with the Nationalists' promises.

For the Nationalists' paternalism, the Communists substituted fraternalism. They presented themselves as liberators, not oppressors. They listened to the common people with respect and promised to learn from them and to join hands with them in efforts to improve conditions. They held elections, they set up "people's courts," and they founded a People's Republic of China. Moreover, they were disciplined and incorrupt. All indications suggest that they won genuine, widespread support and that, since their takeover, the Chinese people generally have fared better in material ways and have experienced more active participation in government than was the case under the Nationalists.

The costs paid for such progress have been substantial; as Mao Tse-tung had warned, revolution is not a garden party. In the name of the common good, private wealth has been confiscated, private property has been collectivized, private thoughts have been exposed, and millions of persons considered enemies of the people have been put to death, assigned to reform-through-labor projects, or subjected to humiliation and vilification. Also, the Chinese people at large have been insulated from the outside world. They have been indoctrinated to fear and hate the West, and steeled for what is presented as an inevitable armed clash with the United States in particular. The people have consequently been required to devote efforts and resources to military activities at some cost to other developmental programs.

As in traditional times, and as in the Nationalist regime, government in Communist China is organized in a vast hierarchical pyramid with power radiating down from the top. The Constitution of 1954, under which the government functions, provides for a strong chairman or president of the People's Republic. Associated with him are two theoretically autonomous specialized organs: A Supreme People's Court, which is responsible for the administration of justice, and a Supreme People's Procuratorate, which is charged with maintaining censoratelike surveillance over the state apparatus and the citizenry to see that the law is enforced. Both of these organs have counterparts at the provincial and county levels. But the chairman of the government manages all matters of both military and civil administration through agencies directly subordinate to him: a National Defense Council and a State Council, the latter headed by a premier who supervises the work of many ministries and commissions. Through the State Council, the chairman's directives move down to councils at the provincial and then the county levels, and even beyond that to village councils and town councils.

The organizing principle of the government is known as "democratic centralism." The "democratic" character is justified by the fact that local councils are appointed by and responsible to local congresses that are popularly elected. The local congresses also designate representatives to county congresses, who in turn designate representatives to provincial congresses, and these in turn designate representatives to an All-China People's Congress, the principal duty of which is to elect the chairman of the People's Republic, confirm his nominees for important posts, and hear his reports on the state of the nation. Thus at each level of government there is a congress elected directly or indirectly by the people, which theoretically establishes policy, and an appointed council (in the case of the central government, a chairman) to administer policy. The centralization of authority is secured by the fact that each council, while answerable to the congress that appointed it, is also answerable to the administrative agency at the next higher level. Moreover, each council has the power to suspend decisions made by congresses at the next lower level and to revise or annul directives issued by councils at the next lower level.

In actual practice, although non-Communist parties are allowed to exist as long as they are cooperative, the Communist Party dominates the People's Republic as fully as the Nationalist Party has ever dominated its government. It has the usual communist-style organization, running from small cells at the bottom of the hierarchy up through local, regional and provincial levels to a National Party Congress, where power is concentrated in a Central Executive Committee and a subordinate Central Political Bureau. All organs of government at all levels are virtually monopolized by party members. Also, all governmental programs have been implemented at the grass roots level by party agents, called cadres. It is to these young, zealous activists that the Communist government owes most of its successes and many of its excesses. It has been their responsibility to translate the ideals of Mao Tse-tung and the general directives of party headquarters into operational reality in the villages and city wards.

Since it was at this level that the Nationalists failed most notably, the Communist Party has selected and trained its cadres with great care, to achieve an optimum blending of almost fanatical party loyalty with common-sense realism and responsible creativity. When the cadres have too zealously implemented the party line, progress has been pushed too far too fast to the point of diminishing returns, as in the so-called Great Leap Forward. On the other hand, when cadres have stressed practical solutions to problems more than party discipline, free thought has flourished to such a degree that the party's basic premises have been threatened, as happened when the so-called Hundred Flowers movement produced a crop of ideological weeds. As the Chinese put it, the cadres must be "both red and expert," not one to the detriment of the other. Above all, morale among the cadres must be kept high, for the cadres are depended upon to give exemplary leadership to the people, and eventually to provide personnel for party and government positions of responsibility and power. Once again, in short, China's public affairs are in the hands of a meritocracy, an elite group of men judged on their merits, these merits being defined largely in terms of dedicated adherence to an orthodox ideology.

Once again, also, the government is totalitarian in that it claims authority over and responsibility for all aspects of Chinese life. As in traditional times, but not characteristically in the case of the Nationalists, no force or group is allowed to compete with the government for power over the people. Either by direct government action or through mass organizations inspired by the party (cooperatives, women's associations, youth leagues, and so on), the Communist Party channels all of the people and all of their activities toward goals established by the state. Although the Chinese people have long been accustomed to being organized and to subordinating their interests to those of the group, they have never before in history been so totally organized as now. Religion, education, business—all have been subordinated to the state, and penetrated by the state to grass roots levels never reached before. Even the family has been subjected to attacks, since familism of the traditional Chinese sort handicaps the development of nationalism; and young people are being trained to look for security and gratifications outside the family, in state-oriented mass organizations.

Even the old universalistic concept of the world order seems to have echoes in contemporary China's attachment to a world revolutionary movement and its effort to assume the leadership of the movement. Although in its early years the People's Republic had no choice but to play the part of younger brother to the Soviet Union, on which it relied for technical aid, it was not long before Chinese arrogance provoked the Russians to rupture these relations; and the Chinese have not hesitated to compete against the Soviet Union openly, and in an increasingly hostile manner, for influence within the communist bloc—in Asia, Africa, Latin America, and even Eastern Europe. The West is envied and to some extent feared, but the Chinese exude confidence that their cause is destined to triumph over the West: "The east wind prevails over the west wind." China's attitude in this regard is not aggressively militaristic. Chinese fought United Nations forces in Korea when they thought China's vital interests were threatened; they heavy-handedly put down rebellion in Tibet; they skirmished with Indian forces along the Tibetan border long enough to demonstrate their superiority and safeguard what they considered their territory; they have talked freely of conquering Taiwan and so reuniting the Chinese nation in its entirety; and they insistently prepare the people to defend the country from anticipated American attacks. But, on the whole, their actions have not been warlike. They expect to triumph by a process of historical inevitability, very much as ancient Confucians serenely and confidently argued that the virtue of a truly kingly ruler would eventually overwhelm the most awesome armies.

The personal influence and mystique of Mao Tse-tung have increased enormously, as if the Chinese find it difficult to accept anything other than the one-man rule to which they were accustomed in traditional and Nationalist times alike. After the Great Leap Forward of 1958, Mao stepped out of the presidency without yielding his party leadership; and for a time it appeared that President Liu Shao-ch'i, a long and faithful aide, was emerging as a second-generation leader with less grandiose and more pragmatic goals. But in 1965 Mao loosed a Cultural Revolution designed to transform human nature and human society so thoroughly that nothing comparable to the de-Stalinization of Russian communism could occur in China. Bypassing both governmental and party organizations, he entrusted his new campaign to fanatically zealous youth groups called Red Guards, and these disruptive hordes virtually took over the country and subjected President Liu and many other public figures now considered anti-Maoists to unremitting abuse, humiliation, and in some cases physical attack. Even more than before, "Father Mao" was publicly credited with infallible wisdom and judgment on all subjects, was spoken of with deference akin to that formerly shown Sons of Heaven, and was made the personal symbol of all China's aspirations. Probably no other public figure in modern world history has been so glorified by his people. But the Cultural Revolution brought China to a condition of astonishing disarray—in domestic politics, social order, economic organization, education and science, and diplomacy. What new adventures Mao might undertake, or how a post-Mao China might be consolidated into a more stable polity, remains to be seen.

Contemporary China faces problems that would strain any government. It is overpopulated, underendowed with natural resources, underdeveloped in technology, politically isolated from possible sources of outside help, and proud of a heritage that will not let it be content with second-rate status. The people are willing to work and willing to be led, and their leaders—notwithstanding the aberrations of Mao Tse-tung—have not been lacking in intelligence and dedication. How China will continue to fare under their guidance will clearly remain one of the great themes of human history in our time.

XIX

The Chinese

Language

BY

YU-KUANG CHU

Chinese is one of the major languages of the world in the sense that it is the mother tongue of more people than any other language, although it does not have as wide a geographical distribution as English or French. In recent years Chinese has been increasingly taught to college and high school students in this country, perhaps in anticipation of the need for large numbers of persons competent in the Chinese language to deal with a resurgent China. Actually, apart from this practical need, considerable theoretical interest and liberal value are derivable from a study of Chinese, because the language, in both its oral and its written aspects, is dramatically different from Western languages. It helps one to appreciate the richness of human thought and civilization to see how a language, with a literature comparing favorably with the best of the world, was created and developed by another part of mankind on the basis of principles strikingly different from those to which one is accustomed.

Because of their differing characteristics, Chinese and English are classified into entirely different language families.[1] English belongs to the Indo-European family, which also includes the Germanic, Romance, Slavic, Iranian, and North Indian languages, while Chinese is a major member of the Sino-Tibetan family, embracing also, according to one reputable scheme, the tongues of Tibet, Thailand, Burma, Vietnam, and Laos. Because Japanese makes use of Chinese characters in its writing system, many people have the misapprehension that Japanese and Chinese are very similar. In fact, Japanese is closer to Korean, and both are classified by some authorities, along with Mongolian, Tungus, Manchu, and Turkish, as members of the Altaic branch of the Ural-Altaic family. Japanese is as unintelligible to a Chinese as English is. This leads to the question, Just what is Chinese like?

The Chinese Language
and Its Dialects

Of spoken Chinese there is a variety. The majority dialect is Mandarin, which has been adopted and called "national speech" in

---

THIS CHAPTER incorporates material in an article by the same author, which originally appeared under the title "The Interplay between Language and Thought in Chinese" in *Topic: A Journal of the Liberal Arts* (Washington and Jefferson College, Washington, Pennsylvania), Fall, 1963.

1. For a general classification of the world's languages, see Mario Pei, *The Story of Language,* rev. ed. (Philadelphia: J. B. Lippincott Company, 1965), Part I, ch. 3.

Nationalist China and "common speech" in Communist China. It is spoken as the native tongue of the people of north China, Manchuria, central, and southwest China, making up about 70 percent of the population of China, exclusive of ethnic minorities. The other dialects are spoken mainly within a strip of land, about 300 miles wide, along the southeastern coast from Shanghai down to the Vietnamese border. These dialects, numbering about two hundred if fine distinctions are considered, may be classified into four or five major groups, i.e., the Wu dialect of the Shanghai area; the Min of Fukien Province, subdivided into Foochow and Amoy dialects; Hakka in several linguistic enclaves; and Cantonese. Fukienese and Cantonese are also the principal native tongues of Taiwan, Hainan, and most of the Chinese communities in Southeast Asia. Cantonese is spoken in the Chinatowns of the United States. The speech of the south central provinces of Hunan and Kiangsi, respectively called Hsiang and Kan, is sufficiently different from Mandarin to be considered by some as separate dialects.[2] All these non-Mandarin dialects are distinct in pronunciation from one another as well as from Mandarin to the same extent as French is distinct from Spanish. A native of Peking cannot converse with a Shanghai person or a Cantonese unless the latter two have learned Mandarin, of which Peking is the standard. However, they could sit down and write out their conversation, since dialects are seldom written and all Chinese use the same system of writing. In spite of their wide divergence in pronunciation and lesser differences in idiom and syntax, these dialects share with Mandarin enough basic common characteristics that they may more properly be called dialects than separate languages.

There are, however, non-Chinese languages in China, which are the native tongues of ethnic minorities such as Mongols, Turkic peoples in Sinkiang, Tibetans, and a large number of aboriginal groups in widely scattered pockets in south and southwest China. These ethnic minorities make up approximately six percent of the total population of China.

2. For a language map of China and East Asia, see Edwin O. Reischauer and John K. Fairbank, *East Asia: The Great Tradition* (Boston: Houghton Mifflin Co., 1958), p. 16.

Characteristics of Mandarin

From this point on we shall concern ourselves with a brief description of Mandarin only,[3] considering four aspects: speech, grammar, written symbols, and manner of writing.

SPEECH

Chinese words are monosyllabic; for example, *chung*[1][a] for "middle" and *kuo*[2][b] for "country." *Chung*[1] *kuo*[2] means "China."[4] Owing to this monosyllabic quality, Chinese speech has a drumbeat rhythm. Since there are about 420 syllables in Mandarin, as compared with about 1,200 in English, and since a full Chinese dictionary contains approximately 50,000 words, there are many words pronounced as the same sound or syllable. As a way to differentiate some of these, tones are used. Every character has a fixed tone. Each stressed syllable in a sentence in Mandarin is pronounced in one of four tones—high level, high rising, low dipping, or high-falling—indicated in Romanization either by a diacritical mark over the main vowel or by 1, 2, 3, or 4 as subscript. An example is the syllable *ma,* which, if pronounced in the first tone, means "mother"; in the second tone, "flex"; in the third tone, "horse"; and in the fourth tone, "scold." So in speaking Chinese one must say each stressed word not only with the correct sound but also in the right tone, or else not be properly understood. This tonal feature of Chinese words gives spoken Chinese a sing-song quality.

The four tones have been compared by Herrlee G. Creel with four ways of saying "yes" in English.[5] The first tone is like the tone of saying "yes" in answering a roll call (a high, level tone slightly prolonged). The second tone is like the rising tone in which one says "yes" in answering a knock on the door while one is still absorbed in one's work. The third tone is similar to that of the "ye-es" said by one who agrees to something doubtful while still questioning it in his mind, the tone being from high to low and rising slightly at the end.

3. For a fuller description of the Chinese language by a distinguished linguist, see Yuen Ren Chao, *Mandarin Primer: An Intensive Course in Spoken Chinese* (Cambridge, Mass:: Harvard University Press, 1948), pp. 3-71.

4. For words Romanized in English in the text, Chinese written forms, or "characters," keyed to the superscript letters, will be found toward the end of the chapter. The subscript numbers with these Romanized words indicate tones, which are discussed below.

5. *Literary Chinese by the Inductive Method* (3 vols.; Chicago: University of Chicago Press, 1939-52), I, 3.

Finally, the fourth tone is like that of a "yes" which is spoken as a brief, sure, and positive reply and comes to a full stop. While most linguistic authorities say that there are only accents but no fixed tones to English words, at least one writer claims to have identified seven English speech tones and equated some of them to Chinese speech tones.[6]

Even with the use of tones, many words are pronounced identically in both sound and tone. In an abridged 5,000-word dictionary, no fewer than forty-one characters are pronounced *yi* in the fourth tone. To name only a few, the words for "easy," "intention," "righteousness," "difference," and "art" are all pronounced yi_4, although they are written in entirely different characters. The abundance of homophones makes it difficult to write Chinese phonetically with certainty of meaning.

In order to further differentiate homophones, Chinese speech has resorted to the device of using compound expressions, consisting of two or more words each, as substitutes for single words. For example, instead of using the single word yi_4 to mean "easy," we say the compound expression $jung_2$ yi_4^c (literally meaning "endure easy"). Similarly for "intention," we say yi_4 ssu_1^d (literally, "intention thought"); for "righteousness," $kung_1$ yi_4^e (public righteousness); for "difference," yi_4 $tien_3^f$ (different point), for "art," yi_4 shu_4^g (art technique); etc. The vast majority of compounds consist of two characters each. There are some with three; for example, $t'u_2$ shu_1 $kuan_3^h$ (atlas book building) for "library." There are more with four, often made up of two binomial expressions. Sometimes the meaning of a compound is entirely unrelated to the meanings of the separate constituent words. An illustration of this is $shou_3$ $tuan_4^i$, the two characters of which taken separately mean "hand" and "section," but taken together mean "method of doing things." Apparently, the meaning of this compound was derived from generalizing the manner of a hand sectioning things to methods of doing things in general. The two characters really make up one word, and in this sense some compound expressions in Chinese may be regarded as polysyllabic words. It should be pointed out that classical Chinese uses far fewer compounds than the vernacular speech of today.

---

6. Sheng-hu Chu (Jee Sane Woo), *The Seven English Speech Tones, Analyzed and Identified with Musical Tones and Chinese Speech Tones* (New York: William-Frederick Press, 1959).

When a compound appears in written form, the characters making it up are not hyphenated. The reader is supposed to know whether a group of characters is to be read with individual meanings or as a unit. The suggestion of hyphenating characters of a compound sounds simple, but actually it is a vexatious one. Linguists have failed to agree on a set of rules clearly defining various types of compounds. It is interesting to note that in machine translation of Chinese into English the machine is instructed to start with the longest lexical unit and, if this does not yield coherent meaning, to search progressively for shorter and shorter units until it reaches single words.[7] This is necessary to avoid errors arising from translating elements of a compound separately.

GRAMMAR

Chinese is a noninflectional language. The words do not change according to number, gender, case, tense, voice, or mood. There is no conjugation or declension. This makes Chinese speech one of the easiest in the world to learn. However, it should not be said that Chinese has no grammar, for there are, in general, three ways to indicate grammatical relationships in human languages. Though Chinese does not use inflectional change of words, so characteristic of Western languages, it does employ the other two methods, namely, word order and the use of auxiliary words. For example, we would say, in Chinese, "Yesterday he give I two literature revolution book." The order of words clearly indicates that "he" is the subject, "I" the indirect object, and "book" the direct object. Since, by rule, all modifiers must precede the words they modify, "literature revolution" must mean "literary revolution" (not "revolutionary literature," though that would also make sense), and the whole phrase must be the modifier of "book."

The other device to indicate grammatical relationships is to use auxiliary words. The use of a time word or phrase suggests the tense of a verb. An action verb followed by the auxiliary word le^j indicates completed tense. "I" followed by ti^k becomes "mine." Plurality is shown by number or plural-meaning words. For example, "I" followed by men^l means "we."

Chinese words are not classified into parts of speech as in English.

---

7. Gilbert W. King and Hsien-Wu Chang, "Machine Translation of Chinese," *Scientific American,* 208 (no. 6, June, 1963), 124-35; p. 130.

A word may be used as a noun, adjective, adverb, or verb, depending on its function in the sentence. However, Chinese words are classified into two general classes: "solid" and "empty." The "solid" words have meanings in themselves, while the "empty" ones are used merely as prepositional, connective, interjectory, or interrogative words.

For example, the Chinese question form does not invert the subject and the verb. In one of the three ways of asking a question, the order of words is exactly the same as that of a statement, but the "empty" word ma_1^m is added at the end. This auxiliary particle, without meaning in itself, transforms the statement into a question. Thus, in Chinese, "You are an American ma_1" means "Are you an American?" "Empty" words like ma_1 often hold the key to the interpretation of a sentence. The significance of this for thought processes will be pointed out later.

WRITTEN SYMBOLS

As pointed out by Reischauer and Fairbank, the modern writing systems of all the rest of the world derived ultimately from a single series of inventions made in West Asia, but the Chinese system is based upon entirely different principles.[8] Chinese is written in symbols, called "characters." The characters are not phonetic representations, but ideographs. Each character consists of a certain number of strokes, which are written in a prescribed order, and is designed to fit into an imaginary square space. In fact, copybooks for children are ruled into columns of squares, into each of which a character is to be written. One must learn by rote memory to recognize the form of each individual character and to write its constituent strokes in the proper manner and order.

In spite of all the dialectal differences in China, the written characters are the same for all dialect groups. Since a character is an ideograph, it has the same meaning or meanings to all readers though it may be pronounced differently in various dialect regions. Partly because of this quality the use of Chinese characters in writing spread to neighboring countries culturally influenced by China—Korea, Japan, the Ryukyus, and Vietnam. In spite of the dissimilarity of speech between Chinese and the tongues of these countries, Chinese characters have been borrowed to serve as elements of their writing systems.

8. Reischauer and Fairbank, *East Asia: The Great Tradition,* pp. 8-9.

The origin of Chinese writing is shrouded in legends.[9] The invention of characters is ascribed by tradition to Ts'ang Chieh, an official recorder to the semimythical Yellow Emperor, Huang Ti (28th-27th centuries B.C.). Observing the marks of birds' claws and animals' footprints on the ground and the shadows cast by various objects, he invented the first pictorial characters. However, archaeologically, the earliest evidence of Chinese writing goes back no farther than about 1400 B.C. in the form of inscriptions on animal bones, tortoise shells, and bronze vessels. But the complexity of the characters then used as well as the size of the vocabulary represented a level of maturity which must have required centuries of previous development.

The original construction of Chinese characters was based on four principles. The first is pictorial representation. The archaic form of $jih_4{}^n$ (sun) is a circle with a dot in the center. Later on it was conventionalized into an upright rectangle with a short horizontal stroke in the middle. (The characters for this and the next twelve examples are written toward the end of the chapter, first in the original form and then in the present form.) A crescent represents "moon."[o] Three peaks stand for "mountain."[p] The symbol for "tree"[q] has a vertical line to represent the tree trunk, two spreading strokes at the bottom to represent roots and two others at the top to suggest branches. The character for "door"[r] is clearly the picture of a pair of swinging doors and has changed very little throughout more than 3,000 years.

The pictorial quality of Chinese characters led Fenollosa, writing at the turn of the century, to assert that it added greatly to the visual imagery of Chinese poetry.[10] It was alleged that when a Chinese reader saw the character for "moon," he not only got the idea of moon but actually saw a crescent moon. This view has been discredited now, for it is simply not true. Most of the pictorial characters have changed their forms so drastically that they no longer are pictures. The Chinese reader simply takes each character as a conventionalized symbol of an idea. However, it remains true that the Chinese treat the written character as an artistic design. It is perhaps no coincidence that Chinese art excels in the visual field.

9. For a brief account, see Florence Ayscough, "Calligraphy, Poetry, and Painting," in Harley Farnsworth MacNair, ed., *China* (Berkeley and Los Angeles: University of California Press, 1946), pp. 334-36.

10. Ernest F. Fenollosa, *The Written Chinese Character as a Medium for Poetry* (San Francisco: City Lights Books, 1936).

The second principle of character construction is diagram. Some ideas cannot be pictured but may be diagrammed. For example, one, two, and three[s] are represented by one, two, and three horizontal strokes respectively. A dot above a horizontal line represents "above,"[t] and one below such a line stands for "below."[u] A vertical stroke running through a circle means "middle" or "center."[v]

The third principle is suggestion. Two characters are put together to form a word suggesting a third idea. The word "hear"[w] is formed by placing an ear between the two panels of a door. Two trees standing side by side suggest "forest."[x] A woman holding a child means "love," and since love is good, the word by extension of meaning becomes "good."[y]

The fourth and final principle is to combine a significative element and a phonetic element. The former element indicates the general category of things to which the meaning of the word belongs, while the latter element gives the sound of the character. For example, the words for "ocean" and for "sheep" are both pronounced $yang_2$. So in order to write "ocean"[z] the character for "sheep" is combined with that for "water," both of which were originally picture words. The combination is to say that the new character has something to do with water and that the "sheep" element is merely a phonetic. A large majority of Chinese words belongs to this type.[11] A present-day trouble with this type of character is that in many cases the pronunciation of the character has departed from that of its phonetic element.

Chinese characters are classified in a dictionary according to 214 "radicals" or identifying parts. Many of these radicals are significative elements indicating general categories of things and ideas. The radicals are arranged in order of the number of strokes they contain. Following each radical, the characters bearing the same radical are arranged in order of the number of strokes in the remaining part of the character or the phonetic element. One must first detect the radical imbedded in a character before he can know where to look for the word in the dictionary. It is a cumbersome and sometimes a difficult process.

In the period of antiquity, the writing must have been fairly close to speech. However, as the language developed and spread over a

11. For interesting stories on the origin of individual Chinese characters imaginatively told and illustrated, many of which are etymologically true, see Rose Quong, *Chinese Wit, Wisdom, and Written Characters* (New York: Pantheon Books, Inc., 1944).

wide area, speech changed more rapidly and became more varied than writing. By about A.D. 600, written Chinese had already become a dead language, but scholars continued to use classical Chinese in all forms of writing, whether literary or practical. From about A.D. 1000, fiction and drama began to be written in the vernacular, but scholars had a low opinion of such writings. This situation lasted until 1919. Classical Chinese provided linguistic continuity with the past and unity among the educated across dialectal differences. The situation was similar to that of post-Renaissance Europe, when scholars of various countries, speaking different tongues, could communicate with one another in Latin. Although the vocabulary, grammar, and syntax of classical Chinese are somewhat different from those of present-day vernacular Chinese, the basic structure of the language and the written characters are the same.

MANNER OF WRITING

The traditional way of writing Chinese is vertically from top to bottom, with the columns arranged from right to left on the page. A Chinese book is open with the bound edge on the right so that the front cover would, if the book were an English volume, be the back cover. Traditionally, Chinese characters are written with a brush on highly absorbent paper in indelible ink, although modern educated Chinese often use a pen and sometimes write horizontally.

The implements for Chinese writing are paper, brush, ink, and inkstone, called the "Four Treasures of the Studio." Prior to the invention of paper near the beginning of the second century, the writing materials used were bones and shells, bronze, stone, jade, clay, pottery, bamboo and wooden tablets, and silk.[12] Paper is an indigenous Chinese invention. It took more than a thousand years for paper to make its journey from China to Europe.[13] Ancient paper was made of tree bark, hemp, and rag. Later bamboo became the principal raw material. There are many varieties of paper in many degrees of quality, depending on the raw material used and the method of manufacture.

When the Chinese writing brush was invented is uncertain. Some

12. For an account of the evolution of Chinese writing material, see Tsuen-hsuin Tsien, *Written on Bamboo and Silk* (Chicago: University of Chicago Press, 1962).
13. See Thomas Francis Carter, *The Invention of Printing in China and Its Spread Westward*, 2d. rev. ed. by L. C. Goodrich (New York: Columbia University Press, 1955).

of the inscriptions on bones and shells (*ca.* 1400 B.C.) were written with a brush. The Chinese brush consists of a bamboo holder, into one end of which is inserted a tuft of hair. The tuft of some of the best brushes is made of rabbit or deer hair as a stiff core, enfolded by goat or sheep hair which is soft. The combination is the most suitable for writing. The tuft of the Chinese brush is much more pointed and far more flexible than that of a painting brush in the West. This has a lot to do with the subtle variations in quality of the stokes in Chinese calligraphy.

Chinese ink, miscalled "India ink" in the West, is made with lampblack. Ancient writings on bones, bamboo, and silk were in black and red. The red was cinnabar or vermilion, and the black, lampblack. Lampblack is produced by burning pine wood, tung oil, or crude petroleum, the best ink being made of pine soot. The soot is collected and mixed with glue, obtained from boiling deer horn, cow hide, or fish skin. The mixture dries into a solid in the form of a stick. To use it one needs an inkslab, which is usually made of smooth stone, on which to rub the stick of ink with a little water. When the fluid reaches the right consistency, the ink is ready for use. Freshly prepared ink is regarded as better than leftover ink or liquid ink and ink paste, which have appeared to answer the needs of modern hurried life.[14]

Throughout the centuries Chinese writing went through many styles. Characters written in the ancient styles were often complicated and cumbersome, and the same character might have different forms. In general, the trend of evolution of styles was toward simplification and standardization.[15] Three of the later styles became established and are in everyday use today. They are the Regular Style, the Running Style, and the "Grass" Style. In the Regular Style, every stroke making up the character is distinctly made, roughly comparable to manuscript writing in English. In the Running Style, separate strokes tend to merge into flowing lines; this style is more "running" than the cursive script of English. Finally, the "Grass" Style is the most abbreviated and speedy. It is something like English shorthand. For example, the character $li_3{}^{aa}$ (ritual, propriety) is written with

14. For a historical discussion of the tools of Chinese writing, see Tsien, *Written on Bamboo and Silk,* ch. VIII.

15. For a description and excellent illustrations of the various styles, see Chiang Yee, *Chinese Calligraphy* (2d ed.; Cambridge, Mass.: Harvard University Press, 1954), ch. III.

seventeen distinct strokes in the Regular Style, which merge into nine flowing strokes in the Running Style, which in turn were reduced to four speedy strokes in the "Grass" Style. Children are taught the Regular Style, and as they grow up, they pick up the Running and "Grass" Styles by encountering them in the handwriting of the people around them. The Regular Style is called for in formal writing, but the other two, being more flowing, are preferred by many as art. Chinese calligraphy is an abstract art, and good specimens are hung up in Chinese homes as paintings are in the West.[16] In fact, Chinese calligraphy and painting not only employ the same implements but also share much the same esthetic standards and are practiced by the same artists. Calligraphy in the form of a poem or colophon often appears in a painting and forms a part of the total composition.

Interplay between Language and Thought

Having summarized the characteristics of the Chinese language as represented by Mandarin, I now proceed to an exploration of the interrelationships between language and thought. That language and culture are intimately related is a common observation of persons who have studied a foreign language. Relatively few, however, have investigated in specific detail the possibility that the structure of a language may condition thought processes and, conversely, that radical changes in thought may lead to reforms of the language.

To demonstrate an interplay between language and thought is one thing, but to say which is the cause and which the effect in any one specific aspect is another. It is like the proverbial question of the chicken and the egg. For convenience of presentation, I will, in the next section discussing Chinese traditional thought, generally assume the point of view that language structure has influenced thought processes, although the reverse might well be argued. In the latter part of this chapter, it will be pointed out how Western ideas which have gained dominance in modern China have led to various language reforms now occurring.

16. For a brilliant analysis of the abstract beauty of Chinese calligraphy, see *ibid.*, ch. IV.

Linguistic Structure and Chinese
Traditional Thought

The relationships between linguistic structure and Chinese traditional thought may be seen on two levels: on a broad level where emphasis on word relations tended to encourage the relational character of Chinese thought and culture in general and also on a more specific level where sentence structure might have influenced Chinese basic concepts in logic and philosophy.

WORD RELATIONS AND RELATIONAL THINKING

The monosyllabic, noninflecting, and ideographic characters provided a congenial medium for relational thinking, which has been a distinctive quality of Chinese thought and culture. By virtue of the language structure, attention is focused on word relations rather than on individual words themselves. While this is in some degree true of any language, it is outstandingly so in the case of Chinese. In English, a noun is a noun and connotes a kind of "substance," imaginary or real.[17] But in Chinese almost any word, excepting "empty" particles, can be a noun, depending on its position and function in the sentence. The English pronoun "him" has an individuality even when standing alone. We know there is only one person involved, this person is a male, and something has been done to him. On the other hand, Chinese pronouns have no gender, case, or number. Their exact meanings cannot be determined except in relation to other words. The reliance on word order and the use of auxiliary words to make meanings clear inevitably stress the importance of word relations and pattern.

This emphasis expresses itself in literature, especially in its highest form—poetry. There is a type of classical poetry according to which a poem is usually composed of four couplets. Each line has either five or seven characters. The intervening couplets between the first and the last of the poem must exhibit parallelism, achieved by careful matching of categories and of tones. Every word in the first line of a couplet is matched by a corresponding word in the second line which belongs to the same category of things, such as astronomical phenomena, plant kingdom, house and garden, food, or any other established

17. Benjamin Lee Whorf, *Language, Thought, and Reality* (Cambridge, Mass.: Technology Press of Massachusetts Institute of Technology, 1956), pp. 140 ff.

category. A word used as an adjective in the first line must be matched by an adjective in the same position in the second line, and so on. Furthermore, a word in the first or second tone in the first line must be matched by a word in the third or fourth tone in the second line, or vice versa. Also, the first and second tones may be matched. No tone may match itself. In addition, the poem as a whole must conform to one of the standard schemes of rhymes at the end of certain lines.

The following is a literal translation[18] of the second couplet of a well-known poem by Wang Wei in the eighth century:

Bright moon amidst pines shines
Clear spring over rocks flows

The sounds and tones are indicated by the following romanized version, according to present-day Mandarin pronunciation:

ming$_2$ yueh$_4$ sung$_1$ chien$_1$ chao$_4$
ch'ing$_1$ ch'uan$_2$ shih$_3$ shang$_4$ liu$_2$[bb]

The two lines of this couplet have been carefully matched in regard to material category, grammatical structure, and tonal pattern.[19] This tendency to match and balance things and ideas not only is required in this type of poetry but also occurs frequently in other types of verse and even prose. It would be difficult, if not impossible, to achieve this kind of parallelism with polysyllabic, inflecting, and nontonal words as in English.

Emphasis on word relations is probably correlated with relational thinking manifested in many areas of Chinese life and culture. A few examples will suffice. Chinese art and architecture are characterized by a strong sense of balance. Attention is centered not so much on separate elements as on the total pattern. Ideas are often denoted by compound expressions composed of antonyms; for example, "buy-sell" for "trade," "advance-retreat" for "movement," and "rule-chaos" for "political condition." The antonyms are not thought of as irreconcilable opposites but as being united to form a complete idea.

---

18. A preposition in Chinese follows the noun instead of preceding it as in English. For the sake of intelligibility, I have reversed the order of the third and fourth words in each line in the translation, although not in the romanized version.

19. For a fuller description of this and other types of Chinese poetry and the literary techniques involved in them, see James J. Y. Liu, *The Art of Chinese Poetry* (Chicago: University of Chicago Press, 1962).

One of the important concepts in Chinese philosophy is expressed in a compound of antonyms, yin_1 $yang_2$[cc]. These two terms denote two opposing but complementary forces in the universe, the interaction of which produces all things and the unity of which reposes in the Ultimate. It is well known that Confucianism, a dominant philosophy in China for more than 2,000 years, is largely a code of ethics governing human relationships. Its focus of attention is not on the individual, but on the web of human relations. Its concern is with order and harmony in family and society and not with the freedom of their constituent members. Thus, the emphasis is on a person's moral obligations to others, not on his own "human rights."

Even Chinese cooking reflects relational thinking. In food preparation the Chinese way is to cut things up and cook ingredients in proper combination and proportion. Long experience has established that certain combinations of ingredients are more pleasurable than others. Even dishes of the same dinner must bear pleasing relations to one another. Whether cooking a single dish or making up a menu, it is a matter of pattern building. With slight exaggeration, one could contrast this with Western cooking. The Western style of cooking ties in well with the modern rationale of a balanced meal, which reflects an analytical mind. Meat and vegetables are cooked separately. One eats meat for protein, potato and bread for carbohydrates, butter for fat, vegetables for fiber; drinks coffee for liquid; and, finally, takes a pill for vitamins!

SENTENCE STRUCTURE, LOGIC, AND PHILOSOPHY

There is a still deeper and stricter sense in which language influences thought. According to Tung-sun Chang, Western logic and philosophy are determined by Western grammar, while their Chinese counterparts are determined by Chinese grammar.[20] The English sentence must have a subject and a predicate. This structure lends itself to the concept of the law of identity, which is the basis of Aristotelian logic. This subject and predicate proposition gives rise to the philosophical concepts of substance and attribute. Study of substance leads to the idea of a supreme being in religion and atoms in science. From the concept of substance is derived the idea of

20. Tung-sun Chang, "A Chinese Philosopher's Theory of Knowledge," *ETC.,* IX (No. 3, Spring, 1952), 203-26. For a somewhat different view, see Chung-ying Cheng, "Aspects of Classical Chinese Logic," *International Philosophical Quarterly,* XI (No. 2, June, 1971), 215-19.

causality, which in turn gives rise to science. So the categories of Western thought are identity, substance, and causality, perhaps all traceable to the sentence pattern in Western languages.

On the other hand, neither subject nor predicate is required in a Chinese sentence, although they may often be found. On many occasions when the subject is clear in context, it is omitted; at other times, the subject simply does not exist. For example, "Drop rain" is a perfectly good sentence in Chinese, while in English it is necessary to say, "It rains." Dispensability of the subject in Chinese makes it easy to think of the cosmos as being in a perpetual circular process of transition without postulating an external agency to actuate or control the process. This is a key concept in Chinese cosmology.

According to Chang, this view reflects a lack of interest in substance, the substratum of things. Written characters are merely signs. But from signs come things. The ancient Chinese did not investigate the substratum of things, but were only interested in signs and their relations. This statement may be a little extreme, but it cannot be gainsaid that Chinese traditional thought was weak in exploring the idea of substance or substratum. The Theory of Five Agents (wu_3 $hsing_2$[dd]) conceived of wood, fire, earth, metal, and water less as physical substances than as metaphysical forces identified with a great variety of things and phenomena, both natural and human. If it was a probe into the substratum, it certainly did not go very deep. Classical Taoism postulated tao_4[ee] as the final reality but asserted that it was unknowable except as manifested in nature, and later neo-Taoism declared it to be vacuity or void. The Confucianist stream of thought was interested in the Will of Heaven, but not the nature of Heaven. The Will of Heaven was revealed in social and political conditions. Hence, Confucius concentrated his attention on human affairs. It is true that later neo-Confucianists did fully develop an earlier concept of li_3[ff] bordering on the idea of substratum,[21] but it came 1,500 years later and then largely as a response to the challenge of Buddhist philosophy.

Furthermore, a Chinese sentence need not have a verb. "Mountain big" is a sentence. It is not necessary to use the verb "to be." In fact, the verb "to be" does not exist in classical Chinese. In an English

---

21. Cf. Wing-tsit Chan, "The Evolution of the Neo-Confucian Concept *Li* as Principle," *Tsing Hua Journal of Chinese Studies,* New Series IV (No. 2, February, 1964), 123-49.

sentence of definition, this verb is absolutely required. In classical Chinese a definition employs two "empty" words, *che*₃ and *yeh*₃.[gg] For example, a definition of *jen*₂[hh] (humanity) would take this form: *jen*₂ *che*₃ *jen*₂ *yeh*₃.[ii] The second *jen*₂ is a different character meaning "man." In other words, the sentence defines by analogy, saying in effect, "Humanity is the quality of man."

Without the subject-predicate pattern in sentence structure, the Chinese did not develop the idea of the law of identity in logic or the concept of substance in philosophy. And without these concepts, there could be no idea of causality or science. Instead, the Chinese develop correlational logic, analogical thought, and relational thinking, which, though inappropriate to science, are highly useful in sociopolitical theory.[22] That is why the bulk of Chinese philosophy is philosophy of life.

If the Chinese sentence does not necessarily have subject or verb, it may be asked, "What is its basic structure?" It should be understood that some sentence types in Chinese resemble in a general way certain patterns in English sentences, but there are some unique ones. As pointed out by Chao,[23] a common sentence pattern in Chinese consists of a topic followed by a comment. The speaker first mentions a topic he is going to talk about and then says something about it. Action is only one kind of comment, and the topic need not be the agent of the action. An example is: "He, heart kind mind stupid." It would not be strictly accurate to translate this sentence as "His heart is kind but his mind is stupid." A better translation would be, "Speaking of him, his heart is kind, but his mind is stupid." Again, "America, many families have two cars" means "Speaking of America, many families have two cars." Chao compares this type of sentence to the road sign in English: "Third Street, keep right." The Chinese Golden Rule also takes this form: "What you don't wish for yourself, don't do to others."

This sentence structure suggests that the topic is broader and more

22. See Harvard University, *General Education in a Free Society* (Cambridge, Mass.: Harvard University Press, 1945), pp. 65-67. This passage analyzes effective thinking into three types which, though not mutually exclusive, have each an area of appropriateness in human thought: logical thinking in science, relational thinking in social studies, and imaginative thinking in the humanities. In Chinese thought, even imaginative thinking is colored by relational thinking.

23. Yuen Ren Chao, "How Chinese Logic Operates," *Anthropological Linguistics,* I (No. 1), 1-8.

inclusive than the comment. This is congenial with the idea that the cosmos is infinitely complex and what we can say about it amounts to tiny comments that distort rather than reveal the truth.

Such a belief underlies the mystical attitude in Taoism, a philosophy which paralleled and interacted with Confucianism in the history of Chinese thought. Also, Taoism considers "being" and "nonbeing" as interdependent and stresses the fact that being derives its utility or function from nonbeing. The usefulness of a bowl lies not in the wall of the bowl but in its hollowness. This emphasis on nonbeing leads to the idea of nonaction in personal conduct as well as in government, to the esteem for quietude and meditation, to the importance of using blank space to balance objects in a Chinese painting, etc. Perhaps this attraction to nonbeing is influenced by the fact that in language the Chinese must pay special attention to the "empty" words which, though devoid of meaning in themselves, play a critical role in the structure of a sentence. Once a student has mastered the common "empty" words, he has overcome the most troublesome part of Chinese grammar.

Modern Ideas and Reforms of the Chinese Language

The above discussion defines, of course, only some of the ways in which the structure of the Chinese language might have influenced the formation of traditional thought in China. Now let us consider the other side of the coin; that is, how Western ideas which have gained dominance in modern China have led to changes in language.

CREATION OF NEW TERMS FOR NEW IDEAS

After the floodgate was opened by China's defeat in the Opium War of 1839-42, the country was inundated by an influx of Western things and ideas, for some of which there were no names in Chinese. New terms had to be created. There were two possible solutions to the problem. One was to use Chinese characters or phonetic symbols to transliterate the sound or sounds of an English term. The other was to coin a new word or expression with Chinese characters to translate the meaning of the foreign word. Both methods have been used in China as well as in Japan but, by and large, China has preferred the second method, while the modern tendency in Japan is to transliterate with her phonetic script. Originally without a phonetic script, China has found it clumsy to transliterate foreign sounds with Chinese characters. So in most instances the method of translation is used. For example, a train is called huo_3 $ch'e_1$[jj] (fire carriage); a fountain pen, tzu_4 lai_2 mo_4 $shui_3$ pi_3[kk] (self coming ink liquid pen); atom, $yüan_2$ tzu_3[ll] (original particle).

"Democracy" is translated as min_2 chu_3 chu_3 yi_4[mm] (people master master meaning). This compound of four characters is really made up of two two-character compounds. The first constituent compound means "people being the master" and the second one means "a master doctrine or ideology." The whole compound of four characters means "the ideology which says the people are the masters of a country." Likewise, "communism" is $kung_4$ $ch'an_3$ chu_3 yi_4[nn] (communal property master meaning).

When uranium was discovered, an entirely new character had to be constructed to name it in Chinese. The construction followed the fourth principle of character formation, previously discussed, by combining a significative element, or radical, and a phonetic element. The radical chosen is the character for "metal," which is written on the left side of the new character, and the phonetic element is a character pronounced u, written on the right. The resultant combination, regarded as a single character, is pronounced u_2.[oo]

THE CHINESE RENAISSANCE

Contact with the West brought into China the ideas of national consciousness, national loyalty, and national independence. These and other Western ideas gave birth in 1917 to a linguistic-intellectual-social-political liberation movement, known as the Chinese Renaissance, which swept the country for a decade or so.[24] One phase of the movement was concerned with the fact that, although China had always had linguistic unity in writing, there was not unity in speech. Considerable numbers of people, especially along the southeastern coast of China, speak a variety of dialects. For the sake of unification of speech, the leaders urged and finally secured the official adoption of Mandarin as national speech to be taught in schools all over the country. Since Mandarin was already spoken as a native tongue by about seventy percent of the Chinese people, exclusive of ethnic minorities, its adoption was a feasible goal. A phonetic script con-

24. For a firsthand description by the foremost leader of this movement, see Hu Shih, *The Chinese Renaissance* (Chicago: University of Chicago Press, 1934).

structed out of parts of Chinese characters was created and used in printing textbooks. It could be placed alongside the characters to indicate their national pronunciations.

The linguistic unity in writing was in terms of classical Chinese, a dead language. Its vocabulary and idiom, grammar and style are somewhat archaic. While it is an excellent medium for poetry and other literary writings, it is ill-adapted to the needs of scientific description, precise reasoning, or even realistic literature. So another phase of the Renaissance had to do with the adoption of the plain speech of the majority of the people (that is, Mandarin) as the all-purpose medium of writing. This proposal, which started the Renaissance, aroused a great controversy. It ended in the victory of the advocates of the vernacular in 1922. Since that time, all elementary school textbooks have had to be published in Mandarin, and classical Chinese has been taught only in high schools and colleges. The aim of this movement was to unify speech and writing and to produce a living literature in a living language. Traditional fiction and drama, which were written in the vernacular, were no longer looked down upon but elevated to a position of prestige.

The linguistic reform did, in fact, bring forth a great liberation of the Chinese mind in literary, intellectual, and cultural realms. It broke away from the rigid conventions of the past and became fascinated with Western ideas and literary expression. Writers experimented with Western forms of poetry and drama, wrote free verse, criticized the Chinese cultural heritage, and extolled Western science and democracy. Hundreds of periodicals mushroomed and a flood of new books, written in the vernacular, helped quench the thirst for new knowledge. Social changes (reform of the family system, liberation of women, increased social mobility, etc.) and political movements (anti-feudalism, anti-imperialism, nationalism, etc.) began to appear and flourished. These aspects of the Renaissance lie outside the scope of this chapter. Suffice it to say here, the linguistic reforms did not take place in a social vacuum but were intimately linked to social and political movements. The effects of the Renaissance have been continuing.

Even English form and style of writing have been imitated. Many writers have adopted the punctuation system used in English. Classical Chinese has no punctuation marks, and quotations are not set off by any signs. It was considered an insult to the reader not to expect him to be able to pause at the proper places in the text or to recognize the source of a quotation. This lack of punctuation sometimes leads to ambiguity. In adopting English punctuation marks, we now err on the side of superfluity. For example, to put a question mark after the character ma_1, which is an interrogative particle at the end of a question, is redundant.

Western influence has affected even Chinese grammar. The subjects of sentences are now more often explicitly stated than before. In statements of identification or definition, $shih_4$,[pp] the verb "to be," is always used as in English. In traditional Chinese usage, the passive voice is rarely employed. In reference to an inanimate object, the active voice means passive. For example, "Cymbal and drum beat loud" means "Cymbal and drum are beaten loud." Referring to a person, the passive voice is indicated by the character pei_4 preceding the verb, as in pei_4 sha_1[qq] (been killed). The passive voice is used only under disastrous circumstance. So a linguistic purist would hardly say in Chinese, "I am invited to dinner." He would say, "Someone has invited me to dinner" or "I have received an invitation to dinner." Now, under Western influence, the use of the passive voice is becoming more general, and it is rather common to say, "He has been elected president" without implying he has encountered a disaster![25]

Another little evidence of Westernism in sophisticated literary writings is to place a dependent clause after the main clause, separating the two by a dash. This construction is contrary to Chinese grammatical usage. It is still not very common in everyday writing but seems to grow in practice. Still another development is the tendency towards printing Chinese in horizontal lines instead of the traditional vertical columns. This is specially common in scientific magazines to facilitate the incorporation of formulas and equations into the Chinese text. Horizontal printing is now the regular practice in all newspapers and periodicals on mainland China.

Since the Communist take-over, there has appeared in the press of mainland China a host of new terms and old expressions in new usage, resulting in a veritable jargon, some of which is incomprehensible to readers of Chinese outside Communist China.[26]

---

25. For other emerging new grammatical usages, see Yuen Ren Chao, "What Is Correct Chinese?", *Journal of the American Oriental Society,* 81 (No. 3, August-September, 1961), 171-77.

26. See the continuing series of *Studies in Chinese Communist Terminology,* published by the Center for Chinese Studies, University of California (Berkeley, 1956-).

LANGUAGE REFORMS TO PROMOTE MASS LITERACY IN COMMUNIST CHINA

Universal literacy is one of the hallmarks of a modern nation, but the ideographic nature of the Chinese characters is a great stumbling block in the path to achieving this goal. Some commonly used characters contain many strokes each, and the misplacement of a tiny stroke even in a character containing only a few strokes might transform it into a different character. Since the form of the character bears only an indefinite relation to its sound in most cases and is composed of elements of almost endless variety, every character must be learned by rote memory. This obviously slows down the rate of learning and impedes universal education. To alleviate this difficulty three kinds of efforts have been made.

1. Selection of Basic Characters. The first effort is to select the most commonly used characters to form a *basic characters* list. These characters are to be taught in elementary schools and classes for illiterate adults. The Language Reform Committee of Communist China published in 1952 a *common characters* list, consisting of 1,010 characters in the first class in point of frequency of use and 490 characters in the second class, totaling 1,500. In addition, there is a supplementary list of 500 characters in the third order of frequency. It has been estimated that a person who has learned the 1,500 basic characters would be able to read about 95 percent of "popular reading matter." This percentage at first seemed too optimistic, but to the surprise of the present writer, when he made sample character counts of three recent issues of the People's Daily, they showed that only about one percent of the characters used, exclusive of those in proper names, were not found in the commonest 2,000-character vocabulary.

Selection of basic characters is only part of a bigger job, because, it will be recalled, modern Chinese uses a large number of compounds, which must be learned as units. In 1958 a list of 20,000 compounds commonly used in Mandarin was published. An enlarged edition including more than 59,000 compounds and short common sayings appeared in 1963. The entries are not ranked in order of frequency of use, and hence there is no suggestion as to which ones should be taught first. Most of the short common sayings included are really expressions in classical Chinese, but they are often quoted in vernacular speech and writings.

2. Simplification of Characters. The second effort towards removal of illiteracy is to simplify complex characters by reducing the number

of strokes in each. This is accomplished by retaining a small part of a complex character, by substituting a simpler element for a more complex one in a character, by adopting a simpler homophone for a complicated character, and in other ways. Simplified forms of many Chinese characters have long been used by tradesmen, but they were frowned upon by the educated elite in old China. Now these forms are officially approved and new simplified forms have been created.

An extreme example of simplification is the character *ch'ang₃*ʳʳ (factory), which has been reduced from fifteen to two strokes. In 1956 the government of Communist China officially proclaimed a list of 515 simplified characters to be used in lieu of the original complex forms in all publications. Since many of these characters serve as radicals in many others, the effect of simplification goes far beyond the 515 officially proclaimed. Analysis shows that the 515 characters in their original forms have an average of 16.1 strokes per character, whereas, after simplification, the average number of strokes in each has been reduced to 8.2—a 50 percent reduction.

3. Working Towards Alphabetical Writing. The third effort in behalf of the literacy campaign is to work out a plan for shifting the medium of writing from ideographic characters to an alphabet. After much study, Communist China announced in 1958 the adoption of the twenty-six letters of the Latin alphabet used in English and a standard system for writing Mandarin with this alphabet—except for the letter *v*, which will be used only to reproduce foreign sounds and in minority languages in China. The system[27] uses single letters or two or more in combination to represent twenty-one consonants, six vowels, and twenty-nine diphthongs. There are four diacritical marks to indicate the four tones and a dividing line to indicate, when necessary, that two adjacent vowels are to be pronounced separately. This system is being used (a) to indicate the Mandarin pronunciation of characters, and as an aid to the learning of Mandarin, the "common speech"; (b) to help those ethnic minorities within China that have no writing systems to create their own written languages; (c) to teach the blind to read and, in combination with a finger-sign

---

27. For an official description of this system, with Wade-Giles equivalents, see "Scheme for a Chinese Phonetic Alphabet" in *Reform of the Chinese Written Language* (Peking, Foreign Language Press, 1958), pp. 55-59. It should be noted that the present chapter uses the Wade-Giles system for romanizing Chinese characters. Hence, the romanizations here should not be taken as examples of alphabetical writing under the new system.

alphabet using one hand, to teach the deaf and dumb to talk; (d) to signal by flag at sea; (e) to transliterate foreign proper names and scientific terms; (f) to help foreigners learn Chinese; (g) to revise the Latinized postal names of Chinese places created by the "imperialists"; (h) to compile indices and improve order in filing; (i) to facilitate the informal writings of newly literate persons who may write a mixture of characters and alphabetical writing; and (j) eventually to replace the characters as the standard system of writing for all. It is the announced policy of the Communist regime to use this system in place of the characters at a later, as yet unspecified, date.

Actually, the replacement of the characters by alphabetical writing at the present time would cause several serious difficulties. One has to do with the existence of a large number of homophones. For example, the characters for "new," "heart," "salary," and "delight" are all pronounced $hsin_1$,[ss] although the written characters are very different. If they are written alphabetically according to sound, they will have identical spelling, and the reader will have to rely on context in guessing the correct meaning.

The tendency of modern Chinese to use compounds, each composed of two or more characters, and thus to become, in a sense, polysyllabic, is a partial solution to the problem of homophones. However, according to a preliminary analysis, among 14,000 compounds, there are about 790 groups with identical pronunciation in sound and tone and, hence, with identical alphabetical writing, involving 1,986 homophonic characters. If the correct meaning of a homophone cannot be inferred through context, the only way to make it clear in a sentence written alphabetically is to insert the appropriate ideographic character immediately after, or in lieu of, its alphabetical spelling. This is done in sending telegrams between railroad stations in Communist China, where much of the content of telegrams has to do with routine operations of the railroad. About five percent of the words in such telegrams have to be in numerical code symbols standing for written characters. However, public telegraph offices do not use alphabetical writing at all; they are still following the traditional method of converting each character into a four-digit number according to an arbitrary code for transmission, to be reconverted into character at the receiving end. This means that, at least under the present linguistic circumstances, alphabetical writing of Chinese is lacking in intelligibility, accuracy, and certainty of meaning as well as hazardous in its consequences.

Another serious problem in alphabetical writing is how to join elements of a compound together and write them as a single word. There are as yet no standard rules for defining or delimiting compounds. This problem is ignored in writing Chinese with characters, as the characters in a sentence are not grouped in any way to indicate compounds. But to write each component of a compound separately in alphabetical writing is to lose the individuality of the written expression. It would look almost as meaningless as writing in English thus: "A mer i ca is a de moc ra cy." The compound for "Chinese Phonetic Alphabet" is han_4 (Han Chinese) yu_3 (speech) $p'ing_4$ yin_1 (phonetic) tzu_4 mu_3[tt] (alphabet). This expression can be written as one long word or as two, three, or four words, depending upon how one delimits the internal components of the over-all compound. Before Chinese can be written alphabetically with intelligibility there must be far greater standardization of the grouping of the elements of compounds in writing than exists now.

A third difficulty in writing Chinese alphabetically arises from the lack of uniformity in pronunciation, vocabulary, and even grammatical structure, not only among dialects but also within Mandarin. The character for "elder brother" may be pronounced ko_1 or ke_1.[uu] "Cement" may be called $yang_2$ hui_1[vv] or $shui_3$ ni_4.[ww] "Unless the majority agree, then we can reach a decision" is at present as good Chinese as "Unless the majority agree, we cannot reach a decision," and means the same. These variations are bad enough when written in Chinese characters, but they would be even less easily recognized in alphabetical writing. Normally, Chinese syntax and grammar are already loose enough to cause frequent ambiguities.[28] Unless there is more agreement based on more uniform usage, confusion and ambiguity may be compounded by alphabetical writing.

It is significant to note that in the Great Proletarian Cultural Revolution the Red Guards have always written their bulletins in large characters, often simplified, but never in alphabetical writing; in June, 1966, the People's Daily, the leading Party-controlled newspaper published in Peking, abandoned its Romanized masthead "Rénmín Ri Bào[xx] on the front page ostensibly to make room for a

---

28. For amusing examples of ambiguities, see Yuen Ren Chao, "Ambiguities in Chinese," *Studia Serica Bernhard Karlgren Dedicata* (Copenhagen: E. Munksgaard, 1959). On difficulties in translating Chinese, see Bernhard Karlgren, *Sound and Symbol in Chinese* rev. ed.; Hong Kong, London, and New York: Hong Kong University Press, 1962), ch. V.

CHINESE CHARACTERS
KEYED TO ROMANIZATIONS IN THE TEXT

			Original form:	Present form:
a.	中	n.	⊙	日
b.	國	o.	☽	月
c.	容 易	p.	⋀⋀	山
d.	意 思	q.	木	木
e.	公 義	r.	門	門
f.	異 点	s.	一, 二, 三	一, 二, 三
g.	藝 術	t.	二 ‧	上 下
h.	圖 書 館	u.	二 ‧	
i.	手 段	v.	中	中
j.	了	w.	閒	閒
k.	的	x.	林	林
l.	門	y.		好
m.	嗎	z.		洋

aa Regular Running "Grass"

禮 禮 礼

bb. Couplet:

明月松間照
清泉石山流

cc. Antonyms:

陰 陽

dd. 五 行

ee. 道

ff. 理

gg. 者,也

hh. 仁

ii. 仁者人也

jj. 火車

kk. 自來墨水筆

ll. 原子

mm. 民主主義

nn. 共產主義

oo. 鈾

pp. 是

qq. 被殺

rr. Complex: Simplified:

廠   厂

ss. 新 (new)   心 (heart)

薪 (salary)   欣 (delight)

tt. 漢語拼音字母

uu. 哥

vv. 洋灰

ww. 水泥

xx. 人民日報

yy. 國語羅馬字

zz. 注音字母

daily quotation from Mao's sayings; and, finally, no one has so far been accused by the Red Guards of being an opponent to alphabetical writing. Does this mean the Maoists have second thoughts about alphabetical writing or simply realize that characters are as yet indispensable if all readers are to have a clear and accurate understanding of what is written?

ATTITUDES TOWARDS LANGUAGE REFORMS IN NATIONALIST CHINA (TAIWAN)

The Nationalist Government, before losing the mainland to the Communists, did favor the selection of basic characters for teaching children and illiterates, and the use of a phonetic script as an aid to pronunciation, but it did not favor replacement of the characters. There were two forms of phonetic script. One was called *Gwoyeu Romatzyh*[yy] (the National Romanization), making use of the Latin alphabet to indicate the Mandarin pronunciation of characters. Since this form looks like Western writing and cannot be conveniently printed alongside characters, its use was never extensive or officially encouraged. The other form was chu_4 yin_1 tzu_4 mu_3[zz] (the National Phonetic Letters), consisting of thirty-nine symbols derived from elements of ancient Chinese characters. This form has been regularly taught in the elementary schools under the control of the Nationalist Government and has proved a very effective instrument in teaching non-Mandarin-speaking people to speak Mandarin with a high degree of accuracy in pronunciation. Since 1937 all elementary school textbooks must be printed in Chinese characters with their pronunciation indicated by National Phonetic Letters to the right of the characters. For fear of incurring a serious break with China's cultural heritage, Nationalist China has not officially encouraged the simplification of characters, although a certain amount of abbreviation is used by most people in everyday writing. It is not found in print. The Nationalist Government has—as is to be expected—vigorously opposed alphabetical writing.

The advocates of reform on the mainland have declared that only Marxist thought could have produced the language reforms.[29] With-

---

29. For a summary of theoretical arguments regarding, and historical antecedents of, language reform in China, see Paul L.-M. Serruys, *Survey of the Chinese Language Reform and the Anti-Illiteracy Movement in Communist China* (Berkeley, Calif.: Center for Chinese Studies, Institute of International Studies, University of California, 1962).

out having to subscribe to this particular view, it is beyond doubt that Western ideas have brought forth linguistic changes in modern China. On the other hand, Hajime Nakamura has demonstrated that the ideology of Buddhism—a common link among Indians, Chinese, Tibetans, and Japanese—has been subjected to various interpretations by these four peoples because of their linguistic differences.[30] If so, will the ideas of Western thought, and of Marxism in particular, be modified in China by Chinese linguistic peculiarities even though the latter are undergoing change?

The interplay between language and thought in Chinese, as in other languages, is real and has many ramifications. Awareness of this interplay liberates a person from a sort of semantic imprisonment and enables him to avoid a pitfall which trapped Immanuel Kant. Kant, not knowing any non-Western language, probably assumed that the categories of thought he formulated were universal in human thinking. Nothing is farther from the truth. An understanding of the interaction between language and thought is clearly one of the essentials of a liberal education.

30. Hajime Nakamura, *Ways of Thinking of Eastern Peoples: India, China, Tibet, Japan* (rev. ed.; Honolulu: East-West Center Press, 1964).

XX

Chinese

Literature

BY
BURTON WATSON

Chinese literature, with a history stretching unbroken over almost three thousand years, represents one of the richest and most voluminous literary traditions in the world. In this chapter I will not attempt to describe all the genres which make up this tradition, or to catalogue its numerous masters and masterpieces. Instead I will try to define some of the characteristics which have made Chinese literature great in the past and insure it a position of importance in the world, and to outline the main course of its development.

Chapter XIX has discussed the language in which this literature is expressed; here I need make only a few remarks on the system of writing used for this language. Much misinformation and sheer nonsense has circulated in the West concerning the immense difficulty of the Chinese writing system. It *is* a difficult and complex system to master, though our present system of English spelling, with its manifold exceptions and eccentricities, at times seems hardly less difficult. Most of the characters, as we have seen, are made up of basic elements which keep appearing in different combinations and which, moreover, give clues to both the meaning and the pronunciation of the character. In addition, though Chinese lexicons contain vast numbers of characters, only a small portion of these are likely to be encountered in ordinary types of writing. It would probably be safe to say that a knowledge of five or six thousand characters will enable one to read nearly all the important works of Chinese literature, and in the case of the older and more difficult texts the Chinese scholars themselves have usually provided commentaries or glosses to assist the reader over the rough spots.

Chinese literature presents enormous difficulties in understanding and interpretation, but these are not due, as is so often supposed in the West, to the Chinese writing system. They are due rather to the nature of the Chinese language itself, and to the great age and continuity of Chinese civilization. From earliest times the Chinese language has shown a marked fondness for economy of expression, and for the use of short, simple, syntactical units, which may, if desired, be strung together or piled up to form more complex structures. As we have seen, number, tense, and mood are often left unexpressed, and the reader must try various interpretations of the syntax in his mind until he discovers the one that seems to fit the context best. In poetry, the use of the caesura and end-stopped lines guides the reader in his comprehension of the meaning, and prose often makes use of similar devices of rhythmical and balanced construction to aid comprehension. The frequent use of strict verbal parallelism, in particular, one of the commonest rhetorical devices in both prose and poetry, helps greatly to make clear the syntax; once one has perceived the syntax of one member of a pair or series of parallelisms, he may be sure that the other members will follow the same syntactical pattern. In addition, Chinese, lacking an elaborate grammatical apparatus, relies very heavily upon linguistic custom and usage to insure comprehension. The great bulk of Chinese literature, at least before the present century, was written by men who had received a thorough education in the Classics and other great works of antiquity, and who could assume a similar education in their readers. As a result their writing is often highly elliptical and allusive in style, and demands for its comprehension a knowledge of the precedents and earlier usages upon which it builds. Such a habit of echoing and building upon the usages of the past permits great elegance and economy of expression, not to mention displays of pedantry. But it also tends to inhibit originality, since a writer who attempts to use words in a new way is often in danger of becoming merely incomprehensible. Perhaps as a result, Chinese literature has, linguistically speaking, tended to evolve rather slowly and cautiously, with frequent periods of consolidation or even reversal; new areas of expression have been opened up not by swift and dramatic conquest, but by the gradual pushing forward of the frontiers of language.

Chinese literature in general is marked by two characteristics: common sense and decorum. One may immediately object that such a statement takes no cognizance of the numerous works of fantasy and imagination which are to be found in both prose and poetry, or of the well-known Ming and Ch'ing novels with their passages that at times can only be called pornographic. It is true that both fantasy and, to a much less extent, bawdiness have at times been important elements in Chinese literature. But, with a few notable exceptions, they have usually been smuggled into the literature, often under at least token disguises of reasonableness and propriety, or they represent conscious and calculated departures from the norm, floutings of convention that are all the more savored because they are not so frequent or so numerous as to become a convention in themselves. The prevailing tone of Chinese literature, both in poetry and prose, is one of quiet reasonableness rather than frenzy or imaginative flight; the emotions are more often those of friendship, sorrow, or despair at the plight of mankind than romantic passion.

This situation is in part due to the fact that most of Chinese literature, particularly that from the earlier centuries, is the product of one group of men, the scholar-officials, whose views and tastes in literature were influenced, often dominated, by Confucian concepts of humanism, rationalism, and propriety. If we had more literary remains from other classes of Chinese society, the picture might be quite different, and in fact the few and imperfect glimpses we get of early popular literature suggest that it was a much lustier and more wonder-filled affair than the literature of the scholars. Certainly the extensive remains of popular literature which have been preserved from more recent centuries are of this type, though many of them have been reworked and polished by the scholars.

Another characteristic of Chinese literature is its tendency to focus upon action rather than ideas. This again may be in part at least a reflection of Confucian ideals, for Confucius and his followers consistently emphasized the importance of right acts over right thoughts or beliefs, of true philosophy as something that is not pondered and elaborated in abstractions of the mind, but acted out in one's daily relations with the other members of society. Chinese literature, both fiction and nonfiction, concentrates upon the narrative of events, the flow of individual acts and their causes and results. Through these acts, rather than in any overt comment or analysis, the personalities of the actors and the moral significance of their story is revealed.

The Chinese treatment of personality tends to be categorical. Human beings may, on the basis of their actions, be classified into numerous, well-defined types, many of which have been clearly recognizable from ancient times and keep reappearing in human history, and by extension, in the world of fiction. The Chinese historian or writer of fiction, therefore, is more interested in summing up, in vivid and economical strokes, the representative of the type, than in constructing a detailed and complex portrait of an individual. He prefers to describe his subject from the outside, in terms of the subject's actions and relations with society, rather than to delve into the subject's interior mental and psychological workings.

If the traditional Chinese writer and his readers do not seem to be much interested in an analysis of the interior life and makeup of the individual, however, they are endlessly fascinated by the variety of acts and incidents through which the individual reveals himself to the outside world. The typical Chinese novel is a lengthy, sprawling affair, the typical Chinese historical work even more voluminous. Both are made up largely of almost inexhaustible recitals of individual acts, linked together in intricate patterns by webs of cause and effect. It is this procession of acts, and the webs binding them, which hold the attention of the Chinese reader and convey to him the moral significance of the story. Poetry, particularly lyric poetry, because of its more subjective nature, would seem to present an exception to these remarks, but here again the revelation of interior states of mind and feeling, as we shall see when we come to the discussion of Chinese poetry, is accomplished almost wholly through the medium of exterior acts and images. It is not that the Chinese writer makes no attempt to probe into what lies beneath the surface appearance of life; he probes, but he believes that, in order to be meaningful, whatever he may find there must be expressed not in abstractions, analyses, or private symbols, but in terms of the known, tangible elements of experience that are familiar to all men.

With these remarks in mind, let us look now at some of the important works of Chinese literature. The history of Chinese literature begins with the so-called Five Classics, the *Book of Odes,* or *Songs* (*Shih ching*); *Book of Documents* (*Shu ching*); *Book of Changes* (*I ching*); *Spring and Autumn Annals* (*Ch'un ch'iu*); and *Book of Rites* (*Li chi*). These are often referred to as the Confucian Classics because Confucius or his disciples were believed to have had a hand in compiling, editing, and transmitting them, though they contain much material that dates from before the time of Confucius.

From the literary point of view the most interesting of these texts is the *Book of Odes,* a collection of some three hundred songs dating from about 1,000 to 600 B.C. and representing works associated with the Chou court and the feudal states of northern China which acknowledged its suzerainty. The earliest pieces are sacrificial hymns and celebrations of dynastic might and glory, expressions of communal faith and sentiment couched in simple, stately, and impersonal language. From a somewhat later period are songs of the nobles dealing with banquets, hunts, warfare, city-building, and affairs of state; they are more impassioned and personal in tone, richer and more colorful in their descriptive passages, sometimes celebrating the joys of the feast, the hunt, or the battle, but at other times complaining bitterly of injustice and misrule. Most famous, and probably of late date, at least in their present form, are the songs of the common people, brief works, often no more than three short stanzas in length, depicting the loves, courtships, marriages, and daily lives of the farmers and their families. Some are lighthearted and joyful in tone—work songs, epithalamiums, or songs of festival time; but more often the tone is one of sorrow as the singer laments a faithless lover or a loved one far away, or cries out against misfortune, poverty, and the griefs of soldiering.

All the songs employ a basic four-character line, which usually comprises a single syntactical unit. The even numbered lines are rhymed, and there is occasional use of alliteration and internal rhyme. Lines are frequently repeated, especially in the folk songs, sometimes with minor variation, forming a refrain. Narrative is important in some of the songs, notably those dealing with dynastic legends, but in most it is subordinate to the lyric element. The imagery of the songs is vivid and concrete, drawn from the sights and sounds of daily life. Many of the poems begin with some image from the natural world—a particular type of plant, tree, bird, or beast—that serves either to symbolize the emotions of the singer, or to contrast poignantly with them, and that sets the mood of the piece. The supernatural figures only slightly in the songs; deities are addressed but never described, and elements of the magical or fantastic are almost totally absent. The focus is on human affairs and human emotions, with an underlying tone of optimism that suggests that most of the ills of mankind are in the end remediable by human means. There is much love and tenderness, but scarcely more than a hint of the erotic. In addition, there are curiously few references to sickness, old age, and death, themes that were to become so important in later Chinese poetry, and few references to children. Perhaps these subjects did not interest the singers, though it seems more likely that their absence reflects some kind of taboo.

Very different in nature are the works in a second anthology of early poetry, the *Ch'u tz'u* or *Songs of the South*. Whereas the *Book of Odes* represents the poetic tradition of northern China, these songs are associated with the state of Ch'u to the south in the Yangtze valley and reflect attitudes and tastes that differ from those of the north. These differences, however, may in part be due less to geography than to the passage of time, since the earliest of the Ch'u songs are probably no older than the third century B.C.

Some of the pieces are shaman's songs in which various deities, described in images of radiance and winged flight, are addressed in ecstatic and sensuous language and invited to a rendezvous with the worshiper. Others, including the longest and most important piece in the anthology, the *Li sao* or "Encountering Sorrow," are associated with legends of a third century poet-statesman named Ch'ü Yüan, who was slandered and exiled and who is believed to have composed many of the poems in the anthology to pour out his grief and give expression to his unswerving loyalty to the state. Much of the language and imagery of the poems associated with Ch'ü Yüan is fantastic in nature and draws upon the same body of religious beliefs and attitudes that inspired the shaman songs; there are fabulous journeys through the sky, meetings with magicians and nature deities, and a lavish use of plant and flower symbolism that at times seems to have erotic connotations and may, as has been suggested, have some connection with hallucinatory drugs. And yet, much of this fantasy and lush imagery seems to be overlaid with allegorical meaning, to be subordinated to a moral or even political conception of poetry in which the final reality is not the fantastic world of the imagination but the sorrowing statesman and his protestations of loyalty. Perhaps the Ch'ü Yüan poems can best be seen as a tentative attempt to graft the sober, moralistic, and human-centered ideals, which we have seen reflected in the *Book of Odes* and the teachings of the Confucian school, upon the fertile and magic-loving poetic imagination of the south.

Most of the pieces in the *Ch'u tz'u* use a line that is longer and freer than the old four-character line of the *Odes,* though certain words were perhaps pronounced very lightly and when the poems were sung or chanted, their lines may have been more regular than they appear to be in written form.

From the principal poem in the anthology, the *Li sao* or "Encountering Sorrow," this longer, freer line came to be called the *sao* form. The *sao* type line was taken over, along with the *Ch'u tz'u*'s fondness for rich, exotic verbiage, in the next important poetic form in Chinese literature, known as the *fu* or rhyme-prose. Some of the works in this form are prefaced by or interspersed with passages in prose—hence the English name rhyme-prose—which increase in intensity and rhythmicality until they pass over into rhymed verse. Occasionally the form is used for discourse or philosophical meditation, but more characteristically it is employed for lengthy and elaborate descriptive pieces, often of imperial hunts or outings or of the great capitals of the empire. The form enjoyed its greatest popularity during the Han dynasty (206 B.C.-A.D. 220); particularly fine are the works of the poet

Ssu-ma Hsiang-ju (179-117 B.C.), which, in their lavish and often fantastic descriptions of the court and its pleasures, succeed splendidly in conveying the richness, exuberance, and variety of Han life. Later poets often preferred to employ the medium for works of more modest dimensions, descriptions of a particular kind of bird, tree, household article, or musical instrument, or evocations of a particular mood. Their works, less fantastic and less fired with imagination and inspiration, often give an impression of lifeless imitation. The genre has been much criticized, particularly in recent years, for its artificiality, its difficult and pedantic diction, and its open flattery of aristocratic pursuits and pleasures. Nevertheless, in its best days it fostered works of dazzling verbal lushness and color, if not often of great depth. It satisfied the desire for a poetic form that would be suitable for rich, detailed passages of description, allowing the lyric forms, by a kind of poetic division of labor, to concentrate upon economy of expression and symbolic depth. And when the enthusiasm that had earlier infused the *fu* form began to wane, the descriptive powers which it had nurtured and raised to such a high level could be adapted and employed to good effect in other types of prose and poetic composition.

So far I have talked about works of poetry; but from the point of view of volume and richness of content, if not of literary interest, prose far outweighed poetry in the early history of Chinese literature. Many early Chinese prose works were designed to preserve and transmit the teachings of various masters of the so-called Hundred Schools of ancient Chinese philosophy. These range in form from the brief utterances collected in the Confucian *Analects* to the elaborate and closely argued essays of the *Hsün tzu* or the *Han Fei tzu*. Of particular importance because of their intrinsic literary value and their enormous influence upon later Chinese literature are two works of the Taoist school, the laconic pronouncements of the short text known as the *Lao tzu*, or *Tao te ching*, and the witty, incisive, and paradoxical anecdotes of the *Chuang tzu*.

Works of history as well as philosophy figure prominently in early Chinese literature, reminders of the abiding interest of the Chinese in the daily flow of events in society. Some, like the *Ch'un ch'iu* or *Spring and Autumn Annals*, traditionally supposed to have been compiled by Confucius, are no more than chronologically ordered notations of happenings; others, like the *Tso chuan*, are rich in anecdote and are cast largely in the form of dramatic speeches and exchanges of dialogue connected by passages of brisk narrative. Works of the latter type, though they are probably based upon sound historical fact, contain a large mixture of fiction and folklore, as well as occasional elements of the supernatural.

These accounts of ancient China, along with the narrative techniques which they display, were taken over and utilized by China's first great historian, Ssu-ma Ch'ien (145?-90? B.C.). His *Shih chi* or *Records of the Historian* in 130 chapters is a history of the entire past of the Chinese people from earliest days to the time of the historian, and includes accounts of all the foreign lands and peoples known to China. Ssu-ma Ch'ien was deeply conscious of the tradition, commonly accepted in his day, that Confucius had compiled the *Spring and Autumn Annals* and had placed great emphasis upon the moral lessons of history, and he no doubt believed that his own work embodied similar lessons, though he usually leaves the reader to discover their meaning for himself. His history contains very little of the outright miraculous or sensational, especially in his accounts of ages nearer to his own; instead he focuses upon the inexhaustible variety of human types who have appeared upon the stage of history, particularly the great statesmen, thinkers, and military men whose actions and ideas have moulded the course of events. The last seventy chapters of his history are devoted to biographies of such men, often grouped together according to the similarities of their lives and personalities. In these chapters he does not attempt to give a detailed account of the lives of his subjects, but to catch the essence of their personalities, usually through the medium of a few well-chosen anecdotes, and to indicate what it is that makes their names worthy of remembrance, correcting the errors of earlier accounts, pointing out the lasting influence of virtue and goodness, and insuring to his subjects the reward of everlasting fame. The warmth, vitality, and interest of his narrative, particularly in these biographical chapters, have caught the imagination of countless generations of Chinese and made his history one of the best read and loved of all prose works, second in influence perhaps only to the Confucian Classics themselves.

Less comprehensive in scope but more detailed is the second major historical work, the *Han shu* or *History of the Former Han* of Pan Ku (A.D. 32-92) in 100 chapters. Somewhat more impersonal in tone and austere in style than Ssu-ma Ch'ien's work, the *Han shu* is, nevertheless, characterized by the same wealth and vividness of incident and skillful delineation of personality, and has been highly regarded through the ages. Later Chinese historical works, numerous and valuable as they are, have never, with a few exceptions, enjoyed the same popularity as these two early works. Some are marred by elements of the fantastic, others are so lengthy and detailed as to swamp the reader in minutiae; particularly in later times, when official histories were compiled by committees of government scholars, they became less coherent literary works than mere repositories of data, unformed by the personality of a single writer or a consistent philosophy of history. Nevertheless, the Chinese have remained through the ages indefatigable readers and writers of history; and works of history, particularly those of great literary interest and excellence such as the *Shih chi* and *Han shu,* have often filled in their lives the place that is filled in ours by great works of fiction.

The old poetic form used in the *Book of Odes,* with its four-character lines, was revived during the Han and continued to be employed from time to time for several centuries afterward. But it had become a stiff, pedantic affair, encrusted with archaic diction, and few poets succeeded in infusing it with any vitality. Meanwhile, a ballad literature had grown up among the people which employed different and often much freer forms, perhaps influenced by new types of music introduced from Central Asia. These new songs, known as *yüeh-fu* or Music Bureau songs from the name of a government agency that was set up in Han times to collect them, are often extremely appealing in their simplicity and vigor. Like the songs in the *Book of Odes,* they are anonymous creations dealing in direct and unadorned language with the daily life of the people, particularly the hardships of poverty and warfare and the vicissitudes of romantic love. In time they attracted the attention of the scholars, who took them up and wrote imitations and variations on the same themes, until the *yüeh-fu* became established as one of the standard genres of Chinese poetry. One theme in particular, that of the neglected wife or palace lady, grieving in perfumed and helpless seclusion, proved of perennial fascination to Chinese poets, who used it sometimes for allegorical expressions of their own personal or political frustrations, sometimes merely for exercises in pathetic or mildly erotic description.

Toward the close of the Han dynasty, in the second century A.D., a new poetic form came to prominence. Like the earlier form used in the *Odes,* it was called a *shih,* but for the old four-character line it substituted a line of five characters, with a caesura after the second character. A second and very similar form, using a seven-character line with the caesura after the fourth character, later joined it in prominence, and together they came to constitute the most popular and widely used forms in all Chinese poetry down to the present century.

The most famous early examples of this new form, using a five-character line, are the so-called Nineteen Old Poems of the Han. Anonymous and of uncertain date, they appear to be products of the late Han, when the great system of imperial rule that had insured peace and security to the nation in earlier centuries was becoming increasingly ineffective, and Chinese society was torn by factionalism and internal strife. The poems, which employ the same type of nature imagery found in the *Odes*, deal with themes of separation, thwarted love, betrayed friendship, the passing of time, and the immanence of death. Unlike the *Odes*, they are dominated by a tone of despair and world-weariness. They are products of a society which is far vaster, richer, and more complex than that which produced the *Odes*, but one which, in the midst of abundance, has glimpsed its own spiritual poverty and realized at last the fearful limitations which chance and time impose upon human aspiration.

The new *shih* form was taken up by a remarkable group of men who wrote during the troubled times that attended the downfall of the Han and the division of China into three contending states. Some, including the greatest of them, Ts'ao Chih (192-232), were members of the ruling families; others were officials at the courts. They lived in the shadow of war, political intrigue, and frequent and terrible outbreaks of the plague, and they employed the *shih* form to describe the grim realities that faced them, now recording the actual scenes of devastation and hunger, now expressing in symbolic language their fears and longing for escape. Their works, combining the nature imagery of the *Odes*, the simplicity and vigor of the *yüeh-fu* ballads, and the descriptive powers of the *fu*, represent a new high point in the development of Chinese poetry, one that was seldom to be surpassed until the great flowering of poetry under the T'ang dynasty.

The poets of the centuries following the end of the Han, as so often in other ages, were at the same time officials, and the fear of giving offense to their cruel and capricious superiors no doubt imposed a restraint upon their writing. In spite of caution, many of the most prominent of them were executed in the violent shifts of power that marked this period of strife and disunion. It is hardly surprising, therefore, that men took more and more to writing in covert and symbolic language or searching for themes that were free of political implication. The poetry of the period, imbued with a profound air of melancholy and nostalgia for the distant past, became increasingly concerned with the possibilities of escape from reality, through spiritual or physical retreat from society, through Taoist dreams of immortal spirits or efforts to discover elixirs of immortality. The life of the mountain recluse became the new ideal, and the natural landscape, heretofore viewed principally as a background for human activities, came more and more to be an object of active appreciation. Elaborately varied descriptions of weather phenomena and of the ever-changing appearances of rivers, lakes, and towering mountains occupied the energies of the poets, who found in these scenes a relief from the sordidness of human society.

The history of Chinese poetry appears to unfold in cycles. A new poetic form or genre develops, usually on the popular level, and is taken up by the literati. For a while it displays great vigor and inventiveness, as poets utilize it to formulate new ideas and to open up new areas of expression. A time comes, however, when interest seems to shift from what is being said to the way in which it is said. More and more attention is paid to refinements of diction and technique, while theme and thought content become stereotyped. Finally, the form is reduced to mannerism and must wait until it is reinvigorated by some new wave of creativity or replaced by other forms that are in the ascendant.

This is what happened to poetry in the *shih* form during the centuries we are describing. After an early period of vigor it became increasingly enveloped in an air of pedantry and overrefinement, and although there were innovations in subject matter, their growth was stifled by the taste for elegance of language. Simple, everyday words were replaced by learned circumlocutions, realistic description gave way to pretty idealization, and poets became engrossed in fashioning ingenious couplets, employing strict verbal parallelism, at the expense of the over-all unity of their works.

Fortunately, there were a few men even at this time who were able to surmount these weaknesses and to produce works of lasting value, the most noteworthy being T'ao Ch'ien or T'ao Yüan-ming (365-427). An official who withdrew early from public life and spent most of his years in rustic retirement, he is famous for his descriptions of the rural scene and of the inner joy and quietude which he found in its midst, and in the solace of wine. Yet his poetry is not simply that of the self-satisfied hermit. Its interest and profundity spring rather from the never-resolved tension between the poet's seemingly calm, Taoist-minded detachment from worldly values and concerns, and his nagging Confucian sense of responsibility toward society. His poems are moving not because he succeeded in conquering despair, but because he fought so long and passionately with it.

At the close of the sixth century the long years of disunion and foreign invasion which had racked China were finally brought to an end. The nation once more enjoyed the peace and security of a strong central government, first under the Sui dynasty, then under the more stable and long-lived T'ang. For a time, poetry continued in the effete style associated with the Six Dynasties period, the period of disunion, but soon it showed signs of developing a new depth and vitality. A group of unusually able poets, some of the greatest in all Chinese literature, in time succeeded in infusing the old *shih* form with new life, in pushing it to new levels of technical complexity, and in achieving unprecedented subtlety and power of expression.

Tones and tonal patterns had been a recognized element of Chinese poetry at least from the fifth century on, and the T'ang poets, while retaining older forms of the *shih* that took no formal cognizance of tones, developed new forms that were characterized by strict arrangement of tones within the line. The older forms were hereafter referred to as *ku-shih* or "old poetry," the new forms as *chin-t'i-shih* or "modern style poetry"; of the latter the most important were the *lü-shih* or "regulated verse" in eight lines, and the *chüeh-chü* or "broken-off lines" in four lines.

The themes of T'ang poetry are essentially those that had been inherited from earlier ages. Nearly all the important T'ang poets were also government officials, and many of their works are occasional, having to do with state functions, official journeys, or formal or informal gatherings at which poems were composed to commemorate the event or to send off a departing member of the group. Others treat folk themes derived originally from the ballad literature—the village maid, the lonely wife, the fisherman, the soldier on frontier duty—and allow the poet, by assuming these various personae, to exercise his imagination and occasionally to make covert social comment, though convention usually prompted him to give the piece an antique setting so that he would not appear to be commenting too openly on contemporary events. Finally, T'ang poetry includes many works of a personal nature, records in verse of the poets' private lives and meditations or expressions of affection addressed to close friends and relatives.

The T'ang took over much of the elegant diction and technical refinement of earlier poetry, but it sought to achieve greater intensity and depth of feeling. Direct comments and expressions of feeling are occasionally employed, but more often the emotion of the poem is conveyed indirectly through careful selection of images. Each line of the poem, usually an independent syntactical unit, presents a separate image or group of images, some visual, some aural, some observed from far off, some from close at hand. These are flashed before the reader in rapid succession, like a series of lantern slides, with a minimum of connectives or expletives. At first they may appear almost random in their diversity, but careful examination will suggest a number of links, spatial, temporal, emotional, or symbolic, which relate them to each other and to the theme of the poem as a whole. And when the reader has perceived these links and followed the movement of the imagery correctly, he will find himself in possession of a whole which, as in all great poetry, is vastly more profound and meaningful than the sum of its parts.

In T'ang poetry, direct visualization is valued over cognition and analysis, and economy of expression is the ideal, resulting in the great popularity of the *chüeh-chü* form with its four brief lines, often totaling no more than twenty characters in length. Two examples will perhaps give some idea of this most typical of T'ang poetic forms. The first, employing a seven-character line, presents a graceful series of images which, one feels, are intended to convey some deep symbolic, perhaps even allegorical, meaning.

> Wei Ying-wu (b. 737) "West River at Ch'u-chou"
> These I love: hidden plants that grow by the water's edge;
> above, yellow warblers in the deep trees singing;
> spring tides robed in rain, swifter at evening;
> the ferry landing deserted where a boat swings by itself.

The second, which uses a five-character line, is admired for its deft evocation of the delights of a cup of warm wine on a winter's evening, delights to which the last line offers a tactful invitation.

Po Chü-i (772-846) "A Question to Liu Shih-chiu"
Green bubbles—new-brewed wine;
lumps of red—a small stove for heating;
evening comes and the sky threatens snow—
could you drink a cup, I wonder?

T'ang poetry reached its highest level of development in the eighth and ninth centuries, when the dynasty was still powerful, though torn for a time by the disastrous civil strife of the An Lu-shan rebellion. Among many competent poets, Li Po (701-62) and Tu Fu (712-70) stand as giants of the earlier century. Li Po, renowned for his drunkenness and his fondness for alchemy and Taoist supernatural lore, wrote poetry that is infused with a spirit of romanticism and a childlike freshness of vision. His language, lush and colored with the exotic, seems to race along effortlessly, and at times appears about to break free once and for all from the tight regularity of the *shih* form. Tu Fu, by contrast, is a much soberer and more responsible figure. Faithful to his Confucian ideals, he used poetry to comment on social and political ills, and some of his most admired works are those which describe the hardships of the common people at the time of the An Lu-shan rebellion, hardships which he himself had experienced in full measure. His poetry is for the most part highly personal and colored with a despair that grew as his hopes for active participation in the government dimmed and he was left with no outlet for his reformist energies other than the indirect one of poetic comment. Unlike Li Po, he did not seem to strain at the formal restrictions of the *shih* form, but rather to welcome them; much of his best work is cast in the most exacting of all Chinese poetic forms, the eight-lined *lü-shih* or "regulated verse" with its elaborate requirements for verbal and tonal parallelism. His work is marked by a denseness and complexity of language unknown in earlier poetry, an attempt to pack the greatest amount of meaning, through the use of allusion, word-play, and deliberate ambiguity, into the smallest number of words. He is regarded by the Chinese as their finest poet, partly because of his sincerity and warmth of feeling, but also because of his brilliant exploitation of the possibilities inherent in the Chinese language for succinctness and density of expression. The very nature of his language, however, makes him one of the most difficult of all poets to translate, and his merits can perhaps never be made fully apparent in a foreign language.

Po Chü-i (772-846), the most important poet of the century following Tu Fu, represents in his work a conscious reaction against the type of dense language described above. Though working within the same poetic forms as his predecessors, he employed a looser, more colloquial style which won for his poems an immediate and widespread popularity. Like Tu Fu, he wrote poetry of social criticism, which he himself considered to be his most significant work; but he is better remembered for his narrative ballads, particularly the famous "Song of Unending Sorrow" which deals with the tragic love between Emperor Hsüan-tsang of the T'ang and his beautiful consort Yang Kuei-fei. Because of their relative simplicity and great lyric beauty, his works have enjoyed immense popularity in Japan; and, thanks to the brilliant translations of Arthur Waley, he is the T'ang poet whose writings have so far been brought over most successfully into English in significant numbers. His poems seem to pass with ease over the language barrier, and to appear as fresh and moving in translation as they do in the original.

A second important poet of the ninth century, Han Yü (768-824), more famous as a Confucian thinker and prose writer, worked to introduce a greater plainness, even harshness, into poetic diction and to free it from the stilted elegance that marred the works of so many minor T'ang poets.

The closing years of the T'ang saw a return to the dense, allusive language we have noted in Tu Fu, often mingled with startling imagery and dominated by an air of eeriness, languishing melancholy, or subdued eroticism. In many of the works of the late T'ang, the language becomes so strange and contrived that it ceases to be intelligible, leaving the reader with no more than a series of vivid and intriguing riddles in verse.

It was not until the eleventh century, when T'ang rule had crumbled into disunion and had been replaced by the Sung dynasty, that poetry in the *shih* form regained its earlier vitality and creativeness. The intellectual climate of the day was dominated by Neo-Confucianism, rational, social-minded, and basically optimistic, and its influence was reflected in the new poetry. Following the earlier lead of Po Chü-i and Han Yü, poets adopted a simpler, relaxed, often almost prosy style, and devoted increasing attention to social and philosophical comment and to the depiction of everyday life. In this last effort they went far beyond what had ever been attempted before, treating subjects that would have been rejected by earlier poets as too commonplace, crude, or intrinsically unpoetic. The number of men writing poetry greatly increased, as well as the volume of their individual works, and poetry became much more a part of the daily life of the educated gentleman, a medium for recording not only the moments of highest emotional intensity, but every passing scene and thought. A second philosophical influence, in some ways complementing and reinforcing that of Neo-Confucianism, was exerted upon Sung poetry, and Sung culture in general, by the philosophy of the Ch'an or Zen school of Buddhism, which, unlike many earlier schools of Buddhism, did not direct the believer's attention away from the mundane world, but trained him to discover the inner spiritual significance—the Buddha nature—that is hidden within all of its phenomena, even the most lowiy and commonplace.

Some of the finest work of the time comes from the hand of the statesman, poet, and painter, Su Shih or Su Tung-p'o (1037-1101), who, though he lived through a very checkered career, in his poetry sought to convey an attitude of calm, even good-humored acceptance, rather than succumb to the melancholy that had enveloped so many poets of earlier times. A second high point was reached in the closing years of the dynasty in the works of Lu Yu (1125-1210), some of them expressions of patriotic fervor, others descriptions of the daily life of the village where he lived in his old age, all informed by the lyricism, if not the intensity, of T'ang poetry at its best.

The history of the *shih* form in later centuries is largely the history of schools modeling themselves upon either the T'ang or the Sung masters, and attempting to recapture the brilliance of their respective models. From time to time it produced significant, sometimes even great, works and writers, but no large body of poetry that could match in quality the products of the past.

Toward the end of the T'ang dynasty, a new poetic form came into existence, known as the *tz'u*. Like most other Chinese poetic forms, it was originally associated with music, in this case mainly new tunes imported from Central Asia. It is characterized by lines of varying lengths and prescribed tonal patterns, the particular form of the lines and tonal patterns depending upon the tune it was designed to be sung to. In time these various patterns, known usually by the title of the tune to which they originally fitted, came to be regarded as purely literary forms and were used for the composition of works that were divorced from music. As with other poetic forms, the language of the *tz'u* was at first quite colloquial, though in later centuries it tended to become as stilted and stereotyped as that of the older forms at their worst. Since the *tz'u* were originally popular songs, often associated with the world of brothels and singing girls, they were mainly romantic or erotic in character. Their variety of line length, so different from the clipped regularity of the *shih*, was especially suitable to the creation of a suggestive, impressionistic effect that enhanced the voluptuous nature of the texts. The indirectness of expression we have already noted in the T'ang *shih* became even more pronounced in the *tz'u;* beautiful women, for example, are described almost entirely in terms of the furniture and toilet articles that surround them, leaving the ladies themselves to be created in the imagination of the reader. In Sung times the subject matter of the *tz'u* was broadened to include many themes hitherto treated only in *shih*, and this expansion of content, along with a greater directness of expression, did much to prolong the vitality of the form. At least one major poet, Li Yü (937-78), wrote exclusively in the *tz'u* form, and many other poets, notably Su Tung-p'o, produced works of great merit in it. The Sung is regarded as the high point of the *tz'u*, but, though the over-all quality and interest of the form declined in later centuries, it has remained popular to the present day, being one of the favorite poetic forms of Mao Tse-tung.

Related to the *tz'u* but longer and freer in form is the *ch'ü* or *san-ch'ü*, the poetic form used for the songs which are such an important element in Chinese drama. Drama seems to have developed relatively late in China, and specimens of complete dramatic texts date back no farther than the Yüan dynasty (1270-1368). Chinese drama is essentially operatic, with extended arias and orchestral accompaniment, though spoken dialogue is used to carry the story forward. For the Chinese, the interest of the drama lies in the lavishness of the costumes, the virtuosity of the actor-singers, and the appeal of the poetry, which is lyric in quality and heavily interwoven with allusions, puns, and displays of wit. The stories are usually well-known ones drawn from history, folklore, or earlier fiction; the characterizations are thin; and the plot development is spectacular rather than convincing. Yet the plays contain much elaborate and beautiful poetry that is only now beginning to receive from translators the attention it deserves.

Having briefly surveyed the major poetic forms, let us now turn back to the Han dynasty and examine the development of Chinese prose. The great Han historians in their narrative used a simple, unmannered prose style that depended for its effectiveness upon speed and economy rather than rhetorical flourish. At the same time there existed a second style, used in memorials, letters, and expository writing, that made extensive use of historical allusion, parallelism, and the neat tailoring of phrases in units of equal length, usually of four, five, or six characters. This tendency toward ornateness became increasingly pronounced until, in the Six Dynasties period, it reached its highest development in the so-called *p'ien-wen* or "parallel prose" style, which not only made use of the devices already mentioned, but borrowed from poetry the additional devices of occasional rhyme and tonal euphony. It was used not only for expository writing, but for all types of *belles lettres,* even including historical narrative and fiction.

P'ien-wen, because of its ornateness, lacks the lucidity that one expects of true prose, and in fact it is often closer in spirit to poetry in the *fu* form. A number of important works were written in the medium of parallel prose, some important in spite of their style, a few because of it; but, for all its surface brilliance, it proved, in the hands of all but the most skillful writers, a literary dead end which expended energies that could have been more profitably applied to the pursuance of simpler, less technically demanding styles of prose.

During the early years of the T'ang, parallel prose continued to be accepted as the standard prose style. But dissatisfaction with its artificialities was growing and in time took shape in the so-called *ku-wen* (ancient style) movement, headed by Han Yü (768-824). As its name suggests, the movement looked for its models among the writings of ancient times, particularly the works of the Han historians, but it did not counsel slavish imitation. As so often in Chinese intellectual history, the call for a return to the past in fact masked the creation of something new, a style that had strength and dignity and drew upon the resources of the past, but one that was free of the furbelows and artificial rhythms that marred the lucidity of parallel prose. Above all, the *ku-wen* movement worked to return prose to the realm of ideas, to ensure that it honored the demands of sense as well as sound.

This new style enjoyed considerable popularity for a time, but the closing years of the T'ang saw a reversion to the use of parallel prose, and it was not until the Sung that *ku-wen* became firmly established as the accepted style for almost all types of prose writing. A large number of fine works were produced in the *ku-wen* style, many of the best and most famous of them being short pieces in the form of essays, letters, prefaces, and other incidental writings. The Sung dynasty in particular is looked upon as the great age of Chinese prose, and the writings of its scholars, statesmen, and historians are among the finest in the language.

The *ku-wen* movement was also important because it provided a medium suitable for the writing of fiction. The early Chinese historical works, as we have noted, placed strong emphasis upon biographical accounts and were customarily enlivened by a wealth of dialogue and dramatic incident. The historians often, no doubt, drew upon popular legend and folk tale for their material, though they were usually careful to omit any of the grosser and more fantastic elements which offended their Confucian ideals of common-sense and decorum. In the centuries following the breakup of the Han in A.D. 220, a growing interest in Taoism, alchemy, and the lore of the supernatural, along with the gradual spread of Buddhism, created a climate that was more congenial to the growth of fiction. An element of the bizarre began to creep into the writings of the period and collections of tales appeared, some of them cast in pseudo-historical form, others unabashed accounts of ghosts and wonders, though most often with a moral attached, good or evil conduct being aptly rewarded. A few were based on models taken from Indian literature, which exerted a certain indirect influence through the translations of Buddhist works, but most drew upon the rich body of native Chinese myth, legend, and spirit lore, which had hitherto been largely ignored by writers of the scholar class. Collections of biographies also appeared, modeled on the biographical chapters of the Han histories but devoted to the lives of particular groups or types of men. They are usually mixtures of fact and wonder, which is hardly surprising, since they deal most often with recluses, Taoist adepts, or Buddhist monks, of the type who are commonly expected to wield supernatural powers.

These beginnings of creative fiction, naïve and technically crude as they often were, in time produced the *ch'uan-ch'i* or "wonder tale," a genre which developed rapidly in T'ang times once the *ku-wen* movement had supplied a suitable prose style that could be used in the writing of fiction. As the name *ch'uan-ch'i* suggests, many of these were simply reworkings of the older tales of heroes, ghosts, and wonderworkers. But others, written by men of learning, partly as diversion, partly as literary exercises, were subtle and sometimes strikingly realistic works of fiction. Usually they combined a brisk narrative style, patterned on that of the historians, with set passages of description; poems and letters to enhance the literary interest were often included. They enjoyed great popularity among the educated class, were widely imitated in later ages, and contributed much in both subject matter and technique to the development of fiction and drama. The last great collection of *ch'uan-ch'i* appeared during the Ch'ing, the *Liao-chai chih-i* of P'u Sung-ling (1640-1715). Containing over 400 tales, it utilizes many of the older subjects (particularly that of the fox-fairy, a spirit who appears in the form of a beautiful woman and saps the strength of her unwitting lovers), but achieves a realism and conciseness of language that surpasses in power all of its predecessors in the *ch'uan-ch'i* form.

In the earliest periods of Chinese literary history, the written language presumably represented a fairly accurate transcription of the spoken language of the time. But before long the written and spoken languages began to draw apart, a result of the educated man's veneration for the literature of the past, his fondness for displays of erudition, and his desire to give his works an elegance that would distinguish them from the folk literature of the vernacular. By the first or second century A.D., a distinct literary language had evolved, known later as *wen-yen* or classical Chinese, that differed increasingly, both in diction and syntax, from the colloquial. *Wen-yen* provided a magnificent *lingua franca* for the educated classes, a medium that was little affected by the drastic dialect differences of the widespread Chinese empire, or by the passage of centuries, and a vehicle for the exportation of Chinese culture to Korea, Japan, Vietnam, and the other states bordering China. All the works of poetry and prose I have discussed so far are written in variations of this literary language, some with significant borrowings from the colloquial, but all couched in a style that differed significantly from the spoken language of the day and that, at least from Sung times on, was intelligible to the eye alone.

For some centuries after the development of this written style, there seem to have been few if any attempts to record the actual spoken language of the time. Remains of a literature written largely in the colloquial language have, however, been recovered which date from the T'ang dynasty. Known as *pien-wen* or "popularizations," these works combine prose and verse and are moralistic in tone, dealing mainly with Buddhist themes or stories from Chinese history and legend. Other passages in colloquial language are occasionally to be found in religious and philosophical works in dialogue form from the T'ang and Sung periods, particularly in the texts of Ch'an Buddhism.

Of much greater literary interest are the *hua-pen* or "prompt books," colloquial language texts of the tales of professional storytellers which date from Yüan and Ming times but which undoubtedly represent a tradition extending back many centuries in its origins. The early *hua-pen* display the conventions of the storyteller's art, a rambling introduction which allows time for an audience to gather, and interspersed remarks designed to hold the interest of the listener, and these conventions were often retained in later, purely literary imitations of the form. Like the *ch'uan-ch'i*, the *hua-pen* tales often deal with ghosts, heroes, and superhuman feats of strength, but because of their popular origin they also afford a much more realistic and intimate glimpse into the daily lives of the common people of the age.

Cycles of stories grew up which dealt with the events of a single period or a particular group of characters, and these in time were worked into the shape of full-length novels. Of such origin is the *Shui-hu-chuan*, translated by J. H. Jackson as *The Water Margin* and by Pearl Buck under the title *All Men Are Brothers*. It is a lengthy collection of episodes dealing with the exploits of a band of robbers, set in the Sung dynasty and provided, like many Chinese novels, with a supernatural framework. The impulsive and heroic behavior of the robbers is contrasted with the corruption of the local officials, whose injustices have driven men to become outlaws. There are numerous vivid and enthusiastic descriptions of cursing, fighting, eating, and drinking, but a severely puritanical attitude toward sex. Of similar origin is the *San-kuo yen-i* or *Romance of the Three Kingdoms*, a historical novel dealing with men and events of the third century A.D.

Another important novel, the *Hsi-yu-chi* by Wu Ch'eng-en (*ca.* 1500-80), translated by Arthur Waley under the title *Monkey*, derives directly from the wonder tales of earlier times. It describes the adventures of a Buddhist priest on his journey from China to India in search of sacred texts, the priest being modeled upon an actual historical figure, the famous monk Hsüan-tsang of the T'ang. But the companions who accompany the priest are of a highly unhistorical nature, notably a monkey possessed with astounding supernatural powers, and the lands they visit and the trials that befall them are equally fantastic. On the surface the novel may be read as a delightful fairy tale, and it has long been enjoyed in the East as such; on another level it functions as a biting satire on Chinese society and the bureaucratic system; and on still another level, as an allegory of religious seeking and salvation.

Another famous Ming novel, the *Chin-p'ing-mei* or *Golden Lotus,* the work of an unknown writer, is very different in subject matter. Though it employs a supernatural framework, the body of the work is devoted to a detailed and realistic description of the lives of a rich merchant and his numerous wives. Its abundance of characters and its grim portrayal of the corruption and hedonism of late Ming society make it one of the most powerful works of Chinese fiction. Ironically, it is best known for its frank depictions of sex, though the total effect of the novel is terrifyingly moral.

The greatest traditional Chinese novel is generally conceded to be the *Hung-lou-meng* or *Dream of the Red Chamber,* begun by Ts'ao Chan (d. 1763) and finished by Kao E (*ca.* 1795). Like the *Chin-p'ing-mei,* it possesses a supernatural framework that gives the story religious overtones, and depicts the life of a large and wealthy household whose fortunes are on the wane. But the focus is upon the adolescents of the family rather than the adults, their childhood innocence and its gradual loss. The characterization is more subtle than anything known in earlier works, and the central love affair between the youthful hero and his two girl cousins is described with a psychological depth that places the novel among the great works of world fiction.

The history of Chinese literary criticism is a complex one and can only be touched upon here. Its beginnings go back to the Han dynasty and, like so much of Han life, were strongly colored by Confucianism. No distinction was made between pure literature and other types of composition; all serious writing, whether in poetry or prose, was expected to be edifying or instructive. Great works of the past that did not seem to meet these requirements, such as the love songs of the *Odes* or the shaman songs of the *Ch'u tz'u,* were given allegorical interpretations that turned them into social or political comment, and later genres such as the *fu* were assigned a didactic role, though in practice they often filled it very badly.

The centuries following the Han saw the appearance of a number of statements on literary theory and practice, some upholding the traditional didactic view, others attempting to break away from it and establish alternative criteria for the judgment of literature. Of these the most important is the *Wen-hsin tiao-lun* or *The Literary Mind and the Carving of Dragons,* a series of essays by Liu Hsieh (6th century) on prose and poetic genres and problems of literary composition which combine a reverence for the Confucian tradition with keen critical intelligence and sensibility. At this time also appeared the most important extant anthology of early literature, the *Wen hsüan* in twenty chapters compiled by Hsiao T'ung (501-31). It omits the Confucian Classics (on the grounds that they are too perfect to be excerpted), as well as the writings of the philosophers and, with minor exceptions, of the historians, but includes a wide sampling of other types of prose, along with poetry from the *Ch'u tz'u* and poems in the *shih, yüeh-fu,* and *fu* forms. Like all anthologies, it can be criticized for its omissions, but it has enjoyed great prestige and its study was long regarded as the very foundation of a literary education.

The T'ang writers, though voluminous in production, seemed little inclined to theorize about literature. The Sung, with its more philosophical bent, saw a revival of interest in literary theory, as well as in the compilation of anthologies, and the appearance of a new type of work, the so-called *shih-hua* or "remarks on poetry." These were in the form of scattered comments and anecdotes on poets and poetry rather than formal disquisitions on literary theory, though the remarks often had important theoretical implications. The gradual spread of printing at this time also had a significant influence on the development of literary taste and theory, aiding the preservation of texts that might otherwise have become lost and providing a wide variety of works of the past and present to satisfy the demands of a rapidly growing reader's market.

The history of literary criticism from Sung times to the present century, like that of poetry, is largely the history of rival schools of poets and prose writers, each vehemently championing its particular ideals and models. One point is important. Although works of fiction and drama written partly or wholly in *pai-hua,* the colloquial language, obviously enjoyed widespread popularity, no school of literary criticism was willing to accord them the status of true literature. Whether literature was to be judged by moral or by aesthetic criteria, it had, according to the definition of all but a few unusually independent-minded scholars, to be something that was written in the classical language.

During its many centuries of development, Chinese literature was almost untouched by outside influence; in the isolation of its growth it is unique in the history of the important literary traditions of the world. The only foreign literature that the Chinese read to any extent was the literature of Buddhism, and that almost wholly in translation, since only a few priests were familiar with Sanskrit or the other Indian and Central Asian languages in which Buddhist texts were written. I have already noted a few incidents of direct Buddhist or Indian influence on Chinese literature, as well as indirect foreign influences that entered China through the medium of music, but these are no more than scattered exceptions to the rule.

In the early centuries the cultural isolation of the Chinese was due less to deliberate choice than to accidents of geography and to the fact that the foreign peoples with whom the Chinese had contact were culturally less advanced than the Chinese themselves. In time, however, China's recognition of its own cultural superiority hardened into a prevailing disdain for, or at least indifference to, the cultures of other nations. The society of T'ang times was in many respects highly cosmopolitan; men from Korea, Japan, India, or the Islamic states visited or resided in China, or even held civil or military posts in the government, and foreign foods, clothing, musical instruments, and other objects of material culture enjoyed great vogue. But the only foreign element that exerted any significant influence on the intellectual level was Buddhism, and that suffered from severe attack, partly on grounds of its mere foreignness. The typical lofty and patronizing attitude of the Chinese toward men and cultures of lands abroad is well illustrated by a poem written at a farewell party for the Japanese envoy to the T'ang court, Abe no Nakamaro (698-770). Abe had lived for many years in China, mastered the language, and made friends among the scholar-officials, and the writer of the poem undoubtedly intended a compliment when he began with the statement: "Superior talent may spring from an inferior land."[1]

This situation has changed radically in the present century. The Chinese have at last become willing, even eager, to learn about the literature of foreign lands, taking up its study as one facet of their quest for modernization. Under its influence, they have reassessed their own past literature, according high value to works in the colloquial language that had been disdained by earlier critics, and have experimented widely in the adoption of foreign literary genres and forms. The old classical language has been largely discarded and

---

1. Poetry of Pao Chi, in *Ch'üan T'ang shih,* ch. 205 (Peking, 1960), p. 2142.

replaced by *pai-hua,* the spoken language of modern China. The history of present-day Chinese literature, the result of this so-called Literary Revolution, is thus a separate subject, and one which is too complex to be treated here in detail. So far, the new literature has proved most successful in its handling of the short story form, particularly in the works of Lu Hsün (1881-1936), though it has also produced novels and poetry of considerable social significance and literary merit. It is still too soon to say what elements and forms from the old literary traditions will survive, or what significant new trends will develop. We can only be certain that the old isolationism has gone forever and that from now on Chinese literature will develop as an integral part of the literature of the world.

XXI

The Role

of Religion in

Chinese Society

BY

C. K. YANG

This chapter deals with the role and structural forms of religion in the functioning of Chinese society. For the present purpose, religion is viewed as a system of nonempirical beliefs, ritualistic practices, and organizations which were developed to deal with the ultimate concerns of human existence such as life, death, and frustrations. The emphasis is on Chinese religious practices and organization; theology will be considered only as it concerns issues of actual religious functions in society. Unacculturated systems such as Christianity will not be treated here.

General Importance of Religion and Its Structural Forms

The importance of religion to Chinese society is indicated by the high density of temples and shrines in all parts of the country. Lacking nationwide statistics, we may cite for north China Wang-tu County (Hopei Province), which had in 1905 an average of 5.7 temples per village, or one temple for every 17.7 families. Also in south China there is Nanching village (Kwangtung Province) which had in 1950 eight temples for its 233 families, or one temple for each 30 families. Different varieties of temples were related to a wide range of functions: integration of the family, protection of the community, operation of the state, maintenance of the moral order, success of economic relations, and the maintenance of health and general personal welfare. In addition to the temples, other forms of religious practices colored every major aspect of social life.

Despite its pervasive role, religion did not enjoy a prominent position in the structure of Chinese society, due to the dominance of diffused religion as compared to institutional religion. Institutional religion is characterized by an independent theology, a separate cultus (rituals and symbols), and a discrete personnel structure. Religion of this type constitutes a *separate* social institution, hence the designation "institutional religion." Diffused religion, on the other hand, has these three elements combined into the concept, rituals, and personnel of the host institution. Traditional institutional religion in China was represented by Buddhism, Taoism, and religious sectarian societies. Diffused religion was found in all major traditional social groups and institutions. Ancestor worship was an example: its belief in the souls of the departed ancestors was a part of the concept of family perpetuation; its mortuary and sacrificial rites formed an important part of the family rituals; and its personnel consisted of the head of the family acting as the officiating priest, with the family members as the congregation. In theological concept, in ritualistic practice, and in personnel structure, ancestor worship was an integral part of the family and the wider kinship system. As a component of all major social institutions, diffused religion affected every significant aspect of social life in China. Hence, the dominance of the diffused structural form made religious influence pervasive, but did not make it a prominent structure independent of other social institutions.

Theological information on Buddhism and Taoism, two of the dominant faiths in traditional China, is available elsewhere, but the content of classical religion requires a brief statement here. Indigenous to China, classical religion developed to a mature form during the classical times of Chinese history (Shang, Chou and Early Han periods). It had four major components: ancestor worship, the worship of Heaven with its subordinate system of naturalistic deities, divination, and sacrifice. While Buddhism and Taoism remained in institutional form, classical religion became largely diffused into the secular social institutions such as the family and the state.

Although Buddhism, Taoism, and classical religion were separate faiths, in practice, they intermingled freely in the religious life of the people. China is a land of polytheism and eclecticism, and the focus of popular religious interest is practical function and not theological identification. Thus, a man would readily pray one day to the Buddhist Goddess of Mercy for the begetting of a son and another day to the Taoist medicine god, Hua-t'o, for the return of health, and on still another occasion might go to a classical diviner to have his fortune told, all without any thought that he might be unfaithful to any single religion. In fact, there have been occasions when even priests in a temple were not sure whether certain gods in it belonged to Buddhism or Taoism. Monotheism and theological absolutism have been foreign to the popular tradition of Chinese religious life.

Ancestor Worship and the
Family System

Largely in its diffused form and its polytheistic nature, religion has served as an integrative force for Chinese social institutions and organized groups. This can be plainly seen in ancestor worship in relation to the family system which has been a structural core in traditional Chinese society. If polytheism stimulated individual divergence in religious practice, ancestor worship enjoyed universal observance for, under the traditional order, failure to practice it would invite moral condemnation or even legal punishment.

The basic function of ancestor worship was to maintain the cohesion and continuation of the family organization by using the memory image of departed kinsmen as an integrative symbol of perpetual kinship tie. Operation of the cult started with mortuary rites at the death of an adult family member. The first act was the reporting of the death to the Earth God (T'u Ti) or the God of Five Roads (Wu Tao), who, as guards at the portals of the underworld, would facilitate the admission of the soul of the dead to the world of spirits. The rites continued for as many as forty-nine days, depending on the family's wealth. There were such rituals as the dressing of the corpse in the best garments available, burning paper money, paper clothing, a paper house and furniture, even paper servants, all for the obvious purpose of serving the needs of the soul in the other world. For those who could afford it, there was the rite, by the chief mourner (the eldest son), of assisting the soul (represented by a paper tablet) to cross the paper Bridge of Sighs (*nai-ho ch'iao*), from which the deceased could take a last longing look at the world of the living before passing into the world of the dead. There were the many scriptural chanting sessions by Buddhist or Taoist priests, who would also perform such rites as helping the soul to pass the ten courts of judgment in the underworld on his way to the eventual destination, the paradise of Western Heaven. Through the psychological process of "acting it out," performance of these elaborate and prolonged mortuary rites had the emotional effect of affirming the belief in the continued existence of the soul of the deceased, thereby setting up a lasting symbol for long-term integration of the family group.

Another part of the mortuary rites was the innumerable sessions of ritual weeping by the mourners. The spouse or children of the deceased wept in genuine expression of grief, but the more distant relatives might weep only as an appropriate gesture. These different kinds of ritual weeping, genuine or formalistic, expressed a sentimental tie between the deceased and the entire membership of the family, and therefore performed the function of demonstrating organizational unity and promoting group cohesion for the family system.

The last part of the mortuary rites was the funeral procession and the main mourning feast. These rites differed radically according to the family's wealth and status. For the poor and insignificant, the funeral procession consisted of probably only a handful of immediate kin, and there would be no mourning feast for the wider kinship circle. But for the wealthy and prominent, a funeral procession of relatives and friends could stretch out for a mile, with flowers, honorific and complimentary banners, bands of musicians, and chanting priests. The mourning feast, attended by hundreds of mourners, would be no less an exhibition of lavishness. Middle-class families often strained their resources to the limit, and even sank deeply into debt, to provide an elaborate funeral and mourning feast. The entire undertaking required maximum exertion and cooperation from the family members, and thus helped to reintegrate a family organization disrupted and weakened by the death of a member, particularly if the deceased had been an important member. Furthermore, the impressive display of the funeral procession and the mourning feast was partly an effort of the bereft family to reassert its status in the community after a major tragedy, and partly an expression of the willingness of relatives and friends to render emotional and material support when the need arose.

Mortuary rites were concluded with the enshrining of the wooden spirit tablet, symbol of the deceased, in the family shrine or in the clan's ancestral temple. With this rite began the second major phase of ancestor worship, namely sacrifice. There were three types of sacrificial rites: daily, anniversary, and collective. Daily sacrifice consisted of burning incense and keeping up the ever-burning lamp in front of the ancestral tablets; this served as a daily reminder of the continued existence of the ancestor's soul as a basic part of the family structure. Anniversary sacrifice took place in front of the family altar at the date of death of each major deceased member. Rites were performed by family members in their proper order according to generational and age priorities, thus rehearsing the hierarchical structure of the family. Sacrificial food, as elaborate as the family could provide, was shared in the subsequent feast attended by all members who could possibly come home. The sharing of good food (symbol of abundance brought by family success) by the entire family in front of the altar periodically reinforced the membership loyalty and solidarity of the group in a sacred atmosphere.

Collective sacrifice took place both at major festivals such as the New Year celebration and, for the clan, at the Spring and Autumn Sacrifices at the ancestral temple. Sacrifice was offered collectively to all the ancestors whose spirit tablets were enshrined in the family altar or in the ancestral temple. In the case of the New Year sacrifice, the portrait scrolls of the major ancestors were hung in the hall as reminders of their continued moral influence on the family's destiny. No major traditional festival, and no major family event such as birth or marriage, passed without sacrificial rituals and the offer of food to the ancestors. The significance of the occasion was to renew the unity and cohesion of the kinship organization.

The ancestor cult was as characteristic of Chinese religious life as the family system was of central importance to traditional Chinese society. The family organization, especially the extended family system, owed much of its solidarity and long continuity to the function of this cult. The secular fact of biological relatedness could serve as a binding force for two or at most three generations, but the cohesion of an extended family beyond three generations, or the solidarity of an extensive clan, had to rely on translating biological relatedness into a sacred social bond symbolized by belief in the continued existence of the ancestors' souls as an eternal overseeing and cementing force for later generations. This would free kinship relations from the limitation of time. In performing the worship, the farther back one traced a family's ancestors, the larger the size of the kinship group thus consolidated with the help of the cultic bond.

Religious Elements in Social and Economic Groups

Chinese traditional society was structurally anchored at the local level by the kinship system and at the national level by the state. In between there lay a limited range of intermediate organizations such as fraternal groups, secret societies, occupational associations, and local communities. As in the case of the family, these intermediate organizations were never purely secular groups, but contained vital religious components. Fraternal and sororal groups, the smallest of the intermediate organizations, comprising generally less than a dozen members, were launched by a vow of loyalty before a chosen deity and by the exchange of information on each member's birth date and hour, a token of complete frankness and mutual trust, since magic could harm a person through the use of such information. These acts were meant to invoke the supernatural forces to help cement and stabilize friendship ties which the members felt eager to perpetuate. Fraternal and sororal groups were important organized means of mutual aid, especially among those who were underprivileged.

Secret societies were among the most extensive and cohesive intermediate organizations. They can be considered an expanded version of brotherhood groups, and their structure and operation relied seriously on the use of religious elements. Secret societies could be a poor laborers' gang, purely religious sectarian groups, or organizations with political ambition. They were all banned by the traditional Chinese government. The danger of persecution compelled the maintenance of secrecy, and the seriousness of the undertaking motivated the members to develop elaborate religious beliefs and rituals such as the blood vow (letting a drop of blood into a cup of liquor from which other members sipped), the sacred pledge of substituting the new brotherhood for one's natural kinship relations, and the burning of a list of membership to signify communication of the names to the invisible supernatural forces. All these acts served to induce organizational loyalty and solidarity for a perilous undertaking. The sipping of each other's blood was to add realism to the simulated kinship tie of brotherhood, as kinship was the strongest group tie known to the common people.

The religious element was prominent among traditional economic activities and organizations. In the prescientific age, the dominance of the uncontrollable element of chance in the hard struggle for a livelihood led people to appeal to the supernatural for attainment of success and security. The importance of the religious element was often in proportion to the risky nature of the economic activity. Gamblers were proverbially superstitious, and so were traditional Chinese sailors, as even the best of captains did not always return safely from the perilous high seas. Until the Communist assumption of power, the goddess of sailing, Tien Hou, enjoyed the most active worship in all southern coastal communities; the celebration of her birthday was among the most exciting communal events, when the sailing population as well as the general populace came to thank her for another year of safety on the high seas which human effort alone would not have achieved.

Every traditional trade had its patron god, piously worshiped in the shops and homes of its practitioners. The birthday celebration of the patron god was a major event with its tradesmen, involving mass worship and community theatrical performances. Generally the guild used such an occasion to hold the annual business meeting, with the proceedings punctuated by religious ceremonies honoring the patron god. During the meeting, fines against members for violating guild rules were imposed as incense and lamp-oil money donated to the patron god, which served as a collective symbol of the trade, transcending divisive personal utilitarian interests. Thus, fines were imposed in the name of the god as a means to avoid antagonism against the group which must enforce rules for common interest. This demonstrates the integrative function of religion in occupational organizations.

Agriculture, which has been basic to the Chinese economy, has had to face the vagaries of the elemental forces, the control of which was mainly beyond the human abilities of a prescientific peasantry. Consequently, the landscape of China was characterized by the ubiquitous sight of temples and shrines dedicated to agricultural deities which governed the atmospheric forces (gods of wind and thunder), regulated water (Dragon God or Lung Wang), and controlled pests (gods of locusts). Due to the broad importance of agriculture, religious activities related to agricultural deities performed the function of integrating the entire community, from a village to the entire nation. Peking had its temples of Heaven and Earth and atmospheric gods, and the annual imperial sacrifices to these deities were impressive symbols of the imperial power in action on behalf of the nation's interest. Similarly, provincial and county capitals had their official shrines for the atmospheric forces, and official annual sacrifices to them symbolized the existence of the political community of the province or the county. The worship of agricultural deities was a part of traditional communal cults.

Communal Worship

The family met the individual's major needs, including economic production, consumption, moral and technical training of the young, recreation, religion. This fact restricted the individual's workaday existence to the kinship circle. But wider community organization was necessary for large-scale collective undertakings beyond the capacity of the kinship group, hence the development of seasonal communal worship in which the sacred element of religion transcended the divergence of individual and family interests and class status, and thus helped to weld the population into larger communal entities such as a village, a neighborhood, a town.

Communal worship took the forms of a variety of "temple fairs." There were the seasonal great trade fairs organized around a temple. There were the regional religious fairs celebrating a god's birthday in some famous temple which was often located on a scenic site, attracting pilgrims from a wide territory. There were the local temple festivals celebrating the birthday of T'u Ti (Earth God) or other deities in an urban neighborhood or agricultural village. The great concourse of people attracted to the different kinds of fairs for religious worship and collective excitements (shows, storytelling, acrobatic performances, gambling) served the function of periodically mustering the population of the wider community beyond the narrow confine of kinship and demonstrating the vivid existence of greater community ties. In addition, there were the unscheduled mass religious observances in times of such crises as drought and epidemics; the great assemblage of people and exciting religious rituals in normally deserted temple grounds impressed the participants with the sudden emergence of the wider community beyond the small groups of daily existence.

The Traditional State and the Mandate of Heaven

Beyond the local groups and communities stood the national political community of the traditional state as the largest unit of social structure. The state, like the local groups and communities, has not been a purely secular utilitarian structure, because religious elements have been woven into the political dogmas and administrative operations.

The importance of religion to the state is clearly demonstrated by the popular belief that the emperor ruled with the Mandate of Heaven. Although the belief can be traced back to the Shang period over three thousand years ago, in the nineteenth century it was articulated by the Manchu ruling house, when its tottering power needed justification during political crises. Under the Republic, the belief was actively exploited in Yuan Shih-k'ai's abortive attempt to restore the monarchy in 1916. It has not completely lost its validity in the popular mind today, as current Communist literature has often raged against the "thought of changing Heaven's [Mandate]" as a rallying point for anti-Communist forces. Deeply rooted in the traditional mind, the belief in the Mandate of Heaven was a forceful support for the ruling power, for it rendered the government institution sacred and awe-inspiring.

But the Mandate, so went the belief, could be retained by a ruling house only on condition of good conduct as defined mainly by the Confucian values. Misgovernment or grave moral violations would disturb the cosmic order and bring signs of warning (e.g., the appearance of a meteor or such an unnatural occurrence as the birth of a two-headed baby). Disregard of these reactions from Heaven would bring disasters like floods, droughts, and wars, and finally the fall of a ruling house which, by then, would be considered to have lost the Mandate of Heaven. This was called the theory of "interaction between Heaven and man," and the interpretation of Heaven's intent in this connection constituted the content of official apocryphal literature and was declared the prerogative of the ruling house in order to stamp out anti-government interpretations.

One function of the theory of the "Mandate" and the "interaction between Heaven and man" was to place ethical responsibilities on the ruling house as a moral restraint on its otherwise unchecked power. This function has been an important factor in the political stability in traditional China by helping to reduce misrule and to make government morally acceptable to the populace. Confucianism espoused the principle of "government by men of merit," who were selected by the civil service examination system. The examinations legitimated the authority of the bureaucracy. Dynastic founders, however, emerged not from the morally imbued examination halls, but from the violence-ridden battle fields. The Confucian orthodoxy offered no rational explanation or moral justification for the origin of dynastic power. Later development of the Confucian tradition accepted dynastic power on a *post facto* basis ("the successful one became an emperor, the defeated one, a bandit"). But might needs right to attain stability, for power without popular acceptance generates constant resistance and instability. Hence the Confucian orthodoxy endowed dynastic power with moral respectability through the theory of the "Mandate," and by doing so put power under moral restraint, especially with the interpretation of "interaction between Heaven and man." Whatever the channel of success, the power contender who won the throne would possess the "Mandate" invested in it by popular belief, but he would also be subject to the rigid moral requirements imposed by the "Mandate."

Cults of Deified Men and the
Local Political Order

While the worship of Heaven was a supportive force for the institution of central government, the counterpart of the local political order was the cults of deified men or the ethicopolitical cults. Physically such cults were housed in innumerable *tz'u* or fanes dedicated to the commemoration of departed men who had exhibited exemplary virtues in the performance of civic or social duties. Fanes could be dedicated collectively to a group of such men, commonly called "fane for the loyal and the righteous," "fane for martyrs of loyalty," "fane for the chaste (women) and the filial (sons)." A fane could also be devoted to a single individual under his own name coupled with a posthumous honorific title like Wang Kung Tz'u (fane for Prince Wang), Wu Hou Tz'u (fane for the Martial Duke [Chu-ke Liang]) or Kuan Ti Miao (temple of Emperor Kuan [Kuan Yü]).

The ubiquitous presence of such fanes led to John Shryock's characterization of China as a land where the worship of heroes was more developed than in any other culture. In the extensive traditional empire without the benefit of modern transportation, maintenance of local political order had to rely heavily on social morality and civic virtues (e.g., filial piety, political loyalty, righteousness), rather than on the tenuous authority of formal law. The ethicopolitical cults served this function by stimulating dedication to civic morals as exemplified by the men to whose memory the fanes were devoted.

Whether a fane stood proudly at the center of a great city or sat forlornly on the edge of a humble village, it inevitably celebrated a community crisis and a hero who met the challenge with extraordinary moral courage and sacrifice. Whether the crisis was a flood, a war, the dangers of banditry, or a family tragedy, it provided the occasion for the hero's outstanding performance of moral duties (e.g., martyrdom in the public interest, or extreme self-sacrifice for his parents). Both the crisis and the hero served to accentuate the significance of moral values needed for the social and political order of the community.

When the crisis was over and after the hero had passed away, the local people or government authority would decide to build a fane to commemorate the virtuous personality, with a sculptured idol or a wooden tablet to symbolize him. The temple building and the image in it were visible reminders to the people and subsequent generations of the hero's great deeds and virtues long after the community had returned to normal life. Without these physical symbols, the memory of the hero and the moral values he demonstrated might have faded soon after the crisis.

Following the construction of the fane and the initiation of the cult, the operation of the ritualistic component which would influence the cult's viability began. Some fanes were well maintained for centuries with periodic renovation and active worship, while others fell into disrepair and neglect in a few decades, and the cult finally disappeared in a heap of ruins. Regularity of sacrificial rites was a determinant in the stability of the cult, but the development of a mythological lore and personal worship in addition to communal sacrifice seem to have been essential for its long-term survival.

A mythological lore developed based on belief in the magical power of the hero's soul, a belief generally inspired by legendary accounts of the hero's extraordinary ability and superhuman deeds. With the belief in the magical powers of his soul, the cult of a deified hero would enjoy not only the formal spring and autumn sacrifices, but also would attract personal worship and supplication from members of the community on ordinary days. While the formal sacrifice symbolized high level civic morals in public matters, personal worship dealt with mundane affairs of the citizens' private existence: requests for an heir, for cure of sickness, for good fortune of one kind or another. Occasional fulfillment of such prayers spread the fame of the deified hero as an efficacious god and led to popularity of the temple as a place of worship. At this point, the hero had entered the common people's memory by giving his blessing to their daily life, and the cult's function underwent a temporary transformation from inspiring ethicopolitical values to general magical efficacy.

This development was vital to the preservation of group memory of the deified man. High-sounding moral values might motivate officials or the Confucian elite to establish the cult and to carry on the formal sacrifices; such values might even guide the common people in the midst of a crisis to recognize the greatness of the hero. But while great men, great deeds and great virtues were prominent elements in a crisis, they retreated to a negligible position in the common people's consciousness during normal times when their daily struggles engrossed them. The passing of a crisis into history meant the gradual disappearance from the people's memory of the prominent men and their great moral lessons. To be remembered by the community over a long stretch of normal times, the hero had to become part of the common people's normal life, standing for humble values and assisting them in the humble events that occasioned their prayers.

In time, a community would face new crises of famine, war, and other forms of mass misery inflicted by overpowering forces beyond the control of the normative rules of routine existence. At such critical times, there would be once more the need for high-level moral values (e.g., loyalty and righteousness beyond the call of duty) to inspire courage and dedication and to organize the community for collective action. Ethicopolitical cults would serve to revivify these values. Often memory of the hero of a cult and his reputed superhuman deeds inspired collective hallucination of his return to the scene to lead the community in its struggle to surmount the new crisis. Apparitions of Kuan Yü (god of righteousness, a third-century hero of war), whose temples were found in every part of China, abound in the historical records of the Ming and Ch'ing periods. Such apparitions reaffirmed vital civic morals in the consciousness of the people, and inspired courage and confidence in them. Without the rich mythological lore of Kuan Yü, and the mass following of the cult based on the belief in his magical efficaciousness, the cult would have long been buried by time, and would not have reappeared in people's memory in recurrent crises over the centuries.

When there was continued belief in the efficacy of a cult, particularly with hallucination of apparitions, it would receive periodic revitalization in the form of temple renovation and imperial decorations with honorific titles reaffirming its ethicopolitical value and its magical efficaciousness. Once more the cult stood out prominently in the view of the community, and its high-level moral value was impressed on the consciousness of the people. But as the new crisis subsided and the community returned to its normal existence, life was guided more by institutionalized routine than by extraordinary moral performance. The people once more practiced the cult for its magical value rather than its ethicopolitical significance, and it entered upon another cycle of development.

State Control of Religion

Although the influence of religion was invoked to support the established political order, it could also be used for opposing the government, because it could be infused with different ethical and political contents. The long history of political disturbances organized by religion attested to this, and the bureaucracy was well aware of it. Hence the persistent policy of state control over religion to ensure that it served as a supportive and not an alienating force for the government.

One form of control was the attempt to encourage the belief that the emperor and his bureaucracy could command obedient service from deities in the pantheon, with the exception of Heaven and Earth. An illustration was the emperor's bestowing of honorific titles on efficacious gods as if they were subordinate members of the bureaucracy. Another form of state control was the ruling house's absolute monopoly over the organized worship of Heaven and the interpretation of heavenly portents. Other measures of political control over religion included the legal requirement of government approval for ordination of Buddhist and Taoist priests. The Ch'ing law also stipulated that priests "must be over forty years of age before giving apprenticeship to a neophyte," and that each priest was permitted to train only one neophyte in his lifetime. These measures were obviously intended to minimize the size of the priesthood. In addition, the central and local governments in the Ch'ing period had special agencies for protecting the priests against subversion by heterodoxies. Convents and temples were under full control of the secular law, with no religious sanctuary rights, and they were warned against harboring fugitives.

The basic motivation for government control of religion was not to convert theological or philosophical deviation from Confucian orthodoxy. The real concern was the possible subversion of the sociopolitical order by organized religion. For officially recognized religions like Buddhism and Taoism, the priesthood was exempt from military and labor conscription and their property was free from taxation. Uncontrolled expansion of such religions would lead to heavy loss of revenue as well as military manpower and corvée labor. This was experienced in the period of disunion and during the latter part of the T'ang dynasty, when the Buddhist church was extensively developed. In addition, powerful local families often placed their property in the hands of the convent or temple clergy to evade taxation. This augmented the wealth and power of the priesthood, raised the specter of political alliance between the clergy and powerful local families against the government, and caused widespread unrest among the common people by shifting onto them a heavier burden of taxation.

Furthermore, the growth of the Buddhist priesthood, which required abandonment of family ties, threatened to undermine the kinship core of the traditional social order.

But the most serious concern of the government was political rebellion by religiously organized groups, especially by unapproved and unsupervised organizations. Ch'ing law laid heavy penalties on unapproved sectarian leaders who formed an organization by training disciples. Those who initiated a sworn brotherhood by the ritual of drawing a few drops of the members' blood and burning to the gods a written oath with a list of the members' names were threatened with the death penalty. The government's fear was the strength of the religious bond among the membership of heretic groups which might harbor rebellious intentions. The earnestness of these laws can be seen from the numerous persecutions of sectarian organizations in Ming and Ch'ing periods.

Rigid control and persecution were a forceful factor in weakening the structural position of centrally organized institutional religion in Chinese society. In this struggle the government enjoyed the advantage of unified power of a continental empire, while religion suffered from the weakness of division among faiths and sects, in contrast to Europe where Christianity was once united while the continent's government was divided among feudal and national states.

The Religious Element in Political Rebellion

As suggested above, religion has been both a supportive and an alienating force in political order. The alienating function of religion is amply evidenced by the example of the Ch'ing dynasty, during which, except for the early decades after its founding, few major rebellions did not involve the religious element to some degree. Thus, there was the series of uprisings which began in the reign of Emperor Ch'ien Lung in the eighteenth century, the height of the dynasty's power: the uprising of the White Lotus sect in 1774, of the Eight Trigrams and the Nine Mansions sects in 1786-88, the Heaven and Earth Society in 1786-89, and the rekindling of the White Lotus forces, in 1794, which affected nine provinces and took eight years to suppress. The nineteenth century was launched with the extensive rebellion of the Eight Trigrams sect in 1813. The middle of the century saw the Taiping uprising which nearly toppled the dynasty, the first major uprising inspired by Christianity. The century terminated with the development of the magical sect of The Boxers' association, which climaxed in the Boxer Rebellion of 1900. And sectarian organizations like the Triads and the Heaven and Earth Society contributed their share to the republican revolution which brought the dynasty to its end.

Under the Republic, religious groups played their part in the general political chaos: the Big Sword and Red Spear societies in the 1920s, which offered their members invulnerability to firearms, and the I-hsin T'ien-tao Lung-hua Sheng-chiao Hui (Single-hearted Celestial Principle Dragon Flower Sacred Religion Society), which set up its own leader as emperor until it was crushed by the warlord of Shantung Province, Han Fu-ch'ü, in 1930. During the eight years of Japanese occupation of the country in World War II, there was the reemergence of a branch of the White Lotus sect, the I-Kuan Tao (Unity Sect), throughout China with antigovernment implications. The early years of the Communist rule saw severe suppression of sectarian movements, as will be pointed out below.

The past two centuries show religion as a constant partner in antigovernment struggles. Unlike Christianity, Chinese religions, especially sectarianism, did not relinquish the claim of temporal power, a claim which led to the development of the traditional suppressive measures against organized religion.

Major religious uprisings grew out of a background of crises and mass misery—widespread famine, war destruction, official oppression, and misgovernment. Thus, an imperial decree of 1817 said of the Eight Trigrams rebellion of 1813: in normal times the society was engaged in worship of the sun and in the magical practice of acquiring invulnerability to weapons, fire and drowning, and when famine and disorder came, it turned to plotting for imperial power. Famine was never out of sight in the Hopei-Shantung-Honan triprovincial area affected by the series of uprisings by the White Lotus and T'ien Li (Celestial Principles) sects in the latter part of the eighteenth and the early part of the nineteenth century. The Hsien T'ien (Prebirth) sect rebellion occurred in Hopei Province in 1835 when "not a drop of rain had fallen there, and all the people were in a state of agitation, anguish and dismay, thus prepared at any moment to be stirred up by evil-brewers." Similar instances could be multiplied.

In the state of crisis and widespread misery, established sociopolitical institutions failed to bring security, and the traditional moral admonitions of filial piety, political loyalty, benevolence, prudence, and hard work, which would earn blessings at normal time, became irrelevant to a population gripped by massive catastrophe. The platitudes of the Confucian orthodoxy could neither explain convincingly why the crises arose nor offer a solution adequate to the unusual circumstances. Searching hard for salvation beyond the tradition-bound Confucian orthodoxy, the people turned to the *i-tuan* (deviating orientation), the classical term for heresy or unorthodox doctrine.

A "deviating orientation" of religious nature could offer deliverance to a crisis-stricken people in many ways. Its brotherhood organization afforded a measure of economic relief or physical safety. The claims of magical power for its gods and rituals raised morale and confidence in a struggle against overwhelming odds at a time when human efforts seemed futile. For the anxious mind, religious doctrines would identify the source of catastrophes and suggest new paths of salvation.

The Buddhist Tripitaka, for example, contains a cosmological explanation of the universe, an ethical interpretation of society, a plan for total deliverance from all human suffering, and a detailed organization and set of rules of monastic life which, if expanded to cover the entire secular world, would transform the earth into a paradise. A doctrine of such comprehensiveness could take over the operation of a government, as in the case of Buddhist theocracies like Tibet. Even the lesser salvational doctrine of the Taiping uprising had an elaborate blueprint for a new society containing items of popular appeal such as nationalized land ownership to alleviate the economic plight of an oppressed peasantry. Sectarian movements built their syncretic salvational plans from Confucian ethics and Buddhist and Taoist theology and cultic symbols. Whatever the brand, salvational propositions have the general revolutionary characteristics of conceiving an unorthodox image of life and a commitment to transform the world in accordance with it. At a time of crisis, when established formulas of life no longer worked, doctrines of revolutionary character would have their popular appeal.

Adding effectiveness to the religious doctrines of political movements were the prophecies accompanying their salvational messages. Prophecies thrived during crises when men were profoundly disturbed by feelings of insecurity and impending disaster. A familiar example is the prophecy of the recent I-Kuan Tao (Unity Sect) which claimed that the supreme force of Limitless Ultimate (Wu Chi) created Heaven and Earth and all things in them and made them operate in cycles of three *kalpa* or cosmic aeons of 125,000 years each. Each *kalpa* was controlled by a Buddha. The transition from one *kalpa* to another was accompanied by great calamities which would strike down all evil men, but believers would be saved. The chronology of historical crises of Chinese history was fitted into the interpretation of the *kalpas* and their transition. Now, it was claimed, the third *kalpa* was about to come, Buddha Maitreya would be in control, and great calamities would be sent down to the world to effect the needed transition. This prophecy was in wide currency during the years of Japanese occupation of the country.

Prophecies used to enlist followings for movements with religious connotations had many points of psychological appeal. First, they provided a sweeping explanation of the dynamic changes of the world by reference to such vague devices as the process of the cosmic aeons. In times of crisis, man was demoralized by chaos and disorder which were beyond his comprehension and control. But according to the prophecy, chaotic events fell into an orderly sequence prearranged by the power of a supreme supernatural being. Formerly incomprehensible tragedies now became explainable, and might even be circumvented under certain moral conditions, and life seemed once more predictable. Second, prophecies almost invariably identified disasters and crises with transitions from one state of affairs to another, and generally threatened worse calamities before things would get better. The prediction of much greater calamities, such as a vast destructive wind, would add anxiety to the minds of an already tortured people, and would drive them to embrace the doctrine in order to be spared. This is precisely what many imperial edicts of the Ch'ing period called "frightening the people and alarming mankind with unfounded heretic talk." Finally, periods of change of cosmic rule of immense dimensions of time and space were set forth to stagger man's imagination, and they were superimposed upon periods of Chinese history in order to dramatize the insignificance of man—a dynasty of two to three hundred years would be an ephemeral episode when measured against a cosmic aeon of 125,000 years. If the established sociopolitical order reaffirmed its own legitimation and power by invoking supernatural sanction, rebel forces in traditional China also made their antigovernment cause a battle by the command of the gods.

Supernatural Influence in Confucianism
and the Traditional Moral Order

Confucianism has characterized Chinese society by giving it the basic values and structural norms, by staffing the state with a Confucian bureaucracy and guiding the community with a Confucian gentry elite. The religious nature of Confucianism has long been a controversy. I have no intention of going into this academic question here, beyond the statement that it was not a *theistic* religion: its doctrine was not founded on supernatural premises. But this fact, together with the much-stressed rationalistic features in the doctrine, would not exempt Confucianism from religious influence. Operating in the prescientific age when the supernatural loomed large in man's mind, Confucianism would not have been able to serve as a guiding orthodoxy without assistance from religious elements persistently present in its development.

Prominent among the religious elements was the acceptance of the almighty anthropomorphic Heaven and the belief in fate as Heaven preordained it. This is illustrated by the concept of the Mandate of Heaven. The Confucian Classics recognized that, beyond human effort, there was the determining power of Heaven in the arrangement of cosmic order and the grand design of history. In the Confucian *Analects* is the familiar expression, "Death and life have their determined appointment; riches and honor depend upon Heaven" (*Lun Yü*, XII, ch. 5), which gave all subsequent generations the final explanation for personal success and failure; and Mencius ascribed to Heaven's prearranged plan the determinant in the rise and fall, peace and order, of the empire (*Meng-tzu*, I, ch. 16). Believing themselves to be the best of men, who had done their utmost for the moral cause of uplifting mankind, the two sages could only point to Fate as the explanation for their personal frustration and for the misfortune of the state.

The belief in Fate led to the development of ritualistic and magical practices of trying to "know fate." The six basic Confucian Classics included the *I-ching* (*Book of Changes*), which, in spite of its metaphysical or protoscientific speculations, served mainly as a book of divination techniques. Later, from the Han period on, the theology of Yin-Yang (negative and positive forces) and Five Elements (metal, fire, wood, water, earth) worked out a standard system for predicting events as predetermined by these mystical cosmic forces. The *I-ching* and the Yin-Yang and Five-Element theory together have profoundly colored the Confucian mind with a predeterministic tenet in their interpretation of the cosmic order, human history, and personal events.

In the centuries after the Han period, the ideal type of Confucian scholar was conceived as one who could interpret personal events and historical development in terms of fate. Thus, Wang Mien, the hero of the famed eighteenth-century fiction, *Ju-lin Wai-shih* (The informal record of the scholars), took one look at the refugees from a Yellow River flood, which forced the current to flow northward, and exclaimed that this [the unnatural phenomenon of the river flowing north] was the omen of general violence and destruction in the empire and that he was going home to hide for safety. Sure enough, as the novel had it, the dynasty collapsed four years later and local strong men arose in every part of the empire to contend for supremacy. Traditional Confucians, including such nineteenth-century figures as the Taiping suppressor, Tseng Kuo-fan, generally believed in the mystical arts of prediction, such as divination, astrology, physiognomy, palmistry, geomancy, and coscinomancy. Many Confucians not only believed in them and used them as guides for action, but also became adept in their practice. Coscinomancy was a popular pastime for small parties among Confucian scholars in the Ch'ing period. The indulgence in geomancy caused many Confucians to delay interring their ancestors for years while they sought a lucky burial plot. Although the imperial examination system was a rational Confucian device of recruitment for the bureaucracy, personal success was regarded as the combined result of human effort and predetermining supernatural influence. Divination and other mystical arts of prediction were in great demand by scholars about to take the examination.

But the belief in predeterminism did not lead to general resignation to fate and a crippling of self-reliance. The Confucian cosmic order was made up of Heaven, Earth, and Man, giving man a high place endowed with a degree of sacredness. Hence the Confucian concept of *li-ming* (establishing fate), giving man the role of forging his own destiny under the ultimate power of Heaven and Earth. Man must rely on his own effort in shaping his course, and those who shunned effort and resigned themselves to fate ("waiting for Heaven to rain rice") would invite community censure and contempt. Should human effort bring success, the belief in "establishing fate" would encourage continued struggle and reduce complacency, since human effort accounted only partially for the success. But should one still fail after utmost exertion, the belief in predeterminism helped one to accept the adverse result as preordained, thus minimizing emotional disturbance or breakdown. Resignation to fate in this situation might either lead to lowering one's goal or encourage one to continue the struggle in spite of disappointment by treating the failures as part of the unfolding process of a fateful moral cause. There was the deep faith that the cause would win eventually, if not in one's own lifetime. This was indeed the view of fate held by Confucius and Mencius and leading Confucians in subsequent generations. Without the belief in fate, the Confucian doctrine might not have reemerged time and again from crushing historical crises.

The Confucian doctrine offered elaborate rational interpretations for the values and structure of the family and the state as core components of social order. But rationality alone could not have brought about the traditional stability of the Chinese family and the state or the effective functioning of the related critical values such as filial piety and political loyalty. Hence the importance of the religious components of the Confucian tradition such as ancestor worship, group sacrifices, the Mandate of Heaven, and ethicopolitical cults of exemplary men.

Similarly, the general moral order of traditional Chinese society, which was dominated by Confucian ethical values, probably could not have functioned without religion serving as a deterrent to deviation. The most prominent form of religious influence in this respect was the belief in Heaven and Hell as guardian authority for the moral order. The organizational image of this spiritual authority was patterned after the traditional temporal Chinese government. There was the Jade Emperor at the apex of a hierarchy of offices, the boards of central administration, and the graded ranks of local authorities, from the Ch'eng Huang (City God) who might govern a province, a prefecture, a county, or a city to the humble T'u Ti (Earth God), who supervised only a neighborhood district.

These spiritual authorities governed as subjects not only all the souls in the "world of shadows"; they also supervised the living man's moral conduct by the threat of both calamities in this life and punishment of the soul after death. Few children were not terrified by the mural paintings of the eighteen purgatories in the City God temples, to be found in every locality, depicting the tortures by fire, sword, and every imaginable form of suffering for sins committed in one's lifetime. The temples of the Jade Emperor, the ubiquitous shrine of the Earth God at every street corner, even the symbol of the kitchen god, who supervised the moral conduct of every household and reported it to the Jade Emperor at the end of every year, suggested to the traditional common man the omnipresence of spiritual authority over his moral life.

The realism of the spiritual authority was enhanced by its pattern, which followed that of the temporal government so familiar to the people. The link between the temporal and spiritual authorities was further strengthened by the belief that the Ch'eng Huang was often appointed from the souls of deceased officials whose spiritual rank frequently depended upon the grade of his temporal office. All this gave people the impression that the system of authority and law enforced the moral order not only in this world but also in the next, and that there was no escape from the pressure of morality, not even in the realm of the spirits.

Reinforcing this belief of Heaven and Hell was the wide dissemination of the powerful Buddhist concept of karma. By this concept, the soul exists eternally, materializing in an endless succession of temporal existences in a variety of forms of life, from insects and animals to different kinds of human beings. As one form of existence is ended by death, the soul will transmigrate to the embryo of another form of life, and moral conduct in one existence determines the form of the next existence of the soul. Each violation of the moral precepts becomes for the next existence the causal seed of retribution in the form of misery. A robber in this life may find his soul reborn as a pig to be slaughtered in the next existence. On the other hand, a moral martyr's soul may be reborn a prince. The revolution of the wheel of causal retribution in the infinite succession of existences of the soul answers questions of the innumerable instances of ethically unaccountable successes and failures, which could seriously undermine men's confidence in the moral order. Why should a lucky crook wallow in riches and power while a morally conscientious servant suffers a lifetime of misery or even a violent death? While rational doctrine could offer no convincing categorical explanation, karma's causal retribution in the succession of existences brings emotional consolation and restores a sense of effectiveness and justice in the operation of the moral order.

Structural Weakness of Institutional Religion

The foregoing discussion has indicated the supportive and stabilizing function of religion for social organization and the moral order. Religion has played this role mainly in a diffused form. In comparison, independent institutional religion occupied a less important place because of its weak structural position in Chinese society.

The classical religion was largely diffused into the concepts, ritual, and personnel of the secular institutions, and its professional priests (diviners, geomancers, sorcerers, and less common types of magical practitioners) were small in number, low in status, and unorganized as a group, serving the needs of individuals and groups as hired practitioners. Buddhist and Taoist priests were also numerically insignificant after the tenth century. In the first half of the twentieth century they numbered between one half and one million, an average of from 0.06 to 0.17 percent of the country's population of 582 million (1953 Communist census). Many local samples showed even lower ratios. This was obviously a consequence of traditional governmental restrictive measures on the size of the priesthood. One illuminating fact was the absence of priests in most temples and convents in the countryside. In normal times local residents maintained the buildings and grounds, occasional worshipers came in to burn incense and pray by themselves, and only on special occasions were priests hired to perform rituals. Even the staffed temples, mainly in the cities, had an average of only one to three priests. Those with large colonies of priests were exceptions.

The temples were administratively autonomous units, lacking any hierarchical structure of authority. An important temple or monastery might be a leading center of theology and worship, and its high priests might hold a limited influence over temples in the same region, but such influence was not stable hierarchical authority.

The financial position of institutional religion was as weak as its organization. The majority of temples had no property endowment as a source of support. To cite two cases: temples having income-yielding property (land and buildings) accounted for 33.6 percent of all temples in the northern county of Wang-tu (Hopei Province), and

3.8 percent in the southern county of Ch'uan-sha (Kiangsu Province). And the majority of those with endowment had property equivalent to that of a poor family; those having the equivalent of a well-to-do family's property were few. Such limited resources were insufficient to support any sizable number of priests in a temple, maintain the buildings, or defray costs of ritual operations. Consequently, temple priests had to rely heavily on worshipers' small donations of "incense and lamp-oil money", on remunerations for rendering ritual services in private homes, and on supplementary occupations such as farming. It was common that priests at normal times would farm the temple land and go on calls for ritual service as in the case of a funeral.

The position of institutional religion was further reduced by the lack of participation by its leaders in community affairs. It was usually the secular community leaders, not temple priests, who formed the core of charity and public welfare work. Priests had neither the financial resources nor the commanding prestige to lead in community welfare activities. The function of education and knowledge, which aided the development of Christianity and some other religions, remained outside the role of Chinese religion. While the elite of the traditional priesthood was generally educated, and occasionally there were a few well-known intellectual priests, the majority of the priests were uneducated, many of them even illiterate. They generally did not conduct secular schools or teach civilian pupils. The function of education was under the firm control of the Confucian elite. Nor were priests or temples involved with the enforcement of justice and moral discipline in a community, an important influence of institutional religion in many other cultures.

Finally, the lack of an organized following or laity was a major source of weakness of the structural position of institutional religion in China. Sectarian societies had organized followings, but persistent persecution kept their membership to a minute proportion of the population, except in short periods of religious uprisings when they collected huge followings. Devotees of Buddhism and Taoism had organizations, but they were numerically insignificant. For the vast majority of the population, religious worship was unorganized individual activity. The individual's relation to a temple or shrine was limited to each occasion of worship; after the worship was over, the worshiper and the temple were not bound by any organizational tie. If there was a priest in a temple, the worshiper discharged his obligation for the occasion by paying him a small donation for the incense and sacred-lamp oil, with no further responsibility.

The absence of priests in most temples meant the lack of an active agent to develop organizational allegiance between a temple and its lay worshipers. The dominance of polytheism also hampered the development of organized congregations, as worshipers went to different temples or appealed to gods of different religions on various occasions. Thus, the tie of worship could not be concentrated on a single temple as an organizational focus. The lack of a regular time (daily, weekly, or monthly) of worship deprived the worshipers of the opportunity of sustained contact and association which might induce the development of an organized laity. Above all, the historical alliance between religion and uprisings led the government to suppress the development of organized religious followings.

Religious Change in the Republican Period

The foregoing picture represents religious life and organization in its traditional form. Changes in many respects occurred under the Republic. In general, traditional religious life persisted among the common people and the Confucian elite who were not seriously affected by science and Western materialistic values. But replacement of the Confucian monarchy by the Republic, the expansion of the Western-minded elite in the government and community leadership, and the rapid growth of the Western type of education among the younger generation seriously eroded the old religious concepts and structure.

The persistence of traditional religious life among the general population was seen in the continued vitality of the belief in the Mandate of Heaven, as previously mentioned. The traditional pantheon was very much alive as indicated by the prosperity of "incense fire" offerings in temples of popular cults in every community, and by the enthusiastic celebration of temple fairs everywhere. The repair of old temples and cosntruction of new ones during the period of the Republic, especially before the "second revolution" of 1926, proceeded at a pace commensurate with that in the Ch'ing period. Temples destroyed in a century of unceasing disturbances and wars were continuously restored, and new ones were added to meet current requirements, especially in localities sharing in the growth of the modern economy, such as areas of expanding urban centers. Many new temples of Lu Pan (patron god of carpentry and masonry), for instance, were constructed in the rapidly urbanizing communities near Shanghai to meet need of religious integration of the fast-growing construction trade which prospered from building the new metropolis. Ancestral temples in the countryside were continuously refurbished and many new ones were built, attesting to the vitality of the traditional kinship system in the rural areas. Where old temples were not kept in repair and few major new ones were built, the probable cause lay with the impoverishment of the community rather than with any change in religious belief among the masses.

The recent century was a period of cataclysmic events buffeting the nation with death, hunger, frustration; neither the traditional institutions nor the Confucian orthodoxy could hold together vital group ties or offer hope for a solution. A time like this was typically conducive to the rise of religious movements.

The first half-dozen years of the Republic were greeted by the "Confucian religion movement," which tried to convert Confucianism into a formal religion as a means of strengthening the faith in orthodoxy in the national struggle against Western influences. Headed by such champions of traditional Chinese culture as K'ang Yu-wei, leader of the Hundred Day Reform, the movement did not go much beyond setting up a system of headquarters and provincial branches, and sporadic performance of sacrificial rites in the local Confucius temples. Without visionary or mystical prophets as leaders, the movement developed no new theology or rituals. Cultically there was no renewed attempt to deify Confucius as a supernatural symbol, and the time-worn sacrificial rites failed to breathe fresh inspiration into a generation which demanded new orientations to face unprecedented challenges. Above all, as will be discussed later, the movement suffered from the disadvantage of being a diffused religion which must rely on the vitality of secular social institutions for its existence.

The short-lived "Confucian religion" movement was confined to the Confucian elite minority. Affecting a wider circle and exhibiting greater vitality was the Buddhist movement, which collected a sizable middle-class following by the 1930s. New national Buddhist leaders like Abbot T'ai-hsü (Ultimate Void) delivered mass sermons and set up national headquarters and local branches of Buddhist associations, some of which had several thousand members. Institutes and schools were established in various parts of the country to study Buddhist theology and to train leaders for the rejuvenation of the religion.

Periodicals and popular tracts were circulated. Organized action of this type would have been persecuted by the imperial anti-heresy law, which was repealed under the Republic. But the movement lacked a modern theology and progressive leadership which could meet the challenge of science and the new values of industrial society. And it was a victim of the historical situation: its mass organizations had less than two decades to develop before its disruption by the total Japanese invasion in 1937. The Communist ascension to power in 1949 put an end to its further development.

Developing extensive followings in the Republican period were the sectarian societies like the I-Kuan Tao (Unity Sect). The many sectarian movements probably had a wider membership among the middle and lower classes, especially the laborers and peasants, than did the Buddhist movement, but there has been no systematic study of their size and structure. In the four decades of chaos and destruction under the Republic, sectarian movements played their role as they had done in the preceding centuries in offering common men hope and a rallying focus to organize themselves against misfortune and oppression.

While religion maintained its virility among people of all classes in times of widespread misery and mass anxiety, it could no longer generate controlling influence over the sociopolitical order of the republic because unprecedented antireligious currents were at work to turn an age of belief and piety into one of skepticism and atheism. Popular theistic movements were but rearguard actions of an era rapidly receding into history.

Although the Confucian religion movement failed to restore new faith in the ancient Chinese culture, it did spark national interest in a new issue: did China need a national organized religion to survive among the modern family of nations, as Western countries have their Christianity and Japan its Shintoism? The ensuing polemics in the years following World War I resulted in unqualified victory for the forces of science and agnosticism. The young intellectual generation embraced wholeheartedly the view brought by Western education and by personal visits from such leading Western scholars of the day as Bertrand Russell and John Dewey. Religion was declared the product of primitive ignorance and incompatible with the spirit of modern science. Another mighty force, the rising tide of nationalism and communism, cast its weight against religion by the now familiar charge that religion was the opiate of the oppressed and the vanguard of Western imperialism. This led to the antireligion movement of the 1920s. First aimed at Christianity, the movement soon widened its target to include other religions, condemning all supernatural beliefs as superstitious. To make China a modern progressive nation, religion was not needed.

The generation educated in modern schools in the 1920s and 1930s was profoundly influenced by these antireligious currents, which soon seriously undermined the religious foundation of Chinese society. The mythological theme and the religious note, an inevitable element in the traditional novel, no longer appeared in the "new literature" as a means of dealing with life crises. The Nationalist Northern Expedition of 1926 left behind a wake of wrecked temples. When the successful expedition set up the Nationalist government in Nanking, the latter lost little time in issuing regulations to purge religious education from the curriculum in missionary schools, and to abolish the occupations of superstition (astrology, divination, palmistry, geomancy, etc.). Regulations against the latter occupations were never enforced, but the general current was unmistakable. Since the turn of the century, temples, especially those in the countryside, had increasingly been converted into schools or devoted to other nonreligious uses. This trend was accelerated under the Republic, as indicated by the fact that Ting Hsien in Hopei Province had 75 percent of its temples converted to secular uses under the Republic, and Hunan Province in the south lost half of all its temple areas to schoolrooms.

One notable impact of the establishment of the Republic was the replacement of the belief in the Mandate of Heaven by the principle of "rights of man" in the formal concept of the government, and the dying out of ethicopolitical cults in the local communities. Although the "Mandate" idea and the magical image of departed exemplary men remained very much alive in the traditional popular mind, the discontinuation of public sacrifices to the powers above doomed them to eventual extinction. Peking's magnificent Temple of Heaven stood in silence as the impressive annual sacrifices no longer returned to breathe life into it, for its identification with monarchical power was incompatible with the democratic assumptions of the Republic. Cults of civic virtues received intermittent attention which failed to resuscitate them. Even the annual sacrifice to Confucius, a grand occasion for the intellectuals, school children, and neighborhood communities in preceding centuries, was abandoned by the Republican regimes. Provincial authorities here and there ordered official sacrifice to cults of men of extraordinary moral rectitude (in political loyalty, righteousness, filial piety), but such sacrifices were as ephemeral as the provincial regimes, and when they were performed, their once colorful rituals recalled only the backwardness and inadequacy of an ancient civilization in the face of the modern world, and failed to inspire new hope and vigor in the young generation. Even in the family, the modern educated young increasingly ignored the rites of ancestor worship. Thus, from the state to the family, social institutions under the Republic rapidly lost the sacred and awe-inspiring character which underlay their past stability and effectiveness.

The failure of religion to gain leading influence in an age of turbulence and insecurity was due partly to the historical weakness of institutional religion, as discussed previously, and partly to the nature of diffused religion which dominated traditional religious life. Previously, diffused religion contributed to the stability of traditional Chinese society not only by imparting an aura of sacredness to social institutions, but also by helping to minimize the divisive effect of the dominance of independent institutional religion, and by sanctifying traditional values in contrast to the requirement of breaking with the past as characteristic of conversion in institutional religion. But the strength of diffused religion depends on the healthy functioning of the secular institution which embodies it. When an institution fails repeatedly to surmount major social crises or to meet social needs, people lose faith in that institution as well as in the religious elements diffused in it. Diffused religion, constituting part of a secular social institution, shared the fate of the institution itself.

Religion under Communism

In the traditional periods when Chinese society was functioning effectively, religion, especially in its diffused form, served as an integrative force for social institutions and groups. The failure of religion to develop decisive influence under the Republic stemmed from its inability to serve the same purpose in a protracted period of chaos, contradictions, and frustrations.

The succession of Republican regimes and a plethora of social and political movements brought neither stability to the social order within nor improved national status without. Instead, the nation's crisis deepened rapidly with eight years of disastrous war against the Japanese invasion and the violent postwar contest between the

Nationalists and the Communists which dwarfed all preceding civil wars under the Republic. In this contest, Communism won the victory not only by superior military force, but also by its appearance as a supreme concern which could transcend divergent interests and claims, command undivided national dedication, and at the same time provide a centered act in which the individual could reintegrate the emotional and rational aspects of his personality and aim at a central goal. Such a supreme concern for the nation and such a centered act for the individual is, as Paul Tillich has said, a faith. Communism thus offered the tortured and divided nation a nontheistic faith as a new integrating force, a function which the traditional religions could no longer serve because of their inability to symbolize modern values needed for fulfillment of the nation's aspirations.

The new faith of Communism established itself as a symbol of two goal values: national power and materialistic progress, which have been China's aspirations for close to a century of struggle for national salvation. Its all-embracing doctrine of materialistic determinism, class struggle, and the millennium of communistic society that would ban want and misery forever gave to the mind of a troubled generation an ecstatic enlightenment in which the once incomprehensible chaotic world suddenly fell into an orderly pattern, explaining with certitude what had happened before and what would happen in the future as mankind's inevitable destiny. It was a "natural law" demanding obedience from all men. The all-embracing quality and a sense of inevitability of Communism bred an attitude of omnipotence, absoluteness, and dedication commonly encountered in religious faiths. Consequently, when the Communists attained power and faced the problem of dealing with religions, it was a situation of "faith countering faith," with ultimacy assumed by both sides. And Communism, as with theistic religion, demanded conversion from all men, with a clean break with the past leading to a new existence.

As the ultimacy of Communism admitted of no competition, and its long-term policy toward religion was one of eventual elimination, its materialistic dogma dismissed all assumptions of the supernatural, which its class struggle theory regarded as the opiate of the exploited. The new society of Communism could find no place for theistic religion. Eventual abolition of religion was implied in the atheistic education for the young and in the purging of mythological themes from the popular stage and other types of folk communication.

But practical considerations led the Communists to adopt a

transitional policy of limited tolerance toward religion under the conditions of subordination and active support for the Communist state. Common people as well as priests were permitted in principle to continue their worship so long as they also participated actively in the Communist programs, including political indoctrination and economic production. For this purpose, the Communist authority even assisted in establishing national organizations for the leading religions with the exception of sectarian societies. Buddhism and Taoism for the first time had functioning national systems reaching temples and convents in even remote mountain areas. Christians, both Catholics and Protestants, had their nationwide associations to carry out the policy of "self-administration, self-preaching, and self-support" so as to sever the ties with the imperialistic West. The national religious organizations obviously facilitated Communist surveillance over the otherwise scattered religious population, aided the indoctrination of them by forming "study groups," helped in the mobilization of priests for public works and economic production, and served as a network of communication for transmitting Communist government instruction. Religious organizations have been formed and operated as instruments for consolidation of the new Communist social and political order.

This does not mean that religious worship was left completely alone so long as the worshipers did not resist the Communist political power. The effort to reduce religion must go on. Thus, religious goods (incense, candles, etc.) were taxed heavily as "superstitious articles" to discourage their use. Conversion of temples to secular uses continued apace to meet the needs of the rapidly growing number of schools and public organizations. While a few prominent ones were preserved and even renovated as symbols of the cultural heritage and national pride, the majority of temples and convents were no longer devoted to religious worship. Temple land and property were collectivized, and the priests, except for a negligible minority, were mobilized for production on the land or in other occupations, as priesthood was regarded as parasitism and exploitation. A majority of them married and returned to secular life.

In general, the Communists had little difficulty in controlling religion. Independent institutional religion had been in a weak position for the past one thousand years, without an organized priesthood or laity. Christianity was an organized force, but its small numerical size minimized its importance. Diffused religion, not being independently organized, posed no threat to Communist power, and it was expected to decline or disappear with the drastic alteration of the secular institutions. Craft patron gods, for example, disappeared when labor unions replaced traditional guilds.

One serious political threat was from the sectarian societies, which the Communists have been suppressing with full vigor and effectiveness. In 1955 alone, Communist police authorities announced the liquidation of 40,000 sectarian "counter-revolutionaries" spread over all parts of the country. But the sectarians continued to emerge sporadically in the subsequent decade as the population went through a succession of crises, including the establishment of the communes, the Great Leap Forward Movement, and the Great Proletarian Cultural Revolution. Communist literature presented sectarian names that echo popular uprisings of half a century ago: Pai-yang Chiao (White Sun Religion), Lung Hua Hui (Dragon Flower Association), Chiu Kung Tao (Nine Mansions Sect), Sheng Hsien Tao (Sages Sect), Red Spears Association, Big Sword Association, I-Kuan Tao (Unity Sect). Some of them, following suppression, reappeared under new names, such as the Unity Sect, which assumed the camouflage of Chung Tao (Middle Sect). And they operated with the traditionalized secret pattern of organization. In the countryside extensive systems of communication tunnels and subterranean chambers (102 of them in Shensi Province alone) served as headquarters of sectarian organizations. There were cases in which an entire collectivized farm had been turned into a sectarian operational base.

Thus, in the initial two decades of Communism, religion continued to exist in the social and political scene. Whether theistic influence will again emerge as a social and political force depends on the success of the Communist system in surmounting new crises and in meeting the basic physical and emotional needs of the population.

Appendix: Maps

General Political and Physical Map of China, with Provinces and Cities
Prominent during the Third Imperial Period and Modern Times

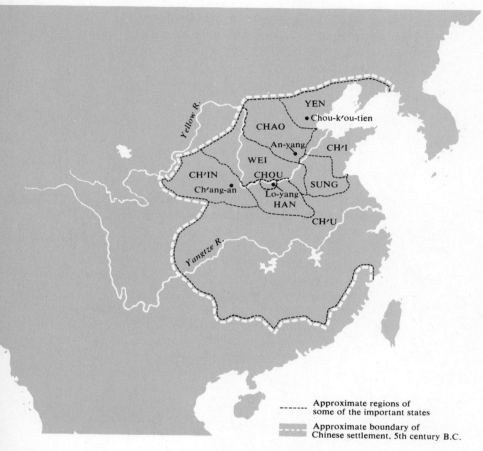

Approximate regions of
some of the important states

Approximate boundary of
Chinese settlement, 5th century B.C.

Sites of the Ancient and Classical Period

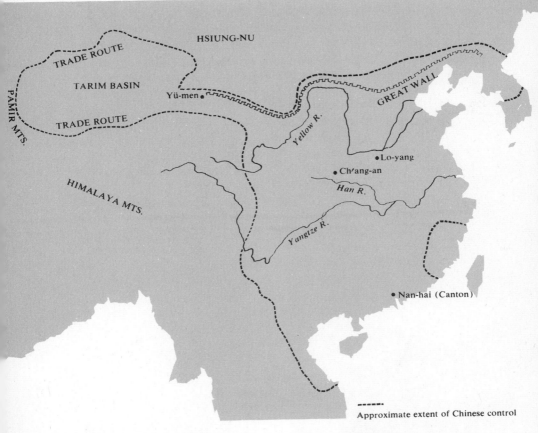

China in the First Imperial Period (Reign of Emperor Wu, 2nd-1st Century B.C.)

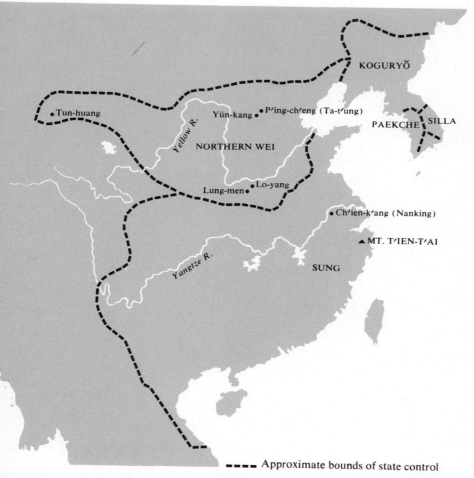

- - - - Approximate bounds of state control

China in the Period of Disunity (Fifth Century; Northern Wei and Sung)

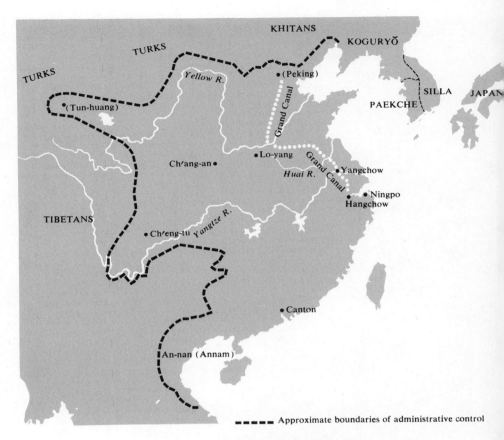

China Early in the Second Imperial Period (7th Century)

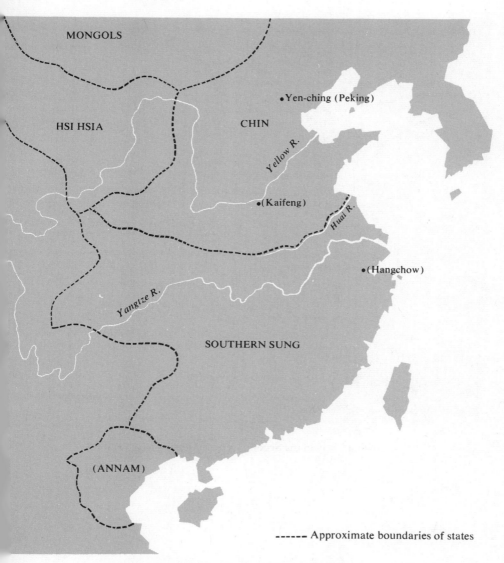

China Late in the Second Imperial Period (12th Century)

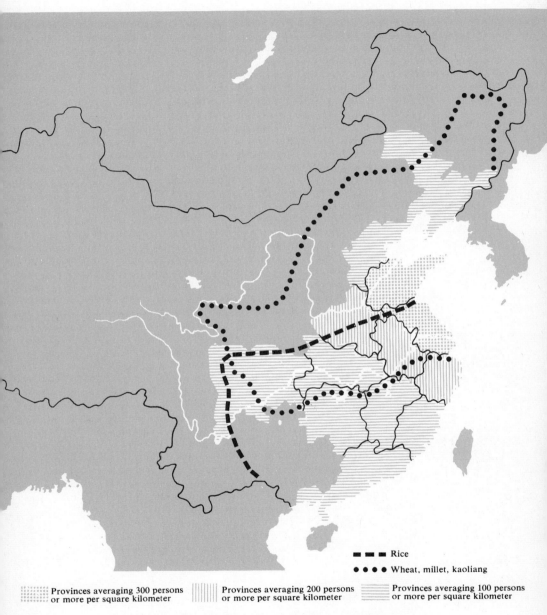

Rice

Wheat, millet, kaoliang

Provinces averaging 300 persons or more per square kilometer

Provinces averaging 200 persons or more per square kilometer

Provinces averaging 100 persons or more per square kilometer

Modern China: Population Distribution and Agricultural Areas

Acknowledgments

Illustrations in Part One: Chapters 1 and 2: Nelson Gallery–Atkins Museum, Kansas City, Missouri (Nelson Fund); Chapter 3: property of Tenri Sankōkan, reproduced in *Tenri Sankōkanzuroku*, published by Asahi Shimbun; Chapter 4; detail, *Ladies Preparing Newly Woven Silk,* courtesy Museum of Fine Arts, Boston; and cave painting, Tun-huang Institute photograph, reproduced in *Buddhist Cave Paintings at Tun-huang,* by Basil Grey and J. B. Vincent; Chapter 5: Metropolitan Museum of Art, New York, Fletcher Fund, 1947; Chapter 6: Collection of the National Palace Museum, Taipei, Taiwan, Republic of China; Chapter 7: *Wan-shou shengtien ch'u-chi,* compiled by Wang Yüan-ch'i and others, chap. 41; Chapters 10 and 11, Wide World Photos.

Illustrations in Chapter XIII: Figure 1: Franz Weidenreich, *Palaeontologia Sinica,* n.s. D, no. 10 (1943), pl. XLVIII; Figure 2: after H.L. Movius, Jr., *Transactions of the American Philosophical Society,* n. s. 38 (1949), figs. 35, 37–39; Figure 3: from *Vertebrata Palasiatica,* 10 (1966), no. 1; Figure 4: H. Boule *et al., Le Paléolithique de la Chine* (Paris, 1928), figs. 30–48 *passim;* Figure 5: An Chih-min, Cheng Nai-wu, and Hsien Tuan-chü, *Miaoti-kou yü San-li-ch'iao* (Peking, Science Press, 1959), fig. 5; Figure 6: *Hsi-an Pan-p'o* (1963), figs. 121-22; Figure 7: Chang Kwang-chih, *The Archaeology of Ancient China* (New Haven, Yale University Press, 1963), p. 71; Figure 8: *Hsin Chung-kuo ti K'ao-ku Shou-huo* (1962), p. 18; Figures 9 and 10: Chang, *The Archaeology of Ancient China* (rev. and enl. ed., New Haven, Yale University Press, 1968), figs. 77 and 126; Figure 11: Collection of Academia Sinica; Figures 12 and 14: Liang Ssu-yung and Kao Ch'ü-hsün, *HPKM 1001* (Taipei, Academia Sinica, 1964); Figure 13: Liang and Kao, *HPKM 1003* (Taipei, Academia Sinica, 1967); Figure 15: Li Chi. *"Chia* Tripods of Anyang," *Archaeologica Sinica,* n.s. 3 (1968); Figure 16: *Hsin Chung-kuo ti K'ao-ku Shou-huo* (1962), p. 61; Figure 17: based on *K'ao-ku Hsüeh-pao* (1965/1), fig. 1, following p. 84; Figure 18, P.C. Kuo, *Shan-piaochen yü Liu-li-ko* (1959), pl. 91.

Illustrations in Chapter XIV: Figure 1: *Kaogu,* 1965, 5, p. 220, fig. 8, no. 13; Figure 2: *Hsin Chung-kuo ti k'ao-ku shou wo* (Peking, 1962), pl. XXIX, 3; Figure 3: William Rockhill Nelson Gallery of Art, Kansas City; Figure 4: Freer Gallery of Art, Washington, D. C.; Figure 5: Nihon Keizai Shimbun, Tokyo; Figure 6: William Rockhill Nelson Gallery of Art, Kansas City; Figure 7: Nihon Keizai Shimbun, Tokyo; Figure 8: Minneapolis Institute of Arts; Figure 9: Metropolitan Museum of Art, New York; Figure 10: William Rockhill Nelson Gallery of Art, Kansas City; Figure 11: Richard C. Rudolph, Los Angeles; Figure 12: S. Mizuno and T. Nagahiro, *Yün-Kang: The Buddhist Cave-temples of the Fifth Century A. D. in North China,* Kyoto, 1954, vol. 15, pl. 16; Figure 13, Museum Rietberg, Zurich; Figure 14: University Museum,

University of Pennsylvania, Philadelphia; Figure 15: Freer Gallery of Art, Washington; Figure 16: Nihon Keizai Shimbun, Tokyo; Figure 17: Benjamin Rowland, Jr., Cambridge, Massachusetts; Figure 18: Daitoku-ji, Kyoto; Figure 19: Charles D. Weber, Los Angeles; Figure 20: British Museum, London; Figures 21 and 22: Museum of Fine Arts, Boston; Figures 23 and 24: Palace Museum, Peking; Figure 25: Palace Museum, Taipei; Figure 26: Museum of Fine Arts, Boston; Figures 27 and 28: Palace Museum, Taipei; Figure 29: William Rockhill Nelson Gallery of Art, Kansas City; Figure 30: Museum of Fine Arts, Boston; Figure 31: Wango Weng, New York; Figure 32: James Cahill, Berkeley, California; Figure 33: Cleveland Museum of Art; Figure 34: Princeton Art Museum; Figure 35: Charles A. Drenowatz, Zurich.

Index

Administration, *see* Government and administration

Agriculture: prehistory, 4-5; Shang, 9, 464, 466; Chou, 18-19, 464-68, 521; South China, 62; T'ang, 99-100, 475; Yuan, 150; Ming, 167, 475; Ch'ing, 193-94, 475, 481; Nationalist, Taiwan, 321; Great Leap Forward, 332-34, 504-5; Ch'in and Ch'ing, 469-71, 475, 481; traditional China, 473-76, 480-81; Han, 474, 475, 522; technical developments in, 474, 480-81, 494, 511-12; Sung, 475; modern China, 494-96, 510-11, 538-41; socialization of, 500-1; communes, 505-7; new policy, 1960s, 508-9; gods of, 650

Aigun, Treaty of, 213

Amoy, 534, 589

Amur River, 213

Analects (Lun-yü), Confucian classic, 24, 31, 661

Ancestor worship, 9-10, 13-14, 645-48, 663, 671

Anhwei province, 62, 210, 409, 426, 537

Animals, 9, 539

An Lu-shan rebellion, 104-5, 106, 108, 112

Annam, 85, 86, 92, 163, 164, 165, 552

Anthropology: physical, 344-47; cultural, 347-78

Anyang, 6, 7, 8, 400-1, 420

Archaeology, 380-415; Peking Man, 4, 384-87; Shang, 6-7, 382 *(table)*, 400-9; Chou, 11, 382 *(table)*, 409-13; important sites, 381 *(table)*, 383-87, 393, 397, 398, 399-400, 402-3, 409, 419, 420, 434, 441; Pleistocene period, 382 *(table)*, 383-90; Postglacial period, 382 *(table)*, 390-91; post-Chou, 413-15

Armies: Hunan Braves, 209-11; Northern, 237, 250, 260; Nationalist, 296-98, 303-4, 309, 316;

Red, 300, 303-5, 313-15; *see also* Military establishment; Warlords

Art, 418-61; Period of Disunity, 78-79, 436; T'ang, 99, 103, 436-37, 447, 448; Yuan, 154, 451; Ming, 171, 453-57; Shang, 404-7, 420-24; Chou, 420, 424-28, 441-42; Han, 428-30; Buddhist, 430-40; Sui, 435-36; Ch'an, 440; Sung, 446; Ch'ing, 458-60; *see also* Bronze work; Painting; Sculpture

Art of War, The (Sun Tzu), 16, 566

Asoka, Emperor, 83

Astronomy, 156; Jesuits and, 173, 182

Bandits, 39, 46, 48, 50, 201-2, 212, 350; Communist, 298-99

Banks, 492, 493-94; nationalization of, 293

Barbarians, 39, 200; Northern Dynasties during Period of Disunity, 58, 59 *(table)*, 60-61, 63

Big Sword Association, 674

Black Pottery culture, 5

Book of Changes (I ching), 29, 661-62

Book of Documents (Shu ching), 29, 39, 621

Book of Odes (Shih ching), 29-30, 39, 621-22, 626

Book of Rites (Li chi), 30, 621

Borodin, Michael, 281, 284, 288

Boxer Rebellion, 233-34, 658

Bronze Age, 6, 410, 418

Bronze work, 8-9, 173, 411, 414, 418-28

Buck, John L., 494-95

Buck, Pearl: quoted, 260-61; *All Men Are Brothers*, 638

Buddha, Gautama, 70-71, 94; sculptures of, 432-34; paintings of, 437

Buddhism, 55, 644, 645, 656; doctrine of, 70-73, 659-60, 664; branches, 72; during Period of Disunity, 73-78, 82; repression of, 75-77, 110-11, 439;

NHON

AN INTRODUCTION
TO CHINESE
CIVILIZATION

Prepared
as one of the
Companions to
Asian Studies

WM. THEODORE DE BARY
EDITOR